EAGLE

EAGLE

The Story of
American Airlines

by Robert J. Serling

St. Martin's/Marek · New York

Library of Congress Cataloging in Publication Data

Serling, Robert J.
    Eagle: The history of American Airlines.

    1. American Airlines, inc.—History.   I. Title.
HE9803.A95S47   1985   387.7′065′73   85-11790
ISBN 0-312-22453-2

First Edition
10 9 8 7 6 5 4 3 2 1

To "C.R."
Because it was Cyrus Rowlett Smith who
gave American Airlines its identity—
and its soul.

Contents

Part IV
1955–1974

Part V
1974–1985

EAGLE

Prologue

On a cold New York winter night early in 1931, a young airline official named Goodrich Murphy sat down to a pre-theater dinner with his wife and another couple.

The fact that they were heading for the theater was unique in itself; in 1931, airline people, even if they were in management, worked for salaries that today would stand several notches below the poverty level, and even then were roughly the equivalent of grocery clerk wages. The chief (and about the only) fringe benefit was an occasional trip pass—which Murphy, who hated to fly, seldom used.

Yet his personal dislike of flying in no way interfered with his enthusiasm for his job. He was divisional traffic manager for a recently formed airline and, like all his underpaid airline brethren, Goodrich Murphy possessed something that helped make up for skimpy paychecks: a deep pride in belonging to the exciting, challenging new world of commercial aviation.

His own company had been forged out of a sprawling, unwieldy, sadly uncoordinated conglomeration of a dozen or so smaller air carriers operating no fewer than twenty-seven different types of aircraft, over routes that on a map resembled hopelessly tangled spaghetti; its pilots didn't even wear the same standard uniform, their varied flight apparel ranging from blue serge suits to leather jackets, depending on which division they flew for and whether they were hauling mail or people.

No matter. It was an *airline,* albeit one with the cohesiveness of watered-down glue, desperately seeking some kind of corporate identity that would establish instant acceptance and recognition as a new transportation giant. As a matter of fact, the very subject of corporate identity came up at Goodrich Murphy's dinner table that night.

Murphy had entered a company-sponsored contest for a new insignia that would go on all letterheads, ticket offices, hangars, and aircraft. The rules limited entrants to a maximum of five designs; professional designers were ineligible, and the employee whose design was chosen would get a $100 prize —a small fortune to the recently married divisional traffic manager.

Deadline for submission happened to be that very midnight, but Murphy already had submitted three entries, one of which he felt had an excellent chance. In between the airline's two initials he had drawn a V-shaped wing that he proudly described to his dinner companions as his best shot at that coveted $100.

"Who are the judges?" someone asked.

An alarm bell clanged, for it suddenly dawned on Goodrich Murphy that he might have a problem with the three most influential members of the judging panel: the airline's president, one of its vice presidents, and a director. All of them had one thing in common: a military background. The president and vice president, in fact, were graduates of Annapolis and West Point, respectively, and the director had been an officer in World War I.

None of his entries, Murphy realized, even remotely hinted at a patriotic motif, an omission he hadn't thought of until just now. He looked at his watch and made an instant decision: he sent his protesting wife and the other couple to the theater and sat down to create a new insignia.

The American bald eagle, he figured, would have to be the focal point of the corporate symbol—it connoted not only powerful flight but patriotism, a natural link between the company and the country it served. At this point he collided with a major obstacle: he wasn't much of an artist and he couldn't find a picture of an eagle in any book, even an encyclopedia. In desperation, he began thumbing through magazines without success until he came across an old issue of *The New Yorker* magazine. His eyes fell on an advertisement for the Gleneagles Hotel in Scotland, a layout featuring a swooping eagle.

Working on the card table that also doubled for the Murphy's dining room table, he sketched his own version of an eagle from the one in the ad, depicting it in flight, talons outstretched and poised just over the upper curvature of the earth. On each side of the bird he put the airline's initials in large red letters set against a blue background. His final touch was a double red-and-white circle around the insignia.

Red, white, and blue—the national colors. The eagle—another national symbol that spoke of powerful, effortless flight. The globe—signifying an air carrier that someday would be known around the world.

Tired but sensing that he had achieved a goal that was more instinctive than real, Goodrich Murphy went to his office in the Chanin Building at 122 East 42nd Street, just across from the Commodore Hotel. There he placed it in a company envelope and time-stamped it before the midnight deadline.

In due time, Murphy was notified that his entry had won over some thousand other designs and would become the official corporate logo. A tall, distinguished, and articulate man, he was to leave the company eventually and go on to important positions at the New Haven Railroad, Eastern Airlines, Matson Navigation, and the Budd Company. But the insignia he created on that card table became one of the most instantly recognized corporate symbols in history, a logo that has lasted for more than half a century, albeit with occasional modifications.

For the initials Goodrich Murphy drew on each side of the bird were A-A. Then they stood for American Airways. Today it's American Airlines, and the symbol of the proud, magnificent eagle signifies now what Murphy hoped it would fifty-four years ago. Like the great winged creature itself, the airline is a national institution, with worldwide acknowledgment of its leadership in air transportation.

But it wasn't always that way, certainly not when Murphy copied the picture from the magazine ad. American in those days was the Rodney Dangerfield of the airline industry, with a hodgepodge fleet, a route system that made no sense, and a corporate structure so tangled as to defy imagination. To paraphrase a classic description of the airplane, American quite literally was a collection of spare parts flying in abysmally loose formation.

Even its ancestry is somewhat uncertain; for the first few years of its existence, it wasn't a single airline but rather a group of small, struggling carriers so unorganized that occasionally they competed against one another. Their only link was a holding company under whose roof they cavorted like a passel of undisciplined children.

Every airline seeking the honor of chronological seniority and historical longevity likes to cite the start of some long-forgotten predecessor company as its own birthdate; United, TWA, and Western have been feuding for years over which is supposed to be America's oldest carrier. American never got into the argument for a very good reason: its genealogical roots are as numerous as the characters in a Russian novel, with more predecessor companies than the rest of the major airlines combined. Figuratively speaking, it knows when its parents got married, but it isn't sure about its grandparents—there were too many of them. And its own files reflect this uncertainty.

The archives trace American's direct ancestry to Robertson Aircraft of St. Louis, a small company that in 1926 won the second air mail contract awarded to a private operator by the U.S. Post Office Department. The date of Robertson's first mail flight, from St. Louis to Chicago, was April 15, 1926, and Robertson eventually became part of American. If this is accepted as the airline's birthday by right of ancestral seniority, then the honor of becoming American's first pilot belongs to the man who made that first flight.

His name was Charles A. Lindbergh.

The majority of aviation historians, however, reject Robertson as the true progenitor in American's complex lineage. Cincinnati, not St. Louis, is most frequently cited as the airline's birthplace. For in that Ohio city, in 1925, was established the Embry-Riddle Company, which operated a flying school, sold airplanes, and ran sightseeing flights. It, too, won an air mail contract over the Chicago–Cincinnati route, although it started service twenty months after Lindbergh's inaugural trip.

But while Embry-Riddle became an airline almost two years after Robertson, it preceded the latter in becoming a part of the giant holding company that eventually merged its numerous acquisitions into one carrier. Thus, the real birth of American dates back to the organization of that holding company.

It was a colossus called the Aviation Corporation, known more familiarly as Avco.

PART ONE
(1925–1934)

1
Family Album

Avco was one of several hundred U.S. companies engaged in various commercial aviation enterprises from the mid-twenties to the early thirties.

This was an era in which the risk factor was no less for the entrepreneurs who built the primitive airplanes and operated the shoestring airlines than it was for the men who flew them; the mortality rate was abysmally high in both categories. One group gambled with money and the other with lives, and each suffered the consequences of trying to sell air transportation to a nation that for a long time had regarded the airplane as simply a dangerous toy.

In the immediate post–World War I period, the United States was the Romper Room of commercial aviation, a strange anomaly for the country where powered flight was born. During the war itself, America's aviation lethargy was only too evident: U.S. industry had failed to put a single American-designed, American-made aircraft into actual combat. Yank fighter pilots flew French Spads and Nieuports; observation crews used British DH-4s. And in commercial application of the airplane, European progress made a mockery of the Wrights' legacy.

Within a year after the war ended, Britain and France were operating scheduled passenger flights between London and Paris. Junkers of Germany had on its drawing boards a design for an all-metal transport monoplane with internally braced wings, and the French began development of an air mail system that dwarfed America's in route mileage and personnel. And by 1923, when the only U.S. airline operating a regular passenger service folded ignominiously—as had a predecessor ten years earlier—Britain was sending thirty daily scheduled flights across the Atlantic, in aircraft that featured upholstered chairs, bar service, and champagne lunches served by jacketed stewards.

As far back as 1913, in fact, Russia's Igor Sikorsky had built a four-engine airliner with enclosed cockpit and cabin, accommodations for two pilots and four passengers, electric lights, and a washroom. Even in Italy, supposedly not a technologically minded nation, an aeronautical engineer named Caproni had created a 100-passenger flying boat powered by eight engines and grossing 30,000 pounds.

All of which contrasted sharply with the bleak picture facing the three thousand U.S. pilots and more than fifteen thousand skilled aviation mechanics returning to civilian life after the Armistice. Theirs was a country that regarded aviation with either fond amusement or outright indifference. To most Americans, the airplane was something to be enjoyed vicariously, in pulp magazines recounting the make-believe exploits of the pursuit pilots battling the hated Hun; in movies like *Wings;* in the barnstorming appearances at county and state fairs. As far as public transportation was concerned, the nation's far-flung railroad was king and the airplane merely a plaything.

For a returning American pilot who wanted to stay in aviation, there were only two games in town, barnstorming or flying the mail—neither of which constituted a prime labor market. The former involved the double hazard of crashing to one's death while in the process of starving one's self to death. And the slightly more prosaic job of carrying mail offered no greater guarantee of life expectancy than did barnstorming; of the first forty pilots hired by the Post Office Department in 1919 to operate the air mail service, thirty-one had been killed in crashes by 1925. During the ten years in which the government flew the mail, there were two hundred crashes and eighty airmen killed or seriously injured, most of them in weary, obsolete DH-4s converted from wartime observation aircraft to mail planes.

Into this environment of pitifully inadequate technical research, starvation funding, and apathetic support, there eventually appeared two catalysts generating galvanizing effects.

The first was the 1925 passage of the Contract Air Mail Act, more familiarly known as the Kelly Act after its chief sponsor, Representative Clyde Kelly of Pennsylvania. The new law turned the entire job of flying the mail over to private contractors, who had to bid on the various routes that were to become the nation's first real air transportation system. A more ironic choice for the father of the U.S. airline industry could not have been made; Congressman Kelly was known in Washington as "the voice of the railway mail clerks." He was the chief spokesman for railroad lobbyists anxious to get the Post Office Department out of mail transportation entirely; not by the farthest stretch of the imagination could Kelly or anyone else foresee the day when the industry he helped create would be carrying not only 90 percent of the nation's first-class intercity mail but fifty passengers for every person who travels by train.

The second catalyst occurred two years later: Lindbergh's dramatic nonstop flight from New York to Paris. Because of the Lone Eagle's subsequent involvement in pre-war isolationist activities and his admitted strong conservatism, too many historians have tended to dismiss that 1927 flight as a foolhardy stunt by a skilled but exceptionally lucky pilot. It was far more than that. In just thirty-three and a half hours, Lindy changed the very attitude of America toward the *potential* of aviation. Literally overnight, the airplane became the tool of future air commerce, exciting and almost limitless in its possibilities. Adoration of Charles Lindbergh was to prove relatively short-lived, but not so the real significance of his accomplishment—making America air-minded. The fact that he flew some three thousand miles in a tiny, single-engine aircraft bespoke unsuspected reliability and safety; it sowed the initial seeds of confidence, not only on the part of the lay public but on those who first grasped the commercial viability of scheduled air travel.

In the two years that elapsed between passage of the Kelly Act and Lindbergh's flight, the airlines already had begun to make some slow, faltering progress. At the time the Act became law, there were exactly three passenger-carrying airlines in the United States. One was a San Diego–Los Angeles route operated by Claude Ryan, whose company would build Lindy's *Spirit of St. Louis.* The second carrier was owned by none other than Henry Ford and carried Ford personnel and freight between Detroit and Chicago; a Detroit–Cleveland route was added later. The third was a one-plane venture operating under the name Pacific Marine Airways; its founder was Sydney Chaplin, brother of movie comedian Charlie Chaplin, and its fleet consisted of a single ancient flying boat that carried passengers on excursion trips between Catalina Island and Wilmington, California.

Of the three, only Ryan's could be called a real airline. Ford, in today's terminology, would be considered a business fleet, and Pacific Marine was not much more than a sightseeing operation. Their combined routes totaled only three hundred miles.

Then came the deluge.

When the Kelly Act was passed, more than five thousand would-be airline tycoons buried the Post Office Department with inquiries on the bidding process for the initial twelve available route segments, officially known as Contract Air Mail routes or CAMs. Fortunately, not all five thousand actually submitted formal bids or it would have taken forever to get the embryonic industry out of the womb. There were still several hundred legitimate applications, however, and it was more than seven months before the Post Office Department began issuing the route awards.

The twelve original CAMs were set up to feed the lone route retained by the government, the transcontinental route between New York and San Francisco via Chicago. Other CAMs were added later, including the transcontinental route that was broken into shorter segments and awarded to private contractors. But those first twelve formed the nucleus of what was to become the world's greatest air transportation system. In numerical order, they were:

CAM 1: New York–Boston
CAM 2: St. Louis–Chicago
CAM 3: Chicago–Dallas
CAM 4: Los Angeles–Salt Lake City
CAM 5: Elko, Nevada–Pasco, Washington
CAM 6: Detroit–Cleveland
CAM 7: Detroit–Chicago
CAM 8: Seattle–Los Angeles
CAM 9: Chicago–Twin Cities
CAM 10: Miami–Jacksonville (later expanded to Atlanta)

CAM 11: Cleveland–Pittsburgh
CAM 12: Pueblo–Cheyenne

Only two of those first dozen routes were flown by airlines that eventually became American's predecessor companies, CAMs 1 and 2. But this was just the beginning of the infant industry's explosive expansion, thanks to these four major developments:

- On May 20, 1926, President Calvin Coolidge—pressured mostly by Secretary of Commerce Herbert Hoover—signed the Air Commerce Act, which created an Aeronautics Branch (later changed to Bureau of Air Commerce) within the Commerce Department. It gave the Secretary of Commerce authority to designate and establish federal airways; install and operate air navigation aids and do research for improving those aids; license pilots; issue airworthiness certificates for aircraft; and investigate accidents. The Act fell short of satisfying aviation enthusiasts who were urging establishment of an independent Department of Air, but it was still a long step forward for civil aviation. The new regulatory authority forced the airlines to grow up a lot faster than they would have if left to an undisciplined environment.
- The Post Office Department began awarding additional air mail routes to successful bidders, expanding the initial twelve to twenty-four by 1928. Six had been started but discontinued, and five more had been approved with operations not yet under way.
- The airlines, while existing largely on mail pay from the government trough, gradually increased their passenger-carrying operations, which, in turn, led to the development of bigger and faster airplanes. And this trend accelerated after Lindbergh's flight.
- The emergence of commercial aviation as a potentially viable enterprise attracted the attention of an increasing number of financiers anxious to capitalize on this new target for investment funds.

The latter factor was the key element in the formation of the Aviation Corporation. It became involved with the Embry-Riddle Company of Cincinnati, which had just won a contract to fly the mail between Cincinnati and Chicago—one of the Post Office Department's subsequent awards.

Embry-Riddle was founded by John Paul Riddle and T. Higbee Embry in 1925. Riddle was a good pilot himself and Embry more of a business type, who furnished most of the capital. What they started was a flying school and an airplane dealership, the latter involving one aircraft in particular, a cabin plane built by the Fairchild Airplane Manufacturing Company.

Sherman Fairchild was the son of a man who in 1915 founded a company from which giant IBM descended. The father, in fact, was IBM's first chairman and president. When his father died in the early twenties, Sherman used part of his inherited wealth to foster various aviation projects, from a new type of aerial camera to the design of a plane reliable and steady enough for air photography missions. (In American's archives, there is a memo from an unofficial company historian suggesting that "American Airlines was born because of IBM"—a fascinating if farfetched claim.)

When Embry-Riddle won its air mail route, the two partners put up $10,000 of their own money and raised another $90,000 from local businessmen. But this wasn't sufficient funding for starting up a new airline and they were about to give up the mail award when Curtiss, a Fairchild competitor, offered to supply additional funds if Embry-Riddle would drop the Fairchild plane in favor of Curtiss aircraft.

Sherman Fairchild had the reputation of not being an especially astute businessman—someone once described him as "a benign Howard Hughes"— but in this crisis he acted fast, with admirable if possibly inadvertent foresight. He had no intention of losing one of his best dealers to Curtiss, so he asked his board of directors to lend Embry-Riddle what it needed to launch the airline.

The directors went beyond merely agreeing to the loan; they decided to form a new subsidiary that would finance another aviation projects. Fairchild lacked the financial muscle to handle such an undertaking alone—the original capitalization estimate was $1 million—but Wall Street was interested and a number of outside investors joined the party.

On March 1, 1929, lawyers filed incorporation papers in Delaware for "The Aviation Corporation," described as a holding and development company in the transportation industry. The new Avco stock, with an authorized ten million shares, was underwritten by two prestigious New York investment banking firms, W. A. Harriman & Company and Lehman Brothers. They sold two million shares at $17.50 per share, raising $35 million for the new holding company, which then began fly-casting for assorted acquisitions.

Over the next few years, those acquisitions were to become so numerous that an exact total is impossible to determine—there seem to have been at least eighty and possibly more than eighty-five. It was a family tree with so many branches and leaves that in the thirties, when air mail contracts were being probed, investigators from two congressional committees and both the Treasury and Justice departments were unable to figure out Avco's corporate structure and the tortuous, hopelessly involved paths of its myriad acquisitions.

One investigator did unearth the fact that Avco apparently owned a company (non-airline), organized in 1927, which nobody had ever heard of. Further digging failed to disclose how or why the firm was acquired, or even exactly what it did. It was typical of the explosive but confused expansion that Fairchild itself wound up as the dog being wagged by the tail; the financing company was supposed to be a Fairchild subsidiary, but instead Fairchild became an Avco subsidiary.

In 1935, American assigned lawyers to trace Avco's ancestry and, ideally, arrive at an accurate, definitive picture. They tried nobly, and in many ways sorted out much of the mess. But their twenty-four-page report to the company included these plaintive words:

On some old organizational charts, the names of some companies are found but we have never been able to find the companies, and in at least one case we have found a company which apparently belongs to us but about which we have been able to find nothing.

Their research added this bit of information about Avco's early years:

A list of former officers and directors of the companies involved in the organization of the Aviation Corporation and its subsidiaries contains approximately 500 names, many of whom are of considerable prominence, including two former Postmaster Generals, one former Commanding General of the Air Corps, numerous prominent bankers and business men . . . and one person, incidentally, now in jail for robbing the mails.

American's airline ancestors are more positively established than those other companies in Avco's Babelesque edifice, but hardly less confusing. Basically, Avco acquired five airlines, three of which were in turn holding companies themselves, controlling eleven individual carriers. To these eleven Avco added two independent airlines.

The biggest acquisition was the Universal Air Lines System, a combination of six airlines. Universal was something of a smaller-scale Avco; it began life in 1928 as Continental Airlines, with a passenger route between Chicago and Cleveland, but changed its name to Universal before service was inaugurated. It then started accumulating an assortment of smaller carriers as the quickest way to expand and also latch onto mail contracts. Of the five airlines it purchased, two had mail authority: Robertson Aircraft, which not only possessed CAM 2's St. Louis–Chicago route but a later award for CAM 28 between St. Louis and Omaha via Kansas City; and by coincidence another airline called Continental, which flew the mail on a Cleveland–Louisville route. (The name was revived in 1938 when Bob Six changed his Varney Air Lines to Continental.)

The three passenger airlines that came under the Universal tent were Northern (Chicago–Twin Cities), Central (Tulsa–Wichita–Kansas City), and Braniff (Tulsa–Oklahoma City). The latter, founded by the brothers Tom and Paul Braniff, was reborn a few years later under the same name and only a few old-timers remember the ironic twist: the carrier that developed into one of American's bitterest rivals was, for a brief time, part of its system.

Universal lasted less than two years as a separate entity, but before its absorption into the Avco empire it was an aggressive, formidable airline with one major historical achievement: the honor of operating the nation's first air/train transcontinental service. On June 14, 1929, the New York Central's crack *Southwestern Limited* left Grand Central Station for Cleveland on the initial leg of the New York–Los Angeles air/rail trip. At Cleveland, through passengers boarded three Universal Fokker F-10 trimotors that carried them to Garden City, Kansas, via Chicago, St. Louis, and Kansas City. In Garden City, on the morning of January 17, they switched to the Santa Fe Railroad for the rest of the way into Los Angeles.

New York's jaunty mayor, Jimmy Walker, launched the historic trip with some typical Walker hyperbole. "You are more than making aviation history," he proclaimed to the audience of five hundred gathered at Grand Central. "You are making Los Angeles and New York suburbs of each other."

Universal's publicity department hailed the new service as "bringing the Atlantic coast within two business days of the Pacific, yet calling for only one day of flying." The cost, a company news release added, was only $85 more than an all-rail trip.

Mayor Walker sent a silver flask filled with water from the Atlantic to Mayor Cryer of Los Angeles, with a request that he pour the contents into the Pacific.

The paying passengers numbered only six, but the three Fokkers were needed to carry the large contingent of reporters covering the transcontinental inaugural, even though the Los Angeles arrival by prosaic train fell somewhat short of the dramatic. It didn't make much difference—in Kansas City more than fifteen hundred people were at the airport to see the Fokkers arrive, and in Los Angeles the intrepid travelers were treated to three days of celebratory breakfasts, luncheons, and dinners in honor of this continent-compressing feat.

The continent actually hadn't been compressed by much, however.

The entire trip had taken sixty-seven hours, cutting five hours off the fastest coast-to-coast train schedule. Only three weeks later, Transcontinental Air Transport inaugurated an even faster air/rail service: forty-eight hours between New York and Los Angeles.

TAT's inaugural was a masterpiece of upstaging the pioneering Universal effort. It featured such public relations gimmicks as movie stars christening the first eastbound Ford trimotor, with Lindbergh flying the initial leg, and Amelia Earhart as a passenger on the first westbound trip. Adding these promotional activities to TAT's speedier service (the twenty-hour bulge was made possible by TAT's flying two daytime legs instead of Universal's one), it is no wonder that Universal's feat has been ignored in many aviation histories.

Universal actually was Avco's third airline. Tiny Embry-Riddle was regarded as the first, through the Avco loan, although it resisted a full takeover for a long time. While its operation of the Cincinnati–Chicago mail eventually was absorbed into the Avco system, its name was to be perpetuated by the founding of the Embry-Riddle Aeronautical University, a fully accredited institution with two campuses, at Daytona Beach, Florida, and Prescott, Arizona.

Next to come into Avco's embracing arms was the fast-growing Colonial Airways Corporation, adding another holding company and three more airlines to the roster. Colonial was launched in 1923 as the Bee Line by New England financiers, including Governor John H. Trumbull of Connecticut. Its name was changed to Colonial Air Transport and it stayed relatively inactive except for flying the governor and his staff on occasional business trips.

But when Colonial won the New York–Boston mail route designated as CAM 1, it became Colonial Airways and was no longer what amounted to the governor's private airline. One of its earliest principals was its general manager, a young Yale graduate named Juan Trippe, who left the company after an angry dispute over Trippe's insistence that Colonial needed bigger planes for passenger business.

Trippe went on to found Pan American Airways, but his brief stint with Colonial raises the tantalizing speculation that if he had stayed with the New England venture, he might have wound up running American instead. His angry departure over the issue of passenger traffic reflected the attitude of many early airline executives—they were convinced nobody could make money carrying people.

Colonial was no exception. It did condescend, however, to try a two-week experiment aimed at determining public demand for air travel between New York and Boston. This was in the spring of 1927 and one of the first paying passengers was James Reddig, a Boston businessman who had startled the airline the day before by phoning to ask if there would be space on the flight.

Mr. Reddig arrived at what was then the Boston airport, looked in vain for something resembling a terminal building, and then heard his name called by the only Colonial employee in sight. He escorted Reddig to a dilapidated shack adjoining an equally dilapidated hangar, the two men having to slog through thick mud en route. The shanty, heated by a smelly coal-oil stove, was filled mostly with engine parts strewn along a wooden bench. The agent (Reddig assumed he was an agent, although he could have been anyone from a mechanic to Colonial's janitor-on-duty) located an ancient typewriter amid the mess and proceeded to write up the passenger ticket.

Said ticket was typed (with two fingers) on a Colonial letterhead, and Reddig noticed later there were several misspellings, including his name. Politely, he inquired as to the availability of ground transportation from the destination airport, Hadley Field in New Brunswick, New Jersey, to downtown Manhattan.

"Oh, New York trains go through New Brunswick every hour," he was assured. This, Reddig was to learn, was the gospel truth—trains *did* go through New Brunswick hourly; unfortunately, very few of them stopped, and Reddig, who had to hitch a ride on a mail truck from the airport to the railroad station, consumed more time getting from New Brunswick to Manhattan than it took to fly from Boston.

This wasn't the first surprise for our brave traveler. When he boarded the flight, he discovered that he was the only one who had shelled out the required $25 for a ticket. The other four passengers were newspapermen riding free.

Once airborne, Reddig got yet another surprise. The pilot came into the cabin to chat, dressed in a tuxedo with a white silk scarf and a derby.

"I'm going to a party in New York after we land," he explained when he got to Reddig. He also confided that the man flying the plane was a Colonial mechanic getting some practice—a bit of information Reddig could have done without.

But Colonial grew up fast, gradually taking on an air of professionalism in developing its passenger traffic. By early 1929, it had merged two sister airlines into the Colonial Airways holding company, both possessing air mail authority on valuable routes. Colonial Western served CAM 20, between Albany and Cleveland via Schenectady, Utica, Syracuse, Rochester, Buffalo, and Erie. Canadian Colonial Airways operated Foreign Air Mail Route 1 from New York to Montreal via Albany.

A stock exchange deal brought Colonial under the Avco banner in May 1929, and after acquiring Universal, the insatiable tentacles reached out to the south and a third holding company: Southern Air Transport.

Southern was a combination of two airlines, Gulf and Texas Air Transport. Gulf was organized initially as St. Tammany–Gulf Coast Airways, providing passenger service between Atlanta and New Orleans before it got a mail contract over the same route (CAM 23). Its partner-to-be was founded by Temple Bowen, a lean, leathery-faced Texan who owned a bus company at the time he started Texas Air Transport. Bowen had latched onto two mail routes —CAM 21 Galveston–Dallas and CAM 22 Dallas–Brownsville—and also was carrying passengers on both routes when he sold his airline to the new Southern Air Transport system.

The Avco network was extended further when the holding company bought out Interstate Airlines, a small but colorful carrier possessing another prime mail route, CAM 30 from Atlanta to Chicago. Adding up the score, the Aviation Corporation by the end of 1929 had picked up thirteen airlines, eleven mail contracts, a fleet consisting of virtually every type of civil aircraft then being manufactured, and a route system that looked impressive on a map but suffered badly from its lack of cohesive structure. Even worse, there was no real leadership at the top, no legitimate central command deciding and dictating overall policy. The largest and most critical gap in the system was the lack of a Chicago–New York link.

In truth, there was no sum to Avco's voluminous parts; it had gobbled up not only its assorted collection of airlines but a conglomeration of other aviation enterprises—flying schools, aircraft and engine manufacturers, makers of airplane accessories from cockpit instruments to seaplane pontoons and aerial cameras, and even two airports—Roosevelt and Curtiss fields on Long Island. It owned stock (but not a controlling interest) in the parent company that formed Pan American Airways. It bought into Alaskan Airways, which never did become part of American, and ventured overseas with the purchase of a company called Cuban Aviation, which, like Alaskan, stayed clear of American's orbit.

Theoretically, a passenger could fly from Boston to El Paso on the Avco system, but it would have been simpler and faster to go by train. There was no attempt to integrate schedules or establish connecting flights, a rather inevitable deficiency inasmuch as the chief subsidiaries—Colonial, Southern, and Universal—had their own officers and boards of directors, with individual operating rules and policies.

The first president of Avco was Graham Grosvenor, a Fairchild executive, who thus might be termed American's first president. This would be stretching the truth a bit, for Grosvenor was presiding over a Chinese fire drill, not an airline with the status of a solid entity. The auditors finally gave Avco Chairman Harriman the bad news: since going on its acquisition spree, the Aviation Corporation had lost $1.4 million—by today's standards not an alarming amount, but in those Depression-plagued days it was massive red ink, with a chilling effect on the Avco hierarchy.

Harriman and the chairman of Avco's executive committee, Robert Lehman, decided on drastic action. They talked their sixty-five colleagues on the parent corporation's board of directors into consolidating all of Avco's domestic airline holdings into a new subsidiary corporation. The machinery was simple: the airlines would sell all their stock to the new corporation and receive in return common stock of the latter, in an amount proportionate to the relative value of each carrier's assets.

Everyone went along except Embry-Riddle, ironically Avco's very first airline; while Embry-Riddle couldn't block the reorganization plan, with Avco holding controlling shares, it stubbornly refused to sell the stock it still owned and hung onto it for another two years. Why Embry-Riddle resisted is a mystery, but it may have been because the company was as mixed up as Avco itself. When Embry-Riddle was dissolved in 1932, lawyers discovered that its management had organized six subsidiary companies for no apparent reason. They existed solely on paper and were never financed.

Embry-Riddle notwithstanding, the Avco board elected a new president, a soft-spoken but tough-minded industrial engineer, Frederic G. Coburn. He was entrusted with straightening out the mess and bringing order to the chaotic 9,100-mile system being operated by a platoon of unconformists.

There is an unsolved discrepancy, however, in the files of Avco and American as to exactly who *was* the airline's first president. American and virtually all historical accounts list Coburn. But Avco's archives contain a brief reference to a James F. Hamilton, identified as head of New York States Railways and the United Traction, "an authority on electric and transportation problems."

Avco's own official corporate history says Hamilton was named president of the newly formed airline subsidiary while Grosvenor still headed the parent corporation, and does not mention Coburn as holding that post. Apparently Hamilton, if he served at all, didn't last long enough to have his name painted on his office door. Coburn definitely became president of both Avco and the airline on January 25, 1930.

On that date, after much haggling by the directors over what to call it, American Airways, Inc., came into existence.

2
Early Birds

In the first three years of American's existence, the noble eagle that Goodrich Murphy designed could more appropriately have been a turkey.

Fred Coburn tried hard to bring order out of chaos and in some ways succeeded. He pruned Avco's family tree from eighty subsidiaries down to twenty, and his economy measures for American Airways cut operating losses from a hemorrhaging $3.4 million in 1930 to $1 million in 1931.

But he failed to accomplish what American needed so desperately—centralized control of its operations, with a single strong leader calling the shots. It wasn't entirely his fault, for Avco named him president of the holding company while simultaneously neglecting to appoint a president of the airline. Coburn was in charge of both, and it didn't work. The other mistake was allowing American to be organized into independent geographical divisions, thus perpetuating the same old weaknesses that had prompted the consolidation of the airline properties.

American Airways started out in 1930 with three divisions—Colonial, Universal, and Southern Air Transport—and the following year increased these virtually autonomous units to four by giving Embry-Riddle divisional status, removing it from Universal. This left American the same hydra-headed monster of old, with separate officers for each division and a crazy quilt of flight equipment maintained and operated under a dozen different sets of procedures. It was no wonder that a Colonial pilot could wear a tuxedo in the cockpit while a brother airman at Interstate came to work in coveralls, and a pilot from S.A.T. showed up in what amounted to an ordinary dark blue business suit with a pair of air mail wings on the breast pocket. Pilot uniforms weren't standardized until 1932.

The aircraft themselves reflected the airline's fragmented structure. Their fuselages carried not only the American Airways name but the division to which the plane belonged and whatever happened to be an affiliate airline of that division. Before the American eagle was born, the company logo was a lighthouse with beams emitting from a glass-globed top. The word "American" appeared just over the lighthouse and "Airways" was superimposed across the base, both in elliptical lettering. At the top of the logo was the division's name, and at the bottom, the subsidiary airline's. Even after the eagle was adopted, most of the aircraft continued to carry the divisional designation above or below the new insignia.

The fleet, incidentally, was geared primarily to handle mail, which represented almost 75 percent of the company's revenues. It included a fair-sized proportion of biplanes such as Pitcairns, Stearmans, and Travel Airs, flown by men who had cut their airmen's teeth flying the early mail schedules. Avco had accumulated more than mail contracts, routes, airplanes, embossed stock certificates, and hangars in building its empire; it also inherited the people who went along with the tools, including pilots whose names would become legendary in American's history, their escapades as colorful as their exploits.

In the Colonial division, for example, there was one Simon Peter Bittner, a man of diminutive stature and enormous humor. He was known to all as Si Bittner, and his peccadilloes during his long and honorable career with American would fill a book. Like so many of his contemporaries, Si was an ex-barnstormer who fell in love with flying at an early age. He bought an old Jenny biplane while still in his teens, and his neighbors used to refer to him as "that crazy Bittner kid."

Bittner joined Colonial fresh out of the famous Gates Flying Circus, where he had served as a stunt pilot, wing-walker, and parachutist—he claimed to have made over three hundred jumps. He didn't have to make any jumps with Colonial, but he recorded quite a few dives into proverbial hot water. One of his earliest transgressions involved a sudden impulse to buzz an Erie Railroad train while flying the night mail on the New York–Buffalo run.

Si spotted the train as it approached a tunnel and dove his Pitcairn mailplane almost down to track level—the train was eastbound and Bittner was flying west. He headed toward the mouth of the tunnel and timed the encounter perfectly. Just as the locomotive was about to emerge from the tunnel, Bittner turned on his landing lights.

It was a single track, and the devastating effects on the startled engineer are best described by a retired American captain, Bill Evans, who knew Bittner well.

"You could have seen the sparks flying for miles around when the poor engineer applied his brakes," says Evans. "He must have flattened every wheel on that train. The railroad raised hell, of course, and Si denied he had done it. We all knew it was him—hell, he had told quite a few pilots what happened, with full details."

Bittner also acquired the reputation of being late on some of his trips. His alibis were most logical—head winds, weather, balky engines, etc.—and not for a long time did the company find out the real explanation: he would occasionally land his Pitcairn at some farm and pick up a few dozen fresh eggs.

Si's heart-rending protestations of innocence were made to Colonial's chief pilot, Willis Heath Proctor, a no-nonsense veteran mail pilot himself, who didn't believe Bittner but never could prove otherwise. Proctor, too, was to become a legendary figure at American, although for vastly different reasons. He was a lumberman and fur trader before learning to fly and joining Colonial.

Well known in every city the airline served, Proctor surveyed Colonial's mail routes and flew the first mail load out of Buffalo for Cleveland.

Proctor was a geography buff, one of his special interests being the story of the Mason-Dixon Line, the boundary separating Pennsylvania from Maryland and part of West Virginia. Established in 1767 by English mathematicians Jeremiah Mason and Charles Dixon, it became the theoretical line dividing the northern and southern states. Milestones were erected along the boundary and some of the original markers are still in existence. Proctor got the idea of photographing them from the air, and in the late 1930s shot a picture from the cockpit of an American plane he was flying on a regular trip. The spectacular photograph showed, for the first time, a clear outline of the markers, and Proctor sold the picture to the then-new *Life* magazine. It wasn't the first aerial shot of the area, but previous pictures of the line had been interpreted as a conventional firebreak.

Heath Proctor retired in 1950, but American regarded him so highly that he stayed on another seven years as head of pilot training in Chicago. His two sons are in the airline industry he loved so much. Bill Proctor is a TWA pilot and Jon a senior TWA flight attendant.

Two names destined to play major parts in the American story did not come from the predecessor airlines but rather from another Avco subsidiary, Fairchild itself. Avco inherited something of a lifelong team in the persons of William Littlewood and Myron Gould ("Dan") Beard, who had started working together as young engineers at Ingersoll Rand. They both joined Fairchild, Beard as a pilot/engineer and Bill Littlewood as general manager of the Fairchild engine plant. Littlewood took Beard with him when they went with American.

They even looked alike, both tall and, in those days, rather slender; Littlewood for years bore the nickname "Splinters." After Fairchild became an Avco subsidiary, Littlewood was assigned to another Avco company that sold insurance and was named safety officer for all corporation properties. Most of his work involved the airlines, and one of his jobs was the investigation of engine and hangar fires. He toured the system, establishing rules and procedures for preventing and fighting fires at every station.

Coburn liked his professional thoroughness and gave him a new task: to develop specifications for an economical passenger plane. Out of this assignment came the Pilgrim, the first commercial transport to be designed according to an airline's specifications. It was a single-engine plane carrying nine passengers and flown by a single pilot. The cockpit was inaccessible from the cabin; messages to the passengers were passed through a sliding glass panel in a bulkhead. Also unique was the compass, also on the bulkhead, with its face printed backwards—the pilot read the instrument via a mirror in front of him.

The Pilgrim was the result of a $35,000 study Avco had commissioned to determine what kind of a transport plane the airline needed. Previous single-engine aircraft were too small and the trimotors were considered too big; the Pilgrim's size seemed to be the ideal compromise.

Its design was largely the work of two men: Otto Kirchner, Fairchild's chief engineer, and project engineer John Lee. Kirchner would later become a member of Littlewood's engineering team at American, while Lee joined United Aircraft. And their joint efforts in creating the Pilgrim produced some interesting innovations. Passenger comfort was a prime goal, so they developed a primitive form of soundproofing, using duck feathers as insulation. They also equipped the plane with soft-pressure "donut" tires, for gentler landings.

Avco ordered fifteen Pilgrims and distributed them among the Southern, Universal, and Embry-Riddle divisions. Complaints from the latter two began coming in with the first seasonal drops in temperature—passengers were freezing because the planes lacked heaters. Kirchner sketched a crude heating system on a piece of paper, chief mechanic Price Arnold built one in the shop, and they tested it in a Pilgrim; the whole development process took not more than three days. That was par for the course in these early days of aeronautical engineering. Only six months elapsed between the decision to build the Pilgrim and its introduction into passenger service.

One of the Pilgrims assigned to Southern Air Transport had its nine seats upholstered in South American snake skins, the idea of a Fairchild official whose brother imported skins. The airplane was a showpiece when it arrived in Fort Worth, but no one had realized what rough snake skins could do to silk hose and flimsy dresses. One woman passenger wearing chiffon nearly lost her dress when she stood up, and the seats had to be reupholstered in less exotic leather after a few trips.

Robertson, too, contributed some memorable characters. One of Lindbergh's favorite fellow air mail pilots was E. L. "Slonnie" Sloniger, who wound up at the top of American's seniority list when all the Avco airlines were merged into a single carrier. There was no union then, and seniority was determined by a drawing. (Heath Proctor was Number Two and "Squabby" Vine of Embry-Riddle Number Three.)

Sloniger was a teacher as well as a superb pilot, worshipped by every young copilot who flew with him. His list of admirers included fellow captains, too, for Slonnie had cut his airman's teeth on those firetrap DH-4 mailplanes and never, in his entire career, scratched any airplane he flew. In later years, he was to recall the days when every Robertson pilot had his own airplane and would paint his name on the side of the cockpit.

"Nobody else was supposed to fly it," he related. "But if you had some seniority and saw some plane with a better windshield or a newer engine, you'd sweet-talk some mechanic into putting your name on it. Every third night I'd go out to the field and fly to Chicago—we had no operations office. On rare occasions we'd take a passenger, but only people who were in desperate circumstances would fly to Chicago, or somebody who was crazy."

Another Robertson pilot and friend of Lindbergh's was Bud Gurney, who seems to have developed the first uniform. He showed up one day in white flannel trousers, a blue blazer, and a chauffeur's cap with the airline's initials. Nobody followed suit, however.

Interstate had some interesting characters in its pilot corps, too. Perhaps the best known was Durwood Wesson Ledbetter; like Bittner, few knew him by anything but a nickname and Ledbetter's was "Duke." He got his pilot's license in 1923, barnstormed for a few years, and was hired by Interstate to fly the mail between Atlanta and Chicago.

The airline paid its pilots five cents a mile for daytime duty and ten cents when they flew at night. Base pay was $166.66 a month. Ledbetter averaged around $500 a month.

"That was big money in 1928," he recalls. "When I started with Interstate, they didn't know it but I would have paid *them* to fly."

Duke was a rather dignified individual whose only complaint was the fact that Interstate's pilots didn't have uniforms; they wore coveralls. So he began reporting for duty wearing spats and carrying a walking cane, a sartorial touch that prompted the other pilots to start calling him "the Duke."

His air mail experiences were typical for pilots of that brave and hazardous era. Forced landings were almost routine, and rare was the man who didn't have at least one a month. Ledbetter was flying the mail eastbound out of Chicago one night and ran into weather so bad that he landed his Stearman biplane in a field next to a farm. He borrowed the farmer's car, took the mail into the closest town to put on the next train, and slept that night in a hotel. The next morning he drove back to the farm only to discover how close he had come to disaster.

"There was no way I could take off," Ledbetter said. "I had landed just under some high-tension wires—I hadn't even seen them and I must have come in no more than ten feet under them. I knew I couldn't get over them and I wasn't about to go under them again, so I called the power company. They sent a crew out to disconnect the wires long enough for me to get out of there."

Ledbetter had a love affair with the J5 Stearman, the plane that comprised Interstate's mail fleet, and on one occasion the little aircraft's amazing stability saved his life. He had been bitten by a rabid dog and was undergoing the then-prescribed anti-rabies treatment consisting of multiple shots in each arm and the abdomen. The pain was as bad as the dog bite itself, but Duke insisted on taking his regular mail trip, with about a dozen shots in him.

On the Evansville–Nashville leg, the pain became so fierce he swallowed a pill a dentist friend had given him, downing it with a cup of coffee from the Thermos bottle the mail pilots always carried. That was all he remembered for a long time. When he came to, he was due south of Evansville, one hundred and twenty-five miles off course, and had been asleep for over two hours—a period during which the Stearman had flown itself. When he landed in Nashville, a reserve pilot was called out to finish the trip and Ledbetter went to the hospital.

The air mail pilots made good copy for the press, reporters and feature writers gravitating eagerly toward these romantic, dashing figures in goggles, leather helmets, white scarfs, and toggled flying clothes. Virtually every plane was described as a "giant craft" regardless of size, and every forced landing earned eight-column banner headlines of the ESCAPES DEATH variety. The same somewhat exaggerated status was accorded the airmen, who were invariably labeled "fearless."

Brave they were, but rarely fearless; most of them flew scared, and for good reason. They understood only too well the inadequacies of their weapons in the never-ending battle against the elements. Colonial's pilots flew through some of the worst winter weather in the nation, and Interstate's routes weren't exactly milk runs. What little space remained in the Stearmans after the mail was loaded was packed with emergency equipment, such as parachute flares fired from a special pistol. Each flare provided one minute of light (200,000 candlepower) over an area of one square mile. Also carried was a 600,000-candlepower flare capable of lighting up five square miles for four minutes.

Interstate's pilots followed a standard procedure when approaching mountainous terrain: they climbed as high as possible in order to gain the maximum gliding distance if an engine quit. But the technique didn't always work. Duke Ledbetter got caught in a storm over Chattanooga one night en route to Nashville. He was climbing to get over Mount Avel, a 5,000-foot peak, when his carburetor iced up and the engine began sputtering.

The almost powerless Stearman went into a spin and by the time Ledbetter could pull it out, he was down to 200 feet over a canyon, with mountains on both sides. Duke braced as the plane plowed into a snowbank and flipped over, pinning him in such a way that he couldn't unfasten his seat belt.

He heard the ominous sound of gasoline dripping out of a ruptured tank onto some metal object—"It sounded like a leaky faucet in the bathroom," he remembered later—and knew he was a goner if it ignited. Then he heard voices and he began hollering.

His rescuers turned out to be an elderly woman and a twelve-year-old boy who managed to dig through the snow for a half hour and help him out. Several farmers showed up and aided him in unloading the precious mail, about two hundred and fifty pounds of it, the farmers lugging the sacks over the rim of the canyon to the nearest house.

The closest railroad station was Oakley, Tennessee, some fifteen miles away, so Ledbetter rented a horse and and buggy for the trip through a snow-covered road. At Oakley, he was told that the next train wasn't due for another four days but that he could put the mail on a train at Cookeville, the next town up the road. It was too far for the tired horse and Duke talked a farmer into driving him to Cookeville, in an old Chevrolet.

En route, the farmer insisted on stopping at every farmhouse on the way so he could tell the occupants about the air mail plane falling out of the sky. At every stop, Duke was offered whiskey, which at first he refused. Then his resolve weakened and he began accepting the hospitality. By the time they arrived at Cookeville, Ledbetter was pretty well smashed, an unhappy state to be in: he was met by the postmaster and a postal inspector—who put him under arrest for drunken flying.

He finally convinced them he had gotten stoned after the crash and not before, at which point they accepted the mail for transfer but refused to cash a $166.66 paycheck—the only money he had on him. The postmaster did agree to send the check on to Nashville via a mail clerk, and Duke got the money two days later.

Ledbetter contacted Interstate officials—they had written him off as dead —and informed them he thought he could fly the Stearman out if they'd send a good mechanic with the necessary repair parts—a landing gear strut, a new propeller, and a replacement carburetor. The mechanic they dispatched was Interstate's best, Abe Hoyt, who in subsequent years became one of American's most beloved employees.

Ledbetter and Hoyt went out to the crash site and found more than a hundred farmers and mountaineers gathered around the crippled plane, waiting to see what this crazy pilot and equally crazy mechanic could do with it.

The biggest initial problem was the landing gear, which had been sheared off. The spectators tilted the Stearman up high enough for them to reattach the gear with its new strut. It took four days to fix that gear and install the new propeller and carburetor, and their worries weren't over. There was enough room for a takeoff, but the snow was too deep, so Ledbetter and Hoyt cajoled their audience into tromping down a path for the makeshift runway.

"If you get it off the ground, would you do a flip for us?" one farmer asked.

At that point Duke would have promised them an outside loop and fifty barrel rolls, so he agreed to the flip. For three hours, the men stomped up and down in the snow, clearing a reasonably firm path about three hundred yards long. Abe climbed into the front cockpit, Duke into the rear while several husky men held up the tail. Ledbetter revved the engine.

They almost crashed again at the end of the three hundred yards, when a wingtip hooked a bush. But Ledbetter wrestled the plane into the air and they headed for Nashville—without doing the promised flip, however. When they landed, part of the bush was still on the end of the wing.

Years later, Duke could laugh about the whole affair, but he adds, "I've always avoided going back to Cookeville or Oakley just in case there'd be someone there who'd recognize me as the guy who broke his promise to do that flip."

He never forgot Abe Hoyt's role in the story, though. The pilots were the dashing heroes of the time, but the Abe Hoyts of the airlines were just as important in their own way. Interstate also had an operations manager named Tom Ridley, "one of the finest operational men I've ever known," according to Ledbetter.

"He had an uncanny ability for predicting weather. He could predict the terminal weather at Atlanta, Chattanooga, or Nashville about as well as the meteorologists we have today. He died some years ago, when he was manager of operations in Fort Worth. But through the years, he saved an awful lot of pilots from sticking their necks out, especially the younger ones who were just coming on the line.

"We weren't too kind to those kids. They had to prove themselves to the older guys. If one of them felt a little cocky, he got absolutely no help from us and it was the survival of the fittest unless he'd see the light and learn from the older pilots. Otherwise the younger ones didn't have a chance. You couldn't survive unless you had been through the mill and you knew all the peculiarities of the weather existing over a particular route. Because then we didn't fly above it, we flew right into it or under it. We got away with a lot of stupid things and in no way could we credit our ability and knowledge— we were just learning, by trial and error."

Many of the veterans were afflicted with certain idiosyncrasies that fascinated the press. Interstate pilot Gene Fricks confessed to a reporter that in good weather, he read Shakespeare and did crossword puzzles. Asked if he ever prayed in the cockpit, Fricks shook his head.

"I don't do any praying while I'm up there," he declared. "I believe in doing my praying on the ground."

The subsequent published interview explained there was no need for Fricks to pray at all because "he has the blue-gray eyes of those who fear nothing on earth."

Gene's wife read this breathless account and told a friend, "He failed to mention that he frequently sings religious songs up there."

Nobody, the pilots included, really objected to florid reporting because in those days any publicity not involving a crash was only too welcome, even if it was pure fiction. Interstate's colorful chief of operations in Atlanta, Colonel W. G. Schauffler, Jr., was the innocent victim of journalistic hype. His official company biography, dutifully supplied to any reporter requesting it, naturally, included the fact that Schauffler had piloted the first American plane to fly over German lines in World War I. It neglected to mention what the mustached operations chief freely admitted: he flew over the German lines only because he was lost. Schauffler did have the distinction of being the first Army officer to parachute from a plane, but the public relations department wasn't satisfied with this legitimate honor. He also was identified as a former newspaperman who scooped the world on the sinking of the *Titanic*—which came as a complete surprise to the *New York Times,* whose brilliant managing editor, Carr Van Anda, was the first to deduce from the early sketchy reports that the giant liner had gone down.

When Interstate began carrying passengers, the news media's tendency to glamorize airline activities was still prevalent. On the occasion of the first inbound flight landing at Atlanta's Candler Field, the six passengers aboard the new single-engine Fairchild included a reporter from the Atlanta *Constitution,* who raced to his office and composed this lead:

"Out of the grey skies into the blue; soaring above a limitless sea of glistening snow-like clouds under a dome of azure; roaring between Georgia pine-clad mountains; gliding in a great yellow-winged blackbird through valleys ordinarily days away from the haunts of man; leaping the great ridges of the Cumberlands to find a city of more than a hundred thousand lying a thousand feet below; dipping here and there to make a brief exploration of mountain-guarded valley communities . . ."

And so on. Such purple prose must be viewed in the context of the times, when a trip by air was more of an adventure than a simple means of getting from Point A to Point B. To mention with false casualness "Oh, by the way, I flew from Buffalo to Cleveland the other day" was the equivalent of one's bragging that "I went two rounds with Jack Dempsey the other day."

Rare was the passenger who honestly sensed the majestic beauty of flight. The average person who boarded an airliner was too nervous to wax poetic about the experience, the *Constitution*'s reporter notwithstanding. The pilots, in fact, were far more appreciative, and it is no coincidence that most of the great literature on flying has come from the aviators themselves, men like Antoine de Saint-Exupéry and American's own Ernest Gann, who could put into words what their hearts and brains were telling them.

"Some of what I saw I can never forget," Duke Ledbetter reminisces. "The beautiful coloring of sunsets, the sunrises, the cloud formations, the changing terrain below. You could never get bored, for even as you were marveling at the scenery you knew the engine could quit in the next sixty seconds and you were always watching ahead for some possible landing area where you could get in without clobbering yourself or tearing up the airplane."

Ledbetter, in fact, used to deliberately fly as much as twenty-five miles off course to seek out thunderheads so he could take pictures. He'd leave the camera lens wide open until it picked up a lightning flash. Duke achieved some sensational pictures this way—until he flew into a thunderstorm one night, hit a downdraft, and saw the wing wrinkle. He never did it again.

Such diversions, of course, occurred on the air mail flights; once the airlines started carrying passengers, some of the informality and individualism went out of the game. Not the risk, however. The dawn of the thirties found most airlines with no radios, no teletypes, and only the sketchiest of weather reports.

Farmers were the pilots' best friends. Weather Bureau forecasts were aimed at rural America, not the airlines, and operations managers at carriers like Interstate used to compile phone numbers of farmers along its routes for weather information. Interstate, which lacked a teletype system, would send warning weather advisories to its crews via Western Union or Postal Telegraph; the telegrams would be wired to the next station to which a flight was heading. All too often the plane would arrive and depart before the telegram got there.

When Si Bittner began flying passenger planes between Dallas and Los Angeles, he noticed a number of isolated ranches in the desert between Phoenix and Palm Springs, some of them not more than large shacks with no electricity. Every time he flew the route, he would tie a string around newspapers passengers had left on the airplane during previous stops and drop them at these little ranches.

This was Bittner's "newspaper route," and he was quite proud of this little gesture.

Most passengers were blissfully unaware of commercial aviation's technical deficiencies—which included the fact that pilots weren't required to take instrument training, had virtually no supervision, and were pretty much their own bosses when deciding whether it was really safe to fly or not. Sometimes that decision rested on the state of their bank account. When the bulk of an air mail pilot's income was based on how many miles he flew, the temptation was great to take a few chances. Night flying, for example, was far more dangerous than daytime, but it paid more.

Embry-Riddle was one of the airlines that paid its crews less than the going rate on the grounds that its mail route wasn't as hazardous as others. Lionel Stephan, an Embry-Riddle veteran who flew many years for American, remembered rather wistfully that the pay scale was a flat ten cents a mile with no base salary, and no differential for night work. "The company insisted a dime a mile was enough because we flew over level country," Stephan explained.

Embry-Riddle wasn't being cheap. Every airline figuratively (and perhaps literally) was counting the company's pencils at night. Air mail was not, at first, regarded as particularly reliable or punctual—a logical conclusion inasmuch as so much of it wound up going by train anyway. The carriers were paid an average of three dollars for every pound of mail flown, which explains why their early salesmen concentrated more on plugging air mail than air travel. Some of the early airline advertising even urged people to "fly with the U.S. mail."

If there wasn't enough mail to pay for the gas on a trip, ingenuity took over. It was a common practice to put wet blotters in the bottom of a mail sack, a soaked blotter weighing more than a dry one. The next inevitable step was to wrap bricks in ordinary paper and send them out via air mail. This lucrative practice, however, foundered when a new agent on an unnamed airline was briefed inadequately on proper brick mailing techniques. He merely tied an address label on a brick, affixed an air mail stamp to the label, and tried to send it to another station. A postal inspector intercepted it, bringing an end to airborne brick traffic.

This, it must be emphasized, was in the *very* early days of contract mail operations. Yet even when the airlines began supplementing mail pay with passenger revenues, station managers looked for ingenious ways to increase the poundage in those sacks. One method was almost universally employed: the station managers wrote letters to other station managers and sent them air mail. The percentage of company mail in a postal sack those days will always be one of aviation's unsolved mysteries.

Flying *with* the mail attracted people with one common denominator: they largely were neophytes, innocents aloft who balanced the asset of excitement against the liability of fear in this totally strange new environment. Lack of technical knowledge was almost a blessing in disguise, although it took some weird turns at times.

Duke Ledbetter was flying a passenger trip in one of Interstate's new Fairchilds shortly after the airplane became part of American. Each passenger had been given the requisite amenities that passed for 1930 in-flight service: a box containing a sandwich, apple, chewing gum, cotton for the ears, and two small ammonia capsules wrapped in tinfoil—the standard (and usually ineffective) remedy for airsickness.

Once airborne, Duke glanced back in the cabin to see if his charges were enjoying their lunch—and did a double take. One of them had just taken the ammonia capsules and was in the process of stuffing them in his ears. The others promptly followed suit.

Interstate's first passenger plane was the Stearman LT, a biplane with four seats in the fuselage. The pilot sat outside, still wearing the helmet and goggles of air mail duty. Not until the Fairchilds did Interstate allow the crews to wear some kind of business suit; the standardized uniforms would have to wait.

In most ways, Interstate was typical of all carriers in the American family. Their colorful personnel were virtually interchangeable, and so were stories told about them. One could find Murphys, Ledbetters, Hoyts, Proctors, and Ridleys at every station on the sprawling AA system, names that form a montage of American's gutsy and glorious past. From management to mechanics, some of the most renowned figures in the airline's history started with the predecessor companies before the eagle was born.

They were men like Paul Kent, who began as a mechanic at Robertson Aircraft in 1929, worked his way up to supervisor of maintenance, and after retirement in 1971 founded American's historical museum in Tulsa—its first and, at this writing, its only curator, a man to whom preservation of the past became a crusade.

The same year Kent went to work for Robertson, a feisty youngster named Jimmy Conner got a job as a mechanic's helper at the Universal Flying School in St. Louis, which was part of Robertson Aircraft. He was paid $60 a month and was in the school's hangar from 6 A.M. to 6 P.M. "It wasn't as bad as it sounded," he recalled later, "because a loaf of bread cost five cents and you could rent a nice house for thirty-five bucks a month." When he retired in 1972, he was manager of facilities and ground equipment maintenance for American in Los Angeles and, in accordance with the nomadic tradition of airline people, had served the eagle in such stations as Chicago, Memphis, Dallas, Fort Worth, Little Rock, Nashville, and even New Zealand during American's short-lived South Pacific service in the 1970s.

The man who hired Conner in St. Louis was Bob Rentz, manager of the flying school at the time. He and Lindbergh had been fellow Air Corps cadets at Kelly Field before they both joined Robertson, Lindy as a pilot and Rentz as operations boss who not only ran the flying school affiliate but supervised the Sunday sightseeing flights that were the principal means of meeting Monday's payroll.

Rentz ended his career at American in 1960, with 26,342 logged flying hours behind him and a unique reputation among passengers. Like Heath Proctor, Rentz was fascinated by the geography, history, and geology of the land that passed under his silver wings. He used to drive his car between the cities American served, picking up historical and geographical information that became part of his cabin PA announcements. He was one of the first American pilots—and perhaps *the* first—to utilize the cabin PA microphone as an informational tool for passengers, and his narrations drew so many raves that in 1949 the airline gave him its highest honor: the Award of Merit.

Rentz, however, was just as proud of another achievement. Along with Duke Ledbetter, Heath Proctor, and a colorful captain named Kit Carson, he founded the organization of senior and retired AA pilots known as the Grey Eagles. Its first national convention was held in Chicago in 1962, and one of its earliest goals was the establishment of a fund to help former comrades who had fallen on hard times, mostly men who had ended their flying careers long before there were generous pension plans. By 1984, the Grey Eagles Foundation had accumulated well over a half million dollars.

It was Proctor who gave the group its name, and Ledbetter remembers that the hottest controversy evolved around its spelling. "We argued for hours over whether it should be 'Grey Eagles' or 'Gray Eagles' and we finally chose the former because it didn't seem as old."

The organization is as much a fraternity as a retiree group, a receptacle for the countless memories of camaraderie and comradeship that began with the predecessor airlines. Each carrier contributed its share of characters. Like Ray Wonsey of Colonial, the pilot who gave a future President of the United States his first airline ride, a momentous event to be described later; Walt Braznell, who flew for Universal and Robertson and rose to the rank of vice president of flight after serving for years as the tough but beloved chief pilot in Chicago; Interstate's Fermon Stone, who flew the first mail trip from Atlanta to Jacksonville and back, a flight involving one forced landing and sleet so bad that when he landed in Atlanta, his face was a mass of red welts.

Southern Air Transport furnished some wonderful individuals, such as Henry "Hank" Myers, who was to fly more than one President. Also from S.A.T. came Vic Miller, who once landed a plane with a lion loose in the cockpit—this incident, too, will be recounted subsequently—and Joe Glass, who may have been the most taciturn pilot who ever flew for American or any other airline. After S.A.T. was merged into the parent airline, Glass was flying a trip from Los Angeles to Dallas and his copilot, looking down at the terrain below them, commented:

"That farm is well irrigated."

Glass said nothing. The next day, on the way back to Los Angeles, they flew over the same farm. Glass peered out of the cockpit window and muttered, "Yeah."

After they landed, someone asked Glass how he liked the copilot.

"Too talkative," Joe growled.

Not all the characters were from the pilot corps. Colonial had a young sales representative named Ralph Maugham, who retired in 1961 as American's director of interline traffic after thirty-three years' service. He is still remembered fondly by old-timers for whom he provided a memorable sight: he always chose to ride in the mail compartment of Colonial's Pitcairns instead of taking the train on company business. Colonial's employees would gape as he climbed out of the cramped compartment, always immaculately dressed in a Chesterfield coat and a derby—dignity superseding discomfort.

They were a hardy breed of courage and determination, these pioneering predecessors. Their one common bond was faith in commercial aviation's future, their only real unity an ability to regard adversity as a challenge to be overcome. Out of this they helped forge an American Airlines that gradually metamorphosed into the recognized leader of the adolescent airlines.

But first American had to endure internal bloodletting at the highest levels of command. For in seeking to unify, expand, and improve the airline's divergent route system, Avco invited a fox into the chicken coop.

He was Errett Lobban Cord, the *enfant terrible* of the industry.

3
Of Coburn, Cohu, and Cord

Mark well the date of April 29, 1930.

On that day, two years before E. L. Cord began his invasion by invitation of the Avco empire, Congress passed one of the most far-reaching pieces of legislation in the history of civil aviation.

It was called the McNary-Watres Act, but its real author was neither of the two Republican lawmakers whose names were on the bill, Senator Charles McNary of Oregon and Representative Lawrence Watres of Pennsylvania. The man who dictated most of its devastating provisions was Walter Folger Brown, postmaster general of the United States.

Brown was a Harvard-educated lawyer and politician from Toledo, Ohio, named by President Herbert Hoover to a job traditionally held by political hacks. Brown was no such animal, however; subsequent events were to portray him to the public as a combination of Attila the Hun and Al Capone, but in truth he was an intelligent, capable public servant with an admirable sense of responsibility toward his duties.

Those duties were outlined in the leather-bound portfolio given to all new cabinet officers on the day they take office, and they included the dictate that the postmaster general was "to encourage commercial aviation."

Brown accepted this quite literally, and also quite freely, even though at the time he couldn't have told the difference between a Curtiss Jenny and a Martin bomber. In appearance, he was a Victorian snob right out of Charles Dickens, his stern face hardened further by steel-rimmed glasses, high-necked stiff collars, and the top hat he insisted on wearing outside his office—a chapeau that required an official limousine with an abnormally high roof.

In his private life, he actually was something of an outdoors man who loved sailing, camping, and barbecue cooking. But only his close friends knew this side of him; on the job, he was a demanding, even dictatorial administrator who became almost obsessed with what he considered the sorry state of the airline industry.

For nearly two years, Walter Folger Brown conducted a thorough study of the U.S. air transportation system, and he didn't like what he found. It was a rags-and-riches potpourri of forty-four airlines ranging from well-heeled giants to shoestring operators, and they all had a single, distasteful common denominator: for the most part, they really weren't interested in developing passenger traffic, and never would be as long as they depended so heavily on mail pay, many of them for sheer survival. And Brown believed sincerely that the industry's future rested on passengers, not postal stamps.

The nation's air map offended Brown's orderly mind, its lack of integration actually feeding indifference toward passengers. There was only one legitimate transcontinental route, United's New York–Chicago–San Francisco service; to fly coast to coast any other way meant circuitous travel, the use of more than one airline, and several plane changes. And forty-four airlines, the postmaster general felt, were just too many. The majority were underfinanced, economically shaky, and unreliable. Furthermore, he was convinced that all mail contract carriers were getting away with murder, thanks to the government's rather lucrative mail pay system.

The pill that Walter Folger Brown concocted to cure all these ailments, in the form of the McNary-Watres Act, would have choked a dinosaur. The new law wiped out the generous $3 per pound average and established a maximum mail subsidy rate of $1.25 a mile regardless of poundage, and regardless of whether the available mail space was filled. The latter was the poison in Brown's pill. The $1.25-per-mile maximum rate would be paid only to the carriers offering the most space; the others would be paid less, at rates low enough to wipe them out.

If this wasn't enough to stagger the smaller airlines, Brown had an even stronger potion. The Act stated that any air mail operator with two years' operating experience could exchange its current authorization for a ten-year route certificate in recognition of its "pioneer rights." This sounded fair, except that the new law defined pioneer rights as belonging to the "lowest responsible bidder who has owned and operated an air transportation service on a fixed daily schedule over a distance of not less than 250 miles and for a period of not less than six months prior to the advertisement for bids." It was a definition that automatically disqualified a number of tiny pioneer airlines flying minuscule routes, many less than 100 miles.

In effect, McNary-Watres was a blank check, which Brown filled out and proceeded to cash. Some of its key provisions were so vaguely worded as to hand the postmaster general more authority than the law intended. He simply gave them his own interpretation, in accordance with the air transportation policy he was formulating. The Act required the Post Office Department to advertise for new bids, and added a new eligibility requirement he had thought up himself: every operator had to have at least six months' experience flying at night, over routes of 250 miles or more. Down the tube went a few more smaller carriers.

Brown did fail in an attempt to include a little item that would have eliminated all competitive bidding for mail contracts, giving the postmaster general total authority to name airlines of his own choosing. U.S. Comptroller General John McCarl raised the roof, and the provision was eliminated. But Brown wasn't unhappy, because the final version of the Act contained a supposedly innocuous sentence that allowed the postmaster general to extend or consolidate routes "when in his judgment the public interest will be promoted thereby."

Those eleven words were all he needed to consummate his grand scheme. To Walter Folger Brown, Big was Beautiful. He envisioned a drastically revised air map of the United States, featuring three competitive transcontinental routes, with all north-south routes feeding into this triple network. Only two weeks after President Hoover signed the McNary-Watres Act, Brown summoned the heads of the large airlines to Washington for a momentous meeting that was to last twelve days and go down in history as the infamous "Spoils Conference."

Uninvited were the smaller carriers, who had no role in Brown's grandiose blueprint. Throughout those twelve days, the postmaster general hammered, cajoled, threatened, and pleaded his case before the giants of the youthful airline industry. His main thrust concerned the three transcontinental routes. He praised United for developing the northern route, but said no single airline should have a monopoly on coast-to-coast air travel. United must have two transcontinental competitors, one operating a central route via such cities as Pittsburgh and St. Louis, and the other a southern route via Dallas and Oklahoma City.

Furthermore, Brown added tersely, he would not approve any route served by a combination of carriers with connecting flights. One route, one airline, and if that meant enforced mergers, so be it. He then told the participants to work out their own consolidation plans and report back to him.

Walter Brown was nobody's fool; he reasoned, quite correctly, that these rugged individualists couldn't reach any agreement if they stayed in session for twelve months. Sooner or later they'd have to come back to him and let him decide. Which in the end is what happened, although not without some hectic backstage maneuvering and verbal brawling that for a time threatened to blow Mr. Brown's intricate scheme into oblivion.

Right from the start, the postmaster general intended to award the central route to Transcontinental Air Transport and the southern route to American Airways. But there were two obstacles endangering this plan. The first involved TAT, which had never flown at night and therefore didn't qualify for the central route award. Brown circumvented this by "suggesting" that TAT merge with Western Air Express, which had plenty of night flying experience. Western's president, Harris "Pop" Hanshue, was furious and refused; he was attending the so-called Spoils Conference under duress anyway, and considered Brown's whole plan asinine. During one meeting, when the postmaster general was outlining his desire for the two new transcontinental routes, he asked Hanshue his opinion.

The stocky, fiery little president pulled out a gold watch, looked at the time, and growled, "I think it's a lot of bullshit. Let's go to lunch."

But Hanshue's battle was doomed. Eventually his own board of directors was to overrule him and force the merger with TAT that formed Transcontinental and Western Air, which in turn was to become Trans World.

An even harder nut to crack, however, was the award of the southern route to American. This collided with the formidable opposition of one Erle P. Halliburton, a wiry Oklahoma oilman who had founded Southwest Air Fast Express, which operated out of Tulsa into Texas, Missouri, and Kansas, a system that sat astride part of the potential southern route.

Halliburton, whose tough, craggy features gave the impression of a gunslinger about to draw, hadn't been invited to the Spoils Conference but showed up anyway. Southwest Air Fast Express (forming the wonderful acronym SAFE) was operating Ford trimotors, and the minute Halliburton heard about Brown's meeting, he called William Mayo, head of the Ford aircraft factory, informing him that if SAFE got a mail contract he was going to order another $600,000 worth of trimotors.

Mayo's boss, Henry Ford, was an avid supporter of President Herbert Hoover, and thanks to this foot inside the White House door, the postmaster general allowed SAFE to be represented. And Halliburton was far more effective than Hanshue in fighting Brown; he had the political clout that Hanshue lacked, and he wasn't afraid to use it. He spent the entire twelve days needling and heckling. At one point he raised so much hell that assistant postmaster general Irving Glover threatened to have him ejected from the building. And Halliburton had a worthy ally in the person of Comptroller General McCarl, who was constantly criticizing Brown for going beyond the intentions of the McNary-Watres Act.

SAFE, Halliburton argued, had just as much right as American to bid for the southern route, and probably more. He kept reminding Brown that SAFE had been willing to carry mail for about one-fourth the going rate, an offer the postmaster general had persistently rejected. Brown considered SAFE typical of the shoestring operators he wanted out of the picture—without a mail contract, it had lost some $1 million since its founding early in 1929, although its passenger service was reliable and highly regarded. Yet Brown knew that Halliburton's unrelenting pressure was the proverbial monkey wrench, and consummate manipulator that he was, he came up with an involved compromise.

First, he suggested that American Airways and SAFE bid jointly for the southern transcontinental route. Then, if Halliburton was willing, American would buy him out for $1.4 million—not a bad deal for the feisty Oklahoman, because that amount was about $700,000 more than SAFE's hard assets. Halliburton would have the same option—to buy out American if the big airline didn't want SAFE. But there was no chance of the rabbit devouring the wolf.

Yet Brown wasn't finished with this complicated finagling. He tossed in another provision to make sure American wouldn't balk at that $1.4 million payoff, one based on the assumption that the TAT-WAL merger would go through. Avco, it seems, owned some 30,000 shares of Western Air Express stock, which would go into the new TWA. So Brown sweetened the deal by proposing that Western pay $1.4 million to American for those shares, American thus acquiring SAFE for precisely nothing. The stock wasn't worth quite $1.4 million but a "half interest in a hangar at Tulsa" was tossed into the complicated transaction. Halliburton promptly sold out, the central and southern transcontinental routes going to TWA and American respectively.

By the time Walter Folger Brown finished rewriting the nation's air map, those two carriers plus United were operating 90 percent of U.S. airway mileage. While United actually received little of Brown's initial largesse, it did benefit from some of his subsequent route extensions, most of them aimed at keeping competition away from the Big Three's territories.

The postmaster general seemed particularly solicitous of American's welfare. This became painfully clear to Temple Bowen, who had gotten out of the airline business temporarily when he sold his Texas Air Transport to what became the Southern Air Transport combine. Only a few days after American was awarded the southern transcontinental route, Bowen started a passenger service between Fort Worth and Houston, under the name of Bowen Air Lines and then expanded the route to Oklahoma City and Tulsa—-right in American's backyard. He used swift Lockheed Vegas, which could fly rings around American's lumbering Fords and the combination of speed and lower fares quickly cut into the bigger airline's passenger traffic.

Vastly encouraged, Bowen applied for a mail contract between Nashville and Fort Worth. Brown's response was to hand American a Nashville–Fort Worth route extension, including mail authority, and Bowen's application was rejected. Late in 1931, Bowen discovered that the postmaster general was openly promoting American in the Houston area by having local mail carriers deliver handbills door to door urging residents to "Fly with American Airways." The circulars mentioned the airline's "new low fares with 10 percent reduction on round trips" and ended with "Fly With the Air Mail."

Bowen stormed into the Houston post office demanding an explanation, and was told by the embarrassed postmaster that "Washington" had authorized distribution of the handbills "to stimulate passenger business for air mail operators"—a curious alibi inasmuch as Houston was the only city to have such promotion. The Texan's angry protests ended the delivery service, and he got some measure of revenge via advertisements featuring Bowen Air Lines' new slogan:

"Fly *Past* the Air Mail!"

Brown interceded on American's behalf in another instance, this one involving Frank and William Robertson, who had sold their Chicago–St. Louis mail route to Universal/American. In the spring of 1930, the Robertson brothers founded a new airline offering passenger service between St. Louis and New Orleans, and after the Spoils Conference asked for a mail contract on the route. Brown blocked this bid by a somewhat liberal interpretation of his authority to extend an airline's routes. He added two spurs to American's southern transcontinental route at Jackson, Mississippi, one from Jackson up to Memphis and the other from Jackson down to New Orleans—both intersecting the transcontinental route at 90-degree angles, which would seem to cast doubt on their legitimacy as true extensions. To finish the demolition of Robertson's application, Brown extended American's Chicago–St. Louis route all the way to New Orleans.

In the two years that followed the Spoils Conference, however, American didn't sit around waiting for Brown's helping hand. One of its major moves was the purchase of Standard Airlines, a Western Air Express subsidiary that operated between Los Angeles and Dallas via Phoenix, Tucson, and El Paso. Its president was one of the most capable young airline executives in the U.S., a personable, curly-haired man named Jack Frye. Coburn wanted him to join American, but Frye opted to go with TWA and eventually became its president. As with Juan Trippe at Colonial, one wonders how American's history would have changed if either of these two industry giants had stayed with the Avco organization.

Coburn's own regime at American was doomed. He was trying valiantly to achieve more efficiency in the zigzagging route system through a number of consolidations and extensions, as well as seeking more cohesion within the airline's clumsy, sometimes even feuding divisions. The additions of Standard and SAFE, both with traditions of fierce independence, made matters even worse.

SAFE in particular was remarkably like the Colonials and Interstates in American's family. Its operations manager was Larry Fritz, a former Ford test pilot who was weaned on the trimotor "Tin Goose," as the Fords were known, and, as did most pilots, groused frequently at what he considered management's parsimonious policies. To save a few dollars, for example, Halliburton had ordered SAFE's Fords without self-starters; before every flight, it took three men to crank the old-style inertia starters by hand.

The airline's communications system was no less primitive than Interstate's. Don Urquhart, who was to become American's top liaison man with travel agencies, started out as a SAFE dispatcher in St. Louis, where one of his chief tasks was to handle the weather observations wired from farmers scattered along SAFE's routes. They were paid twenty dollars a month to perform this task, and generally were pretty accurate. So it came as a shock one day when a farmer telegraphed in a "visibility and ceiling unlimited" report. Urquhart dispatched the flight and a few hours later the angry captain phoned from Tulsa.

"We ran into one hell of a squall line," he complained. "That farmer must have been wearing blinders."

The next day, the same farmer reported "weather clear, visibility unlimited." The flight that Urquhart dispatched encountered heavy fog right down to the ground.

It happened again for the third consecutive day, and Fritz sent his dispatcher out to visit the overoptimistic weather observer. Urquhart returned from this mission, shaking his head when he confronted Fritz.

"Did he have an explanation?" Fritz demanded.

"He wasn't there," Don sighed. "He and his wife went off on a two-week vacation and left fourteen telegrams with their kid to send us, one every day."

But colorful pasts didn't change the realities of the present. Fred Coburn, popular and competent though he was, couldn't stem the flow of red ink. In three years, according to one estimate, American Airways had gone through some $38 million, which was $3 million more than Avco's initial capitalization. On March 10, 1932, a tearful Coburn told his office staff he was resigning at the directors' request.

Exit Mr. Coburn. Enter Mr. Lamotte T. Cohu, the short, powerfully built president of Air Investors, Inc., a participant in the original underwriting of Avco's stock. Cohu gave up that post to become president of American Airways, one of two decisions he was to regret. His other admitted mistake was to go along with the board's decision to buy out two small airlines owned by the redoubtable and controversial Errett Lobban Cord.

E. L. Cord began his career as a bus driver in Arizona. Short in stature but large in ambition, he quit that job to sell automobiles in California, worked his way up to sales manager, and amassed enough capital to purchase control of the Auburn Motor Company, which he later merged with Duesenberg. The famous Cord car that bore his name was America's first front-wheel drive automobile.

But Cord, a restless wheeler-dealer with enormous ability, wasn't satisfied just to be running Auburn. He wanted to get into the airline business, a desire motivated partially by his fascination with technological challenges. The holding company he had organized, the Cord Corporation, included Lycoming engines, and Cord himself had helped design a new aircraft engine lighter and more economical than any other power plant of its time.

Aviation historian R.E.G. Davies suspected that Cord's airline yearnings stemmed from his admiration for and desire to emulate Henry Ford. Whatever the reason, he achieved his ambition in typical Cord fashion: he started not one but two airlines.

He launched the first in March 1931—Century Air Lines, operating a fleet of fourteen brand-new Stinson SM-6000 trimotors between Chicago–St. Louis and Detroit–Cleveland. Three months later his second airline, Century Pacific Lines Ltd., began service on a San Francisco–San Diego route via Oakland, Fresno, Bakersfield, and Los Angeles, again using the new Stinsons, an airplane in many ways superior to the Fords and Fokkers. It was quieter than the Tin Goose and faster by a good fifteen miles an hour, with a roomier cabin that held ten passengers in what was then relative comfort.

His West Coast airline had seven competitors when it inaugurated service; in less than three months, Century Pacific had carried 55,000 passengers and was in the black. Its fares were attractive, less than rail and half of what most of its airline competitors were charging. The eastern service was equally successful, and Cord began adding cities to his upstart network, Century offering through service from St. Louis to Cleveland, and Century Pacific opening a California–Phoenix route.

This was an open declaration of war against American Airways, but Cord suddenly found himself embroiled in a two-front conflict: his pilots went on strike. Cord, in an unexpected economy move, had cut their salaries, and the pilots claimed they were already being paid less than their brethren on other carriers. They had joined the newly formed Air Line Pilots Association (ALPA), and the last thing the young union needed or wanted at this stage of its own organizational difficulties was a strike on a relatively insignificant carrier. But ALPA supported the Century pilots, and the war of words was vitriolic. Cord had an anti-union reputation anyway, and he didn't help clear the atmosphere when he called pilots "a bunch of chauffeurs."

The pay cuts *were* drastic. Century had been paying $350 a month plus $3 an hour for daytime flying and $5 for night duty. Cord reduced Century Pacific's pay scale to a flat $150 a month, and when he threatened to apply the same reductions to Century's pilots, the airmen on both carriers walked out. Cord promptly began hiring replacement crews and after training them, reinstituted service. It was no wonder that the union's official historian, George Hopkins, wrote that "Errett Lobban Cord was to ALPA what Satan was to the early Christian church—both encouraged membership."

The strike, however, went far beyond its historical significance as a labor relations incident; it happened to be the first walkout by airline pilots in the United States. More important was the fact that it led indirectly to Cord's involvement with American Airways. And, once again, Walter Folger Brown got into the act.

Prior to the strike, Brown had been privately urging Cord to bid for mail contracts. He even called him to Washington to discuss the possibility. The independent-minded E.L. balked. "I don't want any air mail," he told the postmaster general. "I'd rather paddle my own canoe."

Brown wasn't particularly pro-labor himself, and when Century reopened with "scab" crews, he still kept pressing Cord to "go into business with the other air mail carriers," saying quite frankly that they couldn't afford to carry passengers at Century's fares. E.L. snapped that he didn't want "any of this government money" nor did he want any involvement with the big airlines. Cord, in fact, years later claimed that Avco had fomented the strike. "Some men came over from Cincinnati," he told an interviewer. "They came out of the Aviation Corporation to organize our pilots and shut us down."

There is absolutely no evidence to support this charge, but Cord apparently believed Avco was out to get him, and this conviction makes subsequent events more understandable. There is reason to suspect that Brown unwittingly played into Cord's hands by informing Averell Harriman there was no way to get rid of the maverick entrepreneur other than buying him out or joining forces with him.

And this Harriman set out to accomplish. His first move was to send Sam Fuller, an Avco executive, to Chicago for preliminary discussions. Fuller informed Cord that Avco was interested in buying him out. When E.L. just laughed, Fuller asked him if he'd be interested in merging Century into American Airways. If so, Harriman would like to see him in New York.

Cord said he'd think it over, and Harriman, scenting progress, dispatched Lamotte Cohu to Chicago for further discussions. Cohu thought him "a personable, intelligent guy, and I was quite impressed with him." He didn't get the same impression when he met a few days later with Fred Coburn in New York. (Coburn was still president at the time.) They argued over Coburn's insistence that no airline could make money carrying passengers, a view that E.L. held in total disdain.

After seeing Coburn, Cord met for three nights with Harriman at the Union League Club and finally agreed on a a deal whereby Cord would exchange the assets of his two airlines for 140,000 shares of Avco. Cord also would become an Avco director.

The agreement was consummated in April 1932. To his dying day, Cord was to insist there was far more to it than selling his two airlines for an exchange of stock and a promise to go on Avco's board. He claimed that Harriman offered to let him run all Avco operations, not only the airline but its other properties. He hinted that he was instrumental in Coburn's dismissal and Cohu's becoming president, that when he asked Harriman what he was going to do about Fred Coburn, Harriman told him he had Coburn's resignation in his pocket—"all I have to do is put a date on it and I'll tell Coburn."

This doesn't jibe with other accounts, which indicate that Harriman had no intention of letting Cord run the whole show. There is agreement, however, that Fred Coburn deserved a better fate. American's troubles were far from his own making, and there was a tragic element to his departure—his son was killed in the crash of an American Airways plane near San Bernardino, California, the day before he was fired.

His successor's seat was barely warm before Cord began making waves. E.L. let it be known that he thought American's operations were just plain sloppy, especially in the vital area of maintenance. Whatever one thought of Cord's rapport with pilots, there is no doubt his tiny airlines were run tautly and well. Cord related one incident when he was at the Newark airport and saw an American trimotor land. When he walked over to the plane, he noticed that several wheel spokes were missing and he also found a thick layer of oil on the cockpit floor. He ordered a mechanic to summon Cohu from American's headquarters in Manhattan, and when the president finally showed up, they got into a heated argument. According to Cord, "That started the fight between me and Cohu."

"He thought I was some punk from out west," E.L. recalled long after he left American. "He played up to Harriman and Lehman, and thought if he was strong enough with them he'd be able to save his neck no matter what happened."

Cohu never had a chance to prove his worth at American. His tenure lasted less than nine months and included only one event of note—the best publicity any airline had gotten to date. On July 2, 1932, an American Airways Ford trimotor flew the just-nominated Democratic candidate for president from

Albany to Chicago, so he could deliver his acceptance speech in person before the convention delegates went home.

Franklin Delano Roosevelt delighted in breaking precedents. In the past, presidential nominees had waited about two months after the convention before the traditional acceptance, at which time a convention committee would officially inform him in person that he had been duly nominated. Then would come the speech.

FDR wanted no part of such moss-bound anachronisms. Even before his nomination was assured, he had discussed with dubious advisors the possibility of flying to Chicago the morning after the nomination and before the convention adjourned. He wanted to get there while enthusiasm was high and the delegates were still there. Roosevelt argued that flying would be a dramatic symbol of bold, fast action in a time of crisis. He also subconsciously may have been trying to demonstrate that a polio-crippled candidate wasn't as helpless as critics claimed.

One of his aides was Guernsey Cross, who happened to be a next-door neighbor of Max Pollet, district sales manager for American's Colonial division in Albany. Cross tipped him off to the governor's possible flight and Pollet informed his immediate superior, none other than Goodrich Murphy.

Murphy consulted the airline's top management, which wasn't very interested at first. Then Cross formally requested that a plane be readied at Albany for Roosevelt's use. The brass still seemed lukewarm, but condescended enough to suggest that the aircraft be one of American's new Pilgrims—Bill Littlewood's first of many contributions to the airline's equipment choices.

Actually, the Pilgrim was a fine airplane, but Murphy argued against using an aircraft with only one pilot. "It's also got only one engine," he pointed out. "If anything happened to Roosevelt, it would ruin the plane, not to mention the airline."

The next proposal was to use a Stinson trimotor, but Murphy opposed this, too. While the Stinson had a metal frame, the wings and fuselage were fabric-covered; Murphy said the all-metal Ford was safer and argued them out of the newer trimotor. Some officers wanted to fly the party free—"Roosevelt would owe us a favor," one remarked. Murphy insisted on a paid charter: $300 for a group of six, one way.

The Colonial division was operating only Pilgrims and Stinsons, so a Ford had to be ferried up from Dallas. It was parked at the Albany airport and word leaked out that a plane was standing by for the governor's use. Two days before the convention, FDR was asked by reporters if it was true he intended to fly to the Windy City. Roosevelt laughed. "I'm going to bicycle out to Chicago," he hedged.

At 8:30 A.M. July 2, a Saturday, the trimotor left Albany with eleven passengers aboard: the governor and Mrs. Roosevelt, their sons Elliott and John, three secretaries, two bodyguards, speechwriter Sam Rosenman, and Max Pollet. Dressed in a borrowed pilot's uniform, he was serving as cabin attendant—in effect, American's first. Ray Wonsey, division chief pilot, was the captain, and Fred Clark, another veteran, was copilot.

Lunch, catered by the Ten Eyck Hotel in Albany, was to be served after the first refueling stop at Buffalo—cold chicken, sandwiches, and chocolate cake. The other refueling point was Cleveland, and the flight plan called for a 2 P.M. arrival in Chicago.

Wonsey did his best, but ran into a combination of headwinds and the almost inevitable low-altitude turbulence of a hot summer day. Fifteen-year-old John Roosevelt was airsick almost the entire trip, but FDR kept sending radio messages ahead to Chicago assuring that despite the delay, it was a fine flight.

The cabin of any Ford trimotor has the noise decibels of a boiler plate factory; the only way to converse was to pass notes back and forth or merely shout. Before takeoff, Murphy and Pollet had prepared a series of questions to be handed the candidate in the interest of future public relations. At various intervals, Pollet passed these to Roosevelt, who scribbled his replies. The first one asked:

"How are you enjoying the flight?"

"My first in a big cabin plane," FDR wrote. "When I was in the Navy we had only open cockpit ships." (Actually, this was his first ride in *any* airplane.)

"What do you think of American Airways' service?"

"Excellent, and very comfortable."

"Do you think aviation has a future?"

"Yes, a definite but probably rather gradual growth each year."

Mrs. Roosevelt was asked if she thought flying "should appeal particularly to women for any reason?"

"I think it should appeal to everyone," was her diplomatic response, although she must have had tongue-in-cheek if she looked in the direction of her miserable youngest son.

Roosevelt also passed a note to Wonsey for radio transmission to Chicago mayor Anton Cermak. It read:

"Sorry—strong headwind makes us a little late but it is a delightful trip and we are getting a fine view. Franklin D. Roosevelt."

"A little late" was an understatement. The plane fell so far behind schedule that Chicago advised Wonsey some impatient delegates had started for home. Rosenman and FDR decided to cut the acceptance speech drastically for fear they'd lose the attention of what delegates remained to hear it. The Ford finally arrived around 4:30 P.M. Chicago time, two and a half hours late, but was still greeted by a huge, cheering crowd and a horde of photographers, most of whom fortunately shot the smiling candidate from angles that also displayed the American Airways insignia on the trimotor.

The precedent-shattering flight wasn't the only interesting publicity American generated that summer. It came to light that a young copilot, hired under the name Charles Howard, actually was an incognito Howard Hughes. The millionaire apparently wanted to get some airline experience, but whether anyone at American really knew his true identity when he was hired is a mystery. There is a strong suspicion that *somebody* knew and was just waiting, with Howard's permission, to break the story when he left.

Hughes stayed only two months, flying mostly a Fort Worth–Cleveland trip for a salary of $250 a month—the only steady job he held in his life. He doesn't seem to have been as incognito as claimed, for several of the captains with whom he flew claimed later they were aware he was Howard Hughes. One of them, Ted Lewis, had "Charles Howard" assigned to him on a night trip from Glendale, California, to El Paso. A photographer showed up before departure and wanted to take a picture of the copilot—a strong clue that his identity wasn't exactly a secret. Howard posed dutifully for a shot showing him loading baggage, a shy smile on his face. He borrowed Lewis' white uniform cap for the picture.

Their aircraft was a venerable Fokker F-10 trimotor, the same type of plane in which Knute Rockne had been killed the year before. En route to El Paso, they hit one thunderstorm after another, had to overfly Phoenix, and finally landed in Tucson, where a ground crew informed them an American F-10 had crashed near El Paso. Their plane was commandeered by a relief crew ordered to fly a medical team to the crash site, so Lewis and his copilot went to a hotel for some sleep.

Hughes registered under his assumed name, but the desk clerk recognized him.

"Mr. Hughes," he blurted. "I worked for you when you had to remake *Hell's Angels* in sound. I dubbed in all the loud German officers' voices."

Hughes said nothing, but the next morning he invited Lewis to breakfast and told one story after another about the making of *Hell's Angels.* When Lewis mentioned they'd be flying back to Glendale that night, Hughes shook his head.

"Not me," he smiled.

"Why?"

"I won't fly that junk again. I'm going to New York as a passenger."

That flight he made with Lewis was his last as an American pilot. Later he reportedly flew for Eastern briefly, also incognito, but this is believed to have been more of a rumor than a fact. He did encounter Lewis at LaGuardia Airport, where he landed after his record world flight in 1939. Hughes' Lockheed Lodestar was being moved into an American hangar and he spotted Lewis, who was watching the action. Howard walked up to him and shook his hand.

"I remember you," he said cordially. "From that trip to El Paso, wasn't it?"

Hughes bought into TWA six years after his stint at American and apparently never gave a thought to American as an alternative investment. But Lamotte Cohu probably would have preferred him to E. L. Cord. (Hughes did hire Cohu years later to replace Frye.)

For Errett Lobban was becoming increasingly irritated with Avco and its money-losing airline. His boiling point was reached when Avco's directors announced plans to purchase certain assets of North American Aviation, a holding company almost as big as Avco itself. North American owned Eastern Air Transport and Sperry Gyroscope, among other properties, and had interests in Pan American, Curtiss-Wright, and Douglas Aircraft. The Avco board, having rid itself of Cord's two airlines and folded most of their routes, had in mind to merge some of Eastern's routes with American's. The plan was to issue two million additional shares of Avco stock and use the proceeds for the North American takeover.

Cord owned 25 percent of Avco's stock and those two million new shares would dilute his interest to 15 percent, a prospect which caused him to declare war. His first move was to obtain a temporary injunction that stopped the directors from finalizing the deal. His second was to acquire as much Avco stock as possible and then launch a proxy fight, which he personally directed from a command post in New York's Biltmore Hotel. Leased telephone wires connected him to aides in Chicago and Los Angeles.

Both Cord and Avco began wooing the company's 28,000 stockholders via full-page newspaper advertisements prepared by hastily hired publicity experts. Each side enlisted support from prominent individuals and institutions. Avco used Captain Eddie Rickenbacker and Congressman Fiorello LaGuardia of New York; Cord had in his corner the E. F. Hutton firm and the National City Bank.

Back and forth flew the charges and countercharges. Avco asked shareholders if they wanted the company dominated by the likes of Cord or "the present management which has brought the company to its position as America's leading air transport company." It charged that Cord, referred to as a "certain maker of airplanes, airplane motors and automobiles," was against the merger because he wanted to sell his own products to American Airways and was afraid of competition from North American's subsidiaries.

Representative LaGuardia brought up the Century strike and claimed Cord would likewise cut the salaries of American's pilots, invite another walkout, and then hire inexperienced pilots. The American Federation of Labor's crusty president, William Green, issued a statement labeling Cord as "hostile to union labor."

Rickenbacker's support for Avco stemmed from his desire for an American-Eastern merger. One of aviation's most forgotten historical footnotes is that Captain Eddie was an American vice president at the time of the proxy war. Harriman and Lehman had hired him away from General Motors in April 1932, shortly after Cohu became president, although his duties were extremely vague and his achievements nonexistent. Rickenbacker liked E. L. Cord—they were both Horatio Alger types who had come a long way with little formal education—and actually tried to serve as a peacemaker between the warring factions. It was his belief that combining Eastern's north-south system with American's east-west routes would solve their seasonal difficulties. American suffered in the winter months, which were profitable for Eastern, and vice versa.

Cord's counterattack hit hard at Avco's poor track record, making much of the fact that under this board the company had lost $38 million since 1929. He accused the directors of everything but wife-beating—"unwarranted speculation, gross mismanagement, extravagance, waste and inefficiency."

Almost from the start, Harriman and Lehman knew Cord held the upper hand, even though one of E.L.'s allies, E. F. Hutton, pulled a boner in the form of a brochure mailed to Avco stockholders. It contained a balance sheet for the Aviation Corporation listing the losses since 1929, and Lamotte Cohu's name was included in the roster of executives responsible. Cohu, of course, didn't become president until early 1932, and he filed a $1 million libel suit over it (he never collected).

Even before this blunder, however, Harriman and Lehman had quietly contacted Cord's lawyers and proposed an armistice. They reached an agreement before a single stockholder's vote was counted, and Cord emerged the victor, with 55 percent of Avco's stock. When all the shooting stopped, Errett Lobban Cord was the new chairman of the board and Avco had become a subsidiary of the Cord Corporation.

The proverbial and inevitable ax flashed, Lamotte Cohu being the first and most prominent victim. Rickenbacker offered up his own head. He went in to see Cord and asked bluntly, "Well, E.L., when do you want it?"

"Want what, Eddie?"

"My resignation."

Cord looked at him, remembering Rickenbacker's reputation for total honesty, his war-hero status, and their past association. They had known each other for years, a friendship dating back to the captain's automotive activities.

Cord said softly, "Eddie, I don't want it."

But Rickenbacker insisted, although he agreed to stay on for a month or so. He was still officially an American vice president when Cord decided to move the airline's headquarters from New York to Chicago, and that was Rickenbacker's excuse to leave. Thus we come to the third "what if": it might have been Captain Eddie of American instead of Captain Eddie of Eastern.

American officials who had opposed Cord had their figurative bags packed when he won. Some had been extremely active in their opposition, such as Julian Lyles, assistant general traffic manager. He had contacted all traffic managers throughout the system, asking them to wire stockholders that Lamotte Cohu was doing a great job. Burck Smith, traffic manager in Austin, questioned the wisdom of the telegram campaign.

"Why are you doing it?" he asked.

"Because Cord is a real son of a bitch," Lyles explained.

After the proxy fight, they happened to meet in Austin at a sales conference.

"I see where that son of a bitch is now in control," Smith observed caustically.

"Yeah," Lyles said, "but now he's a nice son of a bitch."

The one person who more than anyone else expected to be purged was none other than Burck Smith's older brother, the man Cohu had named vice president of operations. This was a tall Texan by the name of Cyrus Rowlett Smith.

4
They Never Called Him Cyrus

Before Lamotte Cohu was run over by the Cord machine, he at least had enough time for his greatest contribution to American Airways—recognizing the talents of one C. R. Smith.

Cohu inherited him from the Coburn regime, which, in turn, had inherited him from Southern Air Transport. By the time Cohu became American's president, the young Texan already had established himself as a comer. But Cohu went beyond regarding him as merely promising. When the proxy fight started, he already was letting C.R. run the airline, and there is strong reason to believe he was grooming Smith as his eventual successor.

Cord's animosity toward Cohu evidently blinded him to the latter's very real achievements, chief of which was his consolidation of the unwieldy four divisions into two: Southern and Eastern, the first headquartered in Fort Worth and the other in New York. Under this arrangement, C.R. headed the Southern division but also commanded both as vice president of operations, based in St. Louis, the post to which he was named just before the Cord takeover.

Cyrus Rowlett Smith had gotten into the airline business not only by accident but under duress. He was assistant treasurer of the Texas-Louisiana Power Co. and reasonably happy in that job when the firm's president, A. P. Barrett, a gambling promoter at heart, bought control of the airlines that merged into Southern Air Transport. Already enamored of Smith's ability in his chosen profession, accounting, Barrett asked Smith to keep the airline's books and generally oversee its operations.

C.R. was horrified. "I'm not interested in aviation," he protested, in what may have been the most inaccurate appraisal of one's future ever uttered.

"You go ahead and take it over," Barrett persisted. "If you don't like it, you can come back here and I'll get somebody else."

"Okay, I'll try it for a while," Smith said grudgingly.

Thus in 1928 began the saga of a man who by all standards of measuring greatness must rank with the handful of giants who built the U.S. airline industry—and there are many who believe he belongs at the very top. Trying it "for a while" turned into a forty-five-year career during which he served not only as American's chieftain, but as a progressive influence on the entire industry, a wartime leader of immense stature, and a cabinet officer.

Quite a list of accomplishments for someone born into near poverty September 9, 1899, in tiny Minerva, Texas. Minerva was just the first in a long roster of towns in which he lived during nine years of wandering around Texas and Louisiana, his father stopping off wherever he could find work and moving on when the job ended. The family finally settled in Amarillo—a traumatic stop, as it turned out. Smith's father was a religious fanatic with a total inability or desire to establish roots. He simply walked out of the house one day and the family—by now consisting of C.R.'s mother Minnie, his two brothers and four sisters—never saw or heard from him again.

At the age of nine, C.R. as the eldest found himself the nominal head of the impoverished, deserted family. Minnie Smith insisted that all her children get an education, but C.R. also wangled himself a job as an office boy for the legendary Panhandle cattleman C. T. Herring. The salary was two dollars a week, and Smith's main task was to tell visitors Herring wasn't in.

Herring usually *was* in; as soon as C.R. got rid of an unwelcome caller, he would pop back into Herring's office and the boss would resume telling the youngster stories of the Old West. Being a naturally impressionable nine-year-old, C.R. instinctively began imitating the storyteller's posture. Herring always talked with his spurred cowboy boots propped on his handsome mahogany desk, and American's veterans forever remembered C.R. doing the same thing in his own office.

He acquired more from Herring than the feet-on-the-desk habit, namely a love of the West that in much later years developed into his collecting Western art, including originals by artists like Remington that are worth a fortune. But this affluence was a long way down the road. He worked for Herring three years, at which point Minnie Smith moved her family to Whitney, where C.R. obtained a series of other jobs, including manual labor.

But he still attended school. His mother had the courage and indefatigable resolve of a commando, and she was determined that all seven children would go to college. She herself supported them by taking in boarders and teaching school, but as soon as each child was old enough to work, he or she did just that. All earnings went into a college fund that Minnie called "The Smith Family Cooperative." She added her own contributions to the SFC as she became active in politics and eventually got to know Texas Governor Pat Neff, who appointed her to several state posts, including census supervisor.

C.R. never stopped working even as the family's fortunes improved. The best description of his boyhood was penned by Jack Alexander in *The Saturday Evening Post* some years ago. "Young Smith," he wrote, "didn't read Horatio Alger books; he was too busy living one." In truth, C.R. never had a boyhood, not of the relatively carefree nature most of us know. He was only sixteen when the First National Bank of Whitney hired him as a bookkeeper and teller at $30 a month.

He quit after a year for a better-paying job as bookkeeper for a cotton mill in Hillsboro, Texas. He was still there when the U.S. entered World War I. The draft depleted the mill's work force and Smith, who was putting in fifteen hours a day, hinted that he deserved a Christmas bonus.

His boss agreed, but the bonus was a box of cheap cigars; C.R. promptly quit, worked briefly for the state in Austin, and then entered the University of Texas, more specifically its school of business administration. Technically, he wasn't eligible for admission because he lacked sufficient high school credits. This didn't stop him; somehow he wangled special permission to enroll on a probationary basis.

To a youth older, wiser, and more experienced than his years, college studies were a breeze. He not only earned high grades but was president of his junior class and elected to two honorary societies. Typically, he wasn't satisfied with just going to school. In his freshman year he obtained a part-time examiner's job with the Federal Reserve Bank. Throughout his college career, he also operated an advertising agency he called C. R. Smith & Co.—a deceptively fancy title for a firm in which Smith was not only the lone executive but the sole employee.

C. R. Smith & Co. actually had New York and Chicago investment firms as clients; C.R. sold them mailing lists of stockholders he copied from corporate records in the state capitol. He branched out by copying the names and addresses of new parents from state vital statistics files and sold these to parents' magazines, infant food companies, and manufacturers of nursery and baby buggy equipment. Between his examiner's salary and the ad agency, he was making some $300 a month when he graduated in 1924—in those days a very respectable salary for someone not quite twenty-five.

In fact, his income dropped drastically when he obtained his first postgraduation job: a junior accountant for Peat, Marwick, Mitchell & Co. in Dallas at $150 a month. This well-known accounting firm was very aware of his unique entrepreneur record in college and wasn't afraid to assign him clients who normally would have been served by more experienced men. C.R. audited hotels, apartment houses, movie theaters, oil companies, cigar factories, and insurance companies.

The latter assignment provided a good insight into his character. Smith knew absolutely nothing about the complex insurance business and with only five days' notice he was handed his first auditing assignment for an insurance firm. He spent the five days in the state library at Austin reading up on the subject, borrowing many of the books to study in his hotel room at night.

Peat, Marwick, Mitchell thought enough of him to promote him to senior accountant, specializing in audits of public utilities. It was in that capacity that he met Barrett, who talked him into joining the Texas-Louisiana Power Co. as assistant treasurer.

C.R. learned the airline business as fast as he learned everything else. When he reported to Southern Air Transport, the vice president and general manager was Tom Hardin, a licensed pilot who seems to have been more of an airman than a businessman. At their first meeting, Smith proposed a deal.

"You know something about flying. I know something about accounting. I'll teach you accounting if you teach me how to fly."

This mutual instruction pact didn't work out to mutual satisfaction; Hardin did teach C.R. to fly, although he was never truly proficient, but Hardin apparently didn't learn enough about accounting—on Barrett's orders, within two years Smith replaced him as S.A.T.'s vice president and general manager, a rank he retained when Avco absorbed Southern Air Transport and C.R. became Cohu's chief lieutenant.

Cohu did far more than advance C.R.'s career. One major accomplishment was engineering the purchase of Transamerican Airlines, a company that started life as the Thompson Aeronautical Corporation. In 1928, Thompson bid successfully for CAM 27, a mail route between Bay City, Michigan, and Chicago. The airline followed this by opening a second route from Bay City to Cleveland via Detroit. A third expansion came with the inauguration of Detroit–Cleveland passenger service across Lake Erie, using a small fleet of Keystone-Loening amphibians, single-engine aircraft carrying six passengers and two pilots.

The ninety-one-mile overwater route took fifty-five minutes and proved popular, although the service was suspended during the winter because the amphibs couldn't land when Lake Erie froze. When they did operate, convenience was their biggest selling point—Cleveland's lakefront terminal was only two minutes from downtown and Detroit's only a little farther.

The Lake Erie inaugural flight featured a publicity gimmick: Amelia Earhart as the copilot. The Loening departed Detroit on schedule, but ran into fog and landed in the middle of the lake to await clearing. The amphibs initially were equipped with radios but they were receiving-only sets. By the time the fog lifted and the flight resumed, the newspapers already were out with banner headlines: AMELIA EARHART LOST IN LAKE ERIE. After the plane landed in Cleveland safely, the press accused Thompson of staging the whole thing.

The airline's traffic manager was Charles Rheinstrom, a brilliant, imaginative marketing man destined to rise high in American's hierarchy. In 1928, however, he was mostly a brash young salesman looking desperately for ways to drum up attention. The hue and cry over Amelia's supposed "fake" disappearance gave him an idea for an even better and legitimate fake—a stowaway.

Rheinstrom had a wealthy friend with a seven-year-old son who was immediately cast as the criminal. The boy arrived at the Cleveland waterfront terminal in a chauffeured limousine two hours before the crew was ready to board, and Rheinstrom stuffed him into a rear baggage compartment. Charlie had tipped off the captain but the copilot wasn't in on the stunt, and after takeoff, the captain complained that the Loening seemed tail-heavy.

"Better go back and check," he ordered.

The copilot's inspection of the rear fuselage disclosed the presence of the stowaway—who, incidentally, was dressed appropriately like an urchin and resembled an underfed refugee from *Oliver Twist.* The copilot bawled him out until the tears came, at which point Rheinstrom's script took an unexpected and extremely favorable turn.

Aboard the plane was restaurant magnate Gordon Stouffer, who interrupted the copilot's tirade by offering to pay the boy's fare. The copilot returned to the cockpit and informed the captain who radioed ahead to Detroit—the amphibs had two-way sets by now—and when they landed, the flight was met by reporters and photographers.

The unsuspecting Stouffer bought the youngster new clothes and took him to his Detroit restaurant for lunch, before returning him to Rheinstrom with earnest instructions to "make sure this poor lad gets back to his parents."

"Oh, I will, Mr. Stouffer," Rheinstrom assured him solemnly. "In fact, I've already located them."

The boys flying the Loenings were called "duck pilots" and they hung up an excellent safety record in the lumbering amphibs. The Lake Erie operation had only one fatal accident, a mishap that occurred when an engine failed. In the process of a dead-stick landing, one wing hooked the water and the plane cartwheeled. The passengers got out alive but copilot Johnny Kasper, who had flown for the German Air Force during the war, drowned.

Investigators blamed the crash on the captain, Cy Caldwell, himself a well-known airman. In 1927, he had flown Pan American's inaugural mail flight from Key West to Havana, although the honor came about quite fortuitously. The new Fokker supposed to make the Havana trip hadn't arrived in Key West yet, there was no other airplane available, and the mail service had to start by a set deadline or the contract would be forfeited. A frantic Pan Am official heard that Caldwell, an itinerant "have-plane-will-travel" pilot, was in the area with an ancient seaplane en route to Haiti. The official paid him a reported $250 to fly the inaugural trip and Caldwell became briefly famous—Thompson fired him after the Lake Erie accident. Thus did Fate prevent Pan American's first pilot from becoming an American Airlines captain.

The amphibian service was never profitable, because of the necessary winter shutdowns. The original one-way fare was $20 and there were subsequent price cuts in an effort to attract more passengers, first down to $15 and finally to $10.25. As with most airlines, mail brought in the bulk of revenues and selling air mail was the main assignment of Thompson's small corps of sales personnel.

The latter included a young man who went on to better things as a key and extremely popular American executive. Charles Speers started out in the banking business after graduating from the University of Minnesota, where one of his classmates was Charlie Rheinstrom's brother. Speers was working for the Illinois Trust Company's bonds department for $150 a month when Rheinstrom popped in one day and offered him a $50 raise if he'd join Thompson. Later Speers was to admit, "while I'd like to claim I had a lot of vision, actually it was that extra fifty bucks that got me into the airline business."

Rheinstrom couldn't have recruited a better prospect. Enthusiastic, and tremendously innovative, Charlie Speers became an airline marketing man respected throughout the industry—albeit ruefully by some of his competitors. He and the tall, rather handsome, curly-haired Rheinstrom formed an instant team that helped establish American's superb reputation in an industry that lives or dies on marketing acumen.

Rheinstrom took Speers to Thompson's general offices on the second floor of the First National Bank of Kalamazoo where he was introduced to the airline's president, Tex Marshall, himself a pilot and a rangy man who might have stepped right out of a Marlboro ad. Rheinstrom had offered Charlie the job of divisional traffic manager in Detroit, subject to Marshall's approval, and the president must have liked Speers because he suggested that he start work immediately.

"I'll fly you to Detroit myself," Marshall said.

When they got to the airport, it was foggy, so Speers took a train to his first airline post—one he had accepted despite some unanimous suggestions that he was out of his mind.

"I talked to my dad about taking the job," he recalls. "He asked me to discuss it with five businessmen whose judgment he trusted and respected. I remember they included a prominent lawyer and the vice president of a bank. They all told me to stay in banking. So I ignored their advice and joined the airline—on March 2, 1929."

Word got around quickly that Speers possessed both imagination and ingenuity in large quantities. In his own words:

"Selling air mail in those days was like trying to sell kosher food in Cairo. We couldn't admit it, but the weather factor made it very unreliable and it was hard to get companies to use it regularly. I started to sell it on the basis that the red, white, and blue bordered envelopes attracted more attention from the recipient. Our pitch was that air mail could be used as a promotional device, and a lot of companies bought the idea."

Speers freely admitted that Thompson, like most airlines, resorted to slightly dubious practices to assure at least minimum mail revenues.

"We made up a daily mail sack for every city we served in Michigan, and there were ten of them. We were being paid sixty-nine cents a pound and every sack plus its padlock weighed three pounds, so all we needed was one letter for each city and we'd get paid for three pounds of mail. Sometimes we didn't have a letter to put in a sack, so one of my jobs was to mail a promotional blotter to every city from the Detroit Statler Hotel. The last pickup was at ten o'clock every night and that was the only one we could use—if I mailed the blotters any earlier, they'd go by train and if I missed the ten P.M. pickup, they'd be held until the next day. I never sent a wet blotter, though, nor did we send out any bricks."

In those days, the word "traffic" was synonymous with "sales" but Charlie never let a definition limit his area of involvement. On days when the lake was flat calm, the Loenings had trouble getting airborne because their boat-shaped hulls needed a few bounces. Speers negotiated a contract with a girl who owned a speedboat service in Detroit right next to the Loenings' waterfront launching ramp. When Lake Erie was glass-smooth—which was rarely—she'd take out one of her speedboats and make waves so the amphibs could get airborne faster.

Early in 1931, Thompson changed the name of the airline to Transamerican as a subsidiary, with Thompson Aeronautical the parent company; the change coincided with expansion of the passenger service throughout the Michigan intrastate system, a new leg into northern Indiana, and a 225-mile extension from Cleveland to Buffalo—the latter a development that was to attract American.

Speers was happy working for an airline that seemed unafraid to try anything. It even experimented with Stinson mailplanes powered by Packard diesel engines, the first time this had ever been tried on a U.S. commercial transport. In this kind of environment, Charlie's innovative mind flourished. He came up with the idea of establishing a schedule pattern that eliminated the necessity of consulting any timetable—in other words, dispatching flights on the hour or half-hour on a regular basis. Years later he would introduce this on some American routes including American's New York–Chicago, one of the most competitive airline markets in the U.S.; after Speers installed it, American's share of that market soared from 25 to 60 percent.

Another Speers novelty with tremendous potential implications was the selling of discounted coupon books. He tried them out first in his own Detroit bailiwick, selling a book of ten Detroit–Cleveland trips at a 10 percent discount. Then he began offering a book of air travel coupons worth $250 for $212.50, a 15 percent discount. They were sold mostly to the big automobile companies, who loved the discount feature but complained about the requirement that a passenger had to have his coupon or "scrip" book with him in order to buy a ticket; they didn't want their employees running around with $250 worth of airline tickets, only to purchase one.

So Speers worked out a plan whereby each company held the scrip books in their possession and issued authorization cards to employees for their use. Charlie designed the ID card himself, a simple form of identification declaring that "I, John Smith, am authorized to draw on the scrip account held by the Duncan Motor Parts Co." Each card carried the bearer's signature and was co-signed by a designated company official.

Nobody at TAC's headquarters objected to the experiment; most officials, with the exception of Rheinstrom, showed indifference until Speers suggested that scrip books be sold throughout the system. This audacious suggestion raised the hackles of Tom Dunnion, the dour Scotsman who was company treasurer.

"Young man, you cannot do it!" Dunnion proclaimed. "You cannot sell air transportation on credit, like it was a piano or an automobile. It's impossible."

"It's not really credit," Speers argued. "The customers are just drawing against money we're holding ourselves."

"The answer's still no," Dunnion snorted. "You can keep selling the damned things in Detroit but nowhere else."

Speers did just that, increasing sales in the Detroit area to the point where Rheinstrom waded into the fray. He went right to Tex Marshall and won his approval to try the plan out systemwide. It worked just as well as it had in Detroit, with a single modification: they established a new price scale of $425 for every two scrip books, still a 15 percent discount; each customer bought another book when the balance dropped to $250.

The only disadvantage was the laborious process of tearing the coupons out of the books when used ticket vouchers came in. So Rheinstrom and Speers decided to handle the operation on an accounting basis, which eliminated the scrip books but retained the required $425 minimum deposit.

This was the genesis of the famed Universal Air Travel Credit Plan adopted by the entire industry in 1936. Speers inaugurated it at American three years earlier under the name "Universal Air Scrip Plan," when both he and Rheinstrom went over to American after it absorbed TAC. Remembers Speers:

"Between 1934 and 1936, American had it exclusively and it became a big competitive tool. We had a hell of a head start with all these companies on our books, and the big advantage was a certain amount of built-in loyalty.

"When it was adopted by the whole industry in '36, it gave American a chance to check the plan's record of sales—it was the record of all our competitors. We kept the 15 percent discount but we added a 5 percent discount for round trips, so card holders actually got a 20 percent discount in return for that $425 deposit.

"I remember our 1936 list included seventy-one companies, ranging from Acme White Lead to Zenith Radio. The plan became our basic sales weapon, because it gave salesmen something tangible to sell instead of just handing out timetables. In fact, in 1936 we changed the name of our department from Traffic to Sales—we weren't just soliciting traffic anymore, we were selling a product."

It is interesting to speculate what would have happened to Transamerican if American hadn't taken it over. Certainly it was an aggressive little airline, thanks to men like Rheinstrom and Speers, and at one time it even had some rather grandiose hopes of becoming an international air carrier. In March 1932, it negotiated a seventy-five-year agreement with the Icelandic government for landing rights in that country. Apparently the purpose was to use Iceland as a refueling stop for an air service to Europe; two years previously, one of Thompson's Loening amphibs actually had surveyed a route from Detroit to Copenhagen via Greenland and Iceland, with the approval of Denmark. In the spring of 1932, Transamerican got $5,000 from Pan American for an option to develop the route and three months later sold its Icelandic landing rights to the same airline for $55,000; this was shortly before American bought out Thompson and thus lost a chance to acquire an international route in the process. It was to take another thirteen years before American ventured into the international arena.

At this point in time, of course, commercial transatlantic air travel was strictly for the dreamers and prophets; American had enough worries trying to plug the biggest hole in its still-uncoordinated system, lack of a direct New York–Chicago route. Purchase of Transamerican, with its strong Chicago–Detroit–Cleveland–Buffalo service was the first step. The next was the acquisition of Martz Airlines, owned by the Martz bus company and possessor of a passenger route from Newark (then the air terminus for the New York area) and Buffalo.

The gap was closed. American no longer had to fly north to Albany and then west to serve Chicago, competing hopelessly against United's and TWA's more direct routing. But Cohu didn't stay around long enough to get credit. He was fired in December of 1932. On December 25, Lester D. Seymour became the new president of American Airways. E. L. Cord's Christmas present to the airline was his choice of a man who was deathly afraid of flying and always took trains.

It is perhaps regrettable that Lester Seymour is remembered mostly for his reputation as a confirmed airplane-hater.

In many ways, he was an able executive, curiously enough with an aviation background. He served with the Army Air Corps, albeit as an engineer who didn't have to fly, and before Cord talked him into heading American he had been a United Air Lines vice president. It remains a mystery, never explained even by Seymour himself, why he was attracted to the airline business, considering his jaundiced opinion of flying as a means of travel.

His selection was not solely Cord's idea. E.L. relied heavily on two men for advice: his chief corporate lieutenant, Lucius (Lou) Manning, and the Cord organization's lawyer, Raymond S. Pruitt. Both recommended Seymour as Cohu's replacement, Manning because he had heard Seymour was a good operations man, and Pruitt because C. R. Smith was the only other real candidate and Ray Pruitt disliked C.R. intensely.

The feeling was reciprocated, in spades. Those who knew both men well always claimed C.R. blamed Pruitt for his not achieving the presidency sooner than he did. It also was rumored that Pruitt was instrumental in getting Smith demoted shortly after the Cord takeover.

Seymour didn't need any help from the lawyer in that respect—he didn't get along with C.R. any better than Pruitt. Their feuding began almost immediately, fueled by C.R.'s habit of popping into Seymour's office and putting his feet on the president's desk while discussing business. During some conferences Smith would take out a magazine in the middle of a Seymour discourse and pretend to read it.

Such violations of corporate etiquette sent Smith back to Forth Worth, stripped of his title of vice president of operations but still holding—reportedly at Cord's insistence—his old job as vice president of the Southern division. It is only too evident that C.R. would have been forced to seek employment elsewhere except for the fact that Cord liked and respected him. When Cord emerged triumphant over the Harriman/Lehman forces, Smith had walked into E.L.'s office and told him he assumed he was now *persona non grata*.

"No," Cord said pleasantly. "C.R., you're just getting started."

But not even Cord's admiration could save C.R. from Seymour's antagonism and banishment to Fort Worth. C.R. seems to have gone out of his way deliberately to irritate and goad American's new president. He addressed him as "Prez" and if he wasn't using that derisive salutation, he'd call Seymour by his nickname of "Bing." Seymour had let it be known that only Cord, Pruitt, and Manning were to use the nickname, but C.R. ignored that order along with quite a few others. He simply regarded Seymour with undisguised contempt.

Seymour had a prizefighter's face, and a short-fused temper that Smith caused him to lose frequently. Once Seymour sent him an angry telegram warning, "If you don't follow orders, I'll take the next train to Fort Worth and fire you."

C.R. would insult him to his face; other officers laughed at him behind his back. The sad truth was that he commanded little respect or affection. Both his fear of flying and his personality were to blame. When he became president, American's engineering department consisted of Bill Littlewood and Otto Kirchner. "We don't need but one engineer," Seymour decreed, and fired Kirchner. Kirchner worked at Stinson until Littlewood convinced Cord he needed Otto back.

In some respects, Seymour deserved sympathy. Littlewood once commented that the president always seemed to be "in the midst of treason."

"The boys in the field would take no orders from him," Littlewood said, "and they wouldn't cooperate with each other. Under Seymour, the airline was pretty much a divided camp."

This was only too true. If C.R. stayed with American only through Cord's intervention, Seymour kept his own job mostly because Pruitt and Manning protected him.

And American did make some progress under its non-flying leader. Three new types of transports were added to a fleet already overpopulated with too many different types, but two of them were improved airliners. The exception was a low-wing Stinson trimotor, called the Model A, which Cord—who owned Stinson—insisted that American buy, to the eventual consternation of every American pilot who had to fly one.

The Model A carried nine passengers and handled like an iron bathtub with wings; the cockpit was so small some pilots couldn't squeeze into it. Byron "Dinty" Moore, who logged more than five million miles flying for American, chronicled the Stinson's many faults in a book, which included this succinct description of just one Model A idiosyncrasy:

"The slightest drizzle, when mixed with the oil on the windshield from the center engine, made it as untransparent as the stained glass of a church window. You couldn't see out the side windows either—the outboard engines were in the way."

For reasons known only to himself, some American official ordered all

Stinson A pilots to refrain from flying on instruments. The order was diso-
beyed unanimously; there were too many times when instrument flight was the
only alternative to crashing.

Cord himself drew up the specifications for the Model A, but it must be said
that he did have some good instincts for aircraft design. The high-wing Stinson
trimotor wasn't a bad plane—some pilots liked it better than the Ford—and
it should be remembered that E.L. was a fairly capable pilot himself, with a
great love of flying even in bad weather. On one occasion, he asked Dan Beard
to accompany him on a flight and Beard refused to take off because of the
weather. Cord overruled him and they went anyway.

The second of the aircraft trio that joined American in this time period
stemmed from another Cord concept. He wanted a single-engine transport
built around the factor of speed, and he talked designer Gerard "Jerry" Vultee
into building the Vultee-1. It carried only eight passengers, but with a powerful
Wright Cyclone engine and a retractable landing gear, it cruised at more than
200 miles an hour—the fastest airliner of its day.

American bought twenty in an ill-considered deal; while the Vultee was a
bargain at $35,000 per plane, by then any single-engine transport was consid-
ered obsolete regardless of speed. Otto Kirchner always thought the swift
Vultee was its brilliant designer's biggest mistake.

"Jerry Vultee had always been a great believer in the superiority of single-
engine performance," Kirchner said. "His studies showed that no combination
of engines could perform as well as a single engine. But one factor was lost
sight of or ignored, and that was safety. The fact was that if one engine of a
two- or more-engined plane failed, the aircraft could still fly. If Vultee had not
clung to the old concept, he might well have built his own version of the Boeing
247 or Douglas DC-1. And the irony was that he was killed in the crash of
one of his single-engine airplanes."

Neither the Stinson A nor the Vultee lasted very long in American's fleet.
The airline eventually peddled some Stinsons to Mexico, and a few were used
as makeshift bombers in the Spanish Civil War. At least seven Vultees also
wound up with the Spanish Air Force, and several served in Turkey. But the
third new equipment choice had C.R.'s name, not Cord's, stamped all over it.

This was the famed Curtiss Condor, the nation's first sleeper plane. In most
respects it was a step backwards in aircraft design—a twin-engine biplane
whose forest of struts and wires provided built-in headwinds. Eastern was the
first airline to operate an early model, and until Smith got interested was the
only purchaser. Curtiss-Wright tried to sell some to Pop Hanshue at Western
Air Express, and Pop summed up his low opinion of the underpowered airliner
with a classic appraisal.

"The only way I'd buy one," he snorted, "is if they built a tunnel through
the goddamned Rockies!"

But C.R. saw something in the clumsy Condor that intrigued him. While
in St. Louis on a business trip, he stopped in at the Curtiss-Wright factory there
to see the firm's president, Ralph Damon. Damon showed him a mock-up of

a Condor fitted out with Pullman-style berths, easily adaptable to the plane's fat-bellied fuselage.

Smith was so entranced he caught the next flight to Los Angeles, where Cord had his home. For several hours he extolled the potential of a sleeper transport on American's transcontinental route. It must have been some pitch, considering E.L.'s feelings toward competitor Curtiss-Wright, for Smith summoned Damon to the West Coast with instructions to bring blueprints and a model.

Damon showed up carrying the model under his arm; it was a beautifully crafted miniature with tiny dolls occupying the berths. He left Los Angeles the next day with a $500,000 order for ten Condor sleepers, and something else: the start of a close relationship with C. R. Smith that would one day elevate him to American's presidency.

The Condor American bought was vastly improved over the twin-tailed early model Eastern was flying; American's had a single tail and more powerful engines, plus such features as seventy pounds of soundproofing material, a retractable landing gear, and a significant new development, variable-pitch propellers with three blades instead of the usual two. The props were set at one angle for maximum takeoff "bite" into the air, and adjusted to a different angle at cruising altitude; it was not only more efficient but quieter, with less vibration. Aware that to the public, variable pitch could have meant anything from baseball to opera, American's publicity explained it as an "aerial gear shift," which in effect it was.

Passengers loved the Condor's roomy comfort. In American's configuration, the big biplane carried eighteen passengers by day and could accommodate fourteen in the surprisingly spacious berths. Compared to the noisy, rattling Fords and cramped Stinsons and Vultees, the Condor interior was palatial and compensated for the airliner's abysmal performance. The top speed was only 145 miles per hour, and this was achieved on extremely rare occasions—even to hit 120 m.p.h. it needed a shallow dive and/or a tailwind.

Pilot enthusiasm for the Condor ran several thousand feet below that of passengers. It wasn't hard to fly, and its chief virtue was its low landing speed, less than 50 m.p.h. It flew like a big box kite and the crews learned to "mush" it in, putting the plane almost on the edge of a stall and then letting it float down to the ground. They also liked the Condor's cockpit visibility; not until the jet age's DC-10 could any transport American bought equal the Condor in that respect.

But the airplane's snail speed was only one of several major flaws. It was exceptionally vulnerable to ice, and the pilots tried to avoid any weather conducive to icing. Duke Ledbetter, who flew Condors between New York and Chicago, was one of the pilots who employed a crude, anti-icing technique called "shaking the grate."

"Ice would form mostly on the guy wires," he recalled. "They'd start vibrating, and if it didn't stop, eventually the wires would snap. We developed the trick of deliberately backfiring the engines, so the heat would melt at least some of the ice."

This in itself could be hazardous, for the plane was something of a flying firetrap. Bill Littlewood hated the Condor with a passion.

"It was a dangerous airplane. The frame was welded steel, but the fuselage and wings were cloth-covered and there was no firewall between the engine and baffle. Two burned up on the ground at Los Angeles. It was phenomenal luck that a Condor never caught fire in the air."

For a plane of its size, the Condor was unusually light, and flying one in turbulence was akin to riding in a roller coaster. Littlewood was aboard one of the early test flights, and the pilot flew into a thunderstorm. The plane bounced so hard that Littlewood's head went right through the cabin's canvas ceiling.

A Condor subjected to icing could be heard fifty miles away, creating a banshee howl that was absolutely frightening. Donald K. Smith, another veteran airman with Condor experience, said the sound could send shivers up his spine.

"It was almost indescribable. I never heard anything as eerie until I retired, moved to Tucson, and heard the baby coyotes howl at night."

Any encounter with ice required a thorough inspection at the first available airport. Paul Kent was a maintenance supervisor at Chicago when a Condor landed one night and Kent noticed that a wing appeared damaged. When mechanics lifted the wing for inspection, every strut fell off.

"Ice vibration had weakened them," Kent recounted. "We examined the rest of the airplane and found the same thing—all that was holding the wings together were the guy wires."

The very first Condor delivered to American nearly came to an embarrassing end. Earl Ward, the airline's operations manager at the time, was flying it from St. Louis to Chicago where Seymour, C.R., and the rest of the brass were waiting for the arrival of their spanking new bird. The takeoff from the factory was delayed; by the time Ward reached Chicago it was almost dark and he couldn't find the airport.

Ward, a former Interstate pilot, flew around for a half-hour before he spotted a school building with arrows on the roof pointing to the airport. He was so overjoyed to find the guiding symbols that he forgot to lower the landing gear. Just before they touched down, Littlewood, who was in the cockpit, noticed that the gear warning light wasn't green, and yelled. Ward pulled up, lowered the gear, and came around again for a perfect landing. Seymour and C.R. thought he had just buzzed the field playfully.

Passengers, of course, were unaware of the Condor's drawbacks. With its distinctive color scheme—orange wings and a blue fuselage carrying an orange lightning bolt from nose to tail—it was the last word in air transportation. Eastern tried to steal a march on American by installing a few hastily improvised berths in its own Condors, but they couldn't equal American's Pullman interior. Admittedly, the berths had one inconvenient flaw: the uppers were fine but the lowers were practically on the floor, and they were always the last ones to be reserved. A passenger had to get down on his hands and knees to crawl into a lower.

Originally, American installed two private berths between the cockpit and lavatory, with the aim of attracting honeymooners. There was a great demand for such privacy, but American discovered that most of the reservations requests were coming from unmarried couples. Eventually the berths were ripped out and replaced with a lounge dubbed "the Sky Room."

Acquisition of the Condors led to the hiring of American's first stewardesses, something United had started three years earlier. The initial class, in April of 1933, consisted of four registered nurses: May Bobeck, Chicago; Agnes Nohava, Londale, Minn.; Marie Allen, Cincinnati; and Velma Maul, Burlington, Iowa—the vanguard of the thousands who would wear the eagle's wings in the future.

Their training consisted of three days of elementary instruction conducted in a Chicago hangar, and they were dispatched on their first flights with one simple admonition: "Treat each passenger as you would a guest in your own home."

For this brave quartet and these who followed them into Condor duty, life was not easy. Making up those berths was guaranteed to bring on backaches; the removable seat cushions were heavy, the curtain tracks frequently stuck, and to make up a lower berth required the muscular coordination of a contortionist. Not a few stewardesses fainted on the job, because of the heavy manual exertions in an unpressurized aircraft. American operated its Condors at a maximum of 12,000 feet, 2,000 feet lower than the government allowed but still an altitude that could cause breathing problems for a girl trying to wrestle with a balky berth.

Applicants had to be age twenty to twenty-eight, not more than five feet, four inches in height, with a weight maximum of 118 pounds and a "pleasing appearance and personality." The registered nurse requirement was kept in effect until 1940, when the supply of R.N.'s began to run low.

The 1933 pay scale for stewardesses started them out at $100 a month following a three-month probationary period. The girls got a ten-dollar raise after nine months of flying at least a hundred hours a month—and a hundred hours on a Condor was a prison term. But there were few complaints, not even when applicants found out they had to buy their own uniforms, which cost 60 percent of the first month's salary. The price broke down to $31 for the double-breasted jacket, $2.25 for a cap, $23 for a winter overcoat, $2 for a white shirt, 75 cents for a scarf, and 55 cents for a tie. Total: $59.55.

To Velma Maul went the honor of assignment to American's first stewardess-manned flight on the Condor's inaugural trip, from Chicago to Newark via Detroit and Buffalo, May 3, 1933. In addition to the three days of training, she and her fellow rookies had taken an airplane ride (the first for all but one) from Chicago to St. Louis, where they visited the factory and got a look at the new plane's cabin. Their in-flight instructions consisted mainly of learning how to serve coffee without spilling it in a passenger's lap. They also included the protocol advice that, when serving meals to the cockpit, "the pilot should be allowed to finish his lunch before the copilot is served."

This bit of priority didn't mollify the handful of crusty airmen to whom the presence of a young woman as part of the crew ranked slightly above engine fires on their scale of unwelcome situations. Fortunately for the stewardesses, the die-hard cockpit chauvinists were in a definite minority; most pilots regarded the girls as hard-working, courageous comrades doing a difficult job, and the Si Bittners on the line found them wonderful targets for practical jokes.

Gradually the pilots and stewardesses began to develop a team attitude toward their mutual task of getting people from Point A to Point B safely, while enjoying the trip in the process. The "first pilot"—they wouldn't be called captains until 1935—was instructed to "make one trip back through the cabin between each station and speak a brief word to the passengers."

"The pilot should confine himself to a pleasant salutation," the 1933 operations manual continued, "perhaps some brief comment as to the trip, unusual speed, or some well-known landmark on the ground."

The manual told stewardesses to "give every possible attention to airsick passengers without embarrassing them by centering attention on them"—a fiat that in actual practice was harder to achieve than making up a lower berth.

Every cabin attendant carried a strip map of the route she was flying, and it was suggested that she "become thoroughly familiar with the map so she can point out objects of interest or at any time be able to give the location of the plane." The latter was a must, for the most frequently asked question in those days was "Where are we?"

The 1933 list of stewardess do's and don'ts covered mostly rules for conversing with passengers. Such as:

Never discuss your own affairs.

Answer all questions positively and quickly, then turn the conversation back to the passenger.

If someone asks, "How do you like Bostonians?" answer "I find everyone interesting."

Always remember people want to tell YOU what THEY think.

Do not voice your own personal opinion about such topics as politics. Instead, turn the conversation back with, "I'm not sure. . . . What do you think?"

No set of rules could cover what neophyte riders might come up with. One stewardess asked a male passenger, "Sir, would you please fasten your belt?"

"I can't," he replied. "I'm wearing suspenders."

The redoubtable but diminutive Si Bittner was dutifully making a prescribed visit to the cabin and nodded pleasantly in the direction of an elderly lady passenger, who frowned back.

She said testily, "Young man, aren't you awfully small to be in charge of this big airplane?"

"Lady," he sighed, "I'm flying the damned thing, not carrying it."

The advent of stewardesses and the accompanying improvements in in-flight service were solid indications that American was maturing. The meal Velma Maul served on the inaugural Condor flight was good even by today's standards. She first offered salted nuts and sweet pickles, then came hot consommé, cold cuts, and three choices of sandwiches—egg salad, Swiss cheese, or olive and nut. A mixed green vegetable salad with dressing was followed by pistachio ice cream, cake, and coffee.

It should be mentioned that Velma had plenty of time in which to serve; the flight from Chicago to Newark took six hours, and the westbound inaugural —worked by Agnes Nohava the same day—involved a six-and-a-half-hour trip. Only thirty-five years later, American's first jets would cross the entire continent in less time.

Condor sleeper service was introduced on the Fort Worth–Los Angeles leg of the transcontinental route, and neither United nor TWA had anything to match it. With the simmering Seymour-Smith feud the only sour note, American was prospering in a modest way, and Cord began to take a less active role in its affairs.

This may not have been a 180-degree turn, but the shift nevertheless was sharp compared with his early dominance. At one time he even expected American's employees to buy his cars, although few could afford an Auburn, let alone a Cord or Duesenberg. His influence over aircraft purchases in several cases was outright harmful—the unpopular Stinson A was one example, and the Vultee another. Even worse was his insistence on the use of Smith propellers simply because he owned the Smith Propeller Co. Littlewood bluntly called the Smith product "a miserable piece of machinery," and prop failures became so common that Cord relented, allowing American to retrofit with Hamilton Standard propellers.

The loosening of Cord's reins was most evident in his acquiescence to the Condor purchase, and that same decision underlined his growing admiration for and reliance on C. R. Smith. It did not escape Cord that the Southern division was being run more profitably and efficiently than its Eastern counterpart.

The 1933 Chicago World's Fair was a welcome traffic booster for American, although it provided the airline with a pair of passengers whose unusual demand required a high-level policy decision. The famous Siamese twins, Violet and Daisy Hilton, were flying from New York to Chicago and insisted that they travel on one ticket. They won this argument and then won a second: for the one ticket, they got two meals.

But the Fair also generated a dark cloud on the horizon. One of its most heavily attended attractions was the display of a revolutionary new airliner, the twin-engine, all-metal Boeing 247, whose 180-mile-an-hour cruising speed rendered all other U.S. multi-engine transports obsolete. It also happened to be available only to United, which had tied up Boeing's assembly line for at least one year with an unprecedented order for sixty airplanes—the largest aircraft commitment any airline had ever made, and one of particular concern to American and TWA, United's transcontinental competitors.

And that wasn't the only gathering storm. The previous summer, a young newspaperman had a casual drink with a minor airline official, touching off a chain of events that in 1933 was to shake the airline industry to its very foundations.

5
What Brown Wrought, Black Teareth Asunder

Fulton Lewis, Jr., worked for the Washington Bureau of Hearst's Universal Service, an idealistic reporter whose beat included the Departments of Commerce and Agriculture.

It was his coverage of the former agency that led to his involvement in what would turn out to be the upheaval of the airline industry. The Bureau of Air Commerce was part of the Commerce Department, and Lewis became acquainted with a number of airline officials in the Washington area. One of them was William Briggs of the New York, Philadelphia and Washington Airway Corporation, more familiarly known as the Ludington Line.

Ludington had been formed in 1930 by two wealthy Philadelphia brothers to offer all-passenger service among the three cities, and rather successfully, too. Its fleet of Stinson trimotors, Lockheed Vegas, and Consolidated Fleetsters operated on an hourly schedule, much like today's Eastern shuttle. Ludington, in fact, was the first U.S. carrier to make money carrying only passengers.

Not a great deal of money, however, and while Walter Brown was still in office Ludington had bid for a mail contract on the New York–Philadelphia–Washington route. Brown rejected it in favor of Eastern; Ludington did not know what Eastern had bid but assumed innocently that it must have been lower than its own. It wasn't, as Lewis was about to discover.

He was having a friendly drink with Briggs when they happened to wander into discussing the questionable viability of operating an airline without mail revenues. Briggs allowed it was pretty tough, and added sadly that no one at Ludington could understand how it was outbid.

"What was Ludington's bid?" Lewis asked.

"Twenty-five cents a mile," Briggs replied.

Lewis did think that twenty-five cents seemed a very reasonable figure, but let it pass from his mind until a few days later, when he was glancing idly at a routine Post Office Department handout listing current airline-by-airline mail payments. He did a double take when he saw what Eastern was getting: eighty-nine cents a mile.

Idealism was not Fulton Lewis, Jr.'s sole virtue; he smelled something extremely unkosher and he was a relentless digger. For weeks he searched Post Office files and records and finally emerged with the full scenario of the Spoils

Conference. It was there in black and white, for the meeting was never any secret, and Brown himself never thought he was doing anything illegal; he did not try to hide anything—including the unhidable fact that he had awarded twenty-four out of the twenty-seven available mail routes to the three giant conglomerates, Avco, North American, and United.

The more Lewis dug, the richer the lode of scandal appeared to be. He informed William Randolph Hearst that he was uncovering a keg of journalistic and political dynamite, and was given permission to devote full time to his probing. It took another six months before he sent the results to Hearst's estate at San Simeon and then waited anxiously for a publication green light, convinced that he was about to break a tale of graft, corruption, and chicanery of monumental proportions.

The green light never flashed, and Lewis did not know why. It may have been Hearst's awareness that Arthur Brisbane, his top editor and columnist, was a close friend of Walter Brown. Perhaps the publisher also hated to furnish the rambunctious new Roosevelt administration with ammunition to be used against the Hoover regime. Whatever his motives, Hearst simply sat on the Lewis report.

But Lewis's investigation was no secret in a Post Office Department under new Democratic management, and its ramifications were leaked to a U.S. senator who in the summer of 1933 was plodding through a prosaic hearing on ocean mail contracts.

Hugo Black, Alabama Democrat, had been a World War I artillery officer, a Birmingham police judge, and an aggressive prosecuting attorney. The role of prosecutor was very much his style. He got first wind of what Lewis had unearthed from Chief Postal Inspector A. G. Patterson, who had been talking sympathetically with the discouraged reporter. And the former artillery officer knew how to load a cannon.

From Patterson Black learned that Lewis had wired Hearst for permission to show his findings to postal authorities, but that there had been no reply. So Black wrote Hearst himself, and the publisher unexpectedly ordered Lewis to comply. The Lewis report wound up in the hands of Black's committee, and the dull hearing on ocean mail suddenly became a full-scale inquiry into Brown's awarding of air mail contracts.

Black, of course, needed more than Lewis's lengthy memo to Hearst. One day in mid October, on the senator's orders, Patterson mustered a small army of investigators from the Interstate Commerce Commission—why he didn't use his own postal inspectors or U.S. marshals was never explained—and stationed them in a dozen major cities where various airline general offices were located. At a prearranged time, with watches synchronized by Western Union clocks, about a hundred men marched into the offices without warning and seized all correspondence and records relating to air mail contracts.

For the next three and a half months, Black kept the air mail hearings on front pages across the country, painting an ugly picture of alleged graft, greed, and collusion that obscured one clear fact: he proved absolutely nothing warranting criminal prosecution. Black's failure to come up with any real scandal was even more remarkable considering his skillful and often brutal interrogations. One of the most fascinating aspects of Hugo Black's personality was its Jekyll/Hyde quality. He could turn a courtroom or Senate committee hearing into the Spanish Inquisition; at home, he was a mild, doting husband and father who used to get up regularly at 2 A.M. to change his infant daughter's diapers.

When he questioned Walter Folger Brown, observers could have gotten the idea that the former postmaster general was up on first-degree murder charges. Yet Brown never broke, never lost his cool, and presented an able if somewhat self-serving defense of the Spoils Conference. He was particularly effective in justifying the action that had led Lewis into the labrynith of postal files, the Eastern/Ludington bids. Brown explained that Eastern's higher bid involved mail service from Florida to New England, whereas Ludington wanted to operate only a New York–Washington segment. It was far more economical and efficient, Brown argued, to have one carrier serve a large region than to chop up the region among a number of smaller airlines.

The machinations and maneuvering that resulted in American's southern transcontinental award came under close scrutiny, but Black was unable to pinpoint any scandalous skullduggery. Brown never let the committee lose sight of motive, even when his ethics were challenged. He insisted, as he put it, "There was no sense in taking the government's money and dishing it out to every little fellow that was flying around the map and was not going to do anything."

He kept emphasizing that the mail contract awards were merely a means toward achieving his principal goal: the development of passenger traffic, which only the bigger, more experienced airlines could accomplish. In effect he was saying, criticize my methods if you will, but look at the results.

"I could think of no other way to make the industry self-sustaining," Brown told the committee, "to make it economically independent, than to compel the air mail contractor to get some revenue from the public. Almost all of them were refusing to carry passengers and were depending wholly on the Post Office Department, and we were getting nowhere in the development of airplanes. They were just using little, light, open-cockpit ships to move mail, with very great dependability, but no progress in a broad sense was being made in the art.

"I believed that it was my duty to force them, if I could under the law, to get revenue from non-postal sources, and the obvious one was passengers. And after we could get the people flying themselves . . . we thought then they would send their freight by planes, and the purpose of it was altogether to help develop an industry that could live on its own."

Brown pointed out something else that Black and everyone else crying for blood apparently never grasped or deliberately ignored. He said the much-maligned Spoils Conference itself was perfectly legal under existing law. Yet throughout the hearings, Black kept referring to the "secret" meeting in language implying it was the worst crime of all. Forgotten was the fact that even if it had been illegal, it was Brown who arranged it, not the airlines; most airline officials hadn't even wanted to attend.

Black's cross-examinations were aided by none other than Fulton Lewis, Jr., who sat near the committee chairman and fed him scribbled notes suggesting questions to be asked of witnesses. And if the Alabama senator failed to shake up Walter Brown, he did have some of the airline witnesses red-faced and squirming. Their hands weren't entirely clean; in one case allegedly incriminating evidence had been destroyed, and some officials had used mail revenues for profitable stock deals.

But the bottom line was whether any mail contracts had been obtained by fraud, and this Hugo Black was never able to prove. In fact, a 1941 ruling by the U.S. Court of Claims was to find no evidence of fraud or collusion either by Brown or the airlines. Nothing stopped Senator Black, however. Late in January 1934, he had lunch with President Roosevelt at the White House and expressed his conviction that all air mail contracts awarded by Brown should be annulled.

He based this advice not only on what the hearings had disclosed, but on what postal inspectors were turning up from the Post Office Department's own files. That internal investigation was under the direction of the Department's chief legal counsel, Solicitor Karl Crowley, once described by *Fortune* as "a rustic Texas lawyer and politician."

Crowley kept Postmaster General James Farley fully briefed on the progress of his in-house probe. At 2 A.M. on Wednesday, February 7, he finished a 100-page report, the gist of it being that Brown's air mail contract awards had been obtained by fraudulent means and should be cancelled. And then he went home to get a few hours of badly needed sleep—he had been working on the case seven days a week for more than a month.

Later that morning, he went to Jim Farley's spacious office, handed him the thick report, and said, "I want you to read this."

"I can't wade through all this," Big Jim snapped. "Just tell me about it."

Crowley gave him an oral condensation, adding that he felt the government would be legally justified in voiding all mail contracts. The next day, Farley conferred with his chief lieutenants, assistant postmaster generals William W. Howes and Harllee Branch, who agreed with Crowley's recommendations. Farley then called the White House and asked for an appointment with the President that same afternoon.

At 4:30 P.M., Farley, Crowley, Howes, and Branch were ushered into the Oval Office, where they sat in a semicircle in front of FDR's desk. Farley gave the President a verbal synopsis of Crowley's report, dwelling heavily on the fact that Brown had doled an overwhelming majority of air mail routes without competitive bidding. This was the main legal point on which Crowley had hung his hat, in the belief that there had to have been a conspiracy among the carriers to prevent all competition, and with Brown's approval.

Of the four men trying to sell Roosevelt on cancellation, only Farley urged caution. He pointed out that voiding the contracts meant the Army would have to fly the mail and he wasn't sure it could do the job. His alternate suggestion was to cancel, but then invite immediate new bids.

His three companions objected to this plan as mere wrist-slapping. Roosevelt agreed but said they still should consult the Army. He also warned that no action could be taken unless Attorney General Homer Cummings approved of its legality.

The quartet drove to the Justice Department and conferred with Cummings, who said he'd have to study Crowley's report overnight. They returned to his office the next morning, and Cummings gave them his verdict.

"Unquestionably adequate grounds," he declared.

Farley, still worried, told Branch to contact General Benjamin "Benny" Foulois, chief of the Army Air Corps. Foulois showed up at the Post Office Department early that afternoon, wondering what was up. Branch asked him bluntly, "Can the Army carry the mail temporarily?"

Foulois, a short, graying man totally devoted to the cause of air power, was backed into a corner. His beloved Air Corps for years had been the stepchild of the armed forces, starved for funds, saddled with obsolete equipment, and incessantly castigated by critics like Billy Mitchell, who was sincerely convinced that Benny's Air Corps was a paper dragon.

Yet in the fateful seconds given him to answer Branch's brusque question, Foulois also glimpsed a golden opportunity to show an entire nation what his fliers could accomplish. If they succeeded, he could foresee bigger appropriations, generated out of new respect.

Tragically, he did not have time to weigh the terrible odds against his young pilots. Because of a parsimonious, short-sighted Congress, the Army's airmen were limited to approximately 175 hours of flying a year, almost every minute of this in good weather; the average airline pilot flew that much every three months and in every kind of weather, day and night. The Army wasn't well trained in instrument flying, had virtually no experience in nighttime operations, and few pilots had ever been exposed to bad-weather flying. There were only three pilots in the entire Air Corps who had logged as many as 5,000 hours.

But Benny Foulois gave Branch the answer he *wanted* to give.

"Yes, sir, if you want us to carry the mail, we'll do it!"

At 4 P.M. that same day—February 9, 1934—Franklin D. Roosevelt issued an executive order cancelling all air mail contracts effective February 19. He cited postal laws that gave the postmaster general punitive authority if such contracts had been obtained by apparent conspiracy, and added that he had been assured the Army could take over. Both the legal justification and the assurance were in the buck-passing category—the former put the onus on Farley, and the latter covered FDR's tracks if the Army failed.

From around the nation came a chorus of condemnation. Prominent aviation figures such as Lindbergh and Rickenbacker denounced the action as punishment without benefit of trial. Lindbergh wired FDR that the cancellation "does not discriminate between innocence and guilt, and places no premium on honest business." He accused Roosevelt of condemning "the largest portion of our commercial aviation without just trial." Rickenbacker went even further by warning flatly that the Army might well "pile up ships all across the continent"—a prediction of grim accuracy.

Amid all the angry outcries, conspicuous by his silence was E. L. Cord, who passed the word that American was to keep its corporate mouth shut. He was sick in bed the day the cancellations were announced and Seymour contacted him. He told Cord everyone at American had agreed on a strategy that called for enlisting the support of Chambers of Commerce in every city the airline served; they would protest on American's behalf, Seymour explained.

"Don't do a damn thing," Cord ordered. "Let everybody else squawk."

Theoretically, American had the most to lose from cancellation. It was operating more mail mileage than anyone else and had received more generous route extensions than any other carrier. Yet the wily Cord had a perfectly logical reason for refusing to make waves. He was a heavy contributor to the Democratic party—it was rumored he had given as much as $1 million to FDR's campaign—and he knew politicians are loath to bite the hands that feed them.

Furthermore, Cord privately agreed with Rickenbacker that the Army was heading for trouble. And his decision to wait out the storm made more sense than anyone realized at this turbulent moment.

With only ten days in which to prepare, the Army was indeed heading for trouble. Foulois's first mistake was to insist that his men could familiarize themselves with the mail routes in three or four days; they could have used three or four weeks. He did ask airline pilots to volunteer for temporary Army assignment, but the military pay was half their airline salaries and few accepted. Foulois finally mustered some 150 planes, about 200 Army pilots, and less than 400 enlisted ground personnel to operate the mail service, truncated from the 27,000 miles flown by the airlines to a 16,000-mile system.

Their antiquated equipment and inadequate training were brutal handicaps by themselves without adding a third: the gallant Army pilots started flying the mail in the teeth of the worst winter weather encountered in years. They were using bombers, observation aircraft, and even tiny fighters, and some of the planes lacked the navigation aids airline pilots took for granted as basic necessities.

The results were inevitable. In the first week alone, five pilots were killed, six seriously injured, and eight planes destroyed in accidents. Between February 26 and March 31, another seven died in crashes.

Accusatory black headlines were their epitaphs. Even Will Rogers, who admired FDR to the same degree he loved aviation, joined the tidal wave of anger and shock that swept across the nation. He compared the cancellation to "finding a crooked railroad president and then stopping all trains."

William Randolph Hearst did more than denounce Roosevelt and Farley editorially. He took Fulton Lewis, Jr., off the air mail story and punished him with a cancellation action of his own; he ordered the stunned reporter to cease writing a Washington gossip column of which Lewis was inordinately proud. Lewis was said to have sobbed when he got the word.

The airlines supplied one final gesture of defiance only hours before the Army took over its ill-fated assignment. TWA's Jack Frye and Eastern's Rickenbacker flew the prototype of a new airliner, the Douglas DC-1, from Burbank to Newark with the last load of privately contracted mail. In the process of this nose-thumbing demonstration of civilian air power, they set a new transcontinental speed record of thirteen hours and four minutes.

Stripped of their mail revenues, the airlines were forced to furlough hundreds of employees, mostly pilots, as schedules were slashed to passenger-only operations. Approximately one out of every seven men were laid off throughout the industry, and scores of aircraft sat idly on the ground. American was no exception, although it did keep its new Condors flying.

(In one of those intriguing footnotes to history, there was a furloughed American copilot who found his "pink slip" a blessing in disguise. His name was Charles Dolson, and he soon found a job at Delta, where thirty-two years later he became its president and chief executive officer.)

Only his attempt to "pack" the Supreme Court brought Franklin Roosevelt a worse press and public reaction than the air mail fiasco. It was the first setback for an administration that had been basking in the public's adoration while cowing a subservient Congress. It mattered little to the President that the airlines, without mail subsidies, were losing their collective shirt—American alone was running about $300,000 a month in the red. FDR, in fact, had been infected by Black's anti-airline venom and might have been willing to let the Army carry the mail indefinitely. The safety record did improve markedly as the pilots gained experience and the weather eased.

But Roosevelt didn't wait for this favorable development. Stung by the spate of unceasingly angry editorials, and furious at Foulois (who had to endure a face-to-face tongue-lashing at the White House), FDR announced he would return the air mail to private operators, but under new rules.

Their real author was Hugo Black, who, like the President, knew it had been a mistake to believe the overconfident Foulois. Black, too, was willing to get the Army off a hook not of its own choosing, but he also wanted the sinners punished.

So he spelled out their sentences in a bill called the Air Mail Act of 1934, and it lowered the boom. The measure reopened all air mail routes to competitive bidding and included these three additional provisions aimed at demolishing Walter Folger Brown's carefully constructed edifice:

1. All aircraft manufacturing companies must divest themselves from their airline subsidiaries—a clause intended to break up the Avco/Cord, North American (by then controlled by General Motors), and United conglomerates.

2. No airline executive who attended the Spoils Conference would be allowed to hold office in a carrier possessing a mail contract.

3. No airline that had participated in the Conference would be permitted to bid for any mail contract.

That last item was not Black's idea but Jim Farley's, and on the surface it seemed to spell the industry's doom. What Black didn't realize until too late was that Farley had talked him into including a slickly technical loophole, one that saved the nation's air transportation system from complete chaos. For another thing that Black didn't realize was Farley's concealed contempt for him. Big Jim regarded Black as a headline hunter who had gotten FDR into political hot water.

Farley had never really understood or even believed in Black's case against the airlines; he had accepted Crowley's and the senator's assurances that evil had been committed and, loyal to the core, he had taken most of the heat generated by the Army's early failures. It was Farley, not Roosevelt, who bore the brunt of the criticism; most of the editorials blamed the postmaster general as the villain, while FDR was portrayed as a man victimized by bad advice.

Big Jim resented this, but his resentment was directed toward Black, not the President. He had gone along with the cancellation mostly because the politician in him loved the idea of throwing mud at the former Republican administration. Once the so-called air mail "scandal" began backfiring, he began to see the investigation in a different light—one with no real substance and one that threatened to wreck the airline industry beyond all repair.

It will never be known whether any airline official, such as Cord or Jack Frye —both of whom Farley liked—influenced the postmaster general's decision to circumvent Black's vindictive measures. It is known, however, that Farley met privately with a number of airlines after the Air Mail Act was introduced and showed them the loophole through which they could escape Hugo Black's wrath.

There was nothing they could do, he said, about the requirement that aircraft manufacturers be separated from airlines—which the carriers themselves were willing to accept. Many even welcomed this provision because it would give them more freedom and flexibility in choosing equipment. Heads would still have to roll, Farley warned; those who had attended the Spoils Conference must be symbolic sacrifices to Brown's well-intentioned ruthlessness.

But, Farley assured them, nobody had to swallow the biggest pill of all, the one he had concocted himself, namely, the ban against new bids from any Spoils participant. Farley simply suggested: change your corporate names and bid under new names.

The Air Mail Act was rushed through Congress in less than two months, while the airlines hastened to follow Farley's advice. American Airways was incorporated as American Airlines, Eastern Air Transport became Eastern Airlines, United Aircraft and Transport changed its name to United Air Lines, and TWA merely added the word "Incorporated" to its initials. They all filed bids for the same routes they had been operating before annulment—a strategy suggested by Cord, who warned both TWA and United, "Don't bid on anything you didn't have when the contracts were cancelled." And they submitted bids as low as they dared, knowing that the smaller airlines, those Brown had ignored, were hungry for their own spoils.

Farley himself opened the new bids on April 20, 1934. The results represented something of a Pyrrhic victory for Hugo Black. American, TWA, and Eastern bid successfully for their existing routes, with a few modifications. United retained everything except its Dallas–Chicago mail contract, for which it was outbid by upstart Braniff. Another small independent, Delta, won a Dallas/Fort Worth–Charleston, S.C., mail route. Those two ostensibly minor victories were the foot-in-the-door for two carriers that would one day become American's bitter rivals.

History and the distortions of time have painted a somewhat lopsided picture of the air mail war. Most Roosevelt biographies portray FDR as an innocent president misled by those who convinced him wrongly that the Army was capable of flying the mail. They also paint the airlines as a bunch of conniving crooks who deserved what they got. Likewise, Hugo Black is regarded by the majority of political historians as a crusader who exposed a nefarious conspiracy between the big airlines and Walter Brown.

Both portraits are sadly retouched. Listening to Benny Foulois wasn't Roosevelt's only mistake; he also listened too readily to Black and Crowley, not to mention Attorney General Cummings, without probing deeper into the key issue: did Black really have a legal case against Brown and the industry? It is painfully obvious that FDR, a great leader but still the consummate politician, grabbed avidly at any chance to embarrass the old Republican administration, and got his fingers burned.

As for Black, he was well-meaning but he uncovered an awful lot of smoke with no actual fire. The only real crusader was Lewis, who honestly thought he was sitting on another Teapot Dome scandal.

The airlines were not totally without guilt, but they did not deserve the drastic punishment Black wanted to levy—and would have, except for Farley's brilliant end run. It was only after the airlines resumed flying the mail that a few previously ignored facts emerged from Hugo Black's thick smoke.

The Army's own audit of its air mail operations disclosed that it cost the government more than $3.7 million for the three-month experiment. Charges that the airlines had gouged the Post Office Department didn't stand up under scrutiny. The audit revealed:

- The Department's average pound-mail payment to the Army during this period was 8.5 mills; American and the other major airlines had offered for years to carry the mail for 2 mills a pound-mile.
- The Army's direct operating costs amounted to an average of $255.50 per hour; the airlines had been criticized for citing operating costs between $75 and $125 an hour as the basis for their subsidy rates.

- The Army carried the mail at an average cost of $2.21 per mile; the airlines flew it for 54 cents a mile and just before the cancellation had agreed to a government request for a reduction to less than 43 cents—a figure that could have been reduced even further, because under the existing Watres Act the postmaster general already had authority to set subsidy rates almost at will. If alleged airline greed had been the sole issue, there would have been no need for new legislation.

Some able airline officials lost their jobs because of the Air Mail Act, although the carnage was not as bloody as feared. Several airlines had changed management after the Spoils Conference and there weren't that many candidates left for Black's chopping block.

The most prominent casualty was United's Phil Johnson, who went to Canada and organized Trans-Canada Airline. The saddest victim was Pop Hanshue of Western, forced to resign from the airline he founded although his only crime was his reluctant attendance at a meeting where he was mugged.

American emerged virtually unscathed; only one minor official present at the Spoils Conference was still around when mandatory resignation became law. The airline's route structure under the new awards was even improved by the elimination of a few circuitous legs. And it won every mail contract it sought. One newspaper accused American of getting its desired routes because it allegedly had given FDR a free plane ride to the 1932 convention. Goodrich Murphy produced the paid-for ticket stubs, signed by Roosevelt in accordance with the practice then in effect.

In contrast to American, United lost a coveted route (Chicago–Dallas), and TWA, while it retained its old routes, had to operate 40 percent of its system without mail contracts for the next five years.

The way things turned out, Cord couldn't have been happier. The provision requiring severance of manufacturing activities from airline operations mattered little to him. His propeller company was a flop, and the only aircraft firm he owned was Stinson, whose line of obsolete fabric-covered trimotors stood no chance against growing competition. Lockheed's fast new twin-engine, all-metal transport, the Model 10 Electra, already was in service. United had stunned the industry with Boeing's 247. And then there was suddenly emerging Douglas; it was not lost on E.L. that the DC-1's dramatic transcontinental flight was the shadow of things to come.

American, Cord felt, had the only real potential, and his only concern was his awareness that Lester Seymour was not the leader it needed. Coincidental was C. R. Smith's glowing performance as head of the Southern division, and his faith in the future of air travel for people, a belief Cord shared. In Errett Lobban's eyes, Seymour's chief weakness was his insistence that no airline could exist without government mail subsidy. In the context of that time period, this was true. But Cord was looking ahead: passenger traffic had a future, whereas subsidy was not only stagnant but vulnerable to political whims; mail pay could just as easily go down as up.

Seymour is said to have signed his own execution papers. Cord owned a yacht that he kept on Lake Michigan, and shortly after American had bid for its new mail contracts, he invited Seymour to go skeet shooting on the boat. In the course of this friendly outing, Cord brought up the subject of reliance on mail pay.

"Bing," he said sternly, "we've got to figure out a way to make money with an airline without depending on a damned government subsidy."

"There's no way to do it," Seymour replied. "As a matter of fact, I'm going to Washington and ask for a larger subsidy—our bids were too low."

Cord may already have decided to replace Seymour, but if not, that little exchange proved to be the proverbial last straw. A few days later, he told Lou Manning, his long-time chief lieutenant, he thought American needed a change of command, and brought up C. R. Smith's name.

"C.R.'s good," Manning conceded, "but you know as well as I do that he doesn't follow orders."

Cord grinned. "He doesn't exactly disobey, Lou. He just disregards orders or alters them to suit his own way of getting things done."

The two men agreed that Manning should summon Smith to Chicago for an interview. "I think he's the right man," Cord said, "but I'll leave it up to you. Ask him anything you want, and then decide."

C.R. flew to Chicago aboard an American Ford trimotor on which he was the only passenger—there was no scheduled flight available at the time he had to leave Fort Worth, so in typical C.R. fashion he simply commandeered an idle plane. He never saw Cord, but Manning grilled him for almost an entire day. So intense was the questioning that Smith figured the whole thing was a charade in which he would wind up fired. But at the end of the grueling session, Manning rose and put out his hand.

"Congratulations, C.R.." He smiled. "You're the new president of American Airlines."

The board of directors formally elected him on October 26, 1934—the start of a new era for an airline that finally could control its own destiny, under the leadership of this poker-playing Texan who couldn't be bluffed, bullied, or bought.

PART TWO
(1934–1945)

6

A $335.50 Phone Call

Corporations are supposed to be inanimate, as soulless as metal, possessing all the lifelike characteristics of dirt.

But not always.

In rare instances, the corporate body acquires a leader of such domineering strength and will, it begins to take on his very personality traits. It reflects his methods, policies, ambitions, even his emotions, until it becomes a mirror image of the man himself—almost as if his genes had somehow been implanted in what normally is an impersonal entity.

It happened most recently at Chrysler, where a flaccid, moribund, demoralized company became synonymous with the dogged resilience and determination of Lee Iacocca. And it happened far more frequently in the adolescent years of the airline industry, when sheer force of leadership personality was a means of survival. At such companies, the leader *was* the airline.

The examples are many.

William A. "Pat" Patterson of United, a cautious, conservative, paternalistic man to whom integrity was almost a religious commitment; in the forty years he headed United, the airline was his clone in philosophy and policy.

Delta's C. E. Woolman, even more of a patriarchal figure than Patterson, who ran his company like a closely knit Dixie family; Delta was stamped with the image of two-way Southern loyalty, to such an extent that even today it is the only long-established major carrier to resist unionization except for its pilots.

The unconventional, flamboyant maverick that was Bob Six of Continental, with a flair for the spectacular; as long as he ran Continental, it was an airline noted for its "pizzazz," from flight attendant uniforms to uniquely colorful aircraft interiors.

Pan Am's Juan Trippe, obsessed by his conviction that only one carrier should fly the American flag overseas; his unflagging efforts to achieve that goal turned Pan Am into an airline with a touch of arrogance born in the days when it *was* the sole U.S. international carrier, so powerful that it acted as its own State Department in its negotiations with other countries.

And Eddie Rickenbacker of Eastern, whose airline mirrored his insistence on a Spartan, close-to-the-vest operation stressing efficiency and economy at the expense of service; Rickenbacker's cavalier attitude toward passengers seeped down to the ranks, and it took Eastern years to rid itself of what he had branded into its corporate hide.

Into this company of benevolent dictators strode the towering figure of Cyrus Rowlett Smith, ready to establish a niche of his own among his peers. He had two goals. He already commanded the largest airline in the United States in terms of routes and equipment; he wanted to make it the best as well as the biggest. But he also wanted to do something for an industry sporting one huge black eye from the so-called air mail scandal: to restore its credibility and instill public confidence in air travel, not merely for American but all airlines.

No more fiercely competitive man ever lived than C.R., yet in pursuing that second goal he stood head and shoulders above the rest of his pioneering compatriots.

As he would consistently demonstrate.

American Airlines in the early days of Smith's regime might be likened to a somewhat flabby giant—huge in stature but still uncoordinated, deficient in competitive spirit, and lacking the professional slickness of United and the technical proficiency of TWA.

C.R. set about to change this in a hurry. On his first day as president, Bill Dunn of Public Relations poked his head into Smith's office. "Congratulations," he ventured.

"Come on in," C.R. growled. Dunn complied, not knowing what to expect. He didn't have to wait long.

"Morale in this company is too damned low," Smith announced. "It's particularly bad among our pilots. I think we'd better order them some new uniforms. Those blue serge suits they're wearing make 'em look like Pullman conductors."

This was a relatively minor move, but most indicative of the way he was going to run the airline—in one word: decisively. C.R. believed fervently in the adage that a camel is a horse designed by a committee. He sought advice, input, and suggestions from others, but not decisions. That was his *modus operandi* from the day he took over to the day he left American. He hated long-winded meetings and, with equal fervor, long-winded correspondence.

C.R. took into the presidency a habit he acquired when he was boss of the Southern division. He insisted on typing most of his own letters, and they were just as pithy, brusque, and abbreviated as his conversation. Through the years, American's people—officers and "enlisted" personnel alike—collected and saved them with the same devotion accorded rare stamps and first editions.

No one ever forgot who was top man, yet Smith was never a martinet. To every man and woman working for American, he was either "Mr. C.R." or just plain "C.R." In the formative years of his regime, when the airline had only about a thousand employees, he seemed to know everyone by name—and if he didn't recognize a person, he'd walk over and introduce himself. "I don't believe I've met you," he'd say. "My name is C.R. Smith." Nor did he ever lose this personal touch; as American grew it was impossible to keep track of every individual, but he tried.

One of his first pronouncements as president was a warning to all officers that they were never to put on the airs of a high-powered executive.

"I'll fire any guy who thinks he's an executive," he told a staff meeting.

His assuming command caused the usual trembling among the brass hats; it is axiomatic that the proverbial new broom can assume the awesome proportions of an amuck bulldozer. But C.R. bided his time before making any drastic changes in the Chicago hierarchy. He even kept Raymond Pruitt's law firm for legal representation, despite his personal dislike of the man, although possibly he didn't want to ruffle Cord's feathers.

With Smith in the driver's seat, however, Cord seemed to lose interest in the airline. He had finally found the right man to run it and was perfectly content to let American go its own way. E.L.'s short figure and tight little smile were seldom seen around the Chicago headquarters after C.R. took office. In fact, Cord left the country around this time and settled briefly in England; he told friends he had received a kidnapping threat against his only child, although it was rumored he was trying to duck a Securities and Exchange Commission investigation into some non-airline stock deals.

He retained considerable stock in American until World War II; as late as 1940 he was the largest shareholder, with 19 percent. Three years earlier, he had sold his Cord/Avco holdings to Victor Emanuel, a young Cleveland financier, for $2 million; in 1938, Emanuel became the new president of a revived Avco that today is one of America's best-run diversified conglomerates, its roots to American withered away until only dusty files of the past remain.

A few veterans are still around who remember Errett Lobban Cord. Hamilton Hale, who joined the Pruitt firm fresh out of law school in 1932, emphasized that not many people knew Cord really well. Reminisced Hamilton:

"He was a fairly small guy, pleasant enough, but he moved around like a shadow sometimes. He was savvy about financial matters. He warned a lot of his friends that the stock market was going to crash in 1929, and he pulled himself out in plenty of time. Tight-fisted, too. He would always ask every job applicant, "How little can you work for?' "

One of the last people at American to see Cord was Jim Gainer, a much respected man who joined the airline in 1937 and retired thirty-eight years later. In the early 1960s, he was American's manager in Los Angeles and made a point of talking to Cord whenever E.L. was at the airport. Gainer encountered him just before Cord moved to Reno, and asked how things were going.

"Oh, pretty good," Cord said. "I just bought into a little electrical company. Don't know if you ever heard of it."

"What's the company?" Gainer inquired.

"Sunbeam."

The conversation drifted into current airline topics and Gainer dutifully asked what Cord thought of American's first-class service.

"There's no such thing as first-class travel in this country," E.L. declared firmly.

"Ours is pretty damned good," Gainer said loyally.

"It's not first class," Cord insisted. "First class to me is being picked up at the front door by a limousine that takes me to the airport. Nobody asks for my ticket or weighs my baggage. When I arrive at my destination, another limo takes me to my hotel, and at the end of the month the airline sends me a bill. Now *that's* first-class service!"

Cord made another fortune in California real estate while he lived in Los Angeles and also profited well from Santa Fe Railroad stock. He remained active the rest of his life, developing L.A.'s Wilshire Boulevard into a high-tone shopping area; the Beverly-Hilton Hotel stands on former Cord property. After leaving California to settle in Reno, he acquired extensive ranch holdings and became a Nevada state senator.

He died in 1974. Most of the obituaries dwelt heavily on the classic car that bore his name and his great wealth. There was scant mention of his brief but strong links with American and the part he played in its history. Which is understandable—he had willfully abdicated the influence and authority he wielded over two short but stormy years, and almost overnight he was totally eclipsed by the man to whom he handed the baton of leadership.

C.R.'s first shake-up involved public relations, then headed by a "Windy" Williams. Smith summoned the entire department, consisting of Williams, Bill Dunn, and two men from Los Angeles and New York respectively, to his Chicago hotel room and questioned them on their work. Then he declared abruptly, "Bill Dunn's gonna take over. He'll run the show from now on."

Williams promptly resigned and Dunn, while grateful for the unexpected promotion, didn't stay in his new post very long. American's principal public relations advisor at the time didn't even work for the airline. He was a hard-drinking, brilliant advertising man named Pete Willis, who worked for a small Chicago advertising agency. He had only two accounts, but one of them was the Cord organization and Willis ranked high in Cord's severely rationed trust. Dunn himself decided to join Willis after an abbreviated stint on the airline's payroll.

It came as some surprise when C.R. relied very little at first on his Southern division cohorts in forming his own executive team. There were two key exceptions, however. One was Melvin D. "Doc" Miller, whom Smith brought to Chicago, where, in due course of time, he became general sales manager. Doc was a workaholic who thought nothing of spending seven days a week in his office—Christmas was the only day he took off regularly. C.R. had known him since college, where Miller had taught him in an accounting course. He was working for Dictograph when C.R. talked him into joining the Southern division.

The other import from Fort Worth was Claude W. Jacob, like Miller a much-beloved name in American's saga. He was "Jake" to everyone and he got into the airline business even more accidentally than C.R. Jacob managed a small men's clothing store in Fort Worth and Smith was one of his best customers.

When C.R. was still running the Southern division, he came into the store one day in an unhappy mood. He wasn't pleased with the division's one-man accounting department.

"Jake, can you keep books?" he asked with impulse born of inspiration.

"Sure. I majored in accounting."

"How much do you make here?"

"Well, it's a pretty good job," Jacob said cautiously. "I get $75 a month."

"I'll give you $150 a month if you'll be my head bookkeeper at the airline."

Thus was born a relationship that was to last three and a half decades. Jake Jacob not only developed into one of C.R.'s most trusted officers but provided American with a future vice president. A letter dated August 10, 1933, addressed to Jacob, reads as follows:

Dear "Jake":

Congratulations to you and Mrs. Jacob on the addition to your family of Mr. Jerry Rowland Jacob. We are quite sure he is going to grow up and be a splendid addition to the personnel of American Airways, Inc.

Yours Truly,
C.R.

The letter wound up eventually in the possession of the vice president of American's eastern region, namely the subject of that accurate prophecy. But Jerry Jacob always remembered there were days when his father wished he was back running a haberdashery. Claude Jacob did get his promised $150 monthly salary—for two months. For the next three, he got $50. C.R. had recruited him in a bleak period; things were so bad that Smith on more than one occasion would meet the division's payroll by using mail revenues to play commodity market futures.

No one can truly appreciate C.R.'s master plan for American without grasping his passion for developing passenger traffic as the only road to airline viability; he never forgot the degrading and dangerous strategy of meeting a payroll by gambling on the stock market. Even before he became president, he was drawing the blueprints. Once in a position of authority, he could act as well as dream. He wasn't the only airline president to have such goals—Rickenbacker, for one, hated government largesse even worse than C.R.—but C.R. went beyond his contemporaries in the scope and execution of his blueprints.

He began constructing an airline edifice that might be compared to a three-spoke wheel. The hub was safety. The three spokes were marketing, service, and equipment. Admittedly, this wheel-shaped concept was far from unique; every major airline followed it, albeit with varying emphasis on the individual spokes. But nobody turned that wheel more effectively than C.R.'s American, and it's still turning the way he intended. You must attract passengers with innovative marketing, put them into modern, clean equipment operated safely and reliably, and keep them in your airplanes with good service. All this could be underlined; Madison Avenue calls it "brand loyalty" and American has no competitor who does a better job in achieving so consistently what Smith envisioned fifty years ago. There would be one bleak period when the airline stumbled badly, but it recovered simply because fresh leadership went back to the basics C.R. established.

There is, of course, one huge difference between 1934 and 1985: the public now takes air travel for granted, and the airlines have to sell themselves individually. This wasn't true when C.R. launched his crusade to make flying acceptable by making it safer. In 1934, fewer than 500,000 Americans had ever been in an airplane—less than one half of one percent of the population. Yet today almost twice that number board the U.S. airlines *every day*. Five decades ago, 99.5 percent stayed away from flying mostly because of fear, and while cost played some role, it was secondary. Nobody could blame them. Most life insurance policies were automatically suspended during the time a policy holder was in any airplane, commercial or otherwise. Premiums for pilots were exorbitant, when available.

So Smith's top priority was safety, for without it no one could sell air travel. He preached this message incessantly, warning one of his first staff meetings, "You wash out safety, you wash out American Airlines."

He ordered the employe magazine to carry under its masthead, in every issue, the time-honored airman's axiom: "Aviation is not unsafe, but like the sea it is terribly unforgiving of any carelessness or neglect."

He sermonized to the pilots, quite naturally, more than any other group and by and large they memorized the Scriptures According to St. C.R., including the most senior, rugged individualists. M.D. "Doc" Ator, who had started flying for Southern Air Transport, used to impart this advice to younger pilots: "Son, if you're flying and it gets too tough for you, just land somewhere. You'll hear some guy flying over you and all you have to remember is that your troubles are over—his are just starting."

Even the carefree pranksters like Si Bittner never let clowning override judgment and responsibility. Some years into the 1940s, Bittner was promoted to chief pilot at the Memphis base and one of his boys mistook a fairly large airport near San Francisco for the regular field. Bittner sentenced him to a week off without pay. A month later, when the base was short of pilots, Bittner flew a trip to San Francisco and landed at the same wrong facility. He, too, took a week off without pay, signing the suspension order himself.

The pilots loved C.R. for his down-to-earth simplicity, frankness, and accessibility. His office at Chicago's Midway Airport was on the second floor of an American hangar located not too far from the northwest runway. It faced the field, so Smith could always see what was going on outside. Any pilot with a problem or some information he thought C.R. might want to hear merely had to park himself under the second-floor window and shout.

"Hey, C.R., you busy?"

"Hell, no," he'd yell back. "Come on up."

Captain Dinty Moore always remembered Smith for the maroon Auburn roadster he drove occasionally—a reminder of the days when Cord wanted the entire airline to drive his cars (he used Auburns as airport limousines for a while). But C.R. didn't really like to drive, and after he became president, he spent an inordinate amount of time trying to peddle the Auburn to pilots, apparently figuring they were among the few employees who could afford one. His price, according to Dinty, was as much as $400 too high. C.R. would meet some new pilot, stick out a big paw, and open fire.

"My name's Smith. Just call me C.R. By the way, what kind of car are you driving?"

Then would come the sales pitch, invariably with the astronomical price. Moore came around to believing C.R. may not have really wanted to sell the car. "He'd point to this fancy maroon job and allow as how he'd let it go for a certain price—way out of line, of course, but deadpan all the time. I don't know if he ever did unload that Auburn, but he must have learned a bit about us pilots from our reactions."

He did, indeed, learn a lot from his airmen—and most of it worried him. He listened to their opinions of the airplanes they flew, good and bad but most of them bad. The Ford and Stinson trimotors were hopelessly outdated. The speedy Vultee, the last single-engine plane American ever operated, flew "like a brick" according to crews assigned to them. And the Condors, for all their passenger comfort features, were too slow, underpowered, and only marginally safe. With anything approaching a full load, no Condor that had suffered an engine failure could stay in the air on the remaining engine.

American did try to eliminate the dangers of Condor engine fires by installing the first in-flight fire extinguishers ever put on a commercial transport, some rather crude carbon dioxide bottles that could be discharged from the cockpit. Extinguishers notwithstanding, however, operations chief Earl Ward passed the word that at the first sign of an engine fire, "get the hell on the ground as soon as possible."

This edict was brought home forcibly to President Smith. He was aboard a Condor one night, having had a pleasant chat with the young mechanic who serviced the plane just before takeoff. The mechanic, Frank Vosepka, was so excited at meeting his new boss that he forgot a rather important item he had left propped up against the right engine's "J-box." His flashlight.

"I was so nervous I was shaking like a dog passing fishhooks," Vosepka recounted later. "I just cowled up the engine and watched them take off for New York—with the damned flashlight still in the engine. I not only had forgotten it but I hadn't turned it off."

The flight was American's popular "Night Owl" and was over Michigan City only minutes out of Chicago when Captain Pat Patterson noticed a glow coming from the starboard engine.

"Fire in Number Two!" he yelled to the copilot. "Pull the bottle!"

The discharged CO_2 fluid apparently smothered the glow of Vosepka's flashlight but Patterson, although thinking the fire was out, decided to return to Chicago. After landing, they opened the cowling and stared unbelievingly at the evidence. Like many mechanics, Vosepka had marked all his tools with his initials, and there on the green flashlight were the telltale initials, FHV.

He wasn't fired, however; in fact, he eventually went to Western in Los Angeles, where he became, with poetic justice, supervisor of maintenance inspection. One of the best nuts-and-bolts men who ever worked for an airline, he always remembered ruefully a mistake he made at Western that dwarfed his flashlight episode. He installed a bird-repellent lighting system in a hangar. The minute it was turned on, an estimated two thousand birds flew in and perched atop a freshly painted plane.

C.R. and his Condor pilots would have settled anytime for false fire alarms instead of the very real emergencies the Condors kept generating. Their Wright engines were not the last word in reliability, and icing remained a constant problem despite all efforts to avoid icing conditions. In 1934, weather forecasting was an inexact science remarkably akin to the accuracy of picking horses. One Condor was lost in an unexpected snowstorm that hit upper New York State in June!

On December 28, 1934, another American Condor made a miraculous forced landing on the side of a snow-covered mountain in the Adirondacks, near Gloversville, New York. The flight, en route from Syracuse to Newark, encountered an unpredicted snowstorm, and one engine quit when the carburetor iced up. It was impossible to maintain altitude on the remaining engine, which also began sputtering.

On board was a single male passenger and a deadheading American copilot returning from a Christmas vacation. The captain was Ernie Dryer, a curmudgeon with the gruff personality of a dyspeptic bear. But he could have flown a boxcar if it had wings, and he pancaked the big Condor onto the mountain slope without anyone getting a scratch.

The radio was damaged and inoperative. Dryer's copilot was his brother Dale and they spent the first night outside the plane, huddled by a small fire they built in vain hope somebody would spot the flames. The passenger and deadheading pilot slept inside the cabin, which wasn't that much warmer.

The next morning, Ernie and the third pilot started hiking north, carrying the airplane's compass, which they had removed from the cockpit. Ernie wasn't sure of their location because he had no idea of how far they had drifted off course when one engine failed—it was almost impossible to fly straight in a Condor minus half its power. For two hours they struggled through snow up to their knees before turning back, completely exhausted.

They examined the radio again and found that the chief damage was a broken antenna. They rigged up a makeshift antenna, got the plane's generators started somehow, and managed to contact a radio operator in Albany. A number of additional calls were made so a radio fix on the signal might be established;

eventually the battery ran down and all they could do was wait and pray.

For the rest of the day, they fashioned a lean-to out of saplings covered with fabric torn from the fuselage and wings. The flimsy shelter was hardly adequate during the daylight hours and that night, another foot of snow fell; the temperature dropped to fifteen degrees below zero. Dryer wanted to stay outside and keep another fire going, but it was impossible to find dry wood. They all slept in the cabin, on seat cushions with the aircraft's window curtains wrapped around their feet. There were only two blankets, which they shared, sleeping as close to one another as possible.

Shortly after dawn, they heard the sound of an airplane engine and rushed outside, waving their arms frantically. They saw the plane, a single-engine aircraft equipped with skis, but the pilot never saw them. For the rest of the day, they could hear the groping search planes, but no one spotted them.

To survive through the third night, they tore off the leather backs of the cockpit seats and made leggings out of them. Further if inadequate warmth came from any material they could find—pillowcases, towels, even the cloth from the luggage racks. There was no food, but later the passenger was to comment that no one seemed conscious of hunger.

On the third morning, discouraged by the failure of the search planes to locate them, Ernie suggested that they all start finding their way to civilization. The four men, bundled in their pitifully improvised protective covering, started out and marched for two hours before giving up and returning to the plane. They had resigned themselves to death when just around dusk they heard a plane making one last search before darkness.

The Dryer brothers managed to get a small fire going and Ernie resorted to what he had been saving as a last-ditch effort. There was a little gas left in the Condor's tanks, fuel Ernie had hesitated to use because he was afraid a bigger fire might spread to the cabin and destroy their only shelter. This time he poured the gas over a nearby tree and ignited it with embers from the fire they had just started.

The flames soared high enough to attract the pilot's attention. He dropped a flare signalling that they had been spotted, and almost five hours later a rescue party arrived carrying hot liquids, food, warm clothing, and blankets. All four survivors recovered completely from their ordeal, and the Dryers were back flying after a brief rest. Dale, unfortunately, was living on borrowed time —he was killed in a crash a few years later.

C.R. was ready to assign the entire Condor fleet to whatever purgatory is reserved for wayward airliners. During the same week of the Adirondacks drama, another American Condor had been involved in a nonfatal landing accident at El Paso. Smith flew there to find out what had happened and was still at the scene when word came that Ernie Dryer's flight was overdue and missing. C.R. went right to New York for a firsthand look at the search operations. If this wasn't bad enough, two more American planes cracked up within minutes of each other while landing at Louisville. Again, there were no fatalities, but the airline seemed to be coming apart.

These horrendous seven days happened to immediately precede the week of a momentous event in Smith's life: he was scheduled to get married. His engagement to Elizabeth Manget, an attractive Dallas Junior Leaguer, had been announced shortly after he became president, and the accident epidemic erupted while he was supposed to be getting ready for the wedding.

Thanks to the rescue of the Dryer party, he managed to make his own nuptials on time but it was a grim portent of a marriage that was to be subjected to strains from the day the couple took their vows. More literally than figuratively, Elizabeth Manget married an airline as well as a man, and she ranked second in Cyrus Rowlett Smith's priorities.

They were just settled in their Chicago apartment when another minor accident took Smith away from his new bride. Nor was it always some crisis that interfered with marital responsibilities. C.R. was in New York when their only child, Douglas, was born in a Dallas hospital, and Smith dutifully grabbed the first flight to Texas. The plane stopped in Nashville and grinning agents informed him he had a son.

He arrived in Dallas that night and the agent who met the plane hadn't heard the news.

"Golly, Mr. C.R.," he enthused. "We didn't know you were coming to our Christmas party. This is great!"

Incredibly, C.R. went to the employee party before going to the hospital. It may have seemed callous, but one of his closest friends remarked by way of explanation, "He simply chose what to him was more important—he couldn't really help much at the hospital, but he figured he could do an awful lot of good at the party."

The marriage ended in an amicable divorce not too long after Douglas was born. They always remained good friends, and Elizabeth later remarried. She explained the break simply.

"I love the man," she said of C.R., "but I can't be married to an airline."

Some of their mutual friends theorized that the marriage might have worked out, or at least lasted longer, if they had waited a couple of years; taking on a wife while simultaneously taking on an airline might have been too much to expect of any man. But this has to be relegated to the category of wishful thinking. Significantly, C.R. never did marry again, recognizing and accepting the restrictions imposed by his single-minded set of priorities. He refused to change because he did not want to change, and what made him a poor husband made him a stronger leader.

It is only too true that he married smack in the middle of crisis, a period in which he had to make one of the most crucial equipment decisions in American's history. American may have been the biggest U.S. airline but it was moon-mileage away from being the best.

Several months before C.R. became president, American had ordered fifteen new DC-2s, developed from Douglas's pioneering DC-1. The production airplane, designed like the prototype to TWA's specifications, carried fourteen passengers in considerably greater comfort than did the Boeing 247. The DC-2 was ten feet longer than its rival, carried four more passengers, cruised nearly fifty miles an hour faster, and had double its range. Almost overnight, United's big 247 fleet was outmoded.

Because TWA's initial interest had prompted Douglas to design and build the airplane, Jack Frye's airline owned the first twenty delivery positions. This gave TWA a tremendous head start in exploiting the DC-2's acknowledged superiority over United's cramped and slower 247 and American's comfortable but lumbering Condors. TWA put its first DC-2s into scheduled service in July 1934, and a month later inaugurated transcontinental service; Dan Beard, by then chief engineering test pilot, didn't start DC-2 acceptance tests until early October, and it was the end of December before American began its own DC-2 service on the New York–Chicago route.

Heavy advertising and press promotion emphasized that TWA now had the only fifteen-hour coast-to-coast service. The ads cited "the atmosphere of the living room with its deeply upholstered, fully reclining and reversible chairs and the spacious cab with its *unobstructed* aisle." The description was a large needle aimed directly at the 247, whose main wing spar ran right through the cabin, so that passengers had to step over a large hump. The needle aimed at American was speed. While the fifteen-hour transcontinental schedule was a bit of hyperbole—the eastbound time was fifteen hours and twenty minutes and westbound flights took between seventeen and twenty hours to cross the country—the DC-2 still was hours faster than the Condor.

All of which chafed and grated on the nerves of Cyrus Rowlett Smith like fingernails on a blackboard. He was president of an airline that for all its size had been the butt of industry jokes from the day he joined it. He had heard too many times a standard pilot crack that the airline was called American "because of its democratic equipment—you can fly anywhere in anything." Employees themselves had been fond of deliberately misquoting the company slogan: "From coast to coast and from Canada to Mexico." Their version went "From coast to coast *via* Canada and Mexico."

And now the opposition could deride American further. Even the acquisition of fifteen DC-2s didn't change the fact that the fleet remained largely obsolete. The Condors actually replaced only the old Fords; Stinson trimotors were still being operated as late as 1938, albeit only on the Nashville–Cleveland route. The DC-2s were a welcome and badly needed addition, but American ran six months behind TWA in introducing them, and C.R. didn't really like the airplane anyway.

It had been ordered, of course, before he became president, which may have been a factor in the historical decision he was about to make. But it definitely was a minor factor. The biggest input into that decision came from C.R.'s deep conviction that the DC-2, revolutionary though it was, fell far short of his standards for a truly great commercial transport. And sharing that conviction was the man on whom Smith had come to rely heavily for technical expertise: Bill Littlewood.

Littlewood had recommended the DC-2 order simply because it was better than anything else then flying. But he also considered it woefully deficient in too many respects. It was vulnerable to propeller and fin icing, and while it could carry an awesome load of ice before stalling, its anti-icing system (flexible rubber boots) was disturbingly inadequate. Pilots liked its ruggedness but not its handling—the DC-2 was abysmally difficult to fly, hard to land, and directionally unstable due to its relatively small fin area that caused it to fishtail constantly.

Speed and strength were the DC-2's chief virtues; it could go by a 247 on only one engine. But ailerons and rudder were extremely heavy. A contemporary critique of the plane described it as having the handling characteristics of "a flying barn door." It had an extremely stiff landing gear, and any smooth landing was 10 percent skill and 90 percent luck. Pilots used to joke that when they logged a DC-2's touchdown time, they usually logged just the last bounce.

Raising or lowering the manually operated landing gear required brute strength, and the sound of a captain's voice ordering "Gear up!" could turn copilots pale. It was bad enough in good weather but in the winter, the gear pump's seventy-two moving parts all seemed to freeze simultaneously.

Taxiing a DC-2 was an art in itself. It was said that while a monkey could be taught to fly the plane, it took a brilliant pilot to taxi one. Pilot/author Ernie Gann, who started flying for American in the DC-2 days, once offered a classic description of its ground-handling idiosyncrasies:

> The braking system in a DC-2 was activated by heaving on a horn-shaped handle protruding from the left side of the instrument panel. By simultaneous use of the rudder and handle, the desired left or right brake could be applied. Since there was inevitably a lag between the motion and effect, the DC-2 was stubbornly determined to chase its own tail on the ground and in crosswinds, sometimes switching ends to the embarrassment of all aboard.

Another problem was the tail wheel, which had to be locked securely while landing or the aircraft would ground-loop. The cockpit windshield had a tendency to leak in rain, resulting in a memorable weather report from one American DC-2 pilot: "Moderate precipitation outside, heavy precipitation inside." DC-2 pilots learned that raincoats were required cockpit equipment.

The DC-2's heating system was nothing more than a modified steam radiator, emitting alarming bangs, gurgles, gasps, and metallic sighs. Passengers often had to be reassured that the plane wasn't about to explode.

Added to all these deficiencies was the DC-2's fourteen-passenger payload, four less than a Condor configured to daytime operation. It galled C.R. more than anything else. He figured rightly that the supposed last word in air transportation should be big enough to make money. And this, more than anything else, was the genesis of the gamble he took.

His chief ally, as already mentioned, was Littlewood. They were in a DC-2 one night flying from New York to Chicago and the plane was caught in an icestorm. C.R. was no white-knuckle passenger, but on this occasion he was gripping the armrests tightly. The DC-2 began to fishtail so sharply that both he and Littlewood could feel their seats swaying.

Smith leaned across the aisle and said quietly to his chief engineer, "I don't think very much of this, do you?"

"No, I don't," Littlewood agreed.

This incident occurred a few days following American's DC-2 introduction, and apparently solidified C.R.'s determination to get a better airplane. He had been talking to Littlewood about it for some time; now the two men sat down and began discussing specifics, Smith supplying the generalized goals and Littlewood the technical requirements for meeting those goals.

First and foremost, C.R. wanted a *viable* airliner that eradicated all the DC-2's bugs without sacrificing its strength and reliability. And viable meant a transport capable of carrying a profitable payload *without* mail revenue. A transcontinental sleeper plane as luxurious as the Condor, Smith insisted, possessing sufficient range to cross the country in either direction with not more than three refueling stops. One of his biggest complaints about the DC-2 was the fact that its advertised 1,000-mile range was more hypothetical than real. Flying westbound from New York to Chicago often required refueling at Buffalo or Cleveland if a fully loaded flight ran into strong headwinds.

While C.R. sketched the broad concepts for his dream plane, Littlewood filled in the specification details. And on a cold December afternoon in the waning days of 1934, C.R. picked up his phone and placed a person-to-person call to Donald Douglas, Sr., in Santa Monica, California.

When Douglas got on the line, Smith wasted no time on pleasantries.

"Don, I want you to expand the DC-2 so it could carry twenty-one passengers in the daytime and sleep fourteen at night."

Douglas was shocked. "You're asking the impossible," he protested. "We can't even keep up with orders for the DC-2."

Smith persisted. He scoffed at technical difficulties. The plane he wanted, he assured Douglas, would be 85 percent DC-2 and only 15 percent new (he was wrong: it turned out to be 85 percent new and only 15 percent DC-2). Douglas argued that the market for such a transport wouldn't justify the development costs. C.R. predicted it would outsell the DC-2. And somewhere in the course of their debate, he tossed every poker chip he owned into the pot: American, he promised, would buy twenty of these planes sight-unseen—ten sleepers and the same number in daytime configuration.

At one point, Douglas pointed out that his engineers had never designed a sleeper plane. This didn't faze C.R.

"I'll send one of our Condors out there so they can study it," he proposed loftily. "And I'll have Bill Littlewood there to help all he can."

Several times Douglas tried to end the discussion, but C.R. refused to let him hang up. The manufacturer kept arguing that Smith was asking too much —a 50 percent increase in payload in what basically would be a DC-2. C.R. said—overoptimistically, he was to concede later—that all he wanted was a "stretched" DC-2 with a little wider fuselage. He never used the phrase "no big deal" but he was implying it, however innocently. He even told Douglas the whole project, from preliminary design to first flight, should take not more than a year. (It was to take a bit longer.)

They talked for more than two hours before Douglas wearily threw in the towel. What convinced him more than anything else was Smith's confidence, his willingness to commit American to buying an airplane that wasn't even on paper yet.

"I'll go ahead with a design study," Douglas allowed. "If my engineers tell me it's feasible, we'll talk further."

"Fine!" C.R. enthused. "At the right moment, I'll send Littlewood to Santa Monica."

Littlewood, informed of the marathon conversation, went into an immediate huddle with his chief assistant, Otto Kirchner, an engineering graduate of Alabama whose first airline job was at Texas Air Transport. Part of Littlewood's unquestioned genius was not only his own ability but his knack of attracting a high-caliber staff. Kirchner was typical of the crack aeronautical engineers who seemed to gravitate toward their brilliant chief. He himself was the first man to show by scientific analysis that low-wing airplanes offered a greater chance of passenger crash survival than high-wing types. And in 1940, Kirchner first conceived the idea of evacuation slides for large-capacity aircraft with tricycle landing gears.

The Littlewood/Kirchner study came up with a preliminary design of intriguing possibilities. It called for splitting the DC-2 fuselage longitudinally down its middle and inserting new strips of cabin floor and ceiling metal twenty-six inches wide. The fuselage would be lengthened by slightly more than two and a half feet. DC-2 seating consisted of seven seats on each side of the aisle; American's initial configuration in the new plane provided more than C.R. had asked for: eight rows of three-abreast seats, two on one side and single seats on the other, a total of twenty-four in the non-sleeper version.

The sleeper plane would have three double rows of berths, twelve in all, with two more berths in a private "Sky Room" on the forward right side of the cabin. These were the day and sleeper layouts Littlewood took to Santa Monica early in 1935, only to be talked into one major modification: Douglas engineers suggested giving up one row of seats in order to provide more forward baggage space, and the final configuration went back to C.R.'s original twenty-one-seat daytime layout.

Of somewhat more concern to C.R. than seats at this stage was how to pay for the twenty airplanes, not to mention an option for twenty more—it was a potential forty-aircraft order C.R. was dangling under the nose of Douglas. At a tentative price of just under $100,000 per airplane, including spare parts and radios, that added up to a $4 million commitment. Many years later, Smith was to recall the enormity of the risk.

"We bought the plane from Douglas without ever signing an actual contract. We did not want to sign one because it was customary to put up a cash deposit when you signed, and we didn't have enough cash to make the usual required deposit."

C.R. knew, of course, that Douglas wasn't going to carry American on the cuff indefinitely. While Littlewood headed west to get the project under way, C.R. flew east to see an old friend and fellow Texan, Jesse Jones, head of the Reconstruction Finance Corporation. RFC was an agency created by the Hoover administration and one of the few the New Deal inherited and kept alive. C.R. obtained a quick appointment and as usual got right to the point.

"Jesse, I've read that the RFC was set up to ward off financial disaster."

"That's right," Jones allowed.

"Well, American Airlines is a disaster if you don't make us a loan."

C.R. left Washington with a $4.5 million loan, an astronomical sum for those days. But it was hardly more significant than what he had spent on that two-hour phone call to Santa Monica, when he talked Donald Douglas into building a plane he didn't want to build. (After Douglas hung up, in fact, he grumbled to one of his engineers, "Who the hell is gonna buy a sleeper plane anyway? Night flying is about as popular as silent movies.")

The phone call, according to the tariff records of Illinois Bell, cost American $335.50. It was, in retrospect, a reasonable price to pay for its consequences.

For with that $335.50, C.R. had launched the Douglas Sleeper Transport program, otherwise known as the DST. The daytime model was the most famous single airplane in the history of commercial aviation.

The DC-3.

7
Not Just the Biggest,
But the Best

The DC-3 concept was somewhat easier than its execution.

On paper, it looked deceptively simple. Widen and stretch the fuselage, install more powerful engines to handle the increased weight, and solve the stability problems of the DC-2 with more wingspan and additional fin area.

But paper airplanes don't always perform as expected when they're transferred from the drawing board into metal reality, and the DC-3 was no exception. Douglas officially began the project May 10, 1935, with the issuance of Report No. 1004, which set forth the aircraft's general design, weight, and performance specifications. During the 412 days that elapsed between that date and the DC-3's entrance into regular airline service, there were enough setbacks to discourage the most incorrigible optimist.

Bill Littlewood figured the engines would give him the fewest worries. Early in 1935, Wright and Pratt & Whitney had come out with two new, very promising power plants they were proposing for American's new plane, and both manufacturers sent technicians to Santa Monica to participate in the DC-3's gestation. The Wright entry was the G-2 Cyclone, a beefed-up version of the 710-horsepower Cyclone that powered the DC-2. Pratt & Whitney had gone the same route, adding more muscle to an existing Wasp engine; like its Wright competitor, the new Wasp R-1830 developed 1,000 hp, or almost a third more power than the engines on the DC-2.

The rivalry between the two engine manufacturers was fierce throughout the development program. There were even occasional fistfights during overheated arguments on the merits of their respective products. Douglas officials finally painted a white line across the hangar floor where the engines were being tested; Wright engineers were ordered to stay on one side and the P-W representatives on the other.

This ended the fisticuffs but didn't stop the incessant insults and taunts flung across the dividing line. The ultimate in promotional needling came one morning when the entire Pratt & Whitney contingent showed up wearing identical turtleneck sweaters with the company name spelled out on the backs.

Littlewood and Otto Kirchner virtually lived at the factory for almost a year, with Dan Beard joining them when the flight test phase began. To Beard, known throughout his career as a pilot's pilot, went the responsibility of

working with Douglas on the cockpit layout, controls, and flight stability—
he was, in fact, the third man to fly the DC-3. An unsung but vital member
of the American team was H. W. "Hobie" Beals; he was assigned as the
airline's factory representative from the first cutting of metal on the initial
airplane to the actual production of every DC-3 delivered to American. It was
a job he was to perform ably for almost thirty years; whenever Douglas built
a transport for American, Hobie Beals was there to make sure the product was
as perfect as possible. His official title was "West Coast factory representative"
but unofficially he was a resourceful, nitpicking mother hen who prowled the
assembly lines like a supervising surgeon ready to pounce on a resident's
mistake.

Littlewood truly appreciated him, and once paid Beals this heartfelt tribute:
"Throughout the years when we were the principal customer of Douglas
commercial aircraft, and they were the largest manufacturer of transport
aircraft, Hobie Beals was the most important link between American and
Douglas. He not only knew intimately the people in the front office from
Douglas, Sr., down, but he also knew all the important people in the engineering and production ends of the business and was able to secure . . . materials,
engineering changes and financial concessions which were beyond the power
of anybody else in our company to negotiate."

Hobie was not above resorting to discreet theft if American needed some
hard-to-get part in a hurry. He knew every inch of that assembly line and the
parts procurement status of every plane being built—those of the competitors
as well as American. If his airline was short, say, of a key landing gear
component for one of its DC-3s, Hobie would quietly appropriate a unit
earmarked for someone else's DC-3.

Hobie's reputation extended beyond his own airline. When Rickenbacker
bought the DC-3 for Eastern, he sent for the man who would be EAL's factory
representative in Santa Monica.

"Now when you get there," Captain Eddie told him sternly, "insist on
getting an office next to Hobie Beals. When Hobie leaves his office, you leave
yours. When Beals raises hell, you raise hell. When he goes down to the
production line, you follow him. You do all this, son, and by God we'll get
our airplanes out of there in good shape!"

"Hobie," Littlewood said admiringly, "knew exactly to whom to go to
abstract material under the noses of competitors, right from the Douglas
manufacturing line."

The first DC-3 began to take shape under the Smith/Littlewood marching
orders that, freely translated, simply said "get rid of everything that's wrong
with the DC-2." Actually, American's DC-2 fleet already had benefited from
modifications Littlewood had insisted on when the plane's numerous bugs
became apparent after it went into airline service.

Five of the first fifty DC-2s built had dropped on their bellies while taxiing
or standing still, and at Littlewood's prodding Douglas had installed mechani-
cal down-latches to prevent gear collapse. Early DC-2 models had landing

lights in the nose, as did the Condors, and pilots complained that in haze, dust, or snow, the nose lights were inadequate. American's DC-2s had landing lights on the leading edge of the wings, along with greater heating capacity for the carburetors, better cockpit lighting (fluorescent supplementing standard lights), and an ice-prevention system for the rudder.

All these improvements went into the DC-3, but they were relatively minor compared to the rest of the design work. American's specifications called for a maximum 1,000-foot takeoff length with a full 24,000-pound gross weight. This required ten more feet of wingspan, five on each wing. Douglas tried to meet Littlewood's demand for improved stability by enlarging the horizontal and vertical tail area, but the early results were unsatisfactory. On one key test flight, Beard was flying simulated instrument approaches, utilizing the common procedure of avoiding sharp banks at low altitude by sideslipping or "skidding" into the desired direction. He found that in such skids, the DC-3 tended to pitch down dangerously.

He took his complaint to W. Bailey Oswald, Douglas's chief aerodynamics engineer, who subsequently informed Beard he had determined the cause of the instability.

"There's a cross-flow ahead of the fin that spoils the depression forces on the horizontal stabilizer on the lee side of the fin during a skid," was his erudite explanation.

"How the hell do we fix it?" was Beard's blunt question.

Bailey's solution, based on wind tunnel tests, was to add a dorsal fin about five feet long to the rear fuselage. The extension was six inches wide at the base of the tail fin and tapered to zero about a fifth of the way toward the front. It eradicated the pitch-down gremlin. But the test flights uncovered other problems.

The braking system proved inadequate and almost caused a fatal accident in an unexpected ground-loop that wound up with the plane's nose only two feet from the side of a hangar. The right wheel brake cylinder had burst from excessive pressure during the landing, and Douglas installed stronger cylinders.

An outwardly minor improvement but one of some importance to stewardesses was a redesigned two-quart thermos coffee jug. The jugs on the DC-2s were vulnerable to a pressure differential as the plane gained altitude, and a stewardess turning the spigot often got a blast of hot coffee on her hand if the pressure inside the jug had built up too high.

Littlewood designed a spigot with two tubes, one to let air into the jug to equalize pressure and the other to let coffee flow at a safe rate. It worked so well that American wound up selling the new two-tube spigot to other DC-3 operators at 25 cents a unit.

Littlewood's biggest concern was engine performance. Both he and Kirchner were leaning toward the Wright G-2, partially because American already was using the earlier Cyclones and its mechanics were familiar with the engine. The new G-2 went into the first test airplane, No. 14988 (a DST version), and began generating creased foreheads on everyone except the Pratt & Whitney delegation.

The new Wright engine failed the most crucial test of all, the ability to take off with a maximum payload within a thousand feet of runway. During one solid month of test flights, every takeoff overshot the 1,000-foot mark by up to 50 feet. Beard could neither believe it nor explain it and was on the verge of advising Littlewood to shift to the P-W Wasp when Bob Johnson, Wright's chief service engineer, asked Dan to lend him the DC-3 for a couple of days.

Three days later, Johnson turned the plane back to Beard and asked him to make another 24,000-pound takeoff test, without telling him what had been done to the engines. This time, the DC-3's wheels broke ground at 970 feet. Johnson confided later that excess lubricating oil had been absorbing about 75 hp; by improving the oil flow via a minor modification, he had achieved delivery of full horsepower.

Until that fix, however, the whole DC-3 program appeared shaky. The P-W Wasps hadn't been tried on the test airplane, and pilots from other potential customers weren't that impressed with the DC-3. TWA's Tommy Tomlinson, in fact, flew 14988 and reported back to Jack Frye that American was buying a lemon. "It's a clunk," he told Frye after witnessing the plane flunk one of the earlier full-load takeoff tests. This jaundiced if understandable view cost TWA valuable delivery positions, for Frye later ordered a batch of DC-3s, including the sleeper version.

So, eventually, did Pat Patterson of United. Saddled with his fleet of out-classed 247s, Patterson had bypassed the DC-2 in hopes of catching up with the DC-3, but he didn't sign a contract (for twenty airplanes) until April 1936, and by that time American was getting ready to accept delivery of its first DST. Ironically, United actually signed *before* American—C.R. and Douglas had no formal contract drawn up for signature until after the first ten DC-3s had been delivered!

Patterson, of course, enjoyed one advantage: his DC-3s would be the beneficiaries of American's bug-elimination program, avoiding all the frustrations and disappointments of the grueling test phases. And the wily United chief, cognizant of American's sizable lead, tried to go his rival one better. UAL's DC-3s were ordered with an even better engine than the Wright G-2 or P-W Wasp, the new Pratt & Whitney Hornet, which would make its DC-3s fourteen miles an hour faster than the Cyclone-equipped plane. The Hornet also provided higher altitude capability, needed for United's more mountainous transcontinental route.

Patterson stayed away from a sleeper DC-3. Instead, he ordered some of his DC-3s equipped with only fourteen seats that were more like the luxurious armchairs in a Pullman club car. The legroom would have done justice to the first-class section in one of today's 747s. To fly in one of United's "Sky Lounges," a passenger would pay a premium of only $2 above regular fare. It was an intriguing gimmick but it didn't last long, for the obvious reason that the $28 extra revenue on a fourteen-passenger plane couldn't match what seven more seats brought in.

Worrying about how the opposition was going to operate its DC-3s was something C.R. put on the back burners for a while. He was far more concerned with the reports from Littlewood on the test flights. As late as May 1936, only a month before the start of scheduled DC-3 service, there were still sixty detailed technical items in dispute—such items as unsatisfactory engine mounts, inadequate oil cooling capacity, and persistent brake problems. Smith flew to Santa Monica May 27 for a showdown; with Littlewood at his side, he met with Donald Douglas and Art Raymond, chief Douglas designer.

During the marathon sessions, held in the Douglas flight hangar, 14988 stayed grounded for three days. C.R. said it wouldn't move one foot until he was satisfied all of American's specifications were met. It was a rather tense situation, for American had already officially accepted the airplane a month earlier. Raymond finally brought drawing boards right into the hangar and worked out the necessary modifications to Littlewood's satisfaction.

One problem was never really resolved. The DST was overweight, considerably heavier than the DC-3 in sufficient proportions to affect performance. But C.R., who had insisted on a sleeper plane over Douglas's misgivings, didn't press the issue.

Those berths furnished almost as many engineering headaches as the engines. True to his word, Smith had shipped a Condor to California. It proved valuable, if only to demonstrate how *not* to put berths in an airplane cabin. Douglas built a DST mock-up that almost became Bill Littlewood's Santa Monica address. He and Harry Wentzel, Douglas vice president and general manager, consumed hours climbing in and out of sample berths trying to arrive at the most comfortable, easiest to make up, and lightest. One thing achieved was a vastly improved lower berth.

"We also," Littlewood recounted, "spent a lot of time on our backs figuring out the best location for reading lamps."

The first ten aircraft delivered to American were DST models; all were flown from Santa Monica to Phoenix to avoid the stiff California sales tax, and American took possession at the Arizona airport. NC-14988, known affectionately around the system as "old '988," was the first DC-3 to fly, but it lost the honor of being the first into service; Douglas continued using it as a test airplane for several months before it began flying commercially for the Eagle.

Of poignant note was its eventual fate. Three and a half months after Pearl Harbor, it was transferred from an American Airlines hangar at New York's LaGuardia Airport to TWA's hangar. As of that hour, it had logged more than 17,000 hours in combined airline and test flights. TWA stripped its interior and flew 988 for two months under a wartime Military Air Transport contract before turning it over to the Army. On October 15, 1942, it was nearing Chicago on a routine flight from Missouri when one engine failed. The aircraft crashed, killing all nine Army men aboard.

Thus ended, in sadly ignominious fashion, the honorable career of the first DC-3. The first of many, it must be added; Douglas built more than 10,000 between 1935 and 1946, when production ended. But old 988 was more than just the grandfather of all DC-3s. As long as it flew for American, it carried the name *Flagship Texas*—the forerunner of what became a unique American Airlines tradition: the Flagship Fleet.

The dawn of the DC-3 era coincided with C. R. Smith's first real efforts to form his own management team.

He had been much impressed with some of the alumni from the old Transamerican ranks, retaining Tom Dunnion as company treasurer and then promoting him to vice president and treasurer. When C.R. made Doc Miller general sales manager, he also promoted Charlie Rheinstrom to be Miller's chief assistant (in just one year, they were to exchange positions, with Rheinstrom becoming vice president of sales). And innovative Charlie Speers succeeded Rheinstrom as divisional sales manager in Chicago.

Bill Littlewood, too, was marked for much-deserved recognition. The year after the DC-3 began operating, he was made vice president of engineering. But Smith's major and most surprising executive selection was the recruitment of Ralph Damon, who left Curtiss-Wright in January 1936 to become American's vice president of operations.

C.R. had liked him from the day they first met at the Condor factory in St. Louis. He knew Damon was a hard worker, so completely dedicated that he and his wife actually slept in the Condor mock-up many nights, to make sure the berths were conducive to slumber. He was more gregarious than C.R. and had Smith's knack of remembering names and faces to an even greater extent. Both were domineering men, a shared trait that eventually would strain their relationship, but C.R. could not have picked a more capable and popular lieutenant.

Everyone liked Damon, including the pilots who at first resented being under a vice president of operations who wasn't a pilot himself—Earl Ward had been more their type. But no airline ever had a more likable and respected officer than Ralph Damon, who was tough yet always fair. One of his few personal weaknesses—one that could drive C.R. up the wall—was his inability to tell jokes. He could never remember a punch line and used to resort to writing them down on a piece of paper, which he'd take out and read at the end of the story.

Only C.R. himself outranked Damon in the affections of pilots, and the margin was slim at that. Donald K. Smith, now a retired captain, was hired at the same time Damon came over to American and happened to be sitting next to him on a DC-2 heading for Chicago. They got to talking and D.K. volunteered, "I'm going to work for American as a pilot."

Damon smiled. "That's a coincidence. I'm going to work for American, too." He finally admitted he was the new vice president of operations and added, "I might as well tell you that one of my jobs will be to take you pilots out of the circus category into professionalism."

It was Damon's incredible memory that awed everyone. He and twelve other passengers were aboard a DC-2 flying between Buffalo and Detroit one winter night and D.K. was the first officer. The cabin heater froze and at Detroit the chilled passengers were transferred to a DC-3 for the rest of their trip to

Chicago. About ten years later, as D.K. recalled it, he bumped into Damon and asked him if he remembered the night the heater froze.

"I sure do," Damon said—and proceeded to name all twelve fellow passengers.

"He could meet fifty new pilots at graduation and call every one of them by name at the end of the evening," D.K. marveled.

Damon was with C.R. when the latter got the idea for a special flag to go with the name *Flagship*. They were on a boat in Lake Michigan, just offshore from the Chicago Yacht Club where C.R. was a member. They were idly watching the CYC pennant flapping in a stiff breeze when Smith suddenly remarked, "Ralph, we oughta have our own flag for the airline."

It already had been determined that the new DC-3s would be called "Flagships," although the exact authorship of that idea is unknown. Some sources credited Doc Miller with thinking up the fleet name, others said it was advertising whiz Pete Willis, and it may have been C.R. himself. Reportedly, it was Smith who conceived the practice of christening each aircraft with the name of a state or city American served.

But there is no uncertainty as to who designed the company flag. Within a few weeks after C.R.'s conversation with Damon, notices went up on all company bulletin boards asking for flag design suggestions. Five student agents in New York saw one of the notices and decided to enter the contest. They started out with the premise that a flagship had to be commanded by an admiral, although nobody had the slightest notion of what an admiral's flag was supposed to look like.

All five proceeded to a public library, where they discovered that admirals' flags had one thing in common: four stars. From this bit of information, they developed and submitted a design with four white stars and the eagle symbol on a field of blue, the flag itself outlined by a red border. For the record, the quintet consisted of Ralph Smith, Wilson Burdett, J. H. Wiseman, Kendrick Kerns, and George C. Wright.

The overall Flagship theme was to be an American Airlines trademark for years to come, and it reflected C.R.'s rather surprising admiration for the nautical. There was nothing in his background to explain it, yet he loved seascapes almost as much as Western art, and boating ranked behind only trout fishing and poker in his affections. So his pilots became captains and first officers, the airplanes were Flagships, and each was named like a ship. But the final touch was another C. R. Smith stroke of genius.

He came back from Forth Worth one day, having just been made an Honorary Texas Ranger—for a Texan, the equivalent of the Congressional Medal of Honor. Proudly he showed his Ranger card to Charlie Speers and Ed Bern, American's new director of public relations.

"You know," C.R. said thoughtfully as they examined the card, "these guys in Texas and the ones in Kentucky, with their honorary colonels, they get a lot of mileage out of those little pieces of paper. Why can't we have something like that?"

From that impulsive remark sprang one of the greatest marketing gimmicks in airline history: formation of the first VIP passenger organization. C.R.'s choice for its name was perfect: the Admirals Club, which tied in with the new four-star pennant that he was ordering to be flown on every DST and DC-3. Flagships, of course, carried admirals, and full admirals sported four stars.

It wasn't a real club at first, and wouldn't be for another three years.

"Nobody at the time envisioned it as anything more than a promotional scheme like the Texas Rangers and Kentucky Colonels," Charlie Speers explained. "The idea was to make certain people Honorary Admirals of the Flagship Fleet. We asked our field offices to send us the names of those special customers, celebrities, or prominent officials who might get a kick out of being an admiral. The first certificates, all signed by C.R., weren't very fancy. We also sent them to airport managers, members of the press, and people like that."

Among the early recipients were hotel porters, as a reward for steering guests to American whenever possible. One porter at the Stevens Hotel in Chicago was so proud of his certificate that he hung it up in the lobby.

Every new DC-3 and DST delivered to American was equipped with a small flagpole socket, mounted just outside the cockpit next to the first officer's window. Into that socket went the four-star pennant; it was the copilot's duty to insert the flag before the boarding process began, remove it just before takeoff, and put it back after every landing, so it could be seen from the terminal as the aircraft taxied up to the gate. The solemn ritual was followed until after World War II, when American began operating pressurized planes.

First officers being only human, they occasionally would forget that "flag removal" before takeoff was part of their checklist, and quite a few flags were lost by being blown from their poles at 180 miles an hour. The original pennants were hand sewn, with four white stars next to the eagle emblem on a blue background. So many disappeared that later ones had the eagle and stars printed on inexpensive felt. The sockets also would collect rain water and when a copilot opened his window to insert the flag, he'd get his arm wet from the splash.

The flagpole sockets weren't the only unique feature on American's DC-3s. Virtually every carrier ordering the plane specified that the passenger door be located on the left side of the fuselage. C.R. insisted that American's DC-3 doors be on the right side, and for years one could always spot an ex-American DC-3 by the location of that door.

There were several explanations for this idiosyncrasy, the most common one being that American's Condors also had right-side passenger doors (as did the Vultees and Fords), and that C.R. merely was seeking fleetwide standardization.

A more interesting theory is that he wanted passengers and terminal spectators (and in those days the latter constituted a sizable audience) to witness the flag-raising ritual, which meant the door had to be on the same side as the first officer's socket. He probably envisioned having a small Stars and Stripes for each Flagship, until he came up with the idea of an American Airlines flag.

The Flagship motif and individual aircraft names were excellent demonstrations of C.R.'s sharp marketing instincts. He had so much faith in the DC-3, he quickly grasped the possibility that it would be operated by most U.S. carriers and would dominate air travel for a long time. Thus, he wasn't satisfied with the honor of being the first DC-3 airline, knowing this lead had to be temporary. If competitors were going to fly the same plane, he wanted American's fleet to be different and distinctive, with a touch of glamour.

Since 1935, American and other carriers had followed the old railroad practice of assigning names to crack trains; popular flights had not only the usual trip numbers but were called "The Niagara," "The Night Owl," "The New Yorker," and "The Manhattan." Now C.R. decided to give special names to the new DC-3 nonstop flights between Chicago and New York (actually Newark). The midday eastbound Trip 22 and westbound Trip 21 were designated "American Eagle." The late afternoon nonstops, Trips 16 and 17, were "American Arrow." When transcontinental sleeper service was inaugurated later that year, the twice-daily schedules didn't even carry flight numbers at first; the crack three-stop trip was "American Mercury," later shortened to just "The Mercury," and the slower seven-stop flight was "The Southerner."

American began DC-3 service after the first three DSTs were delivered, operating all three in a fourteen-passenger daytime configuration. On June 21, 1936, four days before the scheduled inaugural Chicago–New York nonstops, the airline pulled off a publicity stunt that gladdened the headline-hungry heart of publicity chief Ed Bern. NC–16001, *Flagship New York,* took off from Chicago with a full fuel load of 822 U.S. gallons, flew to Newark without stopping to land, and went right back to Chicago's Midway—a nonstop round trip completed in eight hours and seven minutes. The DST landed with 50 gallons of fuel still remaining.

The unprecedented exploit earned a lot of favorable attention although C.R. and Littlewood, who were aboard, knew the spectacular flight was more hyperbole than a true demonstration of the plane's range capability. In actual service over the Chicago–New York route, westbound DST flights with all fourteen seats full couldn't carry a single pound of mail or cargo. The eastbound trips with a full passenger load had enough weight available for almost 500 pounds of mail and cargo. Even on the lighter DC-3s, if mail and cargo were carried on westbound flights, four seats had to be blocked out. These weight restrictions were temporary, however; Douglas eventually increased the allowable maximum takeoff weight from 24,000 to slightly over 25,000 pounds.

The DC-3 era began June 25, 1936—"the most significant date in the first twenty-five years of air transport history," as one aviation chronicler called it. Captain Walt Braznell, who served for years as American's chief pilot in Chicago and became vice president of flight, commanded *Flagship Illinois* (NC–16002) as it took off at noon from Midway with thirteen paying passengers and C.R. himself aboard, wearing a white straw hat and grinning from ear to ear. The DST landed at Newark three hours and fifty-five minutes later.

The westbound inaugural, captained by the legendary Doc Ator, took four hours and forty-five minutes, which was still almost an hour faster than the swiftest DC-2 *eastbound* schedule (which involved a stop at Detroit).

Ed Bern pulled out all the publicity stops prior to the DST's introduction, and so did Pete Willis, who may well have been one of the best advertising men any airline ever had. There were occasional fumbles, however. The first occurred several months before service inauguration when Bern got Douglas to put 988 on display for a few days at the National Pacific Aircraft and Boat Show in the huge Los Angeles Auditorium.

Donald Douglas, Sr., himself showed up the first night to inspect the exhibit. There sat the world's first DST, resplendent in its American Airlines color scheme—gleaming silver except for the traditional orange-and-blue lightning bolt stretching from nose to tail, orange peel markings on the nacelles, and orange rudder and ailerons. It was enough to take one's breath away and Douglas was visibly affected—but not by his airplane. His eyes fell on the large sign in front of the DST. It read:

21 SEATS—14 BIRTHS!

No spelling error was ever more hastily corrected.

One of Pete Willis's early DST ads wound up in the Let's-Forget-It-As-Quickly-As-Possible category. Pete composed it for the *Official Aviation Guide* (now the *Official Airline Guide*), which carried all airline schedules. It was a full two-page spread with a headline extending across both pages: "IS IT TRUE WHAT THEY SAY ABOUT FLAGSHIPS?" Pete's answers strayed somewhat from the truth.

On one page was a photograph of passengers boarding a new DST, and above the picture were cartoonlike "balloons" quoting their ecstatic reactions to the giant airliner. One comment referred to the June 21 nonstop round trip between Chicago and New York and declared that after flying eight hours it still "had two and a half hours fuel left in the tanks!" Willis must have pulled that statistic out of his felt hat—there was no way a pilot could keep a DC-3 in the air for two and a half hours on only fifty gallons, unless through the power of prayer.

Another passenger remark referred to the DST's great speed. "They're faster than any other transport plane . . . 220 miles per hour top speed . . . 190 cruising. . . . Man, that's moving!" The DC-3's actual cruising speed was around 180 m.p.h. and its top speed sans any tail or headwind was about 200. And there were at least two transports operating in 1936 that were faster than the DC-3: Lockheed's single-engine Orion and the L-10 Electra. Even American's old Vultee was swifter, and some pilots claimed the lighter DC-2 was faster. The DC-3's virtue was its greater range, which compressed flying time between far-apart cities and required fewer refueling stops.

Willis could be forgiven for a third "quote" in the *Guide* ad, because he was no soothsayer. He had a passenger commenting, "Say! These new Flagships look like the 'Hindenburg' with wings!" The ad first ran in the July 1936 issue

of the *Guide* and the huge German dirigible wasn't destroyed until the following May. But the mention may not have been accidental. At the time, the
Hindenburg was the talk of all aviation, it drew 100,000 visitors to Lakehurst,
New Jersey, after arriving on its maiden flight to the U.S. in 1936. It made nine
more round trips between Germany and Lakehurst that year, and the ever-
alert C.R. capitalized on its popularity by assigning a DC-3 to connect with
the incoming and departing transatlantic trips. There was a DC-3 waiting for
the *Hindenburg* at Lakehurst on that fateful day of May 6, 1937.

Pete Willis may have colored the facts a bit in that one ad, but overall the
advertising campaign he created for the first few years of the DC-3 era was
masterful. It was largely soft sell, highly original, frequently institutional, and
devastatingly effective—there wasn't an airline in the country that didn't admit
privately American's advertising was the best in the industry. And while Willis
usually was the author, it was C.R. who so often gave him the concept from
which to work. Pete only had to keep in mind Smith's goals for the airline:
sell air travel per se and in the process depict American as the air travel leader.

The speed of air transportation was a favorite theme. I'LL BE HOME TO-
NIGHT, ran one headline. FEWER HUSBANDLESS NIGHTS was another. WHEN
YOUR COMPETITOR HAS NOT REACHED GALLUP, YOU CAN BE IN NEW YORK
went a third.

There were nontechnical descriptions of the DC-3, aimed at instilling confidence—such as calling the plane "relatively stronger than the Brooklyn
Bridge." Which in a sense was true and far more aptly put for the layman than
detailing the advantages of the DC-3's stressed skin and multispar, cellular
wing construction.

One ad asked the burning question: "Shall We Serve Cocktails On Airplanes?" It included a coupon ballot to be mailed in, and the response would
have done justice to the turnout of a congressional election in a large state.
C.R. wasn't surprised at the referendum's outcome—it ran ten to one against
serving in-flight liquor—but he didn't expect the volume of ballot returns to
be so high. It gave American's sales force an exceptionally large list of prospects to be wooed through direct mail and personal contacts.

Not all the ads were successful. One C.R. let slip through—and regretted
later—featured a beautiful blonde in a negligee; she was holding up a telegram
and the caption had her exclaiming: "He Still Loves Me! He'll Be Home
Tonight Via American Airlines." The implication was that American had
saved a failing marriage. But if Willis struck out with this one, he scored
heavily with another that turned out to be the most famous single advertisement in airline history.

This was the controversial 1937 "Afraid To Fly?" ad that stunned an
industry that had studiously avoided the very mention of safety. It was strictly
C.R.'s idea to run such a tell-it-like-it-is ad, and it was aimed bravely and
bluntly at the principal reason most people refused to fly: fear. Unlike his peers,
who considered the subject of safety about as welcome a topic as discussing
sexual techniques in a kindergarten class, Smith felt it was time for the industry

to face up to the fact that fear was a major detriment to the growth of air transportation.

Willis composed the text from a first draft C.R. had hammered out on his ancient Woodstock typewriter. Over the large-type headline AFRAID TO FLY? was the line, in slightly smaller letters, "Why Dodge This Question." The ad began, "We know that fear keeps many people from enjoying the advantages of air transportation. *So why should we be silent on the subject?*" (That sentence was italicized in the ad.)

The third sentence stood the industry on its collective ear. "Regrettable as it is, the records show there *have been* accidents and fatalities in *every* form of transportation." It was considered heresy to admit that airliners crash and kill people. But having conceded that obvious but never-to-be-publicly-discussed fact, the ad concluded that "People are afraid of the things they do not know about" and reminded the reader that "you would be equally afraid of a train if you had never ridden on one."

The full advertisement, signed by C.R., is reproduced elsewhere in this volume. Its impact on a nervous industry, plagued by a series of bad accidents, can best be judged in the context of the times. Most 1937 airline advertising was pretty prosaic, usually featuring a picture of the carrier's newest airliner and an abbreviated timetable. Smith's daring departure from the norm faced an industry problem squarely and, in doing so, benefited all airlines. The ad did not claim that American was the safest or even a safe airline; it merely declared that flying was safer than most people realized.

Admittedly, C.R. was not always so generous to his competitors. He got into an angry feud with United over a series of Willis ads that seemed to imply that flying American's southern transcontinental route was safer because there weren't many mountains along the way. The ad that kicked off the fuss asked the provocative question: "Is There a Low Level Airway Through Southern Sunshine to California?" Other ads proclaimed American as "The Southern Sunshine Route."

The phrases "low level" and "southern sunshine" were to United's Pat Patterson what "Marching Through Georgia" is to a resident of Atlanta. He felt the ads implied that United's transcontinental route, which admittedly was exposed to worse winter weather, was more hazardous. C.R.'s intentions were well meaning. American was at something of a competitive disadvantage with its southern transcontinental route, simply because it was longer than either TWA's central or United's northern coast-to-coast airways. The emphasis on a "sunshine" route was a somewhat questionable effort to offset its longer distance.

At any rate, the ads did violate what *Fortune* observed was an unwritten code among the airlines. "Essentially," *Fortune* noted, "the industry is a collection of independent states that are joined by common interests as well as common hazards. The greatest of these hazards is the ordinary man's fear of air travel and the first commandment of the industry is Thou Shalt Not Do Anything to Reflect Directly or Indirectly on Air Safety."

United counterattacked with ads of its own, denying any inference that its routes were unsafe and pointing out rather sharply that, systemwide, American flew over more mountainous terrain than United. C.R., who hadn't really intended to disparage a fellow airline president he honestly liked and respected, invited Patterson to a quiet dinner where the hatchet was buried. The words "low level" were henceforth banned from American's advertising lexicon, although the airline continued to stress "southern" and "sunshine" in its copy for several years.

And Smith was to prove to his rival that he had the industry's best interests at heart. On February 9, 1937, a United Air Lines DC-3 making a routine night approach to the San Francisco Airport in perfectly clear weather suddenly went into a dive and crashed into the Bay, killing all eleven aboard—eight passengers, the stewardess, and both pilots. The wreckage was hauled out of the water the next day and examined, but there were no clues as to what had caused an inexplicable 45-degree dive.

Investigators were ready to pin the blame on the veteran UAL captain, but five weeks after the accident an American DC-3 was rolling down a runway at Newark and about to take off when the captain found the controls jammed. He managed to abort the takeoff and examined his control yoke, which wouldn't budge. Looking down, he noticed that the copilot's radio microphone had fallen off its hook and become wedged in a small V-shaped well at the foot of the yoke. Shaken yet relieved, he pried the mike loose and took off—but upon landing at his destination, he reported the incident to his chief pilot. Within a few hours C.R. was on the phone to Patterson.

"We think this is what might have caused your San Francisco accident," he told the UAL president.

Investigators hurriedly took another look at the wreckage of the United DC-3, stored in a hangar after it was fished out of San Francisco Bay. There they found the copilot's radio mike, wedged into the tiny well that had turned into a deadly loophole.

Fortune's description of the airline industry as "a collection of independent states . . . joined by common interests" was astutely accurate, and the friendship that always existed between Smith and Patterson was typical of the love-hate relationship that permeated the industry's hierarchy; it is probably less true today but a residue still remains. Not everyone liked C.R., but respect was universal. He, in turn, had strong and varied opinions of his peers. Patterson seems to have been one of his favorites. Conversely, he reportedly considered Continental's Bob Six something of a maverick upstart (ironically, they were very much alike in many respects), and he always showed a kind of amused disdain toward Eddie Rickenbacker.

C.R. was personally fond of the crusty Eastern chief, but he took special delight in needling him on frequent occasions. When the industry's trade organization, the Air Transport Association of America, was founded in 1936, its newly formed board of directors decided that ATA's salaried officers should receive free transportation on member carriers. Only Rickenbacker objected. He was overwhelmingly outvoted but it stuck in his craw, and he later mentioned to Smith that he was going to stop giving passes to ATA officials.

"I don't want them riding around free on Eastern," he grumbled.

"Don't worry, Eddie," C.R. said gently. "They'll only try Eastern once."

Yet top-level feuds were far less numerous than instances of cooperation. Tragedy was a special catalyst that subordinated intense rivalries to mutual sympathy and understanding. Every airline official and employe viewed somebody else's crash as a There-But-For-The-Grace-Of-God-Goes-Us situation, knowing that accidents depressed traffic for everyone. The spontaneous reaction to a radio bulletin that "an unidentified airliner has crashed" instinctively went "I hope it wasn't one of ours," but the second reaction was the sinking realization that any accident was bad for everyone.

American, justifiably proud of its own safety record, was not immune to whatever fate dictates unexpected death. On January 14, 1936, an American DC-2 crashed under mysterious circumstances near Goodwin, Arkansas, killing all fourteen passengers and the crew of three.

The plane was operating as Trip 1 (they were called "Trips" instead of "Flights" until the early 1940s) from Newark to Fort Worth with a crew change at Memphis, where Captain Joe Marshall, copilot Glenn Freeland, and stewardess Perla Gasparini boarded for the remainder of the flight to Fort Worth via Little Rock and Dallas.

Trip 1 was nearing Little Rock when ground observers noticed it was flying at an unusually low altitude—lower than what Marshall was reporting in his radio contacts. His last radio report was at 7:18 P.M. and fourteen minutes later the DC-2 suddenly went 60 degrees off course and dived into the ground.

Vandals and looters hindered the investigation by carrying away some of the wreckage. The Bureau of Air Commerce was never able to determine whether structural failure had occurred, but the evidence was against it. Weather was no factor; it was an exceptionally clear night. The Bureau's official report listed several possibilities but admitted none was provable or even likely. It included such possibilities as the captain being absent from the cockpit and a relatively inexperienced copilot becoming confused with a minor difficulty; slowness in switching fuel from a nearly empty tank, which might explain the 60-degree course change; and the far-fetched likelihood that a passenger being shown the cockpit could have obscured the captain's vision. The accident was never solved, and to this day it comes up at Grey Eagle meetings when the old-timers talk about the days when accident investigation was not the scientific process it was to become. And many believe Trip 1—the first fatal DC-2 crash—was the victim of a pathological killer.

There were rumors, never confirmed but also never flatly denied, that bulletholes were found in the cockpit and that somebody discovered a fired gun in the wreckage that disappeared before it could be turned over to the authorities. Another rumor was that a passenger's body was found in the cockpit. The Bureau's final report mentioned none of this except for this one brief and oblique reference:

"It is possible that a passenger entered the cockpit either by invitation or otherwise and incapacitated the pilot or copilot or both or maliciously interfered with the controls. This, however, is not substantiated by any of the available evidence."

That last sentence consigned the accident to the unsolved files. The report's most curious omission was failure to mention the outcome of autopsies on the pilots' bodies—if any were performed at all. There seems to have been no effort to determine whether any passenger might have a murder or suicide motive; flight insurance, for example, was unavailable in 1936.

It would be soon, however. In 1937, flight insurance became available to passengers for the first time—a $5,000 policy for only 25 cents. It was the same premium insurance companies offered bus and railroad passengers, and there wasn't the slightest doubt that the plane American pioneered was responsible for air travel's newfound respectability and public confidence.

Nor was this superb airliner the only contribution American made to commercial aviation's maturing process. Two of its employees fathered the air traffic control system that essentially is still the one used today.

Up to late 1934, there was no formal ATC system. Then an American Airlines radio operator/dispatcher named Glen A. Gilbert developed a flight-following system for all American planes approaching within 100 miles of Chicago. It worked so well that C.R. agreed to let other airlines serving Chicago—United, TWA, Eastern, and Northwest—utilize American's control system to avoid traffic conflicts and establish landing and takeoff sequences.

Gil Mears, American's director of communications, extended the coordinated system first to Newark and then to Cleveland, and by 1936 the three cities were operating joint "Airway Traffic Control Centers" that handled all airline flights entering or leaving their respective areas. Mears and Gilbert also set up the mechanism for controlling traffic. It consisted of a large map table and blackboard in each Center; markers (called "shrimp boats") represented each flight and were moved across the map table in accordance with a flight's reported position. Onto the blackboard went various flight data—estimated arrival times, etc. Later Gilbert and Mears improved the operation by developing paper flight-holder strips in movable holders to replace the blackboard.

On July 6, 1936, the Federal government took over the three Centers and went on to establish five more around the country under the Bureau of Air Commerce. After World War II, radar eliminated the "shrimp boat" system, but the principles of air traffic control developed by Mears and Gilbert, who worked with Earl Ward, were never really changed.

To get the temperamentally competitive airlines to agree on any common system was a feat in itself. Yet the industry demonstrated to American that it, too, was capable of pushing rivalries aside in face of emergency. And such an emergency struck the week of September 20, 1938, when a killer hurricane swept out of the Caribbean and devastated virtually the entire New England area. Hundreds were injured, thousands were homeless, and New England was virtually cut off from the rest of the nation. Roads and railroads were under water, and the area's transportation system was at a standstill.

With one exception. The air.

American was the only major carrier operating a New York–Boston route then, and C.R. assigned every Flagship available to mercy missions, shuttling back and forth between New York and Boston with medical supplies and personnel. Within twenty-four hours, Smith knew American couldn't do the job alone. Normally the airline carried about 200 passengers a day over the route. On the first day after the hurricane, more than 1,000 persons were pleading for seats, and the demand multiplied with the need for emergency construction and utility crews.

C.R. called Edgar Gorrell, a former Air Corps officer known as "the Little Colonel," who two years before had been named ATA's first president.

"We need help and fast," he told Gorrell.

The ATA president immediately asked United, TWA, and Eastern to divert as many aircraft as possible to New England and then got the government to issue an emergency authorization for these carriers to operate over American's franchised route.

For seven days, the four-airline armada operated an unprecedented airlift in and out of Boston, flying in 60,000 tons of emergency supplies and more than a thousand rescue and reconstruction workers. They also took some 1,500 stranded persons out of the ravaged area. There weren't enough DC-3s, so American and TWA threw their DC-2s into the fray.

One TWA pilot arrived in Newark from a Midwest base and asked an American captain, "How the hell do I get to Boston?"

"Just get back in your airplane and follow us," was the laconic reply.

By the time weary ground and flight crews returned to their normal jobs, they had shown Edgar Gorrell the massive potentiality of air power in a major crisis. It was a lesson he was not to forget when the war clouds gathered.

American spent the 1936–1938 period solidifying its status as the industry's recognized leader. The Flagships dominated the airways, and the best the competition could do was play catch-up ball for longer than they wanted.

Overnight transcontinental sleeper service was launched September 18, 1936, with *Flagship California*'s inaugural "American Mercury" completing the flight from Glendale Airport in Los Angeles to Newark in fifteen hours and fifty minutes; the westbound inaugural's elapsed time was seventeen hours and forty-one minutes. The refueling stops in both directions were Tucson, Dallas, and Memphis; later Nashville replaced Memphis as one of the stops. About a month later, American introduced "The Southerner," also a DST but with four stops.

The faster Mercury was more popular, with a late afternoon departure from Newark that put passengers into Los Angeles before 8 o'clock the next morning. The first flights were sold out with waiting lists, and bookings were being made up to two weeks ahead—unheard of in those days when the average airline reservation was made the day before the flight.

The DC-3 was nothing but pure glamour. It drew huge crowds every time it went on display. In Detroit, for example, American trucked a DC-3 from the airport across town to the state fairgrounds, where it remained on exhibit for ten days. Rain or shine, long lines formed to walk briefly through the cabin and get a glimpse of the cockpit. There was an admission charge of 10 cents, which American turned over to charity. The total sum was more than $11,000; some 110,000 persons saw the DC-3 in that fortnight.

DC-3s also were displayed on the lawn of the Ambassador Hotel in Los Angeles and in Rockefeller Center, where even blasé New Yorkers gaped at the size of what was then a rather enormous airplane. But the impact of the DC-3 can best be measured not by the number of curious spectators at static exhibits but by the number of people who began flying them. In 1936 alone, the U.S. airlines for the first time in their history carried more than a million passengers—double the 1934 total—and the traffic curve was to mount steadily from then on. In 1939, the airlines flew a whopping 42.2 percent more people than the previous year, a staggering rate of growth that had to be credited almost solely to the DC-3, which by then was carrying 90 percent of the nation's air traffic.

Smart marketing played a role, too, and this was the area in which American excelled. If it didn't innovate something, it improved on what somebody else had thought up. TWA and United, for example, upstaged American by offering to fly wives free, and the promotion scheme was a bonanza—until both airlines made the well-intentioned mistake of writing follow-up letters to the distaff spouses asking them how they enjoyed their flights.

The consequences could be embarrassing; not a few wives wrote back asking, "WHAT FLIGHT?" The press gleefully reported an incident in which a taxi roared right onto a boarding ramp area and pulled up next to an about-to-depart plane. Out of the cab stepped a hefty lady who marched into the cabin and emerged a few seconds later, leading her husband by one ear. Just behind the red-faced mate was a slim blonde, unhappily clutching a now-useless free ticket.

American instituted its own "take your wife along" plan, but judiciously refrained from any follow-up letters. It also went the opposition one better by tying the promotion to its fast-growing list of Admirals and credit card holders, a far better demographic roster than anyone else had. This typical Charlie Speers letter illustrates the dignified slickness of an approach aimed at not only easing the fears of wives whose husbands flew, but persuading them to fly themselves—some 95 percent of airline passengers in the thirties were male:

Dear ———

We would like very much to have your wife accompany you on a trip as a guest of American Airlines. . . .
As a holder of an American Airlines air travel card, you have had an opportunity to experience the many advantages of air transportation. You know that air travel not only saves time but that it is also comfortable, clean, pleasant and safe. . . .

As our guest, your wife will have an opportunity to learn first-hand
how entirely safe you are when you travel by air. We want her to see
for herself how strong, sturdy and mechanically and structurally perfect modern airliners are; with what precision and skill airline operations are carried on; the type of personnel that operates and supervises
the operation of American Airlines Flagships. . . .

Similar letters were sent by district sales managers to card holders and
Admirals in their territory. The free trips involved regional flights—say from
Detroit to Buffalo or Chicago—but each letter suggested that "the value of the
complimentary ticket may be applied to the cost of a longer flight."

"The response was great," Speers said, "and the emphasis on safety was
the smartest thing we did. That's why we had to harp so much on our
southern route during the winter months. Just one accident could hurt
traffic, and two or more within a relatively short span hit every airline with
devastating effects. This was true even in the fifties, and it was prevalent
until the jets took over."

By the end of 1936, American had all twenty of the DC-3s it had ordered
originally in operation; United had only ten, and TWA was still waiting for
the first of eight to be delivered. Equally important was a little statistic of no
interest to the public but of vast significance to the airlines: American's 1937
passenger revenues totaled nearly $6.6 million; mail revenues were just under
$3 million. People, not postage stamps, were now the lifeblood of an industry
that finally understood what C.R. Smith had said a long time ago about the
plane nobody else wanted:

"The DC-3 freed the airlines from complete dependency upon government
mail pay. It was the first airplane which could make money by just handling
passengers. With previous aircraft if you multiplied the number of seats by the
fares being charged, you couldn't break even—not even with a 100 percent full
load. Economically, the DC-3 let us expand and develop new routes where
there was no mail pay."

It cost American 67.4 cents a mile to operate a DC-2. It cost 71.6 cents for
the DC-3, but those seven additional seats more than made up the difference.
Before its advent, American had been averaging annual losses to the tune of
$758,000; in 1938, the airline made over $200,000. This would be peanuts
today and a cause for concern, but in 1938 any profit was a minor miracle.

Eventually, American would be operating an all-DC-3 fleet of ninety-four
aircraft, but it was those first twenty that made aviation history. They also
made possible American's first employee bonus. Late in December 1938, each
of the airline's 2,000 employees received a letter from C.R. and a check—$25
for those who had been with the company at least a year and $15 for those
with less than a year's service.

"We know twenty-five dollars is not a lot of money," the letter said, "but
we do not want the books to close for 1938 without sending you some token
of our appreciation."

Maybe it wasn't a lot of money, but the total bonus voted by the board of directors—at C.R.'s insistence—was almost a fourth of the year's profits. The letter concluded:

"American begins the New Year with the finest group of men and women in any airline. We are proud of what you have done and wish you a good Thirty-nine."

They were to have one.

Plus a few things nobody expected.

8
Of Stratoliners and Stewardesses, Pilots and Passengers

To C. R. Smith, status quo was synonymous with stagnation, complacency a first cousin to stupidity, and standing still the same as moving backwards.

He had too much respect for his two chief competitors to think that American could sit comfortably on any lead without being seriously challenged. Pat Patterson, for all his innate cautious conservatism, was an able executive and United was a most professional airline. TWA's Jack Frye had a flair for the dramatic, not to mention his airline's reputation for a technical excellence that matched American's.

Frye, in fact, shared Smith's gambling instincts and, quite appropriately, both were crackerjack poker players. There is no record of their ever having played together, but it would not have been a Hoyle's Super Bowl. More to the point was their mutual refusal to believe there was any such animal as the ultimate airplane. Each was ever alert to whatever might be forthcoming around the next technological corner.

In 1936, just when the DC-3 was being hailed as the last word in air transportation, Frye had committed TWA to a $2 million contract for six Boeing 307s, a plane even more revolutionary than the DC-3. Dubbed the Stratoliner, the B-307 would be powered by four-engines and its cabin pressurized—the world's first commercial transport capable of flying above most weather. Furthermore, its projected range would permit transcontinental flights with not more than two stops. Pan American ordered four of the new giants, and both airlines expected the 307 to achieve at least a 250-mile-an-hour cruising speed.

Range and speed. C.R. knew these were the DC-3's major deficiencies. Potentially, its twenty-one-passenger capacity was another—adequate for the time but not if air travel continued to expand. The Stratoliner would carry thirty-six in a daytime configuration, and there would be sixteen berths in the sleeper version that Frye planned.

Almost simultaneously with Boeing's launching of the Stratoliner project, five airlines had pooled $300,000 to help Douglas develop a new four-engine transport, the DC-4E (E for Experimental). The quintet included American, United, TWA, Eastern, and Pan Am, and all five sent their top engineers to work with the Douglas design team. Bill Littlewood was American's representative, and he had his doubts right from the beginning. It was the old "a camel is a horse designed by a committee" definition all over again.

The initial DC-4E meetings were held in Chicago, and Littlewood was appalled. "Everyone wants everything," he reported to C.R., "so there's no way we're going to get an airplane that meets our specifications."

His gloomy appraisal was to prove only too accurate. The prototype DC-4E that Douglas built met the standards of almost every compromise: it didn't entirely satisfy anyone and it pleased nobody. It first flew in 1938 and quickly demonstrated it was grossly overweight and underpowered, its performance so disappointing that Littlewood had very little trouble persuading C.R. to pull American out of the project.

This was easier said than done. United was unhappy with the plane, too, but unfortunately and unwisely it already had begun to advertise the DC-4E as the greatest aeronautical achievement since the Wrights first flew. And under the terms of the contract with Douglas, American couldn't pull out unless United did. It took a meeting between C.R. and Patterson to solve the impasse, which mostly involved United's wanting to save face. This was accomplished when American agreed that the next Douglas transport either airline bought would be called the DC-4.

Aware that the DC-4E was shaping up as a disaster, C.R. became interested in the Stratoliner, and Littlewood spent several weeks in Seattle conferring with Boeing engineers. His initial verdict was sour. "The plane's underpowered and not worth a damn," he informed Smith. He gave Boeing a shopping list of suggestions, mostly concerning propellers, engines, and seating—the mock-up he inspected had three-abreast seats on one side of the aisle and one long row of single seats on the other side.

Boeing did adopt some of his recommendations, but his lukewarm opinion of the airplane didn't alter. Actually, the Stratoliner was something of a hybrid, utilizing the wings and tail of the B-17 bomber, and it had stability problems of its own—cured, incidentally, by the addition of a dorsal fin just like the DC-3.

At one point, American was on the verge of signing, but three weeks of haggling ended in disagreement, somewhat to Littlewood's relief. He told Smith the Stratoliner wasn't good enough anyway, its chief virtue being its cabin pressurization system.

"If they had built the 307 the way we wanted it," he was to say later, "there never would have been a DC-4."

The Stratoliner failed to become much of competitive threat to either American or United. TWA wound up with only five airplanes and then turned them over to the military when the U.S. entered World War II; the B-307 wasn't in service long enough to make much of a dent in the pre-war transcontinental market.

Yet it *was* a revolutionary airliner, a worthy grandparent of the great Boeing jetliners that were to play such a vital role in American's future. Both the Stratoliner and the even more unsuccessful DC-4E (the prototype eventually was sold to Japan and ended its career at the bottom of Tokyo Bay after a crash) were signposts of U.S. aviation technology's accelerating progress.

There was increasing awareness of that progress from the government, too. The biggest aviation news of 1938 was passage of a new Civil Aeronautics Act that finally ended the clumsy, often quarrelsome system of dividing federal regulatory authority over the airlines among three agencies: Post Office Department (mail contracts and routes), Interstate Commerce Commission (mail rates and passenger/freight tariffs), and the Commerce Department's Bureau of Air Commerce (safety, airways, and pilot/aircraft licensing).

The 1938 Act created an independent, five-member Civil Aeronautics Authority with jurisdiction over all civil aviation with one exception. Accident investigation, a long-time sore point among airlines and pilots alike, was turned over to a three-man Safety Board, which operated independently even though it was part of the CAA. At the head of the CAA was an administrator in charge of executive and managerial duties.

For the airlines, it was their own Magna Carta, bringing stability and reasonable regulation for the first time to an industry that had been walking a shaky tightrope between czarlike controls and competitive anarchy. The Act's greatest accomplishment was the elimination of specified duration for mail contracts, making all route awards permanent. Route certification thus became protected, but the CAA was given the authority to provide competition in markets where traffic justified the services of two or more carriers.

Congress didn't shove this drastic regulatory reform down the industry's throat, either. The airlines themselves asked for such legislation through the Air Transport Association, which not only lobbied hard for its passage but wrote much of it. The Civil Aeronautics Act of 1938 was authored mostly by the young lawyer ATA president Edgar Gorrell assigned to the task, Howard Westwood of Covington and Burling, a Washington law firm handling ATA legal matters.

Westwood was something of a character in his own right, slated to become a dignified, prestigious attorney deeply involved in American's legal affairs for several years. In the late thirties, however, he was a decided liberal who had once campaigned for socialist Norman Thomas. As the youngest partner in doggedly conservative Covington and Burling, he used to walk down its staid corridors defiantly whistling the "Internationale."

His youthful political leanings may have raised a few eyebrows, but Colonel Gorrell considered him indispensably brilliant. Westwood had served as his counsel when Gorrell set up ATA, and it was Westwood who helped convert Charlie Speers's air travel credit card plan into an industrywide system under ATA's sponsorship. But his greatest contribution to the airlines was that 1938 Act.

In its first annual report to Congress following its creation, the CAA described the pre-1938 condition of the industry in such phrases as "near-chaos," "shaken faith on the part of the investing public in the financial stability of the airlines," "uneconomic, destructive competition and wasteful duplication of services." The report noted that "half of the private capital which had been invested in the industry has been irretrievably lost."

Within a year after the Act became law, the majority of U.S. carriers were showing a profit. American's 1939 net was just under $1.5 million—only the third profit in its history.

Yet it should be noted that C. R. Smith turned American around *before* the industry began to thrive in the new and fresher regulatory atmosphere. While American was showing a modest $100,000 profit in 1938, United was losing almost $1 million and TWA $1.2 million. And under the umbrella of protected routes and controlled competition, C.R. was ready to send the eagle flying even higher.

This was the period when his marriage deteriorated to the point of an inevitable break-up. Lawyer Ham Hale of the Pruitt firm was in C.R.'s office late one Friday afternoon when Elizabeth Smith phoned to remind her husband of some social engagement. His face turned red and he roared, "Well, I'm not going to the Saddle and Cycle Club because I'm going to New York!"

"He hung up on her," Hale said, "and muttered something to the effect that she didn't understand his work came first."

He was, above all else, a man's man who was happiest in traditional male relaxations—hunting, boating, fishing, and poker. Some of his airline associates automatically expected defeat when they played cards with him. "I got into a game with him once," Hale recalled, "and in fifteen minutes I was down $300."

C.R.'s social companions often included pilots, and to some of those veterans, going duck hunting with the company president remained among their fondest memories. Or, occasionally, not so fond.

He once invited Fred Bailey, one-time chief pilot in Chicago, to go duck hunting, having been informed that Captain Bailey was an expert. Which he was—he even carried a duck call with him on flights and drove copilots crazy with a soulful rendition of "Old Rugged Cross," apparently the only tune he knew. (Bailey also happened to be a very sharp airman who devised the so-called "racetrack pattern" for holding over airports.)

In a moment of great kindness, Bailey invited a young first officer named Jack Oleson to accompany them on this particular duck expedition. At 6 A.M. on a bitterly cold day, they stationed themselves in two blinds, Bailey and C.R. in one and Oleson in the other. Bailey began blowing his duck call like a virtuoso piccolo player.

They saw plenty of ducks flying south, but they were out of range. For five solid hours, Bailey's duck call sounded away. His face turned blue and a trickle of blood flowed from a split lip, but he never quit. Finally, around 11 A.M., two ducks suddenly wheeled away from a flock and headed their way. Bailey and Smith tensed. "Here they come, C.R.," Fred whispered. "Get ready."

Their guns were poised, fingers on triggers, when a shotgun blast shook the morning air. The unharmed ducks did a fast one-eighty and flew out of danger.

C.R. cursed and Bailey turned in the direction of Oleson's blind.

"Oley, was that you who missed?"

"Yes, sir," Oleson gulped.

"Bailey," C.R. grunted, "I want to see that kid in my office first thing Monday morning."

Oleson wasn't fired, of course, but he never went duck hunting with C.R. again.

Smith's attitude toward American's stewardesses was somewhat indifferent at first; he regarded them rather impersonally, and took little interest in their training. As late as 1935, American had no formal training facilities, but this changed when C.R. assigned young Newton K. Wilson to be the new supervisor of stewardesses.

Wilson, a short, cigar-smoking individual with the same innovative spirit Charlie Speers possessed, seemed to be an unlikely candidate. He was relatively new with American, having been hired more as an office boy than anything else. He worked for T. K. Griffith, who was then assistant to Earl Ward, vice president of operations, but his qualifications were unique. Wilson was a graduate of Northwestern and during the course of his education he had acquired six years of cooking school in both high school and college.

As far as C.R. was concerned, this knowledge outweighed Newt's airline inexperience, and when Griffith brought his name to Smith's attention, C.R. dispatched him on a systemwide observation tour. Wilson took copious notes on Condor and DC-2 in-flight service and returned with the blunt finding that the stewardesses needed closer supervision and better training.

Wilson also had a hatful of suggestions about food service and this, too, became his responsibility. He worked with Littlewood's DC-3 design team and was largely instrumental in choosing the plane's galley arrangements. On the DC-2, cold food was stored in a box under a rear coat rack, but C.R. was determined to serve hot food on the DC-3s. Wilson and Ernest Fuller, another Littlewood disciple, developed a hot food system that consisted of two-gallon thermos jugs that could keep reasonably warm anything from fried chicken to lobster. On each DC-3, there were four food jugs and six liquid jugs holding two quarts each, and as Wilson himself said, "Basically the two-sized jugs were what we used until the jets came along."

The large food jugs cost $70 apiece and were constantly disappearing from the airplanes. "Theft," Newt recalled wryly, "was a problem. Every pilot had his own jug and you could always find them at pilot picnics." Passenger pilferage was another headache, silverware and blankets being the most frequently stolen items.

He was versatile enough to deal effectively with people as well as food problems. In his report to Smith on the cabin attendants, he noted that while American had chief stewardesses, they didn't really supervise. And he also criticized what was then a policy of hiring girls furloughed from United—in the winter, UAL used to cut its personnel in accordance with reduced schedules. In fact, American's first chief stewardess supervisor was supposed to be a girl recruited from United. She got married before reporting to Chicago and Wilson was picked for the job after she cabled from Europe that she was on her honeymoon.

From 1936 to 1942, Newt Wilson had the final say on every stewardess American hired. If an applicant cleared an initial interview with a recruiter, she still had to pass muster before Newt, who had set up selection standards that were to be adopted by many carriers. For example, he preferred girls who came from small towns because he felt failure would be more traumatic to someone who would have to go back to her small community and admit she had washed out. Such girls, Wilson insisted, would work harder. He also favored applicants who came from large families, figuring that a girl with several brothers and/or sisters knew how to hold her own. And above all, he went for personality rather than beauty.

No one subjected to a Newton K. Wilson interview was likely to forget it. Debbie Jeter, who flew for American until 1964, remembered hers only too well. "He was really something. I was interviewed initially in Los Angeles, but then they sent me to Chicago to see Newt. He'd sit there, smoking a big cigar, staring at you as if he was just waiting for you to say the wrong thing."

Vivian Jorgensen, who flew as Vivian Shattuck before she married, was one of some 600 applicants Wilson interviewed for a 1937 class. "Of the 600, he picked six, including me. I'll never forget my interview. It lasted an hour and a half, starting with what was Newt's usual opening question: 'What makes you think you can be a stewardess?' "

Wilson's official title may have been supervisor of stewardesses, but he quickly was dubbed "our bull stewardess." Despite his toughness, he was well liked, and within a few months he had instilled an air of professionalism among what soon became known as "the stewardess corps." Before he picked a single girl, he chose his first instructor, a popular stewardess named Hazel Brooks, whose natural leadership qualities Newt had been observing. She taught her first class in her own Chicago apartment, a situation that Wilson thought was close to degrading. Between the two of them, they decided to do something about it.

When her class finished training, Hazel and Newt suggested that they compose a little song in honor of the occasion and that it be sung in C. R. Smith's presence. The entire class trooped out to Midway and parked under C.R.'s second-floor office window. It was a surprised and slightly startled president who heard the chorus of young voices, more or less out of tune but loud and clear.

> *We've passed our tests, and are finally on our way*
> *With a heart that's light, with a song inside*
> *We're on our way.*
>
> *As passengers come, as passengers go*
> *They know they'll get the best service*
> *The great American way.*

It wouldn't have made any Top Ten list, but C.R. was impressed to the point of inviting the class up to his office and then took everyone to Mickleberry's, a very good Chicago restaurant, for a graduation luncheon.

During the festive meal, Wilson, Hazel Brooks, and the graduates took turns selling Smith on the need for better training facilities. Newt thought he was going to be fired for such temerity. But C.R. nodded solemnly and added, "Well, if you're going to have a school, then you should have diplomas."

For the first time, he seemed to have grasped the magnitude of stewardess input into an airline's image—and that up to now he hadn't really done much about it. That little song may have been corny and amateurish, but it still carried a message of sincerity and comradeship he had never realized existed. From that day on, the stewardess corps had in C. R. Smith its most loyal friend and supporter.

He didn't go overboard on new facilities right away, for reasons he couldn't reveal then, but he did take the classes out of Hazel's apartment and establish them in the Hyde Park Hotel near Midway. And someday he would give American's flight attendants the finest training facilities in the world. Throughout the years stewardesses found him extremely protective and solicitous, and perhaps more lenient than with any other single group of employees. More than one girl had a twenty-,fifty-, or hundred-dollar bill pressed surreptitiously into her palm as C.R. deplaned, murmuring with false gruffness, "You work a pretty good trip, young lady."

Hazel Brooks was one of his favorites. He had met her on a DC-2 flight that was proceeding routinely until Hazel discovered someone had forgotten to put any pillows on the plane. Pillows were used as meal trays in those days, and she figured she'd better tell C.R. about it.

"They can't hold the damned meals on their laps," he complained.

"No, sir. But we have plenty of magazines. I can use those."

"Good idea," he agreed. "And I'll help you."

They served the meals together, half the passengers getting an apologetic explanation from the president of American Airlines on the reason for their impromptu "trays."

Dan Beard had a similar experience. He was check-riding a captain on a DST flight when the stewardess came up to the cockpit and almost tearfully reported there were no clean dishes for the meal service. Maintenance had removed the dirty dishes from a previous leg at Dallas and by accident had reloaded the same dishes. Beard told her to relax, left the cockpit, and laboriously washed the dishes in the plane's lavatory.

Newt Wilson stepped up the training period from five days to two weeks and eventually increased this to as long as six weeks as aircraft and service/safety procedures became more complex and demanding. His aim, in his own words, "was to get a group of girls who could work *without* supervision; to motivate them to have pride in their jobs and the company so they didn't need constant supervision."

He started the practice of holding monthly stewardess meetings around the system, informing them what was going on within the company and listening to their problems and suggestions. The problems often involved the attitude of some of the older captains who resented the presence of girls on their airplanes. About one out of ten, Wilson recalled, regarded them as nuisances and gave them a rough time on virtually every trip.

"I spent hours and hours working with the pilots," he said. "I tried to make them feel proud of the stewardesses instead of just being their immediate bosses. To do everything they could to help them. And most of them finally came around. I got more cooperation from captains than anyone else."

In turn, he insisted that the stewardesses understand pilot responsibilities and problems. One of his innovations was to put every class into Link trainers to give the girls an idea of what flying an airplane was all about. "It gave them confidence," he explained.

He faced one minor crisis when a captain's favorite stewardess didn't show up for a flight and Newt substituted another girl.

"I won't fly with her," the captain announced.

Wilson had only about twenty-five girls in Chicago at the time and he decided, "I was either going to be their supervisor or I wasn't." He called each one of them and told them they had a captain who wouldn't fly with a certain girl.

"I want all of you to stand together and refuse to fly with *him,*" he ordered.

They obeyed. Wilson believes that if C.R. had heard about this impromptu strike threat, he would have been fired. But it worked. The captain relented and, Newt admitted, "he finally turned out to be a pretty good guy."

From a training and job performance standpoint, Wilson was happy with the requirement that applicants must be registered nurses. He thought their hospital training had given them a sense of discipline that was easy to transfer into their airline job. Out of the hundreds of applicants he interviewed and hired, only one non-R.N. slipped through with forged credentials.

"She treated a pilot for a gunshot wound when he shot himself accidentally in his butt, and she did such a professional job that I couldn't believe it when I found out later she wasn't a nurse."

Every graduating stewardess had to be able to remember twenty-one names, or a full DC-3 passenger load. She was taught to take the passenger manifest before every trip and make notes as each person boarded: "Mr. Johnson, Seat 3, has red-striped tie; Mrs. Gillespie, elderly, looks nervous, Seat 12; Mr. Decker, Seat 6, wolf type," and so forth. Occasionally the memorization system would break down, as it did with Vivian Shattuck. She drew tire magnate Harvey Firestone on a trip and dutifully noted "rubber company" next to his name on the manifest. Later, she walked through the cabin and stopped by his seat to say hello.

"Are you enjoying the flight, Mr. Goodyear?" she beamed.

Passengers liked to call the stewardesses by name, so Wilson issued nameplates to be attached to uniform jackets. When a stewardess had a jawbreaker for a surname, or it was too long to put on a nameplate, Newt would let her shorten it for job purposes. Mary Todzonia, for example, became Mary Todd.

The fancier DC-3 service and the growth of air travel didn't change the fact the passengers were still largely neophytes, as both ground and flight personnel could testify. Reservations got a call from a woman wanting to know how long it took to fly from Chicago to St. Louis.

"Just a minute," the agent told her.

"Thank you," she said, and hung up.

At an American ticket counter one night, an agent was putting tags on various pieces of piled-up luggage and asked one young lady, "Are these bags yours, Miss?"

She blushed. "No, they're my sister's, but she said I could use them."

Some of the new stewardesses weren't much more sophisticated than the passengers. Captain L. T. Hansard had one on a late-night flight over west Texas, where the gas flames from the oil fields can be seen from the air on a clear night. The stewardess came up to the cockpit—it was around 2 A.M.— and asked what the fires were.

"Well," Hansard said solemnly, "at this time every year thousands of Indians gather in this area for a two-week powwow. And what you see down there are their campfires."

She thanked him for this bit of knowledge and left, only to return a few minutes later.

"I woke up every one of my passengers so they could see the Indian campfires," she announced proudly.

As the stewardesses became accepted and respected crew members they also became inevitable targets for the likes of Captain Bittner. He was notorious for playing practical jokes on rookie stews, such as the one he scared almost to the point of resigning.

The DC-3 had a flexible rubber tube used for defrosting the cockpit windshield. Bittner was duly advised one day that a brand-new stewardess was working his trip. After takeoff, he attached an old glove to the tube and put the glove on the throttles. Then he rang the cabin call button twice, the signal that summoned the flight attendant to the cockpit.

Before she arrived, Bittner put the plane on autopilot and, accompanied by copilot Ray Newhouse, climbed into the forward baggage compartment, out of sight. The unsuspecting girl walked right by them and went into the cockpit, where the only sign of life was a glove flying the airplane. Bittner had rigged it so the tube itself was hidden.

She turned white and started back to the cabin, panic-stricken. Just as she passed the baggage compartment, Bittner reached out and grabbed her leg. In Newhouse's own words:

"You could hear her scream at the other end of the plane."

Yet there wasn't a stewardess flying the line who didn't love this bald-headed little guy. He teased and tormented them unmercifully, but would go to bat for any of them. Besides, it usually was sheer fun working a Si Bittner trip because nobody knew what he'd pull next. The DC-3 crews flying between

Cleveland and Nashville used to eat box lunches that always contained an identical menu: an apple and a turkey sandwich. One day a stewardess brought Si his lunch. He opened the box, sighed, and said, "Hebrews, thirteen eight."

"What's that supposed to mean, Si?" she asked.

"Look it up in a Bible," he advised. She did and in Hebrews, thirteen eight, she found this:

"Jesus Christ, the same yesterday, the same today."

But the stewardesses learned to hold their own. One girl was called to the cockpit to face an angry captain holding his paper coffee cup as if it contained a live rattlesnake.

"You stirred the sugar with a blue pencil," he scolded. "Look at this goddamned cup. It has blue pencil marks all over it. Don't you ever do that again or you're in deep trouble."

On their next flight together, she brought him his morning coffee and when he emptied the cup, on the bottom, written in blue pencil, were the words: "Oh, shit! I did it again!"

In self-defense, the flight attendants also became adept at handling obstreperous passengers, although their tactics were sometimes questionable. One man got annoyed at a stewardess and snapped, "You're nothing but a witch!"

She retorted, "If I'm a witch, you're a pile of manure."

The passenger reported her and in due time she was called before her supervisor to explain her remark.

"He called me a witch," she said defensively.

"Did you call him a pile of manure?"

"Yes," the girl admitted, "but I don't know why he got so mad. I changed him back before we landed."

As happens with every airline, the pilots generated the most folklore, but it is doubtful whether any carrier had a pilot who matched Si Bittner's status as a legitimate folk hero. He once got into a feud with Tucson controllers who accused him of flying too close to their tower. They threatened to report him to the CAA, and he decided this was a reflection on his professional skills.

He landed in Tucson one day and walked over to an American mechanic who, like all the mechanics, considered Captain Bittner a truly Great Man.

"I'm coming through here again tomorrow," Bittner said, "and I want you to get the biggest sledgehammer you can find. As soon as you see me coming in, stand at the base of the tower. Wait till I get real close and then swing the damned thing as hard as you can."

The script went even better than he planned. The next day, he came in on final approach and flew so close to the tower that the controllers held their breaths. At precisely the moment when the DC-3's wing flashed by only inches away from the structure, the mechanic smashed the sledgehammer against the tower's brick side.

"He's hit us!" screamed one controller and dove for the door—followed by the entire day shift evacuating the building.

Bittner was very democratic in his choice of targets, copilots being among his favorites, especially cocky ones. He drew such a youngster on one trip, and at their layover hotel Si happened to encounter an Army pilot he knew.

"You leaving tomorrow?" Bittner inquired.

"Yeah. First thing in the morning. I'm ferrying a fighter back to my base."

"What time?"

"Oh, about eight."

"Same time we leave," Bittner commented. "Look, how about doing me a little favor?"

The next morning, Bittner graciously let his copilot handle the takeoff. They had just reached cruising altitude when an Army pursuit plane drew up to the right of their DC-3. Just before it came into view, its pilot rolled the plane over and pulled alongside in an inverted position. Bittner, who had been waiting for its appearance, tapped the copilot on the shoulder and nodded in the direction of the fighter.

"Don't panic," he said gently, "but we're flying upside down."

Si was flying from Nashville to New York on another trip and the copilot happened to mention that his wife's birthday was next week.

"I wish I knew what to get her," he added.

"Perfume," Bittner suggested. "As a matter of fact, I know a waitress in New York who wears a perfume that would turn the Pope into Jack the Ripper. We'll eat there after we get in and you can ask her what brand she uses."

Bittner arranged to get to the restaurant before the copilot arrived, and cornered the buxom waitress in question.

"I'm going to be having dinner here with this copilot of mine," he told her. "You're a nice kid so I thought I'd better warn you. He's a sex maniac. The minute he gets close to a well-endowed girl, he tries to bite her breasts."

She thanked him for his fatherly concern and in due time the copilot came in and was escorted to Captain Bittner's table. "Here comes that waitress I told you about," Si said. "Be sure and smell her perfume."

The girl approached and stood there, pad in hand. The copilot leaned toward her, trying to get a whiff of the perfume. She glared and swung a Marvin Hagler right hook, knocking him right out of his chair.

"Touchy dame," Bittner remarked innocently. "Maybe you leaned too close."

One of Si's best friends was Guy Stratton, a pilot with the same sense of humor as Bittner, which spelled trouble every time they got together. On one New York layover, they walked through the hotel lobby facing each other, one arm down and the other up as if they were carrying a huge sheet of plate glass between them. The illusion was so perfect that every person in that lobby stepped aside to let them by. They continued onto the street and walked several blocks in this fashion, giggling as the flow of pedestrian traffic parted to make room for the two men carrying plate glass. The highlight of their excursion came when a policeman stopped auto traffic for them at an intersection.

On rare occasions, Bittner and Stratton would arrange to fly together even though both were captains. Every American pilot who boarded a plane this pair had just flown learned to bring a towel into the cockpit. They always coated the control yokes with lipstick or grease for the benefit of the next crew.

Nor were passengers exempt from Si's pranks. Serving him fried chicken on a flight was guaranteed to inspire the Bittner chicken bone stunt. He would consume the chicken down to the bare bones and attach these meal remnants to a string long enough to reach back to the first cabin window. Then he'd open his side cockpit window and let the slipstream catch the string. Some poor passenger would look up startled as the bones banged against his window.

Si did not confine his shenanigans to the airways. When he was chief pilot in Memphis, he had a farm quite a distance from the city, so far out that its toilet facilities were of the Chic Sale outdoors variety. Bittner took full advantage of this by installing a loudspeaker at the bottom of the privy and connecting it to a microphone located in the kitchen. As soon as a guest went out to the privy, Si would wait for the appropriate minute and then pick up the mike. "Be careful. We're painting down here."

The Si Bittner story that is told most often concerned his second wife's love of bridge, a game he detested. She belonged to a bridge club, and there came the day when the club met in the Bittner home. Si slipped outside unnoticed, took a garden hose, and pushed it through the open window of a bathroom on the ground floor, immediately adjacent to the living room where the bridge game was under way.

He turned on the water but kept the nozzle in the closed position. Then he re-entered the house and walked past the players en route to the bathroom.

"I have to answer a call of nature," he announced politely. Once inside, he placed the nozzle in the commode and turned it on.

The water flowed. And flowed. And flowed.

Until the bridge players finally put down their cards, in total awe at the supposed capacity of Captain Bittner's kidneys.

Simon Peter Bittner died in a Cleveland nursing home in May 1984; his first wife, whom he had remarried, was at his bedside. In his final days he could hardly speak and there were times he didn't recognize her, but he kept whispering, "I love you."

Nine of his fellow airmen came to the funeral. Fred Campbell delivered what they all referred to as the "urology" and his farewell remarks were devoted solely to Si Bittner stories. Laughter sounded through the church and as Walt Gosnell, one of the attendees, put it, "That's the way Si would have wanted it."

Bittner was far more than a happy-go-lucky clown. Like so many of his brethren, he simply laughed at both life and death in equal proportions. Behind all the jokes, laughs, pranks, and generally outrageous activities was a man who wore his wings not just on his uniform but in his heart. He unquestionably was a cockpit clown, but he also was a cockpit professional who used humor as a safety valve against danger. When he retired in 1967, he had flown virtually every type of aircraft American operated and never scratched so much as a wingtip in a career spanning nearly four decades; his employee number was 23.

Nor was he totally unique. American's airmen from the Condor/DC-2/DC-3 era were teachers as well as line pilots, imparting their own hard-earned knowledge to the younger men joining the fast-growing industry. Only a few, if any, achieved Bittner's stature as an incorrigible jokester, but a great many matched his inherent dedication to job and airline. And not a few became legends in their own right.

Jap Lee. He went down in history as the only American Airlines captain who had a high school named after him (in Fort Worth). Don Smith had his first trip with American as Lee's copilot on a Condor, and the experience was branded into his memory banks:

"Jap pushed the throttles forward, then pushed the nose down so far I picked up my feet. I thought he was gonna scrape the nose off. I didn't know that's how you took off in a Condor. Jap had a phobia about radio contacts. In those days, depending on what route you were flying, you made radio contacts two minutes after the hour or two minutes after the half hour, at which time you tried to contact the ground stations and tell them where you were and when you expected to be where you were going. In all the years he flew, Jap never missed one of those contacts; he was an absolute fanatic about them. It was the copilot's primary job to write out the contact message, show it to Jap, and then get it on the air. And God help you if you were five seconds late. He had a wonderful way with kids—absolutely loved them."

Bill Evans was another who cut his pilot's teeth in the right seat next to Lee. "He'd argue either side of a question. We used to have an Esso tank farm near Dallas and one day on the way to Los Angeles I looked down at the tank farm and remarked, 'Boy, that's sure a dead place down there. I never see any trucks going in or out.'

"Jap immediately starts rattling off statistics on how much business they were doing. On the way back the next day, we came over the same tank farm and I said, 'Jap, you were right. That's really a going business down there.' So help me, he turned right around and started telling me how much money Esso was losing on that tank farm."

Lee, who started flying in 1926, died of an embolism after surgery in 1970. Evans went to the funeral, which he described wistfully as "the wettest I ever attended."

Fuzzy Robinson. He ranked almost as high as Bittner in the affections of his fellow pilots. Fuzzy was Si's physical opposite: huge, tough-looking, and pro-fane. He had fired boilers on ships and locomotives before learning to fly, and his formal education reportedly ceased after grammar school. Although he had great natural intelligence, he butchered the English language even as he pretended to be more erudite than he was. Bob McDaniels remembered Fuzzy's best line: "It's like that Latin phrase, *tempus fucksis.*"

Some of his phraseology was brilliantly descriptive, such as: "He ain't got no more chance than a one-legged man in an ass-kickin' contest."

Fuzzy could be rough. Milt Coppage was his copilot on a flight and when the stewardess brought Robinson his meal, he tasted it, opened the DC-3 cockpit window, and threw it out—tray, silverware, and food—muttering, "It ain't fit to eat!"

But he could fly an airplane. Walt Gosnell, a Robinson crony, called him "the smoothest pilot I ever saw. He'd sit there like he was sound asleep but you knew damned well he was flying."

When a buddy of theirs, Elmer Heckel, married an American stewardess named Ginny Elrod, Gosnell and Robinson were invited to the wedding. Elmer was a character himself. He was a used car salesman in Cleveland and took an airplane in on a trade for a Cadillac. The dealer was horrified, so Elmer had to buy the airplane. He then talked Si Bittner into teaching him to fly. Heckel soloed in two hours, and Bittner recommended him for a job with American.

The wedding was held in Ginny's home town of Murfreesboro, Tenn., near Nashville, and before the nuptials Elmer checked in at the local hotel, which happened to house American crews on layovers. To get an airline rate, Heckel identified himself as an AA pilot. The desk clerk looked at him suspiciously.

"Do you know Captains Robinson and Gosnell?" he asked.

"Sure. They're my best friends."

Up went the desk clerk's eyebrows. "Is Miss Elrod aware that you know these kind of people?"

Fuzzy died in Las Vegas, where he had retired. The Grey Eagles were having a directors' meeting there and several pilots went to visit him in the hospital shortly before he died. Gosnell was one, and he asked Fuzzy if there was anything they could bring him.

"Yeah. One of them shrimp cocktails."

"We brought him," Gosnell said, "two of the biggest shrimp cocktails in the state of Nevada. And that was the last time we saw him."

Ernie Cutrell. He was something of a pilot/scientist, whose contributions went beyond a spotless career as an American captain. Cutrell, a lifelong crusader for greater air safety, invented airport centerline approach lighting, a system still in existence.

Like so many airline pilots of his generation, Ernie put a bit of himself in every young pilot who flew under his command. D. K. Smith summed it up best: "After you flew with him, the other copilots would ask, 'What did you learn?' "

Cutrell was Central Casting's version of an airline captain—a tall, broad-shouldered, handsome man with a ready smile and a dry wit. When D.K. was transferred temporarily to the training department, he had to check Cutrell out in a Link; the student had become the teacher. He instructed Ernie to do some "Fade 90s," an approach maneuver that started by picking a course at a 90-degree angle to the final approach leg until the latter was bisected, then turning sharply into it.

Cutrell for some reason hated the procedure. A few months after the Link session, D.K. went back to the line and was assigned as Ernie's copilot on a New York–Boston trip. Smith was flying the DC-2 in heavy fog and became disoriented. Cutrell sat there, calmly watching him sweat, and then suggested slyly, "D.K., why don't you do a Fade 90?"

Someone asked Cutrell how he happened to invent his approach lighting system. Ernie smiled. "Well, I learned a long time ago that if you wanted to find an airport at night or in bad weather, all you could do was look for a spot with no lights."

Except for flying ability, Cutrell had little in common with a free soul like Bittner. But after they retired, they experienced the same phenomenon: when either one walked into a Grey Eagles meeting, every man in the room would gravitate in his direction.

Kit Carson. He had a gut feeling for people that stamped him as one of the most responsible pilots who ever flew for any airline.

Carson was advised one day that his flight to Chicago, the last until the following day, would be carrying a man rushing to see his injured daughter in a hospital about 100 miles from the Windy City. Came the departure time and the passenger hadn't shown up. Kit looked at his watch and walked over to a mechanic.

"Take the cowling off number one," he ordered.

"What the hell for?" the mechanic asked.

"Just take it off."

"But that'll delay the trip a half hour, Captain."

"I know," Carson said. "I need an excuse for that delay. We're waiting for somebody important."

The passenger finally arrived and the flight proceeded to Chicago. En route, Carson went back to the cabin to talk to the distraught father, who told him he was planning to take a taxi to the distant hospital.

"No need for that," Carson said. "I'll drive you there myself."

He did. And for years thereafter, both father and daughter kept in touch with him.

But Kit could be one tough cookie, too. He was flying to Dallas and was warned that the destination weather was foul. Carson landed at Nashville and informed his Dallas passengers the flight would be delayed indefinitely until the Dallas weather improved.

They took the bad news calmly, except for one man who walked up to Carson in a state of fury.

"If it wasn't for you yellow bastards, I wouldn't be missing an important meeting!" he yelled.

Carson pulled out the .38 caliber pistol all pilots carried before the war, ostensibly to guard the mail. "If you want to commit suicide," he said coldly, "I'll give you this and you can shoot yourself."

Expecting the passenger to file a complaint, Carson later went in to see C.R. and told him the story.

"I'm afraid I may have done the wrong thing, C.R.," he concluded.

"Maybe you did," Smith allowed. "You should have shot the son of a bitch!"

Bill Keasler. He had a unique way of landing a DC-3, descending with full flaps as slow as it was possible to fly without stalling. At about thirty feet off the ground, he'd call, "Flaps up!" and he'd grease it on every time.

But one day he drew a brand-new copilot only two weeks out of training. They were landing at Detroit and Keasler got the plane down to thirty feet above the runway. He yelled, "Flaps up!"

"What did you say?" the copilot asked.

John McCarten, another American pilot who was watching Keasler land that day, described it succinctly.

"They must have bounced that DC-3 eight times. Keasler was furious. He tells the kid, 'When I ask for flaps up I want flaps up!' The copilot says, 'Gee, Captain, they didn't teach me that technique in school.' "

Added McCarten: "It was the damnedest landing I ever saw. That airplane was bouncing down the runway like some giant grasshopper."

Keasler, like a good many of his contemporaries, tended to distrust new airplanes. When American began flying pressurized DC-6s after the war, he insisted on flying them at DC-3 altitudes even though the DC-6 was fully capable of cruising at 25,000. The average Keasler trip seldom exceeded 4,000 feet, which exposed his passengers to an exorbitant amount of turbulence. It was a habit that didn't exactly endear him to stewardesses.

Millie Alford, who was supervisor in Memphis before she became director of stewardess training, kept getting complaints from the girls that too many passengers were getting airsick.

American had a Flight 7, a DC-6 that originated in New York and stopped in Washington, Memphis, and Dallas before going onto Los Angeles. It would come into Memphis around 2:30 P.M. and in the summer, if Keasler was flying the trip, the stewardesses would come charging into Millie's office demanding that she come out and see the scores of airsickness bags being taken off the plane.

Si Bittner was Memphis chief pilot at the time and Millie would carry two shopping bags full of used containers into his office. "Si, he's done it again! The girls say he never got over 4,000 feet and they ran into a thunderstorm."

Bittner would curse and storm down to operations, where he'd confront Captain Keasler. "Goddammit, Bill! I told you to fly that airplane where it's supposed to be flown and I'm sick and tired of hearing about those poor sick passengers!"

Eventually, Keasler reformed—when he became convinced that pressurized cabins were here to say.

George Kopf. Another unconventional soul who loved to tell about the first job he ever held, as a teenager working for a Standard Oil station. He was doing fine and might even have stayed in the oil business if it hadn't been for a woman who came into the station for gas. While Kopf was cleaning her windshield, she asked, "Do you have a rest room?"

Kopf thought she said, "Do you have a whisk broom?"

"No, ma'am," he told her, "but if you'll back up to that air hose, I'll blow it out."

He also lost his first flying job, piloting an autogiro for a beer distributor. The owner called him one day. "George, my daughter's getting married and we're celebrating the engagement with a lawn party. I want you to fly over trailing a sign that says *Good Luck Betty And Bob* and just when you get over the lawn, release a cageful of doves."

Kopf followed instructions to the letter, with one painful exception. Ornithology was not within his field of expertise and instead of doves he loaded a cage with squabs—which can't fly. He appeared over the lawn party at the appointed time and proceeded to bomb the spectators with a cargo of thudding squabs.

Those who knew Kopf invariably used one word to describe him: unpredictable. Ray Newhouse was driving with him in Cleveland one day and George suddenly spotted a sign in the window of a hash joint: COOK WANTED. "He stopped the car—we were out of uniform—and went into the restaurant to apply for the job," Newhouse recounted. "He must have spent an hour in there arguing about the salary."

John McCarten was with him on another occasion when George got into a discussion with a stewardess about music.

"I play an instrument, too," Kopf informed her. Out of his pocket came something shaped like an ocarina and he proceeded to play a tune through his nose. McCarten listened respectfully for a few minutes before commenting, "You know, George, with very little encouragement you could play that damned thing in a much more spectacular manner."

(American's pilot musicians were rare, but one of them was famed author Ernie Gann, who used to play a concertina in the cockpit.)

Art Caperton. He was a rather unorthodox airman whose flying career began when he was personal pilot for the Vanderbilt family.

Not until the jets came along did Caperton finally concede that maybe he'd better start flying by the book. Until then, he was the bane of every chief pilot who had him under his jurisdiction. Art was a heavy-set man who wore glasses, which he habitually removed before pronouncing some pearl of wisdom.

He once drew a check ride from a particularly tough assistant chief pilot with a reputation for chewing up captains and spitting out the pieces. After the flight, he was asked how he liked the check captain.

Off came the glasses. "You know," Caperton said quietly, "that man is an aviation enthusiast."

There were many others, of course . . .

Like Marv Althus, who earned a measure of undying fame for the Perfect Alibi. He got into hot water with Walt Braznell for landing at Detroit below limits.

Braznell had tried to land there, too, and decided to overfly the airport and proceed on to Chicago, where he learned that Althus had gone into Detroit, using an unauthorized but frequently employed approach by some DC-3 pilots that allowed them to land with a ceiling as low as 300 feet (the official allowable minimum then was 700 feet).

Marv finally arrived in Chicago, where Braznell was waiting, fire in his eyes. "What the hell do you mean going into Detroit below limits?" he stormed.

Althus looked at him innocently. "Walt, it's a scheduled stop, isn't it?"

Pilots like Marv Althus had uncanny memories of landmarks around airports—they had to if they wanted to survive. One of them was Rocky Kent. D. K. Smith was his copilot on a DC-2 trip into Detroit and when they broke out of the overcast, D.K. saw the towers of the Ford plant *above* them. He gasped and Kent said, "Hey, am I making you nervous?"

"Not if you know where you're going," Smith gulped.

"Oh, sure," Rocky assured him. "We're going up to 34th Street, turn right, go four blocks, and land."

It mattered little that so many of the DC-2/DC-3 pilots never went to college. They could fly anything with wings and an engine—like George Apitz, who joined American after holding down a garbage collector's job. Most pilots considered themselves efficient if they could maintain an assigned altitude within 500 feet plus or minus. Apitz never strayed more than 20 feet and would tell his copilots, "You'd better learn how."

And there were much respected and revered instructors and chief pilots from that era, too—Bill Lester and George McCabe, for example. The former's pilot training center in Chicago became known as "Lester's School of Knowledge" and the young airmen he taught would comprise a Who's Who of American Airlines pilots.

McCabe was chief pilot in Newark, big, fat, and definitely the antithesis of any airman's "Greek God" image. He climbed into a Link trainer once and the whole thing collapsed under his weight. But he was tough and fair with his crews. Among the pilots he hired was Ernie Gann, who showed up for his interview in a car so decrepit that the ground was visible through the floorboard.

But McCabe liked his style. There was no immediate opening, but Gann hung around the Newark base for at least three weeks, flying the Link in an old National Guard hangar anytime it wasn't being used. When he wasn't in the trainer, he'd be reading DC-2 and DC-3 manuals and every book on instrument flying he could get his hands on.

And there also were the curmudgeons. Dean Smith was one. He had been one of the four pilots who flew with Rear Admiral Richard Byrd on his 1928–1929 South Pole expedition. D. K. Smith flew with him many times, and used to dread the assignment.

"He never let a copilot make a takeoff or landing. He'd take off, get about fifty feet in the air, and yell, 'You've got it!' Then he'd take out a book and start reading. You'd get to the next airport, lower the wheels, and think, *My God, is he gonna let me land it?* Then he'd put the book down and shout, 'I've got it!' All he could talk about was mink. He raised them and he could tell you anything you wanted to know about mink."

For the pilots especially, the DC-3 years were halcyon years, a time of comradeships forged out of the common adversities and challenges they faced. A period of learning, maturing, and growing, even though their environment was relatively carefree and informal.

They occasionally winked at rules and regulations, cut a few corners, improvised, and defied the conventional, knowing all the time that this would change, simply because it *had* to change. The DC-3 would be the last simple airplane they would fly. It had fostered an air travel revolution without being a truly revolutionary aircraft in a technological sense. It was safe, reliable, and, for its time, viable, but in the explosive industry the DC-3 had helped so much, the true leaders were always looking ahead.

C. R. Smith was one of them. Which was why, in 1939, he decided to move American's headquarters to New York, where the nation's newest, finest and most modern airport was being carved out of a big sandpit at a place called North Beach, in the borough of Queens.

9
"Never in God's World Will We Ever Fill Three Hangars"

Its official name was New York City Municipal Airport, and it was thus christened October 15, 1939.

But smack in the middle of the dedication ceremonies, a skywriting plane appeared overhead and began spelling out a message that brought a roar from the crowd of some 325,000 spectators and assorted VIPs.

NAME IT LAGUARDIA, the plane wrote, amid thunderous cheers. And less than a month later, a joint meeting of the New York Board of Estimate and the City Council unanimously passed a resolution changing the name to New York Municipal Airport, LaGuardia Field—in the words of the resolution, "as a testimonial to the Mayor of our city who conceived the idea of this great airport and who was solely responsible for its development."

Not quite true. Someone else had a beefy hand in bringing Fiorello La-Guardia's greatest dream to fruition, and the feisty little mayor privately admitted it. He happened to be a swashbuckling, earthy ex-pilot and politician who only a year before had been elected an American Airlines vice president. LaGuardia Airport would have been built without his help, but he unquestionably aided the embattled mayor in overcoming countless obstacles—not the least of which was considerable opposition to its being built at all.

"The Little Flower" also owed a large debt to C. R. Smith, who alone among airline presidents supported LaGuardia when he first proposed a new airport to serve the nation's biggest city. In fact, Smith's interest was the main reason he hired Orval McKinley Mosier in the first place. The first assignment he gave him was to explore American's potential in New York and in the process to cooperate with its firetruck-chasing mayor and his airport project.

Like C.R.'s own life, the red-haired Mosier's career was of the Horatio Alger variety, except that Alger's fictitious heroes were Pablum-bland by comparison. Red was born in 1897 in Pawnee, Oklahoma, when it still was Indian Territory, and in his teens achieved a hell-bent reputation as a bronc buster, brawler, and rifle marksman. He saw his first airplane at a 1912 county fair and five years later earned his wings as an Army pilot.

It was during World War I that he first met LaGuardia, who was in the Army himself as a pursuit pilot, although reportedly not a very good one, according to those who served with him. He was courageous to the point of

133

being foolhardy, and he was said to have cracked up more planes than he shot down. Yet Red Mosier liked him for his spirit, and a friendship was born that would someday serve American well.

Mosier left the Army in 1919 and spent the next three years barnstorming throughout the Rocky Mountain states. Some of his biographical files at American have him attending the University of Texas either before or after the war, but actually little is known of his formal education. His best friend for years was Sherman Billingsley of New York's famed Stork Club, and Billingsley always insisted that neither he nor Mosier ever got past the eighth grade. He once told Bob Tuttle, Mosier's assistant at American for a time:

"We finished eighth grade only because the teacher was Red's mother."

Any lack of formal education notwithstanding, Mosier was street-smart, with the personality of a born politician. He left aviation briefly, in fact, to become secretary to Oklahoma Senator J. W. Herrold and spent 1922 and 1923 in Washington, where he renewed his friendship with the then Congressman Fiorello LaGuardia. Then he returned to aviation as "Flying Sales Manager" for the Spaulding Sporting Goods Co., a job that took him into most of the forty-eight states.

A burly, lusty, and likable man, Mosier possessed insatiable energy. He trained polo ponies, played semi-pro baseball, and coached football at Capitol Hill High School in Oklahoma City. One of his players was John "Pepper" Martin, who went on to become one of the famed St. Louis Cardinals' "Gashouse Gang."

He always seemed restless and he left the Spaulding job to become chief pilot for an outfit called Pikes Peak Air Commerce, one of those Have-Planes-Will-Travel companies. He was flying for Pikes Peak when he won headlines by guiding three lost Navy fliers to safety when they were caught in a Colorado blizzard, a feat that earned him honorary membership in the Navy's famous High Hat squadron.

In the early thirties, Mosier flew as a test pilot for an aircraft manufacturer, piloted seaplanes in Cuba, married an Oklahoma belle named Frances Colcord, and in 1933 finally cashed in on his growing political connections by landing a post as city manager of Oklahoma City. He had been two years in this job when an obscure inventor, Carl Magee, wangled an appointment with him and disclosed that he had perfected a device that would bring in great revenues to Oklahoma City.

"What kind of a device?" Red asked.

"A parking meter," Magee replied.

"What the hell is a parking meter?"

Magee explained how meters installed at urban curbsides would require drivers to pay for valuable downtown parking space and enrich city coffers, not only from the meter collections but from fines on those who parked over a meter time limit. Further conversation disclosed that Magee had tried unsuccessfully to sell the idea in a number of cities.

"We'll try 'em out," Mosier decided, and thus launched an experiment that eventually put meters in every U.S. city. But despite such successes, Red missed aviation, and in 1937 he became vice president and general manager of Braniff Airways.

He lasted at Braniff only a year, resigning after an angry argument with Tom Braniff. C.R. wasted little time contacting him and offered him a vice presidency at American; he joined the airline March 15, 1938, and was to serve it loyally for the next quarter century.

Mosier earned his keep in the very first year, capitalizing on his friendship with LaGuardia when C.R. dispatched him to New York to sound out the mayor on his airport plans. Even before Mosier came with American, Smith was considering a move to New York, whether a new airport would be built or not, for he had not been that happy at Chicago's Midway Airport.

The land at Midway was owned by the Chicago School Board, which banned the sale of liquor on airport property even though the surrounding area was populated heavily with cheap bars. The city finally obtained a long-time lease on the land and took over the airport's operations, immediately issuing a series of rules and rental rates that drove the airline users crazy. Mosier was with Braniff at the time and was selected to represent all the carriers in opposing the city council's new regulations.

Red was at his best dealing with politicians and much to the surprise of everyone got the council to reverse itself. C.R. offered him a job shortly after this victory, and Mosier became a major ally in LaGuardia's pet airport project —though not without some rocky moments.

Almost from the day he took office, the stormy little mayor had considered it disgraceful that his beloved city didn't have a major airport of its own. Not too long after he was sworn in, he staged a publicity stunt that in effect launched his airport campaign. It was typical of the way he could manipulate the press.

He boarded a TWA DC-2 in Chicago and his destination was Newark. But his ticket, of course, read "Chicago–New York," which was exactly what he wanted. He had tipped off the New York press that they might find it interesting to cover his arrival at Newark. When the DC-2 landed, a horde of reporters were rewarded by the spectacle of New York's mayor throwing a carefully staged tantrum. He refused to get off the plane.

"My ticket says Chicago–New York," he shouted at the flustered stewardess. "This is Newark. I demand to be taken to New York!"

"There's ground transportation," she pleaded. "We don't fly to New York."

"The hell with ground transportation!" he yelled in his high-pitched voice. "I paid for a ticket to New York and that's where I'll get off this airplane."

By this time, the DC-2 was filled with gleeful reporters taking down every word. The captain entered the debate, got nowhere, and retreated to the terminal, where he passed the buck to TWA's station manager. He called the airline's headquarters in Kansas City, and the brass hats finally threw in the towel. "Take the s.o.b. to New York," the station manager was told.

This necessitated a renewed debate: where in New York? LaGuardia solved this impasse by suggesting Floyd Bennett Field, in Brooklyn. And that's where TWA finally flew him, accompanied by a half-dozen reporters whom he lectured on the need for a new airport.

For some time, Floyd Bennett appeared to be at least a temporary solution. In 1935, at LaGuardia's urging, the city had acquired slightly over 100 acres of North Beach property that had once housed Glenn Curtiss Airport, a private landing field used by wealthy Long Island sports fliers. But 100 acres fell far short of the facility LaGuardia was envisioning and there were no funds available for buying up additional North Beach land.

So the mayor began trying to get the airlines to operate some flights at Floyd Bennett. He hosted several luncheons there, making a pitch for what he overenthusiastically described as "the finest airport in the U.S." In truth, all Floyd Bennett had was a new administration building and not much else.

He might as well have suggested that Pan Am land its giant flying boats on Fifth Avenue. The carriers wanted no part of Floyd Bennett, and the Air Line Pilots Association regarded it as only marginally safe because of short runways and a prevalence of fog. With no funds for a new airport and Floyd Bennett rejected, LaGuardia was treading water until American suddenly tossed him a rope.

C.R. Smith, once again uncanny in his instinct for knowing the right thing to do, informed the mayor that American was willing to operate its New York–Boston schedules out of Floyd Bennett for a trial period. The only trouble, C.R. said, was ground transportation between the field and midtown Manhattan; he pointed out that it took an hour and a half compared to the one-hour limo schedule between Newark and Manhattan.

This was no problem, the ebullient mayor declared. On April 4, 1937, American's Boston–New York service shifted to Floyd Bennett and, as LaGuardia had promised, ground transportation was no problem. He proceeded to provide police escorts, lights flashing and sirens screaming, for the Floyd Bennett limos. Passengers, many of them terrified, were treated to the experience of careering through the city's streets at breakneck speeds, running red lights as if they didn't exist.

The police escorts did cut the running time to an hour, equaling Newark's, but too many passengers complained about the hair-rising rides. The Floyd Bennett experiment lasted only two weeks, and even the mayor admitted its impracticality. But it did achieve one thing: it planted in Fiorello LaGuardia's volcanic mind some tiny seeds of goodwill toward American. And more seeds were planted the following year, after Mosier joined the airline.

By then, LaGuardia had decided to seek federal help for his ambitious dream. The original cost estimate was $23 million and in the end it would require at least twice that sum. He wangled an agreement out of the Works Progress Administration that called for WPA to pay 60 percent and the city of New York the rest. And he wanted the airport opened simultaneously with the first day of the 1939 New York World's Fair, scheduled for that May.

The obstacles to such a demanding schedule were mountain-sized. For one thing, LaGuardia's plans involved expansion of the original 100-acre North Beach site to nearly 600 acres, much of it under the waters of Flushing Bay. This would require landfill from the city's huge dump on Riker's Island, and the only way to move the fill from the dump to the airport site was to build a drawbridge between Riker's and the old Curtiss airport. Even this landfill wasn't enough. In the end, they had to level a ninety-foot hill not far from Flushing Bay.

President Roosevelt approved the WPA funding September 3, 1937, and six days later the mayor was at the controls of a steam shovel lifting the first load of dirt. But at this stage, with a completion deadline less than two years away, LaGuardia had no airline customers for what threatened to be a multi-million-dollar white elephant.

Of Newark's five tenants—Eastern, United, TWA, Canadian Colonial, and American—only the latter showed any interest in locating at the new airport. The most adamantly opposed was Eastern's Rickenbacker, who called the project "folly" because it would merely duplicate Newark's facilities. There was some logic in this argument, but only if one could assume that Newark was adequate for the future as well as the past.

It wasn't, of course, and in terms of passenger convenience it wasn't even that adequate for the present. More than 50 percent of people using Newark originated in or were traveling to New York City itself. Inevitably, the airlines' antagonism had to weaken, a process hastened by the realization that American was carving itself a position of dominance if the airport turned out to be as good as LaGuardia hoped. The last holdout, as might be expected, would be Rickenbacker, who stubbornly refused to use LaGuardia until a year after it opened. The motive behind his mulish attitude was never clear, although C.R. was one of many who suspected that Captain Eddie simply didn't like New York's very liberal mayor. In political philosophy, Rickenbacker stood several miles to the right of Calvin Coolidge.

In April 1938, a month after Mosier had joined American, LaGuardia managed to alienate his potential airline tenants by imposing a tax on the Carey Limousine Service, which handled most of Newark's ground transportation. It was a perfectly legal fee because it already was being levied on interstate bus companies serving New York, and Carey's New Jersey limos were operating interstate.

Carey immediately wired the airlines, asking that they send telegrams to LaGuardia protesting the tax as discriminatory. All complied, except for American. C.R. handed the Carey telegram to Mosier and suggested that instead of protesting, it would be smarter to send Red to New York to see the mayor.

"And while you're there," he added, "check into the airport itself. I want to know if we'd be doing the right thing going in there."

Mosier went to New York, accompanied by someone Smith *hadn't* suggested. His traveling companion was Dave Behncke, president of the Air Line Pilots Association, a dedicated but abrasive man not too far removed from

LaGuardia's own personality. The crafty Mosier wanted Behncke along for two reasons: the ALPA president would do anything to get his pilots better airports; and, like both Mosier and LaGuardia, he was a former pilot himself.

It took Red very little time to establish the legality of the interstate bus tax, and he phoned Smith to urge that no protesting telegram be sent. Then he and Behncke went to the ancient City Hall, where they walked into the mayor's office without bothering to ask for an appointment with His Honor, blithely assuming that he'd welcome a friendly chat with a couple of fellow ex-airmen. After all, Mosier had known him during the war and Behncke had met him at Quiet Birdmen meetings (the QB was an organization of retired pilots).

They were wrong.

LaGuardia's secretary went into the mayor's office to announce their presence. From those august quarters came a five-megaton blast of profanity. If voices could be measured like earthquake intensity, His Honor would have shattered every Richter scale in New York City.

"YOU TELL THAT SON OF A BITCH NO! I WON'T SEE ANY OF THOSE GODDAMNED AIRLINE PEOPLE! AND FURTHERMORE . . ."

The torrent of invectives continued, amid sounds of fists crashing on furniture. Mosier and Behncke lost track of the time, marveling at the extent of the mayor's four-letter vocabulary, most of it directed in a screeching falsetto at "those "##&$$#*# airlines!"

The secretary finally emerged, white-faced and shaken. "I'm terribly sorry, Mr. Mosier," he managed to gulp, "but the mayor is very busy today. Maybe if you could call him in a few days, his schedule would be lighter."

Red Mosier was nothing if not gutsy. Behncke was ready to leave, but Mosier told the secretary, "Don't give me that crap. I know the Major" [he deliberately used LaGuardia's wartime rank] "thinks we've come to see him about that street loading ordinance. You go in and tell him that's not what we wanted to see him about. He's right about that ordinance. You go back in there and tell him that Behncke and I have come all the way from Chicago to see him about the new airport and that we want to help him any way we can."

It took considerable courage, but the secretary complied. A few minutes later, LaGuardia himself emerged, his hand outstretched, but his voice hoarse from his oral output. "Come right in, Red and Dave," he wheezed. "Good to see you again!"

Once inside, he mopped his sweating brow and started to apologize for his outburst. "For a minute I thought you were sent to intervene for those *$$ +###&&$ airlines." Just the mention of the airlines touched off another explosion. Mosier remembered later that while it was impossible to keep track of the adjectives he used, they included such compliments as "cheap, conniving, chiseling, short-sighted, cripple-brained, and deceitful."

The mayor finally calmed down and Mosier assured him that he wasn't representing anybody but American, and that Behncke was speaking for airline pilots who wanted safer airports. He informed LaGuardia that C. R. Smith had no intention of joining the Carey protest and reminded him that American had been the only airline willing to try Floyd Bennett.

"Frankly, Major," he concluded, "we'd like to see that airport site."

LaGuardia, grinning broadly, called in his secretary, told him to cancel all appointments for the rest of the day, and within five minutes all three men were in the mayor's black Chrysler Airflow speeding uptown toward the 59th Street bridge that led to Queens. They toured the site, examined the plans, and despite the denuded confusion of any unfinished construction project, they were impressed.

Mosier flew back to Chicago and laid out the facts before C.R. and American's ten-man board of directors, including Damon and Rheinstrom. He stressed the traffic potential of a modern airport strategically located only seven miles from midtown Manhattan. He praised the architectural plans for an attractive, spacious terminal building with room for shops, a good restaurant, and an observation deck for sightseeing. And more than anything else, he urged the directors to move fast.

"If we negotiate now for rental and landing fees," he pointed out, "we can get nominal rates and the choice locations before the other airlines wake up."

Mosier was authorized to contact LaGuardia and advise him that American was ready to talk business. There was no immediate response, and when one did come, Red could have strangled the mayor. The second Louis-Schmeling fight was scheduled for Yankee Stadium in June 1938; Mosier was a member of a large party C.R. had arranged, starting with a steak dinner aboard a chartered boat and then going to the Stadium. Just as Mosier was about to leave his hotel room, LaGuardia reached him with a phone call.

"Red, about that airport lease. I want to have all your figures in my office first thing Monday morning."

"For Christ's sake, it's Friday afternoon," Mosier protested. "It'll take me a week to get our proposals together. And I'm going to the fight tonight."

Loud and clear came back the mayor's voice, pitched several octaves higher in the Little Flower's Condition Red level.

"I DON'T GIVE A GOOD #%*$'& HOW YOU GET THOSE FIGURES BUT IF YOU WANT TO DO BUSINESS WITH THE CITY OF NEW YORK, MAKE SURE AMERICAN AIRLINES HAS THE INFORMATION ON MY DESK IN CITY HALL AT TEN A.M. MONDAY! DO YOU UNDERSTAND?"

"Yeah," Mosier sighed. He trotted down to C.R.'s room, broke the news, and received much sympathy but no comfort.

"Guess you'll have to see the fight in the newsreels," Smith said. "Better catch the five o'clock nonstop back to Chicago and get something together."

Before rushing out to Newark, Mosier phoned Carlene Roberts, his secretary, a remarkable young woman whom Mosier had met after she graduated from the University of Oklahoma. Blond, attractive, and as efficient as a computer, she had accompanied Red to Chicago when C.R. hired him and put him in charge of airport leases and properties. She never batted an eye when, on this hot June weekend, he warned her there were a rough two days ahead.

They went without sleep for more than thirty hours, but by Sunday afternoon they had hammered out not only American's official proposal but a suggested schedule of fees for all airlines, aimed at giving the city a fair return on investment. Mosier had supplied the raw data: a sliding scale for hangar rental based on how many American would need, estimated income for the city over a ten-year period, and projections of American flights at the airport over the next decade. It was an incredibly complex layout that Carlene typed into a smooth, comprehensive format; it was placed on an American flight to New York that afternoon, and hand-delivered to C.R., who personally handed it to LaGuardia at 10 A.M. Monday.

A week later, Mosier received a letter from the mayor, ominously addressed to "Dear Mr. Mosier"—LaGuardia had been calling him "Red" for months.

"I have your letter relative to North Beach," it said. "Your proposition together with information which I have received is unsatisfactory. Yours truly, LaGuardia."

Mosier was thunderstruck, but that same day he got a phone call from John McKenzie, head of the New York Dock Commission, which at the time was assigned jurisdiction over the new airport.

"The mayor's very pleased with your proposed leasing arrangements, Mr. Mosier," he said. "He wonders if we couldn't meet here in New York to discuss certain points."

"What the hell's going on here?" Mosier demanded. "I just got a letter from him telling me it was unsatisfactory."

"You know our mayor," McKenzie murmured. "I'll explain that letter when you get here."

It turned out that the mercurial LaGuardia had dictated the letter during one of his patented rages. A minority of the New York press had been viciously attacking his airport plan, the New York *Sun* in particular, with such headlines as MAYOR IGNORES EXPERT ADVICE ON CITY AIRPORT and an even more damaging one: DUMPS MILLIONS INTO BAYS TO DEVELOP DEATH TRAP AT NORTH BEACH. Apparently he saw one of those stories just as he was about to write Mosier.

Formal negotiations began in July and continued for two months, punctuated by heated exchanges between the fiery Mosier and the equally flammable LaGuardia. The mayor's mood wasn't helped by the attitude of the other airlines; McKenzie had invited them to participate in the negotiations and only TWA responded, albeit with somewhat lukewarm interest at first.

But by August, in pure self-defense, they began coming around. Mosier, at C.R.'s suggestion, invited the chief pilots and flight superintendents of all five carriers aboard an American DC-3 to make an aerial survey of the airport site, inspecting the layout of runways and any potential hazards in the form of towers, bridges, and tall factory chimneys. The flight was followed by appointment of American's George McCabe as chairman of a pilot advisory committee, which wound up recommending that the NW-SE runway be lengthened

NEVER IN GOD'S WORLD . . .   *141*

to 6,000 feet and the shorter E-W runway be stretched to 4,500. Both suggestions were adopted, and McCabe's final report predicted that the new airport would be as safe as any in the U.S.

On October 6, 1938, American became the first carrier to execute a lease, its provisions approved by Ralph Damon and American's young counsel, Hamilton Hale, who represented the Pruitt law firm that C.R. still retained. The lease included occupancy of three hangars, plus ticket counter and other space in the terminal, for a ten-year period, with an option to renew every ten years up to a total of thirty years.

The terms were exceptionally favorable. Hangar space rental was set at a modest twelve cents a foot, and terminal space fees were two dollars a square foot—a bargain even in those days. Landing fees were reasonable, too; there would be no charge for test or ferry flights, nor for the sightseeing flights over the World's Fair that American promised to provide, in a unique provision that called for the city's getting 10 percent of sightseeing revenues.

One clause looked into the future. The landing fees applied to DC-3s or any aircraft weighing less than 25,000 pounds. When larger planes came along, the carriers would have to pay a dollar extra for every thousand pounds over the 25,000-pound limit.

With torturing, frustrating slowness, a great airport rose out of muck and mud. By January 1939, more than $40 million had been spent, with no completion in sight. The Little Flower was bristling like a cactus, knowing there was no way the airport could open in conjunction with the World's Fair. To this day, no one knows the exact cost of building LaGuardia Airport.

Much of the trouble was sheer inefficiency. The walls between Hangars 1 and 5 were put up before the heating boilers were installed and had to be torn down when the boilers arrived. Workers poured the entire concrete floor of Hangar 1 over the plumbing system for the sprinkler system—which the plumbers had forgotten to test. When they finally got around to testing it, the pipes all leaked and the floor had to be ripped up and repoured.

Things were so fouled up that C.R. turned to his vice president of engineering, Bill Littlewood, and asked him to send a troubleshooter to New York to protect the airline's interests. Littlewood's choice was Elmer Sittner, an unflappable jack-of-all-trades who seemed to know every phase of construction work. Sittner moved into a small office on the North Beach site, not much bigger than a couple of telephone booths hitched together.

He had no say on the overall work, but he had plenty of authority over any installation involving American. By the time LaGuardia opened in October, he had supervised construction of the offices on the south side of American's hangars, maintenance shops, the fuel supply system, lighting for all hangars, and the terminal facilities. Later he was joined by Delos W. "Del" Rentzel, who had started with American as a radio operator. (Years later he would hold several high government posts and serve as chairman of Slick Airways. One of his sons was football star Lance Rentzel.)

To Rentzel went the task of overseeing communications installations for all the carriers. In addition to what went into the airport, he had to lease a small island in Jamaica Bay for a radio transmitter station. A receiver station was erected on Riker's Island after the city dump was removed for landfill; it was still being tested when the circuit failed. Rentzel discovered that huge rats, for which Riker's was famous, had chewed through the lead shielding protecting the cables. He reported this to a WPA official, who scoffed at the idea that any rat was capable of gnawing through lead.

"These are," Rentzel said grimly. "They're big enough to put saddles on 'em."

Once the lease had been signed, C.R. committed American to the headquarters move, a task that in a human sense was no less formidable than the physical challenge of building the airport itself. American was no General Motors nor U.S. Steel in size, but it still was the largest airline in the United States, and no carrier, let alone many other companies, had ever faced the job of uprooting nearly 800 employees and their families—a total of more than 2,000 persons—and settling them in a new city 843 air miles away.

Smith figured the planning job belonged in Mosier's department, and Red passed the buck to the person he trusted most: Carlene Roberts. She was more of an administrative assistant than a mere secretary, and in many ways his alter ego. And she did a superb job, so capably and smoothly handled that four decades later it became the basic blueprint followed when American moved corporate headquarters from New York to Texas.

Carlene began by choosing two assistants, a pair of youngsters who had applied for jobs as reservations agents, Morris Shipley and Curtis Shields. She had noticed in their applications that both had real estate experience, and she launched their airline careers by sending them to New York early in 1939 for a survey of housing conditions.

Shields did much of the leg work and Shipley, who one day would become a Delta vice president, composed a 100-page illustrated brochure that included everything from available houses to furnished rooms. The brochure went to every employee on the move list; at a glance, he or she could find information on churches, schools, housing prices, commuting times, shopping areas, and even the location of recreational facilities such as bowling alleys. One broker called the brochure "one of the most amazing documents in real estate history."

Long before the exodus from Chicago got under way, American flew small groups to New York, usually on weekends, so they could inspect prospective living areas with Carlene, Shipley, and Shields serving as guides. The for-real eastward trek began in early October 1939, and was completed before the end of the year, an undertaking so deftly performed that one admiring magazine article described it as "humanity in business."

More than a thousand rooms of employee household furniture were involved in the move. Clarence Clark, who coordinated the door-to-door freight transportation, couldn't believe the final results: except for a few cases of minor breakage, not a single major loss was reported. There was one instance in December when a Chicago mechanic ended his regular day shift and flew to

New York that evening to meet his already-moved family. He reported to LaGuardia the next morning and found his tools waiting for him in the hangar.

American's people were ready for LaGuardia long before the new airport was ready for American or anyone else. It didn't open for business until December, because on Dedication Day in October, the runways weren't finished. But at 12:03 A.M. December 2, a TWA DC-3 operating as Flight 18 from Burbank landed and officially inaugurated LaGuardia Field. Actually, the plane had landed first at Newark, but this information fortunately was withheld from the Little Flower, who was there to greet the flight.

To American went the justified honor of dispatching the first scheduled departure, the popular "Night Owl," which operated as Flight 7. Takeoff time was 12:30 A.M., and hundreds of off-duty AA employees were on hand, many with wives and children.

P.R. director Ed Bern had pulled out all the stops. Huge floodlights illuminated the gleaming silver *Flagship New York,* commanded by Captain Tom Hill. The cabin door was sealed by a huge red silk ribbon, and shortly before 12:30, Mayor LaGuardia, with C.R. at his side, marched up the small aircraft steps and cut the ribbon.

The door opened and out stepped red-haired stewardess Helen Flynn. The photographers yelled at LaGuardia, "Kiss her, Butch!" and he did, amid loud cheers and applause.

Everything was set for the on-time departure.

Except that the right engine refused to start.

Mechanics, working nervously under the accusing glares of the airline's entire corps of brass hats, tried in vain to nurse it to life. Present were C.R., vice presidents Mosier, Damon, and Rheinstrom, operations chief Hugh Smith, and station manager Harold Palmer—all of them afflicted with an onslaught of rising blood pressure. Finally, someone thought to bring up a battery cart, and they got the engine started.

Flight 7 took off at 1:15 A.M., forty-five minutes late.

But the ignominious beginning was soon forgotten. There was too much pride in what had been accomplished. To most of the people who had transferred from tiny, cramped Midway, LaGuardia seemed like the wide open spaces.

Mechanic Paul Kent, one of the "migrants," was being shown around his new working area by Joe Martin, manager of maintenance at LaGuardia.

"It's sure nice," Kent commented.

Martin snorted. "This company's crazy! Never in God's world will we ever fill three hangars. I don't know why they built them."

Two years later, American was building an addition to one of the hangars. For that matter, in a little more than a year after "the world's finest airport" opened, it was already considered obsolete.

One of the largest rooms in LaGuardia's terminal had been set aside for the mayor himself as a combined office and VIP lounge for his guests. It was luxuriously furnished and he loved to hold press conferences there.

He held one too many. He was holding court for reporters shortly before the official opening, with both Red Mosier and Charlie Speers present; the latter had been named district sales manager in New York. The newsmen were questioning LaGuardia rather belligerently about the enormous cost of building the airport.

"How are you going to ever pay it off?" a reporter asked.

The mayor's short fuse was sputtering in the openly hostile atmosphere, but he controlled his temper.

"Well, for one thing," he growled, "we're charging two dollars a square foot for every inch of space in this building."

He had left himself wide open. Someone asked, "Does that include this fancy room, Mr. Mayor? Are you gonna rent this out, too?"

Backed into a corner, LaGuardia blurted, "Yeah, we'll lease this out, too."

Up jumped Mosier. "We'll take it!" he yelled.

At two dollars a square foot, it was not only a bargain but an historic occasion. For Fiorello's handsome office/lounge became the site of American's first Admirals Club airport facility, the forerunner of the twenty-one clubs now serving members at twenty airports in fifteen cities. Until Mosier's impulsive gesture, the Admirals Club had been a rather meaningless honor. But from now on a membership would mean access to comfortable facilities where one could relax before or after a flight.

Mosier didn't intend for the LaGuardia room to be part of the Admirals Club, and neither did C.R., although they probably would have come around to the idea of club facilities eventually. They first envisioned it as merely a lounge for VIP passengers. It was C.R. who decided it would be nice to serve free drinks.

This required some legal research, and the task was handed to Bob Howlett, another of the young Pruitt attorneys shifted to New York when American moved. He was told to look into the process for obtaining a liquor license and discovered licenses came in two categories: commercial and membership club. Commercial licenses required that the establishment have a glass door at the entrance, and Mosier didn't want any such privacy invasion. This meant the LaGuardia lounge would have to be a membership club. The next obvious step was to use the already existing if nebulous Admirals Club.

"You need a minimum of nine members to incorporate and sign the license application," Howlett informed Mosier.

"We've got a lot more than nine Admirals," Red remarked, "but which ones do we use?"

"Don't use any," Howell suggested. "Just make nine employees members here in New York and they can sign the papers."

This was done, but Howlett ran into a snag. When he presented a corporate application in the name of "The Admirals Club," the judge refused to approve. "It's the name," he objected. "People will think it's a club for Navy admirals. You'll have to come up with another name."

Howlett thought quickly and suddenly remembered what American called its airplanes.

He said, "Suppose we call it Flagship Clubs, Inc. Would that be all right?"

The judge nodded, Howlett redid the documents and obtained the same nine signatures. Once officially and legally organized, however, Flagship Clubs, Inc., had to obey a New York statute requiring membership clubs to meet at least once a year, and that the annual meeting be published in advance. For several years, Howlett ran an advertisement in the *Irish Echo* duly announcing the annual meeting of Flagship Clubs, Inc. The paper was published in the Bronx but met the statutory requirement for "a newspaper of general circulation."

"I figured it unlikely that any Admiral would read the *Irish Echo,*" Howlett explained. "The nine employee Admirals would troop to LaGuardia once a year, elect directors, and the directors would then elect officers. Then they'd adjourn until the following year. This went on until we were advised that the procedure was no longer necessary."

The girls assigned as receptionists ("skippers") at LaGuardia and subsequent clubs were generally ex-stewardesses, and when C.R. decreed that drinks would be served, the LaGuardia facility got its first bartenders, John Gavin and Bill Grunberg. The latter was built like a Prussian, looked like a Prussian, and talked like a Prussian, in a thick, guttural German accent delivered with the decibels of an itinerant hog caller. When the club began charging for drinks, heaven help any member who might accidentally leave a bar bill unpaid. It didn't matter how famous the Admiral happened to be, Grunberg would try to nail him.

Occasionally, his zeal was embarrassing. A frequent inadvertent offender was John F. Kennedy when he was a senator. The skippers would wince as Grunberg's bellow bounced off the club walls: "Vere iz de zenator? He didn't pay for hiz drinks!"

Most members naturally preferred Gavin, not only because he wasn't as intimidating as Grunberg but because of his generosity in mixing drinks. A Gavin shot would have fueled an automobile for ten miles of driving.

The second club facility was at Washington National Airport, starting up almost simultaneously with the opening of the field in mid 1941. Its first steward (C.R. preferred that title to "bartender") was a slim, pleasant young man named Joe Comnillo; he was still chief steward there in 1985, and his assistant, Ray Metcalf, had been in the Washington club for twenty-three years.

The National Airport club started out with two ice cube trays in a tiny refrigerator. The airport was in Virginia, then a dry state, and no liquor could be sold. So the club operated on a BYOL basis, each member being charged $12 a year for the privilege of storing up to four bottles each. There was an ironclad rule, established by C.R. himself, that no Admiral could have access to another's bottle, even if they were close friends. The list of bottle holders at National included virtually every big name in Washington—Richard Nixon and JFK, for example. At one time, the club had over 8,000 bottles stored and labeled with member names. In 1970, the Virginia law was changed and the Washington club went on the same basis as the others.

C.R. was extremely proud of them, donating valuable original oil paintings, mostly seascapes, and beautiful sailing ship models to supplement their decor. The LaGuardia club housed his prized collection of old bourbon whiskey, displayed in a glass case; more than one Admiral licked his lips at the sight of a 100-year-old bourbon.

Until 1967, membership in the Admirals Club was by invitation only, and complimentary. A dress code was strictly enforced—jackets and ties were required for men; shorts or slacks on women were frowned on. There were no exceptions, although the clubs used to keep a few jackets and ties on hand so skippers wouldn't have to refuse admittance to a member they knew.

Juan Trippe was in an Admirals Club one night, waiting to meet C.R., and took off his tie. Smith walked up, took a look at the president of Pan American World Airways, and barked, "Put that goddamned tie back on! You're in an Admirals Club."

In the 1960s, American asked three lady magazine editors to review the club dress code for women. All three voted against slacks. Then one of them showed up at an Admirals Club wearing slacks and was refused admittance; having been hoist by her own petard, she took it gracefully.

Skippers were forbidden to keep any item of office equipment on the reception desk. Shirley McManus, a skipper at LaGuardia, said the rule stemmed from C.R.'s insistence that the clubs were "a place to relax and not think about business. He wouldn't let us keep even a stapler in sight."

To Smith, especially after his divorce, the clubs became almost a home away from home. The skippers all knew him, of course, but if he didn't want members to see his name on the receptionist's mandatory sign-in sheet, he would write "Mr. Kelly," a pseudonym he employed occasionally on flights.

The LaGuardia club was an instant hit, and as the airline gradually added new facilities at other airports, every department dealing with the public was under constant pressure from would-be Admirals pleading for admission. Los Angeles and Washington, with their greater proportion of celebrities, were particularly bothersome. It made little difference how famous the supplicant in his own right, being named an Admiral was a status symbol. Richard Nixon was vice president of the United States when he asked Don Campbell, American's sales manager in Washington, to make him an Admiral.

American's sales and public relations personnel created their own ceremonial presentation speeches when delivering one of the coveted Admirals Club framed certificates to a recipient. Burck Smith, C.R.'s brother, had many such assignments when he handled sales in Los Angeles. He'd open up with, "Now hear this!"

Another Los Angeles veteran, Schuyler "Sky" Dunning, used a less nautical approach: "This is in appreciation for your interest in aviation and in American Airlines in particular."

"It didn't matter how famous the Hollywood personality was," Dunning recalled. "They'd all stand there as if you were presenting them with the Congressional Medal of Honor, and some of 'em would have tears in their eyes.

And I gave those certificates to some of the biggest, like John Wayne, Bob Hope, Jack Benny, and Bill Wellman."

Bill Hipple, American's p.r. chief in Los Angeles for years, once couldn't resist a sly ad lib at the end of his presentation speech: "And having been made an Admiral, do you now agree to forsake all other airlines?"

"I sure do!" the recipient blurted.

Actually, the beauty of the Admirals Club concept was its subtlety as a subliminal sales weapon. It fostered inbred loyalty to American without an iota of high pressure. If a member happened to be traveling on another airline, he still was an Admiral of the Flagship Fleet and the club skippers treated him accordingly. Yet the loyalty was so deeply implanted, many members would apologize to skippers if they weren't flying American.

The selection process for Admirals would have been envied by a State Department protocol expert. For example, C.R. issued standing orders that no vice president of any company should be offered a membership unless the president of the firm already belonged. There is no telling how many bruised egos and subsequent ill-will were avoided by this policy.

Imitation being the sincerest form of flattery, other major carriers eventually established their own VIP clubs. TWA created the Ambassadors Club, United had its 100,00-Mile Club (later changed to Red Carpet Club), Eastern set up Ionosphere Lounges, Pan Am started its Clipper Club, and Delta came up with its Flying Colonels. Even the smaller airlines like Continental, Western, and Braniff soon got into the act.

But American had led the way, and its Admirals Club remains not only the first of its kind but the largest. The exact membership total is something the airline prefers to keep private, but 200,000 would be a ballpark guess. (It was 4,200 in 1953.)

There was one competitor, however, who had started something the canny Newt Wilson envied: United.

It took a combination of guts and foresight to confront C. R. Smith with the notion that United had *anything* American should emulate, but Wilson did it. He told C.R. that American should follow United's example of establishing its own flight kitchens.

In 1939, UAL had five of them, located along its transcontinental route at New York, Chicago, Iowa City, Cheyenne, and San Francisco. American, Wilson said, needed its own food service at seventeen different locations because its route system was so spread out. He brought up the obvious arguments —better control of quality, more economical, wider variety of menus, etc.— but he also went beyond what United or anyone else was doing. He urged Smith to establish, as part of the flight food service, a systemwide chain of airport restaurants.

"I had been hearing of Fred Harvey's restaurant chain all my life," Newt said. "I had an uncle who wrote a history of the Santa Fe Railroad and I got the idea that we could have a system of airport restaurants just like Harvey had along the Santa Fe's routes."

His timing was perfect; C.R. was well aware that airport food service was abominable. Only twelve of the thirty airports American was serving in 1940 had any restaurants at all, and they fell far short of even minimal standards of service. Newark had the first airport restaurant in the U.S., but it wasn't even on airport property. Midway had one, too, but it was so inferior that passengers—including Eleanor Roosevelt, a frequent American customer—complained to C.R.

Smith was intrigued, but he was leery of getting the airline involved in a field its people knew nothing about.

"I'll buy your idea, Newt," he said, "but only if we can get somebody with restaurant experience to run the operation."

The most likely partner was the Dobbs House organization, and C.R. sent Wilson and Mosier to Memphis for a meeting with Jimmy Dobbs. They reached agreement on a deal in which Dobbs and American would each hold 49 percent interest in the proposed chain, with the remaining 2 percent held in escrow in the event either partner wanted to buy majority control.

Mosier presented the proposed contract to American's board and it would have been approved except for the opposition of one man, Amon Carter, Sr., of Fort Worth, the most influential director of them all.

Carter, an old friend of C.R.'s and as tough and decisive as Smith himself, always expressed his opinions freely at board meetings and everyplace else; he once bawled out C.R. for removing the footrests from the DC-3s. He hated Dallas as much as Georgians hated General Sherman; when he had to fly from Washington to Texas, he would take a two-stop American flight direct to Fort Worth rather than the far faster nonstop to Dallas.

On this occasion, he demolished the Dobbs deal in one sentence.

"If we're gonna operate restaurants," he growled from behind the smoke of a fat cigar, "we should run 'em ourselves."

And thus was born Sky Chefs, one of the most successful airline subsidiaries in the industry's history. It may well be *the* most successful; it was launched in 1940, lost $49,000 the first year, but has operated in the black ever since. There were some years when it was the only segment in the company turning a profit.

Given a green light, Newt Wilson began touring the country, acquiring airport concessions and establishing clean, modern restaurants that served good food at reasonable prices. The concessions included not only eating facilities but gift shops and newsstands. Food kitchens for providing in-flight meals on American's planes also were set up at strategic locations. Between 1940 and 1942, Wilson held down two jobs. He was still running the stewardess department while he organized Sky Chefs.

By 1942, American had nine restaurants in operation and on February 1 of that year, Sky Chefs was officially incorporated as an American Airlines subsidiary, with Newton K. Wilson as its first president. He was to serve in that capacity until his retirement in 1971. The year he started Sky Chefs, it grossed $700,000 and had 213 employes; in the year he left, it grossed $80 million with 6,000 employes.

Wilson's influence on C.R. was greater than a lot of people ever imagined. A good example occurred in 1936 when American was planning for the DC-3's introduction and Treasurer Tom Dunnion came up with the recommendation that the airline charge passengers for their meals. Both Smith and Damon were most interested, but the latter suggested that before they adopted the idea, "let Newt look into it."

Newt did, and bluntly knocked Dunnion's plan into the bleachers. "American," he informed his superiors, "can't afford to sell meals on planes."

The cost of accounting for the receipts, he warned, would run higher than the receipts themselves. If passengers had to pay for their meals, they'd demand a wider choice—through most of the DC-3 era, the entrees were either fried chicken or a swiss-type steak (lobster was tried but flopped). Airsick passengers probably would ask for refunds. He said tipping stewardesses might become a problem, and that increased stewardess workload could be another. Wilson emphasized there already was concern whether one girl could serve twenty-one passengers satisfactorily!

His final rebuttal was simple but conclusive: what happens, he asked, if United and TWA decide to serve free meals?

That did it. A few years later, when the Civil Aeronautics Board tried to get the airlines to charge for food service, the industry pointed out that the cost of those meals already was written into its tariffs—which was what Wilson's 1936 report recommended.

By the time Newt retired, he was known as "Mr. Airline Caterer," quite an honor for a man whose first job, as a teenager in Pawnee City, Nebraska, was cook in a local hospital to earn money for his college education. The entire industry relied on him heavily in the design of new aircraft galley equipment, and at Sky Chefs he pioneered procedures and hardware adopted even by his catering competitors: kitchen conveyor belts, the first radar ranges, dry-ice makers, and large-volume automatic dishwashers were just a few examples.

Yet he remained prouder of his work with stewardesses than what he accomplished at Sky Chefs. In his own words:

"I may be prejudiced, but I think the quality of American's in-flight service and the performance of its flight attendants has been sustained at a higher level than at any other airline, in both attitude and discipline. We set the background for establishing American as a *service* company. From stewardesses we went to airport personnel training and reservations. The training programs began to establish themselves. And this all started with stewardesses. I'm prouder of that than anything I've ever done."

His pride and prejudice seem justified. Wilson's training and supervision standards permeated the industry. The first chief stewardess supervisors on such airlines as Delta, Northwest, Western, Eastern, Pennsylvania Central (later Capital), Colonial, and Frontier were girls on loan from American, all Newt Wilson disciples.

The spread of his training concepts to other departments was a cornerstone in American's history, and nowhere was this more marked than in reservations. Coincidental with the move to New York was the transfer of the main reservations office and the simultaneous creation of a reservationist school, the latter at the new airport.

The reservations center was at 45 Vanderbilt, the present site of the Pan Am building. The most modern of its time, it featured the so-called "Tiffany Desk," named for the man who devised it. Howard Tiffany was a flight superintendent in Boston who took his idea to Karl Day, American's director of flight control —"the toughest cookie who ever existed," to quote one of his contemporaries. Tough or not, Day grasped the merits of what Tiffany was proposing, and the Tiffany Desk became the axle around which the reservation system revolved.

It consisted of a huge stand-up desk with a sloping top, originally manned by four people, each controlling one of American's four major routes including all transcontinental flights. Overhead was a battery of telephones suspended from the ceiling and linked to a 100-line switchboard. In another section of the room was Space Control, where huge lined charts listed every flight and the number of seats available on each leg for any given day.

The Tiffany Desk would get a space request and yell to Space Control, "Need one seat New York–Chicago on the fifth!" Control would check its charts and write down space availability on a small card, which would be rushed back to the Tiffany Desk. The youngsters dashing around with those cards were known as "card boys"; one of them, Chris "Buzz" Whalen, eventually became a senior vice president of Continental. (Card boys later were replaced by less hectic conveyor belts.)

To have worked in the din-filled madhouse that was the Tiffany Desk was the equivalent of a soldier surviving a commando course. Yet it was surprisingly efficient for its day, the fastest in the industry; it was capable of handling twenty space confirmations every minute. Some great old-timers were part of that reservations operation, men like Andy Newcomb, Dave Currie, and Glen Boylan, who helped refine the system until a more sophisticated means was developed.

The reservations school, located in hangar 3 at LaGuardia, opened in April 1940. Vice president Charlie Rheinstrom came out to greet the first class and delivered a pep talk that turned out to be prophetic. "You are in the greatest industry in the world," he told them. "In this room are future vice presidents who in ten or fifteen years will be running American Airlines."

Nobody really believed him, including a pair of would-be agents named Walter Johnson and Walter Rauscher; they both were slated to become vice presidents. Rauscher always had fond memories of the school, even though he said, "It was like going to West Point and the training lasted a full five weeks.

"There wasn't much time to fool around. We stayed at the Kew Gardens Hotel on Queens Boulevard, where we were picked up every morning and driven to the airport. There wasn't much about the airline business they didn't teach us. It was a great approach to training that started those many years ago and still exists today."

Rauscher and Johnson weren't the only future officers and aviation greats whose careers at American started in the immediate pre-war years. F. J.

"Jack" Mullins began as a res agent at Midway in 1938 and retired as American's vice chairman. Malcolm MacIntyre, who once served as Eastern's president and was one of C.R.'s top legal advisors, joined American in 1939 as a lawyer when Smith decided the airline should at least have the beginnings of its own legal staff.

There was Otto Becker, a Tiffany Desk graduate, who retired in 1980 as senior vice president of field sales and services; Dixon Speas, who started out as a flight analyst in Dan Beard's office and matured into one of the world's leading aviation consultants; Gene Taylor, whose first airline job was weather observer for American in Rochester—he rose through the ranks to vice president of maintenance and engineering and later was senior vice president at Capital, United, and USAir.

One of Taylor's predecessors as vice president of maintenance and engineering was Marvin Whitlock, another Bill Littlewood disciple, who went to work for American in the mid-thirties as a part-time mechanic and draftsman. Another youngster whose glittering future began with the eagle was Art Lewis; C. W. Jacob hired him as a research analyst after reading a brilliant masters thesis on commercial aviation Lewis had sent around to several airlines seeking post-graduation employment. He became president of Eastern years later.

A common denominator among these successful men is their memory of certain individuals they knew at American when they were uncertain, nervous rookies launching careers in an industry that was basically as immature as themselves. Anyone connected with maintenance remembered an old mechanic named Arthur Teeple; he was a foreman in St. Louis and his theories about supervising men did not come out of any business school textbook.

"When you get a hard job," Teeple used to say, "always give it to the laziest man because he'll find an easier way to do it."

One of Jack Mullins' favorites was a lovable, gentle little guy named Houston Silliman, known as "the dean of station managers." In many ways, Silliman personified the airline people of his day. He joined American as a mechanic's helper in 1932 and for thirty-six years climbed the company ladder —stock clerk, mechanic, dispatcher, ramp agent, radio operator, station manager, and finally a regional vice president in Chicago. When he retired in 1968, virtually every brass hat from C.R. down attended the farewell party.

At the opposite end of the personality spectrum was Rod King, for many years supervisor of reservations and ticket offices. He was an electronics genius whose I.Q. must have gone off the top of the scale. He actually built with his own hands a primitive reservations computer that was the ancestor of SABRE. This was just before World War II when King was so far ahead of his time that every company he showed it to told him it was a great idea but there was no way to make it work.

King built the device on his kitchen table, a crude computer that could keep track of seat space inventory, pushing one set of buttons to reduce inventory and another set to re-establish inventory. He showed it to Jack Mullins one night. "It was a kind of a box with a lot of buttons and lights," Mullins recalled. "A real Rube Goldberg contraption, but the damned thing worked."

It not only worked but during the war was developed into American's Reservisor system, the industry's first electrical/mechanical device for controlling space inventory. And Reservisor, introduced in 1946, evolved later into IBM's SABRE.

Like so many brilliant people, King was a perfectionist, demanding, impatient, intolerant of mistakes, and as abrasive as sandpaper. Mullins used to dread sending him copies of memos because they'd come back with red crayon marks correcting everything from grammar to spelling.

"He was very critical and never complimented you," Mullins added, "but I learned more from him than any man I ever worked for."

Cut somewhat out of the same bolt as King was Tom Brooks, superintendent of stations, although his gruffness evaporated once he got to know and respect a man. More of a Silliman type was W. Nelson "Bill" Bump, who spent virtually his entire career in Boston and became known as American's "Mr. New England." There was a "Mr. Washington," too—Herb Ford, who was American's sales representative for many years; Jack Tompkins, "Mr. Detroit"; Bob Noble, "Mr. Nashville"; and Al Bone, "Mr. Los Angeles."

The eagle was flying high in these euphoric years. Between 1939 and 1941, American's ranks almost doubled, from 2,795 employees at the end of '39 to more than 4,000 at the start of 1941. By 1940, the airline was carrying 32 percent of the nation's air traffic in the industry's largest fleet, sixty-four DC3s and fifteen DSTs. Profits in the 1940–41 period totaled more than $4 million, and C.R. felt bound to enlarge the vice presidential ranks. Among the new appointees was Max Pollet—the same Pollet who had once served lunch to Franklin Roosevelt on a Ford trimotor.

It was so easy to look at present and future through rose-tinted glasses. Ralph Damon summed up American's confidence and optimism in a speech, telling the audience, "There is never a time during any twenty-four-hour period that American has less than nine Flagships in the air!"

Like the ominous rumble of a distant thunderstorm, however, something else was in the air.

War.

10
The Eagle Goes to War

C. R. Smith's first New York office was at LaGuardia, on the second floor of Hangar 3.

It featured two items of some consequence: a new desk, the first he had ever acquired, and a secondhand globe mounted on a stand in one corner of the unpretentious room. Red Mosier had ordered the desk from W. J. Sloane of New York when the move to LaGuardia was decreed. It contained a swing-out receptacle for C.R.'s overworked Woodstock, and Smith was to use that same desk for the next thirty-five years, although he finally did change typewriters.

Visitors occasionally would see him twirling the globe, half-playfully and half-thoughtfully; he seemed to regard it as a symbol of what both nation and airline faced as they approached inevitable involvement in a global conflict. Actually, the airline industry had demonstrated more vision than the government, especially Congress, when it came to anticipating the worst.

As early as 1936, ATA president Edgar Gorrell had presented the carriers with a plan to mobilize their resources in the event of any national emergency such as war. With the aid of farsighted leaders like Smith, Patterson, and Frye, he had kept updating the plan to conform with the industry's rapid growth and the development of new transport aircraft. In a sense, the response of the Big Four—American, TWA, United, and Eastern—to the 1938 New England hurricane crisis was a dress rehearsal and Gorrell, one of the most underrated figures in aviation history, had the foresight to recognize it as such. What he had begun formulating in 1936 was creation of a civil air reserve that could be turned over to the military on virtually twenty-four hours' notice, providing not only planes but flight crews and ground personnel.

Even as C.R. wrestled with the problems of running an airline in peacetime, he knew he had to plan ahead for the convulsions of war. And what fascinated him the most every time he looked at that globe in his office was the Great Circle route between the U.S. and Europe.

The year 1940 saw another regulatory reform: transferring the functions of the Civil Aeronautics Authority and its five members to a new Civil Aeronautics Board. At the same time, President Roosevelt abolished the three-man Safety Board and assigned the job of accident investigation to a Bureau of Safety within the CAB. The Civil Aeronautics Authority became the Civil Aeronautics Administration, retaining its responsibility for air traffic control, plus aircraft and pilot certification.

While the original 1938 Civil Aeronautics Act lasted only two years, it did contain a provision that bore fruit in 1941—authorization to build a new airport serving the nation's capital. And Washington needed one even more than New York. Old Hoover Field was one of the worst facilities in the country, as any American employee who worked there could testify.

Its biggest drawback was a runway so short that not even the versatile DC-3 could land there safely. American hung onto a handful of DC-2s until mid 1941 solely because there were no airports between Washington and Cincinnati capable of handling the bigger plane—and this included not only Hoover but Huntington, Charleston, and Elkins, all in West Virginia.

Hoover was located on the site of an old dump, just east of where the Pentagon now stands. A road went right through the airport, bisecting the runway; when planes landed or took off, guards would lower railroad gates to halt the automobile traffic. Red Mosier used to say it was a miracle that American never had an accident there. Even by the most liberal safety standards, Hoover Field was a public menace.

At that, it was slightly preferable to the old Newark Airport, built on a salt-water swamp so the hangars had to rest on pilings. Their macadam floors would settle as much as five feet. AA mechanic Charlie Dunbar remembered the time a maintenance crew was jacking up a plane and both jacks went through the floor. The rats were so bad that the mechanics founded an honorary organization they called "Old Swamp Rats." The rodents came out of the cracks in the hangar floors every time it rained, and maintenance work came to a halt while the mechanics grabbed shovels to go after them.

"They burned trash at Newark in the nearby dumps at night," Dunbar recalled. "I don't know which was worse—the stink from the dumps or the mosquitoes. Probably the latter. We used to light smudge pots at the end of the hangar, and we wore large cloth drapes over our heads. We looked like a bunch of Arabs. Everyone carried a Flit gun and we'd spray each other regularly."

It was no wonder that the airlines so fervently welcomed the new LaGuardia and National airports. American didn't even wait for National to be finished before station manager Sam Solomon moved the reservations office from Hoover to the still uncompleted terminal building at National. Jack Mullins was the first airline employee to work there, supervising eighteen agents.

When National did open officially, it was a traumatic experience for public relations director Ed Bern. The time set for the great event was just after midnight, June 19, and a check of airline schedules showed that American had a flight due to arrive in Washington around this time and thus was awarded the honor of inaugurating service at an airport touted to surpass even La-Guardia.

National was the first federally owned and operated civil aviation facility in the United States; located only four miles from the heart of downtown Washington, convenience was (and still is) its outstanding virtue. By today's standards, National is a shoebox disliked by most pilots, but in 1941 the government was boasting that its main runway was as long as the distance between the Washington Monument and the U.S. Capitol.

Bern's counterpart at Eastern was a profane, fast-thinking, and publicity-wise man named Bev Griffith, who took a dim view of American's selection as the first airline to use the new airport. There was nothing he could do about American's incoming flight other than shoot it down, but he had a contingency plan in his pocket.

The "just in case" happened: American's DC-3 was delayed, and Eastern had a flight scheduled to land just behind American. Griffith ran up to the control tower the minute he heard about the delay and began badgering the controllers.

"You can't make Eastern wait just because American screwed up!" he shouted. "Let us go ahead and land!"

The chief controller tried reason. "We promised American . . ." he started to explain.

"The hell with American! Captain Rickenbacker won't stand for this injustice!"

Whether it was Bev's insistence or the mention of Rickenbacker (who was recovering from near-fatal injuries suffered in a crash) that did the trick, nobody knows. But the chief controller sighed, "Okay, tell Eastern they can come in."

It was bad enough for Bern that Eastern's DC-3 stole the show, but this wasn't the only ignominy. Griffith's ace-in-the-hole consisted of packing the EAL plane with chorus girls from a New York show, figuring they'd draw some photographers away from American's inaugural landing. The cameramen never bothered with American at all. They were still photographing the girls when American finally came in.

Bern took such defeats to heart. In many ways he was a capable, ingenious p.r. man but somewhat on the flaky side. After the move to New York, he bought a cabin cruiser, along with such sartorial necessities as a yachting cap and blazer, probably to disguise the fact that he was about as nautical as a Bedouin tribesman. On one of his first voyages he took a party out on Long Island Sound and spotted a large log in the water. Bern promptly radioed the Coast Guard.

"I want to report a hazard to navigation," he announced importantly.

"Thank you, sir. What's its position?"

"Right here in front of my boat."

Bern's wildest promotion scheme was his involvement in Douglas Corrigan's famous wrong-way flight from New York to Dublin in July 1938. Corrigan always insisted that the twenty-eight-hour, thirteen-minute transatlantic hop was just what he said it was at the time—a mistake. He had flown from Long Beach to Floyd Bennett in his 1929 Curtiss Robin and was supposed to fly it back to California—except that he went east instead of west.

What has never been revealed is that Bern, apparently with C.R.'s blessing, arranged to have American underwrite part of Corrigan's expenses. In American's files is a letter from Bern to Corrigan, dated about a week before he went the wrong way, congratulating him on the successful completion of the California–New York trip and adding, "in . . . using the southern transcontinental route, you have done a great job in publicizing that route for American Airlines."

After noting that C. R. Smith "is very desirous of doing a good turn for you," Bern went on to offer this interesting deal:

> If after you complete your East to West flight, you will put the cities
> of the southern transcontinental route on the side of your airplane and
> state underneath, "This is the southern transcontinental route as flown
> by American Airlines," we will pay to you $500.00 in cash for expenses
> including gasoline, oil and maintaining your ship.

After the Ireland flight, Corrigan returned to the U.S. for the traditional New York ticker-tape parade and then toured the country. A letter from Smith to Corrigan, dated August 22 and addressed to "Dear Doug," noted that the tour up to then had been at Corrigan's expense. "You cannot be expected to continue your visits to other cities, with all expenses to be borne by you," the letter continued.

C.R. then offered him a one-year promotional contract, retroactive to August 1, calling for Corrigan to be paid $200 a month covering expenses for any visit to a city American served. The thirty-one-year-old pilot accepted and also expressed interest in another suggestion Smith made.

"When you are able and ready to devote all your time to a job in air transportation," C.R. wrote, "we would welcome an opportunity of talking with you concerning your employment by American."

Corrigan himself, seventy-eight years old at this writing and living in Santa Ana, California, with his son, said he was on American's payroll for a year "as a copilot" but never flew a trip.

"I was on a book tour and I also made a movie," he recalled. "The American job sort of petered out. It was just as well. I never did get along with that Ed Bern fellow."

He did meet once with C.R. and also Smith's brother Burck. The latter said Corrigan "wanted a contract with American like Lindbergh had with TWA and Pan Am—in other words, to be American's technical advisor."

Many years later, when Bill Hipple was running the airline's public relations office in Los Angeles, his secretary announced that he had a visitor. It was Corrigan, wearing the same old leather jacket he had on his flight and carrying a beat-up helmet and goggles in his hand.

"For a minute I couldn't believe it was him," Hipple remembered. "But you couldn't mistake that Irish grin of his. He said he still had that old Curtiss

Robin in a barn at his ranch near Fallbrook and he wanted to know if American could use him and the plane for some kind of promotion. I had to tell him no, but I felt bad about it."

Ed Bern went to his grave a few years after the war without supplying the answer to a provocative question: did he know in advance that Corrigan was going to attempt that unsanctioned flight to Ireland, and was the crazy stunt his idea in the first place? Considering Corrigan's dislike for Bern, and the fact that the pilot never actually admitted he flew the wrong way deliberately, the odds are against it. Yet those who knew Bern wouldn't have put it past him. His enthusiasm for publicity, however farfetched, was unlimited.

He bumped into Dan Beard and Dixon Speas at LaGuardia one day and slapped Beard on the shoulder.

"Dan, I've got the most wonderful news—the greatest thing that has ever happened in the history of this or any other airline!"

"What's the news?" Beard asked.

"American Airlines," Bern said proudly, "carried more babies today than any other airline in the world!"

He was more of a Hollywood-type p.r. man than airline; without meaning to, he could seem insensitive. He once went into lawyer Ham Hale's office to show him a letter he had received from a widow whose husband had been killed in a crash. She was threatening to sue because the wrong body had been put in the casket.

"She has no right to get mad," Bern declared. "Hell, I even threw in a couple of extra ties."

Bern hated Damon and eventually his relations with C.R. deteriorated; he left American shortly after the war. He would have appreciated a 1945 publicity stunt credited to Stan Washburn, a promotion-minded member of the p.r. staff, when the fuselage of a new DC-4, *Flagship Manhattan,* was towed through the streets of downtown Manhattan by a bevy of circus elephants. The wings then were reattached and the big plane was displayed at an empty corner lot at 52nd Street and Sixth Avenue.

American actually ordered the drastically revised four-engine Douglas before the war, but like TWA's Constellations—another pre-war design—all DC-4s would go to the military for the duration. Bill Littlewood had approved of the changes Douglas engineers had made from the unlamented DC-4E, including a switch to a single-tail aircraft instead of the triple tails on the experimental plane. And Littlewood had a hand in the design of another pre-war transport suggested by Curtiss-Wright, the twin-engine CW-20, a large thirty-passenger transport, and the brainchild of Curtiss-Wright's chief designer, George Page. A prototype was built and flown, but Littlewood rejected it for the airline; it was over-sized for its intended engines. But the CW-20 became the Curtiss C-46 Commando, next to the DC-3 World War II's most frequently used two-engine transport.

Selective Service, Lend-Lease, the London air raids, and the apparently unstoppable Nazi war machine were grim reminders of what was coming.

Edgar Gorrell transferred ATA's headquarters from Chicago to Washington. He wanted the industry's trade association to be closer to the source of regulatory activities, but more than anyone else he also knew the airlines' business-as-usual days had to end.

Of course, it wasn't quite business as usual, the unpredictable aspects of airline life being what they were. There was the unforgettable experience of American Captain Vic Miller, who wound up with a lion in his cockpit. He was flying a DST to Los Angeles, having taken over the trip at Nashville, where he was told he had an extra passenger.

In the companionway between the cockpit and cabin was a fair-sized cardboard box, and inside the box was a lion cub. An agent explained that MGM was shipping it to Hollywood as a possible replacement for Leo, the aging lion whose roars and snarling visage introduced every MGM film.

Everything was peaceful after takeoff until copilot Charlie Curry found the cub in his lap, purring. Twice they put it back on the box, and twice it got out again. Miller finally put two suitcases on top, and two minutes later the cub had its head between the rudder pedals. Curry finally tied its leash to a corner post. The friendly feline reappeared a few minutes later and climbed right back in Curry's lap. In desperation, Miller removed all passengers from the Sky Room lounge and locked the lion inside for the rest of the leg to Dallas, where he requisitioned a more secure box.

Using the Sky Room as a lion's cage wasn't the only time the DST configuration solved a crisis. Shortly after Washington National opened, a vicious storm hit the capital area and left the airport an island, cut off from adjacent Virginia communities and the District of Columbia by high water that flooded all access roads. National itself was fully operational, but hundreds of passengers were stranded there for two nights.

Jack Mullins and a handful of other American airport personnel were among the stranded, and it was Mullins who came to the rescue. American had stored in its hangar a number of blankets, mattresses, pillows, and bed linen for use on the sleeper planes. Mullins commandeered a few trucks and transferred the whole lot to the terminal building so passengers would have something to sleep on other than hard chairs or the floor. On the first night, when he found the airport's then-only restaurant closed, he somehow located a key and opened up the kitchen so people could be fed.

C.R. was spending more and more time in Washington in the immediate pre-war years. Route cases before the CAB were proliferating—American's big one was an application to serve Mexico—and C.R. began seriously thinking of building up his Washington staff. An airline could get involved even with a non-aviation federal agency, as American inadvertently did with the Federal Trade Commission.

The manufacturer of Sunbeam electric razors started advertising that its product had been tested by American Airlines and found to be the best on the market. The FTC took a dim view of that claim after discovering that the testing consisted of giving electric razors to a few American pilots, who dutifully informed the company their razors were pretty good.

The Commission filed a misleading advertising complaint against both Sunbeam and American, and C.R. sent Bob Howlett of the Pruitt firm down to Washington to settle the matter. It was resolved by Howlett agreeing that the airline wouldn't plug the razors anymore—a heart-breaking turn of events for pilots who had their supply of free electric razors suddenly cut off.

When Smith decided the airline needed better representation in the nation's capital, he turned to Mosier for advice on staffing the Washington office. Red had only one recommendation.

"Send Carlene Roberts down there," he urged.

It was an excellent and natural choice. As Mosier's secretary and administrative assistant, she had received more on-the-job training in airline economics and government relations than if she had graduated from Harvard Business School. She began making frequent trips to Washington in October 1941, and three months later was officially named head of the administrative staff there.

In New York, C.R. lived in a duplex apartment on 57th Street near the Queensborough Bridge. Ham Hale, whom the Pruitt firm had transferred to New York when American moved, visited there many times and always admired its unusual decor. It was Smith's beloved southwest transported to the middle of Manhattan.

His bedroom featured a bed and dresser made of cactus wood, and the window drapes were in the shape of leather chaps. On the night stand was a lamp whose shade was attached to a genuine antique Colt pistol. Also in the room was a phonograph and a record library of cowboy songs. The one he played most frequently was "The Crying Cowboy"; he told one interviewer, "They're so sad they make me laugh."

The bed in the guest room had a real wagon wheel as a headboard, and the footboard was an oxen yoke. The apartment walls were studded with bleached cattle skulls, stuffed buffalo heads, and Texas steerhorns, plus Western oil paintings by Remington, Russell, and Schreyvogel. There was an old-fashioned Western bar with silver dollars implanted in the top and, inevitably, a well-stocked gun rack. Even the curtain rods fitted the motif—they were branding irons. The only non-Western items in the apartment were his collection of Victorian music boxes, a hobby he started before he got seriously involved with Western art. Hale remembered that Smith sometimes would play all the boxes simultaneously, filling the living room with the tinkling melodies of a half-dozen songs.

For a time, his brother Bill lived there with him, although how much they saw of each other was another matter. He traveled around the system constantly, and no employee could know when he might pop up unexpectedly—including those who wished he hadn't.

Late one night he walked into American's airport office at Knoxville unannounced. Only one man was on duty, and he had his feet on the desk, reading a newspaper. The phone was ringing when C.R. came in, and the employee just kept reading, never looking up.

"Doesn't anyone answer phones around here?" Smith growled.

"That's a sales phone, buster. I'm with operations."

C.R. picked up the phone—it was someone asking for information on American's schedules to the West Coast. Smith, who knew the timetable by heart, politely provided the information and hung up. The man behind the desk finally put down his paper.

"From the way you answered that phone," he observed, "you must be with American."

Smith gave him a look that would have burned through six inches of asbestos. "*I* am but *you're* not," he said coldly. "You're fired!"

He prowled the system without ever worrying about what was going on "back at the ranch." He knew he had an executive staff that may have been the best in the industry: Rheinstrom in marketing, Littlewood in engineering, Damon running operations, and Mosier handling public affairs. They were relatively young, capable, and dedicated. American's bright future was reflected in their own.

And then came December 7, 1941.

Seven days after Pearl Harbor, fifteen American DC-3s flying routine trips received identical radio messages ordering them to land at the nearest airport and disembark all passengers.

The mystified pilots complied. After landing, each crew was handed another identical order: take your plane to Fort Lauderdale, Florida. At that airport, they found some 300 Signal Corps communications specialists ready to be flown to Natal, Brazil, already designated as the jump-off base for a transatlantic airlift to the war zones.

This was the first of American's many wartime missions. It would be a foolish boast to say that it did more than any other carrier; the entire industry came of age in meeting the greatest challenge air transportation had ever faced. But in one respect, American did contribute something extra: it gave to the war effort its own leader.

C. R. Smith didn't put on a uniform right away. He was too busy trying to run an airline plunged into chaos that threatened to get worse. The Gorrell blueprint for a civil air reserve was ready and waiting to be implemented, and when that happened, C.R. knew the Flagship Fleet would be decimated.

He had been more involved in the updating of that plan than any other airline president. Almost a year before Japan hit Pearl Harbor, Gorrell had told Smith the most recent emergency blueprints were three years old and had to revised. He asked C.R. for help, and Smith assigned trouble shooter M. P. Stallter, one of Damon's crack operations specialists, to the task. Stallter's precise, detailed study of what the airlines could provide the military, while still serving their own routes, was in Gorrell's hands when the first bombs dropped on the Pacific fleet.

Incredibly, the ATA plan came micrometers away from being scrapped. Shortly after the outbreak of war, FDR summoned Gorrell to the White House and showed him a *signed* executive order nationalizing the airline industry for the duration. The stunned Gorrell protested. He reminded Roosevelt that the civil air reserve plan could be implemented immediately and that there was no reason for the government to seize the airlines.

Fortunately for the ATA president, present in the Oval Office was General H. H. "Hap" Arnold, chief of the Army Air Corps, who was far more impressed with Gorrell's impassioned arguments than FDR was at first. When Roosevelt asked Arnold for his opinion, Hap sided with Gorrell. He bluntly informed the President that only the airlines had the equipment and skilled manpower to run a global air transportation system, as a civil adjunct to the military but under military orders.

Gorrell added, rather slyly, that World War I had provided a good example of why any transportation system suffered when it was nationalized. The railroads were taken over by the government in 1917 and almost collapsed under the weight of bureaucratic inefficiency and red tape. FDR had the grace to smile at this gentle needle and, with Gorrell standing there, holding his breath, tore up the executive order.

In Hap Arnold, the airlines had a friend, a man who believed firmly that air transportation is a vital component of air power. He was, in fact, one of four young Air Corps officers who in 1925 drew up a prospectus for a U.S. airline that would serve Central and South America. As a major in Air Corps Intelligence, Arnold had been watching the development of a German-backed airline called SCADTA that had been organized in Colombia and reportedly was ready to expand as far north as the Panama Canal. His proposed airline was devised as a countermeasure to this potential menace.

The four officers had just started raising investment funds when three of them, Arnold included, became embroiled in General Billy Mitchell's court-martial. Because they testified in Mitchell's defense, they received official reprimands. With this stigma clouding their records, they decided to stay in the Army and continue Mitchell's crusade for an independent air force.

Reluctantly, they stepped out of the airline venture and some of the men they had attracted as investors took over the project under the same name they had used in their prospectus: Pan American Airways. If Billy Mitchell had been acquitted, Juan Trippe's career might have taken an entirely different course.

The seeds of what would become the mighty Air Transport Command of World War II were planted six months before Pearl Harbor when Arnold, under Presidential orders, established a Ferrying Command for the purpose of flying Lend-Lease aircraft to seaports in the U.S. and Canada, where they would be transferred to freighters.

Colonel Robert Olds was the first chief of the Ferrying Command, starting the operation with only six officers and a civilian clerk. It was in full swing by March 1942 when the overworked Olds collapsed at his desk and was forced to go on emergency sick leave. Arnold summoned another trusted officer, Colonel Harold Lee George, to replace Olds temporarily.

The temporary status lasted only a week, when Arnold informed George that Olds's recuperation would last longer than expected.

"I've had to relieve him of his command," Arnold said reluctantly. "I want you to take over, Hal."

George, whose specialty was strategic bombing, was shocked. He had expected an overseas command in what he knew best, and he told Arnold exactly how he felt. But for several minutes Hap lectured him on the importance of the airplane not only as a combat weapon but a means of expediting vital tonnage and personnel to the war theaters.

George tried one last way to get out of the assignment. "I realize the importance of air transportation, but if you'll permit me, sir, I know nothing about the problems of creating a worldwide air transport system. And I'm sure there's no one in the Ferrying Command with that kind of knowledge."

Arnold said nothing for a moment, then asked, "Do you know C. R. Smith?"

"I know he's president of American Airlines. I don't know him personally."

"Well, I do. I'll call C.R. up and have him fly down here. You meet him and if you two can get along together, I'll make him a colonel." Arnold's eyes twinkled and he added, "I'm recommending you for brigadier general."

Hal George and C.R. met the next morning in C.R.'s hotel room. As Arnold suspected, they hit it off immediately, although George learned quickly that Smith never went around end when he could go through center faster. He was telling C.R. that what they needed was a cadre of experienced airline executives and administrators to set up a global system.

Smith took a pencil and wrote down about twenty names on a piece of hotel stationery. He showed George the list.

"I don't know any of them," George said.

"They're the best in the industry. We'll send telegrams to the presidents of their airlines telling them that these people are absolutely essential to the war effort and that they must be released for service."

Smith composed the telegram text himself and George said later it was phrased so strongly that he warned C.R., "There's only one person who can sign that kind of message and have it mean anything to the recipients, and that's General Arnold."

"I agree," C.R. said laconically. "We'll sign his name and get these wires out."

"Wait a minute," George protested. "We can't put his name on those telegrams without his approval."

"The hell we can't," Smith shot back. "He can't shoot you for doing it."

The telegrams went out under Arnold's unauthorized name. With some trepidation, George confessed to Arnold what they had done. "You might be getting some telephone calls from a few airline presidents," he added.

The general just laughed. "I'll handle them, Hal. They've got to realize this country's at war. By the way, if you and C.R. can work together, take him to the Adjutant General's office and have him sworn in as a colonel."

Thus did the three-year military career of Cyrus Rowlett Smith begin, as George's deputy commander. He went in a colonel and came out a major general in an ATC numbering more than 300,000 men. The man by whose side he worked during those critical war years, Hal George, summed it up best:

"I have had close relationships with a number of people during my many years in the military service and in civilian life. I have never had such admiration and regard for any individual as I developed for C. R. Smith. He was not only a remarkable personality but an outstanding executive."

Just about the time C.R. donned a uniform over his 6'1" frame, the Ferrying Command changed its name to the Air Transport Command. The new nomenclature coincided with a bitter intraservice feud involving a sister Air Corps unit, the Air Service Command, which was responsible for transporting men and material between domestic air depots and military air bases. When war came, ASC insisted it should continue this task, ATC limiting itself to overseas operations.

Arnold made the mistake of appointing a committee to work out a compromise. Its recommendation was that the Air Service Command take over all air transportation within the Western Hemisphere and ATC everything outside that Hemisphere. Hal George's opinion of this decision was that, "If confusion and inefficiency were the objectives to be obtained, no plan could have been proposed that would better accomplish it."

Once more, Hap Arnold came to the rescue. Furious at his own committee, he went straight to Chief of Staff George Marshall and came out with a directive giving the Air Transport Command *sole* responsibility for air transportation within the U.S. and to all war zones. And C.R. found himself helping to run an "airline" that soon dwarfed the one he had left.

He immediately proved himself impatient with military protocol, most of which he regarded as military red tape. Much of it eventually he had to learn to live with, such as adhering to the Pentagon policy of multicopy memos, reports, and correspondence.

According to Carlene Roberts, who had frequent contacts with him during the war, for a while he continued his practice of using his own typewriter for pithy notes, which he often sent directly to the person who was supposed to carry out his order. Nobody was marked in for copies.

For the record, C.R. himself denied that this was his sole method of communicating with subordinates and superiors. His own explanation:

"I knew from long experience that the outfit would not function well unless the top hands knew what the others were doing. I worked out a typewriter that operated on a perforated roll with six copies. I sent one copy to each of the various departments with responsibility. It worked like a charm; no other outfit in the bunch had such a smooth operation."

It is true that he used that fancy typewriter—Carlene Roberts saw it—but one of his wartime associates swore that C.R. once sent an important order all the way to Casablanca, brusque and self-typed, with no copies.

"The Pentagon found out about it," this associate said, "and raised hell with C.R., who ignored all the protests. But it was after this that he got the typewriter with the perforated rolls."

Those who thought Smith might favor his own airline in any dealings it had with ATC were wrong. Hamilton Hale testified to that.

"He made it clear that he wanted to avoid as many contacts with American as possible. He felt he would be dealing with all airlines and he wanted no suggestions that he was favoring American or any intimation that he was still running the company. He really lived up to it, too."

But the biggest surprise that came out of C.R.'s decision to join up was his selection of a temporary successor. He picked a man with no real airline experience, and one few people at American even knew.

Alexander N. Kemp was a grandfatherly, pleasant, and even-tempered gentleman who had spent most of his adult life in the insurance business. He was president of the Pacific Mutual Life Insurance when C.R. put him on American's board of directors early in 1941.

C.R.'s reasons for choosing him to run American during the war have never been really explained. Kemp—his friends called him Ned—certainly was a capable executive, as his record at Pacific Mutual demonstrated. But why Smith went to the board for an interim president—and a very junior director at that—was and still is a mystery.

Ralph Damon would have been an obvious selection, but he took a leave of absence from American about the time C.R. went into the Army, to become president of Republic Aviation, manufacturer of the P-47 Thunderbolt fighter. That still left two competent candidates: Charlie Rheinstrom and Red Mosier. Mosier really wanted the job; it was no secret around American that he had been competing with Damon for the unofficial rank of C.R.'s crown prince.

But Smith, when he informed the directors he was leaving, asked them to elect Ned Kemp president. One theory, very understandable, is that he didn't want too strong a man in the job, who might achieve too much power and influence by the time the war ended. Such a development was not farfetched; that is precisely what happened at Continental when Bob Six joined the Air Corps (other than C.R., the only airline president to wear a uniform in WW II) and left his airline in charge of Terry Drinkwater. While Six was still in service, Drinkwater tried to gain control of Continental and was foiled only when Six was tipped off, obtained emergency leave, and walked into the secret board meeting at which Drinkwater was about to oust him.

There is no indication that Rheinstrom, Mosier, or anyone else would have attempted the coup that Drinkwater tried to pull off. It may well be that C.R. figured, like so many did, that the war wasn't going to last very long and it didn't make much difference whom he left holding the fort. There isn't much doubt he would have chosen Damon. Although Damon and Mosier were theoretically equal as vice presidents, the former had more authority and this was with Smith's approval, as the following incident shortly before the war showed.

Mosier had asked some mechanics at LaGuardia to build him a prop for a Saints and Sinners Circus show—an outhouse. It was parked in a corner of a hangar, waiting for Red to ship it downtown, when Damon happened to walk into the hangar and spotted it.

"What the hell is that and whose is it?" he demanded.

"We built it for Mr. Mosier," the shop foreman said.

"Get it the hell out of my hangar and remember you're not taking orders from Mosier or anyone else but me!" Damon yelled.

He then stormed into Mosier's office and the two men had an argument loud enough to be heard by C.R., whose office was only a few feet away. He never said a word.

But it was Ned Kemp, not Damon, who took over the airline, and whether he was more or less of a figurehead president is a matter of opinion. Ham Hale said flatly, "He never got the credit he deserved." Certainly he presided over some momentous events during the war, including the acquisition of American Export Airlines and the inauguration of service to Mexico (to be described in Chapter 11). But if he ranks as a kind of "forgotten president," it was mainly due to C.R.'s own towering personality. Smith was always a hard act to follow.

In the terminology of today's youth, Ned Kemp probably would be classed as "nice but square." He was kind, always dignified, and just a wee bit pompous in a Victorian sense. When Dixon Speas decided to get married during the war, Kemp heard about it and called him in.

"Boy," he intoned, "I understand you are about to take a wife."

"Yes, sir."

"Wise, my boy. Very wise." Then he nodded. And when Kemp nodded, you knew the interview was over.

Ham Hale's fondest memory of him involved the time the young lawyer had just finished arguing against a CAB proposal to make a new and lower wartime mail rate retroactive, which would have meant American's giving a huge chunk of money back to the government. Hale was in Illinois visiting his parents when the CAB decided to withdraw the retroactive provision. He received this wire from Kemp:

CONGRATULATIONS ON OUTCOME OF YOUR RAPE CASE.

Patrician and rather private, Kemp had difficulty adjusting to airline informality, an atmosphere in which there were few secrets. One day he found on his desk the current issue of *American Aviation,* the industry's news magazine, which was delivered regularly to every American officer. He was horrified to discover it contained a story listing the salaries of every airline executive in the U.S., including his own; he hadn't realized that in a regulated industry, executive salaries are a matter of public record.

Kemp summoned his secretary and sent her through the building collecting every copy—some of them in the process of being read.

In one key respect, an airline in wartime was easier to run: nobody had to sell air travel, simply because virtually every flight ran full. Before the war, the airlines had talked about establishing some kind of emergency priority system; one proposal called for reserved space being subject to cancellation if a government or military passenger needed a seat. But when war actually came, this one never got off the ground. It was far too mild.

The Air Transport Command itself, through its Priorities and Traffic Division, dictated a tough pecking order for all airline travel. It set up these four priority categories:

1. Persons traveling on direct orders of the White House, War, or Navy departments (this one was generally known as "White House priority")
2. Military pilots en route to aircraft ferry bases or military stations
3. Military or civilian passengers traveling on essential business related to the war effort
4. Military cargo

There were surprisingly few instances of airline agents violating a priority rule, even though some bribe offers were astronomical and the sob stories capable of flooding an 8,000-foot runway. American's Washington agents in particular were prime targets for threats, harassment, and heart-rending pleas, but Jack Mullins was a tough boss who would have thrown his own mother off a plane if she lacked a priority.

"We took all sorts of people off our airplanes," he reminisced. "Usually the bigger and more important a person was, the more understanding and easier to handle he was. It invariably was the little guy who just thought he was important who gave us the most trouble."

The highest-ranking VIP Mullins ever removed from a flight was Eleanor Roosevelt. She was going to New York and held a Priority 3. At the last minute, an Army pilot showed up clutching a Priority 2 and Mullins had to tell the wife of the President of the United States she must give up her seat, everyone else on the plane had Priorities 1 and 2.

But when he broke the news, she merely smiled. "My goodness, young man, of course I'll get off. There's no question those pilots should go ahead of me."

It was especially tough for Mullins, and not just because she was the First Lady; Eleanor Roosevelt also happened to be one of American's best customers and remained that way all her life. She was good friends with C.R., who frankly adored her. He had unabashed admiration for her boundless energy and once remarked, "She could always stay up later than I could and be fresher-looking the next day."

Smith was noted for brevity. Someone once asked him to describe his mother and his answer was, "I liked her." But when it came to Mrs. Roosevelt, he gushed. He told one interviewer:

"She was one of the most unusual women I ever met, in intelligence, in energy. She was always interested in doing for someone else instead of someone doing for her. A generous woman and a prodigious worker."

For a while, the Admirals Club had an unofficial "men only" membership policy; C.R. waived it for Eleanor Roosevelt to the extent of telling

Charlie Speers to send her a guest card. Speers still has the letter she wrote in return:

> Dear Mr. Speers:
>
> My son John, has given me my Admirals Club guest card. I am very pleased and honored to have this privilege extended me, for I realize that it is not essentially a woman's club! I do not think that I shall very often avail myself of the Club privileges, but it is nice to know that I can do so if I wish.

Burck Smith told the classic story of this magnificent if admittedly rather homely woman whose real beauty was her compassion and dignity. She had boarded an American DST in Los Angeles and climbed into her assigned lower berth after takeoff. She was restless and began to toss in her sleep, constantly kicking the man in the berth above her.

He finally leaned over and said loudly, "You can stop kicking me, lady. I saw you when you got on."

Not all the priority-displaced passengers were as understanding and cooperative as Mrs. Roosevelt, although the priority system ran smoother than anyone expected. Eastbound flights were a little easier to get on; westbound trips were usually booked solidly with Priority 2s, ferry pilots who had just returned from flying planes to Europe and were heading for the West Coast to pick up more aircraft.

In retrospect, it was a near miracle the airlines did as well as they did, especially in the first two years of the war when they were operating full schedules with decimated fleets. Under the ATA's civil reserve plans for aircraft allocation, the Army requisitioned 183 planes out of the industry's total fleet of 359. That left only 176 aircraft to do the same job performed by nearly 400.

American released all its DSTs first; they didn't carry as many passengers as the standard DC-3 and were more expendable. But by mid 1942, the Flagship Fleet had been reduced from 79 to 41 planes. Utilization soared to an average of more than 13 hours a day per aircraft or nearly 5,000 flying hours a year, about 30 percent above a typical pre-war year.

With half the fleet went almost half the flight crews plus hundreds of mechanics, assigned to the Air Transport Command under the contract American had with the War Department. And while the people they left behind to run their beloved airline did a superb job, it paled by comparison to what American's ATC contingent accomplished.

On a chilly day in February 1942, *Flagship Cleveland* waddled to a stop at LaGuardia, discharged the last regular civilian passengers it would carry for a long time, and then was taxied to hangar 5 for transformation.

Out came the upholstered seats. Stripped from the silver fuselage were all vestiges of airline insignia, and onto the shiny aluminum went the dull olive drab colors of the Army Air Corps. For weeks, maintenance crews swarmed over the plane, installing equipment that had never been on a DC-3 before. Extra fuel tanks. A radio room. Survival equipment from snowshoes to a pair of rifles. Parachutes and life rafts. Fishing lines and medical kits. A plywood table for a navigator.

On April 24, the former *Flagship Cleveland* took off for Presque Isle, Maine, one of the old Ferrying Command's first bases. Aboard was a hand-picked crew starting with a pair of million-mile pilots, H. G. "Robby" Robinson and Frank Bledsoe. At the navigator's table was C. H. McIntosh. The mechanic assigned to the flight was chosen by Frank Ware, chief of American's maintenance; he selected himself. Nobody argued with him because it was said that Ware and Dan Beard were the only men in aviation who could start a balky engine without invoking the name of the Deity.

The rest of the seven-man crew consisted of chief meteorologist C. E. "Doc" Buell, Dave Davidson, who was assistant chief pilot at LaGuardia, and Beard. He was in overall charge of an expedition that seems to have been the work of one C. R. Smith.

One of his last acts as a civilian had been a trip to Washington, where he tried to sell Hap Arnold on the feasibility of an airlift across the North Atlantic via the Great Circle route. The Ferrying Command already had a string of hastily constructed bases from Presque Isle to Iceland, but some experts insisted the North Atlantic was too hazardous for a regular operation. The safer route was over the South Atlantic out of Natal.

All Arnold gave C.R. was a green light for a survey flight. Smith flew back to Washington, assembled his technical staff, and announced, "We're going to Iceland—figure out a way to do it."

Beard and Ware did the technical groundwork, mostly involving the DC-3's conversion. Dixon Speas of Littlewood's engineering department was an all-around "Mr. Fixit" assigned to the planning team. McIntosh wanted to use a $500 drift indicator designed for the Army but the military refused to let him have one. So he and Speas built an improvised indicator out of a ruled celluloid disk they mounted in the floor near the navigator's table. They spent five dollars on the homemade device, and McIntosh claimed it worked better than the Army's $500 model.

Enough was learned from the survey flight to demonstrate the practicality of a North Atlantic airlift, and within weeks the first of thousands of flights, manned by ex-airline crews assigned to ATC, were spanning the Great Circle route. "American's Northeast Passage," it was dubbed by Stan Washburn of public relations. By midsummer of 1945, American alone had made some 7,000 North Atlantic crossings; at the peak of operations, its DC-4s (C-54s in military nomenclature) were averaging almost 500 flights a month.

Between the first survey flight and the airlift armada of the later war years, however, lay countless tales of adversity and adventure that would have filled the pages of a Manhattan telephone directory. The most publicized story involved an American ATC plane commanded by Captain Owen "Chuck" O'Connor, a westbound flight over the North Atlantic.

The aircraft was a C-87, one of the B-24 Liberator bombers the Army had converted into a cargo plane when it needed four-engine equipment for long-range flights. DC-4s were just starting to come off the Douglas assembly lines and the only other four-engine transports ATC possessed were the nine Boeing Stratoliners obtained from TWA and Pan Am.

O'Connor had the usual ATC crew of five aboard—himself, a copilot, navigator, radio operator, and flight engineer/mechanic—plus seventeen soldiers returning to the U.S., seven of them for medical treatment and rest. Almost the entire trip, they had been belabored by stiff headwinds and ice, the latter so severe that O'Connor was forced to descend from 18,000 feet to 3,000. At the lower altitude, however, the C-87 was gulping fuel voraciously and as they neared the Canadian coast, O'Connor knew they were in trouble.

At 3,000 feet in an overcast, the navigator had only two brief glimpses of the stars, and in those fleeting seconds he had been unable to take bearings. Their bag of worms was opened further when the freak weather conditions produced false radio navigation signals. O'Connor was homing in on a station far west of the one he thought he was contacting.

By this time, they had reached landfall, but the fuel was almost exhausted. He sent one final radio message before deciding he'd better gamble on a forced landing:

"Low on gas. I've got to land the ship. Landing on uncharted lake."

He put the C-87 down at dusk on an ice-covered lake somewhere in the wilds of northern Quebec Province. Nobody got a scratch and the plane was unharmed, but they were to be marooned there for thirty-two days in an incredible saga of survival.

What happened was a grim application of Murphy's Law: everything that could go wrong did. They came down February 4, 1943, and the next day O'Connor and his navigator took solar sights to establish their position. They didn't realize that the bitter cold had damaged their octant and the position they radioed to ATC was miles off.

Their signal, however, was picked up by two search planes, whose pilots ignored the erroneous position report and homed in on the C-87's battery transmitter, using their unerring radio direction finders. The ordeal might have ended right then and there but before the planes reached the forced landing site, O'Connor's battery failed. The searchers, low on fuel, had to turn back without spotting the downed plane.

A third search plane stumbled on the lake a few hours later and dropped supplies. Again, their troubles should have been over—except that a blizzard swept into the area and grounded all rescue efforts for another three days. When the search was renewed, the C-87 was covered with snow and almost impossible to spot from the air.

Not until February 10 did the air probes sight the marooned party. A plane piloted by Ernie Gann and Breezy Wynne dropped fresh supplies and radioed the position to the rest of the searching aircraft. O'Connor and his frozen charges figured they had it made. After Gann's welcome report, more planes arrived and began circling the lake.

One of them was a C-47 commanded by Fred Lord, who decided to land and fly the whole party out. If a C-87 could get down on that lake, he reasoned it should be duck soup for the smaller aircraft. But Lord hadn't taken into consideration the snow that had fallen. He landed safely, but came to an abrupt stop after rolling only a couple of hundred feet.

"I'm stuck," he radioed helplessly. Now "Lac O'Connor," as it was later dubbed, had two stranded airplanes and three more marooned men.

Six more inches of snow fell the following day. Lord figured out a way to fashion a makeshift snowplow out of assorted parts from their planes and they staked out a runway outline. Eight men tried to clear the snow, pulling the improvised plow, but even working in shifts they made little headway. The men were terribly weakened by exposure to temperatures that at one point dropped to 70 below.

Each morning, O'Connor had sick call and treated mushrooming cases of frostbite as best he could. All that saved them was the fact that at least ATC knew where they were, although all the frustrated rescue pilots could do was continue dropping survival supplies and equipment, including sleeping bags, tents, stoves, warm clothing, axes, shovels, boots, and even blow torches. The sleeping bags were especially welcome; it was so cold that each man used two.

O'Connor appropriated the C-87's cabin as a storage place for the food the planes kept parachuting down—beef, ham, bread, beans, and flour for hot cakes. It was a vast improvement over their fare in the first few days, when a typical meal consisted of one can of soup in a pot of boiling water to which had been added the defeathered carcasses of small birds. One soup pot contained an owl one of the men had shot.

Nourishment and better protection from the freezing weather did the trick. By February 26, enough men had regained sufficient strength to clear what passed as a runway. On that day, a ski-equipped C-47 managed to land and take off again with the seven wounded soldiers. But weather continued to harass the rescue attempts and it was not until March 6 that the last of the men were taken off the frozen lake. O'Connor was among them.

Miraculously, there were no serious medical consequences; O'Connor, whose courage and discipline had played such a large role in their survival, had only one complaint: he got sunburned. A few weeks later, Breezy Wynne returned to the lake with a crew, filled up the C-87's tanks, and flew it back to New York for an overhaul. When the ship returned to its ATC transatlantic duties, it carried a new name under the cockpit windows:

Lac O'Connor.

There was a further sequel to the ordeal of Captain O'Connor and his men. Ernie Gann turned this true story into a novel, *Island in the Sky,* which also became a movie.

* * *

Gann was one of those rare men who seemed to excel in anything he tried. An accomplished musician and a skilled, sensitive writer, he also was a talented artist. Not coincidentally, he happened to be an excellent pilot as well, a kind of latter-day Antoine de Saint-Exupéry.

One of the wartime tasks assigned to Dixon Speas was the preparation of operating manuals for American's North Atlantic pilots. When the ATC began acquiring C-54s, Speas worked forty-eight hours without sleep getting the manuals for the new plane ready. The morning after he finished, he encountered Gann, who was standing in front of his locker at LaGuardia operations. They knew each other well—Speas had been the instructor in C-54 ground school and Ernie was one of his students.

With pride of authorship, Speas handed him the manual. "Ernie, we've got the C-54 emergency manual all done. Here it is."

"What's this all about?" Gann asked.

"It tells you what to do in case of an emergency, dammit."

Ernie smiled. "You gave us all that stuff in ground school, Dix."

"Sure, but this is all written down."

Gann thumbed through the pages, glancing at some complicated graphs and charts. "And what's all this stuff?"

"Well, it tells you what to do if you lose an engine—how far you can go, fuel management, power settings, and so on."

Gann grinned again. "Do you suppose we can go up to flight control, and you give me the power settings for four segments of about three hours each, assuming everything's working right?"

"Sure."

"Fine. Now we can put this manual where it won't do any harm." Ernie opened his locker, tossed in the manual, and closed the door. Then he put his arm around Speas. "You know, Dix, that damned thing could hurt somebody. If I can get into an emergency, I'm not going to have time to look something up in a book. I've got to remember what you've already told me or I'm lost."

Si Bittner was one of the pilots who requested and got assignment to ATC's North Atlantic crews, but not even global war could suppress his sense of humor. He got off a C-54 at Prestwick, Scotland, and started pulling a long pole out of a cargo hatch. A mechanic asked him what the pole was for.

"Well," Bittner explained, "I've heard about those British women who wouldn't touch an American pilot with a ten-foot pole so I brought along an eleven-foot pole."

The same Captain Robby Robinson who flew the survey trip had a hand in saving the lives of two merchant seamen whose ship had been torpedoes. Robby was in a C-87 over the mid South Atlantic, at 4,000 feet, idly watching the ocean below when he spotted a white object that didn't look like a white-capped wave.

"Lemme take it," he told copilot Bob Dietz. "I think I just saw something down there." He disengaged the automatic pilot and went into a descending left turn. What he had seen were two men in a lifeboat frantically waving a white shirt they had rigged to an oar. Robinson ordered his radio operator to start sending their position and flew even lower, until they were only twenty feet from the water.

From that altitude, they threw out most of their own emergency equipment —a waterproof radio, water canteens, radio generator, food, fishing gear, tools and a bright yellow rubber boat. The two men eventually were picked up by a ship.

One of American's most dramatic wartime missions occurred during the battle of Midway. After most of the Japanese fleet had been turned back, part of it headed for Alaska and the alarm bells rang. The Pentagon asked the airlines to pull every available plane off regular schedules and rush troops and war materials to Edmonton in case the Japanese intended to invade. American was one of ten carriers contacted, with orders to muster its aircraft on the West Coast if possible because it was closer to Alaska.

It was 6 P.M. on a Saturday when American operations reached Ted Lewis, flight superintendent at Burbank—the same Ted Lewis who had once flown with Howard Hughes.

"Round up all the aircraft and crews you can find," he was told, "and get them up to Edmonton as fast as possible. Mechanics, too."

Lewis started phoning every American station between Fort Worth and Burbank. Then he realized nobody knew how long the pilots would have to stay in Alaska and they would need money to live on. He raced to American's Burbank ticket office and emptied the till, which had only $300. Then he remembered that Sears, Roebuck's Burbank store stayed open Saturday nights. He telephoned the manager and explained his problem.

"Come right over," the manager said.

From Sears he obtained $6,500 in cash. By Sunday morning he had scrounged up nine DC-3s with pilots to fly them, and at 9 A.M. they took off, one by one, heading north. Bill Miller, Ted's counterpart in New York, followed the next day with two more planes and took over American's Alaskan operation, which lasted one month. During that time the pilots spent twenty hours a day on duty, and so did the mechanics. The DC-3s flew a round trip between Seattle and Alaskan cities daily. The beloved Abe Hoyt was one of the mechanics stationed there, supervising the maintenance work side by side with crews from the other airlines.

The fraternalism of airmen was as evident as it had been when the airlines responded to the New England hurricane crisis. Northwest's pilots, already acclimated to flying conditions in Alaska, willingly and thoroughly briefed their brethren on how to stay out of trouble.

The pilots had most of the glory and glamour, not to mention the dangers, but something should be said about the hardy mechanics who uncomplainingly worked in conditions that in peacetime would have sent them straight to their grievance committee. It was particularly bad at the North Atlantic ATC bases, where the winters could be brutal.

The maintenance men volunteered for duty at these outlying stations. American personnel opened many of them on the North Atlantic route under the direction of Robert "Pop" Handley and Dick Callahan. Handley met virtually every plane that landed at one of his stations and worked at almost every base from Presque Isle to Prestwick. Together with senior mechanics A. L. Robinson and Ed Lawrence, this quartet collectively had eight years of foreign service, crossed the ocean thirty times, and worked in thirteen different countries.

Goose Bay, Labrador, was known as Station 685; the closest rail head was at Moncton, 550 miles away. The station was opened the day before Pearl Harbor with a single dirt landing strip, and anyone who worked there deserved a medal. During the summer, it was possible to bring in supplies by boat, but in the winter, everything had to be flown in. There were no hangars and the mechanics worked in the open, with temperatures dropping to as low as 40 below.

Station 765 was at Stephenville, Newfoundland, which became the hub of North Atlantic operations. American had seventeen men stationed there, who compiled an on-time dispatch record that compared favorably with domestic flights. The station's general foreman, R. M. Smith, had been one of the first six men sent to Presque Isle and was told he could expect to come home in about six weeks; he stayed overseas for four years.

Meeks Field in Iceland was Station 720. It was heaven in the summer, when the sun shined twenty-four hours a day, and hell in the winter; not even the low living costs (25 cents for a steak or chicken dinner and 15 cents for a haircut) could make up for what the men had to endure. Lead mechanic George Stoneking painted this picture of Station 720:

"Did you ever see *horizontal* rain and snow? Did you ever have to dig your way out of a Nissen Hut—a fancy name for a dark alley with doors at both ends? The wind starts blowing at 45 miles an hour, with gusts often reaching 120. You start walking up the road against that wind, rain or snow blowing in your face, and before you've gone a hundred feet you feel as though Joe Louis has given you a ten-round beating."

On the other side of the world, at Tezpur, India, was an American Airlines operation known as Project 7-A.

It began in July 1943, when General Arnold asked American to divert ten C-87s and 150 pilots and mechanics from its South Atlantic operations and fly them to Tezpur. Ted Lewis, who had just been transferred from Burbank to Natal, suddenly found himself in charge of organizing the latest emergency expedition to another place the eagle had never known before.

Arnold's directive mentioned that the men would probably have to camp out in tents but that spare engines weren't needed because there were plenty on hand in India. Lewis took that last bit of assurance with a baseball-sized grain of salt—he put new engines in all ten aircraft and begged, borrowed, or stole every C-87 spare part he could locate in Brazil and Africa. Many of the pilots, however, were drawn from the North Atlantic crews.

Nobody knew much about the mission except what Arnold's terse orders had spelled out briefly: they were to take enough supplies and equipment to operate the fleet for ninety days, and that it involved flying the infamous, dreaded "Hump" over that part of the Himalayas that formed a barrier between India, Burma, and China.

Gene Taylor of operations was the overall coordinator for Project 7-A at LaGuardia; with Lewis mustering planes and pilots at Natal, Taylor finished the planning at his end in unbelievable time. Project 7-A had been activated July 18 with a phone call from Arnold. On August 1, only fourteen days later, Captain Toby Hunt landed the first C-87 at Tezpur with a contingent of twenty-five men. The next day Hunt took the same plane over the Hump; three months later, American's crews had set a cargo-carrying record for the China-Burma-India (CBI) theater, and they did it with fewer planes than the Air Corps was using for the Hump operation.

Bill Evans, one of the American pilots assigned to Project 7-A, had sympathy for the military pilots. "I have to give them a lot of credit. Those guys came right out of advanced training and most of them had never flown the C-46s and C-47s they threw at them. They were terribly inexperienced at first. We had ADF (Automatic Direction Finder) stations along the route and if one of the kids got lost, they'd ask you to recite poetry or start counting so they could get a fix.

"One Air Corps pilot bailed out over what the maps said was unexplored territory. He found his way to a mission, and the priest was a guy who had lived a half block away from him in Chicago—they had grown up together.

"When we got there, the Army pilots were getting the Air Medal for fifteen trips over the Hump and the Distinguished Flying Cross for thirty flights. They never flew it at night. We were making three round trips a day, and when we started flying the Hump at night, that ended the Air Medal and DFC awards."

As might be expected, the ubiquitous Captain Bittner turned up as a Project 7-A pilot, but generally behaved himself—there wasn't that much to laugh at.

There was no indoor plumbing at the Tezpur base, and the toilet facilities consisted of a six-hole Chic Sale which the British army built and sold to American for $10,000. Wild animals abounded in the area—in fact, Tezpur was where Bring-'em-Back-Alive Frank Buck did much of his hunting. Nobody ventured very far from camp.

The C-87s Ted Lewis had scrounged may have had new engines, but they were far from new airplanes. All ten, plus two more that followed later, were former B-24 bombers that had been damaged in accidents and converted into the cargo version. The crews had a love-hate relationship with them, as Evans explained:

"They could fly with more things wrong with them than any airplane I ever saw. But they had to, because they also had more things wrong with them than any airplane I ever saw. We had one that wouldn't climb higher than 12,000 feet. We finally found it had been built with a negative stagger in the tail section."

There were no scales for weighing cargo loads; weights were guessed at by the amount of depression in the landing gear struts. Evans came out to his plane one day and gaped. The struts were so flat they were practically on the ground. A rookie enlisted man had put railroad ties through the cabin and loaded the cargo on top of the ties.

How a C-87 was loaded was important. The nose wheel wasn't steerable, and the pilots steered by using the right or left brakes and jockeying the engines on each side. If the plane was tail-heavy, Superman couldn't have budged it.

It was bad enough having to fly airplanes that no sane pilot would have tolerated in an airline operation, but to cross the Hump in these battered, temperamental aircraft was the epitome of bravery. American's crews sympathized with the younger, inexperienced Army airmen who started showing up in greater numbers as American's ninety-day assignment progressed. The airline pilots often used their regular days off to fly with the rookie military crews, imparting the knowledge they had acquired flying the treacherous Hump.

Sometimes even that knowledge didn't help. American lost several pilots during Project 7-A, including the man who flew the first trip: Toby Hunt. He had made sixty-four crossings and completed the sixty-fifth successfully, but when he reached China the weather was too bad to land. Hunt turned around and was heading back to India, still carrying a heavy load of small-arms ammunition, when an engine quit and another lost power. It was impossible to maintain altitude, and Hunt ordered his crew to bail out through the cockpit escape hatch. All four did, but Hunt stayed with the plane, whether by choice or because he couldn't get through the hatch—he was a huge man—no one ever knew. Ted Lewis believed Toby tried to reach an airport, and at that, he almost crash-landed safely. He was heading for a rice paddy and struck a small hill at its edge. If he had cleared that hill, he might have walked away.

Two of his crew landed on a mountain and the other two on another mountain so close they could holler at each other across the ravine. But the terrain was so rugged it took them two days to join forces. They got back to Tezpur safely, in spite of a broken leg, two sprained ankles, and an assortment of bruises. The Chinese found the C-87's wreckage and carried Hunt's body out of the mountains in a hand-hewn coffin so heavy that when Ted Lewis and other pilots arrived to claim it, they needed ten men to lift it.

His comrades flew Toby Hunt's body back to India and buried him in the shadow of a small Buddhist temple, next to the five bodies of another American crew killed during Project 7-A. Their C-87, commanded by Captain Harry Charleton, lost power on a takeoff and crashed, killing all aboard. The copilot, in grim irony, was Bob Dietz, who was flying with Robby Robinson the day they saved the two merchant seamen.

It was part skill and part luck that these were the only two fatal crashes.

Flying the Hump was regarded as the most dangerous noncombat assignment of the war.

The delivery point was at Yunnanyi, China, apparently home port for every thief in the Orient. The crews were losing so much stuff out of airplanes that they started drawing lots to see who would stand guard at night on layovers. The first night takeoff out of China was made when a captain drew guard duty and announced, "The hell with it. I'm going back to Tezpur." There were no lights, but an Army officer drove a jeep to the end of the runway and on takeoff, they just headed for the lights.

On one Hump trip, a C-87 carrying boxes marked SIGNAL CORPS EQUIPMENT hit a thunderstorm and some boxes were jarred open. A crew member happened to look inside and discovered the box was full of lipstick, nylon hose, and other feminine items—consigned to Madame Chiang Kai-shek.

By the time the allotted ninety days were up, American had flown the Hump more than a thousand times, carrying some five million pounds of cargo, from bombs and aviation fuel to medical supplies and spare parts for tanks and trucks. Passengers were infrequent, but one was a Singer Sewing Machine Co. salesman who somehow had wangled authority to make regular trips into China.

When the Army took over the Hump job completely, an engineering officer inspected American's C-87s and condemned every one as unairworthy.

"We were supposed to deadhead home in style," Bill Evans related, "but when they condemned the airplanes we had to fly them back ourselves. We finally got 'em as far as Charleston, South Carolina, and called New York to find out what they wanted us to do with a dozen C-87s. They told us, 'We don't care what you do with the goddamned planes but just don't bring 'em to LaGuardia.' There wasn't any other place to go, though, so we flew to LaGuardia anyway and parked them on some grass. What finally happened to those C-87s I never found out."

Thus ended Project 7-A, but with a small sequel. The men who served those ninety days used what remained out of their mess fund to buy a memorial plaque honoring the comrades who didn't return. For several years it hung on a wall at LaGuardia operations, and later was moved to the Flight Training Center at the Dallas/Fort Worth Airport.

C.R. never did manage to visit his boys at Tezpur, but he did get to the CBI theater once, where some of his ex-pilots now flying for the Air Corps gave him a royal welcome. Chuck Foerster was one, and so was Cotton Johnson, who in the midst of a festive party took a machete and chopped off C.R.'s tie.

Many years later, Smith was on Johnson's plane flying from Dallas to New York and Cotton asked if he remembered him.

"I don't remember your name," C.R. said, "but I remember that goddamned machete!"

How much he missed the airline during the war no one really knew; C.R.'s sentimentality was carefully hidden. He tried to keep posted on what was happening, often through Carlene Roberts, but his policy toward American was strictly hands-off. Yet some of his friends suspected that figuratively speaking, his uniform didn't fit him.

Bill Dunn, his old public relations director, was on General MacArthur's staff and dropped in to see C.R. while home on leave. They went out to lunch, and Dunn noticed that Smith looked miserable when he had to return a salute —and there were plenty of them, because C.R. had just made brigadier general.

Bill made some reference to all the saluting, and C.R. frowned.

"This general business isn't for me," he said unhappily. "In business, if you're smarter than the other guy you'll get ahead. In the military, if you're smarter than some other general you'd better watch your step or you'll wind up in some place like Samoa."

Dunn was scheduled to return to the Pacific theater in a freighter and figured it would be better to fly. He called Smith.

"Any chance of getting me on an ATC plane, C.R.?"

"No!"

End of conversation. To C.R., the Air Transport Command, not American, was now his airline and he deliberately avoided doing favors for anyone even remotely connected with the company.

He did take notice, however, of the job Carlene Roberts was doing in the Washington office. Smith was no rock-hard chauvinist, although he did have his generation's attitudes concerning women in business. Someone once asked him why he thought so highly of Carlene and he grunted, "She thinks like a man."

Miss Roberts was a fine example of women who prove themselves when given a chance, and the war was giving plenty of them that chance. By 1944, half of American's station managers were female (the 1943 total was 20 percent). Holding down Newt Wilson's old job as supervisor of stewardesses was Hazel Brooks. She replaced Dudley Rice, who went into the Air Corps.

Stewardesses were enlisting, too. The military needed nurses, and the airlines' flight attendants were a gold mine for recruiters. C.R.'s last official act as president was to abolish the requirement that a stewardess had to be a registered nurse. He had to, for too many of his girls were donning lieutenant's uniforms.

A number of American's pilots held reserve commissions and were recalled to active duty. Among them was Henry "Hank" Myers, who, with two other pilots, went to Washington for assignment in May 1942. He was wandering around the Pentagon trying to find out what he was supposed to do when he was summoned to C.R.'s office.

"You're going to be an aide to General George," Smith informed him.

"The hell I am," Myers retorted. "I want to work."

"You'll get plenty of work," C.R. assured him, and took him in to meet George.

"I understand you're going to be my aide," the ATC chief said.

"Look, General, all you need is a fourth for bridge and I don't like to play bridge. So get some other boy for an aide."

Hal George chuckled. "You like to fly, don't you? You'd like to see the world, wouldn't you?"

"Sure, but—"

"So we have bases all over the world and I need someone to take me there. And C.R. tells me you're a hell of a pilot."

From then on it was Colonel Henry T. Myers. From 1942 until 1949, he flew not only George but two Presidents, many other generals, and quite a few congressmen, senators, and assorted statesmen to virtually every country on earth. He was to remark once, "There were some sixty of them and I think I got to all but three."

His biggest assignment was flying President Roosevelt to the Yalta summit conference with Stalin and Churchill. It was the only time FDR used the specially built C-54 that became the first Air Force One. The new Douglas plane, equipped with an elevator for the polio-crippled President, wasn't actually the first transport plane designed specifically for White House use. That honor went to a brand-new C-87 with an exceptionally luxurious interior including a sofa, complete electric galley, and Pullman-style berths.

It was an ATC aircraft and General George chose its command pilot: Hank Myers. Unlike most pilots, Hank honestly loved the C-87 and he adored this particular one. He christened it *Guess Where II*. But while it flew many missions under his command (Eleanor Roosevelt was an occasional passenger), it never carried a President.

Guess Where II was supposed to fly FDR to the Tehran summit conference, but while the trip was being planned the Secret Service became concerned that C-87s were having too many problems and insisted that ATC use one of its C-54s. The plane chosen was a TWA C-54 being flown by the airline under an ATC contract.

Myers was retained as command pilot at George's request. He was not only unhappy about the switch in aircraft but deeply resented the fact that the White House wanted a TWA captain to be his copilot—Otis Bryan, who happened to be a Roosevelt favorite.

There seems to have been no love lost between Myers and Bryan. Hank was still loyal to American (he had started with the airline in 1932, pasting weather reports on a blackboard because there were no immediate pilot openings) and to him, TWA ranked slightly below the Luftwaffe in his affections. On the Tehran flight, he treated Bryan more like a passenger than a copilot, and one crew member commented later, "Hank never let him touch the controls."

As America's military might expanded, so did American's involvement. The base at Natal became an operation as big as the one in the North Atlantic— bigger in the winter, when North Atlantic flights had to be reduced. The number of smaller stations blossomed into a global network. Employees who once thought it an adventure to travel 500 miles in the States found themselves working in far-off places they couldn't even spell.

There was a station at Marrakech, Morocco, where temperatures soared to 130 degrees and tools couldn't be left on the ground. Picking up a wrench in that heat could burn the skin off a man's hand; the mechanics learned to put their tools in a pail of water.

Sometimes they reported to stations so new that hangars hadn't been built yet, and sometimes never were. Maintenance work had to be done in the open regardless of weather. Tezpur was like that in the first few weeks. There were no lighting facilities, work stands, or rain shelters.

By 1944, American was the second largest international air carrier in the world, its ATC operations topped only by Pan American.

But the airline's involvement went far beyond ATC flights. Throughout the war, it trained Air Corps mechanics at schools set up in New York, Chicago, Fort Worth, and Burbank. In peacetime, American's mechanics had to go through a four-year apprentice program; the wartime schools turned out a new class every twelve weeks. One graduating class of more than fifty men had only one student who had ever worked on an airplane before.

One of American's tasks was the creation of an experimental shop known as "Department X" in Hangar 5 at LaGuardia. There, under maximum security conditions, engineers, draftsman, and mechanics worked with General Electric technicians on a secret project: modifying an XB-23 twin-engine bomber into a flying test bed for high-altitude flying. Marv Whitlock was American's chief aircraft engineer on the project and supervised the development of a pressurized cabin that eventually went into Boeing's B-29 bomber. Dan Beard did the test flights in the XB-23, dubbed the *Robert E. Lee,* and took the plane to as high as 36,000 feet. Department X's next mission was a bit more prosaic: it figured out a way to put pontoons on a DC-3.

American's engineers and mechanics also worked on a modification program involving hundreds of military aircraft the Army wanted converted or improved for cargo operations, mostly turning B-24s into C-87s but also modifying C-54s into hospital planes and the toughest job of all: ironing the bugs out of the fat-bellied Curtiss C-46 Commandos that American had almost bought as an airliner.

Thirty C-46s, tagged for domestic military cargo work, came into American's hands straight from the Curtiss factory. By the time Littlewood, Beard, Whitlock, and the others got through with them, they had undergone more than 180 engineering changes and Littlewood was recommending about 180 additional modifications that the Army rejected because there wasn't time. Bill Evans test-flew a C-46 a few times and was forever grateful to Littlewood for not buying the plane.

"They were nightmares," he said. "You'd start trimming the damned thing and nothing would happen. Then all of a sudden the hydraulics would kick in and you'd be standing on your nose or tail."

Evans was one of the many ATC pilots who kept being shifted from one theater to another. From the Hump he went to Natal and started flying the South Atlantic. He was on one trip with Ernie Gann, who was complaining that the smoke bombs they used for checking wind drift over water didn't work half the time.

"The government's charging American two hundred bucks for every bomb," Gann observed sourly. "I'll bet I could make one a hell of a lot cheaper and better."

A few weeks later, he proceeded to build a prototype. It looked so promising that he wrote the War Department he could produce a $20 smoke bomb and guaranteed it would work 90 percent of the time. Much to his surprise, the War Department sent him a contract and told him to go ahead. Gann was too busy flying, however, and never did anything about it.

Such technological improvisations were not rare in wartime. One has only to think of the Army sergeant who came up with the idea of attaching bull-dozer plows to the front of Sherman tanks, a device that flattened every pesky hedgerow obstacle in France. Yet on a far vaster scale, it is impossible to calculate the effects accelerated technology under the pressures of war had on the airline industry. Radar is just one example.

Four-engine transports like the C-54 and Lockheed Constellation were weaned on ATC operations, especially the former. The big Douglas transport that would become commercial aviation's DC-4 was the backbone of the Air Transport Command's long-range assignments, carrying thousands of young Americans who had never flown before but who were becoming, without realizing it, future airline passengers. In effect, they were learning to take air travel for granted, to accept it not as a risk-ridden gamble but as a normal and preferred means of getting from one place to another.

Military-trained pilots, youngsters who before the war were clerks and salesmen and college students, would form an immense pool of skilled man-power from which the airlines would draw their postwar flight crews. If war's legacies included death and tragedy, they also included lessons applicable to the coming peace, from aircraft maintenance to the beginnings of all-weather operations.

That, hopefully, was what the nearly 2,000 American Airlines employees on military leave and the some 1,000 on ATC duty were coming home to.

PART THREE
(1945–1955)

11
New Wings for the Eagle

Seventy-five did not come back—fifty-seven killed in combat and eighteen who died in ATC operations—and seven were still missing at war's end.

Those who did return found an airline far bigger than the one they had left. As of V-J Day, American was operating ninety-three DC-3s and personnel had nearly tripled since 1940, from slightly over 4,000 to 11,450.

The increase in fleet size stemmed from aircraft the military had turned back to the airlines as Douglas assembly lines spewed out some 10,000 C-47s specifically designed for military cargo work. American started getting planes back in the summer of 1944 and discovered they had to be almost completely rebuilt.

During the two years they had flown for ATC, there had been some 140 modifications to the DC-3s in the existing Flagship Fleet, and these had to be applied to the returned aircraft. Virtually every ship needed new flooring and in some cases new outer skin. Each had to be weighed carefully to determine the exact center of gravity, without which no airplane can be flown safely. Standard fleet weights were useless because wartime repairs to ATC aircraft frequently changed their balance.

It had taken only four days to convert a civilian Flagship into military configuration. To convert one back to a Flagship consumed twenty-one days, an expensive process that consumed much of the $2.75 million the airline had set aside from profits for reconversion costs. (American netted $16.5 million during the war but not one cent of this came from its ATC operations; all war contracts were performed at cost.)

Some of the returned DC-3s had won a measure of fame, such as a former Flagship that went back into service in 1944 as N-26658. In wartime, it had flown two daily trips between Presque Isle and Goose Bay carrying mail and supplies. It was so reliable that the lonely GIs at Goosebay dubbed the plane "Old Faithful."

Charlie Rheinstrom came up with the idea of turning several reconverted DC-3s into twenty-eight-passenger aircraft. Wartime inflation had sent operating costs soaring, and Rheinstrom became convinced that American couldn't make money with a twenty-one-passenger airplane. The DC-3s had been profitable during the war, with load factors (percentage of available seats occupied by revenue passengers) averaging an incredible 90 percent. But as costs increased, a 90 percent load factor came close to the break-even point. Rheinstrom felt the seven additional seats would provide most of the profit margin.

Rheinstrom got some static on the twenty-eight-seat configuration from those who said it was impossible to jam that many seats in a DC-3 without turning passengers into sardines. But he also got welcome support from Dixon Speas of engineering, who was ecstatic about the idea. Speas had proposed it in 1937, before he was hired by American.

He was an MIT student then and was writing a thesis on low-cost air transportation. Part of his research consisted of standing at the New Haven Railroad Station interviewing passengers on why they used trains instead of airplanes. The majority said flying cost too much.

Speas had interviewed about seventy people when a railroad detective tapped him on the shoulder.

"What do you think you're doing?"

"I'm conducting a passenger survey," Speas replied.

"Get out!"

Bill Bump, American's "Mr. New England," had heard about the survey and Dix's eviction. He called a vice president of the New Haven, who thought it was funny and told Bump, "Let the kid finish his interviews." Bump passed the news onto Speas, who said, "Thanks, but I've got enough data already."

He sent his finished thesis to United, which replied "not interested." But Bump saw it and was impressed enough to hire him. When Rheinstrom asked Littlewood's department if it was feasible to put twenty-eight seats in a DC-3, Speas thought of his old thesis and backed him up. If frugality as well as fear was a major detriment to air travel, as he had argued in 1937, then greater seating capacity would lower operating costs and possibly fares, too. (Actually, the Speas thesis had called for *thirty-two* seats in DC-3s, a configuration Littlewood refused to even try.)

American's last major domestic wartime mission was to take part in a massive four-carrier transcontinental airlift from the East to West Coast after Germany began to collapse. American, TWA, United, and Northwest were allocated eighty C-47s for the redeployment flights, which lasted seven months. American alone carried 60,000 troops, who loaded and unloaded their own baggage and ate box lunches.

The eagle's final transatlantic flight for ATC didn't take place until January 1946. It was number 9,442. Long before that, however, American had become a *civilian* international carrier, first with service to Mexico in the fall of 1942 and then in March 1944 with the purchase of controlling interest in American Export Airlines.

Melvin "Doc" Miller, who spoke Spanish fluently and liked the Mexican people, was in charge of the Mexico operation. He went down to Mexico City in May 1942, to start hiring native Mexicans for American Airlines de Mexico, the subsidiary C.R. had established. Miller had problems; there were not only no sales or ticket offices, but a total void in such vital items as airport office facilities, radio navigational aids, and emergency landing fields—all this with inauguration of service set for the following September.

The resourceful Doc managed to arrange for all but the last two essentials: the navigation aids and emergency fields. This problem he turned over to the politically savvy Red Mosier, who was faced with an ultimatum from the pilots. They refused to fly the route without range stations and some places to land if everything hit the fan.

Somehow, Mosier latched onto some secondhand range station equipment and installed five stations between the Texas border and Mexico City, plus four landing fields. He was warned that "As soon as you leave, they'll steal the works," but not one radio nav aid was ever touched. Red explained later how he accomplished this.

"I know the Mexicans," he elucidated. "The first thing I did was find a local head honcho and make him a present of the station in his bailiwick. He didn't know what the hell it was, but he sure wasn't gonna let anyone come within five miles of the damned thing."

Later, American set up a communications network within Mexico for the use of all airlines serving the country. It then donated the facilities to a Mexican-owned company and in return had its landing fees waived for several years. Considering all the trouble the airline had encountered before inaugurating service, it was a generous gesture.

American's certificate called for a route from Fort Worth to Monterrey and Mexico City and a second route from El Paso to those two Mexican cities. Monterrey, known as "the Pittsburgh of Mexico," lacked an airport, and American had to build one, plus the four emergency fields. Most of the airfield construction came under the supervision of Tull Rea, who drove his family from Fort Worth to Monterrey and spent the next five years in Mexico.

Heavy construction equipment, such as bulldozers, was hard to come by in wartime, but the airline scrounged what it could. Not only the emergency strips and sites for the range stations had to be carved out of the wilderness but roads leading to them as well, along with water wells and electric lines. At the Actopan strip, Indian superstition created one crisis. Rea's workers had built a fence along the runway without realizing it cut off a natural native trail to a nearby Indian village. The Indians cut the fence down, and it took a Mexican army detachment to convince them they must go around the fence. But this rerouting took them across a path established by another tribe, and it was considered bad luck for one tribe to cross another's path. The two tribes met at one corner of the runway and waged a bloody machete battle until troops broke it up.

Communications between American's New York headquarters and the airline's new Mexico City office were subject to wartime restrictions, including mail and phone call censorship, and it usually took hours to get a call through. One week before the first flights were scheduled to land, the Mexican government informed Miller it wanted numerous changes in the cargo tariffs. There wasn't time to correspond with New York by mail and Doc spent three hours trying to get J. D. Hungerford, assistant vice president of schedule development, on the phone. Then it took another six hours for them to work out the required changes.

Doc also had to solve a language impasse: there was no word for "stewardess" in Spanish and he finally had to coin one, coming up with "estuardess." The Mexicans loved this pot-bellied, hard-drinking American who always tried to understand and live with their customs. He was never afraid to sample a native dish, and this included a delicacy called "gusanos de maguey." Doc's assistant in Mexico City, Tom Brooks, who later became director of stewardess service, shared a hotel room with Miller, and Doc came home one night with a dish of gusanos de maguey, which he put on the nightstand next to Tom's bed.

"What are they, Doc?" Brooks asked.

"A famous Mexican pastry," Miller told him.

Brooks ate several and remarked how good they were. There were still a few left and the next morning, Brooks saw in broad daylight what he had eaten the night before in semidarkness.

"My God," he remarked, "they look just like worms."

"That's what they are," Doc confessed. "Fried worms from the maguey tree."

Brooks turned green and sprinted for the bathroom.

Service was inaugurated September 6, only a day later than scheduled. Duke Ledbetter flew one of the two inaugural trips and was forever after an enthusiast about Mexico; Mexican cooking became his hobby. One of the last trips he commanded as an American captain was a 707 jetliner that went nonstop from Chicago to Mexico City in a record three hours and ten minutes; the flight marked the twentieth anniversary of American's service to Mexico.

If the Mexico route involved a bit of improvised maneuvering, the acquisition of American Export Airlines went in the other direction—some very high-level wheeling and dealing.

AEA's history had been brief and rocky. It began life in 1939 as a tiny subsidiary of American Export Lines, one of the largest U.S. shipping companies, which wanted to start a transatlantic airline to supplement its ship service. It took another five years for the CAB to award the subsidiary a temporary certificate, and it was five years of bitter opposition from Pan Am. Juan Trippe wanted no competition, and his lobbying strength in Washington was awesome. Trippe at one point had even talked the Senate Appropriations Committee into rejecting a modest mail subsidy for AEA that was favored by everyone from the CAB to the White House.

Pan Am almost scuttled its tiny competitor when Trippe's lawyers challenged the right of a shipping company to operate an airline. They cited the Civil Aeronautics Act of 1938, which forbade one common carrier to acquire control of another common carrier in a different area of transportation. The CAB, in awarding AEA its original certificate, had zeroed in on the word *acquire;* the Board said American Export Lines was *starting* an airline, not acquiring one.

Pan Am took that interpretation to court and won. The shipping company was forced to divest itself of the airline subsidiary although it was allowed to retain a sizable percentage of stock. AEA was cast adrift on its own, struggling to stay alive against the most powerful international air carrier of them all. It began by operating three Vought-Sikorsky flying boats between New York and Ireland, carrying mostly mail and freight, and toward the end of the war it was flying C-54s to Lisbon under an ATC contract.

In 1944, when both Congress and the CAB were looking ahead to postwar international competition, Pan Am suffered its first major defeat. Trippe had fought long and hard for a "Chosen Instrument" policy—the selection of a single U.S. flag carrier for all international air service. Sensing that he couldn't win such a monopoly, he proposed a compromise: establish an "All-American Flag Line" in which all airlines would hold stock. The fine print in his plan, however, called for Pan Am to be the operating carrier, and this drew the entire industry's opposition with one exception: United. Pat Patterson had decided to stay away from the international field.

Congress rejected the All-American Flag Line bill twice, and the CAB in mid 1944 began hearings on applications for international route certificates. But Juan Trippe wasn't finished. He knew competition was inevitable, especially in the transatlantic market, which promised to be the most lucrative, so he suggested another compromise. There should be transatlantic competition, he conceded, but only between *two* U.S. airlines, because traffic wouldn't warrant more than two. And his choice for Pan Am's competitor was little American Export Airlines.

Throughout the Chosen Instrument and All-American Flag Line debates, both Patterson and Trippe had argued that not many people would want to fly overseas anyway. Patterson said twenty-three planes could handle all the transatlantic passenger traffic at least up to 1955; Trippe said Patterson was being over-optimistic—twelve planes could do the job.

How clouded were their crystal balls is almost laughable. By 1957, airplanes were carrying more people between the U.S. and Europe than ships. Even in 1944, their dour predictions were ridiculed. CAB member Josh Lee said, "It would be just as logical to have determined how many people crossed the American desert by stage coach, projected this figure, and announced that this is the number of passengers who may be expected to cross the United States by rail."

Another scoffer was Hal George, whose ATC carried nearly three million passengers during the war. He predicted that postwar international air travel would "stagger the imagination."

Yet it was hard for many people to visualize what was still very much in the future: the airplane's almost total dominance over international traffic. Trippe's contention that two airlines could handle all the transatlantic business in the foreseeable future worried a number of industry officials, who felt the

CAB might well buy this argument. And one of them was John Slater, executive vice president of American Export Airlines and the real boss of that carrier.

Slater thought there was a real chance of Trippe's proposal being adopted and he had no intention of feeding his small airline to the Pan Am wolf. Quietly, he initiated negotiations with another applicant for a permanent transatlantic certificate, one he respected and admired:

American Airlines.

The man he sought out was Ralph Damon, who had returned to American late in 1943 after straightening out Republic's production problems. The Thunderbolts were rolling out on schedule, and Damon accepted with alacrity Kemp's invitation to come back as executive vice president. He welcomed Slater's overtures, feeling it would be better to merge with another international applicant than go through the expense of establishing what amounted to a brand-new airline.

On July 5, 1945, the CAB simultaneously approved American's control of American Export Airlines and granted the merged carrier routes across the North Atlantic to the United Kingdom, Scandinavia, the Netherlands, and Germany.

The decision settled a somewhat embarrassing dispute between the two new partners. The CAB's so-called "North Atlantic Route Case" had put three transatlantic routes up for grabs: northern (the one American got), southern to Spain and Rome, and central to Paris and beyond.

American Export, without knowing whether its acquisition by American would be approved, had applied separately for only the southern route, over its future partner's objections; it already held a temporary certificate for the southern route and had flown it as an ATC contract carrier. American had carefully phrased its own application in such a way as to express preference for the northern route but also its willingness to take either of the others.

Kemp and Ham Hale, who was helping Red Mosier steer American's application through the regulatory shoals, always favored the northern route because of its London gateway. They tried to persuade Slater to file an application identical to American's but failed.

Hale reasoned that the conflicting applications put the CAB on the spot. It was being asked to approve a merger between two airlines seeking different transatlantic routes. The granting of the northern route solved the dilemma in American's favor, but Slater wasn't happy about it.

For that matter, neither was C.R. He wasn't in on these wartime negotiations, of course, but when he returned to American he told Hale he thought they should have sought the southern route as the most desirable, and according to Hale, he blamed Mosier for not getting it.

Smith was always sensitive, even touchy, on the subject of American Export. Publicly, he said nothing, but there was a memo, written in August 1959, to then vice president of public relations Willis Player, in which C.R. hinted, albeit obliquely, that he might have done things differently.

"Just to keep the history straight," it began, "American went into the overseas business while I was in the Army. . . . It is possible that I would have done the deal—who knows?—but the facts of the situation are that American made the decision while I was absent from the company."

The price tag for the "deal" was $3 million, with American obtaining 51.4 percent control via stock purchase. American Export's assets were relatively small, consisting mostly of six C-54s that the Army had turned over to AEA at the conclusion of its ATC contract. With those aircraft, converted quickly into DC-4 Flagships, American became a full-fledged international carrier operating AEA as a separate subsidiary under a new name: American Overseas Airlines.

AOA's inaugural flight took place October 23, 1945, originating in New York on a DC-4 christened *Flagship New England* in honor of the jump-off city, Boston. It was big news in the Hub; the Boston *Traveler,* in a page-one headline whose type wasn't much smaller than the one used on V-J Day, announced HUGE AMERICAN AIRLINER DUE TO FLY AT 5 O'CLOCK. The accompanying story by aviation editor Bob Sibley began, "The first commercial trip linking Boston with London is due to take off this afternoon from the Hanson Airport at Bedford."

The menu for the inaugural passengers was specially regional for the occasion: celery, olives, New England clam chowder, lobster thermidor, green salad, and Indian pudding with ice cream as dessert. Passengers on the Philadelphia–London inaugural a month later ate even better: fresh fruit cocktail with assorted iced relishes, breast of turkey and Virginia ham on rice, sweet potato, fresh Julienne string beans, homemade biscuits, tossed greens on tomatoes with French dressing, ice cream, and layer cake.

By this time, however, C.R. had returned, and neither fancy inaugural could match in scope what was going to happen.

Unlike so many executives who took off uniforms but insisted on being called by their former military rank (this was particularly prevalent after World War I and continued to a lesser degree after WW II), C. R. Smith became a civilian again in a hurry. It was still "C.R." or "Mr. C.R." More important, to most people he hadn't changed one bit.

There were a few who thought he seemed a little more arbitrary, even dictatorial, but this may have been due to the contrast with the easygoing Kemp and the personable Damon. In most ways, C.R. always had been arbitrary; for a strong leader, that went with the territory. And there was no doubt who was in charge the minute he sat down at his old desk.

He spent the first few days getting briefed on American's current problems and then began to act, starting with a decision that surprised some. He named, with board approval, Ralph Damon as American's president, becoming board chairman himself and also president of American Overseas.

With Ed Bern gone, C.R. picked an ex-newspaperman named Rex Smith as his successor, with vice presidential status. He had served with C.R. in ATC, and while they were not related, they might as well have been; Rex Smith became a trusted advisor, a close friend, and a man generally regarded as one of the best at his job in airline history.

During the war, C.R. had come in contact with a number of able men whom he envisioned as possible recruits for American. Throughout his career, he had a habit of scouting for executive talent, which he hired almost on impulse, with no specific job in mind. He was always looking for capable officers and figured he'd eventually find some niche for them.

One such man was Richard E. S. Deichler, a former hotel executive who had been a colonel in the Pentagon under Smith. C.R. hired him after the war and, as he was to do on more than one occasion, made him a vice president with no real assigned area of responsibility. In effect, he told Deichler to stick around until he found something important for him to do, although Deichler's title was vice president of administration.

Something did come up, sooner and in a manner Smith did not expect. He had talked Pete Willis into severing his relations with the advertising agency and joining American as vice president of advertising, a newly created title. Advertising was under Charlie Rheinstrom's jurisdiction, as part of the sales department.

Willis, his brilliance notwithstanding, was not that well-liked at American —C.R. was one of the few exceptions. Rheinstrom and Willis Lipscomb, one of his top assistants, disliked Pete intensely. Lipscomb once called him "a brilliant advertising mind but vicious and vindictive." When C.R. announced that Pete Willis was going to take over all advertising, Rheinstrom was not only hurt but furious.

He confronted C.R. face to face. "I've got to have advertising under sales," he told Smith, "and I can't have Pete Willis as vice president of advertising. This job won't happen, C.R."

"This is the way it's gonna be, Charlie."

Rheinstrom went for broke. "I'll resign if you take advertising away from me."

Smith thought he was kidding and laughed. "I'll tell you what I'll do, Charlie—I'll match you for it."

Rheinstrom ignored this. He said quietly, "I can't conduct the affairs of my sales department without advertising."

He returned to his office and wrote a brief letter of resignation. Charlie Speers, who had just come out of the Army as a lieutenant colonel and was his closest friend, was stunned when Rheinstrom confided what had happened, but there was no way he could have talked Rheinstrom into changing his mind. Rheinstrom was as strong-willed as Smith himself.

Rheinstrom had no trouble finding another job. His reputation was such that he could have gone with any airline, but he chose instead to join Dillon, Read, a big New York investment firm, as a consultant on airline affairs. It was C.R. who was now faced with a problem: one of the best marketing men in the industry had walked out, leaving Goliath-sized shoes to fill.

The obvious choice was Willis Lipscomb, assistant vice president of sales, but he was passed over possibly because he felt the same way about Willis that Rheinstrom did—and he also worshipped Charlie. Lipscomb's days at American were numbered, anyway; not too long after Rheinstrom left, Lipscomb was offered a vice presidency at Pan Am and went in to see Smith.

"I just wanted to tell you about the offer," he said. "I don't want to leave American."

C.R. said rather coldly, "Well, maybe that's what you should do."

It seemed evident from his refusal to dissuade Lipscomb that Rheinstrom's resignation still rankled Smith. Lipscomb had been with him since 1929, when he went to work for Southern Air Transport as a salesman; he had been selling coal in Virginia before he married a Texas girl, a relative of SAT's founder, A. P. Barrett, who offered him a job. But the longevity of his ties with American made no difference, and Lipscomb went over to Pan Am, where he rose to the rank of senior vice president.

Charlie Speers, a newly made regional vice president, had learned the airline business from Rheinstrom and could have replaced him, but C.R.'s choice was Dick Deichler—intelligent, capable, but an airline neophyte. He was easy to work for, well liked, and he tried hard, but he was no Charlie Rheinstrom. Lipscomb himself always believed that Rheinstrom's role at American was underplayed.

"The one thing that contributed most to American's sales leadership," Lipscomb said, "was Charlie Rheinstrom's personality, imagination, and inspiration."

Ironically, the man whose hiring caused the Rheinstrom furor, Pete Willis, lasted less than a year in his job. C.R. fired him for reasons never made public. Speers, one of the few who tolerated him (which was typical because Charlie liked about everybody and the feeling was mutual), said Willis went downhill after leaving American and died in near-poverty. "A fascinating guy but a tragic case," was Speers' gentle epitaph.

Deichler's ascent in American's hierarchy was accompanied by several other changes on the executive level. Ned Kemp returned to relative obscurity in California, although he continued on American's board until his death in 1954 —the same year pioneer directors Amon Carter and Silliman Evans passed away. C. W. Jacob, already the corporate secretary, added vice president to his title, and a new addition was Terry Drinkwater, fresh from his unsuccessful attempt to unseat Bob Six at Continental. He actually joined American late in 1944 but when C.R. returned, he gave Drinkwater increased authority and respected his counsel.

Terrell Croft Drinkwater was a crew-cut lawyer who preferred the airline business to the legal profession. At American, he was a jack-of-all-trades and also served as an AOA vice president.

To run American Overseas, C.R. picked a fellow ATC general, Harold Harris, who had been his chief of staff at the Pentagon. Harris did not earn his own wings flying a desk; he began his career with the Army Air Service in 1917 and at one time held ten world records in speed, altitude, distance, and duration. He also happened to be a well-qualified airline executive. He had broken into commercial aviation as a crop duster for Huff Deland, Delta's predecessor company, and then helped establish the first U.S. airline in South America, a carrier that eventually become Panagra. Smith named him AOA's vice president and general manager.

The new vice president of operations at American was Larry Fritz, the former TWA flight supervisor who also had served under C.R. during the war as an operations commander. Fritz was a pilot of the old school, a cigar-chomping martinet. Gene Taylor became his assistant, and had difficulties with him at first. "We had a learning curve for several months," he recounted. "Larry had been away from the airlines so long that he had gotten used to military ways."

C.R. spent more time in Washington immediately after the war than in New York—in fact, American's headquarters were divided between New York and the capital for a couple of years. Smith wanted to stay on top of regulatory developments, and there were plenty of them as the CAB was flooded with postwar route applications. American had a few of its own in the hopper, but the one application C.R. wanted badly to get through was American's bid to acquire Mid-Continent Airlines. This was a carrier 60 percent of whose routes involved cities American didn't serve, and these included Minneapolis/St. Paul, Des Moines, Omaha, Kansas City, and New Orleans.

The merger application was filed with the CAB late in 1945 but failed to win approval, and in 1952, Mid-Continent was absorbed by Braniff. Nor would this be the only merger defeat American was to suffer.

C.R.'s infatuation with Washington soured eventually, and the command post was shifted back to New York, where he moved headquarters to downtown Manhattan. LaGuardia, he felt, had become inappropriate for the main corporate offices of the nation's largest airline. The man most pleased with this move was that transplanted Westerner Red Mosier, who loved New York City and Manhattan in particular with a passion.

Red might as well have been a native New Yorker. He knew every head waiter and maitre d' at every posh restaurant in town. The Stork Club was his favorite. He was so well known there that no one ever bothered to give him a check for his trademark, a white Stetson cowboy hat.

Celebrities gravitated toward him like steel slivers attracted to a magnet. Eleanor Roosevelt called him "my adorable Red." Jack Dempsey was a close friend, and so was New York's official "greeter," Grover Whalen. He made Walter Winchell's column more frequently than most movie stars, and his friendship with Fiorello LaGuardia was deep and sincere; the mayor trusted him implicitly.

It was Red Mosier who helped LaGuardia pick out the location for New York's second major airport. Together they selected a 6,000-acre site in the remote, virtually uninhabited Idlewild section of Queens, largely a salt marsh occupied only by a few hundred families living in shacks built on piles. It would one day become John F. Kennedy International Airport.

His friendship with the Little Flower was one of American's major assets.

When LaGuardia first opened, the airport manager was Elmer Hazlitt, who for some reason harbored a grudge against the very airlines using the new facility. The original runways were macadam, and after a few months' use the airlines complained that the deteriorating surface was throwing stones against propellers and fuselages.

Hazlitt refused to do anything about the situation, but Mosier showed up one day with LaGuardia in tow. With Bill Littlewood accompanying them, they went out to inspect the runways, Hazlitt insisting loudly that any damage was minor.

"Shut up!" the mayor snapped. "I'll decide what's minor."

He took one look at a single runway and turned to his airport manager. "Fix this, Hazlitt," he barked, "and I don't want to hear another word about it!"

When C.R. moved corporate offices to 100 East 42nd Street, Red's office on the seventeenth floor was as large as Smith's (more than 400 square feet) and just as impressive. It had wall-to-wall carpeting in solid blue, walnut paneling, pastel draperies, plush armchairs with a leather sofa, and a massive desk. Oil paintings of Western scenes adorned the walls, and adjacent to his desk was a matching table six feet long. That was where his assistant at the time, Bob Tuttle, worked.

Tuttle (C.R. always called him "Tootles") had started with American as a reservations agent in 1940 and was in the properties department when Mosier offered to double his salary to become Red's assistant. Tuttle held that job for three and a half years and got to know Mosier better than most, being constantly exposed to his violent temper tantrums and equally intense gestures of kindness.

"Red Mosier," Tuttle said, "had only two people in his whole life for whom he had 100 percent respect. One was C.R. and the other was his wife Frances —and there were no exceptions."

Mosier's sense of humor was bawdy, but he was such an excellent raconteur that no one took offense at his raunchiest jokes. It was a quality Ralph Damon envied, and he was not exactly a Mosier fan. For one thing, Red was known for submitting expense accounts that could have sold as great fiction.

That sense of humor led to the creation of a unique airline organization known as the Bone Club sometime in 1946. (It may have been called the Bonehead Club—American's historical files are totally void of any references to the club and some veterans remember it by both names.) But Mosier definitely founded the group, getting his inspiration from a boner pulled by a sales promotion manager named Charles Stevens.

Stevens had arranged for the printing of a number of 1946 calendars in both English and Spanish, with a little New Year's greeting from C.R. attached to the top of each calendar. Unfortunately, the translation to Spanish was done in New York instead of Mexico and nobody caught the error in the hundreds of calendars shipped to American's friends and clients south of the border. As near as anyone could figure out, C.R.'s attached greeting in Spanish closely approximated "Happy Asshole."

Mosier decided a boner of such proportions deserved special recognition, and he conceived an award to be presented annually at a dinner to the officer who had pulled the biggest goof of the year. Stevens was the unlucky first recipient. In subsequent years, previous winners served as the nominating committee.

Red designed the "trophy" himself. It consisted of a large cow or steer bone mounted on a wooden base, with the winner's name engraved on a metal plate. Mosier got the original bone out of the New Yorker Hotel kitchen, where he lived before moving to the Belmont Plaza. The mounted bones were at least eighteen inches long, and to the winners the trophy must have looked like something off a brontosaurus skeleton.

Terry Drinkwater won a Bone Award in 1947 for his decision to leave American to become president of an ailing Western Airlines (he got the job thanks to Charlie Rheinstrom's recommendation). Another winner was Walter Johnson, who for months had ignored Deichler's demand that Walt move his office from the Chanin Building to the general offices. He came to work one morning and discovered that his desk had been moved during the night to where Deichler wanted it.

Dixon Speas was nominated one year for an incident in a crowded men's room. He was standing in front of a urinal when Ralph Damon came in. Gallantly, Speas stepped aside to let the company president go first. But Speas considered himself lucky to have been an also-ran, for the awards ceremony, held around Christmas time, could be embarrassing. When Kirk Rulison, the corporate treasurer and a very proper, dignified man, won the trophy for some unrecorded boner, the award presenter was a former dog show judge. He made Rulison get down on his hands and knees and be judged like a canine.

Each Bone winner was responsible for the following year's dinner, which was much like Washington's famed Gridiron Club dinner—there were original songs and skits, with costumes and lyrics set to current popular tunes. The specific nefarious deeds were never recorded officially, and retired officers from that era don't remember all the winners' names and what they got their award for. It isn't even known exactly how many years the Bone Award lasted. Johnson thought it was around ten years, while others said it wasn't more than five. At any rate, C.R. himself reportedly ordered its demise. According to Jack Mullins, "It had gotten a little too serious and embarrassing as the boners got bigger and bigger."

It was too bad, however, that the club was not in existence when an unnamed official would have been a unanimous choice for the Bone Award. Exactly when he performed his monumental mistake is not certain, but it deserves mention in American's annals. He ordered, at an extremely favorable price, some 50,000 ice cream containers which he figured would make excellent air-sickness bags. When they were delivered, it was quickly decided to throw away all 50,000.

On each container were printed the words:
"Thank You—Come Again."

* * *

With Damon running the airline on a day-to-day basis, C.R. concentrated on the biggest postwar task American faced: modernization of the Flagship Fleet.

The first priority was to decide on a replacement for the now-outmoded DC-3. Almost as important was the selection of a long-range aircraft for the transcontinental market. American was getting fifty DC-4s, but both C.R. and Littlewood regarded this unpressurized aircraft as not much more than an oversized DC-3, merely an interim piece of equipment.

During the war, Littlewood and his engineers had drawn up specifications for a DC-3 replacement and, as the conflict ended, submitted them to seven airframe manufacturers: North American, Curtiss-Wright, Douglas, Lockheed, Martin, Boeing, and Consolidated-Vultee, the latter an Avco subsidiary. North American showed no interest, but the other six came up with varying proposals.

Douglas presented the most radical design, a commercial version of its Mixmaster bomber, an unconventional aircraft with two Allison engines hooked to a huge pusher propeller in the tail. Its main virtue was speed; one of the two bomber prototypes had flown coast-to-coast in less than six hours. Littlewood rejected the design on sight. Propellers were known to fail, and he had a horrified vision of a Mixmaster transport losing its only prop.

Lockheed, Curtiss-Wright, and Boeing submitted high-wing designs. The Lockheed entry was called the Saturn and tentatively priced at an attractive $85,000, but its sixteen-passenger capacity killed any chance of the plane ever becoming a Flagship. Boeing's proposed transport was bigger, but Littlewood didn't like high-wing airplanes. This also eliminated Curtiss-Wright. (Boeing sold its design to Fokker, which developed it into the successful F-27 prop-jet of the 1950s.)

The "paper airplanes" that interested Littlewood the most were the more conventional CV-110 and Martin 202. They were almost twins in every respect —size, performance, and appearance—with one important difference: the CV-110 would be pressurized. The selection process boiled down to these two airplanes, and the stakes, as we shall see, were extremely high.

Littlewood conducted a unique survey among employees. He distributed the general details of all five aircraft and asked them to rate the designs. He couldn't believe the results of some 1,250 responses: the first choice was the Mixmaster, which Douglas called the DC-8 (the same designation it would give its first jetliner). But the 110 ran a close second, and Martin was third.

Engineering's analysis of the five designs were ready for C.R.'s inspection when he returned and he quickly agreed with Littlewood's recommendation: the CV-110 appeared to fit American's needs best. Negotiations with Consolidated-Vultee began immediately, and they were not easy. The company was having financial problems and would soon be sold to the Convair division of General Dynamics. Furthermore, the 110 design was strictly preliminary, and the changes Littlewood demanded amounted to almost an entirely new airplane. One of his own ideas would be incorporated into the transport when it was actually built: folding boarding and deplaning stairs that were an integral part of the forward fuselage, the first ever put into an airliner.

Even the name was changed. The CV-110 became the CV-240 and this, too, was at Littlewood's suggestion. He said the "40" represented the number of seats American wanted—and those forty seats, incidentally, represented almost a 100 percent increase over the DC-3's passenger capacity. The "CV" also fit the name of the company that would eventually manufacture the plane, Convair.

On December 26, 1946, American announced it had signed an $18 million contract for 100 CV-240s, up to then the largest single aircraft order in the history of commercial aviation. But months before that official announcement, C.R. already had committed the airline to a far greater fleet expansion: 50 DC-6s and 20 Republic Rainbows, the latter to be flown by AOA in transatlantic service. The Convairs, DC-6s, and Rainbows, plus the 50 DC-4s, added up to some $90 million worth of airplanes—220 aircraft that multiplied the seating capacity of the DC-3 fleet five times. American, indeed, was betting on the postwar future.

The DC-6 was a joint venture with archrival United, which also ordered a DC-6 fleet simultaneously. Of all his counterparts in the industry, Littlewood was closest to United's Bill Mentzer. They were not only friends but often collaborators in various engineering projects, and it is significant to note that C.R.'s intense rivalry with United never prompted him to interfere with that friendship. Both Littlewood and Mentzer provided huge inputs into the DC-6 development program.

The new four-engine Douglas airliner was American's and United's joint and urgently needed answer to a plane that throughout 1946 was clobbering their DC-4s in the transcontinental market, TWA's Constellation, queen of Jack Frye's postwar fleet. The DC-6 would be faster and, thanks to an experiment that failed, would have something hitherto unknown in the Flagship Fleet: air conditioning.

This development was brought about shortly before Rheinstrom resigned. He had heard or read somewhere that painting the top of an aircraft fuselage white could cool the interior by as much as fifteen degrees, and that United and Pennsylvania Central Airlines actually had a few planes painted that way. He asked Littlewood to check into it, and Bill turned the matter over to Dixon Speas.

Speas ran some tests on metal parts placed under a hot sun and discovered that the white paint actually did provide a cooling effect. Littlewood was so intrigued that he informed C.R. about the experiment; unfortunately, he also mentioned that United was trying it out on a real airplane. This was a mistake. Smith allowed that he wasn't interested in any crazy idea that United had pioneered.

"That's it for the white paint," Littlewood told Speas. "If United did it first, we can't try it."

Speas agreed, but a few days later he came across a book on ocean liners which disclosed that the heat-reducing qualities of white dated back to 1857, when ship builders began painting superstructures that color. He showed the book to Littlewood, who rushed into C.R.'s office to assure him United hadn't invented the idea.

This cleared the way for Rheinstrom's proposal: paint one DC-3 white and show it to C.R. Charlie urged Speas to make a really strong pitch. "Now, when he comes out to look at it, you spend about fifteen minutes explaining the technical details—how it really cools off the cabin and why. Then we'll take him into the hangar and show him the airplane."

"He'll never sit still for a fifteen-minute technical discussion," Speas said dubiously. "Maybe two or three minutes?"

Rheinstrom agreed, and soon came the day for the great unveiling. Smith listened to Dixon's technical data for about twenty seconds and grunted, "Lemme see the damned airplane."

The DC-3 was in Hangar 3, which had been cleared totally except for the repainted plane, gleaming under the overhead lights. "God," Speas recalled, "we all thought it looked beautiful."

The hangar doors opened dramatically. C.R. stepped inside. He looked at the DC-3 for not more than a minute, then turned to the anxious Rheinstrom and Speas, his heavy face glowering.

"If you want to cool it," he snapped, "do it some other way."

End of experiment.

"And that," Speas recounted, "is why American bought the DC-6 with air conditioning."

The DC-6, at about $650,000 per aircraft, was the most expensive transport American had ever ordered. But C.R. got a bargain in the 240. He signed at a unit price of only $195,000 and then picked up hundreds of war surplus Pratt & Whitney R-2800 engines for $5,000 each. They were in excellent condition, and the price was $32,600 less than what PW was charging for a brand-new R-2800.

Pratt & Whitney's unhappiness, however, was diluted considerably when at Littlewood's urging American ordered new R-2800s for the DC-6s, one of the most astute decisions an airline ever made. Putting the same engine on both the 240 and DC-6 meant enormous savings in maintenance costs.

The Republic Rainbow turned out to be an "almost" airliner—a promising design that never materialized into an operational airplane. On paper, it looked like a winner, and aesthetically, it may have been the most beautiful transport aircraft ever built. Officially designated the Republic XR-12, the Rainbow was a sleek, needle-nosed speedster whose specifications called for a 400-m.p.h. cruising speed, nonstop transatlantic range, a then unheard-of altitude capability of 40,000 feet, and a passenger capacity of forty-six.

Ralph Damon had envisioned the Rainbow as the ultimate Flagship when he headed Republic. He had become close friends with the XR-12's chief designer, Russian-born Alexander Kartveli, who created the superb Thunderbolt fighter, and when American took over American Export, Damon was convinced that the Rainbow was the plane AOA needed.

He wasn't the only one enamored. Juan Trippe ordered twenty-five Rainbows for Pan Am, and the Air Force signed for twenty more, to be used primarily as a photo-reconnaissance plane. It must be said that Littlewood and his engineers weren't that optimistic about the Rainbow. Its perfect streamlining resulted in a relatively narrow, cramped cabin; Marv Whitlock recalled that "the lavatories were particularly small." Littlewood thought the plane was too small to be economically sound. And its chief technical fault was the engine chosen as its power plant: the twenty-eight-cylinder Pratt & Whitney R-4360, which had powered the B-29 bomber and hung up an unenviable reliability record.

The Rainbow's main Achilles heel, however, had nothing to do with its performance. Republic badly underestimated development and production costs and stood to lose a fortune on the sixty-five aircraft on order. Troubles with the R-4360 engines were cropping up in the test flights on the two prototypes built, and there was some speculation that Republic might be considering scrapping the entire project.

These rumors started about the same time C.R. was having doubts about the wisdom of that $23 million Rainbow commitment. He met with Littlewood's engineering department and announced he was ready to cancel, even though it would cost a $150,000 penalty to pull out.

No one objected, but Marv Whitlock had some advice: "Don't cancel yet, C.R.," he urged. "Wait another month and they'll come to you and pay *us* to cancel. I guarantee it."

"I don't think we can wait that long," Smith said. "We've got a progress payment due within a month. Have you heard something?"

"Just a feeling in my bones. Nothing specific to go on, but I do have a very strong hunch."

C.R. was a strong hunch player himself, but in this case he decided it would be cheaper to get out immediately. He notified Republic American was canceling, and at the meeting where the papers were signed, he handed over a $150,000 check. A Republic official grinned.

"C.R., I had a check for $325,000 all written out to American, for letting *us* cancel."

"That goddamned Whitlock," Smith muttered.

The Rainbow never flew for Pan Am or the Air Force, either, and both prototypes were destroyed. One crashed on a test flight when an engine exploded at 20,000 feet; six of the seven-man military test crew bailed out but the seventh died when the burning plane crashed into the ocean off Fort Walton Beach, Florida. The only other Rainbow built ended its career as a ground target for artillery.

Except for C.R.'s generosity, the Convair 240 might have gone the same route as the Rainbow. As had Republic, the 240's manufacturer underestimated development and production costs to such an extent that Mack Laddon and Jack Nash of Convair came to Smith in a state of panic shortly after production got under way.

"We can't build that plane for $195,000," they told him. "We'd like to stop production and give you back the advance payments. We'd lose less money that way."

Smith made one of those snap decisions for which he was famous. "We need the 240," he said, "so I'll make you a counteroffer. We'll cut our order from one hundred to seventy-five, and you can sell those twenty-five we're giving up at a profit."

The offer was accepted, and although the 240 itself was never a financial success for Convair, the overall program was profitable—including subsequent versions as well as the original 240 (the 340, 440, and prop-jet 580); more than 1,000 were sold. The 240 was victimized by a disease the airframe industry refers to as "versionitis": the inability of airline customers to agree on a standardized model. In the 240's case, the chief culprit was the built-in forward stairway that American had designed; some carriers wanted a rear staircase and others insisted on no staircase at all, a divergence of preferences that simply increased production costs.

Before American ordered the DC-6, Consolidated tried to sell the airline a four-engine transport called Model 39. Actually, it was an extensively redesigned B-24/C-87, with a wide-visibility cockpit encased in a hemispherical nose closely resembling that of the B-29 bomber and upcoming Boeing Stratocruiser. It was supposed to carry forty-eight passengers with a 2,500-mile range, but Bill Littlewood, as always, wanted no part of any high-wing airplane.

Only one Model 39, dubbed the Liberator Express, was built and American operated the plane briefly as a freighter before turning it back to Consolidated for eventual scrapping; even as a cargo plane it was far too slow. But its temporary employment in freight service underlined the airline's growing interest in all-cargo operations.

American had pioneered the concept during the war. In 1943, it jammed priority mail and express into a standard DC-3 and flew it across the country in what was touted as the first all-cargo service. A year later, it inaugurated the first scheduled domestic airfreight service between New York and Los Angeles. And after the war, C.R. decided to go into the airfreight business all-out.

The initial move was to select a site for cargo headquarters, and Dixon Speas was assigned this task as the newly appointed director of cargo maintenance and engineering. Originally he was supposed to also head cargo flight operations, but Damon yanked the rope on this one: "He's only twenty-nine years old and you can't have him running both," he told Smith.

Speas investigated possible sites and finally picked Oklahoma City as headquarters for the new "contract air cargo division." Then, at C.R.'s request, he phoned Bill Hooten, a veteran supervisory pilot who was an Air Force colonel on leave from American and stationed in Hawaii, where he was awaiting discharge.

"Bill, C.R. wants you to be director of flight operations for the new cargo division," Speas said. "Would you accept it?"

"Sure. Where are you gonna put it?"

"Oklahoma City."

"Have you looked at St. Joseph, Missouri?"

"No, I haven't," Speas confessed.

"Well, you should."

Speas marched into Smith's office at LaGuardia. "Mr. C.R., Bill Hooten says he'll take that job but he wants us to look at St. Joseph as the base."

"You tell Hooten to go to hell," Smith said. He got up to get a glass of water, came back to his desk, and grinned. "Dix, Hooten used to be commanding officer at Rosecrans Field in St. Joe—he's probably got an ulterior motive. Furthermore, you've already made a tentative agreement with Oklahoma City, haven't you?"

"Yes, sir."

"So you have to live up to that agreement. If you want to go out to St. Joe and look around, go ahead, but we have to honor that agreement."

"It's verbal," Speas reminded. "There's nothing on paper."

"Makes no difference. It's still an agreement."

(Speas commented many years later: "It was typical of C.R. that he insisted on living up to every commitment even it was only verbal. He was a straight arrow all his life.")

So Dixon inspected the St. Joseph situation and tried C.R. once more. He reported, "They're really anxious to have us out there and actually St. Joseph's closer to the middle of the country than Oklahoma City." (The location was geared to the best refueling point for the DC-4 cargo planes flying transcontinental.)

Smith said sternly, "You still can't locate there unless Oklahoma City turns you down."

Speas flew to Oklahoma City, accompanied by Jim Wooten, who had been designated as head of the cargo division—it was Wooten's enthusiasm for freight potential that had convinced C.R. to expand its operations. They were scheduled to have breakfast with the city manager and the president of the Chamber of Commerce and had all the papers ready to sign.

The first cups of coffee hadn't been consumed when the city manager launched a tirade against American. "You're a bunch of gouging chiselers," he announced. "This deal is completely unacceptable!"

The Chamber of Commerce man was stunned, but Speas and Wooten could hardly hide their glee—Wooten preferred St. Joseph, too. They informed Smith what had happened and he dispatched them to St. Joseph, where the local newspaper devoted its entire front page to American's choice for its main cargo base. They were still there arranging final details when Speas got a phone call from the president of the Oklahoma Chamber of Commerce.

"Mr. Speas, I'm sitting here with the publisher of the Oklahoma City newspaper and I'd appreciate your telling me the whole story."

Speas did—including something he had found out from Red Mosier after the unpleasant breakfast session. The city manager detested Mosier, who had preceded him in that job.

A few days later, Speas received in the mail the front page from the Oklahoma City paper. The headline read: CITY MANAGER INSULTS AMERICAN. The next day's headline said: CITY MANAGER FIRED.

Six DC-4s modified into all-cargo planes were assigned to the St. Joseph operation. Three were stationed on the West Coast and the others on the East Coast; the aircraft flew nightly to St. Joseph, where loads were transferred among the six planes according to their destinations—Los Angeles, Atlanta, Chicago, Washington, New York, St. Louis, etc. In effect, St. Joseph was a hub, instituted years before the hub concept became a way of life throughout the entire industry.

"If we had possessed the vision," Speas believed, "we would have stayed in St. Joseph and we would have wound up with a Federal Express kind of operation. We were literally doing, at St. Joe, what Fred Smith of Federal Express finally started in Memphis."

The contract cargo division was launched early in 1946, but lasted only about a year. The airline was having financial problems. It lost $252,000 in 1946; the amount may have been modest, but it was the first red ink in almost a decade, which worried C.R. Introduction of the DC-6 and CV-240 was coming up, and cargo, while growing fast, wasn't that profitable. He ordered the contract cargo division disbanded and shifted freight shipments to the passenger airplanes—the same decision American would make nearly forty years later when it sold all its 747 freighters.

Engineering tried hard to save the cargo division. It came up with the ingenious idea of turning the six DC-4 freighters into convertible aircraft, cargo planes by night and passenger planes by day. The passenger seats would be folded against the cabin wall and cargo nets lowered to protect them when freight was boarded. Wooten and Speas begged C.R. to let him modify the cargo fleet, and Smith finally relented partially. "Do one," he said, "and I'll look at it."

The modification work was done in Van Nuys by an aircraft conversion company. Speas phoned C.R.: "It's ready," he said. "Can you come out here and look at it?"

Smith flew to California and inspected the modified plane, walking back and forth through the cabin without uttering anything except a few noncommittal grunts. He emerged and went to his waiting limo, Speas trailing in his wake.

"C.R., we're going to have a meeting," Dixon said as Smith climbed into the car.

"What meeting?"

"Well, we've got all the engineers here to listen to any suggestions you might have—any changes and so forth."

"There won't be any meeting, Dix."

"Why not?"

"Because it won't work." He closed the door and was driven away. All six DC-4 freighters were converted into passenger planes.

But Speas was one of many at American who thought that the airline's pioneering efforts in airfreight were abandoned prematurely. He believed all-cargo operations never reached its full potential because the airlines devoted the overwhelming majority of their time, efforts, and funds on passenger service. He added: "I don't think cargo failed. The industry never gave it the attention to reach the kind of potential that Fred Smith of Federal realized."

A longer-lasting postwar venture was the opening of a huge training center at Ardmore, Oklahoma, on the site of a former Army bomber base.

It was mostly Ralph Damon's baby. When he was vice president of operations, he had wanted to centralize pilot training instead of spreading flight instruction among the major bases. The need for centralization and standardized training procedures became more acute with the advent of sophisticated planes like the DC-6 and 240, and Damon had little trouble persuading C.R. to acquire the Ardmore facility.

Ardmore, chosen after two years of site-searching, was primarily for pilots when it opened in June 1946. Captain Donald K. Smith was chief instructor during most of the school's twenty-nine months of existence. At its peak, he had fourteen instructors under him, checking out newly hired first officers, flight engineers for the DC-6, and captains transitioning to new equipment.

Prior to Ardmore, the training process varied from base to base, and rules and procedures depended on which chief or check pilot was doing the teaching. As D.K. put it:

"The guys out of Los Angeles would fly one way, the ones out of Chicago another way, and the crews based in Fort Worth would have their own ideas. My job was to make sure all fourteen instructors were going down the same highway in the same direction."

The trainees, rookies, and upgrading veterans alike were exposed to an ordeal few had ever faced before: ground school.

"What had passed as ground school before," D.K. recalled, "consisted of showing us the airplane, teaching us how to put on a uniform jacket one arm at a time, and how to fold airway maps. At Ardmore, we began teaching 'em everything about the airplane they were going to fly before they ever got into one—systems, engines, cockpit familiarization, the works. Our first ground school class lasted five days and the guys were complaining, 'My God, what'll they throw at us next?' "

The training center was located sixteen miles north of Ardmore, nestled in a broad, shallow valley. American occupied what had been the Army's hospital unit—an administration building with nine dormitories, a cafeteria that Sky Chefs operated, and a medical unit. There also were two big hangars, a fire station, and two warehouses. The four runways used for flight training were each 7,200 feet long.

Ardmore gradually was expanded into a general training center for mechanics, reservations and cargo agents, and stewardesses. When the first stewardess class was assigned to train there, D.K. was asked if the girls would present any problems.

"No," he allowed, "but if they wear short skirts into the dining room and I lose pilots from sticking their forks into their eyes, *then* we're gonna have troubles."

In just under two and a half years, some 4,000 pilots, stewardesses, mechanics, agents, and contract students passed through Ardmore's classrooms. At the height of its operations, the center was staffed by nearly 190 instructors, averaging 135 students a month. The latter category included pilots from Sweden, Argentina, Venezuela, Brazil, Peru, the Netherlands, China, and several domestic airlines. All told, Ardmore trained 470 DC-6 copilots and flight engineers, 296 DC-6 captains, 688 Convair pilots, 399 DC-4 pilots, and 560 stewardesses.

The decision to close it was purely economic; hastily constructed wartime military bases were expensive to maintain. And the need for such a large facility diminished sharply as the airline filled its personnel requirements during these expansion years. By the beginning of 1947, American's payroll numbered more than 14,000 employees.

Coincidental with the gradual phasing out of Ardmore was the growing emergence of Tulsa as a major maintenance base. During the war, Douglas had operated a modification plant at Tulsa for B-25 bombers, and American picked up the facility for a song. The Douglas hangars and shops were in excellent condition and the city's location—just about in the heart of American's route system—made Tulsa ideal for aircraft overhauls. The base opened in 1946 almost simultaneously with Ardmore, and what began as a fairly modest operation steadily evolved into what today is one of the world's finest airline maintenance centers.

When Ardmore shut down, all training except for stewardesses reverted back to the individual bases. With few exceptions, flight attendants were the only new employees being hired. The stewardess school was transfered to Tulsa. Millie Alford was chief instructor there and managed to obtain for her trainees the first training mock-up, a simulated DC-6 cabin open on one side so instructors could watch the students serve make-believe meals and perform other in-flight chores. Only the seats were real, the mock-up being constructed largely of wood.

Millie had to pull some strings before she got her hands on this valuable training tool. It had been built in Los Angeles, where Bill Hipple of public relations had been renting it out to movie studios who needed an ersatz aircraft cabin for interior shots on a sound stage. There wasn't much demand for the mock-up, and Millie went all the way to C.R. for permission to have it dismantled and trucked to the stewardess school. (The cabin mock-ups for the jets would cost as much as a full-sized DC-6.)

The DC-6 beat the Convair 240 into service by fifteen months—Convair was having production line problems—even though American had ordered the two planes about the same time. American inaugurated DC-6 schedules between New York and Chicago April 27, 1947, and as more of the big Douglas airliners joined the Flagship Fleet, they were assigned to transcontinental service, knocking almost an hour off TWA's eleven-hour coast-to-coast schedules with their Constellations.

American configured the DC-6 to carry fifty-two passengers. This represented a Bill Littlewood concession—he didn't want that many people on any airplane. The airline recently had suffered a DC-3 crash near London, Ontario, on a flight from Buffalo to Detroit, in which there had been no survivors. Littlewood suffered the tortures of the damned in any accident, and this one hit him particularly hard because there never was any explanation for it.

Eyewitnesses had seen the plane go through some peculiar maneuvers. It kept circling, and the minute it tried to come out of the turn, the nose would go up. This continued until the pilot simply ran out of altitude and stalled; the impact compressed the sixty-five-foot fuselage into fifteen feet of crushed aluminum. Some kind of control malfunction was suspected, but investigators could find no evidence of it.

DC-6 planning was well along when this crash occurred, and Littlewood unexpectedly remarked to Dixon Speas, "Dix, we must never put more than fifty people on any airplane."

"Bill, we're configuring the Six for fifty-two," Speas gently reminded him.

Littlewood was silent for a moment, then said, "All right, but fifty-two is the limit."

He had to renege on that pledge, of course, as the growth of air travel made even fifty-two-passenger airplanes inadequate. But the incident demonstrated the compassion and sensitivity of this remarkable man.

Aviation historians often have referred to the 1946–1955 period as "the Golden Age of the Pistons," and perhaps rightfully so. In going from the DC-3 era to the Connies, DC-6s, DC-7s, and Boeing Stratocruisers, the industry figuratively was taking off knickers and donning its first pair of long pants.

But if this time slot represented great progress, it also was a decade marked by tragedy, setbacks, and controversy. And American was not immune.

The long pants were, initially, merely a superficial improvement. First the industry had to learn how to wear them.

12

A Queen Gets a Black Eye

In accordance with a gentlemen's agreement between C.R. and Pat Patterson, American and United put the DC-6 into service simultaneously, the inaugural flights occurring on the same day.

Passenger acceptance was immediate. It was the most comfortable, roomiest airliner of its day, thanks to what aeronautical engineers referred to as its "constant width" fuselage. Cabin width was the same from the first row of seats to the last. By contrast, the rival Constellation's fuselage narrowed sharply in the forward section and tapered again at the rear. The DC-6's interior was not only roomier overall, but more flexible.

The two airlines flew their DC-6s without incident for six months, wiping out the early lead TWA had built up with its Connies. The lead actually had partially evaporated long before American and United launched DC-6 service; on July 12, 1946, a TWA Constellation on a training flight caught fire in the air and crashed, killing four of the five crew members aboard. When investigators found evidence of faulty electrical connections on the destroyed plane and the same flaw in almost half of the Connies then in service, the CAB grounded all Constellations until new wiring could be installed. They weren't restored to service until September 20, sixty-nine days in which TWA had to operate DC-4s overseas and DC-3s transcontinentally.

There was no glee at either American or United over TWA's setback. The airline industry's one unbreakable axiom, rule, and solemn truth is, simply: "It could happen to us." In the case of the DC-6, proud queen of both carriers' fleet, it did.

On October 24, 1947, a United DC-6 operating as Flight 608 from Los Angeles to Chicago caught fire at 19,000 feet approximately one minute before its estimated arrival time of 12:22 P.M. over a radio checkpoint at Bryce Canyon, Utah.

The crew radioed that a fire had broken out in a baggage compartment and was out of control. Two minutes later, the flight messaged: "The tail is going out. . . . We may get down and we may not."

At 12:26 P.M., another radio contact reported that they were trying to find some place to land. The final message, at 12:27 P.M., said: "We may make it . . . approaching a strip."

It wasn't to be. The burning DC-6 disintegrated before the crew reached the strip; all fifty-two aboard perished. CAB accident investigators could find no reason for the in-flight fire, but there were two chief areas of suspicion: seepage from hydraulic lines (a factor in the Connie fire), and possible accidental lighting of one or more of the magnesium emergency flares all DC-6s carried. DC-6 operators were told to check hydraulic lines for leaks and to remove the flares. These precautionary measures were ordered while the crash "detectives" were still examining the wreckage of Flight 608.

Exactly seventeen days after the Bryce Canyon tragedy, an American DC-6 commanded by Evan Chatfield left San Francisco bound for Chicago via Tulsa. About two hours after takeoff, Chatfield began the routine process of transferring fuel from one tank to another, a procedure that maintained stability by keeping fuel tank levels equal as fuel was consumed.

The time was 11:57 A.M. and they were still engaged in the fuel transfer when the cabin temperature began to rise. Stewardess Evelyn Apitz tried to adjust the cabin temperature control, but the heat kept rising and she informed the captain. Chatfield turned off the heater system with no effect, so he switched from automatic heat control to manual, figuring the thermostat had malfunctioned.

This resulted in such a sharp temperature drop that they turned the heater back on. Once again, the cockpit gauge registering cabin temperature began to climb. It was still climbing when a warning light flashed, indicating a fire in the heater compartment.

Chatfield suspected they were in trouble even before the fire warning. He already had begun a fast turning descent toward the nearest airport—Gallup, New Mexico—and they were in that steep emergency descent when a second fire signal came from a forward baggage compartment. By now, smoke was seeping into the cabin and cockpit. It was so thick in the flight deck that Chatfield couldn't see either the instrument panel or through the cockpit windshield.

Copilot V. B. Brown opened the cockpit window on his side, leaning out until he could see the Gallup airport runway dead ahead. For two desperate minutes, he served as Chatfield's eyes, talking him into the landing—a voice linked to the captain's hands.

Airport fire trucks surrounded the burning DC-6 as it rolled to a stop, passengers tumbling down the emergency evacuation chute (an American innovation, incidentally). The crew, including stewardesses Apitz and Marilyn Humphreys, also got out safely, and firemen managed to extinguish the flames before they could devour the fuselage. Thanks to Chatfield's decision to land at the first sign of trouble, and to some pure luck, not only were all lives saved but a virtually intact DC-6 was left for investigators to inspect—an apparent mirror image of the United disaster.

The inspection, however, came up with precisely nothing until there arrived on the scene an American pilot named Glen Brink, one of Littlewood's engineering staff and an assistant test pilot under Dan Beard. Brink was based in

Los Angeles, commuting between Santa Monica and San Diego on both the DC-6 and 240 projects. He was at the Douglas plant, picking up his paycheck, when a phone call informed him that an American DC-6 had landed in flames at Gallup, and that he was to get there as fast as possible.

Brink flew to Gallup with a man from the CAB's Bureau of Safety—a rather brusque, uncommunicative character, as Glen remembered him—and Jack Grant, an American DC-6 maintenance specialist. Otto Kirchner, representing the airline on the investigation group, met him and briefed him on what they knew—which was nothing.

A CAB official said Brink could see the plane but warned him not to talk to anybody. It was sadly apparent that the government investigators were a bit touchy about their prerogatives, unusual in most crash probes, when mutual cooperation is encouraged. The accident investigation procedures called for the formation of specialized teams (engines, structures, systems, weather factors, etc.), each headed by a CAB representative but composed of experts from the airline, aircraft manufacturer, pilots' union, and so forth. But Kirchner, sensing animosity and even arrogance on the part of this particular CAB group, told Brink:

"Don't get on any committee, Glen. Just stay with me. You can get a lot more done that way."

Brink poked around the crippled plane without noticing anything significant. But later that day, he was at an informal meeting when mechanic Abe Hoyt came in and asked a CAB official for permission to drain one fuel tank.

"Why?"

"We've got some fuel leaking out of one tank and I want to drain it," Hoyt explained.

The CAB official told him to go ahead and the meeting resumed, the topic of discussion being the heating system. There were no flares on the American DC-6, and the hydraulic lines were intact.

That same night, after conferring with Kirchner, Brink called Bill Littlewood in New York. "I think we should ground the airplane," he advised. "There's something wrong with it and until we found out what, we shouldn't be flying any DC-6."

Littlewood contacted C.R., who immediately notified Patterson. Within a few hours, both airlines had voluntarily grounded their DC-6 fleets. All DC-6 operators followed suit. Meanwhile, a curious Brink was questioning Hoyt about that leaking tank.

"Which tank was it?" he asked.

"The one nearest the fuselage," Hoyt replied.

Brink said nothing, but a vague suspicion had dawned. Two days later he was back on the West Coast and the vague suspicion suddenly sprouted into a definite theory, which he promptly confided to Douglas engineers. Brink suggested a special flight to test his theory, after first phoning Gallup to confirm one key point: were Chatfield and his crew transferring fuel just before the fire warnings began?

Armed with this information, he started fitting the pieces of a deadly puzzle together. Gene Beatty of American had a brand-new DC-6 available for what was supposed to be a routine acceptance flight; Brink asked to go along. The flight turned out to be far from routine.

He requested and received instant permission from the Douglas DC-6 chief project engineer, Ed Burton, to find out whether an overflow from an inboard fuel tank could be sucked into the heater air-intake system. The airscoop for that system was located close to the tank vents.

Precautions were taken just in case Brink's theory turned out to be right. They took along on the flight portable fire extinguishers so big that they were mounted on wheels. The DC-6 heater was disconnected by shutting off all electrical circuits. To determine the exact path of overflowing fuel from an inboard tank, they glued cotton onto the front of the airscoop and also painted whitewash around the belly area adjacent to the air intake.

Beatty and Brink flew the airplane, with Douglas engineers aboard. At the same altitude Chatfield's DC-6 had been flying when the trouble began, the two pilots re-enacted the sequence of events. They turned on the fuel transfer valves and the booster pump, pouring fuel from outboard to inboard. They deliberately kept the pump on until overflowing was inevitable.

Then they landed. Brink never forgot that tense moment when they inspected the the fuselage belly in the area of the airscoop. "The gas was dripping from the belly, all the whitewash had been erased by fuel, and the cotton was saturated with fuel," Brink said.

After the UAL crash, Douglas had made some changes in the DC-6 heating system, hoping to prevent possible ignition from some electrical malfunction; a short circuit was considered a possibility. But when the Douglas heating technicians saw that fuel-covered belly, one of them murmured to Brink:

"Glen, all these changes we've been making in the heater—that wasn't it at all."

It wasn't. Ed Burton immediately notified Donald Douglas, while Brink called Littlewood. "We know what caused the United crash and what happened to our plane at Gallup," he said tersely, and then went on to describe the test flight.

The CAB's subsequent hearing on both the fatal accident and American's near disaster should have been a mere formality, but incredibly, the government tried to wreck Brink's flying career. The CAB and CAA accused him of conducting an unauthorized test flight and implied that he hadn't really proved anything. They were threatening to lift his pilot's license when their case against Brink collapsed.

It was disclosed that the CAB's assistant Bureau of Safety director, George Haldeman, was advised of Brink's test flight and had asked the CAB officer in charge at Gallup to fly to Los Angeles and go with Brink and Beatty. The official, the same dour man who had gone to Gallup with Brink, told Haldeman that Glen was on a wild goose chase and the test flight a waste of time.

The CAB and CAA also had criticized American for letting one of its employees run tests without official permission—even though, as Brink bitterly pointed out, "Hell, we had invited the guy and he refused."

Glen was criticized further for failing to get authority from the Douglas control tower at Santa Monica to conduct a weekend test flight. This charge seemed to have been substantiated when Donald Douglas, Jr., testified that the tower hadn't cleared the flight, but he turned out to be wrong. One of his own engineers told the hearing that permission had been granted by phone.

Brink still might have been crucified except for further testimony from Douglas, Jr., totally confirming his challenged solution. He disclosed that Douglas technicians had repeated the Brink test flight, using dyed water instead of fuel as an additional safety measure. There was absolutely no doubt, he informed the hearing, as to what had caused the two in-flight fires.

Brink's final absolution came when Douglas witnesses denied another CAB charge, that he had run a dangerous test flight without proper precautions. They listed the measures he *did* take, and except for the use of actual fuel, they were the same ones Douglas used in its own test.

The CAA's motive in trying to get Brink was decidedly suspect. This was the agency that had certificated the DC-6 in the first place, and its own certification requirements specifically stated: "It shall not be possible for fuel to flow between tanks in quantity sufficient to cause an overflow. . . . Vents and (fuel) drainage shall not terminate at points where the discharge of fuel will constitute a fire hazard."

Those supposed safeguards dated back to the DC-4, the first transport aircraft with fuel transfer capability. The DC-6's fuel transfer design was similar to the DC-4's, but with different locations for both the number three (right inboard) alternate tank vent and the cabin heater airscoop; on the DC-6, the latter was directly behind the vent. The CAA's certification inspectors had approved that location, apparently assuming that no pilot would permit an overflow.

It was a dangerous assumption, because it was only too easy for a busy cockpit crew to leave the booster pump on and the vent open a little too long. Fuel overflows had occurred on the DC-4, too, without causing any problem because the "dumped" gas simply evaporated. But on the DC-6, the overflow didn't have a chance to evaporate; it was sucked instantly into that airscoop. In attacking Brink, the CAA seemed to be trying to duck its own culpability, while the CAB official at Gallup apparently was suffering from a bad case of bruised ego.

At one point, Brink's outlook appeared so dark that American's lawyers advised him to appear at the hearings to defend himself. But when Douglas shot down the government's case against him, his appearance was unnecessary. C.R. was so angry that he called the CAA administrator in Washington and warned, "If you lift his license, we'll put it on the front page of every newspaper in the country!"

Every DC-6 in the U.S. and abroad stayed on the ground until the location of the heater air-intake was changed, a major structural revision that kept them out of the air for a little over four months. At the time of the grounding, American's DC-6s were providing about 50 percent of the airline's total passenger capacity; substituting DC-4s reduced that capacity by 30 percent, and the loss of revenue amounted to a staggering $7 million.

American's modification work was done partly in Tulsa and the rest in Santa Monica, one more indication of the Oklahoma maintenance center's increasing importance. When it opened in 1946, it had only 250 employees hired out of 3,000 applicants interviewed in a former automobile showroom. Marv Whitlock rode herd on the modification work at Douglas; under pressure from C.R., he kept prodding Douglas to speed up until one Douglas official told him his presence wasn't exactly desirable. (Privately, Marv didn't blame him. Douglas couldn't show favoritism to any carrier no matter how much C.R. was yelling.)

Not until May 1948 were all of American's DC-6s back in service. To the grounding costs were added the heavy training and orientation expenses involved in the DC-6's 1947 introduction and those of the Convair 240 in 1948. It was no wonder that American in those two years lost nearly $6 million.

There were two tragic and ironic sequels to the miracle at Gallup, one involving a catastrophic crash and the other coming perilously close to the same fate.

After the DC-6 and Constellation fires, the government ordered the airlines to install more sensitive smoke and fire detection systems in aircraft baggage compartments, along with mandatory CO_2 (carbon dioxide) extinguishers. Unfortunately, the carriers were given relatively little time in which to comply, and the new systems went in without much testing.

In June 1948, a United DC-6 was cruising placidly in the area of Mr. Carmel, Pennsylvania, when one of the extremely sensitive new detectors flashed a warning of fire in a forward cargo bin. The crew immediately discharged the CO_2 bottles in the compartment. The captain was giving Air Traffic Control a calm report of the incident when his voice began to slur and then became incoherent.

The DC-6 went into a slow, sweeping spiral and crashed; there were no survivors. The investigation revealed that in closing one safety loophole, an equally deadly new loophole had been created. First, there was no fire in the baggage compartment; the new detector had given a false alarm. Second, in hastily designing the new system, engineers had not taken into account the possibility that carbon dioxide fumes could leak into the cockpit. Both pilots and the flight engineer were probably unconcious when the plane hit the ground.

The other sequel to Gallup concerned the maintenance specialist Jack Grant, who had accompanied Brink to New Mexico. He left American and in 1950 was a laboratory technician in Los Angeles. One pleasant day he put his wife and two children on a United flight and kissed them good-bye; in his wife's suitcase he had planted a bomb. At the last minute, Grant lost his nerve and screamed a warning to baggage handlers. Arrested and convicted, he told authorities he had fallen in love with another woman.

Defense attorneys had asked Brink to testify as a character witness, but Glen refused. The Jack Grant case was one of his few bitter memories of the Gallup miracle.

It seemed to be a time for miracles, that year of 1947.

The remarkable story of American Flight 203, scheduled from LaGuardia to Nashville with several interim stops, began prosaically with a 5:34 P.M. takeoff on January 5. The DC-3, commanded by John Booth, had three and a half hours of fuel in its tanks.

The LaGuardia–Baltimore leg was completed routinely, and Booth intended to add fuel at the next stop: Washington National. What he and everyone else hadn't counted on was an unexpected blizzard that hit the entire eastern seaboard just as he left Baltimore, shutting down every airport between New York and North Carolina.

He had only forty miles to cover between Baltimore and Washington, but in the time it took to cover that short distance, the cloud cover dropped 7,500 feet as the heavy snow swept in. Incoming National traffic began to back up, and ATC told Booth to hold over Anacostia.

At this point, his radio communications began to go bad, precipitation static interfering with both transmission and reception. He decided to return to Baltimore to refuel; Baltimore advised it was swamped with a flight of military planes coming in low on fuel and that he'd be number twelve to land.

The snow static worsened, and Booth found himself unable to read any ground stations. He managed to contact an American DC-4, clear of the static at about 10,000 feet above him, and asked Captain Paul Clough to get him the weather at Philadelphia, Flight 203's alternate. Clough informed him Philly was getting heavy snow with visibility deteriorating fast.

"How about LaGuardia, Paul?"

"Same thing, but it's still above limits."

Booth figured LaGuardia was his best bet and continued heading north until he was virtually over the New York airport. Still unable to raise ATC, he managed to contact a company dispatcher who gave him more bad news: LaGuardia was now closed.

"I'm down to forty-five minutes of fuel," Booth reported. "Can you give me any airport that's still open?"

The dispatcher hesitated and in a choked voice voice said, "Johnny, I'm sorry but there isn't anything open within your fuel range."

Booth summoned stewardess Margaret Murphy to the cockpit. She already knew things were going badly, from all the wandering up and down the East Coast, and when she answered Booth's call she brought along another stewardess, Elsie Looper, who was deadheading on the trip. Neither girl knew how serious the situation was, however, until Booth told them:

"We don't know exactly where we are, we've lost contact with ATC and we're about out of fuel. You two go back there and sit down."

"Should we advise the passengers?" Margaret asked.

"No," Booth decided. "I think they'd panic and that's the last thing we need. I'll leave the no smoking and seat belt signs on and that's about all we can do for them."

(At the time, there was no cabin p.a. system in the DC-3, nor were there any pre-ditching or emergency landing instructions for domestic passengers.)

Booth was faced with the kind of command decision for which airline pilots earn their pay. He had three alternatives: try to land somewhere and risk running out of fuel over the middle of New York City; ditch in the ocean; or try to find some beach area where they might crash-land. Ditching would be the last resort. It was a cold night and they wouldn't last ten seconds in that freezing water.

They were at 2,000 feet, five minutes northeast of LaGuardia, and now they were down to thirty minutes before fuel exhaustion. Booth looked at copilot Tommy Hatcher. "Tom, can you think of anything we could do that we haven't done already?"

"I can't think of a single thing," Hatcher replied.

Booth took a deep breath and said, "Well, I figure about all we can do is head out over the Atlantic and drop a flare."

They flew southeast for fifteen minutes, descended to 300 feet, and Hatcher dropped one of the magnesium flares. All they could see below was angry whitecaps. They opened the side windows and turned on the landing lights, both men peering through the snow ahead of them. They couldn't see more than forty feet beyond the plane.

By now they had emptied the auxiliary tanks and one main tank; the engines were running on the remaining main tank. Hatcher suddenly called out, "Johnny, fuel gauge is down to zero!"

From the time they dropped the flare to Hatcher's warning that they were out of fuel, twelve minutes had elasped. They were resigned to ditching when the landing lights suddenly illuminated a stretch of flat beach ahead. Booth put the DC-3 into a wild split-S turn, trying to spot any obstacles, and then made a couple of passes in an effort to line up with the beach. When the engine died just as he was landing, the right wing dipped and dug into the snow and sand, slowing the plane down but causing a violent turn to the right.

Booth's face hit the windshield, the impact shoving his teeth through his lower lip. Hatcher was thrown to the left against the control yoke, driving one eye a quarter of an inch into its socket.

The careening plane came to a stop.

"Tommy, are you all right?"

Hatcher muttered, "I think so."

Booth opened the escape hatch above the cockpit, crawled out, and jumped to the ground, checking first to see if there was any sign of fire. There wasn't —because there wasn't enough fuel left to ignite with a blowtorch. He walked back to the cabin door and unlatched it; the door came off in his hand. After ordering the twelve shaken but uninjured passengers to stay in the plane, Booth told the two stewardesses to give Hatcher first aid.

Booth had no idea where they were and asked two husky male passengers to start walking down the beach, one in each direction, to find help. Then he returned to the cockpit, where the two girls were administering to a groggy Hatcher. Booth tried to get the radios working, but the generator was dead. Angrily, he kicked it—and it started to hum.

He raised some station—it was either Washington or Boston but he never was sure which—and advised that they were down somewhere on the south shore of Long Island. He was told to hold down his mike button so they could take an ADF bearing and repeat, "M.O. . . . M.O. . . ." A few excruciatingly long minutes went by until the voice of the American dispatcher at LaGuardia came through loud and clear.

"Johnny, you're on Jones Beach about a quarter of a mile from a Coast Guard station."

"That's really spotting us," Booth said gleefully. "I see headlights coming down the beach now."

It was a Coast Guard truck, alerted by one of the two passengers he had sent for help. The man had gone into the station, told the startled sailors what had happened, and then figured he'd better advise the airline. The only listed number for American was reservations, which he dialed. A woman agent answered.

"This is John Smith " [not his real name], he announced. "I'm a passenger on your Flight 203 and we've just landed on Jones Beach."

"I'm sorry, sir," she said politely, "but American doesn't serve Jones Beach."

"Well, young lady," he sighed, "you sure as hell do now."

There were aftermaths to the miracle.

Hatcher suffered double vision for six months and was grounded until doctors repaired the damage. He went on to fly for the eagle another thirty-three years, retiring as a captain in 1980.

Booth's wife Edie went through an ordeal of her own. She heard radio reports that a plane had crashed in New Jersey, killing both pilots. When American notified her that Flight 203 had landed on Jones Beach and that Booth was safe, she didn't believe it—she kept connecting the two crashes. And she didn't see her husband for another two days.

Booth himself stuttered for several years after the accident. His own intensely personal recollections were most appropriate:

"You find out a great deal about yourself in such situations. For example, under extreme stress you burn up a tremendous amount of body fluids. Never in my life have I been as thirsty as I was in the last thirty minutes before the landing and immediately afterwards. At one point I was in the cabin and noticed a pint of whiskey on an empty seat. I picked it up and started to take a drink when I thought, 'What a stupid thing to do—they'll think we got lost because I was drunk.'

"I remember asking God for help when dispatch told us there was no place to go. The prayer made me feel better. I seemed to steady down and stay calm.

It made me decide on a course of action instead of moaning 'What am I going to do?' "

American gave John Booth a Distinguished Service Award for bravery; he retired in 1975 as a senior captain. Even the traditionally cold, impersonal CAB report on the Jones Beach incident praised him. "It must be noted," the Board said, "that the pilot exercised commendable judgment and skill in completing a safe emergency landing under difficult circumstances."

The DC-3 Booth put down on that beach, N-21746, never flew for American again. Most of the interior was salvaged, including the seats and radio equipment, but the rest of the battered plane was sold to a scrap company, which came out to Jones Beach and hauled it away.

Booth always expected to hear from at least some of the passengers whose lives he had saved, but it didn't happen.

"I know that nine of the twelve went out to LaGuardia the next day and got on another plane," he said, "and that's the last I ever heard of any of them."

It was no surprise that American made no attempt to repair N-21746. The airline already was phasing out its DC-3s to make way for the Convair 240s. Convair service was inaugurated June 1, 1948 (the first 240 was christened *Flagship San Diego),* and by that time American was down to forty-three of its one-time queens.

Missing from the Flagship Fleet by then was *Flagship Alpha,* a DC-3 used mostly for experimental work. On August 8, 1947, *Alpha* was pressed into service as a cargo plane, carrying a spare engine to a stranded DC-3 in Buffalo. Aboard were Captain Walter "Scotty" Davidson, first officer Walker Zundel, and three mechanics who would help install the new engine at their destination—Howard Hickey, James Till, and Chester Ball.

Six minutes after takeoff, one engine failed. Davidson turned around to return to the airport, but the visibility was poor and he overshot the runway. He tried to go around again, but the DC-3, whose single-engine performance was notoriously marginal, stalled in the turn and crashed into Flushing Bay.

Both pilots and Hickey were killed, but a police rescue launch fished Till and Ball out of the water. The subsequent CAB hearing was perfunctory and cleared Davidson of any blame. But *five weeks after* the hearing, the New York City medical examiner announced that an autopsy on Davidson showed he had been intoxicated, with evidence of a large amount of alcohol in his liver.

His finding was completely contrary to testimony at the CAB hearing, which heard from two toxicologists and forty other witnesses, including Ball and Till. Also ignoring that testimony was a Queens County grand jury, which ruled that the crash was caused by a drunken captain, and cited the medical examiner's report.

Ralph Damon was furious. He demanded a second CAB hearing, and when this was quickly granted, he hired two of the nation's most distinguished toxicologists, Doctors Howard Haggard and Leon Greenberg of the Yale

Laboratory of Applied Physiology. They demolished the medical examiner's verdict permanently.

Haggard pointed out that the examiner hadn't checked the brain, blood, or stomach, adding rather sarcastically that "the liver is the one organ of the body that cannot prove intoxication."

Greenberg reminded the hearing of what already had been brought out by CAB investigators: *Alpha,* used frequently for de-icing experiments, had been carrying a ten-gallon tank of de-icing fluid hanging directly over the captain's seat; the tank ruptured when the DC-3 crashed and, the toxicologist added, this was the source of the alcohol found during Davidson's autopsy.

Case closed.

Damon's swift defense of a dead pilot who couldn't defend himself was typical. If anything, his relations with the flight crews were better than C.R.'s. Smith was sadly disillusioned when AOA's pilots struck their airline in the fall of 1947 and stayed out for thirteen days, a dispute that added more red ink to that year's financial woes.

C.R. still got along fine with pilots as individuals, but his attitude toward their union, ALPA, was something else. He detested ALPA president Dave Behncke, the latter's support of Mosier and LaGuardia Airport notwithstanding, and blamed the AOA strike mostly on the union chief. Smith thought he had a deal with the pilots all worked out except for some differences in phrasing certain provisions of a tentative agreement. He was stunned when Behncke unexpectedly ended the negotiations, declaring that "an impasse" made further talks useless, and called the pilots out.

The strike also may have had an effect on relations between Damon and C.R. Damon always was closer to the international division than Smith. He had helped bring it into being even though in the chain of command he had little to say about how AOA was being run. Occasionally he clashed with Harold Harris, an admittedly mild feud that began when American Overseas was getting a new DC-4. This was during the days of the cargo contract operation and Jim Wooten wanted to borrow the DC-4 over the weekend to pick up a *Newsweek* press run.

Damon called a meeting to discuss the request, with Wooten and Dixon Speas pleading their cause and Harris representing AOA. For nearly two hours, Wooten and Speas talked about the need for this particular mission, which would demonstrate to an important magazine how efficient American's cargo division really was. Damon kept nodding agreement, or siding with them verbally.

Harris sat there smoking a pipe, saying not one word during the entire discussion. Finally, he took his pipe out of his mouth.

"If you bastards have finished talking," he growled, "I'll tell you what's going to happen with that airplane. You're not gonna get it." Back in his mouth went the pipe, and exit Harold Harris.

Damon was tough but unusually compassionate. Otto Becker was a young agent and decided that the only way to get ahead at American was to take night courses. He asked Tom Brooks, head of field offices during Damon's presidency, if he had any advice on which courses would be best.

"Hell, I'm not qualified to give that kind of advice," Brooks allowed. "Go talk to our personnel man."

Becker did, and personnel suggested he see Damon. With some trepidation, Becker got an appointment with the airline's president and showed up on schedule. He waited in an outer office and almost left when Damon's door opened and out came Red Mosier and a half dozen other vice presidents. But Damon greeted him warmly, and for almost an hour they talked. Damon began by telling him about the history of the railroads, how they developed from the pioneering days to their being run by financiers and lawyers, and that the airlines one day would take the same path.

He recalled his days at Curtiss-Wright. "I was twenty-nine years old and I had 600 people under me. I look back and you know, Otto, I feel sorry for them. They were working for a man who didn't really know how to deal with them. My advice to you, my young friend, is not so much what you can learn from any course but to learn how to run people."

Becker emerged from the meeting starry-eyed and went in to report to Brooks.

"Well, I had my conference with Mr. Damon."

"How long were you in there?"

"Almost an hour."

"An hour?" Brooks exploded. "Hell, we can't get five minutes with him and he gives a goddamned agent an hour."

Not even C.R. worked any harder than Damon. Dixon Speas remembered him as a man "who wanted more than anything else to succeed. He was an achiever, a professional devoted to getting the job done, a no-nonsense guy who eventually worked himself to death. He loved to talk about the old Curtiss-Wright period, when he'd stagger down the aisle of the Condor mock-up as if he were a drunken passenger and throw himself against a berth to test its strength."

Speas thought C.R. and Damon always kept the growing friction between them well hidden. But at least one officer wasn't surprised at the rift; Bill Littlewood said he could see it developing.

"Ralph Damon," Littlewood told a close friend, "was a man who was never content in a room full of people unless he was top dog. And generally he was top dog everywhere except at home—his four kids ran the house. There had to be an eventual break between C.R. and Ralph. They were simply strong men, both of whom wanted to be in charge."

If the friction did involve mutual ego and jealousy, it was to their credit that neither blamed the other for American's slumping fortunes. Both realized that factors beyond the airline's control were largely responsible. The entire industry was having serious problems. The euphoric dreams of a postwar air travel boom had given way to public disillusionment and distrust. A series of bad crashes had eroded passenger confidence. Etched in sharp symbolism was *Life* magazine's 1947 photograph of a fifty-passenger DC-4 cabin just before takeoff, with only three people in its seats.

Manufacturers, the government, and the airlines alike shared the collective black eye inflicted by the Constellation and DC-6 grounding—a black eye whose shading turned even darker in the summer of 1948 when the new Martin 202 was grounded for major structural deficiencies. A Northwest 202 lost a wing in flight and when the CAB inspected the rest of the airline's Martin fleet, investigators found metal fatigue cracks in the wings of five of its seventeen planes. Three of the five had cracks in *both* wings.

Airline payrolls became grossly top-heavy as anticipated traffic growth not only failed to materialize but dropped far below predicted levels. Returning veterans had rightfully claimed their old jobs, and the casualties were those hired during the war. American alone had furloughed more than 2,000 low-seniority employees by the end of 1947, a drastic 15 percent slash that dropped the 1946 peak of some 14,000 to a little over 12,000.

C.R.'s state of mind during the dismal 1947–1948 period might be described as grimly optimistic. He was confident that things would get better. By mid 1949, he intended American to be the only airline in the U.S. with a completely modern fleet, and that included AOA, for which he had ordered sixteen Boeing Stratocruisers to replace its DC-4s and a handful of early-model Connies.

Safety remained a top priority, and the best example of this commitment was his insistence that every new Flagship be equipped with the capability of utilizing the Instrument Landing Systems (ILS) being installed at the major airports.

But new airplanes and greater safety didn't guarantee profits. Getting costs down was a goal he sought with the zeal of an evangelist, and this involved not only operating expenditures but the long-range problems of financing American's future fleet needs. Finance always had been handled rather amateurishly by the still-young industry, and C.R. was gutsy and intelligent enough to recognize it was not within his field of expertise.

To fill a gap Smith felt was hurting the airline, he went outside the industry for a man with financial acumen of the highest order. He hired William J. Hogan as American's new treasurer, and less than a year later—in a promotion reflecting his judgment of Hogan's ability—added the title of vice president.

Hogan was an unusual and controversial person. He came to American from the H. J. Heinz Company, where he had served with distinction as treasurer, comptroller, director, and member of the Heinz executive board. Previously he had been on the comptroller's staff at the Firestone Tire and Rubber Company for fifteen years.

Brilliant was the adjective universally ascribed to Bill Hogan; irascible, autocratic, difficult, and ruthless were other adjectives. He was not easy to work with or for. He got into a fierce feud with Red Mosier almost from Day One, and during his twenty-year career at American he came into conflict, sometimes angry confrontations, with virtually every officer in the company. With the sole exception of C.R., there were no sacred cows at American for

Hogan—not even a much beloved figure like Littlewood, whom Hogan regarded with admitted contempt.

While Hogan could be extremely gracious on rare occasions, he wouldn't have won any popularity contest—nor did he ever want to. Yet there also was grudging respect for the man. At his job, he was simply the best. Smith actually borrowed him from Heinz for six months, a period in which Hogan was supposed to look over the airline's financial situation and advise on possible courses of action. When the six months were up, C.R. talked him into staying, and from then on, Hogan's influence on company policy progressed to the point where he was answering only to Smith himself. At one stage, confronting Bill Hogan on an "It's-you-or-me" basis was a one-way ticket out of American, as one senior vice president was to find out.

He was Mosier's *bête noire.* Red's major weakness was his cavalier attitude toward expense accounts, and Hogan was an intractable believer in the straight and narrow when it came to guarding a company's money. Add this to their totally different personalities—the boisterous, extrovertish Mosier and the stern, often abrasive Hogan—and it was inevitable that they'd clash.

And clash they did, frequently and loudly, in arguments of gargantuan proportions that put C.R. right in the middle. He was too fond of Red and respected Hogan too much to want to take sides. Hogan came to him one day in a cold fury.

"Are you aware that Mosier has been drawing big advances and hasn't been submitting any expense accounts?" Hogan inquired in the tone of an avenging prosecutor.

"No," Smith admitted, "but I'll look into it."

He called Bob Tuttle, Mosier's assistant. Red was out of town and the loyal Tuttle hedged. "Well, yes, C.R., but he's been real busy and he just hasn't gotten around to turning them in."

"When he gets back, I want those expense accounts and I want 'em fast."

Mosier called in later that day and Tuttle broke the news. Red was furious, but not at C.R. or Hogan. He bawled out Tuttle for not submitting the expense accounts, conveniently forgetting that he hadn't made them out yet. Tuttle calmed him down by promising that he and Tabba Reynolds, Mosier's secretary, would put something together and have it ready for him when he returned.

"Tabba and I cheated all over the place," Tuttle said, "but no matter what fiction we concocted we still couldn't get the total to match the advances he had drawn. Finally we decided to pad the taxi fares and wound up with Red spending $500 a week on cabs. My God, there must have been at least a year of unaccounted-for spending—ten or twelve expense reports a month. We finally got them all ready for him to sign, and he never uttered one word of praise or thanks. He signed them and they all went in to Hogan, who took them right to C.R. And don't think C.R. didn't know it was all just one big lie. He just smiled and told Hogan to okay them."

Strangely, neither Tuttle nor Tabba Reynolds resented Mosier's lack of gratitude; it was just the way Red operated. Tuttle knew him better than anyone else and realized that when Red raised that syrupy voice of his and screamed at people, it was usually bluster that he really didn't mean. Nor was he dishonest; he simply had no idea of what he was spending.

"He had a big heart and tried to hide it," Tuttle explained. "You'd go out with him at night and he'd entertain you lavishly. Lots of drinks and lots of laughs. The next morning he wouldn't talk to you. He acted as if he was mad as hell at you. It was all his way of keeping you in line.

"I know a lot of people asked C.R. how he could put up with Hogan, but then a lot of people asked him how he could put up with Mosier. I never heard C.R.'s answer myself, but I've been told he simply said it was because of the service both men were performing for the company.

"Red stepped on a lot of toes, but in an entirely different way than Hogan. Bill Hogan didn't like anybody. Red liked 90 percent of the people he dealt with and the other ten percent he just walked over. He was a master negotiator. He could negotiate anything, and that's where C.R. used him so often. And Red had one understanding with C.R. from the very beginning: he had absolute authority to act. He could commit the company to anything, because he knew C.R. would stand behind him. Mosier could even tell someone like Rickenbacker off. And if Rickenbacker complained to C.R. about 'that son of a bitch Mosier,' C.R. wouldn't do a damned thing about it. He'd never mention it to Red. That's the relationship they had."

Mosier wasn't really an ungrateful person. He may have used Tuttle as an occasional whipping boy, but he recommended him for a major promotion when one of C.R.'s brainstorms bore fruit. Tuttle was chosen to head the new East Side Airlines Terminal, a $6 million project that was strictly Smith's idea.

For a long time, carriers serving New York City had maintained expensive City Ticket Offices scattered throughout Manhattan—American's CTO was at 45 Vanderbilt Avenue, opposite the Biltmore. But in 1939, five airlines (American, TWA, Eastern, United, and Pan Am) decided to put all CTOs under one roof; the site picked was at 42nd Street and Park Avenue, where a handsome new building was constructed. (It was at this facility that airline porters first acquired the name "skycaps.")

The consolidated operation, which included airport limousine service, worked well until 1948, when automobile traffic in the heart of Manhattan became so congested that even emergency vehicles were suffering sometimes fatal delays. The airport coaches, carrying a third of all airline passengers, added to the arterial clogging to a point where the city finally had to take action. It informed the carriers that unless they could come up with a plan of their own to relieve the downtown congestion caused by the frequent airport bus schedules, the coaches would be banned from certain streets.

The city's proposed restricted area included the central airline ticket terminal, and this posed a thorny problem for the carriers. American would be the most severely affected—it was then handling 40 percent of metropolitan New York's air traffic—but it would hurt the other airlines as well. Joint meetings to solve the crisis got nowhere and Smith, impatient with the lack of industry action, decided on a bold move.

Very quietly, he arranged for American to purchase most of the property in a block running from East 37th to East 38th Streets, and from First Avenue to Second Avenue. It was outside the restricted zone and adjacent to the Queens Midtown Tunnel linking Manhattan to Long Island and its two airports, LaGuardia and the forthcoming Idlewild. After completing the transaction, he advised the airlines that if they didn't join American in creating a new downtown terminal on the acquired site, American would proceed on its own.

They joined the project hastily, but it was Mosier and Tuttle who developed and refined it. Funding was underwritten by the Triborough Bridge and Tunnel Authority with American, Eastern, TWA, United, and Pan Am each holding 15 percent of the stock and Capital, Colonial, National, Northwest, and Northeast holding 5 percent apiece. Braniff, Allegheny, and Mohawk came into the East Side Airlines Terminal Corporation later.

It was an ambitious undertaking. Incorporated in 1948, the complex opened in 1953 and remained self-supporting for the next twenty years. At its height, the terminal served twenty-two carriers, including a dozen foreign airlines. Two years after it began operating, a second facility—the West Side Airlines Terminal—was opened at 10th Avenue and 42nd Street to serve Newark Airport; located near the Lincoln Tunnel, it also was outside the restricted zone. Bob Tuttle was president of all three downtown facilities until 1966, when he resigned.

These three monuments to public convenience reflected C.R.'s belief that the airlines would be a lot better off if they cooperated now and then. In the same year he launched the East Side Terminal project, he came up with the idea of pooling all ground equipment—baggage handling, fueling, dispatching, aircraft cleaning, etc.

His plan was to form a corporation in which all carriers would hold stock, and he insisted it would save millions if they consolidated not only ground equipment but personnel. He finally sold the concept to the Air Transport Association, which agreed to put it into effect on a trial basis under the name of Airlines National Terminal Service Company (ANTSCO).

Cincinnati and Detroit's Willow Run were the guinea pigs for what turned out to be an ill-fated experiment. ANTSCO was discontinued at the Ohio airport after only two years, because of friction among the carriers serving it. Willow Run lasted a few years longer, but ANTSCO passed into limbo there, too, for the same reason. The constant interline bickering was why Tuttle eventually resigned from the terminal corporations; he told C.R. he couldn't take the feuding anymore.

It was just as well Smith had Damon and Harris to run American and AOA respectively; he had his hands full with such peripheral ventures as centralized terminals and ANTSCO. Shortly before he conceived the East Side Terminal project, he became embroiled, along with the rest of the airlines, in an angry battle with the executive director of the Port of New York Authority, Austin J. Tobin.

Tobin was a dictatorial character whose disposition fell somewhat short of Dale Carnegie's formula for winning friends and influencing people. His PNYA had assumed jurisdiction of LaGuardia, Newark, and Idlewild airports as a bi-state agency in 1947; previously its operations were confined to the bridges and tunnels linking New York and New Jersey. Tobin assured the airlines that PNYA would honor their leases at the three airports for the next fifty years (until 1997), but the minute the Authority took over, it raised rentals and landing fees and also issued a series of petty new rules and regulations.

Tobin argued that PNYA had to be self-supporting or it couldn't market its bonds. The airlines announced their collective intention to sue, and then discovered they couldn't: by an act of Congress, PNYA was immune from lawsuits. Their litigation reprisal stymied, the airlines then announced they would boycott Idlewild, a $250 million investment (its total eventual cost) that now threatened to fit the first four letters of its name.

Both sides stubbornly refused to budge. There was no doubt Tobin's somewhat arrogant personality was not conducive to calm discussion, but the airlines' own attitude was of the dog-in-the-manager variety—they needed Idlewild badly. It took Governor Thomas E. Dewey to end the impasse. He met around the clock with Tobin and industry representatives, who finally agreed on a compromise: the carriers would accept new leases with PNYA, and the Authority, in turn, had to surrender its immunity from future suits.

According to Tuttle, C.R. never spoke to Tobin again. Mosier was American's liaison man for all future dealings with PYNA, and he used to needle the humorless Tobin unmercifully. They were at lunch one day and Tobin happened to remark that as a boy, he used to swim in the Flushing Bay area where the garbage from the city dump was dropped to build LaGuardia.

"It figures, Austin," Mosier snorted. "You've been up to your neck in crap all your life."

Damon and Harris notwithstanding, C.R. never could sever himself completely from matters that theoretically were no longer his responsibility. The self-typed memos continued to stream from his then-new Remington, such as an unusually lengthy missive addressed to Al Bone and Gage Mace in Los Angeles, with Damon and Deichler marked in for rare copies. It suggested "putting some showmanship into the Los Angeles end of our principal transcontinental services." His suggestions ranged from making sure every DC-6 was well polished to using "distinctive and colorful" ropes to direct passengers to and from the planes—mounted on movable brass standards, which, he added, "should always be bright." The memo continued:

> I should think you could procure from some of the studio outfitting companies some red carpet of durability which we could unroll and lay out to the airplane.
> I would put in a high-quality public address system on the ramp, where music without the rasp of the low-quality sets can be played. I would play the tunes . . . when the "name" airplanes are arriving and

departing. I would try to have the music fit the area—perhaps Spanish would be a good background; you decide it.

On the airplanes coming in, orange juice is what the average Joe expects when he crosses the Colorado and arrives in California. I would discuss this with Sky Chefs; I assume they would be glad to do the work if we pay for it. The objective is to give each passenger on each of the name flights a hell of a big glass of orange juice. This will be most appropriate at breakfast time but if the airplane does not come in at that time you might think of supplying it when they do come in. You might have to ship the oranges to Tulsa or wherever they put on the meals, but I should think there would be plenty of space (time) to get it done.

Get all of this under way and send the bill to me for approval. Send details of what you decide to do to Messrs Damon and Deichler.

When American began selling DC-6 lounge seats to accommodate oversales or demand overflows, C.R. found out about it and raised the roof. The lounge had always been marketed as an extra touch of luxury of which Smith was very proud.

"We're going to stop this practice," he decreed. Art Lewis led a volley of objections, pointing out that selling six more seats added up to about $1 million a year in additional revenue.

"I don't give a damn," C.R. retorted. "We're selling fifty-two seats on an airplane advertised as a fifty-two-seat airplane and if we sell the lounge we're not fulfilling our responsibility to the passengers."

He kept the ban in effect for six months, until he was finally pressured into resuming the sale of lounge seats—and then only to handle oversales.

The Convairs lacked the DC-6's glamour but they proved to be a worthy successor to the gallant DC-3. The pilots were suspicious of the 240 at first. Veteran Captain Ralph Long, a Convair-lover from the start, remembered that, "The pilot group really mistrusted them."

The common impression was that the 240 was too fast and too light on the controls. It also had stiff wings, in contrast to the DC-3's flexible wings—so flexible that crews could see them wave in turbulence. One DC-3 pilot had remarked, "I don't mind when the wings bend up and down, but when they clasp hands over the fuselage, I get nervous."

Yet the 240 was even stronger structurally than the DC-3. Long considered it the most honest airplane he ever flew. It had beautiful aileron, elevator, and rudder control, which made it easy to handle in the stiffest crosswind. It had few if any bad habits, with good stall recovery performance. And it could fly off snow and ice, something not even the ubiquitous DC-3 could do very well.

C.R. once estimated that American saved some $25 million by ordering the DC-6 and 240 as early as he did. The bulk of other airline orders for the two planes came later, when their respective prices had increased considerably. And Smith was equally proud of the fact that the totally new Flagship Fleet was paid for in less than three years.

The 240's tricycle landing gear gave the mechanics at LaGuardia an idea for a new game. When a Convair was ready to leave, they'd choose numbers, which they chalked onto the side of the nosewheel tire. When the aircraft returned to LaGuardia, the winner would be the one whose number stopped closest to the nose bar.

Martin Streicher, than a mechanic and at this writing manager of airport services at Washington National, recalls that it cost a dollar to play.

"Everyone got in the game," he said, "agents, stewardesses, pilots, and mechanics. I think it lasted as long as we operated Convairs. I don't recall who thought it up. It might have been a mechanic named Harry Silverman. He was a handsome, friendly guy who used to ignore union rules and help load baggage.

"It was a lot of fun in those days. I was making thirty-six bucks a week and earning every cent. And we all worked like hell. It was a matter of pride to have a twenty-five-minute turnaround time on a Convair and get the plane off in ten minutes if it was running behind schedule. You had fun, but in the end you did your job, which meant putting the passengers first. American was like one of Vince Lombardi's championship teams. First you became a team and then you became a family, and that's when you've got it made. Once you're a team *and* a family, you can go away for a year and know the job's still getting done."

By March 1949, American was down to only three DC-3s operating two daily schedules—a four-stop trip between Chicago and Windsor, Ontario, and a similar four-stopper between Fort Worth and El Paso. Convairs replaced them on these two routes a month later, and the era of C.R.'s great gamble ended. Yet the DC-3 actually outlasted the younger DC-4 in American's passenger service. The last DC-4 to carry people was retired in December 1948, and only a few were retained as cargo planes.

Most of the DC-3s went on to varied and honorable careers elsewhere. The story of N-16015, one of the first delivered to American, was representative of them all. After serving as a Flagship for five years, N-16015 flew the Hump during the war as an Air Force cargo plane, returned to American briefly, and then was sold to a Miami used aircraft dealer. Bonanza, a Las Vegas–based local service airline, bought it in February 1955, and operated it for five years under a new registration, N-492. In 1960, Bonanza sold the plane to another dealer, who peddled it to the Japanese government. N-16015's last known operator was the Civil Aviation Bureau of Japan.

American's DC-3 service officially ended when Flight 794, inbound from El Paso, pulled up to a gate at the Fort Worth airport April 1, 1949. It also was the last time the four-star flag was flown from an in-service Flagship. The symbolic practice, so close to C.R.'s heart, was abandoned with the advent of pressurized aircraft.

Shortly after the final scheduled flight, American held a decommissioning ceremony at LaGuardia for the last DC-3 in the fleet, with C.R. in attendance. The pennant was rigged so it could be lowered like the flag at dusk; Bill

Littlewood and Dan Beard performed this honor while a Marine Corps bugler played "Taps" and a Marine color guard stood at attention. In the background were several antique cars, and Walt Rauscher of the sales department, dressed in a Keystone Kop uniform. The whole motif was one of "farewell to an ancient warrior," and this didn't sit well with airlines still operating a sizable number of DC-3s.

Rex Smith normally would have been overjoyed at their outraged protests, but they were made not only to American but also to the Port of New York Authority, which was just as angry as the carriers. No one had bothered to ask the PNYA for permission to hold the ceremony, because no one had thought it necessary.

Rex wasn't through rubbing salt in open wounds, however. He had the entire public relations department contacting museums around the country with an offer to donate a DC-3 to anyone interested. Incredibly, there were no takers—not even the Smithsonian, which later acquired one from Eastern. A DC-3 in mint condition today would be a showpiece for any transportation exhibit.

So the first airline to operate the DC-3 was the first to retire it. C.R.'s decision to buy the plane sight unseen had been controversial, yet in sheer controversy it ranked below one he made fourteen years later.

He began secret negotiations to sell American Overseas Airlines to Pan American.

13
All the VPs Were in Europe

There were almost as many explanations advanced for C.R.'s decision to sell American Overseas as the number of planes in AOA's fleet.

Which was understandable, because there really was no single reason. Rather, the decision was based on a number of factors that had been gnawing at Smith for almost four years, starting with the fact that buying AOA hadn't been his idea in the first place.

Yet this had to be the most minor reason of all. He was too big a man to let pure ego play such a major role. It would have played no role whatsoever if American Overseas had been very successful, dominating the transatlantic market the way American dominated the domestic.

But its profitable years were rare, and even its black-ink periods more of a gray shading. It *was* well run, considered equal in service to TWA and superior to Pan Am. As a competitor, however, it still had flaws. Until the Stratocruisers were delivered, its equipment was inferior. And AOA's small size was a definite handicap. Furthermore, the airline had something of a split personality; operationally it was independent, but its reliance on American was heavy.

C.R. recognized these weaknesses, and the judgment call he made stemmed not so much from AOA's faults but what it would take to correct them. American was having its own troubles.

American owned 62 percent of American Overseas, and one solution would have been to merge the two carriers into a single entity. Smith felt the parent airline didn't have the financial resources to go that route, and yet AOA was too small to really stand on its own feet. While it had its own board of directors, a sales force in Europe, and almost total autonomy in its flight operations, it depended heavily on American in two vital areas: domestic marketing and financial help. The simple truth was that C.R. considered this an unacceptable drain on American.

Nor was he alone in this view. His own officers complained that they were spending too much time on AOA's affairs, and Smith was in total agreement. At a staff meeting one day, he brought up the matter in a way that left no doubt he wasn't happy.

"Every time I look around for one of my key officers to get something done around here," he remarked, "I find he's off somewhere in Europe working on

225

some AOA problem. Management is spending 90 percent of its time on an operation that's producing only 10 percent of our revenues."

He hadn't plucked that 90-10 ratio out of thin air. It came from a special economic planning committee he had established to balance revenues against cost in making major decisions. The initial committee consisted of Art Lewis, J. D. Hungerford, and Oliver Wilson. As Lewis described its function, "Sales was concerned with revenues, operations with cost and safety, and you needed someone to balance them."

The planning committee didn't go so far as to recommend disposal of AOA; it merely set the facts on the table. Those facts were supported by a second group Smith set up to specifically study American Overseas' future viability, and this committee's report was even bleaker. It said there wasn't much chance of AOA ever contributing more than 20 percent of the overall revenues, and it particularly emphasized the effects of a CAB overseas mail rate decision that had set AOA's mail subsidy at 42 cents a mile, compared to TWA's 56 cents and Pan Am's 72 cents.

The study group also cited the diversion of American's management skills and talent into the international division, not to mention the diversion of resources. It noted the proliferation of foreign competition from carriers like BOAC, Air France, SAS, and Swissair. Again, the study committee didn't actually recommend that American dump AOA, but it certainly provided C.R. with ammunition.

He told no one at either American or AOA he was going to sell—not Harold Harris nor John Slater, who was still on AOA's board, and not even Damon. The only person he did tell was Malcolm MacIntyre, who had become American's general counsel. C.R. had long since severed relations with Ray Pruitt, and Ham Hale had formed his own law firm, his long service representing American ending amicably.

MacIntyre had joined the Air Transport Command's legal force at Smith's request and worked in the ATC for four years. After he was discharged in the spring of 1946, C.R. told him he had given Pruitt the gate and urged MacIntyre to start a law firm, adding, "You can be our general counsel."

C.R. already had retained Howard Westwood of Covington and Burling to represent American in CAB cases. But it was Mac to whom he turned when the AOA dilemma came to a head. He summoned the general counsel to his office, closed the door, and said quietly:

"Mac, we're going to make a deal with Juan Trippe to sell AOA to Pan Am. I want you to help me with the negotiations."

The secret talks began late in November 1948. Whether it was Smith or Trippe who initiated the negotiations is uncertain; Trippe was generally believed to have been the instigator but the matter is moot—both had willing ears. The almost nightly meetings were held in Smith's apartment at the Hotel Marguery on Park Avenue; C.R. had moved there from 57th Street. Only four men were present: Smith, MacIntyre, Trippe, and Henry Friendly, Pan Am's legal counsel in Washington.

Considering the unbending personalities of the two main participants, Smith and Trippe, the talks went smoothly. Trippe was a tough negotiator, with a habit of speaking with painfully cautious slowness. Between his usual intransigence and his molasses-paced voice, he irritated C.R. at times. After one session, when C.R. happened to be alone with Friendly for a few minutes, he confessed that Trippe's slowness was driving him crazy. Friendly nodded sympathetically and told him about a CAB hearing at which Trippe was testifying. A CAB lawyer asked him, for the record, where he lived.

"Uh . . . uh . . . uh," Trippe crept verbally.

Friendly, sitting next to him, whispered, "It's all right, Juan—it's in the phone book."

The final meeting was in the Chrysler Building, where Trippe had a private office. The two parties had informed their respective heads of public relations that an agreement was pending—Rex Smith and young Willis Player of Pan Am, who in his own words considered Rex "the ultimate authority on airline public relations." The meeting at which the papers were signed took place on a Sunday afternoon, and Rex was told to stand by at American's executive offices to wait for word that an agreement had been consummated. Player kept a similar vigil in an anteroom next to Trippe's office in the Chrysler Building.

The meeting began shortly before noon, and Rex kept phoning Player, asking what was holding up the announcement. Both he and his Pan Am counterpart had joint releases ready to roll. From the frequency of his phone calls and his increasing impatience, Player got the idea that Rex had better things to do on a Sunday afternoon. It was close to 3 P.M. when Rex Smith decided it was time to act.

"Look, Willis," he advised, "you go in there very confidently and you tell those guys, 'Gentlemen, if you want to see your names in tomorrow's newspapers, you'd better have a signed announcement in the next fifteen minutes.' "

Player felt like a battered fighter whose manager has just told him, "Go out there and kill the bum—he can't hurt us." But he revered Rex, so he mustered his courage and poked his head into the inner sanctuary. He gulped and repeated Rex's instructions.

C.R. glared. Trippe, who had the stare of a hungry cobra, just nodded. Whether it was a nod of agreement or curt dismissal, Willis couldn't tell, but he retracted his head and closed the door, wondering what kind of solecism he must have committed. Much to his surprise and relief, Friendly emerged five minutes later with the signed papers, and then took the time to brief Player on the details.

The agreement was signed December 13, 1948, but nearly two years were to pass before American Overseas joined its own Valhalla. During that time, to the everlasting credit of every man and woman who worked for AOA, they never stopped trying to make it the best international carrier in the world, even though they knew it was doomed as an airline with its own identity.

C.R. felt for them, he truly did. One of the biggest stumbling blocks to agreement was his insistence that Pan Am retain as many AOA employees as possible. It was Trippe who kept balking, until even Friendly supported C.R. There were some 800 AOA employees Pan Am considered surplus, and almost half (383) were maintenance and stores personnel covered by a TWU-CIO union contract with American.

Only five of the 383 volunteered to go with Pan Am; the union wanted all 383 hired, and threatened a strike. Under the sales agreement, C.R. had wrenched a concession out of Trippe: Pan Am would absorb 200 of the 800 employees declared surplus, 110 of them in maintenance and stores, selection to be made on the basis of seniority and immediate qualification, all to be credited with their AA/AOA status in seniority, wages, sick leave, vacations, and severance pay. To anyone still not wanting to go with Pan Am, Smith offered two alternatives: exercise your seniority in American's system, or take severance pay.

In the end, only some 300 lost their jobs, thanks mostly to C.R.'s persistent badgering of Trippe even after the agreement was signed. But while his efforts helped ease much of the bitterness, this didn't apply to Harris and Damon. Harris was hurt. And Damon was more than hurt—he was infuriated.

For both men, it was a case of loyalty to C.R. colliding with conviction and emotion. They were on AOA's board, which had to approve the agreement, and some directors were opposed to selling. The main reason C.R. insisted on a sale—technically the transaction involved the sale of AOA's assets—instead of an outright merger was his knowledge that AOA's board probably would turn down a merger. A sale of assets required approval by only 50 percent of the directors; a merger called for a two-thirds majority.

John Slater had promised Smith he'd vote for the sale, and Damon's and Harris's votes weren't considered crucial. Nevertheless, they went separately to MacIntyre just before the AOA board meeting and expressed their dilemma in almost identical language.

"Mac," they each said, "I don't want to vote for this thing but I hate to go against C.R. I know my vote won't stop it, but I can't vote for it, either."

MacIntyre advised them to simply abstain. "In that way," he said, "you won't be voting for it, but on the other hand you won't be trying to stop it."

They took his advice and abstained. Harris, who went with Pan Am as vice president of its Atlantic division, had no hard feelings. He did discuss the sale with C.R. after it was consummated.

"He explained it logically," Harris said. "There was too much competition and AOA couldn't fill its seats. You have to remember that American didn't own AOA outright—American Export still had almost 40 percent of the stock. C.R. told me that to combine American and AOA, which is what he really wanted to do, he'd have to buy out American Export's shares, and this would have been too costly. No, he didn't sell AOA down the river. He just felt it wasn't going to work. AOA was a drag on American, and he didn't want two companies to go down the drain."

Damon didn't share those sentiments. He was convinced that AOA, despite its current struggles, would someday share the inevitable growth of international air travel and eventually might well be more profitable than American. Exactly one month and five days after the agreement was signed, and after considerable soul-searching, he resigned as American's president and also as a director. C.R. replaced him as president and abolished the position of board chairman, although later he was to restore it.

Damon told friends he was tired and after a long vacation planned to teach at a small college. But there is strong reason to believe he had in his hip pocket an offer from Howard Hughes to run TWA long before he left American, an offer first made as early as 1946, when he showed Ham Hale an actual Hughes contract and told Hale:

"Ham, I never wanted to work for anybody but American and C.R. Smith, but I can't anymore. I want you to take a look at this contract I've been offered."

Obviously, Damon did resist that particular temptation, and whether he received further offers from Hughes over the next two years Hale did not know. He probably did, for Hughes was a persistent recruiter who never learned to accept the word no. Damon became TWA's president only six days after resigning, and C.R. himself was convinced Damon had made a deal with Hughes prior to the AOA sale and used the deal as an excuse to leave.

Damon retained a soft spot in his heart for American, however, and it was reciprocated by many employees. He was in Boston on a business trip and at the airport stopped to see some of his old associates, who formed an impromptu reception line as soon as his presence became known. He halted in front of a black skycap.

"Charlie, aren't you about to get your ten-year pin?"

The skycap grinned and nodded.

Damon handed him a $20 bill. "Now you go out tonight and buy your wife a good dinner."

He served as TWA's chief just shy of seven years and died in harness. He had gone to the roof of a New York hotel on a cold December night, without wearing a coat, to attend a lighting ceremony for a new TWA sign that looked down on Times Square. He caught a cold that developed into pneumonia—fatal for a man whose resistance already was weakened by a succession of weird self-prescribed diets he followed in violation of medical advice; one involved nothing but ginger sticks and coffee, on which he subsisted for several weeks.

His relations with Hughes didn't help his health, either. Dixon Speas saw him two weeks before he died, and Damon unburdened himself.

"You know, Dix, I never thought I would work for a man and refuse to take his calls. I've refused to accept any call from him after midnight. He'd call me at one or two o'clock in the morning, talk all night, and then expect me to work all the next day."

His unhappiness was as evident as his deteriorated health, yet it is a known fact that of all the TWA presidents who served under the eccentric billionaire, Ralph Damon was the only one he truly respected. In that, Hughes had a lot of company. When Damon died, he was mourned by two airlines.

* * *

Some historians claim Trippe shafted C.R., obtaining American Overseas for a price far lower than its real value. The final sale figure was slightly over $17.4 million for AOA's assets and assumption of its liabilities. The assets were evaluated at around $13 million and the debts totaled just under $4.5 million, about a fourth of that amount owed to American.

Physical assets were rather slim, consisting mostly of AOA's outmoded fleet —seven 049 Constellations and several DC-4s. But Pan Am also acquired the rights to those sixteen new Stratocruisers; in the nearly two years it took for the sale to run the regulatory obstacle course, American Overseas operated only eight of them and Pan Am picked up the rest on its own.

The value of AOA's biggest asset, its routes, was rather intangible. Both sides arrived at an approximate figure of $10 million, which may, indeed, have been a bargain, considering that Trippe got rid of a tough competitor on routes that would prove lucrative in the explosive surge of transatlantic traffic during the 1950s. He also received a tax rebate and retroactive mail pay owed AOA, amounting to some $5 million.

Yet MacIntyre always considered the deal fair, noting the circumstances under which it was made. AOA seemed to be getting nowhere, and it *was* draining American, which itself was financially strapped from its huge DC-6 and Convair order. The original agreement signed that December 13 called for American to acquire a large chunk of Pan Am stock instead of cash, but this was changed to a straight cash deal. An airline could acquire stock in another carrier so long as the shares didn't involve majority control of the latter. But MacIntyre and Friendly had second thoughts, fearing that the CAB would never let it go through, it looked too much like a potential merger.

MacIntyre's sharpest memory of the sale was not of the actual negotiations but of an incident that occurred right after the agreement was signed. He and C.R. left the Chrysler Building and were walking up Lexington in the direction of Smith's apartment when C.R. remarked, "This is a great day, Mac. Look at this."

He pulled out of his pocket a check and handed it to the lawyer. "I just sold my half-interest in a Nevada ranch to E. L. Cord."

MacIntyre examined the check—it was in six figures—and handed it back. "C.R., that's great. Except Cord didn't sign it," he said gently.

"I thought he was going to faint," Mac remembered. "He turned three different shades of white. Cord signed it later, of course, but he almost gave C.R. a heart attack."

The irony of the AOA sale was that by the time Pan Am finally took it over, in the fall of 1950, American Overseas was a better airline than the one for which Trippe had paid $17.4 million.

It accomplished this feat in spite of some pretty stiff odds, not the least of which was maintaining morale on a carrier facing extinction. AOA had established a tradition of excellent service, and its people maintained it right to the end.

AOA's aggressiveness made up for its handicap of size, and American was a major help in this respect. Its sales personnel worked as hard for AOA as they did for American. A key figure was Walter Johnson, an ex-Marine destined to rise high in the executive ranks; he was made a regional vice president after the war, and AOA's marketing efforts in the New York area were largely his responsibility.

Johnson organized an ethnic sales effort that no airline had ever tried, and he aimed it squarely at a Pan Am miscalculation: its belief that only the wealthy and famous were interested in flying abroad. As he explained it:

"Juan Trippe's idea of building Pan Am was to fly movie stars and the upper levels of the business, legal, and investment communities. When we got involved with AOA, the elevated still ran on Third Avenue and it was manned exclusively by Irish trainmen who, like Irish cops dominated the police force, ran the IRT for fifty years. We had one salesman who did nothing but work the police stations, the IRT, and the Third Avenue saloons, including Tim Costello's. We wound up with a 92 percent share of the market between New York and Ireland. Hell, we *owned* the Irish business, because we went out and mined it.

"Same thing with the German market. We did all our sales work on 86th Street in Yorkville, and we held our presentations and travel agent meetings in the *brauhaus* at the Ruppert Brewery. We'd have sixty German-speaking travel agents belting down steins of beer and singing German drinking songs like they were in downtown Berlin.

"We carried the charwomen who cleaned the office buildings at night, all the Irish cops—in other words, we developed the first market for ordinary people who had never traveled by air. There never was a time when AOA couldn't outsell Pan Am by ten to one between New York and Germany and Ireland, because we knew where the business was while they were still working on high-level contacts."

The Scandinavian market was AOA's biggest headache. Not many Americans traveled to Norway, Denmark, or Sweden in those days, and SAS, an extremely efficient and popular carrier, dominated what business there was. Part of C.R.'s negativism toward AOA's chances could be traced to his belief that it was almost impossible to operate profitably in the North Atlantic without government subsidy, and he hated any government handout. He kept pointing out that the foreign competition was mostly subsidized by their respective governments and didn't have to worry about the black-ink bottom line so important to any U.S. overseas airline.

Smith also wasn't too sanguine about the Stratocruiser, officially designated the B-377. Pan Am, which had ordered twenty, began operating its Stratocruisers in September 1948, almost a year ahead of AOA. But the early reports on Juan Trippe's new queen were disturbing. The 377 appeared to be afflicted with more than a new plane's share of ailments.

The four-engine Stratocruiser, like its predecessor Stratoliner, had bomber ancestry. It was designed during the war as a transport version of the B-29 and utilized the latter's wings, tail, landing gear, and engines. Only the fuselage was new, and this was the best part of the 377. It was a double-deck design, the upper section featuring an unusually spacious cabin, wider and higher than the DC-6. The lower deck had excellent cargo and baggage space plus a feature never before put on a transport aircraft: a cocktail lounge, with a spiral staircase leading to the upper cabin.

Roominess plus the unique lounge made the Stratocruiser a passenger's dream, but for the airlines it was a plumber's nightmare. It used the same powerful but temperamental R-4360 engines that had proved so unsatisfactory in the Rainbow and had given the Air Force's B-29s an abnormally high rate of engine failures. To save weight—the 377 was 25,000 pounds heavier than the DC-6—Boeing equipped the huge engines with hollow-blade propellers.

Instead of being solid metal, the props had a spongy batting material inside that could work loose, shift to the blade tips, and cause an imbalance capable of failing the propeller. The Stratocruisers for several years suffered so many engine and propeller malfunctions that AOA's crews began calling the 377 "Boeing's trimotor."

But the big bird had its virtues. Structurally it adhered to the Boeing tradition of immense strength. Stratocruiser pilots always said they'd rather fly one through a thunderstorm than any plane they knew. Cockpit visibility was superior to that of its Douglas rivals, and for all its great weight the 377 was easier to handle than AOA's old Connies and the trucklike DC-4.

American Overseas introduced the Stratocruiser August 17, 1949, and operated its eight-plane fleet for a year with a perfect safety record before turning them over to Pan Am. They carried the names *Flagship Europe, Holland, Ireland, Scotland, Denmark, Sweden, Norway,* and *Great Britain,* the latter being changed later to *Scandinavia.*

The inaugural, New York–London on *Flagship Europe,* also happened to be the first commercial flight operated out of the new Idlewild Airport. The Stratocruiser, carrying forty-three passengers, took ten minutes under thirteen hours—the 377 wasn't much faster than the early Connies, and slower than the DC-6.

But comfort, not speed, was the Stratocruiser's greatest attraction, and that lounge was something else. It was advertised to hold fourteen passengers (two more than the entire cabin of a Boeing 247), although fourteen people made it pretty cramped. Rex Smith used the lounge for a publicity gimmick; he had a 150-pound Powers baby grand piano installed in the lounge of *Flagship Scotland* and got a young singer to give a concert on a flight to London. The artist was Frank Sinatra.

The Stratocruiser's introductory promotion included an "American Discovery" flight that carried European writers and editors to the U.S., where they visited several cities, including Los Angeles. Rex had been a Hollywood publicist at one time and he put on a memorable luncheon in one of the major studio commissaries for the European visitors. Among the stars present were Clark Gable, Cary Grant, Elizabeth Taylor, and Humphrey Bogart.

Rex's sense of humor and his apparently bottomless reservoir of publicity ideas were a tonic to his boss at a time when the AOA–Pan Am deal threatened to come apart. The monkey wrench was being wielded by none other than Ralph Damon's TWA, trying hard to convince the CAB that approval would strengthen Pan Am to the point where through sheer size it could smother any competition. Howard Westwood represented American and Henry Friendly appeared for Pan Am at the CAB hearings on the sale; they were considered the best aviation lawyers in Washington. But Trippe's absorption of AOA was opposed by virtually the entire industry, a formidable phalanx to argue against.

In the fall of 1950, the CAB by a 3–2 vote rejected the American–Pan Am agreement, the majority finding that it would increase Pan Am's dominance of the international market and put undue hardship on TWA. The decision, however, was not final; by law, any CAB decision involving international routes had to be approved by the President of the United States.

The current occupant at 1500 Pennsylvania Avenue was Harry Truman, who most observers figured was close to Kansas City–based TWA—a belief with considerable validity. Whereas American had enjoyed a good relationship with Franklin Roosevelt and his family, Truman really did prefer TWA and traveled on it frequently before he became President. His only connection with American was his insistence that Hank Myers stay on as commander of Air Force One; he was really fond of this particular American Airlines captain.

Someone once reminded Truman that Myers was a registered Republican.

"I'd rather have a Republican who can fly than a Democrat who can't," Truman retorted.

When the Air Force decided to retire the DC-4 known as the *Sacred Cow* and acquire a new Presidential aircraft, Myers was said to have played a role in the choice. Jack Frye was still president of TWA at the time and lobbied hard in behalf of a Constellation as the new Air Force One. C.R. heard about his efforts, reportedly from Myers, and wrote him a scorching letter that, in effect, told Frye to stay the hell out of the decision-making process.

How much influence Myers actually had is uncertain, but the aircraft chosen was a DC-6 originally intended for American and diverted off the assembly line to the Air Force. It was christened the *Independence,* and this was the plane Hank Myers was flying the day Truman talked him into buzzing the White House—a sin that normally would have cost Myers his license permanently.

Unfortunately, Truman didn't consult his flying pal when it came to judging the merits of the CAB decision. The Board's verdict went to the White House, and there ensued one of the wildest controversies in airline history.

According to most accounts, Truman first approved the CAB decision, then changed his mind under pressure from Speaker of the House Sam Rayburn and okayed AOA's sale to Pan Am. Rayburn was known to be close to one of C.R.'s best friends, lawyer Raymond Buck of Fort Worth. It was said by one political veteran that "Sam Rayburn owned Lyndon Johnson but Raymond Buck owned Sam Rayburn."

There were rumors that Truman actually had sent a signed document to the CAB upholding its decision before announcing that he would reverse that decision. Damon dispatched Tom Taylor of TWA's Washington office to check the CAB files; he reported back that there was such a document—*with Harry Truman's signature erased.* And he testified to that effect in court, under oath, after TWA filed a lawsuit charging illegal altering of a legal document.

The litigation went all the way to the U.S. Supreme Court, which upheld the sale, but to this day TWA officials believe their airline was robbed through political pressure bordering on skulduggery. Yet while the evidence Taylor saw may support that political pressure theory, someone else may have been just as influential as Speaker Rayburn in getting Truman to change his mind.

And that person was Carlene Roberts.

Aware that the President might well be leaning in TWA's direction, she kept in close touch with White House sources as soon as Truman began deliberating the case. And Carlene Roberts had as good contacts there as any airline representative in Washington. She wasn't alone in that regard, of course; the law requiring presidential approval of international route decisions had turned such cases into political footballs, and airline lobbyists worked their beats hard.

"Someone at the White House indicated," she related, "that the President wanted to approve the sale but with a competitive route structure, and that the President had been given to understand that it would have been impossible to achieve this without further proceedings, and that he had been told he could do nothing to accomplish this objective except to disapprove the AOA sale at this time."

The "someone" obviously was referring to a compromise that had been suggested during the hearings. The CAB had indicated it might approve the sale if Pan Am would agree to let TWA compete against it on certain routes. But this solution ran afoul of a provision in the sales agreement that allowed either American or Pan Am to withdraw if the CAB insisted on more competition from TWA for Trippe's airline.

Roberts dropped broad hints, albeit in deliberately cautious language, that this provision was no longer an obstacle. "I suggested," she said, "that the nature of the available courses of action on the record of the case as it stood then could readily be explained (to the President) by persons at the CAB familiar with the record."

C.R., of course, wouldn't have cared if the CAB had given TWA the key to Juan Trippe's private bathroom—that provision was Trippe's idea. But faced with the distinct possibility of losing AOA, Trippe agreed to eliminate it, and Carlene Roberts did the rest by giving Harry Truman the out he needed. The charges of illegal tampering and claims of back-door politics were rendered moot when the President issued his official approval of AOA's sale: he simultaneously gave TWA authority to serve London (which Damon wanted badly) and Frankfurt, and put Pan Am into Paris and Rome, which made everybody reasonably happy.

Except, perhaps, the loyal troops of American Overseas. The pilots in particular, traditionally close-knit, were the unhappiest of them all. They were leaving behind them a proud record. In its entire existence, AOA suffered only one fatal accident, a DC-4 that hit a mountain at Newfoundland just after takeoff. A last-minute 90-degree change in wind direction was the key factor in the crash.

Jim Flynn, the stern but popular taskmaster who ran AOA's flight operations, required all copilots to fly at least once with virtually every captain on the airline's roster. When it came time for a copilot to be upgraded to the left seat, Flynn would gather reports on him from the captains the candidate had flown with. Then he would ask certain captains one question: "Would you be willing to let your family fly with this guy in command?" And it was Flynn himself who gave the final upgrading check ride.

He was one of the few AOA pilots who declined to don the white uniform caps of Pan Am; he opted instead to go eventually with Collins Radio. He was proud of many things in his AOA carreer, but uppermost was the airline's performance during the Berlin Airlift of 1948–49. For 274 tension-ridden days, more than two million West Berliners cut off from all coal and food supplies by a Soviet blockade were supplied entirely by air. AOA was a comparatively small airline, but during that time it flew more than 28,000 passengers and nearly 13 million pounds of cargo between Frankfurt and Berlin.

AOA had its own Award of Merit system; one went to Eric Bleich, who was in charge of flight operations for the airlift. Another was given to stewardess Mary Jane Hinckley, who helped deliver a baby at 19,000 feet over the Atlantic —a single life just as important, in its own very personal way, as the 2.1 million lives AOA helped save in the airlift.

But these were deeds of the past. There was no future for American Overseas. Truman's approval came in July 1950. On September 25, this notice went on every bulletin board in the AA–AOA system:

> The sale of American Overseas Airlines to Pan American World Airways was completed tonight.
>
> > C. R. Smith

All that remained were pride . . . and memories.

In years to come, one of the most frequently asked questions of C.R. was whether he regretted the sale. He usually ducked answering it, but he told one interviewer it reminded him of a story about a football quarterback who went into a barbershop for a haircut. Continued Smith:

"The barber says to him, 'You know, I don't think I would have thrown that pass Saturday.' And the quarterback says, 'I don't think I would have thrown it either, if I had until Monday to think it over.'

"On the basis of the situation at the time of the decision, we did right, I believe. On the basis of the situation many years later, the decision is debatable."

* * *

Two years of nail-biting over AOA didn't mean that American had been standing still, waiting for the outcome.

In 1948, the airline had come up with one of those innovative marketing plans for which it has always been famous. It implemented the industry's first family fare plan, a rather daring idea at a time when the airlines generally were trying to raise fares.

The family fare originated in American's economic planning committee and was the direct result of a question C.R. kept asking: Would lower fares generate enough additional traffic to more than make up for the reduced revenues? The usual answer he got was negative: There wasn't enough elasticity in the air travel market to get back what was lost with reduced fares.

But when Smith kept asking the same question, the committee launched an unusual study. For six months, it tracked load factors for each day of the week, and an interesting pattern emerged. Traffic was extremely high Friday and Sunday. It dropped much lower on Monday and dipped even more Tuesday through Thursday. And the lowest load factors occurred between Saturday noon and Sunday noon.

C.R.'s original suggestion to fill empty seats was to offer "space available" at a 50 percent discount. The committee argued him out of it, pointing out that too many passengers would simply wait around to see if a seat was available; at a 50 percent discount, the lower yield would offset the higher load factors. But the committee was intrigued by that weekly load factor pattern, and under the direction of Art Lewis, the family fare plan was developed.

Initially it offered wives a 50 percent discount if they flew with husbands paying full fare between Saturday noon and Sunday noon. This was considered too restricted, so the plan was extended to the low-traffic weekdays, Tuesday through Thursday. Every industry survey showed that few women were flying anyway, so the increase was incremental, not a diversion of male traffic to low-load periods.

The family fare was an instant success, both in public reception and financially, although American was exclusive with it for only two months when United led other airlines in adopting similar plans. Lewis found out, however, that United had conducted the same load factor study as American, but its immediate response was to cut schedules, not fares, Tuesday through Thursday. Once more, American had beaten its competition to the punch.

It also came very close to being the first airline in the world to operate a jet-powered airliner. Not only is that a little-known fact, but the airplane involved has been almost forgotten, a mere footnote in the history of commercial aviation.

The story began in the summer of 1949, shortly after Dixon Speas became C.R.'s special assistant, a post whose duties frequently involved technical matters. Smith had heard about a jet-powered transport designed by Avro of Canada, a subsidiary of Britain's Hawker-Siddeley; Sir Roy Dobson, head of the parent company, was a friend of C.R.'s.

The plane was the Avro Jetliner, officially the C-102, powered by four Rolls-Royce Derwent turbine engines. The prototype's maiden flight was August 10, 1949, only two weeks after Britain's much publicized de Havilland Comet, which was being touted as the most revolutionary transport ever built. Both jets were about the same size, but the Avro was designed to serve shorter domestic routes; the Comet was aimed at the international market.

"Go up to Toronto and look it over," C.R. told Speas, who spent several days in Canada inspecting the new jet and taking a demonstration ride. He returned to New York and informed Smith he was greatly impressed.

"It's quite an airplane, C.R.," he said, "and frankly, they've asked me to join Avro as U.S. manager. I'd be in charge of marketing, final development, and certification."

Smith frowned. "You don't have to answer them today, do you?"

"No, sir."

"Well, think about it tonight and see me tomorrow."

Speas went home and discussed the offer with his wife, Minette, who urged him to accept. The next day, he told C.R. he had decided to go with Avro, and braced for the expected explosion.

"Dix, I think it's a good opportunity not only for you but American," C.R. said calmly. "There are going to be jets without question, and the experience will do you a lot of good. So why don't you just take a year's leave of absence and come back to us?"

Speas agreed and began a twelve-month tour of duty with Avro, spending most of his time demonstrating the Jetliner to U.S. airlines, including American, United, TWA, National, and Eastern. It *was* quite an airplane, too. It cruised at 500 miles an hour, with a full payload range of 1,240 miles; passenger capacity was forty to fifty-two, depending on what configuration an airline wanted.

The Avro's most impressive demonstration flight was from Miami to New York in a record two hours and twenty-three minutes, at a cruising altitude of 35,000 feet. National's president, Ted Baker, was aboard and later signed a contract for three Jetliners plus an option on three more, contingent on Avro going into production.

American's demonstration flight was from Indianapolis to Washington National. When they landed, Speas found the entire U.S. Navy high command at the airport waiting for the arrival of a plane carrying the body of an admiral who had died at sea. Speas, who had been trying to sell the Navy some Jetliners, invited the gold-braided brass on a ride.

They were airborne and thoroughly enjoying the flight when an admiral asked Speas, "This aircraft's been certified by the CAA, I assume?"

"No, sir," Dix confessed. "It's experimental."

The admiral roared, "Get this goddamned thing on the ground! You've got the whole Navy Department on board!"

Speas didn't sell any to the Navy or, with the exception of National's tentative order, to any airline. C.R. told him, "We aren't buying any airplanes right now, Dix," and Speas was disappointed but not surprised. American already had ordered eleven DC-6Bs, a stretched version of the DC-6 equipped with the finest piston engine ever developed, the Pratt & Whitney R-2800-CR17, which had 400 more horsepower than the standard R-2800 on the Six and became the most reliable reciprocating power plant in history. The 6B was five feet longer than the Six, forty m.p.h. faster, and had several hundred miles greater range. Overall, the DC-6B was rated the best piston transport that ever flew.

C.R.'s optimism for the DC-6's big brother was only one reason why Speas's solid one-hour sales pitch got nowhere. He knew the jets were coming, but he didn't think they were just around the corner. And he was suspicious of such radically new designs as the Comet, a feeling shared by Littlewood. Even if he had bought the Avro, however, the chances are that American never would have operated it. The Korean War began in 1950 and Hawker-Siddeley ordered Avro to concentrate on military aircraft; the Jetliner never went into production.

With the project scrapped, Speas was about to return to American when General Electric commissioned him to do a study on adoption of military jet engines for commercial use. When he got a second consultant assignment, he decided to start his own aviation consulting firm;' it was Smith who helped him get established by recommending him to a number of airline and aviation firms. Dixon Speas & Associates became one of the world's outstanding consulting companies, but its founder never lost his affection for American and the man who headed it.

The Avro Jetliner was an airplane ahead of its time, but it is fascinating to speculate on the course of events if C.R. had succumbed to his gambler's instinct and bought it. If American had been the "launch" airline, given its leadership reputation, this alone might have triggered a follow-the-leader impetus and the jet age would have begun years before it actually did. It is difficult to measure the C-102's real worth from the performance and record of the one prototype that was built, but aeronautical engineers say it was a better airplane in every respect except range than the tragic Comet, especially in the vital area of structural integrity.

In retrospect, however, C.R.'s rejection can't be faulted. The last thing American needed at that time was the headache of introducing a revolutionary transport plane when it was just beginning to adjust to its new family of conventional pistons. The industry as a whole was emerging from the postwar doldrums, and the eagle had plenty of beaks pecking at its tail feathers.

There is no doubt that Bill Hogan, for all his difficult personality, contributed much to the airline's maintaining its front-running status. In 1949, for example, American's operating costs were the lowest in the industry, an achievement attributed largely to Hogan's insistence that every department stay within its allotted budget. This was anathema to freewheelers like Mosier, but he was outclassed in any head-to-head butting contest with Hogan; Red's great influence with C.R. turned flabby when the chief was forced to take sides.

A few officers did get along with Hogan, although it frequently was more in the nature of an armed truce. Malcolm MacIntyre liked him, in spite of an argument they had when the new treasurer first joined American. Hogan thought Mac should report only to him on certain legal matters, and MacIntyre bluntly said, "No way."

"He yelled and slammed the table," MacIntyre laughed, "but after that we worked well together. I know he was one tough cookie, but I would have to say that Bill Hogan, in all my years of airline experience, was the finest financial officer any carrier ever had. Without question, he was the most imaginative, and a hell of a good accountant. He wasn't just a good bookkeeper —he *understood* finance like no one else."

It was Hogan as much as Littlewood who engineered the decision to order the DC-6B, an aircraft so superb in its testing phase that American wound up with twenty-five. And his influence on the purchase of new airplanes grew in direct proportion to his stature in C.R.'s eyes. Nor was Smith's trust misplaced. Walt Johnson, whose own star at American was rising fast in the late forties, pointed out that before Hogan, American considered mostly the input of engineers and pilots in buying planes. "Hogan," Johnson said, "injected for the first time the principles of financial analysis, revenue capability, and profit potential."

But, Johnson added:

"He was one of the most competent men I ever knew, but also one of the most disagreeable. He made his career by climbing over people, by downgrading them without cause as if that was the only way he could make progress. Jake Jacob was one of the finest, most lovable men I ever met and Hogan badgered him mercilessly. I heard him say terrible things about Jake and Mosier, but Red was as tough as Hogan and stood up to him.

"Everybody was at a disadvantage in dealing with Hogan. It was a big, happy family then, both professionally and socially, and Hogan was the one jarring note in an atmosphere of mutual respect. With the exception of Mosier, none of us was psychologically geared to meet in combat every day a guy who every day was after your balls."

Hogan used to call officers he didn't like or respect—and his list seemed to be longer than the names on a DC-6 passenger manifest—by their last name, never the first. Johnson finally got fed up with Hogan's snarled greeting of "Johnson!" and began snarling back with "Yes, Hogan?"

One of the first times they met, Hogan growled disdainfully, "You're one of those guys with a daily expense account."

"It's part of my job," Walt retorted. "I'm *supposed* to take important people to lunch."

But the explanation did no good. Johnson, a vice president at thirty-one and highly regarded throughout the industry, became one of Hogan's favorite targets. Another was Wayne McMillan, American's first real economist. He was an honor graduate from the University of Illinois and was hired in the late thirties when C.R., that indefatigable recruiter, heard about a thesis he had written on air express. Smith not only gave him a job but made him his personal assistant—the assignment Dixon Speas took on when McMillan was promoted to director of economic planning.

Wayne was smart and hard-working; his future at American looked bright until Hogan arrived and the new chain of command dictated that McMillan report to him. They clashed almost immediately, and for several years McMiilan endured Hogan's invectives before he got fed up and left for a responsible post at a New York bank. Bob Tuttle, a good friend of McMillan, said Hogan actually fired Wayne. If true, it would be indicative of Hogan's power within the airline and C.R.'s reliance on his skills.

Disliked and even feared, yes. But no account of his unpleasant characteristics is complete without also mentioning what even his worst enemies invariably conceded: American badly needed a William J. Hogan as it moved into the decade of the 1950s and neared the greatest revolution in the history of aviation technology:

The jet age.

14
The Last Stand of the Pistons

From cockpit to cocktails, each new generation of Flagships brought greater complexity.

Airborne weather radar was one development in which American had played a pioneering role. As early as 1946, a test unit was installed on *Flagship Alpha* and Dan Beard's enthusiasm for this important safety device led to an improved model going into one of the DC-4s flown by the contract cargo division for further testing.

In-flight weather radar was an offshoot of World War II technology. The principle was simple: the device projected a radio beam ahead of the aircraft, and when the beam encountered precipitation, such as that generated by a thunderstorm, it bounced back to the plane a signal measuring the amount of that precipitation. The signal appeared in the form of a pattern on a radar screen in front of the pilot.

The tests on American's DC-4, *Flagship St. Joseph,* were promising, but also revealed an unacceptably high degree of unreliability and misleading signals. Regretfully, even Beard had to admit that radar needed further refinement, and it was put on the back burner for several years. But by the mid fifties, newer models had eradicated all the bugs and United became the first carrier to equip its entire fleet, preceding a government order requiring it.

American followed suit, and while United was justly praised for adopting radar voluntarily, everyone forgot Beard's frequently dangerous test flights years before. He had flown around deliberately looking for thunderstorms to penetrate.

It cost some $5 million to equip all the Convairs, DC-6s, and DC-6Bs with this turbulence-avoiding device, but it was money well spent. Before radar, which measured turbulence by the amount of precipitation the beam was recording, an airline the size of American and United was spending almost $1 million a year to repair aircraft damage from hail, turbulence, and lightning strikes, and to pay for the extra fuel consumed when a flight was delayed or had to detour around storms.

Sophistication extended to the cabin, too. For short-haul passengers, the 240 provided them with their first carry-on luggage racks. And gone were the old meal jugs that were still being used on DC-3s after the war. All Flagships had individually heated entrees, developed by Newt Wilson and his Sky Chefs technicians.

At the stewardess school, shifted from Tulsa to Chicago, trainees had liquor service added to their curriculum. The industry had begun serving alcoholic beverages simply because the majority of passengers wanted it, particularly on longer flights. United was the last holdout. Pat Patterson said serving booze would turn his stewardesses into cocktail waitress. But even Patterson had to cave in eventually when all the trunk carriers adopted liquor service.

C.R. wasn't that happy about it, either, although he was no teetotaler himself—he liked good bourbon. He didn't have Patterson's moral objections, but he felt free cocktails were an added expense the airlines could do without. And he was a little surprised at the shift in public opinion, because a 1946 survey by American showed an eight-to-five sentiment *against* liquor being served on airplanes.

That survey was one of the most extensive ever conducted by an airline. It represented more than 27,000 individual responses to a questionnaire on what people expected and wanted from postwar air travel. Their opinions went into American's planning for its Convairs and DC-6s. Asked what they desired in the way of "extras," for example, an overwhelming majority gave pressurized cabins as their first choice—a preference that helped dictate American's decision to put pressurization on the Convairs as well as the DC-6s.

(Other suggested extras included individual radios with earphones, illuminated trip progress panels, in-flight telephones, a library of current books, and a teletype news service.)

Nearly 70 percent said they'd be willing to pay extra for faster flights. Almost 75 percent turned thumbs down on paying higher fares for a flight that gave them more space by providing fewer seats. Two-thirds preferred reserved open seating rather than specific seat assignments, and more than 70 percent said they were against a no-reservations service on frequently scheduled, short-haul "commuter" flights. (Remember, this was fifteen years before Eastern launched its Shuttle.)

Three out of four opted for female cabin attendants over male stewards, while about the same percentage said they'd rather check all luggage instead of carrying it onto the plane. And by a four-to-one ratio, they voted against an extra charge for a choice of more than one entrée.

By the fifties, of course, that survey was outdated in most respects. Yet the preference for speed—which meant saving time—didn't change as a key factor in transport aircraft design. This was especially true in the transcontinental market, where as little as a twenty-minute advantage seemed important to passengers. The DC-6's speed bulge over the early Constellation led to the development of faster Connies, which, in turn, prompted Douglas to build the DC-6B. The competition was a never-ending war in the golden age of the pistons, as American was to demonstrate before long.

Technology, however, didn't reduce American's supply of cockpit characters; there still was room for pilots like Dan Henry, who became almost as famous as Si Bittner, though for different reasons. Henry was a good pilot, but somewhat eccentric, to the point of driving his supervisors to drink. Before joining American, he ran a shoestring air taxi operation and he also owned a small bus on whose front fender was Henry's trademark: a machinist's vise welded to the metal. Its purpose was unknown except to Henry himself, and he had so many explanations that no one could figure out which one, if any, was the true story. He welded the same vise to the fender of every car he ever owned from then on.

American's chief pilot at LaGuardia during the fifties was a corncob-tough old airman named Harry "Red" Clark. Of all the pilots who tested his patience, Dan Henry led the pack. His colleagues lost count of the number of times Clark fired him, only to have Henry somehow squirm out of his clutches and win reinstatement.

Came the day when Red really did fire him and Henry was brought before a formal CAA hearing with lawyers present representing American, the government, and the errant airman. Walt Braznell, system chief pilot, was on the stand testifying and ALPA's attorney, defending Dan, asked, "What's wrong with Captain Henry?"

"Well, I think the man's unstable," Braznell declared.

"Give me an example of this so-called instability. There's nothing on his record to that effect."

Braznell frowned. "I think any man who welds a machinist's vise onto the fender of a brand-new automobile could be called unstable," he said firmly.

Henry jumped to his feet, demanding that he be allowed to explain this alleged idiosyncrasy. Captain John McCarten, who was a spectator at the hearing, said the next few minutes were unbelievable.

"Dan was fascinating," McCarten remembered in awe. "He was so logical that he had the whole damned hearing convinced it would be idiotic NOT to have a machinist's vise on all cars. The most dramatic part of his argument came when he claimed he had used the vise to locate a gas leak in his apartment and thereby saved the lives of everyone in the building. He never did really explain how the hell a vise on a car fender could locate a gas leak, but he had everybody so hypnotized he got away with it."

Among Henry's newly won supporters was Braznell. After the hearing, he walked up to McCarten, shaking his head. "Jesus, Mac, I think I'll go out and have one welded onto my Cadillac."

Having won this reprieve, Henry resumed his role as the bane of Red Clark's existence. Inevitably, he got into hot water again and Clark fired him again. This transgression happened to be relatively minor, however, and several pilots, including McCarten, talked Red into taking him back. They informed Henry they had just saved his butt and told him, "Look, we got your job back, including the retroactive pay you've lost, so we'll all go in and see Harry and we'll assure him you're going to behave."

One pilot added a word of caution. "But remember, Dan, don't say anything. Just keep quiet. It's in the bag. We'll just let Red make his little speech and you've got no problem."

The delegation accompanied the repentant sinner to Clark's office and one of the pilots representing ALPA went through his prearranged charade, a heart-rending plea for mercy.

Red listened judicially and finally held up his hand like a benign bishop. "Well, fellas, I don't want to be unreasonable. Actually, I've only fired one copilot, and that's because he was a fairy."

Henry stepped forward and shook an accusing finger in the chief pilot's face. "What right do you have interfering with a man's personal life?" he demanded.

Red turned purple. "All right, you son of a bitch!" he roared. "This time you *are* fired, and you'll stay fired!"

The ALPA man turned to McCarten. "I don't care if the guy pays double dues," he sighed. "I'll never defend him again."

But once more Henry managed to escape execution and make it to honorable retirement. Not without further demonstrations of eccentricity, however. He was flying with a new copilot who casually lit a cigarette. Henry reached into his "brainbag" (the bulky pilot briefcase containing manuals, maps, etc.) and pulled out a NO SMOKING sign. The young copilot hastily doused the cigarette.

Henry said nothing, but a few minutes later, out of the captain's brainbag came a flask, and Henry took a healthy swig. The copilot grumbled, "Goddammit, if there's going to be drinking in the cockpit, I'm gonna smoke."

"It's my orange juice," Dan said in a hurt tone.

It really was orange juice. Henry didn't drink or smoke and actually was rather a straight-arrow kind of person. Retired Captain Ray Newhouse, a good friend of Henry's, said he just couldn't resist acting flaky.

"He was flying with a rookie copilot to Boston and the weather was terrible," Newhouse recounted. "Every so often he'd take out that flask and swig. By the time they got to Boston, the poor copilot was a quivering wreck. Sometimes Dan would do things with tongue in cheek. He used to carry raw carrots in his pocket. He'd let the copilot make a night landing, and just as they were on final approach, he'd hand the guy a carrot."

Another Harry Clark nemesis was a captain named Desmond Shipley. He always wore black leather gloves and a wine-colored scarf. Both Newhouse and McCarten knew him well.

"I've never forgotten him," Newhouse said. "He'd park himself in the left seat, pull on those black gloves, and glare at you. He was a terror on copilots."

"You had to go right at him," McCarten added, "and then he'd like you. He used to have Red Clark foaming at the mouth. Shipley was a damned good pilot, but he hated authority and chief pilots represented authority.

"Shipley was a good ALPA member and a tough negotiator for the union, but he never got very far with Clark. He led a union delegation into Harry's office once and before he could open his mouth, Red says, 'Get the hell out of here, Shipley.' "

Added to Clark's list of pilots-I-could-do-without was one Jack Keller, a very methodical captain who could have flown halfway from New York to Boston in the time it took him to read a pre-takeoff checklist. He was dawdling over his checklist at LaGuardia one day and Clark, check-riding in a Convair right behind him, got impatient. He called Keller on the radio, fuming, "For Christ's sake, are you gonna take all day?"

Back came Keller's hurt voice. "Gee, Red, now you're yelling at me through closed windows."

In his spare time, Keller was a cruise director for a shipping line, an avocation that frequently disrupted his flight duties. Clark would phone him, screaming, "When in the hell are you coming back to work?"

Keller once pranged a Convair nose gear landing at Richmond. Red flew down there to interrogate him and opened up with the natural question, "Okay, Keller, what the hell happened?"

Jack looked at him innocently. "Well, to begin with, Harry, it was a piss-poor landing."

Clark left American eventually to go with Flying Tiger. When he died some years ago, he was mourned by pilots who remembered what a pushover he could be—a barnacle-crusted exterior that fooled nobody. John McCarten summed it up best:

"He was a good man and he ran a good office. What you saw was what you got. If he had to discipline a pilot, he knew what really mattered. There probably were some guys he should have fired, but basically when it came to giving deserved boots in the ass, Harry could do it."

American had one pilot with the unusual monicker of Fay Reay—pronounced just like the actress who was King Kong's unattainable love. Everyone was always asking him, "How's the gorilla?" Reay was flying copilot on a Convair trip one night and the captain was Bob McDaniels. It was a miserable flight right from the start. The weather was foul and so was the stewardess who, according to McDaniels, "had enough paint on her face to cover three barns." They landed in Albany in a freezing rain and McDaniels announced, "I think we'll cancel."

They went to their layover hotel and McDaniels registered for the two of them. Reay, a big man who looked more like John Wayne than Fay Wray, stood in the background out of the desk clerk's sight.

The clerk said, "Captain McDaniels, I'll put you in Room 204 and Miss Reay in 310."

"The hell you will," McDaniels protested. "Fay's gonna sleep with me."

The fifties were the apogee of Rex Smith's public relations career.

There was general consensus that American and TWA had the best p.r. staffs in the industry, although no one who saw Rex at work would have suspected it. Anyone going by his office invariably would see him reading a newspaper, feet propped on desk, and giving the distinct impression that he was just plain lazy.

He *was* a bit lazy, but there wasn't one of his airline colleagues and counterparts who didn't envy his ability to conceive publicity gimmicks guaranteed to get into print. In today's more circumspect world of journalism, Rex's stunts would be considered cornball; in his day, the press went for them like fish after surefire bait. And he also was receptive to ideas from others.

He marked the introduction of DC-6 coach service to Boston by renting about fifty horses and re-enacting Paul Revere's ride. All the ersatz Paul Reveres were reporters he had finagled into taking part and it was a wonder nobody got killed. Yet from his own background, few would have thought him capable—or guilty—of thinking up such flamboyant affairs.

Willis Player's father was his boss at one time and taught him much about journalism. Rex started out as an Associated Press correspondent in Peru, and served as an editor on *Newsweek* and the Chicago *Sun* before joining the Air Force in World War II. C.R. met him when Rex was a colonel in public relations and convinced him to become his p.r. chief. It was significant that C.R. regarded public relations as a function of company policy, and he set that policy. As long as he headed American, he insisted that public relations report directly to him and he brooked no interference from marketing or any other department. Rex Smith operated independently, enjoying an autonomy that few airline p.r. directors possessed.

He also had the total respect of his rivals. He was Willis Player's mentor, a neat twist inasmuch as Player's father had been Rex's teacher. Player first met him at a 1947 meeting of airline p.r. directors in Norway, the participants representing member carriers of the newly formed International Air Transport Association (IATA).

It wasn't exactly a brotherly convention—Pan Am, TWA, and AOA were at one another's throats. Rex wasn't supposed to be there, but he was on a European trip and came to Oslo as a gesture of courtesy. Ralph Cohen of IATA thought it would be appropriate for American's new vice president of public relations to make a short speech, and that was when Player decided Rex Smith was a man to emulate.

"He had style," Player recalled. "He got up and established, in a few easy words, a unified U.S. position on international p.r. problems. He complimented Trippe and Frye. His whole speech was in perfect grace, and it made sense."

It is highly probable that placed in today's more worldly and cynical environment, when the news media often seems to have an adversary relationship with airlines, Rex Smith still would dominate his profession—he was that good.

At a time when the airlines were expanding so fast, route and new equipment inaugurals were the rage, and Rex had few peers in staging fancy and well-publicized inaugurals. Most aviation writers of that era thought American and TWA were best at that sort of thing. Rex relied heavily on an exceptionally able staff. One of its colorful members was Joe Harty, a dapper Irishman who worked out of the airline's Los Angeles office; Hollywood was the battle zone he covered most frequently.

Harty was a graduate engineer who found himself unemployed after the war and landed a job with American promoting air freight. His first assignment was

Three decades span these two photographs, but while the uniforms changed, the traditions did not. Top shot is that of American's first stewardesses. From top to bottom: May Bobeck, Agnes Nohava, Marie Allen, Velma Maul.

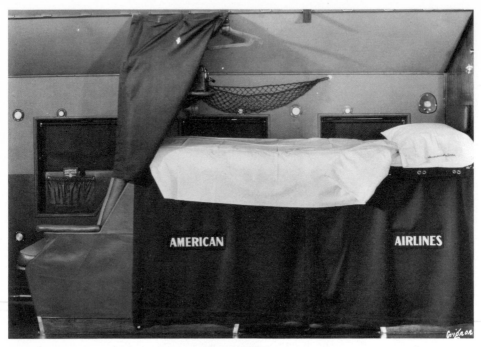

Air travel luxury a half-century ago. This was what a Condor berth looked like—note the hammock for sundry items.

The main (and only) terminal at old Hoover Field, serving the nation's capital. The "belfry" structure at the top was the control tower.

Typical ground transport in the fledgling days of commercial aviation—the late twenties and early thirties.

E. L. Cord insisted that his airline limos be the Auburns he made. Century became part of American.

Above: Charlie Speers tried to sell air travel in planes like this. The "TAC" was Thompson Aeronautical Corporation, which merged into AA.

Right: Air travel at its best —American's famous 747 piano bar.

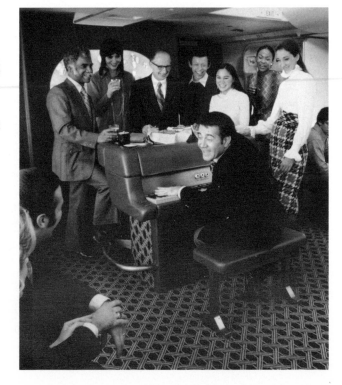

WHY DODGE THIS QUESTION:

Afraid to Fly?

C. R. Smith
PRESIDENT
AMERICAN AIRLINES, INC.

WE know that fear keeps many people from enjoying the advantages of air transportation. So *why should we be silent on this subject?* Regrettable as it is, the records show there *have been* accidents and fatalities in *every* form of transportation. What we do not understand, is why some people associate danger with a transport plane more than they do with a train, a boat, a motor car, an interurban, or a bus. Is it because airline accidents have received more publicity?

The fact is, there *are* risks involved in *all* kinds of travel. It is also a fact that the *air transportation industry has shown greater progress and achieved a much higher standard of efficiency in a shorter span of years than any other form of transportation the world has ever known.*

Why quote statistics? They are not always conclusive. They are often only controversial. I could show you figures to prove that you would have to fly around the world 425 times — or make approximately 14,365 flights back and forth between New York and Chicago — before you would be liable to meet with an accident. Do these statistics overcome your fear of flying? I think not. There is only one way to overcome that fear — and that is, to fly.

Many of our regular passengers, who now prefer air travel to any other form of transportation, admit they were very timid about their *first* flight. Perhaps you say: "It is my business if I want to go on being afraid and confine myself to

slower forms of transportation." No one questions that. The question is: "Is it good business?" Maybe your competitor is flying. Many people lived and died who never rode on a train because *they* were afraid. Today we smile at those old-fashioned fears. And today, to, the more than a million airline passengers of last year, the fear of air travel is just as old-fashioned.

American Airlines, Inc. has carried more than a million passengers. These people travel by air for the same reason they use the telephone, send telegrams, and ride in elevators. It is a quicker, more modern, more efficient way to accomplish what they want to do.

Are airlines safer than railroads? You can find intelligent people to take both sides of the argument.

Whether you fly or not, does not alter the fact that every form of transportation has *one* thing in common — risk! No form of transportation — on the ground, on the water, or in the air — can guarantee its passengers absolute immunity from danger.

This whole subject of fear about flying can be summed up as follows: PEOPLE ARE AFRAID OF THE THINGS THEY DO NOT KNOW ABOUT. You would be equally afraid of trains if you had never ridden on one.

As soon as you become acquainted with air transportation your fear will be replaced by your *enjoyment of the many advantages of air travel.*

AMERICAN AIRLINES INC.

Left: The most controversial advertisement in airline history.

Below: Historic inaugural: Flagship *Illinois* introduces DC-3 service on the New York–Chicago route. That's C. R. Smith in the straw hat, hand in pocket. Note the white uniform caps.

Mr. Smith goes to war, and that's A. N.
Kemp—American's least-known president—
wishing him well.

"I wonder who's catching it now?" C.R. at
his typewriter, probably taken in the late
thirties.

A Few of the Famous . . .

C. R. Smith

C. W. Jacob

William J. Hogan

Charles Rheinstrom

George Spater

Charlie Speers

O. M. "Red" Mosier

George Warde

The difference between $55,000 and $5 million was 35 years. The trimotor taxiing by the 707 is now on display at the National Air and Space Museum.

Three generations of generals. *Left to right:* Al Casey, C. R. Smith, and Bob Crandall.

the Los Angeles garment manufacturing district, where he invariably was told, "Sure I'll ship my stuff on American, provided you get me a seat next to some star like Greer Garson."

Equal if different difficulties were encountered when he made a pitch to Adrian, MGM's chief designer. He ordered Harty out of his office with a remark Joe never never forgot: "My creations are all handmade and I'll never risk them on one of your airplanes."

Harty finally struck pay dirt with a manufacturer who sold dresses to Macy's in New York. Joe suggested a joint promotion effort and thought up an accompanying slogan: "Created on the West Coast yesterday; on display in New York today!" Both Macy's and the dress company were delighted, and their praise reached the ears of Ken Frogley, then regional p.r. director in Los Angeles.

Frogley was something of a character himself. He started out with American in New York before the war and ran afoul of Mayor LaGuardia when an American DC-3 washed out its landing gear at the Little Flower's beloved airport. With the innocence of a rookie p.r. man, Frogley let photographers take pictures of the plane, and the mayor went into orbit. He thought this cast aspersions on his airport, and tried to get Frogley fired.

Ken was a major during the war and became mildly famous for being the last man at American to take off his uniform after the war ended. For weeks he walked around still wearing it. But he was considered a good p.r. man, and when he heard about Harty's feat, he discussed it with Rex Smith.

"Put him in public relations," Rex ordered.

"So Ken and I picked up my little desk and moved it from freight to p.r.," Harty related. "For a while I was lost. I didn't know anything about Hollywood, public relations, names of columnists, studio publicity officials, or anything else."

But he learned fast. Rex Smith stationed him in a small office at the Beverly Wilshire Hotel, where American had just established a new ticket office. Harty worked the Hollywood beat from there, although his early experiences with the studio publicity bigwigs were highly unsuccessful. He would call someone like Howard Strickling of MGM and start out, "This is Joe Harty at American. I see where Greer Garson's going out to New York with us tomorrow and I'd like to put out a little story on why she's going and—"

"We do our own publicity, Mr. Harty," Strickling would growl, and hang up.

The studio cold shoulders went on for several months, until Harty scored a breakthrough. American had just started an interchange arrangement with Delta to provide through service to the West Coast from Miami, New Orleans, and Atlanta. Both airlines operated DC-6s; Delta would fly passengers from those three cities to Dallas, where American crews would take over the same aircraft and complete the rest of the trip.

Harty got a call one day from Perry Lieber, p.r. head at RKO, which was then owned by Howard Hughes.

"Joe, Bob Mitchum's flying from Miami to LA on your interchange. He has some important contractual documents to sign in connection with Hughes selling the studio. Is there any way he can fly incognito? We don't want anybody to know he's on the plane."

"Sure," Joe agreed. "I'll pass the word to Delta and I'll make sure our guys protect him."

Mitchum arrived in Los Angeles unnoticed. Harty never did understand the reason for all the secrecy, but at any rate, Lieber called him to express his gratitude.

"If there's anything you ever want, Joe," he said, "just call me."

Harty's relationships with the studios improved immediately. The toughest nut to crack was Harry Brandt, 20th Century's publicity boss, who regarded Joe with the same haughty disdain he'd display toward a reject from Central Casting. But it so happened that Harty, long before the war, had worked for a couple of New York City radio stations and got to be good friends with a struggling actor named Tyrone Power. Harty, in fact, talked the hesitant Power into accepting a screen test offer.

He hadn't seen Power after that until the actor had become a big 20th Century star and was going out of Burbank on an American flight. Harty was at the airport on some inconsequential business when Power spotted him.

"My God, Joe," he yelled, "what the hell are you doing in L.A.?"

They shook hands with obvious delight and Brandt looked stunned. Power explained they were old friends and Brandt muttered, "Anytime you're at 20th, come in and see me."

"Up to then," Harty reminisced, "Harry Brandt wouldn't give me the time of day."

It was hard for any airline operating out of Los Angeles to compete with TWA's influence in the movie capital. TWA had served California long before American, and when Hughes took over Jack Frye's pride and joy, the competition became even harder. Howard packed a lot of clout around town and was frequently doing favors for studio moguls like Darryl Zanuck and Harry Cohn, not to mention the two gossip queens, Louella Parsons and Hedda Hopper. Hughes arranged to have those two picked up by a private limousine that drove them to their flights—fortunately not at the same time.

Bill Hipple once got fed up with the number of times TWA appeared in Hopper's column, and went to see her. He asked bluntly, "What can we do at American to get a few plugs?"

"When you do for me what Howard Hughes does," Hedda responded, "I'll mention American every day."

Sky Dunning in sales had as many good contacts as Harty, and it didn't hurt that at one time he was married to actress Celeste Holm. It almost broke Dunning's heart when his wife accepted Hughes's invitation to take TWA's inaugural Constellation flight to Washington. He tried to talk her out of it, short of threatening bodily harm, but she went anyway.

The one major studio executive who favored American was Louis B. Mayer, powerful ruler of MGM. He was very friendly with C.R., who visited him frequently when he was in Los Angeles. Dunning accompanied Smith to Mayer's office on one occasion, and after Smith and the studio chief had a pleasant chat, C.R. asked, "L.B., is there anything American can do to make your trips with us more comfortable?"

"As a matter of fact, there is." Mayer smiled. "You know, on your DC-6 we always reserve the four seats up front facing each other because I like to play gin rummy. The stewardesses put meal trays into the slots and cover them with a blanket, but it's pretty wobbly. What we need is a small table or something."

"I'll see what I can do," Smith promised.

Outside Mayer's cavernous office, C.R. told Dunning, "Sky, see if you can devise some kind of portable table Mayer can take with him on trips."

Dunning had a rather cynical attitude toward film moguls. He once remarked about Mayer and Cohn: "They both worked in their shirtsleeves but with their pants pulled up almost to their lower chests, so they could hide their potbellies." But C.R.'s request was a command, and Dunning took the matter up with Stan Markham, MGM's transportation director.

This led to a conference with the studio's carpentry department. Its craftsmen designed a table made out of light wood with hinges in the center, so it could be carried like an art portfolio. The legs unfolded and could be inserted into the seat sockets where the meal trays normally fitted. On one hinged top was the Leo-the-lion logo and on the other American's eagle. The whole table could be folded into a handsome leather briefcase. "It was a thing of beauty," Sky said. "I never did find anyone who saw Mayer actually use it, but I was told he showed it to everyone who came into his office."

C.R. always stayed in the Beverly Wilshire and never failed to visit the reservations and ticket office on the lobby floor. He came down one morning before the nine o'clock scheduled opening and knocked on the door. Agent Jeannie Hall had just come on duty and when she heard the knock called out, "We don't open until nine."

Smith kept banging away, and she finally unlocked the door.

"I'm C.R. Smith," he announced.

Jeannie turned pale. "Oh my God," she breathed. "I'm fired."

C.R. just chuckled and went inside to use a typewriter.

Even out of town, he'd use the local American office to type out a few of his renowned memos. He'd tell Harty, "Joe, send this out."

Joe's most vivid memo-memory concerned one that read: "Why don't our planes have automatic coffee makers?" And this was in the DC-6's heyday.

When E. L. Cord was still alive, C.R. used to fly over to Elko, Nevada, where his old boss had his ranch. "I don't know what they talked about," Harty remarked, "but when C.R. got back to L.A., things always seemed to happen."

Rex Smith was another frequent Los Angeles visitor. He seemed to know every celebrity in Hollywood and always held court in his hotel suite. Harty would tend bar while Rex regaled his guests with stories. His favorite topic was bull fighting; he was a buff on the sport and even wrote a book titled *Biography of the Bulls.*

He loved being with the famous, a trait that didn't help his domestic life. Harty got involved innocently with one of Rex's marital quarrels when Joe was in New York on vacation and accompanied Rex to the 21 Club for lunch. They had lost track of time when Rex heard his name being paged.

"Take it for me, Joe," he asked.

It was June Smith, his third wife, who wanted to know where her husband was.

"He's at the bar having a drink," Harty said. "We're just about to sit down and have lunch."

"Lunch?" she screamed. "It's eight o'clock at night!"

Rex's p.r. staff didn't quite share his fascination with the film famous. "They all gave us trouble," Sky Dunning remarked, "because they all wanted the same thing—the same flight, the same lower berth when we had sleepers. And it was always hard to determine the pecking order."

One big-name star was flying American to some vacation spot and called Harty before he left.

"Joe, I want absolutely no publicity," he said firmly. "I want to get a good rest and I don't want to see anybody from the press either going or coming."

Harty followed his orders. When the actor returned to Los Angeles, Joe met his flight and was greeted with an angry glare.

"Where the hell are all the photographers and reporters?" he demanded.

But one famous actress to whom American owed a large debt was Jane Wyman. She played the lead in a 1951 MGM production called *Three Guys Named Mike;* Bill Hipple once labeled it "the only ninety-minute commercial in history."

The story behind the film was more interesting than the movie itself, which, by today's more exacting entertainment tastes, had enough corn to have been filmed in Kansas. An American stewardess named Ethel "Pug" Wells had producer/director William Wellman on a flight to Los Angeles and got talking to him, the main thrust of her conversation being that nobody had ever made a decent movie about stewardesses.

Pug picked the right target for voicing this opinion. Wellman was an ex-World War I fighter pilot who had made the classic *Wings* in 1926 and eventually would film Ernie Gann's *The High and the Mighty.* She was based in L.A. and was in her apartment after the flight when she got a phone call from someone at MGM inviting her to the studio for a discussion about "that movie idea of yours."

She figured it was either a joke or maybe the old casting-couch ploy and called Harty for advice.

"Joe, will you go with me?" she pleaded.

"You'll be fine," he told her. "Just go out there and see what it's all about. When you're through, call me."

Pug went to MGM and was ushered into the office of Louis B. Mayer's assistant production chief and his eventual successor, Dore Schary. He questioned her for more than three hours about her job and her ideas for a stewardess movie and finally said, "Miss Wells, I think we'd be very interested in making such a film. We'll get back to you."

Pug briefed Harty on the meeting and he called public relations in New York. Kay Hansen, Newt Wilson's original secretary and at that time assigned to p.r., said delightedly, "We know all about it, Joe. Dore Schary's already called us."

Rex was understandably excited. Schary had assured him that not only did MGM want to make a movie about stewardesses, it would be about *American* stewardesses. Rex warned Harty, "You ride herd on this, but make sure nothing's done that'll hurt American."

The producer assigned to the project was Armand Deutsch, and Harty met with him to discuss what the studio would need: plenty of Flagship footage, authentic stewardess and pilot uniforms, and Convair/DC-6 cabin mock-ups. Rex pulled Joe off the assignment after a few weeks, however, worried that it was taking him away from his regular duties. American's subsequent liaison with MGM was handled first by Gerry Tierney and later Dick Fisher. They were given an office next to Deutsch.

Harty did attend a meeting in Schary's office to discuss casting. The original choice to play "Marcy Lewis," the young girl who becomes an American stewardess, was June Allyson, but it was decided to cast Wyman instead. She was perfect for the part. The day Harty was at a casting session, mostly to pick girls for the bit stewardess roles, one name mentioned was actress Nancy Davis. She didn't get the part, but she did go on to marry Ronald Reagan.

For some reason, MGM didn't assign the film to Wellman, whose interest had prompted the whole thing. Charles Walters was picked to direct *Three Guys Named Mike*. One wonders what Billy Wellman would have done with it. He loved aviation, and the two airplane films he did make were noted for their realism and authenticity.

The screenplay was the work of a young writer who later became very famous and very rich from far better efforts: Sidney Sheldon. His script was fashioned from a story line concocted by someone else, and Sheldon admittedly did the best he could with a lighthearted but thin plot; Marcy goes through stewardess training, commits all sorts of boners as a rookie, eventually turns into one of American's finest, and falls more or less in love with three men whose first names are Mike. One is an American captain (Howard Keel), who's competing with a millionaire (Barry Sullivan) and a poor but honest college professor (Van Johnson).

In the end, Marcy chooses the professor, which surprised every stewardess who saw the film; either the pilot or the millionaire would have been a more likely selection for most of them. Pug Wells had nothing to do with the plot, but she got screen credit as a technical advisor and also played herself in a bit role; the credits at the start of the film contained the line, "From an idea by

Ethel 'Pug' Wells." The best thing she did for the movie was her coaching of Jane Wyman on how real-life stewardesses do their jobs.

The airplane footage was spectacular, especially a landing sequence shot from a camera mounted in the nose wheel well of a DC-6. The effect put viewers right onto the runway. There were enough shots of Flagships taking off, landing, cruising, and boarding passengers to make every airline in the U.S. jealous. Never before or since was a single carrier given so much exposure.

C.R. was delighted and gave Pug an Award of Merit, along with a lot of time off for publicity tours to seventeen cities American served. The only sour note for him was the casting of the character who played C. R. Smith in the movie. He was about ten years older and a foot shorter than the real McCoy.

For all its faults, the film did re-create an era that ended when the jets came. Viewed today, *Three Guys Named Mike* is simply a wonderful chunk of nostalgia, recalling the days when the girls wearing wings worked in a far simpler, more carefree environment. Discipline was stricter—a stewardess could get reprimanded for a crooked seam, the wrong shade of lipstick, or a nonregulation hairdo—but the job demands were less and crew camaraderie was one of the fringe benefits.

They weren't strongly unionized then, simply because most of them didn't stay around long enough to make a union very effective. The average tenure was only eighteen months, and it was unusual to find a stewardess who had been with American for as long as five years. C.R. discouraged longevity; he instituted a rule that required cabin attendants to quit flying at age thirty-two, believing that the older girls lost their enthusiasm and became somewhat careless in personal appearance. He once complained to another officer on a DC-6 flight that "the stewardesses look like grandmothers."

The rapid turnover resulted in a whole new generation of stewardesses joining American in these last years of the pistons. Two of them deserve special mention. One was Pat Patterson's daughter and the other became a legend.

Patti Patterson would have been perfectly willing to fly for her father's airline, but the president of United had this thing about nepotism. She really wanted to be a stewardess, however, and at Chicago's Midway Airport one hot August day in 1950, she was walking by American's personnel office there and saw a sign: STEWARDESS APPLICANT INTERVIEWS TODAY.

On impulse, she went inside. She said later, "I guess maybe it was because the office was air conditioned." The man who interviewed her came to the standard question, "What does your father do for a living?" and Patti hesitated.

"Uh, he works for an airline," she finally answered.

"Oh? Which airline?"

"United."

"What does he do at United?"

"A little bit of everything," she said desperately; she was afraid that revealing her father's identity would ruin her chances.

Two weeks later she got a letter telling her she had been rejected. She was still looking for another job and was about to accept one at Elizabeth Arden, when she happened to read in a newspaper that American was seeking stewardess applicants again. Patti had no sooner put down the paper than her phone rang. The caller was the same man who had interviewed her.

"Miss Patterson, I'm happy to advise you that we've reconsidered your application and decided to accept you."

"That's pure malarkey," she said. "I was just reading that you seem to be desperate for stewardesses. I have a hunch you're scrounging up rejects and you're down to the bottom of the barrel."

He laughed and admitted it was true. But she accepted anyway and graduated on Valentine's Day, 1951. Her father was there to pin on her wings; C.R. wanted to attend but had to be elsewhere. He was on several of her trips, however, and they became good friends. For years they kept up a correspondence, even after she left American, and C.R. never wrote Patterson a business letter that didn't end with the P.S.: "Give my love to Patti."

She flew for less than a year before resigning, a decision prompted by a United pilots' strike. Patti belonged to the stewardess union, and when she saw UAL crews picketing her father's office, she decided that her loyalties were too divided to keep flying. Even today, she remains more emotionally involved with American than with United. She was president of the San Francisco chapter of the Kiwis, an organization of former American stewardesses (it now includes current flight attendants) started nationally in 1951, and her closest friends are ex-American flight attendants. She never tried to keep her relationship to UAL's president a secret. "American apparently found out I was Pat's daughter shortly after I began training," she said.

Preceding Patti by a few classes was a trainee named Harriet Henderson, who had wanted to be a stewardess since childhood—and not for any airline: just American. Cleveland, her hometown, was a major American station in those days, and she never gave a thought to any other carrier.

Before she was old enough to apply, she was involved in an automobile accident that left her face scarred. Knowing that the disfigurement would turn off any interviewer, she went to work for a plastic surgeon, who agreed to deduct from her salary the cost of repairing the damage. The surgical scars hadn't quite healed when she had her first interview in Cleveland and was rejected. The same recruiter turned her down twice more. He said first that she was too thin, and then told her she was too tall.

She was desperate enough to take desperate measures, and started writing letters—about ten in all—to John Ewing, head of stewardess recruitment in Chicago, assuring him that in her American would have the greatest stewardess who ever flew for an airline. Only she used a different name; the letters were signed "Harriet Bryan." She figured "Harriet Henderson" must be on American's don't-call-us-we'll-call-you list.

Ewing still wasn't impressed, but shortly after her last letter, a number of accepted applicants changed their minds and a scheduled class was short several trainees. Ewing remembered Harriet Bryan, the most eager would-be stewardess he had ever encountered, and sent her a telegram telling her to report for training in Chicago.

She would have been home free except that the recruiter who had rejected her three times was advised of that class shortage and also sent her a wire of acceptance. Thus did Harriet Henderson/Bryan become the first applicant to be hired under two different names.

She had to confess, of course, and was promptly fired before she could start training. Ewing said her deception demonstrated dishonesty and untrustworthiness. She put on an act of Academy Award stature with enough tears shed to flood a DC-6 cabin and Ewing relented, largely because of one final remark she made.

"If you don't take me," she sobbed, "you'll lose two people."

She was a marked woman throughout training. Director of the Chicago stewardess school was Mildred "Jackie" Jackson, one of the finest, most gung-ho flight attendants ever to work for American, and a C.R. favorite. She carried her own dedication, enthusiasm, and self-discipline into her administration of the school. A stickler for rules and regulations, she was looking for an excuse to terminate the notorious Miss Henderson, and only one week before graduation she found a reason.

Jackie had been inspecting her application and saw something indicating she must be mentally unbalanced at worst and a prevaricator at best. Harriet had answered the question "Are you related to any famous person?" by writing down "Winston Churchill." To another question, "Have you done anything unusual?" she had replied, "I wrote a newspaper column."

Director Jackson figured she had her nailed, and called her in.

"I want proof you're related to Churchill and that you were a newspaper columnist," she said sternly. "And you'd better come up with the evidence before graduation or you won't graduate."

Harriet called her mother in Cleveland. By special delivery the next day there arrived on Jackson's desk the family genealogy, showing that Churchill's mother, Jennie Jerome, was the sister of Harriet's grandmother, so the imperiled trainee and the British prime minister were third cousins. Also enclosed were copies of her columns printed in a small Cleveland weekly newspaper, with her picture.

Jackie wasn't the only one after her hide. Ewing sat in the back of the classroom every day, staring at her. But she kept her nose clean, achieved a 99.8 grade average, and was the undisputed class leader. She wrote all the skits for graduation.

Ewing was present the day she graduated. Jackie had just called out, "Harriet Henderson, Cleveland, Ohio," as the next recipient for the coveted wings, when Ewing jumped to his feet.

"Just a minute, Jackie," he said.

Harriet thought, "Dammit, he got me at last." But Ewing was smiling and announced, "I'd like to pin on Miss Henderson's wings."

He was a short man and he had to look up at her as he fastened the emblem on her uniform jacket. Then he winked.

It had taken three years from her first letter of application to that precious moment.

She had been flying for only a short time when she acquired the nickname that stuck with her all through her thirty-five-year career with American. She was in Cleveland operations getting ready for a flight when a copilot made some remark about women lacking physical strength.

"You're wrong," she corrected brashly. "Take me, for example. I happen to be a judo expert." (Which she was.)

"I'll bet you can't throw me," the pilot challenged.

Five seconds later, he was flat on his back, nursing both a bruised arm and a bruised ego. Someone murmured, "Clancy just lowered the boom." From that day on, she was Clancie Henderson, and literally hundreds of her comrades at American never knew her real name.

As a rookie stewardess, she committed every gaffe known to commercial aviation. Landing in a Convair at Cleveland one night in the midst of a blizzard, she disembarked forty passengers into the middle of a snowbank at the end of the runway. The pilot had stopped, trying to locate the snow-covered taxiway; Clancie thought they had arrived at the ramp area, so she lowered the stairs and bade everyone a friendly farewell.

She staggered through the required six-month probation period, escaping termination mostly because her supervisor kept getting complimentary letters from passengers and glowing reports from the pilots she flew with. The cockpit crews loved her sense of humor and cheerfulness.

Her sharp repartee was known throughout the system, and one story told about her became an airline classic. A captain invited her to the cockpit on a night flight so she could see a landing from this vantage point for the first time. The Convair passed over a radio beam as they went into final approach and the ADF needle (Automatic Direction Finder) did its required 360-degree revolution.

Clancie pointed to the ADF dial. "What's that thing?" she asked.

"That's our virgin indicator," the captain explained. "It reverses every time a virgin comes into the cockpit."

Clancie frowned. "If you're using it for navigation," she suggested, "you'd better get it repaired."

After ten years flying the line, she was promoted to management and for years served as chief supervisor at Washington National. Like so many good supervisors, she was tough yet tolerant. As a line stewardess, she herself had broken about every rule in the book and she could spot a phony excuse eight blocks away. She learned to strike that delicate, fragile balance between natural compassion for another woman and the need for company discipline and loyalty.

An excellent public speaker, she was once asked to address an audience of businesswomen—some 2,000—and memorized a speech that included this climactic line:

"Go ahead! The world's your oyster. You can be an astronaut, a top government official, and, yes, a stewardess. Charge ahead. Don't let anyone stop you!"

She arrived at the auditorium and found there wasn't anyone in the room under fifty. When it came time to deliver that socko line, she ad-libbed, "Encourage your daughters and your younger sisters to go ahead! The world's their oyster. . . ."

Clancie was at her best teaching. When the jets arrived, the airlines were required to put flight attendants through recurrent emergency procedures training twice a year, to refresh what they were taught in stewardess school. She could be bawdy and irreverent at times, but she got her message across. She opened every recurrent class with a solemn reminder: "Remember, never has an American Airlines stewardess let her crew down in an emergency."

She mixed humor with hard facts, often spontaneously. At one recurrent session, a stewardess asked why passengers weren't told about the emergency evacuation ropes installed just above the cockpit windows.

"Because," Clancie explained with a straight face, "when all hell breaks loose those windows are gonna be full of pilot asses."

She was a special favorite of C.R.'s; in his later years, she seemed to be a link with the past, a nostalgic reminder of the days when romanticism and sentiment were so much a part of airline life . . . when American was more like a big family than a corporation. Those days had to end, of course—it was the price paid for technological progress.

And Clancie's own career, spanning three and a half decades, had to end. When she retired early in 1985, virtually the entire Washington base turned out for her farewell party, plus scores of friends from around the system, past and present. A lot of them remembered Clancie's mother, who fed more flight crews than Sky Chefs.

Under her wisecracking personality was a very thick layer of loyalty to the airline she served for so long. In so many ways, Clancie *was* American Airlines.

Crisis came with the territory in the airline industry. When one was solved, another was waiting around the corner.

The scheduled carriers were just recovering from such headaches as postwar chaos, aircraft groundings, and the enormous costs of fleet modernization when a new challenge arose: the sudden emergency of the so-called "non-skeds"—uncertificated carriers offering low-cost air transportation at a time when the trunks were trying to raise fares so they could pay for their new equipment.

The newcomers were known by different names: irregulars, supplemental, non-scheduled, or charter airlines. The established carriers called them other names, mostly unprintable. As aviation historian R.E.G. Davies wrote, airlines like American, TWA, United, and Eastern regarded them "as an infection which could become dangerous if not cauterized."

The anticipated postwar air travel boom had brought more than 2,700 self-styled "airlines" into being, most of them shoestring operations founded by ex-military pilots who often had only one war-weary surplus C-47 or C-46 on whose fuselage was painted whatever fancy airline name the entrepreneur had dreamed up.

They flew charter trips under contract, and by 1950, the majority had gone down the drain. Their safety record was poor (and one crash could wipe out an entire company), and public confidence was nil. But the better-run, more adequately financed irregulars survived to become a real competitive force. They were operating DC-4s and old model Connies whose age and crowded cabin configurations were offset by such attractions as a $99 transcontinental fare.

The Civil Aeronautics Board from time to time tried to curb or at least exercise some control over their activities without violating the precepts of free enterprise. There was no law against starting an airline so long as it wasn't operating regularly scheduled flights. Yet in essence, that was exactly what some of the larger ones were doing. Operating thinly disguised "charter flights," they invaded the lucrative long-haul domain of the scheduled trunk carriers, "skimming the cream off the top," the ATA charged. As uncertificated charter operators, they could fly anywhere they pleased.

The CAB stepped in at one point and ordered the irregulars to limit the number of their flights to no more than eight to twelve a month between the same two points. Many of them circumvented this restriction by operating under a different name each month.

The infighting in Washington between the scheduled airlines and the non-skeds was bloody, as Carlene Roberts remembered so well. In 1951, C.R. named her a full vice president in charge of American's Washington office— the first woman to achieve such status in the trunk airline industry—and she was heavily involved in the battle against the irregulars. And it was uphill combat because there was a case to be made for the non-skeds: they were forcing the conventional carriers to reshape their thinking. They may have been competing unfairly in some respects, but they also were applying significant lessons.

First, they were stimulating air travel with their low fares; a sizable percentage of their passengers had never flown before. Second, they were developing air cargo on a broader scale; among the large trunks, only American was making a real effort in this area. And finally, they had introduced the concept of group travel, something the regular airlines eventually would adopt.

The U.S. military certainly wasn't anti-irregulars. During the Berlin Airlift, the larger non-skeds carried 25 percent of the passengers and a whopping 57 percent of cargo tonnage. And during the Korean War, 50 percent of the commercial air tonnage carried to the war zone was in aircraft operated by the non-skeds.

That last statistic was an eye-opener for C.R. Smith. When it became apparent that the Korean War was no mere "police action," Stuart Symington, then chairman of the National Security Resources Board, asked C.R. to set up some kind of airline equipment and manpower pool similar to the one he had helped the ATA establish before World War II. With Art Lewis as his staff assistant, Smith developed the concept of the Civil Reserve Air Fleet (CRAF). It still is in existence.

The Air Transport Command had been replaced by the Military Air Transport Command (MATS), combining both Air Force and Navy transport operations, and C.R. moved quickly with the new CRAF. The airlines began signing MATS contracts and providing aircraft and crews for the Korean airlift; American alone assigned about half of its sizable DC-4 freighter fleet to CRAF.

Yet the non-skeds were doing as much and even more than CRAF, which had gotten started a little late. Most of them were launched primarily as freight carriers anyway, and while their DC-4s were cattle cars to the average passenger, they were ideal for cargo. And the non-skeds knew how to operate them.

The irregulars pointed with pride to their Korean War achievements in defending their right to compete against the industry's giants. But in the end, they were defeated by an ancient rule: "If you can't beat 'em, join 'em."

In November 1948, Capital Airlines had introduced the first scheduled coach service between New York and Chicago, charging 4 cents a mile instead of the established 6 cents. To operate profitably with the lower fare, Capital packed sixty seats into its fifty-passenger DC-4s and operated the coach flights during off-peak hours, mostly at night.

American and TWA jumped on this bandwagon a month later, also with DC-4s, offering coast-to-coast service for $110 one way. But in 1950, with their DC-4s needed for MATS, both airlines launched coach service with pressurized planes. American used DC-6s converted to eighty-one-passenger capacity, and TWA utilized some of its older Connies.

As usual, cautious United hesitated. Patterson thought low-fare competition could wreck the industry. And when UAL did get into the act, it was on a very limited basis at first: a DC-4 service between Los Angeles and San Francisco for $9.95. (United was really the first scheduled carrier to offer coach fares; in 1940, it operated its old 247s between the same cities, with intermediate stops, and charged only 3.5 cents a mile. The experiment was abandoned when war came.)

Now the non-skeds were being beaten at their own game. As late as 1951, only 7 percent of American's passengers flew coach. But it was 13 percent a year later, reached 23 percent by 1954, and would continue climbing from then on. Still to come was a new wrinkle: two-class service on the same airplane. TWA introduced dual configuration in 1955, a concept that would be carried into the jet age.

Gradually, the irregulars began fading from the scene. A handful survived and some, like World and Trans-Caribbean, eventually became scheduled airlines and even joined the ATA. But there is no doubt that non-sked competition, however unfair it may have been at times, pushed the established airline industry sooner than it wanted in the direction it would have to go someday.

Certainly C.R. saw what was coming. He was not really a low-fare advocate —actually, he thought first-class fares were too low, and he was extremely careful to avoid fare cuts that might divert revenues from first class. The family fare plan was designed to block diversion, and the same principle of restrictions was applied to American's early coach efforts. But he also recognized, albeit privately, the accomplishments of the non-skeds. They had, indeed, tapped a new market.

Surprisingly, the CAB's initial reaction to the scheduled carriers' wave of coach service was unfavorable. It even cautioned the airlines that it did not intend "to permit a general debasement of the existing passenger fare level." But C.R. sensed that this mood wasn't going to last, and his crystal ball was crystal clear. In later years, the CAB gave the impression it might have granted a certificate to a Mafia-owned airline so long as it promised lower fares.

Bolstered by American's financial turnaround (starting in 1949, the airline had three consecutive years of profits, totaling $27.4 million), late in 1951 C.R. ordered another round of new aircraft. It happened to be a plane nobody else wanted and one that Douglas, its manufacturer, tried to talk Smith out of buying. It was the DC-3 gamble being repeated, only this time it was called the DC-7.

C.R. had two motives for going against the grain.

First and foremost, he was worried about TWA, which had introduced a new member of the Constellation family, the Super-G. It was not only faster than the DC-6B but could fly nonstop on eastbound transcontinental trips. Both its range and speed advantage galled C.R. He wanted an airplane that could leave the Super-G eating engine exhaust and be able to go coast-to-coast nonstop in *either* direction.

His second motive was recognition of the trend toward coach travel, and he reasoned that a sizable fleet of DC-7s would release now-aging DC-6s, and perhaps some DC-6Bs as well, to the burgeoning coach market. He was to fulfill both goals, but not without a struggle and a few stumbles along the way.

It was Dan Beard who first conceived the idea for the DC-7.

Beard had taken over for Bill Littlewood, who suffered a heart attack in 1950 and henceforth was to serve more as a consultant, although typically, C.R. refused to take away his vice president's title. Shortly after Littlewood was hospitalized, Beard got one of C.R.'s cryptic notes:

"What would you boys suggest for an airplane that could develop coast-to-coast nonstop service?"

Beard, Kirchner, and newcomer Frank Kolk in engineering went to work on the answer. They were still formulating their ideas when Beard picked up a rumor that TWA was dickering with Curtiss-Wright to beef up the R-3350 engine by converting it to a turbo-compound engine, a relatively new design that fed normally wasted fuel exhaust back into the engine, thus boosting usable horsepower and increasing both speed and range.

Beard called C.R. and asked, "Can I see you?"

"Meet me in the Cloud Club [in the Chrysler Building] for lunch tomorrow."

Bill Hogan was there with Smith when Beard arrived. They ordered food and Smith said, "Well?"

Beard talked for eight minutes without interruption. He described the new engine, warned that TWA was almost certain to put them on its new Connies, and said there was a way to clobber TWA even if they did.

"The answer is to put a turbo-compound engine into the DC-6 and make it a bigger airplane," he continued. "My boys figure we'd have a considerable speed advantage, say fifteen to twenty miles an hour, over a Connie with the same engine. That's because the Six is a cleaner airplane all the way through."

C.R. and Hogan sat there, imitating sphinxes. Smith suddenly slapped his knee. "We don't want United in on this, but Pan Am might be interested. Juan Trippe's over there having lunch. I'll go talk to him."

While he was gone—for only about five minutes—Hogan questioned Beard further about a stretched DC-6/DC-6B; for some reason, Hogan respected Beard more than he did Littlewood. C.R. came back from his brief talk with Trippe and told Beard, "I want you to be in Don Douglas's lunchroom by tomorrow noon. I'll phone him and tell him you're coming."

Beard was in that private dining sanctuary the next day, facing not only the president of Douglas Aircraft but a platoon of vice presidents, including the number-two man, Ted Conan, a hard-nosed negotiator with some influence on the number-one man. The Cloud Club scene was repeated; they ordered lunch and it was Douglas who opened the discussion.

"C.R. said you had something to tell us, Dan."

Beard reiterated what he had outlined to C.R. and Hogan—that something had to be done with the DC-6 if American was to compete against compound-equipped Connies that would be twenty-five miles an hour faster than even the DC-6B, let alone the basic Six. When he finished, he knew he hadn't convinced anybody. Halfway through his presentation, he had caught Conan shaking his head and frowning. The only encouraging signs had come from chief designer Art Raymond, who at least was taking notes, and Ozzie Oswald, the chief aerodynamicist, who had once solved the DC-3's early stability problems; he was smiling.

Beard was at dead center judging the majority's negative reaction. This was in August 1951; from then until November, Douglas was adamant in his refusal to produce another "stretch" on the DC-6, just as he had argued seventeen years before that the DC-3 wasn't needed because the DC-2 was good enough. He had a bit more logic on his side this time, however. Both Douglas and Boeing already were thinking about jets, and Don Douglas believed sincerely there wasn't room for another piston transport between the DC-6B and the inevitable jetliners—the latter involving astronomical development costs.

C.R., Hogan, and Beard made the trek from New York to Santa Monica four times during those three months, without budging anybody. Pleas turned into arguments, and arguments turned into animosity. At one point, C.R. reportedly threatened never to buy another Douglas plane unless it built the DC-7.

C.R. was under pressure from Pat Patterson, too. Pat, as close to Don Douglas as Smith, told C.R. it would be foolish to spend money on another piston aircraft regardless of TWA. The UAL chief knew only too well that if American bought the DC-7, United would have to follow suit. There was no way Pat Patterson was going to order Connies, no matter how fast they were.

Trippe had cooled off a little, although eventually he would order an even larger version of the DC-7, called the DC-7C. C.R. seemed to be fighting a losing battle, until he fired his last and most effective shot.

In late November, he, Hogan, and Beard held one final and futile meeting with Douglas. They were getting absolutely nowhere, and C.R. turned suddenly to Beard.

"Dan, go over to Lockheed and see what they'll do for us." With that, he got up and walked out of Douglas's office, followed by Hogan and Beard. Not one word of good-bye was uttered.

"Dan, I'll see you back at the hotel after you've talked to Lockheed," he said.

For some reason he never could explain—possibly pure intuition—Beard did not leave with them. He went back to Douglas's office and quietly opened the door. No one noticed him, but he saw and heard plenty. Don Douglas was delivering a lecture to about fifteen of his top associates.

"There, boys, goes our best customer," he was saying loudly. "Now if you guys have driven him off, that's *your* responsibility. I think we ought to build that damned airplane for them."

Beard gently shut the door. He didn't bother to go to Lockheed; he raced back to the hotel and informed C.R. what had happened. The American contingent was back in New York for only a day when Douglas phoned C.R.

"We'll build the DC-7," he promised.

American originally ordered twenty-five of them. At $1.25 million apiece, it was a $31.25 million contract for which Hogan arranged the financing. (Some sources say that with spare parts the figure was closer to $40 million.) To this day, there are veterans from that era who think Smith made a mistake, that he gambled unnecessarily knowing the jets were coming, and that the DC-7 turned out to be something of a disappointment. What's more, he later ordered another thirty-three, fourteen of them as late as 1955, which meant that American was operating fifty-eight DC-7s with the jet age looming over the horizon. It might even be said it was a lot closer than the horizon—the Comet went into service in 1952.

The DC-7 served American for only ten years, a comparatively short lifespan for a transport aircraft. When it came to retire them, the going rate for a used DC-7 was only $175,000—one of the fastest depreciations in commercial aviation history.

(Dixon Speas always believed that if American had bought the Avro Jetliner, there never would have been a DC-7. Just before the program was cancelled, Avro had decided to expand the prototype's thirty-two-passenger capacity to fifty in the production airplane. "It could have gone coast to coast with two fuel stops and still beaten the DC-7 by an hour," Speas insisted.)

Yet in C.R.'s defense, he had no way of anticipating the DC-7's flaws, nor the problems it would cause. That it was preceded by Avro's jet and the Comet is beside the point; both those planes were simply too small to be viable in a time of rapidly expanding air travel. And the Comet turned out to be tragically ahead of its time, designed beyond the existing state of the art; the original model was grounded permanently in 1954 after only three years of service.

As for the additional DC-7 orders, it must be pointed out that C.R. needed more capacity to handle the exploding coach market. He filled those seats, too, with the aggressive marketing that was American's trademark. Finally, when the Comets were grounded, a lot of experts were predicting gloomily that jet travel might be at least ten years away. Both the 707 and DC-8 were in the developmental stage, with a lot of questions still unanswered.

While preparing for the DC-7, Smith was active on another front: the composition of his high command. In late 1950s, he had commissioned the management consultant firm of McKinsey & Co. to study American's executive structure. Out of that study, which took several months, came a major reorganization in 1954. Hogan, Mosier, and Jacob all became senior vice presidents of finance, operations, and administration/government affairs. To that list was added a fourth name: Charlie Speers as senior vice president of sales. It was a long jump from the old days in Bay City, Michigan, when Charlie wired the mailbox outside his office building for sound and from his desk would broadcast to startled pedestrians his air travel sales talk.

The quartet, whose offices on the seventeenth floor were known as "Mahogany Row," was answerable only to C.R. Under them were ten vice presidents, reporting to the seniors and five regional vice presidents. The vice presidential ranks included three new ones: Dan Beard, who headed equipment research; Marv Whitlock, who was assigned to Tulsa as vice president of maintenance; and Walt Johnson, who served as Speers's assistant.

It was a well-deserved promotion for Johnson, too. He had attracted C.R.'s attention with a clever stunt he pulled at the 1948 Republican convention in Philadelphia. Every morning he sat in the press gallery listening to Chairman Joe Martin make his daily announcements, and this gave him an idea.

He bribed an usher to deliver a note for Martin's litany of delegate information. On it he had typed, "American Airlines wants you to know that when the convention is over, it will have ample space on all flights out of Philadelphia. For reservations, call . . ."

The next day Martin, who never looked at anything until it was put in front of him, dutifully repeated Johnson's commercial word for word. Walt delivered the same message twice more before the convention ended.

Of those four top bananas, Hogan and Mosier wielded the most power and influence with C.R., which was only to be expected. Speers and Jacob were team players, content with doing their jobs and lacking the intense ambition of their two colleagues, not to mention their volatile personalities. (Jack Mullins would say years later that Charlie Speers might have become president of American if he hadn't been such a nice guy.)

Jacob was cut out of the same mild-mannered cloth as Speers. He was rather shy and soft-spoken, with a crinkled, leathery face, gray-black hair cut short, and a smile that could light up a dark room. He kept his real feelings to himself, and Malcolm MacIntyre, who admired him tremendously, remarked that Jacob "could be in turmoil inside but no one would guess anything was wrong. He seemed to have no outlet for his emotions, even though things might be tearing him apart."

He was a calming influence on Hogan and Mosier, although calming those two down was like trying to pull a DC-6 with a bicycle. The four senior vice presidents formed a "senior council," a title suggested by the McKinsey experts. Whether it really worked is another matter. As Speers put it, "We met once a week in the Cloud Club and we had a lot of fun, but C.R. wasn't a very good government-by-committee man. He liked to decide things for himself."

Speers was one of the handful of officers who didn't regard Hogan as something like the devil incarnate. Another was Dixon Speas, who may have been among the few who got an insight into the real Bill Hogan. When Hogan first came with American, Speas heard some scuttlebutt that the new treasurer had made some disparaging remarks about him. He confronted him with the rumors.

"I hear you don't like me," Speas said bluntly.

"Hell," Hogan replied with rare equanimity, "I don't get along with anybody. Don't take it personally."

C.R. gave everyone who complained about Hogan's belligerence the same advice. At a staff meeting one day, someone made a humorous remark and Hogan laughed.

"Remember it well," Smith commented wryly. "It won't happen again for another fifty years."

There was nothing to laugh about on January 22, 1952, when an American Airlines Convair approaching Newark suddenly lost altitude and crashed into several dwellings in Elizabeth, New Jersey, a suburb located directly on the approach path. All twenty passengers and the crew of three were killed, as were twelve people on the ground. One of the victims on Flight 6780, en route from Rochester and Syracuse, was Judge Robert Patterson, former Under Secretary of War in the Roosevelt administration.

It was the first fatal 240 accident and was never solved officially. The best guess was carburetor icing; weather was marginal in light rain and fog, with near freezing temperatures. It could have been even worse, because the plane just missed hitting a school building. One wing sliced into a candy store, killing the mother and son who ran it; if the crash had occurred fifteen minutes earlier, there would have been about thirty children inside the store, a popular after-school hang-out.

Only a little over a month before, a non-sked C-46 with one engine out had crashed in the same area. And three weeks after the American accident, a

National Airlines DC-4 with propeller problems hit an Elizabeth apartment building, killing four residents and twenty-nine of the plane's sixty-three passengers and crew members. Public protests forced the temporary closing of Newark Airport until the approach path over Elizabeth was changed.

The deadly trilogy was a traumatic experience for young Walt Rauscher, Walt Johnson's protégé. He was New Jersey sales manager and worked without sleep at the American crash scene for two days. After the National accident, American sent him out to the site to help.

C.R. happened to know Judge Patterson and his wife. When an insurance company was settling claims, a representative came to see MacIntyre.

"We've got a problem," he told the general counsel. "*Who's Who* gives Patterson's age as sixty-seven, but we found his birth certificate, which shows he was seventy."

Those three years made a difference in the amount of settlement; the insurance company was paying off in accordance with remaining life expectancy. MacIntyre took the matter up with C.R., who settled it his own way.

"You tell 'em to pay according to his real age," he ordered MacIntyre. "American will make up the three-year difference."

Smith had a rough time in 1951. In addition to the New Jersey tragedy and the controversy with Douglas, he was recalled to active duty with the Air Force early in February. He had maintained his reserve status after the war ended, but never expected to be called up. It took him away from American for three months, time he could ill afford.

He came out to California just prior to his reporting for duty in Los Angeles and met with the airline's L.A. staff at his hotel until almost midnight—the witching hour for Brigadier General C. R. Smith. He glanced at his watch, excused himself, and went to his room. He came down a few minutes later in full uniform, and Joe Harty was just one of those present who gulped.

"God, he was an imposing sight," Harty remembered.

The DC-7's introduction in 1953 was preceded by another profitable year, a $12.5 million net for 1952. And American needed a good financial performance: the biggest, fastest, longest-legged aircraft it had ever operated was about to make its bow, amid applause that turned to boos.

The old baseball expression "good field, no hit" could be paraphrased for the DC-7: "Good airplane, lousy engines."

United, which ordered the DC-7 in self-defense, had warned there was going to be trouble with the R-3350 turbo-compound. Curtiss-Wright was promising that it would deliver 1,800 horsepower—600 hp more than the DC-6B's R-2800, making it the most powerful engine ever put on a commercial transport. But United's engineers felt that to attain such horsepower, the R-3350 would produce too much back pressure and be subject to cylinder failure.

Unfortunately, Beard believed Curtiss-Wright. United's concern became fact. The rate of engine failures on the DC-7 proved to be downright embarrassing, and this was the case even before the plane carried a single paying passenger.

Rex Smith had arranged to launch the DC-7's introduction with two spectacular promotions: a special nonstop New York–Los Angeles inaugural flight for the press, and a huge party in Hollywood. Both turned out to be mild disasters.

The press plane lost an engine and had to land in Colorado Springs; Rex, who was on board, nearly wept. Here was American's proud new bird, *Flagship California,* rendered hors de combat. Mercifully, the press took pity, and some reporters even wrote stories praising the pilot's judgment in making the precautionary landing.

Rex had Bill Hipple in charge of the Hollywood bash, hoping it would match the one arranged for the DC-6 introduction. Joe Harty had borrowed radio magnate Atwater Kent's estate for that previous occasion. Kent's mansion and lawn weren't available this time, but Harty talked a wealthy real estate developer into letting him use his Beverly Hills home. It was built on the side of a hill, and the interior would have made Hugh Hefner envious. When Harty inspected it, he found spigots in several rooms that produced beer, champagne, and scotch.

"How big a crowd do you think this place can handle?" he asked the owner.

"Oh, not more than 400."

Harty thought he meant 400 couples, not individuals, and made his plans accordingly. He invited every politician and celebrity west of Palm Springs and a list of stars, producers, and directors that read like a Who's Who in Hollywood. The invitation produced about 95 percent acceptance, and Harty had the whole Los Angeles staff working the phones to handle the reservations.

One secretary answered an acceptance call and keeled over in a faint. Revived, she explained in an awed tone, "That was Cary Grant."

Four hundred did come—400 couples, that is. The mob was so great that traffic was backed up all the way to Sunset Boulevard, and the expense account Hipple submitted to New York resembled the national debt. But there were no complaints—that's the way the big airlines did things in those days.

American even used a toy company in the DC-7 promotion. The plastic model industry was just getting started and one of the firms was Revell, in Venice, California, which had been producing plastic antique automobile kits. Rex agreed to help pay for the molds if Revell would turn out a DC-7 kit with American's markings. It was the start of a long relationship between the airline and the model manufacturer. Revell subsequently produced kits for the Electra, 707, 727, 747, and DC-10. That first DC-7 kit, originally priced at a dollar, is now a collector's item; one in good condition brings between $50 and $100.

Scheduled nonstop transcontinental service in both directions was launched successfully November 29, 1953, but from then on, the DC-7 fleet was plagued with engine failures. The Tulsa base spent exorbitant time performing surgery on those R-3350 prima donnas. Marv Whitlock once walked into a schedule planning meeting in New York and informed them, "We have a hundred sick engines in Tulsa right now."

Denver, which American didn't serve then, became almost a scheduled stop, and Whitlock finally resorted to keeping spare engines there. Retired Captain

Chick McBath, who used to fly DC-7s, told the story of a passenger who boarded a DC-7 and asked the pilot, "What time do we get to Los Angeles?"

"I don't know," he sighed. "We've never made it."

Whitlock thoroughly despised the R-3350. "We were blowing cylinder heads about every other trip," he remembered, "and there was a 50-50 chance of getting a fire."

Despite its engine shortcomings, however, the DC-7 was far from a total flop. In the decade American operated it, the plane compiled a perfect safety record—not a single passenger or crew member was ever so much as scratched in a DC-7 Flagship. And the big plane *was* fast. On March 29, 1954, Captain Joe Glass took *Flagship Illinois* from Los Angeles to Idlewild in six hours and ten minutes, an official transcontinental speed record and a time not too far removed from that of a jet trip.

Glass suspected he was going to set a record; strong tailwinds were predicted and he alerted American to have an official National Aeronautics Association timer in the eleven-story Idlewild control tower to verify his elapsed time. Fred Williamson of NAA was in the tower when approach radar called and inquired, "Do you see him yet?"

"No, he's not in sight."

"Well, keep your eyes open, because somebody's going across Central Park like a bat out of hell."

The next day, Captain Jim Ingram flew the same eastbound trip, Mercury Flight 2, in five hours and fifty-one minutes, the first time a commercial transport had cracked the six-hour mark. Ingram's record, however, wasn't official because no NAA observer was present. Operations hadn't expected the tailwinds to hold up for two successive days.

C.R. got a letter from a passenger on Ingram's flight, claiming he had been inconvenienced.

"You should have notified my wife you were coming in so early," he complained. "I told her the plane would be on time and I had to wait more than an hour before she met me."

The heavy DC-7 needed an airport like Idlewild, although the terminal facilities were temporary and almost primitive. The spectacular terminal complex at today's John F. Kennedy Airport (Idlewild was renamed after his assassination) was still seven years down the road when American began DC-7 service there. And that concept, in which the larger carriers built and operated their own individual facility, was an American Airlines' idea.

In Idlewild's initial planning stages, the Port of New York Authority wanted a single terminal building almost a mile and a half long. American came in with a proposal for individual terminals, built by the larger carriers (American, TWA, United, Pan Am, and Eastern), who would share them with smaller airlines that didn't need much space.

Walter Johnson was chairman of the joint airline negotiating committee that went to the mat with PNYA's Austin Tobin over the issue. Tobin was adamantly opposed to individual terminals because they would violate his conviction that the only way for Idlewild to make money was the income from centralized terminal concessions—shops, newsstands, snack bars, restaurants, etc. The traffic in an individual terminal, he argued, wouldn't be enough to turn a profit.

Johnson produced a study American had done at Detroit's Willow Run, which American at the time was running for all airlines under its still-existing ANTSCO contract.

"Total carrier traffic at Willow Run is about the same as what we're projecting for ourselves at Idlewild," Walr said. "And our study shows that Willow Run makes a good profit. So would the Port Authority as the landlord of an individual terminal built by American. If you insist on a central terminal of the size you propose, passengers will have to be marathon runners to catch a connecting flight."

His airline cohorts backed him up, and Tobin surrendered. American's Idlewild terminal was in the architectural planning stage when the DC-7 began service, but when it opened in 1960—the first to be completed—it ranked as one of the most spectacular in the world. Architect Bob Jacob, who designed it, got his inspiration for its huge, multi-stained windows from the facade of the University of Mexico's administration building. Only one other Idlewild structure surpassed it in architectural beauty, and that was Eero Saarinen's gull-shaped TWA terminal, and although some critics think American's is warmer, both are truly magnificent.

Johnson also got involved in a second attempt to convince C.R. that American should have white airplanes. He allied himself with Marv Whitlock, and neither was aware of the earlier and very futile efforts by Rheinstrom, Littlewood, and Speas. It was Whitlock's idea, prompted by the knowledge that virtually every airline in the United States was going over to white fusleages.

Whitlock first approached Johnson on the subject, knowing it was C.R. who would have to be sold and apparently figuring that a sales expert could do better job on the boss. Walt listened to Whitlock's justification for the program and suggested they talk to Smith.

Marv's opening remark was no waste of words: "C.R., we'd like to paint our airplanes."

"I've been through this before," Smith growled. "And we are *not* going to paint our airplanes."

Whitlock kept pressing and finally said, "Well, I'd at least like to test the idea."

More in a tone of dismissal than agreement, C.R. grunted, "Okay, go ahead and run some tests, then come back with the results."

Marv went back to Tulsa, and over almost an acre of ground at the maintenance base, he spread scores of fuselage pieces. They were painted, unpainted, polished, and unpolished; he tried every shade of white known to civilized man and quite a variety of other colors, too. He used different types of paint, from acrylic to epoxy. And for nearly a year, they took daily temperatures under each piece of metal. Johnson said the experiment must have cost American at least $100,000, but added, "I didn't want C.R. to know so I never bothered to ask."

A proud Whitlock showed Johnson the results, and a meeting with C.R. was arranged. They brought four thick books to the president's office, filled with data from the study. Bravely, Whitlock launched his presentation and wound up by declaring, "In brief, C.R., everything I've given you demonstrates without any doubt that white paint will keep our cabins warmer in the winter and cooler in the summer by a significant amount."

"Screw it," Smith said. "We aren't gonna do it."

"C.R., I guess you didn't understand the data and their conclusions. I'll go over it again."

"I guess you didn't hear me. I said screw it, we are not gonna paint our airplanes."

"C.R., if you don't mind, in the face of all these facts, why *aren't* we going to do it?"

"Because I don't like it."

End of meeting.

It wouldn't have helped the DC-7's problem if they had painted the planes purple, pink, green, or red. The engine headache was never really cured until the DC-7C came along and Pan Am deliberately downrated the power, sacrificing speed for greater reliability. Yet with all its troubles, it was smart marketing that made the DC-7 more of a success than a failure. Between 1953 and 1957, American gradually implanted in the public's mind an image of airborne luxury that only this monarch of the piston era could provide. The premier DC-7 flights were something special.

Smart marketing boosted the DC-6, too. Out of Charlie Speers's department came a new special amenities service called "The Captain's Flagship," offered on certain DC-6 routes. It was a throwback to the old steamship days when a liner's captain had the role of host as well as commander, and this was applied to DC-6 captains. They greeted passengers at the top of the boarding ramp, gave everyone small souvenirs, and put them in the mood for enjoying a trip that was out of the ordinary. Sky Chefs meals on the Captain's Flagship flights were above average, too, served on satin damask tablecloths. The service was so well received that, years later, American revived it for the 747 with "Captain's Table" fare, including roast beef carved in front of each passenger.

When more DC-7s were added to the fleet, many were assigned to a new kind of coach service, "The Royal Coachman," started in 1956 and continued well into the jet age. C.R. himself came up with the name. His favorite form of relaxation was trout fishing, and when Speers and Johnson were trying to think up what to call the new service—Thrifty Service, Royal Scot, Tartan Flights were some of the names being considered—Smith suggested Royal Coachman, which happened to be the name of his favorite fishing fly. Speers got one of his patented one-line notes, which said, simply: "Charlie: call it the Royal Coachman."

The name alone dispelled the cattle-car image so many people were applying to the proliferating, increasingly crowded economy flights. This wasn't anything new. When the major carriers were being battered by competition from the non-skeds, Walt Johnson used to send subordinates out to ride their $99 transcontinental flights.

"They'd come back with horror stories about being bumped off in Kansas City with no refunds," Johnson recalled. "When we decided to really go after the coach market, we wanted to make passengers feel they were still appreciated."

The service couldn't approach what first-class passengers enjoyed on the Mercury or Captain's Flagship, of course, but it was better than what most airlines were offering coach customers. To publicize Royal Coachman, American hired a British actor named Billy Clark and had a London tailor outfit him in an authentic coachman's uniform. The airline even purchased the original coachman's horn from the old London-Brighton stage. The actor was offered some other job and quit before American's promotion got into high gear. The second one hired was Eddie Nugent, a veteran thespian and producer who was the airline's Royal Coachman for most of the time the service lasted.

Photographs of the fully uniformed Nugent appeared in advertisements and on television, but his most impressive appearances were at Royal Coachman inaugural flights, when he'd show up at the airport and blow that antique horn just before passengers boarded. It was pure showmanship. Walt Johnson called it "the biggest single success of its kind in the airline industry," adding: "Yeah, we ran the hell out of the idea, but it was C.R.'s choice of that name that really made it work."

It wasn't the only marketing idea Smith had at a time when solid United and aggressive TWA were counterattacking on every sales front. He involved American in a radio program that was to endure for more than a decade and win coast-to-coast acclaim for its quality, including a Peabody Award.

"Music 'til Dawn" began in 1953, and stories vary as to its exact origin. Joe Harty thought the concept was born when C.R. was on a flight with William Paley, head of the Columbia Broadcasting System. According to Harty, C.R. conceived the idea when Paley remarked that radio stations were looking for an inexpensive radio program to fill the network's early morning hours, and that Smith suggested American might be willing to sponsor an all-night show emphasizing easy-listening music.

Charlie Speers had a different account. He said "Music 'til Dawn" was, indeed, Smith's idea primarily, but that it was carried out with the help of Bill Smith, C.R.'s imaginative brother, who was with a New York advertising agency and actually proposed it to a number of stations, mostly CBS affiliates.

A third, and the more widely credited, version is that C.R. and CBS president Frank Stanton were having lunch or dinner at the 21 Club and started talking about their respective "down times"—the lack of passengers and advertisers in the late-night hours. Once given the concept, Bill Smith did much of the organizational work and helped sell it to individual stations, not all of which were CBS affiliates.

Which story is correct is inconsequential; regardless of its actual genesis, "Music 'til Dawn" proved to be popular, durable, and one of the most cost-effective forms of advertising in airline history. Smith is said to have bought the time dirt-cheap, getting a program that started out in six major markets and reached nine at its peak. How many passengers it attracted to American was hard to establish, but the show had a loyal audience numbering in the millions.

"Music 'til Dawn" was produced locally, with different hosts in each city and local control over the selections played. The format was simple: music played nightly from 11:30 P.M. to 6 A.M., with an occasional soft-sell commercial as soothing as the music itself. Every program opened and closed with the song "That's All," which achieved instant identification with the sponsor. No one could hear it without thinking of American Airlines.

C.R. got some intra-company static when he approved the project, several officers asking the obvious question: "Who the hell listens to radio after midnight?" But, it turned out, a great many did, in sufficient quantity to keep "Music 'til Dawn" on the air for fifteen years. Speers said it was dropped when American went with a new ad agency, Doyle Dane Bernbach, who advised C.R. that his advertising dollars could be spent better elsewhere, television in particular.

The agency probably was right; nighttime radio's audiences diminished in direct proportion to the growing popularity of television, with its late-night talk shows and movies. It was said around Madison Avenue that by 1966 "Music 'til Dawn" fans had dwindled to all-night diner customers and cab drivers.

This wasn't entirely true. When the program finally went off the air, hundreds wrote American pleading that it be reinstated. And to this day, "That's All" stirs sweet nostalgia and memories of commercials that were subtly persuasive and always in good taste.

"There were," remarked one AA veteran, "a hell of a lot of courtships conducted to that song and that program."

But if "Music 'til Dawn" resulted in a few romances, the DC-7 caused an estrangement.

Only the AOA pilots' strike had marred American's long history of relatively peaceful labor relations. American had even gotten along fairly well with Mike Quill, the cantankerous, colorful head of the Transport Workers Union, which represented the mechanics.

Quill and C.R. understood one another, with a great deal of mutual respect. Not that Quill was easy to deal with, as Malcolm MacIntyre could testify. He was participating at one negotiating session when Smith offered the mechanics a sizable wage increase with one condition: half the money would go to skilled workers, the effect being that these men, who made more to begin with, actually would receive the greater percentage.

"No way," Quill objected.

MacIntyre observed, "Well, Mike, that's giving mediocrity the benefit. A guy who can tear down an engine and put it back together is really the heart of an airline. You can get ship cleaners any day of the week."

Quill glared. "We represent mediocrity," he said pointedly.

Quill had established an inviolate rule: no contract, no work. If a company didn't reach agreement by the exact hour the existing contract expired, a strike was automatic. There were no extensions. American and the TWU locked horns one year, and the negotiations approached a midnight deadline. At around 11:30 P.M., agreement was reached and everyone was shaking hands when Quill announced, "Excuse me, gentlemen, but I have to go on the radio."

"Announcing the settlement?" MacIntyre asked.

"No. I'm going on the radio at 11:45 to call you all bastards for not agreeing to anything, for holding everything up and taking food out of the mouths of babies and bread from the tables of mothers and fathers."

"For Christ's sake," a management negotiator protested, "we just reached an agreement."

"I know," Quill smiled. "At 11:59 I'll go back on and announce that American has capitulated."

MacIntyre once said of Quill: "He was tough, and a real politician. But there are very few union leaders you can trust with just a handshake. Mike Quill was one of them—a man of his word."

Unfortunately, in 1954 the Air Line Pilots Association didn't have a Mike Quill. Its president at the time was calm, erudite Clarence "Clancy" Sayen, who two years earlier had ousted Dave Behncke. C.R. didn't know him very well, and a residue of the ill-will that had existed between Smith and Behncke apparently still colored his attitude toward ALPA.

Whether that influenced what was about to happen is pure guesswork. The real problem lay with the DC-7 and the difficulties any airplane encounters when it has to buck headwinds flying westward. On the DC-7, the slower westbound speeds were crucial, for in them lay the seeds of a bitter dispute.

ALPA's contract with American limited the pilots to a maximum eight-hour duty time in any twenty-four-hour period. And the CAA had an identical regulation: no airline pilot could fly more than eight hours at a stretch. Then along came the DC-7, which had no trouble crossing the continent eastbound in eight hours and usually made it in less time. But the westbound flights rarely could achieve such speed. When that happy event occurred, it resulted from zero headwinds or a following wind, and getting a tailwind on a westbound flight occurred about as often as Halley's Comet.

American's DC-7 crews were in violation of the eight-hour rule from almost the first day the plane went into service, on virtually all of their westbound trips. For several months, both the pilots and the CAA turned the other way. It was a brand-new airplane, it was *supposed* to fly coast-to-coast in under eight hours in either direction, and all the engineers kept asking for patience while they worked out the kinks of those #*&#%* R-3350s.

Gradually, it became apparent that nothing they could do with the engines was going to solve the problem. One crucial mistake had been made when proposed DC-7 transcontinental schedules were being planned: everyone had underestimated the average westbound headwinds at the altitude the plane would be flying most of the time. The airline had painted itself into a corner.

The pilots were getting restless, and in the late spring of 1954 formally demanded that all westbound flights land at some designated city, with a fresh crew taking over. They pointed out that not only were they in violation of their contract, they also were breaking the law.

The company pleaded for more time. Engineering was still nursing slim hopes it could coax more speed out of the R-3350, which already had been subjected to about a dozen modifications. Once again, the pilots agreed to sit tight for a while. And it was at this point that the CAA threw the overalls in ALPA's chowder:

It waived the eight-hour rule for all transcontinental flights.

The pilots were furious, convinced there had been collusion between American and the CAA. They demanded that the company renegotiate their contract, which still obligated the airline to observe the eight-hour limitation. C.R., who considered the matter closed when the CAB waived its rule, simply took off on one of his rare vacations with the feud starting to boil.

With C.R. gone, the pilots had to deal with the senior vice president of operations, and this didn't clear the air one iota. Red Mosier was a master negotiator with anyone *but* pilots. He seemed to share E. L. Cord's attitude that they were overpaid bus drivers, and Smith couldn't have left a more inappropriate official to deal with the situation. Mosier bluntly informed ALPA there would be no reopening of the contract.

The pilots voted to strike. C.R. cut short his vacation and rushed back to New York, but he wasn't in any more of a conciliatory mood than Mosier by now. Thanks to his previous experience with Behncke, he already had a jaundiced view toward ALPA, and he felt betrayed. He had spent millions trying to maintain American's leadership with the first nonstop transcontinental service, and in his mind, the airline was being sabotaged by a handful of greedy union leaders.

Grudgingly, he agreed to meet with ALPA representatives and a federal mediator. But when he showed up, he found only the mediator present. ALPA's absence wasn't deliberate—there had been a misunderstanding as to time. But Smith didn't know this. Being AWOL for a scheduled negotiating session had been one of Behncke's old maneuvers, and C.R. immediately interpreted this affront as history repeating itself. He dug in his heels, and on July 31, 1954, American's pilots walked out.

As so frequently happens, it was a strike nobody really wanted. The unhappiest ALPA pickets were the DC-7 pilots, mostly senior, who had bluntly told Clancy Sayen they were perfectly willing to fly in excess of eight hours; they loved the nonstops as the sweetest, least-demanding schedule they could bid. Sayen, conscious of his role as a yet-untested successor to the legendary Behncke, said the issue was not so much the eight-hour rule but American's refusal to renegotiate a contract that had been technically violated.

If one can understand the union's stand, one also can understand C.R.'s anger. His airline had been shut down over an issue involving only 5 percent of his pilots, most of whom didn't want the strike in the first place. The contract violation amounted to forty-five minutes of additional flying time five times a month for each DC-7 pilot. And C.R. believed that once he sat down to discuss this single issue, ALPA would make further demands that had nothing to do with the eight-hour rule. He remembered bitterly that when the dispute first arose, he had promised the pilots *in writing* that DC-7 pilots would be the only ones who had to fly more than eight hours per trip.

The pilots thought the company had betrayed them. C.R. thought it was the other way around. And with this collision of convictions, the strike went on for twenty-five days, paralyzing the airline right in the middle of the busy summer season.

When settlement was reached, American had won a waiver of the eight-hour rule as it affected DC-7 crews. The pilots had won what Smith feared would happen: some money and a few fringe benefit concessions that had nothing to do with the main issue. But this was partially his own fault.

He had assigned Mosier to represent the company in the negotiations, and Red was out of his league. His greatest admirer, Bob Tuttle, said Mosier was the worst choice C.R. could have made.

"To begin with," Tuttle pointed out, "Mosier thought it terrible that anyone would dare argue with management. He simply wasn't used to dealing with a union, and when he went to bat against the pilots, he never knew what hit him. They knew how to get to him. He'd get tired after hours and hours of negotiating and he'd go back to his hotel room for some sleep. A few minutes later they'd be pounding on his door, demanding that he go back to the negotiating table."

The strike ended August 24, and the DC-7s began droning westward unfettered by any duty-time restriction. They also were flying toward oblivion.

As of that August date, American was only thirteen months and sixteen days away from ordering its first jetliners.

PART FOUR
(1955–1974)

15

The Return of Charlie Rheinstrom
. . . and a Few Other Surprises

American's planning committee started thinking seriously about jets as far back as 1952, the year the ill-fated original Comets went into service.

Art Lewis, representing the committee, went out to the West Coast to talk to Donald Douglas about turbine-powered transports and found him ambivalent. United already had discussed the subject with Douglas and had shown little enthusiasm for what the manufacturer was proposing, a 100–120-passenger jetliner. United considered such a plane too large and suggested an aircraft about the size of the DC-7.

Art reminded him that all through history, each new generation of commercial transports was larger than its predecessor. Even then, American was operating eighty-one-passenger DC-6s and Eastern eighty-passenger Constellations. When Douglas pointed out the required length of a cabin capable of seating more than 100 persons, Lewis said C.R. already had talked to his engineers, who had suggested six abreast seating in coach and five abreast in first class.

"How the hell can United say that jets shouldn't start out with more than eighty seats?" Art demanded.

But Douglas, still feeling the effects of the cold water United had thrown, remained doubtful. Lewis reported to C.R. and the planning committee that Douglas seemed to have been infected with UAL's traditionally cautious "think big but start small" philosophy. Whether that was entirely true matters little, for subsequently Douglas *did* drag its heels on an all-out commitment to jet transport development, and by doing so gave Boeing its long-awaited chance to grab supremacy.

At this early stage, neither American nor any other airline was really concerned about who was going to build what kind of jetliner. But C.R. *was* thinking about an *interim* airplane, one that would bridge the gap between the already doomed pistons and the revolutionary but far-down-the-road jets. A turbine-powered aircraft with the engines hooked to conventional propellers, and one that would be not only "interim" but a replacement for the Convairs, DC-6s, and DC-6Bs.

It was no wild concept. Nor was it his. Such an airplane had been flying since 1948 and would be in scheduled service by 1953 on British European Airways.

This was Britain's Vickers Viscount, the world's first propjet transport, not much bigger than the Convair 240 (forty-four passengers to the Convair's forty), but capable of cruising more than 355 m.p.h.

Smith was intrigued enough to fly to England and look at the Viscount, accompanied by Frank Kolk of engineering, who was beginning to wield considerable influence in aircraft selection. Kolk was a perfectionist, rather impatient and unforgiving, but indisputably smart. With Littlewood virtually semi-retired in Washington, where C.R. had provided him with a little office, his immediate superior was Harold Hoben, who was cut out of the same abrasive cloth. When Marv Whitlock left Tulsa to become vice president of equipment planning around this time, he got to know Kolk and Hoben well.

"Both of them were extremely intelligent," Whitlock said, "but Frank was especially abrasive. If he could have been a little more diplomatic in his presentations, he might have sold more of his ideas. He was apt to treat anyone he was talking to as having inferior intelligence, and if you asked him a question, he'd answer in a way that made you sound stupid. He'd talk way over your head. Yet the people who knew him—the guys at Boeing, Douglas, and Lockheed—they could ride with him because they understood him."

So it was Kolk who went to England with C.R. After examining the Viscount, he told Smith to forget it. Its Rolls-Royce engines were superb, but the airframe was of single-spar construction, in contrast to the U.S. practice of building multispar transports for greater structural strength. In 1954, Capital Airlines was to order sixty Viscounts and then pit them against American's and United's pistons in two key markets: New York–Chicago and Washington–Chicago. The little propjet won hands down, but that sixty-aircraft order was too much for Capital to swallow. It fell far behind in payments to Vickers, which threatened to repossess the entire fleet. Capital was forced into a merger with United in 1960, and thus did the propjet that C.R. rejected indirectly cause the merger that made United, not American, the nation's largest carrier.

But that traumatic event was still in the future when C.R. began casting about for another propjet. Engineering drew up a set of specifications that Smith sent to Douglas, Boeing, Convair, and Lockheed. What the specs amounted to basically was a stretched 240 with four Dart engines like the Viscount—that Rolls-Royce product had impressed even the dour Kolk.

C.R. told the four manufacturers that if they could come up with the right airplane, he'd order 100 of them—in other words, American would be the "launch" customer, as it had been so many times. The responses weren't encouraging. Boeing, already involved heavily in jet transport design, wasn't interested. Convair was, but balked at the development costs involved in such a major propjet. Douglas, like Boeing, didn't think the airlines needed an interim airplane but suggested, a bit half-heartedly, that maybe they could put turbine engines on the DC-7 and turn it into a propjet. Only Lockheed had something concrete to offer.

They called it the L-188. Eventually it would be known as the Electra.

* * *

The bird factory at Burbank had been approached by Capital several years earlier on the subject of propjets, but the airline wanted a short-haul airplane and Lockheed's engineers weren't enthusiastic. But they perked up when they saw American's specifications for a turboprop that would:

- Cruise easily at 400 m.p.h.
- Operate profitably on flights as short as 100 miles and as long as 2,700 miles
- Take off fast enough and land slow enough to serve any of the nation's 100 major airports, particularly those that wouldn't be able to handle the forthcoming big jets.
- Carry at least sixty-five passengers

Lockheed had dipped its toes rather gingerly into the waters of turbine transport design with the L-193, a relatively small aircraft with two aft-mounted engines, much like today's DC-9 series. But customer interest was nil, and the L-193 never got off the drawing board. American's proposal, however, fascinated chief designer Hall Hibbard and his top aide, Clarence "Kelly" Johnson, whose famed "Skunk Works" (nickname for the design building) had created the Connies that had given C.R. so many headaches. In considering Capital's propjet request, they already had a tentative design ready when American knocked on the Burbank door.

The question of the Electra's desired range would generate a bitter controversy. In 1960, the Electra would become the most damned and pilloried transport in history after two catastrophic crashes in which wings came off in flight. Eddie Rickenbacker would charge later that the Electra's structural problems could be traced to American's demand that the plane have true nonstop transcontinental range. The captain claimed that when Lockheed found the L-188 couldn't meet that requirement, American insisted that the aircraft's structure be lightened. According to Rickenbacker, the total pounds Lockheed took off the plane to give it transcontinental capability were almost identical to what had to be added on later to correct the structural deficiencies.

The evidence is to the contrary, and the only inference that can be drawn from Rickenbacker's accusations is that they were intended as a cheap shot at C. R. Smith. It is true that when American's planning committee first began studying the possibility of a propjet airplane, transcontinental range was seriously considered. This was long before American ordered any pure jet, and in that time period—1952–1953—no one knew when the real jet age would dawn. At that stage of advance planning, they were talking about the propjet concept in general, not the Electra specifically.

Art Lewis was present at a meeting in Bill Hogan's office when the topic under discussion by the planning committee was where to use a turboprop. Route segments like New York–St. Louis, New York–Chicago, Washington–Dallas, etc., were mentioned, but Hogan interjected the issue of a longer-range plane.

"How in the hell can American bring in what will be its premier airplane and not have it capable of transcontinental range?" Lewis remembered him asking.

Mark well Hogan's use of the word "premier." At that point in time, the proposed propjet was intended to be the new queen of the Flagship Fleet, but this potential status ended long before the Electra's design was finalized. Even while that design was being formulated, C.R. already was wrestling between the 707 and DC-8 as American's replacement for transcontinental DC-7 non-stop service, *not* the Electra; the L-188 was never intended to be a transcontinental airplane, but rather a short-to-medium-haul transport replacing American's pistons, and aimed mostly at the New York–Chicago market. The 2,700-mile range requirement was never exercised, and for that matter wound up as 2,500 miles in the production aircraft. Nor did American ever insist that the Electra's structure be lightened. Lockheed did institute some weight-reduction measures, but not to the extent nor for the reason Rickenbacker claimed.

Eastern, in fact, became a co-launch customer with American and ordered forty—five more than American. The captain was to boast later that Eastern's Electras didn't require the same major structural modifications as everyone else's because he had had the foresight to beef up the plane beyond American's specifications. After his death, his own chief engineer admitted this wasn't true. Except for a few minor differences, some of them cabin cosmetics, both airlines operated identical aircraft.

Eastern's forty-plane order would have been eclipsed if C.R.'s original plans had gone through. He thought American could use sixty Electras, but it was Hogan who talked him into reducing the commitment to thirty-five planes; he reminded Smith American still had its decision on jets to make.

That decision was made exactly four months after American, on June 9, 1955, signed the Lockheed contract. On November 9, the airline ordered thirty Boeing 707s, at a cost of $5.5 million each. For C.R., it had been no easy choice. His emotional ties with Douglas were strong, and the 707 marked the first time in Smith's career at American that he had picked another manufacturer over Douglas as the builder of a Flagship queen.

It must be admitted that Douglas himself had weakened those ties somewhat by his delay in deciding whether to produce a large jet transport. The DC-8 existed only in blueprints and cabin mock-ups when Boeing was test-flying the 707 prototype, an almost incredible procrastination on the part of the world's leading airframe manufacturer. Overconfidence on Douglas's part may have been a factor, too. Boeing's previous efforts in air transport design—the 247, Stratoliner, and Stratocruiser—had been money-losing flops, and the tendency in Santa Monica was to look northward toward Seattle with some condescension. Even the Douglas salesmen, pitching what amounted to a paper airplane, were assuring their prospects, "Wait for the DC-8. It'll be worth it to sit tight for a better airplane."

But C.R. couldn't wait. In the first place, he was not a little miffed at Douglas, whom he had been pressuring for at least a year to give his jet a green light; he actually preferred the DC-8 in comparing the two designs. To this resentment was added an even more important factor: C.R. didn't know in which direction United and TWA were heading. If his two chief rivals bought the 707, he wasn't going to be left holding a DC-8 bag. As he told Littlewood, Whitlock, Frank Kolk, and Harold Hoben in engineering, "On this round of airplanes, I don't want to be first necessarily but I'm sure as hell not going to be last."

The domestic Big Four—American, TWA, United, and Eastern—were still uncommitted when Juan Trippe fired the starting gun for the big jet race. His order for Pan Am stunned Boeing and put more condescending smiles on the faces at Douglas: twenty Boeing 707s and *twenty-five* Douglas DC-8s. After he announced the record $269 million contract, he explained that Pan Am considered the 707 merely an interim jet, purchased solely because it would be available sooner than the superior DC-8.

Only twelve days after Trippe's October 13, 1955, announcement, United signed for thirty DC-8s. But in choosing Douglas over Boeing, Pat Patterson inadvertently had done C.R. a big favor. While deliberating over his choice of jets, Patterson had his engineering department construct a unique hybrid cabin mock-up. One side represented the still-on-paper DC-8 and the other the fuselage of the 707 prototype, which was not only already in its testing phase but breaking every transport speed record on the books.

In outward appearance and promised technical performance, the two competitors appeared almost identical. The 707's wings swept back thirty-five degrees, the DC-8's sweepback would be only thirty degrees; the five-degree difference gave the Boeing about a 20-m.p.h. cruising speed advantage, but also meant slightly less stability at low altitudes. The big difference was fuselage width. When Patterson studied that hybrid cabin, the DC-8 side was fifteen inches wider. Boeing's narrower cabin would mean going to five-abreast coach seating and smaller capacity.

Still leaning toward the 707 because of its earlier availability, Patterson asked Boeing to widen the fuselage by fifteen inches. Boeing refused on the grounds it would mean excessive retooling costs, but offered to stretch the prototype's fuselage in the production airplane. This wouldn't give United its desired capacity, however, and Patterson opted for the DC-8. He remained in the dark as to American's and TWA's intentions, but he apparently assumed his two chief competitors would do what he was doing: wait about a year for a better jet, instead of spending millions on one that would be outclassed the day the DC-8 went into service.

What he hadn't counted on was Boeing's swift reaction to the United order. Seattle quickly informed C.R. it was planning to widen the 707's fuselage by *sixteen* inches, and that was all he needed. Reportedly, Boeing also sweetened the financial package. Although this was never admitted officially, it would have made sense because without American's huge order, the 707 project might have been doomed.

Counting a number of DC-6A freighters bought around this time plus the last flurry of DC-7 orders, American in 1955 signed contracts for 105 new aircraft, 65 of them jet-powered. The airline netted a record $18.6 million that year, but this paled next to the $310 million it was going to spend for the planes, supporting equipment, and some new building projects.

Hogan was the undisputed brain behind the necessary financing. He arranged for a $75 million loan from Metropolitan Life at a rate that would bring tears to the eyes of today's airline finance officers: 4 percent interest, repayable in thirty years, commencing in 1967. Only a year later, as American bought more new jets, he swung a deal with several insurance companies for a $135 million line of loan credit. The terms were only slightly different: $75 million was at 4 percent and the rest at 4¼. The new loan also involved promissory notes repayable in thirty years.

It is tempting to speculate whether Bill Hogan might well have been the only one who could have pulled off such advantageous loans from hard-nosed lenders. He bullied insurance company executives and bankers just as he did subordinates and fellow officers. One of the latter was in Hogan's office at a time when American was trying to get banks to take over the mortgages on some of the surplus aircraft it was selling. A banker called Hogan to say, "We've taken a long and careful look at these airplane mortgages, and I'm afraid we wouldn't want to get involved."

Hogan roared, "You son of a bitch! When I deal with a bank, I want something more than a goddamned safe deposit box!"

His fearsome temper was even worse than Mosier's, and violent temper was perhaps the only thing these two combatants had in common. Red's at least was verbal; Hogan's was also physical. He once threw a flower-filled vase out of his office window and was lucky it didn't hit some pedestrian on the street many stories below. Gene Overbeck, at this writing American's senior vice president of government affairs in Washington, joined the airline in 1959 as a young lawyer. He became involved in the legal aspects of surplus aircraft sales and saw more than one five-megaton Hogan explosion.

"For some reason," he related, "Bill took a liking to me, but that was a rarity. He used to slam doors so hard after one of his temper tirades that we had to repair the frames. I've seen guys go pale when they had to walk into his office. He didn't seem so tough until he lost his temper. He was a medium-sized man with a very Irish face, and I remember he always wore blue suits."

Said another contemporary: "I hated his guts, but when it came to finance, Bill Hogan was in a class by himself."

Hogan's value to American in this time frame is underlined and capitalized by this one statistic: a single 707 cost $1 million more than what C. R. Smith had to borrow from the RFC to finance the *entire* original purchase of twenty DC-3s only two decades before. And included in the initial $75 million Metropolitan loan was funding for a very special C.R. project: the building of a Stewardess College in Fort Worth, Texas.

*   *   *

It was more than a long-time dream, it was one of his patented gambles. He was betting that a $1 million capital investment with absolutely no tangible rate of return on that investment would somehow pay off.

He literally even gambled to get the land where he wanted to build the Stewardess College. The property was owned by his old friend Raymond Buck, and C.R. kept pressing him to sell without success. Smith was visiting the Fort Worth Club and got into a gin rummy game with Buck. In the course of the game, C.R. suddenly turned it into a high-stakes wager.

"Tell you what, Ray," he said with a tight George C. Scott smile, "I'll play you one game of gin rummy for that land I want. If you win, you gotta sell it to us. If I lose, I'll stop bothering you."

Buck would have laughed at anyone but Smith for making such a bet, but he agreed, and the cards were dealt, while everyone within hearing distance gravitated to the table, awed by C.R.'s audacity. It was over in ten minutes. American had acquired the right to purchase more than fifty acres of totally undeveloped land situated about halfway between Dallas and Fort Worth.

What its true value was in 1955 when Smith played that gin rummy game is guesswork, but if American bought those same fifty acres today it would have to mortgage to the hilt every plane in its fleet. The Stewardess College is still on that site, but its name has been changed twice. When male flight attendants were first hired in the 1970s, it became the Flight Service College. Now it is known as the Learning Center, and houses not only flight attendant training facilities but also serves as a training complex for outside users.

Adjacent to the Learning Center is the Flight Academy for pilot training; nearby are American's new corporate headquarters building, whose construction was started when the airline moved to Dallas/Fort Worth, and the huge new Reservations Center. The former is on airport-owned land protected by a long-term lease, and the entire complex is only minutes away from the Dallas/Fort Worth Airport.

The College was C.R.'s personal project, and not even a Bill Hogan could dissuade him from spending a million dollars at a time when the airline was going into hock for Electras and 707s. Years later, someone asked him, "C.R., was it worth a million bucks?"

"Hell, yes," he replied. "We got at least $10 million worth of publicity out of it."

But publicity wasn't the reason he wanted a stewardess college—far from it. He was motivated almost entirely by his conviction that cabin attendants were the front-line troops in the war of competition, literally the infantry of the airlines. He believed deeply that no matter what any department did before a flight, from marketing to meteorology, in the end the bottom line was how a stewardess worked that flight. He wanted his girls—and *"his* girls" was how he viewed them—to have the finest training in the industry.

It was strictly his idea to call the new facility a "college." It gave the school a more dignified image, implying that a flight attendant's profession was no menial job capable of being performed by any dimwit with a pretty face. He deliberately sought a college-style atmosphere and environment, with attractive dormitory quarters, modern classrooms, and the finest recreational facilities, all in a self-contained complex on grounds that even looked like a college campus.

It was that concept on which he spent the $1 million.

The Stewardess College was dedicated November 21, 1957; it was the finest airline facility in the world, putting all stewardess training under one roof—sleeping quarters, mock-ups, meals, classrooms, recreation, and counseling. The College even had a house mother, Mrs. Ronnie Anagnostis, whose husband Nick served as facilities superintendent in charge of building and grounds upkeep. That was his official task; unofficially he was house "father." Nick was a former AA mechanic whose first job with the airline in 1939 was putting the rubberized de-icer boots on DC-3s in the fall and taking them off in the spring.

The school's first "dean"—the titular nomenclature was director of the Stewardess College—was Millie Alford. She began her new duties before the school opened, and her first office consisted of an orange crate with a phone on top. She also had a frequent visitor—Cyrus Rowlett Smith, who insisted on flying in from New York to check on the architect's plans and the construction progress. If he wasn't satisfied with the way things were going, he'd dictate changes right on the spot. Millie remembered one weekend when he drew some architectural revisions in pencil on a piece of scratch paper and announced, "This is how it's gonna be."

Smith insisted that the trainees go first class. Sky Chefs operated the meal service, and Newt Wilson's Dallas staff was told to furnish only the best meats and vegetables available—steaks, for example, were the same American served first-class passengers. "The food quality," Nick Anagnostis said, "you couldn't buy in a supermarket."

The dormitory was on the second floor. All other facilities were on the first, and a handsome spiral staircase connected the two levels. It became a tradition to pose each graduating class on the staircase, and this has been followed ever since. Each dormitory room accommodated four trainees, and until male applicants were accepted (in 1972), the beds were only seventy-two inches long.

The first class was flown in from Chicago where it already had received two weeks' training, and finished the final four weeks at the College. For the first four or five years, the College operated with traditional curfews: 11 P.M. weeknights and 1 A.M. Fridays and Saturdays. Trainees had to sign out and sign in, and while there were no regular bedchecks, Millie would pull an occasional surprise raid if she suspected flagrant violators. There is an eight-foot wrought iron fence around the building, and for a brief time it was electrified—not to shock anyone out of her libido but to keep out unwanted visitors by setting off an alarm. It was disconnected when squirrels began triggering the alarm, sending poor Nick Anagnostis out of his bed to intercept some supposed boyfriend trying to get over the fence.

Millie neglected to publicize the disconnection. She never told trainees it was electrified, but she hinted at it broadly in the orientation lecture delivered on the starting day of each class. "If you try to go over that fence," she'd warn, "well . . . [dramatic pause] let's just say you'll be sorry."

Most of them believed right up to graduation that the fence's wiring was operational, and AWOL intendees or their dates tried the front gate, which invariably was a tactical mistake. Nick and Ronnie lived in a house right next to the entrance and could see most of the attempts. Ronnie caught one young man trying to help a trainee over the gate. He had parked his car next to the entrance and was standing on its roof boosting her over.

The majority of transgressions involved curfew violations, not escapes. One or two offenses didn't mean dismissal, but repeated occurrences did. Millie said the worst part of her job was terminating a trainee. "I remember only one in my years as director who talked me out of dismissing her, and I was never sorry. I made a practice of following up on the marginal graduates—a kind of feedback from supervisors on how they were doing—and I found there were about 50 percent we should have let go before they graduated. The rest were doing fine."

For trainees, Millie remembered, the most traumatic experience occurred the first Sunday of each new class. That was hair-cutting day; in those days, specified hair length was subject to ruler measurement, and it was one of the first regulations a rookie learned. The entire day was turned over to professional hairdressers who came out to the College from their regular beauty parlors in Dallas and Fort Worth, and the sound of protesting squeals drowned out the scissor clips.

No men were allowed on the second floor except for maintenance workers. When a plumber or carpenter had to climb the staircase, the public address system would blare out, "Man on Second," followed by the thuds of scurrying bare feet and the swish of hastily wrapped towels.

Curfews were abandoned during the sixties, corresponding to the relaxing of rules throughout the nation's schools. But the Stewardess College continued to be the most concentrated system of education in any institution of learning; in effect, it was four years of college compressed down to six weeks. And it got even tougher when the jets came along.

Hundreds of on-line stewardesses went back to the College for jet qualification, most of them as nervous as the new trainees. As the jet age drew near, the rumor mill went into high gear. *"The jets will give you varicose veins. . . . Your menstrual cycles will go completely haywire,"* etc.

The most startling rumor—"Apparently started by pilots," Millie Alford commented dryly—was that constant exposure to jet flights would result in girls becoming sterile. This widely spread canard sent one panic-stricken stewardess in to see Walfrieda McAssey, Flight Service manager in New York.

"Is it true, Mac?" she asked. "I mean, about the jets making us sterile?"

Walfrieda looked up from a pile of papers. "Don't count on it, honey."

Millie Alford spent more time than she wanted to knocking down the scare stories. To her, the 707 represented "the biggest thrill and the biggest change in my career."

"I brainwashed everyone on how great it was," she recounted. "Before it was introduced, I helped write the manuals and procedures we'd use."

In the years she served as director, she was a kind of Mother Superior to every trainee who climbed that spiral staircase—drill sergeant, confidante, teacher, and friend. She was tough but popular, and fully capable of deflating the cocky. One brand-new trainee told her, "You look pretty good for somebody your age."

Millie smiled. "I'll remember that when I pin the wings on your flat chest."

In Nick and Ronnie Anagnostis, she had a pair of valuable allies. For a quarter of a century, this couple was as much a part of the college as the concrete in its foundations. Nick was far more than a maintenance supervisor. His duties also included accompanying trainees to the airport for evacuation training on real airplanes and making sure nobody got hurt going down the chutes, rushing sick girls to the hospital in the middle of the night, and—the most unpleasant memory of all—notifying the parents of one trainee that she had been killed in an auto accident.

C.R. was present, of course, the day the Stewardess College opened. The dedication speech was delivered by Sam Rayburn, who showed up late. He was driving an ancient green Pontiac and not only got lost but almost froze because the heater didn't work. The ceremony was held outside by the pool, the weather was blustery and cold, and Rayburn was miserable until someone offered him some bourbon. He downed the contents of a water glass two-thirds full and proceeded to deliver a bell-ringing oration.

Smith came to many graduations, as often as four to six times a year, and never lost interest in the school. For years he made the graduation addresses himself, but when male trainees began to appear, he refused to recognize their presence. His speech would open with, "Ladies . . ."

Anagnostis asked him on one graduation visit, "Mr. C.R., doesn't it bother you that we spend all this time and money training these girls, and in eighteen months most of them will be gone?"

Smith shook his head. "Nick, this is the cheapest advertising investment we ever made. They'll sell American airlines for the rest of their lives, and so will their children and grandchildren."

There was more truth than sentiment in that remark, as evidenced by the fast-growing Kiwi organization, named after the flightless bird of New Zealand. It started with a small New York City chapter in 1946 and held its first national convention in Chicago in 1954, with 150 attendees and 17 official delegates. Thirty years later, there were sixty-five chapters nationwide with more than 2,000 members, including flight attendants still flying. The first honorary member was Kay Hansen, who had helped the group organize nationally. (Jane Wyman was a guest at the 1960 Kiwi convention.)

The Kiwis were proud of the new Stewardess College, and someone suggested presenting the school with a statue of a kiwi bird as a permanent display.

The idea collided with the club's $150 bank account, but one brave member happened to mention their dilemma to a certain American Airlines vice president.

"We have in mind a kind of large plaque attached to a nice base, with a kiwi bird mounted on top," she told him, "but we don't have the money."

"Hell, I'll pay for the damned thing out of my own pocket," he offered, "but God help you if you ever tell anyone where the dough came from."

The name of the donor can now be revealed. It was Red Mosier.

The Kiwi monument was placed next to a small wishing well outside the College, and for a long time, graduates followed a tradition of marching to the Kiwi statue and dropping good luck coins in the well—American's version of the Naval Academy's famed statue of Chief Tecumseh. Eventually, the graduation ceremonies had to be shortened as the airline expanded. They were shipping girls to new bases almost as soon as their wings were pinned on, and tradition went with them.

College fraternities in the Dallas/Fort Worth area would send initiates to steal the bird from its perch. The kiwi had to be replaced so many times that American finally decided to move the monument to a less vulnerable location at the Learning Center.

C.R. provided the inspiration for another kind of permanent display. Millie Alford first heard about it via a phone call from his brother Bill, who was Smith's sounding board for some of his ideas.

"Millie, C.R. wants a portrait painted of the ideal stewardess. He wants to hang it in the College's lobby."

She asked the obvious question. "Bill, how are we going to choose the girl who'll pose?"

"That's your job," he said cheerfully.

Millie was considering a contest, with each base sending in pictures and nominations, when she encountered C.R. at a meeting in New York.

"How you coming on that portrait idea?" he inquired.

"Mr. C.R., we're having quite a bit of difficulty picking the right girl. We don't want her to be a professional model."

"Hell, no." He thought a moment. "Millie, it should be someone like . . . like, well, Julie Redmond."

Bingo! Julie Redmond, exceptionally attractive and also a superb stewardess, happened to be an instructor on Millie's own staff. It was her portrait that was hung on the wall next to the spiral staircase, and it turned out so well that Smith began scouting for other candidates.

Once a year, he would hold a directors' meeting outside New York City, sometimes at one of the resort cities the airline served, and this particular year the board was meeting in Mexico City. Millie Alford received another call from Bill Smith.

"Millie, just talked to C.R. and he wants a portrait painted of the pretty little Mexican girl who was working our flight down here. Her name's Mary Diaz. Set it up."

The third such call came from C.R., who had just held a press conference announcing American's application to serve Japan. Several stewardesses of Oriental heritage had been present, and he had spotted one in particular.

"We should have another portrait painted," he told Millie. "This littie Bernice Chan is a doll."

The fourth selection was American's first black stewardess, Joan Dorsey. She was hired in the mid-sixties when American became one of the first carriers to break the color barrier in this category. Walt Kistler, for years in charge of flight attendant recruiting, called her at her home in Flagstaff, Arizona, after picking her name from a file of previous black applicants.

"Happy birthday," he greeted her, after identifying himself.

"How did you know it was my birthday?"

"It's not because I'm a mind reader," Kistler confessed. "I have your application in front of me. Do you still want to be a stewardess?"

She did, but because she was setting an important precedent and would be exposed to above-normal attention (and prejudice), the airline deliberately set out to prepare her. Explained Alford:

"Joan was approved by everyone but God. They really groomed her. She was put to work in the recruitment office first, then assigned to the reception desk at the College before she finally began training."

She established not only an important precedent but set an example for the many black stewardesses who followed her. C.R. picked her out for the fourth portrait not just because of her color, but from the way she worked a trip he was on. She and the first black flight attendants on other carriers did much to gradually erase the bigotry that actually dated back to the industry's early years. In the thirties, some airlines used to discourage blacks from flying and even had a code to identify blacks requesting reservations: "Ruby Hart."

If a black showed up at an airport holding a ticket and confirmed space, there was nothing anyone could do except try to avoid seating him next to a white passenger. If an airline knew a black passenger would be boarding, it was common practice to block out the right front seat, a single on the DC-3; putting one in the double-seat row was a no-no. The real discrimination began at reservations. If a call came in from a known black neighborhood, or if the caller sounded black, they were told no space was available. The code "Ruby Hart" came from the name of a black woman who slipped through this screening process. The practice was so widespread that one wealthy black businessman used to send his white chauffeur to pick up his ticket.

American had one captain who was suspended for refusing to fly a trip when he learned that a black girl would be the stewardess. But even the most prejudiced pilots came around when the girls began proving the color of their uniform was more important than the color of their skin. The same captain who was suspended was seen one day showing a little black boy the cockpit, and holding him on his lap so his parents could snap a picture.

Later, of course, the barriers were lowered for pilot applicants from all minorities, and women as well. Bonnie Tiburzi was American's first female pilot, one of more than a hundred now flying for U.S. carriers.

Retired Captain John McCarten emphasized that while American made a decided effort to hire minorities, "to its credit the airline never unbent its qualifications."

He was at a union meeting where a management representative was explaining the need for minority pilots and the qualifications they'd have to meet. A captain raised his hand. "Suppose I can get you a black, Spanish-speaking female," he wanted to know. "Would that count for three?"

"I'll tell you one thing," McCarten continued. "If the qualifications he laid down that night had been in effect in my day, not a guy in that room would have been hired."

Until Joan Dorsey's portrait was hung, no one realized that C.R., apparently by accident, had selected an ethnic cross section (or maybe it wasn't a coincidence, knowing C.R.). So it was decided to commission a fifth painting, and the model was Carol Akers, a Jewish stewardess. All five portraits are now in the Learning Center's dining room, next to one of C.R., painted by Western artist Tom Lea.

When Smith showed up for the College's fifth anniversary, he brought along several distinguished guests to help celebrate the occasion. Present were Congressman Jim Wright of Texas, the mayors of Dallas and Fort Worth, Raymond Buck, Tull Rea, representing American's Dallas base, and Amon Carter, Jr., son of C.R.'s old friend and long-time director. Smith was showing them the recreation room and Carter, who owned the only Fort Worth television station then transmitting programs in color, noticed the black-and-white TV set.

"C.R.," he needled, "why don't you buy the girls a color TV set?"

"Why don't you buy 'em one?" Smith countered. "You've got the station."

They argued about it briefly, until C.R. suggested they play a hand of gin rummy or poker, the loser to buy the new TV.

"Not on your life," Carter protested. "I heard how you got this land."

"Name a game you think you can win," Smith challenged.

"Okay. Dominoes. I see a set over there on that table."

The next morning, C.R. stopped at Nick Anagnostis's house to say good-bye. "By the way, Nick," he added, "Amon's gonna be sending out a color TV set for the rec room."

In 1967, when the Stewardess College was celebrating its tenth anniversary, American began a massive expansion program that added a new dormitory, cafeteria, more classrooms, and the Flight Academy for pilots. All but the latter were added to the original College; the Academy was a separate building. Nick Anagnostis was named manager of facilities maintenance and support, the title reflecting his increased responsibilities.

Millie Alford, who left the College in 1962 to become director of stewardess service in New York, asked to be transferred back after a time and continued to serve as its director until her retirement in 1980.

It was during her second tenure that she began emphasizing to C.R. that the College's facilities, if expanded, could be used for other training programs, such as reservations agents and lower management classes, and perhaps utilized by outside groups.

C.R. listened. He not only authorized the expansion, but hired a consultant firm to study what could be done to attract outside users. Its recommendations were implemented, although, as Millie put it, "They got all their ideas from American Airlines people who could have told management what could have been done in the first place."

One result of the increased outside utilization was the selection of the overall name "Learning Center." Alford said this was done to avoid any static from wives who might object to husbands being sent to the American Airlines Stewardess College. In actuality, the use of an airline's training facilities by non-airline companies (a big accounting firm is one of the users at this writing) merely reflected American's long-standing reputation for training employees.

Years before the College opened, Stanley Marcus of Neiman-Marcus called Doc Miller, then American's manager in Dallas.

"Your employees do by far the best job of any service people I've ever encountered in my travels," Marcus said. "If we could get our employees to be as pleasant and accommodating as yours, I'd be very pleased. Would you consider putting on a training program for our people?"

In Dallas, a Stanley Marcus request was the equivalent of a C. R. Smith command. Miller turned the suggestion over to Jack Mullins, who set up a training program based on courses given to American's agents—how to be friendly and courteous, and how to handle upset or angry customers. It was not only successful, but led to a number of joint American/Nieman-Marcus promotional efforts, such as sending the airline's timetables to a selected list of the store's best charge customers.

In 1980, the huge training facility finally got the new name it deserved: the C. R. Smith Learning Center.

It could be classed as a minor miracle that C.R. could become so heavily involved in such projects as the Stewardess College while preparing the airline for the jet revolution.

He was aided in this juggling act, however, by the fact that American in 1956 enjoyed a year of relative calm, even in the usually turbulent atmosphere of the upper echelons. American's and C.R.'s biggest loss was Carlene Roberts. She had resigned in 1954 to get married, her strong sense of duty dictating the difficult choice she had to make in an era when few women tried to combine career and marriage.

She was missed. C.R. didn't even think of her gender. Once when Wayne McMillan was his assistant, he issued a series of verbal orders to be relayed to various officers and the final one went, "Oh, and tell Mr. Roberts to make sure . . ." When McMillan told her what C.R. wanted, he added, "Carlene, you've arrived."

Jake Jacob, as a senior vice president whose responsibilities included government affairs, took over most of her duties, but he lacked her Washington contacts and experience. And this was a time when the regulatory wheels in the capital seemed to be square-shaped instead of round. All airlines were trying to expand their route structures, and some applications were about as economically practical as bidding for a route to the moon. Everyone wanted the more lucrative long-haul markets, even when those markets obviously couldn't absorb additional competition.

The CAB, too often populated by political hacks who didn't really grasp the intricacies of air transportation, moved with excruciating slowness. The airline industry was and may always be cyclical, terribly vulnerable to the periodic ups and downs of the roller-coaster national economy. The CAB usually was running at least a year behind the economy; by the time it got around to deciding a case it had been deliberating for as long as two years, economic conditions had changed drastically and the decision no longer made sense.

Furthermore, by the mid fifties the CAB was entering a long period in which most of its decisions favored the expansion plans of the smaller carriers. Airlines like American were regarded with a kind of "you're big enough already" attitude. The philosophy of helping the little guys may have sounded great on paper, but some of the little guys were like children being given a $20 bill as they entered a candy store. Both Northeast and Capital were examples of carriers who couldn't cope with expansion and eventually became victims of mergers.

Merger was one way to detour around the Civil Aeronautic Board's roadblocks of procrastination. Jacob and Walt Johnson heard little Colonial Airlines was in trouble and up for grabs, and urged C.R. to buy it. Colonial's biggest asset was authority to serve Bermuda from both New York and Washington, although it was a Montreal-based carrier with predominantly Canadian routes. It was Bermuda, a prime tourist market, that put the gleam in Jacob's and Johnson's eyes, but for once C.R.'s gambling instincts were taking a nap. He said no and Colonial eventually fell into Eastern's willing arms. Johnson believed C.R. felt a merger application would hurt American's chances of getting new routes.

If 1956 was a year of calm, it was a proverbial calm before the storm that was to break on several fronts before long. Particularly deceptive was the peaceful air around 100 Park Avenue, to which American had moved corporate headquarters. There were always periodic changes at the executive level, usually in response to retirements and the shifting of assignments. One example was Marv Whitlock's being brought to New York as vice president of equipment planning. His replacement in Tulsa was former Major General John B. Montgomery, whose credentials were impressive. C.R. had met him during the war when Montgomery was commanding the Eighth Air Force and he also served as secretary to the Joint Chiefs of Staff.

Smith first made him assistant vice president of operations under Mosier and then shipped him to Tulsa, where he is best remembered as the only American

Airlines vice president who insisted that staff members rise when he entered a meeting room. This carry-over from his days as a two-star general didn't affect his competence, however; he knew jets and that's why C.R. picked him. Tulsa as well as the rest of the airline was getting ready. But "Monty," as everyone called him, didn't stay very long. He resigned to go with General Electric's jet engine division and Gene Taylor took his place.

It was Taylor who was running the Tulsa base when a third attempt was made to paint the airplanes. This time it was American's advertising agency that reportedly originated the idea. "I don't really remember whose idea it was," Gene related, "and as a matter of fact I doubt whether anyone would admit authorship, but it was decided that we had to do something for our image on the eve of the jet age. So the agency, public relations, sales, and a few other departments, plus outside consultants, finally agreed on a new color scheme, and it was put to C.R."

They were risking his wrath. Only a few months before, the same ad agency had created a modernized version of the eagle, insisting that the existing one was too old-fashioned. Rex Smith showed C.R. a sketch of the proposed new insignia.

"It looks like a goddamned Airedale!" C.R. fumed. "Get it to hell out of my sight and tell those bastards to stop fooling around with our symbol!"

Somewhat to Taylor's surprise, however, Smith agreed to let them paint one airplane and promised that he'd look at the finished product. "But for Christ's sake keep it confidential," he warned.

There are no known photographs of the aircraft chosen; Taylor remembered it was probably a DC-6 and that there was "a lot of blue involved with some new striping that basically did away with the all-silver airplane." A special non-airline crew of painters was hired to do the job behind a huge curtain draped across one end of a Tulsa hanger. Sandy Underwood, one of Gene's maintenance superintendents, was in overall charge, and he was extremely proud of the results. Except for Taylor, he was the only one in the hangar when C.R. arrived to inspect the new color scheme.

C.R. walked around the plane without comment, Underwood and Taylor following him. Finally, he turned to Gene.

"What do you think of it?"

"I don't like it?"

"Why?"

"It's not very distinctive. We've covered up the one thing that makes us different from every other airline. Hell, everyone's painting their airplanes one color or another. If we keep the metal, we'll be the only one left, and if you're looking for distinction, that's the way to go."

C.R. grunted, "I don't like it either. Take it off."

He accompanied Taylor back to Taylor's office, where representatives of the agency and various American personnel were anxiously awaiting C.R.'s verdict. They hadn't seen the airplane yet.

"Gene, you tell 'em," Smith said.

Taylor did, and was greeted with protests. "We should have seen it ourselves. . . . We should at least discuss it. . . ."

· "If you want to see it," Taylor suggested, "you'd better hurry. The paint strippers are out there right now and that airplane will be back in the fleet tomorrow."

One of C.R.'s greatest concerns was not paint but something far more personal: Rex Smith's health was visibly deteriorating, to the point where he was simply going through the motions. His heavy drinking didn't help; some of his fellow officers privately expressed surprise that he wasn't fired. But it wasn't alcohol that was affecting his work. He was in the first stages of a painful and terminal cancer, and C.R. must have known, because even after he hired Willis Player as the new vice president of public relations early in 1957, he allowed Rex to stay on as a kind of vice president without portfolio: his duties for almost a year were virtually nothing except to give Willis occasional advice and guidance.

Player had left Pan Am and was head of ATA's public relations when C.R. asked him to join American, explaining at the same time what Rex's situation was—in effect, Willis was being invited to step into another man's shoes while those shoes were still occupied. It was typical of both men that absolutely no friction developed between them during the time that American technically had *two* vice presidents of public relations. Player believed, in point of fact, that Rex recommended him to C.R. And when Rex finally decided to retire, early in 1958, Player was the only one who could have replaced him in C.R.'s heart as well as in his job.

Joe Harty, who had been transferred to New York as head of special promotions, saw him just before he left American. He had brought some promotion contract to Rex's apartment to be signed, and was shocked at his appearance.

"His face was blood-red and he was drenched with sweat," Harty remembered. "I never saw a man in such pain. He didn't seem to know where he was."

Harty showed him the contract, but Rex shook his head. "Joe, I gotta trust you on this one. I'll sign it without reading it."

In the spring of 1959, he flew to Albuquerque for last-ditch surgery at the famed Lovelace Clinic. He then went to Los Angeles, where Bill Hipple put him on a nonstop to New York, and then phoned Harty.

"He's in pretty bad shape, Joe," Hipple warned. "I'd appreciate your meeting his flight."

Harty brought him back to the apartment and noticed the furniture already had been covered with sheets. He offered to spend the night there, but Rex said, "No, I'll be fine."

That was the last time Harty saw him. He died three weeks later, mourned by every airline p.r. man in the United States but most of all by C. R. Smith. It was at C.R.'s suggestion that American established a journalism scholarship in Rex's name. Walter Cronkite and Bob Considine were on the original selection committee.

In person, he was rather short, and unusually quiet much of the time. "He knew exactly what he wanted and there was no fooling around with him," Harty said. "He knew whether you were producing."

Some of the great names in American's p.r. history either cut their teeth under Rex Smith's tutelage or learned from those who did. But occasionally Rex tripped over his better judgment and picked a turkey.

One of the rookies he hired was a youngster who was privately wealthy and took the job solely because he loved the airlines and its people. Rex had arranged to fly a planeload of celebrities from Los Angeles to Tucson for the world premiere of a 20th Century-Fox film called *Chicken Every Sunday,* starring Celeste Holm. He arrived in Tucson from New York accompanied by his new assistant, to whom he had entrusted the task of photographing the welcoming ceremonies.

The plane carrying the junketing VIPs landed and Rex looked over at the youngster to make sure he had his camera ready.

"You gonna take pictures?" he asked in a tone implying utter disbelief.

"Sure thing, Rex."

"Well, it's gonna be one hell of a shot. You're pointing the damned camera at yourself."

As Rex Smith, basically a showman at heart, would have said: "Leave 'em laughing."

Willis Player assumed his new duties just in time to witness another round of corporate convulsions.

The figurative seismographs at 100 Park Avenue first began jiggling with the news of another top-level reorganization: Mosier and Hogan were elevated to new ranks as executive vice presidents, and in the revised pecking order Speers and Jacob, who remained senior vice presidents, were no longer their equals.

But the biggest surprise was the addition of a third executive vice president: Charlie Rheinstrom. He was with the J. Walter Thompson advertising agency when C.R. asked him to come back to American. And, according to one former officer serving at the time, "C.R. practically got down on his hands and knees and begged."

It is doubtful whether C.R. would have assumed this imploring position before any mortal, but there is no question he wanted Rheinstrom badly. There *was* some loss of face involved on Smith's part, and C.R. didn't like to lose face. His motive was simple: he wanted Rheinstrom's acknowledged ability and input for jet-age planning, and the reorganization was to accommodate his presence.

Some interpreted Rheinstrom's unexpected recruitment as a slap at Charlie Speers. But it should be remembered that Speers was not only Rheinstrom's protégé almost from the airline's dawn, but admittedly lacked his toughness. Speers's easygoing, friendly nature, a strong virtue in most men, was something of a handicap in the rough-and-tumble world of airline politics.

So Charlie Rheinstrom was back and what Speers, Jacob, Mullins, Johnson, and many others feared would happen did: he clashed immediately with Bill Hogan. They had their own version of the Hogan-Mosier feud. Instead of shouting at one another, they refused to speak to each another, and this began not too long after Rheinstrom returned.

Officially, Rheinstrom was executive vice president in charge of sales, Hogan ruled the financial and planning departments, and Mosier continued to run operations, which included engineering and maintenance. Even in normal times, this would have involved inevitable overlapping in some areas of juris-diction. Engineering couldn't select a new plane, for example, without some input from finance. But even the enormously greater complexity of jet plan-ning, in which jurisdiction became more blurred than usual, shouldn't have resulted in such friction. American's planning performance was superb, as subsequent events would prove, but this was *despite* the feuding—a major achievement in itself.

The infighting was on an intensely personal level, a clash of egos, wills, and personalities that is still fresh in the memories of officers from that era. Speers was just one.

"It was ridiculous. Charlie wouldn't even come to Hogan's floor and Hogan refused to go to Charlie's. There may have been policy disagreements between them, probably over budgetary controls. That was always a sore point among American's marketing people because Hogan always insisted on maintaining very tight budget controls."

For a while, Jacob tried to be the peacemaker between these warring corpo-rate gladiators, for C.R. deliberately tried to stay out of the battle zone. Jerry Jacob said his father once told him that Hogan, Mosier, and Rheinstrom "had guys assigned to spy on each other, so if anything got fouled up they'd go tell C.R. who was to blame."

Walt Johnson, like Speers a Rheinstrom protégé, had an interesting footnote on the feud, namely that for some reason, Rheinstrom began acting *like* Hogan. He recalled the early days when Charlie was an extremely warm, gregarious man who loved to have his young staff out to his home in Great Neck, Long Island, where he'd barbecue steaks and be the personification of a genial host.

"He seemed like a different man when he returned," Johnson said. "He criticized everybody and was harsh on people. Just another Hogan. I was one of his targets, and maybe because I was in a different role than before; I had become a vice president not too far removed from his own level."

Johnson made a speech to the American Association of Travel Agents convention in Madrid and a couple of weeks later, Rheinstrom sent him a note that took issue with his remarks, without specifying why he considered them harmful. "You used very bad judgment," it concluded. Johnson went to Rheinstrom's office, steaming.

"I got your note about that Madrid speech."

"Yeah, like I said, you used bad judgment."

"Charlie, did you read it?"

"No," Rheinstrom admitted.

"Then how do you know it's bad?"

"I've heard some bad reports."

"Charlie, I've got a file of complimentary letters three inches thick telling me it was the finest talk ever made at an ASTA meeting. Letters from all over the world."

"Makes no difference. From all *I've* heard, it was a bad speech."

The furious Johnson went back to his office, got a copy of the speech, and took it to Rheinstrom.

"Read it, Charlie. And by the way, ASTA thought enough of it to make 12,000 reprints."

Rheinstrom returned the text a few days later with another note: "I still don't like it. Hereafter, clear all speeches with me."

Once again, Johnson confronted him. "Look, I'm a damn good speaker, but I don't write my speeches out in advance. I just make an outline and talk off the cuff. So from now on, I won't make any speeches."

"Fine," Rheinstrom retorted.

But two weeks later, it was Rheinstrom who was asked by some important organization if Walt Johnson could address their annual meeting. Charlie relayed the request to Walt, who told him he'd do it if he wasn't required to submit an advance text for approval. Rheinstrom agreed, and the matter was closed. To Johnson, it was a relatively petty argument but indicative of the "new" Charlie Rheinstrom.

Sooner or later, the simmering volcano had to erupt in a showdown between Rheinstrom and Hogan. The latter already had established his supremacy in any argument serious enough to reach C.R. for settlement. There had been an eyeball-to-eyeball shouting match between Hogan and Mosier over one of Red's expense accounts.

"I'm not going to pay it!" Hogan yelled.

"The hell you won't!" Mosier roared. "I'll meet you in C.R.'s office."

A witness said Mosier emerged from the office later, wearing a crestfallen look.

Rheinstrom had no better luck. He hadn't finished the first year of the three-year contract Smith had given him when he presented C.R. with an "it's me or Hogan" ultimatum. Smith fired him.

To Charlie Speers, it was a question of Smith choosing which man meant more to American's present and future. "I think C.R.'s respect for Bill's financial ability outweighed his respect for Charlie's sales ability—it was as simple as that. I remember the day, after Hogan arranged that big loan with the insurance companies to finance the jets, when C.R. called me to his office to see him present Bill with a beautiful Revere bowl; on it was an inscription expressing his appreciation."

But maybe it wasn't that simple. Willis Player, who knew Rheinstrom was going to be fired before Charlie did himself, said the Hogan-or-me ultimatum was only the climax of what amounted to Rheinstrom's self-destruction. Explained Player:

"Charlie may have misunderstood or overestimated C.R.'s willingness to let you do whatever you were doing so long as you were doing it right. And Rheinstrom did something that in C.R.'s eyes was very, very wrong."

Player was referring to something that happened prior to that ultimatum. Rheinstrom's specialty was advertising, the same area of expertise that had led to his earlier resignation. When he came back as executive vice president of sales, he decided he wanted complete control over advertising and assumed he had such authority as part of his job.

He proceeded to fire the agency that had been handling American's advertising for a number of years and turned the account over to another firm. Almost unbelievably, he did it without consulting C.R.; the account executive who had been handling American's advertising was none other than C.R.'s brother Bill. Certainly Charlie Speers couldn't believe it. He had worked with Bill Smith for years on that account and never dreamed Rheinstrom would make such an error in pure common sense. Player put it more bluntly:

"A lot of people might think it funny that the brother of the chief executive officer is the account executive, but on the other hand, if you have a chief executive officer who takes a personal interest in your advertising programs and really wants to run it himself, it's not an unsensible arrangement. Charlie fired Bill Smith without consulting C.R., and when I heard about it, I knew it was going to cause trouble."

Only a few minutes after seeing C.R., Rheinstrom walked into a meeting of officers involved with the 707's introduction—he was the overall coordinator —and conducted the session as if nothing had happened. After about twenty minutes, however, he whispered to Player, "You know what's going on here, don't you?"

"Yes, I do," Willis murmured. Smith had told him first so he could handle the announcement, and because C.R. confided in him just as he had confided in Rex Smith.

The word got around 100 Park Avenue fast, but it was typical of Charlie Speers that he was the one who walked his old mentor to the elevators for the last time. Speers was acutely sensitive to people's feelings under such circumstances; he remembered only too well the day Dick Deichler called him in to inform Charlie he was now senior vice president of sales and that from then on Deichler would be working for Mosier. (Deichler resigned during the reorganization upheaval that brought in Rheinstrom.)

Speers would not disclose what Rheinstrom said to him as they shook hands at the elevator; others said Rheinstrom was naturally bitter and never forgave C.R. But Speers knew how he must have felt; being a senior vice president, let alone an executive vice president, was a heady altitude for any man. When Speers was admitted to the senior council, one of the first things Smith did was invite him to go fishing at the Southside Club on the east end of Long Island, an exclusive 3,000-acre trout fishing facility that had only a hundred members. Only the senior council was invited there, C.R. giving each man a beautiful rod.

Rheinstrom didn't dig his own grave because of any insatiable thirst for power, although control over advertising *was* a phobia with him. In truth, he could be quite reasonable, as Player himself would testify.

When Willis joined American, it was with the understanding he would report directly only to C. R. Smith. But just before Rheinstrom returned, Rex Smith, who was still around, tipped off Player that he would be reporting to Charlie instead. Rheinstrom believed that public relations was a close relative of advertising.

Player marched right to C.R. and recited a long list of reasons why he thought this was a bad idea.

"I agree with you," Smith allowed, "but you'd better talk to Rheinstrom."

Much to Player's surprise, Charlie didn't put up even a token fight. "I think you're absolutely right," he told Willis. "If the other senior officers thought you were my creature, they wouldn't trust you."

Rheinstrom's departure, as unexpected as his return, was just one more instance of the "revolving door" atmosphere so prevalent in an industry whose lifeblood is change. Executive stability is sought but not always achieved. For years, American's stability lay mostly in C.R. himself. He provided the bulk of the leadership continuity every airline needed and still does.

Nevertheless, he never stopped looking for fresh executive talent or potential talent within the company. Marion Sadler, who started with American in 1941 as a ramp agent in Dallas, was one young member of management C.R. had kept his eye on for a long time. In 1959, Sadler made vice president, with no idea that he was heading to the very top of the ladder. A new vice president a year earlier was Forwood "Bud" Wiser, one of Smith's many "warehoused" officers and also one of his better choices.

Wiser was a former Navy commander and a good operations man, but when C.R. recruited him, he had no specific job in mind. Smith turned him over to Mosier, who brought him to Whitlock's office.

"This is Bud Wiser, Whit," Mosier announced. "Break him in."

After Mosier left, Wiser sat down, looking a little bewildered.

"Welcome to American, Bud," Whitlock said. "What's your job going to be?"

"Hell, I don't know," Wiser confessed. "I thought you might."

For a month, they shared the same desk, changing sides every other day. Eventually they did find a spot for Wiser. He succeeded Mosier as vice president of operations when the ailing old warrior became C.R.'s assistant; like Littlewood, Mosier actually went into semi-retirement. Later, Wiser moved on to become president first of Northeast and then of TWA.

C.R. was thinking these days of another change, one that eventually would involve himself. He was good at the job of infusing the board of directors with fresh blood as older directors died or retired. Three exceptionally capable new directors had been added to the board around this time. Two were lawyers, Manly Fleischmann of Buffalo and Francis Hooks Burr of Boston. The third was Dallas banker Jim Aston, who had served with C.R. during the war and became a director several years before the other two.

This trio was destined to play important roles in American's future. They were the type of independent-minded director C.R. consistently sought. He naturally wanted men who agreed with his views in general, but he avoided a rubber-stamp board. However decisive C.R. was, he did not think decisiveness was synonymous with infallibility.

Another new director was Carter Burgess, fresh from the not-unique experience of being an ex-TWA president who did not get along with Howard Hughes. But while Smith unquestionably was strengthening the board, he still felt it lacked cohesive leadership. It had been without a chairman since Ralph Damon left American and C.R. declared the chairmanship vacant.

Sometime in the summer of 1958, Smith flew to Washington for a meeting with Malcolm MacIntyre, who a year earlier had agreed to serve the Eisenhower administration as undersecretary of the Air Force. MacIntyre had no idea why C.R. wanted to see him, but he found out in a hurry.

"I've been thinking about succession, Mac," Smith said. "I'd like you to come back to American right now as vice president and general counsel. If everything goes right, you'll move into executive vice president within a year."

MacIntyre interpreted this only one way: Smith was willing to designate him as his eventual successor and presumably would move up to board chairman when Mac was named president. ("He didn't spell it out," MacIntyre said, "but the implication was there.")

But honor overrode temptation. MacIntyre told him, "I'm sorry, C.R., but when I took this job I promised Ike I'd stay here at least two years. I've got another year to go, and I don't see how I can go back on my word."

Smith, a little irritated, according to MacIntyre, said, "Well, if you won't or can't, I don't have any option. I'll go ahead and hire George Spater as vice president and general counsel."

MacIntyre's account of that conversation was confirmed by another officer, who said he got it from C.R. himself. And there was, in that single incident, more than one shadow of things to come:

- Only a year later, MacIntyre became president of Eastern and would play a reluctant role in blocking an American-Eastern merger. If it had gone through, he would have been president of the merged companies.
- Spater not only became executive vice president and general counsel in 1959, but subsequently succeeded C.R.
- MacIntyre's major accomplishment at Eastern in an otherwise unhappy and unsuccessful regime was to launch the famed Shuttle service on the New York–Boston and New York–Washington routes in 1961, establishing a stranglehold on those two markets that not only defied C.R.'s attempts to break it but eventually was partially responsible for American

abandoning both markets. And no one realized at the time that the whole concept of a no-reservations, commuter-type operation with hourly departures had been dreamed up by American in the late forties.

As usual, it had been the product of C.R.'s ever-busy mind. American was being plagued even then by the "no show" problem that cursed every carrier serving the Eastern seaboard corridor between Boston and Washington. Typical example: a businessman would fly from New York to Boston early in the morning, booking space on the 5 P.M. return flight. But often he'd finish earlier than anticipated and would catch a mid-afternoon flight back to New York —without cancelling his space on the 5 P.M.

There were so many no shows that at one time American, Eastern, and Northeast established joint ticket counters at the airports so they could control space better. But this was taking an aspirin for pneumonia, and C.R. furthermore was galled by the high cost of operating a reservations system for this short-haul, low-yield market.

He had his staff study the feasibility of a no-reservations service aimed at the New York–Washington route, and the proposed project got far enough down the road to warrant the tentative assignment of three DC-6s and four still-in-service DC-3s to a shuttle operation. C.R. was ready to inaugurate the experiment until his officers almost unanimously talked him out of it. The most vociferous opponent was Art Lewis, who ironically later became Eastern's president and thanked the Lord for the money-making Shuttle.

Their objections were sound at the time. Lewis argued it would be impossible to handle a no-reservations system during peak hours, and that overall load factors would be lopsided: strong in the morning and late afternoon but weak the rest of the day. What no one, including C.R., thought of was the gimmick that made Eastern's Shuttle so successful: back-up planes during peak periods, which made guaranteed space possible.

The staff that studied the concept and then recommended implementation to C.R. included two key names: Frank Sharpe, assistant director of reservations, and his top aide, Bob Winn. The latter was the real brain behind the plan that C.R. came so close to adopting. It so happened that Rickenbacker's grudging admiration for American's reservations system led him to raid that system for some of its best men. Sharpe and Winn were among them (Rod King was another), and when MacIntyre asked his own staff at Eastern to look into a possible Shuttle service, Winn had his original data in his desk. History took it from there.

If the contents of American's 1958 Annual Report were turned into one-day newspaper stories, they couldn't be packed into a single front page.

In that one year, the airline:

• Suffered another pilots' strike.
• Asked for nonstop New York–San Francisco authority.

- Ordered twenty-five Convair 990 jets, which turned out to be the only poor equipment choice C.R. ever made.
- Entered the CAB's Southern Transcontinental Service Case, which also wound up in disappointment.
- Discontinued round-trip discounts and reduced the 50 percent family fare discount to one third, both moves the result of the CAB's reducing C.R.'s requested 15 percent fare hike to only 4 percent.
- Accelerated the phasing out of the piston fleet, signing contracts for the sale of twenty-five DC-7s and twenty Convairs.

The latter event brought forth a classic remark by Smith on the difficulties of selling DC-7s. *U.S. News & World Report* asked him what the market was like for such planes.

"It's pretty thin," he replied. "I might trade you one for a subscription."

That didn't apply to the Convairs. The first ten American sold, in 1957, brought $3.1 million, $1 million more than what American had paid for them brand-new. Bill Hogan was behind that deal, and he swung another one with Texaco. In the fall of 1958, he signed a contract for four *billion* gallons of kerosene that would be used to power the 707. It was the largest single aviation fuel order to date, and Hogan got the low per-gallon price he wanted.

At long last, the eagle was ready to go jet.

16

Turbines—and Troubles

The cover story in *Time* magazine's issue of November 17, 1958, concerned the just-arrived jet age.

That date was twenty-three days after Pan American World Airways inaugurated Boeing 707 service across the Atlantic, thus giving the first U.S. carrier to order jets the equal distinction of being the first U.S. airline to operate them.

Yet the face on *Time*'s cover was not that of Juan Trippe, but the likeness of Cyrus Rowlett Smith, and just above his jowled, square-jawed countenance was a turbine engine carrying American's orange-peel markings. No finer or more significant tribute could have been paid an airline president and his company; it was simply another acknowledgment of industry leadership.

The honor was richly deserved. Yet not even the magazine's scrupulous research had uncovered a little-known fact about its cover subject: it was C.R., exercising his considerable influence within the Air Transport Association, who had mustered unanimous airline support for the creation of the Federal Aviation Agency. In its own way, this 1958 legislative development ranked in importance with the introduction of the jets themselves.

"If we don't build our own regulatory environment," he warned the industry, "others will impose one on us." This was his chief argument when he got ATA to begin studies on the possible revision of the outmoded Civil Aeronautics Act of 1938.

For Smith was the first airline mogul to express concern that the industry was heading for the jet age under the regulatory authority of a federal agency possessing a DC-3 mentality. The creaking, timid Civil Aeronautics Authority, born two decades before, had outlived its usefulness; as a weak "subsidiary" of the parent Commerce Department, consistently starved for funding and flabby in its disciplinary and monitoring authority over the airlines, it was a model of bureaucratic ineptness. The CAA's air traffic control system was almost a scandal, expected to handle 500-m.p.h. jets with radar that had once tracked 20-knot warships.

ATC's obsolescence was exposed sharply in the summer of 1956 when a TWA Constellation and a United DC-7 collided in clear weather over the Grand Canyon, taking the lives of all 128 persons aboard the two planes. Both were flying off-airways because the undermanned ATC centers had cleared them to go VFR (Visual Flight Rules). The airways themselves were inadequate for the mushrooming traffic, and the air traffic control regulations were the same ones that had been used in the DC-3's heyday. When TWA was given permission to climb to "one thousand feet above the clouds"—a dangerously imprecise clearance—the Connie went to 21,000 feet; TWA was advised United was at the same altitude, but nobody told United of a clearance that had put TWA at an identical altitude on two converging paths that bisected over a radio checkpoint.

The aftermath of that tragedy was legislation introduced by Senator Mike Monroney of Oklahoma establishing an *independent* Federal Aviation Agency, as had been recommended by the ATA's studies, with sufficient funding to start ATC's modernization. Until C.R. began making waves among his ATA peers, the industry's support had been lukewarm at best.

Time demonstrated its usual penchant for factual accuracy down to the most minute detail. The cover portrait was finished and ready to go to press when researcher Gayle Williams (who later joined American's p.r. department) phoned Willis Player.

"Our artist has C.R. with blue eyes," she said. "We want to make sure he's got the right color."

Player, who saw Smith almost daily, couldn't remember and went right to the source. "What color are your eyes?" he asked C.R.

"I didn't know you cared, dearie," Smith chuckled, "but they're brown."

The cover portrait came out with brown eyes.

Time very accurately described Red Mosier as "sugar-voiced," which may have been a slight understatement. His voice oozed, as if his words were being propelled out of an oiled larynx. The magazine's layout also featured a photograph of a smiling Bill Hogan; someone at 100 Park Avenue remarked, "They must have retouched it."

The excellent publicity was dissipated somewhat by the fact that American wasn't even the first domestic carrier to introduce jet service. Tiny National beat the eagle to the punch by leasing two 707s from Pan Am for the 1958–59 New York–Miami winter rush.

But at that point, C.R. didn't care who was first. He was wondering if American would be getting *any* of its new Electras and 707s off the ground as scheduled. On December 19, 1958—just before the busy Christmas season —American's pilots staged their second strike.

The issue this time was one that would harass all jet operators: ALPA's demand that flight engineers assigned to all-turbine equipment should be pilot qualified. ALPA insisted it was a matter of safety; the union referred to its policy as the concept of a "fail-safe crew." The airlines said ALPA's alleged concern over safety was a red herring, that all the union really wanted was to increase its membership. Flight engineers had their own union, and requiring them to be qualified pilots would force them to join the pilots' union.

As so often happens in labor disputes, both sides were simultaneously right and wrong. It made sense to have the third man in the cockpit of an unforgiving jet know how to fly the airplane. But ALPA did have an ulterior motive, and it was exactly what management claimed: the so-called "third man controversy" was simply a device to win for ALPA bargaining jurisdiction over all cockpit crew members.

The strike lasted twenty-two days and ended with a temporary, unsatisfactory, and totally uneconomical compromise: American agreed to a four-man jet crew, of three pilots *and* a flight engineer. The airline caved in partially to protect the latter group. Most of its flight engineers were veteran ex-mechanics, not young would-be pilots serving as a kind of cockpit apprentice. And ALPA's timing was devastating. The strike not only wrecked Christmas traffic but was called less than two months before the scheduled introductions of both the 707 and the Electra. Management took its lumps and accepted the loss of holiday business, but the pressure to settle in time for the new equipment was immense.

There was about as much need for a four-man crew on the Boeings (or DC-8s) as for a fifth engine, and eventually a government fact-finding commission, whose decision would be binding on all parties, settled the issue permanently. It ruled that all flight engineers must be pilot qualified; those who didn't want to be trained or couldn't qualify were to be given generous severance pay. Before this went into effect, however, the badly wounded flight engineers union staged a series of crippling strikes over the third-man issue. In 1961, it shut eight airlines down almost simultaneously for a week, and United, which long ago had settled the crew complement dispute with an agreement along the lines of what the fact-finding commission would rule later, was the only major carrier unaffected.

In one respect, however, ALPA's 1958–59 strike against American was a case of being hoist on its own petard. The walkout was symptomatic of airline unions' growing strength, accompanied by increasing militancy. There were ten strikes in the industry during 1958 alone. Labor was trying to solidify its position in anticipation of the expected jet-age travel boom. Over the next five years, there would be twenty-five airline shutdowns by various unions, with some carriers being hit more than once.

C.R. saw it all coming; when it came to peering around distant corners, he seemed to possess a right-angled telescope. In 1958, he proposed that the industry adopt a means of self-protection against the swelling power of airline labor. By 1962, he pointed out, the airlines would be spending $2.6 billion on new aircraft and improved ground facilities and could not afford either crippling strikes or equally crippling settlements. The unions, he told his ATA colleagues, held all the high cards unless . . .

The "unless" culminated in the controversial Mutual Aid Pact. Signed by virtually every scheduled carrier in the U.S., it established a complicated formula whereby airlines benefiting from a competitor's strike would turn those strike-generated extra revenues over to the shut-down carrier. The Pact didn't stop strikes, but it eased the financial pains of an affected airline, and it also increased management's bargaining power.

Its effectiveness can best be judged by labor's reaction to it. The unions used every oratorical and legal weapon in their arsenal trying to abolish the Pact. By the mid seventies, it had begun to lose steam. Several carriers had dropped out under union pressure, and the Pact itself ended when the airlines were deregulated in 1978.

But for a long time, it worked. It served the same purpose in airline labor negotiations as mud on a football field—Mutual Aid was management's equalizer at the bargaining table. Northwest, which used to have more than its fair share of labor disputes, actually made money during strikes thanks to the revenues it received from competitors who were fellow Pact members.

Not many people outside of ATA itself knew C.R. was Mutual Aid's principal author, and there was a certain irony in his role: of all the major carriers, American drew the least benefits. In 1966, Mutual Aid proved to be a boomerang; mechanics struck five airlines—United, TWA, Eastern, Northwest, and National—leaving American as the only transcontinental carrier for forty-three days. But while its flights were packed during that time, under the Pact's complex formula, most of the revenues above what American normally would have received over a forty-three-day period were turned over to the five idle airlines.

ALPA officials always insisted that Mutual Aid tended to prolong strikes, rather than shorten or prevent them. While there is some merit in that criticism, there isn't enough evidence on the record to bear it out entirely. Yet the Pact did offer just one more demonstration of C.R.'s stature. Again, he had thought in terms of the entire industry, while continuing to maintain his own airline's front-running status.

He had once remarked to Carlene Roberts, in a tone of mild scolding, "Miss Roberts, you're spending 60 percent of your time on industry problems and only 40 percent on American's."

"So are you," she reminded him.

One decision C.R. made prior to the jets, at Hogan's urging, was to lease the initial 707 engines instead of buying them. This saved some $80 million in capital outlay and was one more reason why American had positioned itself on the inside rail. Carriers signing up for jets after American looked with envy on that 4 percent financing package Hogan had arranged; TWA's jet financing loan, for example, was at 6 percent.

The eagle and the jet rendezvoused January 25, 1959. On that date, American pioneered transcontinental jet service between New York and Los Angeles. Two days earlier, American had put the Electra into service between New York and Chicago, an inaugural that was at least a month behind schedule; production line problems had delayed Electra deliveries. Eastern was a little luckier and inaugurated Electra service ten days before American.

No one at 100 Park Avenue really cared, for throughout the 14,000-mile system, some 21,000 employees aimed far more attention and pride in the direction of the 707. Only operations and engineering mixed frowns with smiles. The 707's Pratt & Whitney JT-3 engines were underpowered, and everyone in those departments knew it. The power deficiency was particularly crucial on a takeoff under maximum gross weight conditions, and to boost thrust at this critical phase Pratt & Whitney had developed a system for injecting cold water into the JT-3's air intakes during the takeoff roll. The water reduced the engine temperature, making the air within denser and providing about a thousand pounds of additional thrust at the moment of maximum need.

The water injection system gave the early 707s the nickname of "water wagons," and American's first twenty-five Boeings were water wagons. Even with the additional takeoff thrust, the safety margin was thin, especially on hot days at high-altitude airports like Mexico City. American was fortunate not to be serving Denver in those days.

The only reason American accepted the JT-3 was the fact that it was the only engine available for the first 707s to come off the production line. Both United and Eastern had ordered their DC-8s with Pratt & Whitney's more advanced and powerful JT-4—of which C.R. was only too well aware.

But the old poker player had the proverbial ace up his sleeve. Since 1954, both Dan Beard and Frank Kolk had been preaching the gospel of the fanjet engine, first cousin to the turbo-compound principle in that it also utilized wasted exhaust to boost power. Unlike the turbo-compound, however, the fanjet refunneled air, not fuel exhaust. It separated the air being drawn into the spinning turbines, sending part of it into a huge fan located behind the turbine section. The utilization of this otherwise unneeded air produced several dividends: drastically increased power and speed, greater range, reduced fuel consumption (literally more miles per gallon, to use an automobile analogy), and less noise.

No thoroughly tested fanjet was on the shelf when American placed its first 707 orders. But Pratt & Whitney had one ready even as the early water wagons began lumbering down the nation's runways with heart-stopping (to the pilots, anyway) slowness. With one eye on these marginal takeoffs and the other on the forthcoming DC-8, C.R. ordered another twenty-five 707s—all fanjets and slightly larger than the initial model—and at the same time signed a contract to convert all twenty-five original 707s to fanjet aircraft.

The announcement came less than six months after American's inaugural 707 flight. He already had American racing ahead of the competition. TWA, badly handicapped by Hughes's difficulties in arranging financing, inaugurated its own jet service almost two months behind American—San Francisco–New York—and for the next month had to operate with a 707 "fleet" consisting of one airplane, because Boeing refused to deliver any more 707s until Hughes could pay for the ones he had ordered.

United was even farther behind. Its DC-8s wouldn't go into service until September 1959, and faced with the impossible task of pitting its DC-7s against 500-m.p.h. competition, Patterson suspended nonstop transcontinental service until he could get his DC-8s into the air. When United did begin its belated jet service, it launched an advertising campaign aimed at disparaging the 707 while extolling the virtues of the DC-8. The effort was wasted; any criticism of the Boeing—and much of it was justified—applied only to the water wagons. By shifting to an all-fanjet fleet, C.R. had made even the fine Douglas jetliner an also-ran. (DC-8 customers, too, all went the fanjet route as quickly as possible, but as usual, C.R. had gotten in his licks first.)

The water wagons weren't exactly slow once they got airborne. Flight 2, the Los Angeles–New York inaugural commanded by Captain Charles Macatee, set a record, carrying 112 passengers and eight crew across the continent in four hours and three minutes. In terms of time, the nation had shrunk by almost 50 percent. Captain Hamilton Smith flew the westbound inaugural.

Flight 2 was N–503, *Flagship California.* In its first three years of service, it was to carry nearly 200,000 passengers, gross some $26 million, compile 9,900 flight hours in flying five million miles, make more than 2,500 scheduled trips landing at 35 different cities (its 627 visits to Los Angeles being the most frequent), undergo 1,058 maintenance and inspection checks plus two major overhauls in Tulsa (cost per overhaul: $50,000) with 72 routine engine changes, and provide the working environment for 300 different pilots and some 9,000 stewardesses.

(The original *Flagship California,* a DC-6, ended its career as a cocktail lounge in Germany.)

N-503's initial configuration, if applied to today's air travel market conditions, would raise enough eyebrows to create a windstorm. The 112 seats were divided equally among first class and coach passengers, 56 in each section. N-503 was converted to a fanjet in 1961 and the configuration was changed to 44 first-class seats and 74 coach for a total of 118; the reduction in first class added 6 more seats to coach. When American retired its last 707 in 1981, first-class capacity was down to 12.

Getting the water wagons off the ground before they ran out of real estate wasn't the only problem American had with the early 707s. Engine starting was another.

The component haunted by this particular gremlin was the starter mechanism that activated the turbines. Pilots would flip the starter switch and nothing happened—it was like trying to start a car with a dead battery. But the resourceful mechanics discovered they could break loose the starter by giving it a hard whack with a wooden mallet. Until Pratt & Whitney supplied an improved starter, those five-dollar mallets often were all that got a $5 million jet moving.

At Los Angeles, the jets took off to the west because of the prevailing wind. A local ordinance banned easterly departures that took them over a populated area, but one morning the winds shifted freakishly and made westbound takeoffs impossible. American's Flight 2, with a full load, was about to cancel when Jack Mullins—then in L.A. to help get jet operations started—called chief pilot Tex Melden.

"Is an eastbound takeoff safe?" he asked.

"Sure, but it's illegal because of that ordinance."

"The hell with the ordinance," Mullins said. "I'll take the responsibility."

Melden said he couldn't ask one of his captains to violate the law, but finally offered to fly the trip himself. So Flight 2 departed with Melden in command —wearing a business suit and being very careful to stay out of the passengers' view.

Jet travel is taken for granted, almost mundane and definitely routine, by the more than 340 million people who fly the U.S. scheduled airlines annually. But that wasn't true in 1959. Going by jet was a brand-new experience, as exciting an adventure as a 1930 trip on a Ford trimotor. Public interest in jets began building long before jet service was launched. American had twenty-five requests for space on the inaugural east- and westbound flights three and a half years before N-503 took off.

John Q.'s breathless anticipation notwithstanding, American took no chances in making sure that the new experience wouldn't be a frightening one. Willis Player remembered this was an area of great concern.

"A great deal of our planning was on the premise that the public would be afraid of jets. We were aware of a Lou Harris poll indicating that people really *were* nervous, particularly women. So we developed a large part of our public relations and sales campaign around that premise, trying to emphasize the positive rather than doing it in a defensive way.

"We paid a lot of attention to women's organizations and even staged special demonstration flights, inviting opinion leaders who included women. And believe me, we heard some weird questions on those flights."

Player was sitting next to a woman television talk show host on one such flight. Red Sutherland of Player's staff had gone through the plane handing out explanatory brochures, with carefully prepared pictures and text aimed at these white-knuckled neophytes who couldn't understand how a collection of aluminum, upholstery, and plastic grossing 247,000 pounds could get off the ground without propellers. After giving everyone ample time to read the brochure, Sutherland got on the p.a. and supplemented the printed material with verbal explanations of the principles of jet propulsion.

The 707 was rolling down the runway when the woman next to Willis asked nervously, "Mr. Player, aren't they even going to use the propellers for takeoff?"

It took only about six months for the public to accept jets as something to be enjoyed, not dreaded. But the precautionary measures against fear continued for several years, including the required cabin p.a. reassurance by the captain or senior stewardess on every takeoff and landing: "The noise you hear is the sound of our landing gear being raised (or lowered); it is perfectly normal and there is nothing to be alarmed about."

That sound wasn't always normal in the early days. Both the 707 and DC-8 were plagued for a brief time by incidents of stuck landing gears, and although the incidents were annoying rather than dangerous, a jammed nosewheel on

a jet generated black headlines and radio news bulletins every five minutes until
the plane landed—always without a scratch, because the 707 and DC-8 had
adequate back-up systems.

Somewhat hysterical press coverage was to be expected. The jets were more
than just another type of new airliner, and they were introduced with the
greatest fanfare in commercial aviation history. They were revolutionary in
every facet of flight, from size to speed, operating in a high-altitude environment hitherto reserved for daring test pilots. They were unforgiving great
beasts that had to be flown by the book. A handful of American's pilots had
trouble transitioning from piston to jet, although there were always the unflappable veterans like Duke Ledbetter who treated the 707 as just another
airplane.

Duke's seniority made him eligible to be one of the first to start 707 qualification training. He had no qualms, but enough doubts to prompt a visit to C.R.

"I don't know whether I should check out on this thing or not," he told
Smith. "I hear it'll cost American $10,000 to transition a pilot. Dammit, C.R.,
I only have three and a half years to go before I retire and I'm not sure you'd
get value received."

"Do it," C.R. said simply.

Most of the 707 instructors were relatively young pilots, wary of veterans
with ingrained flying habits. They'd invariably warn transitional trainees,
"Boy, it's gonna be different from anything you've ever flown." The most
crucial test involved recovery from the so-called (and widely feared) "Dutch
roll"—the tendency of a sweptwing aircraft to swing unchecked, like a hammock allowed to rock too far. The Dutch roll could be induced by overcorrect-
ing in turbulence, but also could occur in steep bank and turn recovery. The
707, with its greater sweepback, was more vulnerable to the unwanted oscillation than the DC-8.

("The Dutch roll," explained one 707 captain, "is everything you'd want in
a woman but not in an airplane.")

Ledbetter sailed through 707 ground school. On his first transitional ride the
instructor warned, "Now I'm going to put us into what we call the Dutch Roll,
and let's see how you recover from it."

He began rocking the wings until the Boeing's rolling motion threatened to
flip the giant jet on its back. Duke gently and calmly nursed it back to level
flight like a rider soothing the wildness out of a frisky horse.

"I'll be damned," the check pilot marveled. "Have you ever flown a 707
before?"

"Nope. First time."

"That's hard to believe, Duke. You fly like you have."

"Well," Ledbetter said laconically, "I used to do that maneuver in a JT-5
Stearman when I was barnstorming the state fairs. Only then we called it the
falling leaf. You call it the Dutch Roll."

Gradually the pilots began to accept the 707 with the same attitude as
passengers—it was new, exciting, and challenging, but nothing to be afraid of.

Some rated it the best airplane they ever flew, and this in spite of the fact that the crews knew something about the water wagons that the passengers fortunately didn't. The first 707s were not only underpowered, but suffered from instability problems that weren't cured until Boeing added three feet to the rudder area.

Probably not one passenger in a thousand noticed the external difference. Most of them couldn't tell the difference between a 707 and DC-8, let alone a modified Boeing. The layman's acceptance of jet travel rested on two factors: (1) his knowledge that no commercial transport to date had ever gone through such rigorous testing as the jets, and (2) the incredible effects of word-of-mouth advertising. Those who flew a jetliner for the first time simply raved about the experience, generating curiosity and interest that not even the best literary creations of Madison Avenue could match.

There were few if any complaints about the $10 surcharge all carriers added to the price of a jet ticket for a couple of years. The compressed travel time, smoothness, and greater comfort were worth an extra ten dollars. And the main reason the surcharge was dropped eventually was the industry's happy discovery that jets cost less to operate and were more profitable than anyone had expected.

They lived up to their advance billing as insatiable fuel guzzlers. A fully loaded 707 taking off on a transcontinental flight consumed more fuel in the first three minutes than Lindbergh did in his entire thirty-three-hour transatlantic hop. True, the average cost of kerosene in 1959 was only ten cents a gallon, but the fuel capacity of a 707 or DC-8 could have powered the family automobile for twenty-five years of nonstop driving. By 1963, the fifth full year of American's jet operations, the airline's $65 million annual fuel bill was almost equal to 1946's *total revenues*.

Two things made the jets viable: greater productivity stemming from their capacity and speed, and the reliability of the turbine engine. In the vital area of productivity, a 707 did the work of at least two DC-7s or DC-6s; it could make two transcontinental trips while a DC-7 was completing one, and be halfway across the country on a third before the DC-7 finished its return trip. The fact that a 707 was five times thirstier than a DC-7 was immaterial.

American had hoped the jet engine would prove more reliable than the piston. Simplicity was the turbine's chief virtue and the key to reliability. The DC-7's R-3350 had thirty-two temperamental cylinders whose incessant pounding produced both vibration for passengers and constant headaches for maintenance. The jet engine basically was nothing but a giant vacuum cleaner that sucked in air, mixed it with fuel in a combustion chamber, and propelled the hot exhaust rearward. It had about a hundred fewer moving parts than the average piston.

Marv Whitlock admitted, "We all underestimated the reliability and safety of the jet engine. I used to make a lot of speeches on how good it was going to be, but I didn't really believe everything I was saying—until we saw what those damn turbines could do."

What they could do was go thousands of trouble-free hours, these giant blowtorches whose combustion chambers generated 1,600 degrees Fahrenheit —hot enough to melt lead in a split second and turn aluminum into boiling liquid. When the jets began carrying passengers, the FAA required every turbine engine to be overhauled as soon as they had compiled between 800 and 1,000 hours of operation. By 1968, the TBO (Time Before Overhaul) regulation was up to at least 8,000 hours. And today, there is no such thing as a TBO. American, for example, maintains its engines in accordance with a regular monitoring schedule that determines whether one or two components must be replaced or an entire engine removed and overhauled. Some turbines have gone 17,000 hours without requiring major overhaul.

The jets had teething problems, but this was not a contradiction of boasts that no previous airplane had been subjected to such ruthless testing. The boasts were challenged by press and public alike in the wake of some thirty incidents of jammed landing gears, but what a layman couldn't grasp was an aeronautical fact of life: no test program could duplicate the wear and tear, the unsuspected stresses, encountered in daily airline operations. The first fifty 707s Boeing delivered to the airlines compiled more flight time in less than one year than the Air Force's similar-sized fleet of KC-135s, a virtual twin of the 707, did in three years!

Bill Littlewood's input into the 707 and Electra programs was limited; the DC-7 was the last American Airlines plane to involve his full-time attention. But when C.R. was raising hell about the DC-7's engine difficulties, Littlewood made a remark applicable to both that time period and the future.

"Something happens to a plane when it completes its testing phase and goes on the line," he said. "It becomes a different creature."

Of all the aircraft ever to bear the eagle's proud symbol, the Lockheed Electra fitted that description the closest.

There were those at American who insisted the L-188 was a better all-around airplane than the 707, and the number of people holding this opinion was not small.

The pilots were the staunchest Electra admirers. Those who flew the propjet during its testing and pre-introduction crew qualification phases gave it rave reviews. "It flies like a fighter" was a commonly heard appraisal. And it did, for the Electra had more reserve power than any transport aircraft built to date, and some pilots claim nothing designed since is any better.

Marv Whitlock accompanied Si Bittner to Burbank for one of the pilot familiarization flights. Bittner was flying the airplane from the left seat, with Lockheed test pilot Herman "Fish" Salmon as the copilot. Fish had just finished demonstrating how easily the Electra flew with two engines out when he suddenly told Bittner, "Feather three."

"Feather three?" Si choked. "Are you nuts?"

"Feather three," Salmon repeated.

"I ain't gonna do it!"

Fish hit the number-three feathering button himself, and Bittner turned pale. But flying on one engine, the plane didn't lose a single foot of altitude.

"First time I ever saw Bittner shaken," Whitlock laughed. "When it came to safety, he was no carefree clown. His only deviation from rules was his reluctance to put maintenance complaints in an aircraft log. He'd tell mechanics about something that needed fixing but he refused to write it up officially. I used to accuse him of not being able to write, but even that didn't budge him."

Bittner's own account of the incident, made later to one of his cohorts, was typical: "Only my laundry knew how scared I was," he sighed.

Another vastly impressed American captain was Art Weidman, one of the first check pilots assigned to the Electra training program. The first time he saw the plane, he asked, "Where the hell are the wings?"

The wingspan was only five and a half feet shorter than the fuselage, but Weidman had been fooled by the size of the four huge Allison engines, whose large exhaust nozzles extended to the trailing edge of the wings and thus hid much of the wing area. Contributing to the short-wing illusion were the monster thirteen-and-a-half-foot propellers, which swept a mighty airstream over all but nine feet of the wingspan. American's specifications had called for an aircraft equally adept at short- and long-haul operations, and the engine/prop combination allowed the Electra to manufacture its own lift in unprecedented proportions.

Fish Salmon took Weidman on a demonstration flight that convinced him of the plane's fantastic performance. Salmon brought the Electra in for a landing, flaps partially extended, wheels down and locked. This normally is a moment of some tension, for Salmon ostensibly had committed the propjet to the landing.

The wheels had just touched the runway when Fish suddenly added power and pulled back on the yoke. When they passed over the *other* end of the runway, the Electra already was going through 3,000 feet and still climbing.

"I had never seen this done with any other aircraft in the years I had flown," Weidman reported. "If I hadn't seen it with my own eyes, I wouldn't have believed it possible. This was the 'wave-off' capability that pilots had dreamed about but never enjoyed. An airplane that never really was committed to a landing, an airplane in which you could make as many passes at a field you wanted, without ever worrying about emergency climb power."

The Electra was a pilot's airplane in very respect, from cockpit visibility to its sports-car handling. The "panic button" for an engine fire was a single fire-control lever. One pull automatically feathered the prop, shut off the fuel and oil supply, armed the chemical fire-extinguishing unit, and discharged the CO_2 bottles. Emergency response time: one second. On American's piston aircraft, those four separate fire-fighting procedures took as long as ten seconds.

It was a passenger's airplane, too—roomy, fast, and vibration-free, although it wasn't as smooth as the 707 in that latter category; no propeller-driven plane could be. American put it into service with an all-first-class, sixty-eight-passenger configuration.

Only twelve days after the propjet's inaugural, an American Electra approaching LaGuardia went into the chilling waters of the East River, nearly 5,000 feet from the end of Runway 22, where it was supposed to land. Of the sixty-eight passengers aboard, only five survived. Captain Albert Hunt DeWitt, a fifty-nine-year-old veteran with some 28,000 logged flying hours, also perished, along with one of the two stewardesses; DeWitt drowned before the copilot could reach him. The flight was 320 from Chicago.

The subsequent Civil Aeronautics Board's investigation verdict, issued more than a year after the crash, attached mixed blame. It accused DeWitt of failing to monitor essential flight instruments during an approach in extremely poor weather, but it cited a number of contributing factors that took at least some of the onus off a dead captain who couldn't defend himself.

"The Board concludes there is no one factor so outstanding as to be considered the probable cause of this accident," the CAB report said. Among the "contributing factors" mentioned were the crew's limited experience with a new type of airplane, an erroneous altimeter setting, possible (the pilots said it was more probable than possible) misinterpretation of a new kind of altimeter radically different from the one DeWitt had been using for years, the fact that the airline had used conventional altimeters in its Electra training, the lack of adequate approach lights to Runway 22, and the sensory illusion suffered by many pilots in making a poor-weather approach over water at night—under those conditions, a pilot often had the illusion of being higher than he actually was.

Nothing in the CAB findings blamed the Electra. As far as American was concerned, the main culprit was that new altimeter, and the airline quickly removed them from every Electra in the fleet, replacing them with the older, familiar instruments.

Seven months later, a Braniff L-188 cruising at 15,000 feet in clear, turbulence-free weather over the little town of Buffalo, Texas, lost a wing and plunged to the ground, killing all thirty-four persons aboard. The CAB was still trying to solve the Braniff mystery when a Northwest Electra also lost a wing on a Chicago-Miami flight, diving 18,000 feet into a soybean field near Tell City, Indiana. The impact, estimated at 618 m.p.h., telescoped the 100-foot fuselage into one-third its original length. There were sixty-three fatalities.

The date was March 17, 1960—St. Patrick's Day.

The Electra crisis had begun.

Structural failure was a rare but not unknown occurrence, even on modern airliners. Previous incidents had involved two factors: the violent turbulence associated with severe thunderstorms, or some design weakness, as in the case of the Martin 202. The Braniff plane couldn't have been flying in smoother air; Northwest's Electra was in an area of reported clear air turbulence, but this weather phenomenon possessed nowhere near the destructive force of the worst thunderstorms. The only possible conclusion: there was something wrong with the Electra.

But what? The L-188 had passed with flying colors every structural strength test known to aeronautical science. The CAB's dilemma was starkly simple. It was faced with a single unpleasant fact: a wing had come off two brand-new airplanes. It also was faced with numerous other facts, all of which said it was well-nigh impossible for those wings to have failed.

Investigators explored every conceivable possibility and ran into a brick wall each time. The discarded theories and explanations included wing damage during refueling, induced abnormal stress from a collision-avoidance maneuver, a runaway autopilot, some kind of control difficulty in which attempted recovery strained the wing beyond design limits, violent flutter from a runaway propeller the pilot couldn't feather, a rocket strike fired accidentally or unwittingly from a missile base, a sonic boom generated by a nearby military plane, and—the most farfetched solution—collision with a UFO.

At various stages of the probe, the CAB looked into such further ideas as inadvertent prop reversal (discarded because the Electra had a reverse-pitch lockout to prevent any in-flight reversal), and a theory involving the proximity of certain electrical units to the center wing section fuel tank. Almost as wild as the UFO proposal was a suggestion that the CAB look into the Electra lavatory as an area of suspicion. There had been reports of large ice balls accumulating in the toilet drains and breaking away from the airplane through leakage, although how an ice ball could destroy a twenty-eight-ton airliner was beyond anyone's comprehension.

There was no conclusive evidence to back up any theory; other than wing failure, the two crashes didn't even seem to have anything in common. The planes had been at different altitudes and the Northwest Electra, aided by a strong tailwind, was cruising about 100 m.p.h. faster than Braniff.

At the suggestion of its technical staff and Lockheed as well, the FAA clamped temporary speed restrictions on all Electras operating in the United States. The "red line" was 275 knots, the speed at which the Braniff plane had begun to break up. But the CAB was urging something more drastic: grounding the airplane until the two accidents were solved. So were several members of Congress.

On March 23, FAA administrator Elwood R. "Pete" Quesada summoned all Electra operators to a closed-door emergency meeting at the agency's Washington headquarters. The announced general topic was the Electra. The unannounced subject everyone knew would be discussed: Should the L-188 be grounded?

Pete Quesada had gone to Tell City and personally seen the graveyard of Northwest Flight 710, a muddy crater forty feet wide and twelve feet deep. The pressure for grounding had been mounting daily, and when he called the meeting, that's what everyone expected would happen.

It was held in a large room that had once been the patients' solarium of the old Washington Emergency Hospital, the only building the new air agency had been able to acquire in the space-short capital. A current crack was that Quesada's office had once been the operating room—a backhanded tribute to his tough-guy reputation.

He was not the most popular official in the Eisenhower administration by a long shot. In the two years he had served as the first boss of the Federal Aviation Agency, he had managed to alienate virtually every segment of the aviation community. The one thing the airlines and ALPA could agree on was their mutual dislike and distrust of the FAA administrator.

Quesada was a former fighter pilot, and like so many of that breed, he was something of a maverick. Even as a World War II general, he frequently winked at rules and regulations. He was sharply criticized once for taking an unauthorized passenger on a ride in a P-51 fighter. The passenger he squeezed into the little plane happened to be a fellow general named Dwight Eisenhower.

His unorthodox reputation made his tactics at the new FAA even more startling. It was not unlike having a former juvenile delinquent suddenly appointed police chief and turning out to be one hell of a tough cop. Unquestionably, civil aviation needed a tough cop after all those years of the CAA's slack enforcement of civil air regulations. And given a clean broom and almost unlimited authority, Quesada proceeded to use the broom not only for cleaning but spanking purposes.

Violation notices filed against the airlines and their crews, business and private pilots, and manufacturers mushroomed to unprecedented proportions. A Pan Am captain who pulled a 707 out of a dive when the autopilot went haywire was hailed as a hero until Quesada socked him with a $1,000 fine for being out of the cockpit when the dive began. Airline pilots were told to stay in their seats except for calls of nature; his inspectors held stopwatches on captains to make sure their lavatory visits didn't exceed a specified time limit. It was Pete Quesada who instituted mandatory retirement at age sixty for all airline pilots—a ruling that ALPA fought for years in vain.

Like so many reformers who are handed what amounts to a blank check of authority, Quesada demonstrated one weakness: he assumed for himself and his powerful new agency virtually the sole judgment of right and wrong as applied to air safety. He was more often right, but he also could be unreasonable, arbitrary, and very wrong. His fast-flailing broom sometimes swept out the good with the bad, went into corners that didn't need cleaning, and ignored corners that did. And in his zeal for strict enforcement of regulations, he occasionally slapped the innocent along with the guilty.

In brief, the quick-tempered, ruddy-faced Quesada was both feared and respected, hated yet grudgingly admired. If his long military career had imbued him with some of the qualities of a martinet, it also had given him a sense of duty, and at the FAA he regarded it his duty to protect the public. Every action he took, right or wrong, was taken in the name of public interest and welfare. Inasmuch as being for the public's safety was like standing four-square against sin, it was hard to question his decisions, and even more difficult to overrule them.

It was this creed that had led Quesada into actions that might better have been exposed to consultation or compromise. But it was a quality ideally adapted to a major emergency requiring swift and courageous decisions.

And on March 23, the Electra mystery had become a major emergency. A superb new airliner, pride of the U.S. aviation industry, was under a cloud of fear and suspicion of unprecedented proportions. Already passengers holding reservations on Electra flights were beginning to cancel.

Representing American at the meeting were C. R. Smith and Bill Littlewood. Eddie Rickenbacker was there for Eastern and a badly shaken Don Nyrop was present for Northwest, along with the other presidents or vice presidents of every U.S. carrier flying Electra. Also on hand were officials from Allison, the Navy (which was operating a submarine-hunting version of the propjet), the full CAB, and Robert Gross, Lockheed's husky board chairman.

Quesada had ordered his aides not to admit anyone who was not a current Electra operator. One of those refused admittance was the chief pilot of Avianca, a South American carrier scheduled to take delivery on three Electras the next day. Quesada personally ejected a lawyer representing an airline; when the attorney conceded he was not a bona fide employee, Quesada snapped, "Out!" waving his thumb like an umpire dismissing an overargumentative manager.

The solarium doors were closed and locked. The FAA chief opened the meeting by stressing that this would be an informal, off-the-record discussion of the Electra situation. No minutes were to be taken, and he emphasized there were no reporters present and all could speak freely. He wanted to hear their views. But, he added, he would assume full responsibility for whatever action he took.

He revealed he had asked the National Aeronautics and Space Administration to put its experimental wind tunnels at Langley, Virginia, at Lockheed's disposal. He then announced the precautionary measures the FAA would put into effect immediately for all U.S. operators of the L-188.

Maximum Electra operating speeds would be reduced from the already existing 275-knot limit (315 m.p.h.) to 259 m.p.h.

All Electra autopilots were to be disconnected until it was proved the autopilot was not responsible for either or both accidents.

Operators were to follow Lockheed's recommended fueling procedures to the letter.

FAA inspectors were to make thorough structural checks of L-188 wings on every plane, and the carriers were to conduct daily checks of the engine reduction gears (which keep the props from spinning as fast as the turbines).

Any Electra that had gone through severe turbulence or experienced a hard landing was to undergo a complete structural inspection before being allowed to resume flying.

Lockheed was to launch a program of engineering research so vast in scope it amounted to a complete reevaluation of the aircraft.

In effect, these measures were based on all the conjecture and speculation as to what *might* have happened at Buffalo and Tell City. They fell short of what many in that tense solarium wanted; he hadn't mentioned grounding at all.

Sunlight, bright and cheerful, streamed incongruously into a room filled with grim silence as Quesada concluded his marching orders and asked for questions or comments. Littlewood rose and read a formal statement defending the Electra and opposing any grounding. When he finished, Quesada snapped that formal statements weren't welcome in an informal meeting. C.R.'s big jaw tightened, but he said nothing.

Gross of Lockheed lurched to his feet, his usually jovial face showing the terrible strain of recent events. He described the test flights Lockheed had commenced that very day in specially instrumented Electras. The company also would test an Electra wing to the point of deliberate destruction, and was calling back a Northwest L-188 with approximately the same number of hours as the Tell City plane, to be tested for any evidence of unsuspected weaknesses. Lockheed, he added in a choked voice, did not think grounding was necessary because the speed restrictions and inspection program furnished an unusual margin of safety.

Quesada looked around the room and asked CAB chairman James Durfee if he had anything to say. Durfee, blithely ignoring the FAA chief's nettled reaction to Littlewood's prepared-in-advance remarks, sailed into a formal statement of his own. The CAB, he declared, thought grounding should be considered seriously. He listed a number of arguments in favor of such drastic action.

When Durfee finished, the meeting erupted into a chorus of airline executives clamoring for the floor. Quesada recognized Nyrop of Northwest. The room hushed as the brusque Nyrop, himself a former CAB member, began speaking quietly but with undisguised emotion. Only a few days before, he had asked Lockheed to return the Stratocruisers NWA had traded in on its Electras; it had been apparent that he expected a grounding order. Now he was to make it clear he wanted one. He was on the verge of tears as he disclosed that Northwest's Electras would be grounded immediately, regardless of what the other airlines did.

A roar of protest greeted this announcement. Rickenbacker shouted angrily that Eastern would continue to fly its Electras. C.R., who normally wouldn't have agreed with Captain Eddie on the time of day, said American sided with Eastern. He calmly reminded Nyrop that if Northwest grounded the propjet, everyone would have to follow suit. It would be impossible to explain to the public why one airline grounded the plane and the others didn't.

Nyrop was surrounded by angry colleagues reiterating Smith's argument, but he refused to back down. Then the tension was suddenly broken by the only woman in the room, Jean Friedkin, the blonde, attractive wife of Pacific

Southwest Airways president Ken Friedkin. PSA had only four Electras at the time, but she figured her tiny intrastate carrier had a voice in the proceedings.

"We're opposed to grounding," she called out loudly.

Quesada looked at her as if she had stood up wearing a press badge.

"Just who the hell are you?" he demanded.

"I'm with PSA."

Quesada glared. "Only Electra operators are supposed to be here."

Jean Friedkin glared back. "I'm vice president of PSA," she said icily.

Pete Quesada did something unusual for him. He apologized, so humbly that it drew laughs. And suddenly he had the unruly session under control. He said it was Nyrop's privilege and right to say and do what he wanted, but that he still felt grounding was unnecessary. All available evidence indicated that the new speed restrictions provided an adequate margin of safety until the mystery was solved.

Once more, Nyrop was surrounded by other airline officials asking him to relent, but this time they were calmer and even sympathetic. He finally gave in and promised that Northwest's Electras would continue flying. Within forty-eight hours, the ninety-six L-188s then in U.S. scheduled airline service began plodding along at DC-6 speeds. Then came the first results of the emergency inspections, and the crisis erupted again.

Early in April, the CAB was advised that of the first forty-one planes to be inspected, thirty-nine were found to have cracked wing-clip rivets—small metal rectangular tabs that tied the ribs and cross-members of the wings together. Nobody at FAA, Lockheed, or any airline pushed any panic button over this revelation. There were 2,754 clips in each Electra and inspectors hadn't found more than 7 sheared clips in any single airplane. (American's engineers, informed of the CAB's concern, pointed out that inspectors could have found the same proportion of cracked clips if they had checked at random any DC-6, DC-7, Convair, or Constellation.)

But the CAB thought the location of the Electra cracks might indicate a developing pattern of clip failure leading to serious structural problems. On April 13, the Board voted unanimously to recommend grounding the Electra until all ninety-six planes could be inspected and the clips repaired. It was not an all-out grounding request, as the CAB's own Bureau of Safety would have preferred, but it was drastic enough, and Quesada, informed of the recommendation, asked the full Board to meet with him secretly.

Once more, he refused to ground the airplane. He also asked them to keep their recommendation confidential. If it were leaked that one federal agency had asked for grounding and the other refused, the public would be looking at one large, open can of worms. To a layman, a cracked wing clip would imply impending doom.

But the CAB's grounding plea leaked anyway, presumably from an unknown source within the CAB. And it was leaked to the one person most likely to make it public: Indiana Senator Vance Hartke, who had been making his own grounding demands since Tell City. He phoned Quesada.

"Is it true the CAB recommended grounding?"

"Yes."

"What are you going to do about it?"

"Nothing," Quesada snapped.

Hartke called an immediate press conference, revealed the grounding recommendation, and demanded a Congressional investigation. He accused Quesada of deliberately risking innocent lives and implied that the FAA chief was trying to protect Lockheed because Quesada had once worked for the Burbank firm.

Publicly, Quesada didn't bother to comment. Privately, he blew his stack. His opinion of Hartke, according to one of his FAA aides, was that the senator seemed to regard an Electra falling on Indiana soil as a personal affront. It was Bob Gross who issued a statement designed to offset the CAB-FAA disagreement.

"Of all the wing clips examined," Gross pointed out, "only five-hundredths of one percent have been found damaged. Such finds are not unusual at the traditional overhaul period of airplanes in service, and there is nothing unusual in this one, either."

His calm, completely factual statement was a Ping-Pong ball fired at an approaching tank. Led by Hartke, Congressional demands for grounding increased. A fair-sized proportion of editorial opinion demanded it, and even some Braniff and Northwest pilots backed away from their previous support of the embattled aircraft called "a pilot's airplane." A delegation of NWA pilots asked Nyrop to reconsider, but he had given his word at the March 23 meeting. Meanwhile, Electra loads continued to tumble, and in New York on a warm day in mid May 1960, C. R. Smith called his own secret meeting.

It was held against a grim backdrop of evidence that public confidence in the Electra had eroded to the vanishing point. The wing-clip controversy and the CAB-FAA feud had spawned wild rumors and scare stories that were being translated into an actual boycott. It didn't help that the Braniff and Northwest investigations, now combined into a single probe, had to be conducted under some semblance of secrecy. The continuing mystery nourished additional fears and rumors.

"Did you hear that American is gonna sell all its Electras?"

"Did you know that Douglas and Boeing have forbidden their employees to ride in Electras?"

"I happen to know it's a fact that Lockheed paid Quesada $50,000 not to ground the airplane."

Whispers. Unfounded reports. Even sick jokes, like the disc jockey in Miami who told his audience one morning, "Did you hear about the guy who said to a ticket agent, 'I'd like a ticket on the next Electra flight to New York?' The agent says, 'We don't sell Electra tickets, we sell chances.' "

Electra "jokes" flew around the nation faster than the plane. "Have you joined the Electra crash of the month yet?" Or, "Don't miss that new aviation play: *Mourning Becomes the Electra.* " And, "Have you read the new Electra book, *Look Ma, No Wings?*"

Far more serious than comedians' attempts at humor was the unorganized but massive boycott. It will never be known how many companies actually ordered their officials and employees to stay off Electra flights. But one former CAB official said that as late as 1962, when the Electra crisis was over, about a dozen large corporations still had an Electra ban in effect. One of them was a general aviation manufacturer.

There was an individual boycott, too. From every Admirals Club on American's system came reports of passengers asking skippers not to book them on any Electra flight. Electra load factors dipped as much as 35 percent on some carriers, a catastrophic loss of revenue in an industry where a 10 percent load factor drop is damaging.

Lou Davis, an aviation writer, was preparing a story for *Flying* magazine on the local service airlines. In the course of interviewing ten passengers on one "feeder line" flight, he casually asked why they were taking this particular flight, which happened to be an ancient DC-3. Eight of the ten passengers told him they didn't want to ride an Electra heading for the same destination. And these were all businessmen, presumably better versed in aviation than most passengers. Davis's impromptu survey showed that the anti-Electra prejudice was festering where it hurt most—among those who supplied the airlines with the bulk of their traffic.

Some carriers went so far as to remove the very name "Electra" from their advertisements. Braniff began referring to the plane as the "L-188" on the logical supposition that few people knew what an L-188 was. Eastern put emphasis on "Golden Falcon" service without mentioning the aircraft itself. Others simply plugged "propjet service" and avoided mentioning the Electra. American was one of the few exceptions.

Even stewardesses were affected. Several airlines—and American was among them—began to experience resistance from girls who refused to bid Electra trips, and some who did were openly reluctant about the whole thing. Not in front of passengers, obviously, but colleagues to whom they admitted fear and misgivings. These reports, too, had reached C.R.'s ears by the time he called that meeting, to which he had summoned most of the top brass.

His eyes swept the room in a silent roll call. Bill Hogan, Marv Whitlock, Bill Littlewood, Red Mosier, Charlie Speers, Marion Sadler, Frank Kolk, Willis Player, and one or two others. C.R.'s office was relatively small and unpretentious, unlike some of his airline peers who had quarters like Mussolini's famous 747-sized office. Player remembered there were about nine or ten men in the room that day, sitting almost shoulder to shoulder. There were six men on a sofa that normally held three.

Prior to the meeting, C.R. had distributed copies of a confidential report Littlewood had received from Lockheed on the progress of the investigation. The gist of it was that Lockheed was almost sure of what was wrong with the

Electra, that it was serious enough to require a mammoth and lengthy modification program, but that the plane could continue to operate safely under its current speed restrictions.

Smith asked every man in the room if, based on Lockheed's still tentative findings, and even more tentative corrective measures, he considered the Electra safe to fly and Lockheed's proposed "fix" program feasible.

The response was unanimously affirmative. In a typical gesture, C.R. leaned back, his hands clasped behind his head, and announced, "All right, we'll keep flying 'em." He turned to Player. "And it's your job, Willis, to persuade the public they're safe."

It was no easy assignment, because Player couldn't disclose the most important fact of all: the Electra mystery *had* been solved. The killer of ninety-seven persons and two magnificent airliners was a rather obscure phenomenon of physics.

Lockheed gave its own investigation an official name: Lockheed Electra Achievement Program. With the American propensity for acronyms, it was quickly boiled down to "LEAP."

Operation LEAP got under way even as the wreckage of the Buffalo and Tell City planes was being shipped to Burbank. Lockheed test pilots, sometimes with CAB and FAA technicians aboard, began a series of hair-raising experimental flights in which they not only braved destruction but sought it. They crammed an Electra full of instruments that measured every stress from every motion of every key part on the airplane. Then they headed for the direction of the Sierra wave, a California mountain area known for violent, almost terrifying perpetual turbulence, where updrafts were like miniature tornadoes and twisting wind shears knifed their invisible paths across the sky.

They flew with loads ranging from light to beyond what an Electra was designed to carry, and at speeds covering the spectrum from slow to past the red line. They simulated emergency collision-avoidance maneuvers. They went looking for the worst turbulence by flying low over the mountain ranges until the instruments told them where the air was roughest, then made repeated runs back and forth through this area at successively increasing speeds. The bouncing was so bad that a camera plane following the flights couldn't keep the test Electra in focus.

One crew dived the Electra until the indicated airspeed hit almost 500 m.p.h., and with a full gross load of 83,000 pounds pulled back sharply on the yoke to see if the wings would come off. The test crews worked two ten-hour shifts seven days a week, accumulating more than three million stress readings in sixty-nine flights.

Both Lockheed and the CAB suspected that the two destroyed Electras had been victims of some kind of unknown flutter problem. Flutter is present in every airplane; it is caused by the movement of turbulent air over an aircraft's fast-moving surfaces. The trick is to keep flutter from going unchecked into an uncontrolled, continuous cycle that eventually will fatigue even new metal, like bending a wire back and forth until it breaks.

The ability of an airplane to absorb and control flutter is called damping, and the Electra's original test flights had shown it to have excellent damping characteristics. Even when turbulence "excited" the wing, a slight speed reduction would remove this external driving force and flutter would dissipate. Like every aircraft wing, the Electra's was designed to recoil and flex, thus absorbing the energy of flutter's oscillations.

Clear air turbulence was present in the Northwest crash, but not at Buffalo, so it was reasonable to assume that turbulence could not have been the primary "exciting" source. But what else could have caused destructive flutter in a plane supposedly immune? Examination of both wreckages eliminated control surfaces—elevators and/or ailerons—and NASA's wind tunnels supported this exoneration.

From the LEAP flight tests came the first clue. Instrument data began to reveal that the the outboard nacelle structures, under extremely heavy motion loads, were taking more of a beating than anyone thought possible. The Sierra wave tests indicated that severe and extreme turbulence put a bending force on the outer wing section, from the outboard nacelles to the wing tip, that was ten times greater than that on the rest of the wing.

This discovery sent the crash probers back for another look at the outboard nacelles of the two planes. They were searching for evidence of destructive flutter, and they found it, particularly in the Northwest Electra. The metallurgists centered their attention on the wings that had failed first—Braniff's left and NWA's right—along with the Braniff's number-one nacelle structure and the number-four from NWA. These were the outboard engine packages under suspicion.

The Northwest wreckage provided the strongest evidence. The right wing structure showed numerous indications of damage progression during rapid reversals of loading. In simpler terms, the wing had been subjected to uncontrolled and massive flutter. The area at which separation from the fuselage had occurred showed a type of metal damage that could have only been caused by the wing folding rearward instead of upward; it could not have failed from a violent up or down motion. Another wing structural area displayed sawtoothed diagonal fractures that told metallurgists one thing: there had been powerful oscillation loads occurring in a repetitive cycle, consistent with catastrophic flutter.

Flutter evidence also was found in the number-four nacelle structure. There were scratches of a vibrating nature on the outside of an air inlet called the "sugar scoop" because of its shape. The engine mounts that held the huge Allison in the nacelle had "bottomed" fifty to sixty times at a rate of 2.5 times a second for up to twenty seconds—further proof of destructive flutter.

The engine's torque housing, which had been separated from the compressor case, bore marks of repeated cycles in the area of the bolt attachments. So did a vane located near the engine exhaust. It was scarred with elliptical scratches that could have come only from violent movements of that portion of the engine casing.

The Braniff wreckage contained less conclusive but still significant similarities. Now the investigators were asking: What was the source, the triggering element, of the mysterious flutter, and what was the nature of the flutter itself?

Douglas supplied Lockheed with a special wing vane designed to induce flutter. It was mounted on the Electra test plane that tried (and failed) to produce flutter at speeds of up to 550 m.p.h. Boeing sent down a team of aerodynamic specialists assigned to interpreting laboratory and test flight data. The cooperation of Lockheed's two bitterest rivals underlined the seriousness with which the entire industry viewed the Electra's misfortunes. Where safety begins, competition ends, for an unsolved crash was a burr under everyone's saddle.

From Lockheed's Georgia plant and from its missiles-and-space division came a fresh influx of technicians, scientists, and engineers. Computers were yanked unceremoniously from other projects and assigned to LEAP. Flight test data analysts went on three shifts a day, seven days a week. Some engineers were working eighty-four hours a week.

They all were looking at more than 100 different kinds of flutter—"modes" was the technical term. And by now, they were getting close to locating the guilty one. This time it was the Braniff wreckage that supplied the chief clue. The damage marks on the number-one propeller showed signs of violent wobbling. And in the early stages of the investigation, there had been clues whose significance no one had grasped at the time.

The CAB's witness team had contacted every known person who either saw or heard Braniff Flight 320. The interviews contained these responses:

"The clapping of two boards together."

"The sound of thunder."

"The roar of a jet breaking the sound barrier."

"A whooshing, screaming noise."

"A creaking noise like a big bulldozer."

"Just an awful explosion."

But one farmer mentioned something else. "When the sound came," he remarked, "every coon dog for miles around started howling."

Further interrogation confirmed this. Every nearby farmer owning a hound reported that the animal began howling shortly after 11 P.M., the established time of the Braniff midair breakup. The CAB then recorded twelve known noises of unusual intensity and played them back to a number of witnesses. Jet aircraft. Sonic booms. Propellers whirling at supersonic speeds. Electras in normal flight. Electras diving and climbing. And also intentionally random noises not having the remotest connection with an airplane.

The witnesses picked two tapes that came the closest to what they had heard. One was the sound of a prop at supersonic speeds, and the other was the sound of a jet aircraft.

All this—the howling dogs and the identification of the overspeeding propeller noise—was remembered when the probers looked at the Braniff number-one prop.

At the Allison plant in Indianapolis, in Burbank, and in NASA's Langley wind tunnels, they tried every form of flutter mode in the book that could be linked to an overspeeding propeller. They found one.

On May 2, 1960, a Lockheed engineer stood up at a meeting of CAB and FAA officials and spoke six words:

"We're pretty sure it's whirl mode."

Whirl mode was not an unknown force, but that it could be deadly was a shattering surprise. It is a form of vibrating motion inherent in any piece of rotating machinery such as oil drills, table fans, and automobile drive shafts. Its application to airplane propellers was no secret as far back as the 1930s, and it was a subject occasionally discussed in technical journals. Scientists also referred to it as propeller auto-precession, propeller-nacelle flutter, and gyro-flutter.

Whirl mode was a simple phenomenon. A propeller has gyroscopic tendencies—in other words, it will stay in a smooth plane of rotation unless it is displaced or agitated by some strong external force, just as a spinning top can be made to wobble when a finger is placed firmly against it. But the moment such a force is applied to a propeller, it reacts in the opposite direction.

Suppose the force drives the prop upward. The stiffness that is part of its structure promptly resists the exciting force and pitches the prop downward. Each succeeding upward force is met by a protesting downward motion, and a battle of vibration begins. The prop continues to spin in one direction, but the rapidly developing whirl mode is vibrating in the other direction. The result, if the mode is not checked, is a wildly wobbling gyroscope whose violent motion eventually is transmitted to a natural outlet: the wing.

But this didn't solve the Electra mystery. Whirl mode occasionally developed in piston aircraft, but it always was smothered by the stiffness of the engine/nacelle structure before it could spread to the wing. In the rare instance when the violence persisted, the prop would finally separate from the engine before the violence could spread.

Supposedly, the same thing would happen in an Electra; even with turbine engines, it still was a propeller-driven airplane. What was there in the L-188's engine package that lowered the barrier to whirl mode? The investigators went back to examining the number-four nacelle structure on the NWA plane and the number-one of the Braniff Electra. In both they found evidence that the *entire* nacelle and engine structure had been subjected to vicious oscillations, so violent that the propeller reduction gearbox had been fractured.

The crash detectives' next step was to determine whether a weakened nacelle structure could create whirl mode. NASA put a scale model of the Electra into a wind tunnel and tried to induce whirl mode, without success. Then, in one engine it deliberately weakened the struts and braces that held the engine in the nacelle and "flew" the model at speeds equal to or exceeding those of the Braniff and Northwest planes. At those speeds, they created a sudden jolt that agitated the weakened nacelle. Whirl mode started, spread, and devoured the wing itself. The time that elapsed between the jolt and the wing separation was only thirty seconds.

The NASA tests showed that whirl mode could not develop in an engine/nacelle structure unless there was previous damage in the package. Such prior damage in the two lost Electras was never determined. In the case of Northwest, a previous hard landing was suspected, and with Braniff, the damage may have occurred during a training flight a few weeks before the crash.

But whatever the birth of such damage, there was no doubt as to what it could lead to. It reduced the nacelle's protective stiffness to the point where it could not keep whirl mode from spreading. And the fact that the Electra was jet-powered as well as propeller-driven added to this vulnerability. Its turbine spun at 13,820 revolutions per minute and the props turned at more than 1,200 RPMs. The entire package was nothing but one huge gyroscope that would break stride and wobble if jolted by some strong external force.

As the agitated engine began to wobble, so did the prop, with its normal plane of rotation suddenly disturbed. As the prop wobbled, its violently uneven motion was transmitted to the wing, which also began to flex and flutter. This, in turn, sent the discordant forces back to the oscillating prop and engine package, which began wobbling even more wildly. By now, whirl mode was well into its deadly cycles, each feeding the mode fresh energy.

The next step in this thirty-second chain reaction was the tendency of uncontrolled whirl mode to slow down in frequency even as it increased in violence. That frequency was measured at about five cycles per second at the start, but unchecked, the frequency dropped to three cycles per second. And the NASA/Lockheed tests showed this to be the same maximum frequency at which the Electra wing would flutter.

The moment those two frequencies touched the same level, the effect was comparable to a sustained high note breaking a glass tuned to the same vibration level. It is called harmonic or dynamic coupling. Applied to the Electra, it could snap a wing like a matchstick.

The "fix" involved a $25 million modification program, for which Lockheed picked up the tab. The entire engine/nacelle structure was strengthened (almost doubled), and the wings beefed up. The changes added up to about fourteen hundred pounds of metal reinforcements.

One test in particular demonstrated the effectiveness of the nacelle improvements. It had been determined that the worst condition during whirl mode was failure of the gear-reduction box housing, which diminished nacelle strength to only 17 percent of normal. Lockheed induced whirl mode in a LEAP-modified nacelle with the housing box fractured in advance. Even with this mass flopping around like a spaniel's ears, nacelle stiffness remained within 96 percent of a totally undamaged nacelle.

Four modified, company-owned Electras were subjected to one hundred hours of test flights involving every violent maneuver possible to inflict on an airplane, from 500 m.p.h. power dives followed by sharp pull-ups to turbulence penetration at beyond red-line speeds. In one test, engineers removed the entire gearbox unit from the outboard engine of a modified plane, which simulated in-flight failure and sent the turbine's enormous torque forces spinning unchecked. In this weakened condition, the Electra was put into a succession of power dives, with whirl mode developing each time, only to be swallowed by the strengthened nacelles.

On December 13, 1960, chief LEAP engineer Jack Real flew to Washington for a meeting with Oscar Bakke, FAA's director of Flight Standards.

"We're satisfied," he told Bakke, "but we want to know if there's anything more Lockheed can do to prove we've licked the problem."

Bakke said, "There is. Have you got the guts to deliberately weaken the engine mounts on a modified Electra, take it into extreme turbulence at speeds exceeding the red line, and see if the beefed-up wings and new nacelle struts can dampen whirl mode?"

What Bakke was asking was the intentional reenactment of Tell City, with an actual airplane and live guinea pigs. But Real didn't hesitate. "I said we were sure, and we are," he said quietly.

Real went back to Burbank, called a meeting of his test pilots, told them what the FAA wanted, and asked for volunteers. Every pilot raised his hand. The next day, engineers went to work on a LEAP Electra, but did more than what Bakke had wanted. They removed the two original side struts from not only one outboard engine but the other three engines as well. Then they took out the reduction gear and torque shaft from the number-four outboard, to simulate a broken engine. To make the number-four prop windwill uncontrolled with no engine power, they disconnected the pitch lock.

When they had finished this brutalization, they had come as close as possible to re-creating the conditions that must have existed at 18,000 feet over Tell City on March 17. The only thing lacking was clear air turbulence, and the two test pilots chosen for the mission—Fish Salmon and Roy Wimmer—supplied this easily. They took off and headed for the Sierra wave.

The cockpit emergency evacuation door was rigged with a special switch for instant opening if a wing failed. The pressurization system was deactivated so the escape door could be used at 20,000 feet, and both pilots wore oxygen masks and parachutes.

They headed for their rendezvous. The Douglas-designed vanes were on the wing tips, ready to excite flutter. The Electra began to buck as it hit the first wave of turbulence. One hundred and eighty knots. The vanes were tilted. No abnormal flutter. Two hundred knots. Still no unusual flutter.

Two hundred and twenty knots. Two-forty. Two-sixty. Two-eighty. Past the speed of Buffalo. Three hundred. Three-twenty. Past the speed of Tell City. Three-forty. Three-sixty. Now they were beyond the never-to-be-exceeded red line.

The windmilling prop was vibrating. The outboard nacelles trembled. Both wings were flexing as if they were made of rubber, in an ominous cycle.

Whirl mode was under way. A faint buzz, a slight shudder—the only audible and physical manifestations of the death mode.

Vanes were now tilted to an angle designed to excite maximum flutter. If whirl mode was going to spread, this was the time. Once the deliberately weakened nacelles gave way, their vibration frequencies would instantly couple with those of the wings. Tell City again. Disintegration.

Salmon and Wimmer glanced at the wings. Flexing and moving, but no runaway flutter. The nacelles were pitching but holding firm, even without those side struts. The fourteen-hundred pounds of strategically placed reinforcements were doing their job; a $2.5 million research prayer was being answered. The stiffer and stronger wings, the additional supports within the nacelles, were damping whirl mode before it could spread and couple.

They put the Electra into a high-speed dive—the suspected last maneuver of the Braniff plane. At more than 400 m.p.h., Salmon applied full back pressure on the yoke. Wings bent as the G forces clamped a stranglehold. Nacelles pitched upward. But no fatal flutter.

They shook hands and headed for the Burbank barn.

Six more times, Lockheed test pilots accompanied by FAA inspectors repeated the Salmon-Wimmer mission. Six more times they failed to induce nacelle flutter that would couple in frequency to wing flutter.

On January 5, 1961, the Federal Aviation Agency announced approval of the LEAP modification program. But by that time, C. R. Smith and American Airlines had already done their own bit to restore the Electra's shredded reputation.

Eight months and three days had elapsed between the determination of whirl mode as the cause of the two tragedies and the FAA's green light for LEAP. It was too long a period to keep the Electra in the public's good graces, even though the tentative solution was disclosed by early summer.

Harmonic coupling and whirl mode were too hard for the layman to understand, anyway. What mattered far more was the Electra's "jinx" stigma, fed not only by continued rumors but by two more crashes that occurred after the mystery's solution was made known. All the technical explanations in the world for Buffalo and Tell City couldn't compensate for two additional accidents.

The first involved an American Electra. On September 14, 1960, the propjet was making an approach to LaGuardia when the landing gear hit a dike at the end of the runway and the plane flipped over. There were no casualties, but there was considerable controversy over why it happened. The captain, a veteran supervisory pilot, said he encountered a downdraft just before passing over the dike. The CAB said he came in too low and too short, and tagged him with pilot error. Inasmuch as downdrafts leave no residual evidence of having existed, the embittered captain was stuck with the blame. But LaGuardia itself—a frequent breeding ground for pilot error—also was criticized for not having warning lights on the dike. In addition, the runway had been shortened because of construction, which may have caused the pilot to subconsciously compensate for the abbreviated length.

As was the case in American's first Electra crash, this was an accident that could have happened to any airplane. Had it not been for the Electra's past history, the propjet probably would have come out of the second LaGuardia mishap with an enhanced reputation; after all, the fuselage stayed remarkably intact, nobody was killed, and it was noted by one rescuer that he had trouble getting the crew out of the cockpit because he couldn't break a flight deck side window even with a heavy ax.

But still, the airliner involved was an Electra and the word "jinx" was heard again. It was front-page news if an L-188 so much as blew a tire. And on October 4, another Electra crashed—only this time there were fifty-nine new fatalities to further blacken the propjet's name.

It was an Eastern Electra, Flight 375, taking off from Boston's Logan International Airport for New York with sixty-two passengers and five crew aboard. Exactly 47.5 seconds after the flight informed the tower, "375 rolling," the aircraft was under the waters of Boston Harbor, with only ten survivors.

The plane took off normally, but a few seconds after becoming airborne seemed to falter as it struggled to climb. The left wing dropped, and the Electra fell into a half roll and crashed into the Bay.

The official verdict was a bird strike—a massive ingestion of starlings sufficient to cause a complete power failure on one engine and partial loss of power on the remaining three, just long enough for the pilot to lose control. That finding stood unchallenged for six years, until litigation on the crash finally came to trial.

Testimony disclosed that six weeks before the accident, a mechanic was assigned the task of replacing a defective rod in the mechanism that adjusted the roll of the copilot's seat either forward or backward. Instead of using a new rod, he substituted a too-short strand of wire that made it impossible to lock the seat in any position. Somehow, the mistake went unnoticed and unreported. At the trial, an expert witness theorized that if the copilot was flying the airplane—although this was never confirmed—the seat may have slid backward just as he was trying to correct the yaw caused by the power failure on one engine. In doing so, the witness added, he probably inadvertently pulled back on the yoke when the seat moved and was still clutching the yoke when the seat moved. A yoke pulled back at that altitude would result in a stall.

That explanation, even if valid, was not available in 1961, however. This was the fifth Electra crash, four of them involving heavy loss of life, and the mutterings of "jinxed" became louder. The appellation was even given credence by *Time.* In an otherwise fair account of the propjet's tribulations, the magazine recalled that Electra, daughter of King Agamemnon, was one of the most tragic figures in Greek mythology. The article, read by millions, contributed to the "jinx" stigma that was hanging from the plane's neck like an albatross. To make even the Electra's name part of the unhappy legend being woven around the propjet seemed to be stretching the point too far. Anyway, the Electra was named after a star, not a mythological character.

A few weeks after the Boston crash, American conducted a survey of eleven cities its Electras served—New York, Rochester, Philadelphia, Washington, Boston, Buffalo, Detroit, Chicago, St. Louis, Dallas, and Cincinnati. Its purpose was to ascertain the effects of the Boston accident on traffic, and it covered the ten-day period immediately following the Logan tragedy. The results were jolting: the survey disclosed that 2,298 passengers canceled or refused reservations on American's Electras and cited the Boston accident as the specific reason.

That was all C.R. needed. He had on his desk a note from Red Sutherland of public relations suggesting an all-out campaign to clear the Electra's name. Sutherland had proposed sending a team of experts around to various cities where they'd hold news conferences and explain why American had complete faith in the controversy-ridden airliner.

Only C.R. could have taken that suggestion and not only run with it but expanded it into an *industry* effort. He told Will Player to set up a meeting with the public relations directors of every airline operating Electras and invite their cooperation.

Player ran into some opposition. Some of his opposites on other carriers were telling him, "What's the use? You can't save the Electra; it's a dead airplane." And one remarked, "Hell, *we* don't even trust it. We're afraid of the damned thing."

C.R., too, encountered defeatism when he discussed the proposed campaign with other Electra operators. Several argued that a frontal attack was a waste of time and money, that it would be best to let time take its course and hope that the public would eventually forget what had happened. Smith, with nearly $90 million invested in an Electra fleet flying half-empty, said, in effect, "The hell with hiding our heads in the sand. This is still a damned good airplane, so let's go out and fight all the phony rumors and grounding demands."

In the end, most carriers went along with the campaign. It goes without saying that C.R. would have waged it on his own if he had to. On November 1, 1960, the first of four "Fact Teams" began the most unusual crusade in aviation history.

The first team was composed of Bill Littlewood, Player, Captain Art Weidman, Captain Warren Schultz of Northwest, and Captain Jack Isbill of National. The team hit New York, Washington, and Chicago on its first swing, not only holding news conferences but briefing local civic groups, and conducting question-and-answer sessions with airline sales and operating personnel. In two months, the Fact Teams covered eighteen of the twenty-six major cities served by Electras. Each meeting opened with the team leader reading a hard-hitting statement of policy by C. R. Smith—one that also appeared in newspaper and magazine ads:

"We operate American Airlines on the basis that *we* are responsible for the safety of our passengers. While the Federal Aviation Agency has equal responsibility and equal determination to have safety in air transportation, we consider the basic obligation to provide a safe operation to be our own, and we are responsible for our judgment and our decisions.

"The good reputation of American Airlines is more valuable than the property rights in a fleet of airplanes. If we believed the Electra to be unsafe, we would ground it."

That statement, pure C. R. Smith, set the stage for what followed. The team leader would relate the Electra's history, discuss the causes of the Buffalo and Tell City crashes, explain the "fix" in King's English, and emphasize that the other three Electra accidents could have happened to any airplane—along with assurances that, pending modifications, the speed restrictions made the Electra as safe as anything flying.

Next would come the pilots, to give their opinion of the Electra. Then the team would open the meeting to questions, and not one was left unanswered or dangling in vague evasions.

"In general," Player recounted, "we talked to three different types of people: the press, travel agents, and community leaders. In almost all instances, we couldn't find anyone who'd admit they were afraid of the airplane. But likewise, almost everyone said they had friends or wives who were afraid to fly it. We knew they weren't telling the truth because all our studies showed they *were* afraid themselves—or at least a high percentage of them.

"After we left a city, I can't recall a single case in which the local American sales manager didn't report an immediate upswing in Electra business. And it was an alert and sensitive news media that contributed to the Fact Teams' success. I learned that if you give them something constructive to write, they will. Once you get a distinction between a working journalist and a performer, you're going to get a story fairly told."

One such story was written by *Flying*'s Lou Davis. Reporting on the results of the unprecedented campaign, he said it "brought American closer to the passenger and fortified its own personnel with confidence, producing answers to questions on which they, themselves, may have nursed secret concern."

But American didn't stop with the Fact Teams. It took out of mothballs a confidence-winning gimmick almost as old as air travel itself: the sightseeing flight. At New York, Chicago, and Washington, the airline offered a thirty-minute ride in an Electra for $6.50 and aimed its promotion and advertising at two specific categories: first-timers and those who feared the Electra.

Stewardesses passed out questionnaires asking each passenger why he or she had taken the flight. A surprising 50 percent replied they had never flown before and were just curious.

The sightseeing flights turned out to be airborne parties. Children were given junior pilot or stewardess wings. Every passenger received promotional material, including a brochure on the Electra. Picture-taking was encouraged, and Revell's model Electra kits were awarded to youngsters guessing closest on the plane's current speed and altitude. The popularity of the flights was so overwhelming that they were extended to Boston, Nashville, Syracuse, Buffalo, Detroit, Hartford, and Philadelphia.

Every marketing survey American conducted in relation to the Electra situation showed that many businessmen were avoiding it because their wives were worried about the airplane. So the airline invited one of the nation's leading women pilots, Jerrie Cobb, to fly the propjet. She had never seen the inside of an Electra cockpit, let alone flown one, but with a wire service reporter along as a witness, she made three takeoffs and landings. The third landing was so smooth, it wouldn't have cracked an eggshell attached to the landing gear. Art Weidman was in the cockpit with her. On one takeoff, he told her to leave the throttles at full power after they were airborne; the Electra hit 4,000 feet in sixty seconds.

American also invited Arthur Godfrey to fly the plane, and he told his sizable audience to stop being afraid of a superb machine.

All the promotion and publicity, most of it generated by the unique Fact Teams, had the desired effect, not just on American's Electra traffic but on all operators of the propjet. By mid 1961, American's Electra load factors were higher than those of the 707, and maintenance reliability was the best in the fleet.

LEAP's modification program took twenty days per aircraft, with nine airplanes being worked on simultaneously. American's first modified aircraft, which it called the Electra II, went back in service April 30, 1961. All its restructured propjets were flying by August, with a mixed configuration of fifty-four first-class seats and seventeen coach.

The crisis was over. When a Northwest Electra crashed on takeoff from Chicago's O'Hare Airport that September, the airlines held their collective breath. But the accident had no effect on the public's restored confidence. It was regarded as something that could happen to any airplane (the cause was a maintenance error in which a disconnected aileron cable was not reconnected), and that was the Electra's finest vindication.

C.R. always gave Pete Quesada full credit for saving the propjet from early extinction. If the FAA had grounded the airplane, it would have been out of service so long that a viable comeback might have been impossible. Quesada's stubborn courage and faith earned him American's gratitude. C.R., in fact, named him to the board of directors in 1961, after Quesada left government service.

But Smith also was grateful to Player and his p.r. staff for the success of the brilliant Fact Team project. When Willis returned from the final Fact Team mission, he encountered C.R. in the corridor.

"I knew you could do it," Smith remarked, "but I didn't know you could do it so fast."

Player refrained from saying what was really his own appraisal of the Electra comeback—that it was C.R.'s doing more than anyone else's.

"It was part of American's spirit," he reminisced. "Only this airline could have pulled it off, and it was because C.R. had given its people a feeling of being something special, a kind of elite. Years later, when I returned to Pan Am, they asked me how Pan Am appeared to the rest of the industry and the public. I said, 'You look haughty.' American was different. It had the same self-assurance, but it had more exuberance, a pride in being a part of an airline that had style and class. And that again was Cyrus Rowlett Smith."

Player wasn't the only one who felt that way. An executive with another airline once told Art Lewis, "When I walk into an industry meeting, I can tell who's from American before I'm introduced to anyone. There's just something about them."

If C.R. had heard that compliment in mid 1961, however, it would have sounded painfully empty.

On June 1, American lost its rank as the nation's largest airline. United had absorbed Capital, in the biggest merger in U.S. airline history, and one that presented the eagle with a far greater challenge than the salvation of an airplane.

17

Farewell to the Flagships . . . and a Few Other Friends

To the surprise of the entire industry, American didn't even try to fight the merger that dislodged it from its thirty-year reign as the nation's biggest airline.

It was about the only trunk carrier that abstained from the battle that erupted when United, number two in size, proposed a marriage with fatally ill Capital, number five among the majors. This was strictly C.R.'s decision; he believed mergers were inevitable and not necessarily evil in an industry having troubles digesting the financial stresses of transitioning to jets.

"The trouble with people in this industry," he told Willis Player, "is that they keep on saying mergers in general are necessary, but they always find some reason for trying to kill every one that comes along. We're not going to oppose this merger because I think it's a good thing for the industry."

American had a shot at courting Capital, but it was more of a casual flirtation than an all-out job of romancing. Neither C.R. nor Hogan were that enthusiastic about acquiring an airline with Capital's huge debts and its heavily mortgaged, predominantly Viscount fleet. And most of Capital's northern routes duplicated American's. Before United made its merger pitch, American and several other carriers had proposed making a joint purchase of Capital's routes and divvying them up among themselves.

Smith wasn't really ecstatic about this plan, either, mostly because a route sale without actual merger would have left Capital's 7,600 employees stranded. He had enough respect for Pat Patterson to concede, albeit privately, that merging with United was the best and perhaps the only way of protecting them.

C.R. had no reason to harbor any warm sentiments toward Capital itself. In 1959, the Washington-based carrier had raided 100 Park Avenue and made off with three of American's most promising executives—Walt Johnson, Marv Whitlock, and Ward Hobbs, the latter a former Air Force colonel and a good friend of Johnson's. All three knew Capital was having problems, but they didn't realize its illness was terminal.

"We went there to work a little miracle," Whitlock said wryly. "We all wanted the challenge of working for a smaller airline that we thought still had a bright future. We figured we could hold it together for maybe five years, but we ran out of time. Capital had such a high debt-to-equity ratio there was no way to keep it going. It took us about a year to realize it wasn't going to work."

Johnson became senior vice president of marketing at Capital, Whitlock went in as vice president of maintenance and later was promoted to senior vice president of operations, while Hobbs held the same post at Capital as he did with American. After the merger, they joined United, where all but Hobbs ended their airline careers. He went on to become FAA's director of federal airports and also served as a Delta vice president.

"Ward was the only guy I ever knew who wound up collecting five pensions," Johnson commented. "He was drawing retirement pay from American, United, FAA, Delta, and the Air Force."

Johnson and Whitlock never lost their affection for American. "I never saw a company like it," Walt said. "Its people worked and played together. Your friends were American, your associates were American, your whole life was American."

Whitlock agreed. "I had no quarrels with American, no complaints or hard feelings when I decided to leave. I had been with the airline twenty-five years, I was forty-five years old, and I figured if I was ever going to make a move, I had to do it then. And I'm glad I had the privilege of working for those two giants, C.R. and Patterson."

Smith missed them both. Whitlock was regarded as having one of the finest engineering and maintenance brains in the industry. And C.R. had relied heavily on Johnson for more than his marketing skills. He was used frequently as a witness in CAB route case hearings, often spending eight hours a day, five days a week testifying. He was articulate and fast on his feet under cross-examination, and American could have used his skills during the southern transcontinental route hearings in which the airline was seeking nonstop authority from Atlanta and Miami to the West Coast. The subsequent CAB decision made Delta a transcontinental carrier and put Braniff into New York, while American got nothing except the dubious distinction of having its only two unduplicated routes—Dallas–New York and Dallas–Los Angeles—open to competition.

Those three capable officers left American before another high-altitude shakeup at corporate headquarters, one of stunning significance because it established a dark horse as C.R.'s probable successor. Next to G. Marion Sadler's vice presidential title were added the words "general manager," which meant only one thing: he had been given the job of running the airline on a day-to-day basis, and it was obvious that Smith—as he had hinted previously to MacIntyre—was thinking again about moving up to board chairman, where he could concentrate on broad policy matters.

The pecking order in 1960 seemed somewhat confused. Hogan, Spater, and a fading Mosier remained as executive vice presidents and thus theoretically outranked Sadler. But in naming Sadler general manager, C.R. literally promoted him over everyone's head in the line of potential succession.

The strongest evidence to support that conclusion came to light when, as part of the latest reorganization, Mel Brenner was promoted to vice president of scheduling and was told to report directly to Sadler. Hitherto, scheduling had been under Hogan's financial and planning department; this was the first sign that C.R., as much as he admired Hogan, did not regard him as a successor.

"Hogan was really bitter about the reorganization," Brenner recalled. "He felt that Sadler's being named general manager had diminished his own role. When I worked for him, he had a very high regard for me. The day I learned I was being made vice president of an upgraded department, I went into Bill's office to thank him for all he had done for me. I felt as if an invisible barrier had come down between us. I was no longer part of his team, and if you weren't part of his team, you were automatically suspect."

Brenner had an unusual encounter with C.R. that illustrates the humility and compassion that so often was hidden under his curt, sometimes even rude manner. Shortly after he became vice president, Mel was making a slide and chart presentation to C.R., Sadler, and Hogan. Smith kept making snide, sneering remarks throughout the meeting, all directed at Brenner.

"I didn't know whether something was bothering him," Brenner recalled, "but I never had C.R. treat me as he did that morning. I was on a real spot. Nobody two levels down could talk back to him. I left the meeting very upset and hurt."

That same afternoon, Brenner got a note from Smith.

"Don't pay any attention to the things I said to you today," it read. "You're still the greatest scheduler in the industry."

It would be difficult to challenge that praise. Mel Brenner was one of the first—probably *the* first—to make a science out of scheduling, and this is not to disparage the skills and contributions of other airline schedulers, most of whom would have agreed with Smith's commendation. Brenner recognized the fallacy that high aircraft utilization meant someone had done a good job of scheduling. He turned it around, establishing the principle that aircraft utilization meant nothing *without* a scheduling pattern that filled airplanes.

He was always a relentless foe of overscheduling—the practice of smothering the competition under a sheer volume of flights. Rickenbacker was the leading exponent of using schedule frequency as a competitive weapon, and also the leading example of overdoing it. He simply hated to see any airplane sitting on the ground, and insisted that Eastern keep operating flights even at hours when no one wanted to travel.

And that was the prime key to Brenner's success. He had his department constantly monitoring the all-important relationship between schedules and load factors, the effects of a schedule change on traffic, and the delicate, almost fragile task of balancing public departure and arrival preferences against aircraft utilization.

In that respect, he was among the first to integrate the needs and objectives of all departments into the building of an efficient, profitable scheduling pattern, to recognize that the time a flight leaves or arrives is dependent on numerous factors that must be taken into account—gate space, connecting times, availability of ground equipment, sufficient allowances for food service and baggage transfers, adequate station staffing, the demands of flight crew duty limitations, reacting to or anticipating competitors' efforts, predicting traffic growth or decline in any given market, positioning aircraft for the most efficient utilization, maintenance requirements, new route awards, judging the impact of new equipment in accordance with performance and capacity, and working its delivery timetable into schedule timetables.

Brenner taught American the importance of traffic flow, or backup traffic support, as it is sometimes called. For example, he got some raised eyebrows when he scheduled two nonstop Electra trips from New York to Nashville daily, in addition to several one-stop and multi-stop flights. Those two nonstops provided a total of 136 seats, and Mel was informed they were averaging only 48 local passengers a day between them—"local" meaning people going solely between New York and Nashville.

True, Brenner said, but more than half the passengers on the nonstops were not local but people who either connected at New York from other flights, or were going to destinations beyond Nashville. Traffic support made the flights profitable.

Scheduling was sometimes an unfeeling ogre to station managers, who naturally objected to any schedule change that affected their own city. Because of an equipment routing problem, American shifted a Louisville–New York flight from a 5:15 P.M. departure to 5:35. American's city manager in Louisville complained the shift would lose about ten passengers a day to Eastern's 4:45 flight. That a twenty-minute change in departure could have such an effect may be hard to understand, but it could matter a lot to a passenger. One man who had always flown American on that original 5:15 P.M. flight wrote that he was switching to Eastern because a twenty-minute-later departure caused him to miss his preferred commuter train from New York to Westport.

Brenner had been a staff expert with the CAB and several other agencies before joining American in time to participate in jet planning, although his first job was in route development. The system schedule for the fall of 1961 provided a perfect example of how one of those aforementioned factors could cause havoc. Brenner's department had that schedule almost finalized by August, when American was advised it was getting four new 707s ahead of their original delivery dates.

"Each of those jets started a chain reaction," he recounted. "It affected gate space, connections, etc., throughout the system, and by the time we got through adjusting for those four planes, there was scarcely a flight left untouched in our schedule pattern."

Introduction of additional jet service by competitors wrecked traffic in markets American was still serving with props; not even the Electra could hold its own against a pure jet. American had a nonstop, midday Electra flight from Boston to Chicago that was averaging sixty-one passengers daily. United ran in a DC-8 flight that left about the same time; in four weeks, the

Electras were averaging only thirty-six passengers. Experiences like this were the main reason American, in mid 1961, began phasing out the Electra fleet by selling five propjets to a South American airline and at the same time ordered twenty-five Boeing 727s—the airplane that proved to be the most versatile transport ever built and the jet-age successor to the Convair 240 and the DC-3.

One scheduling decision could involve a million-dollar shift in revenues, up or down. "Attract one additional passenger a day through an improved schedule pattern," Brenner said, "multiply it by 365 days, and it's worth at least $100,000 a year, and a half million if you can get five more."

Shortly after the jets began flying, Brenner was attending a meeting in San Diego that finished about 11 A.M. American didn't have a late eastbound flight out of San Diego then, so he flew up to Los Angeles to catch the "Red Eye" (11 P.M. departure) nonstop to New York.

"I was sitting in the Admirals Club from about noon on," he related, "and got to thinking that there must be an awful lot of people like myself who couldn't make our morning 707 nonstop to New York and didn't really want to wait for the Red Eye, which got into Idlewild around 7 A.M. I figured if you could catch a jet around 4 P.M., you'd get to New York about midnight—not the greatest, but better than waiting hours for the 11 P.M.

"So when I got back, I told our sales people I thought there'd be a pretty good market for a late-afternoon 707 departure out of Los Angeles. I got a lot of opposition at first, but we tried it and it worked. The flight never had tremendous load factors, but it was profitable enough and did a lot of people a favor.

"I came into scheduling at a time when the airlines were just beginning to recognize its importance, and as competition increased scheduling became a critical make-or-break factor. When you had three guys flying the same route, if the preferred departure time was 5 P.M. and you were leaving at 5:30, you were dead. In the Washington–Los Angeles market, American had a 707 leaving Dulles at 5:15, United a DC-8 at 5:30, and TWA a 707 at 5:45. So TWA rescheduled to get a 5 P.M. departure and the result was $750,000 a year increased revenues just by being first."

Brenner instituted the practice of getting input from the regional field offices for every scheduling pattern before it was adopted. And this liaison also underlined the increasing influence of those offices on company policy. The first McKinsey management study had urged C.R. to let field personnel make appropriate decisions without having to consult New York constantly.

Jack Mullins's appointment as the new vice president of field activities, part of the latest reorganization, underlined Smith's acceptance of this policy. Mullins was a tough, peppery, and extremely competent individual who wasn't afraid to do battle with the New York brass and at the same time keep his collection of regional vice presidents in line. The city managers reported to them and they reported to him. And those regional officers included some veteran rugged individualists like Al Bone, American's "Mr. Los Angeles" for

years, and Elmo Coon in San Francisco, who started out as a traffic manager
at Tucson in 1930.

Mullins, who could fight for them as well as with them, was the type of
leader cast in C.R.'s own mold: decisive, often abrupt, but fair. Walt Rauscher,
one of the several young officers who learned their trade in the F. J. Mullins
School of Practical Knowledge, described him this way:

"You never went into Jack's office and told him, 'Yeah, I know all about
that matter' when you really didn't know a damned thing about it. If he found
out you were bluffing or lying, he'd chew you up and spit out the pieces. We
used to fight and argue, but he was the kind of guy who'd let you argue without
taking it out on you. He didn't want yes men around him."

The shakeup that put Mullins in charge of the field organization also produced one casualty: Bill Bump, "Mr. New England," left American. His
epitaph was uttered by Rauscher: "Bump had American Airlines tattooed on
his heart." Also leaving was Stanley King, regional vice president in Chicago
and another veteran.

The seemingly unending management shifts merely reflected C.R.'s determination to keep American the best even if it was no longer the biggest. United
always was the main enemy. TWA was respected, but too often inconsistent-
aggressive, and in many ways brilliantly innovative, but handicapped by Howard Hughes's reluctance to let TWA's management run the airline.

It took some time for the competition to catch up to American's fanjet
program. Every carrier recognized—belatedly, in most instances—the enormous technical superiority of fanjet power. And American made sure the
public realized it, too. Frank Kolk and Red Sutherland of public relations
orchestrated a series of dramatic demonstration flights for the news media,
travel agents, and civic leaders at Chicago, Dallas/Fort Worth, San Francisco,
Los Angeles, New York, Washington–Baltimore, and Cleveland.

"Dramatic" is a word chosen deliberately. At each city, prior to the demonstration flight, Kolk, Sutherland, and/or others would outline the advantages
of the new engines, emphasizing such features as greater power, less noise, and
more responsiveness. Then the guests would board a 707 Astrojet for a flight
that made the briefing come alive.

Commanded by Captain Walt Moran, the 707 would take off at an angle
of 24 degrees, nearly twice as steep as the normal takeoff attitude. In less than
ten minutes, they'd be at 30,000 feet, with the p.a. system advising that it took
a conventional jet about twenty minutes to attain this height. The demonstration of climb-to-cruise ability was followed by Moran's reducing thrust on the
engines, one by one, to zero. The jet glided like a giant sailplane for miles before
Moran applied thrust and went into a series of thrilling maneuvers.

First, a sharp turn that exerted a force of two G's (twice the weight of
gravity), pressing the passengers against their seats. Legs became heavy, and
a camera seemed to weigh at least fifty pounds.

Next a speed run in a shallow dive up to 630 miies per hour, fast enough
to activate a "mach warning" bell installed in the cabin to alert passengers the

jet was approaching the speed of sound. The final maneuver was a steep, simulated emergency descent repeating the G forces. It was all perfectly safe, yet exciting enough to impress anyone with the performance characteristics of the Astrojet. The fanjet demonstration flights were one of American's most successful promotional efforts.

Fleet modernization was just one way to keep American in the first-place position that meant more than size. The 727 was intended primarily as the Electra's eventual replacement, but this exceptionally fine airplane was a few years down the road and was being ordered by everyone, including United, TWA, and Eastern. The new jet on which C.R. was betting quite a few chips was the Convair 990, which turned out to be his most disappointing equipment decision.

Only the Monday morning quarterbacks and second-guessers could have blamed him. If Convair (General Dynamics) had met American's specifications, the 990 would have been a winner. It fell far short of those specs, including the most important one: General Dynamics guaranteed a cruising speed of more than 600 m.p.h., almost 100 m.p.h. faster than any other jetliner flying. Speed was the primary reason American ordered the 990, whose very name represented the 990 kilometers per hour (615 m.p.h.) the manufacturer was promising.

C.R. envisioned using the 990 for a nonstop, all–first class transcontinental express service that, if the jet had lived up to its advance notices, would have clobbered TWA's 707s and United's DC-8s; American's own 707s would have been predominantly coach-configured. But the 990 proved to be slower than either the 707 or DC-8, lacked transcontinental range, and couldn't ever be used the way C.R. intended.

American originally ordered twenty-five CV-990s, with an option for twenty-five more if the airplane met guaranteed performance. When the test program uncovered serious problems, Smith canceled five of the first twenty-five planes and all the options, then hoped for the best, which never came. To achieve the promised speed, Convair's engineers had developed ingenious antishock "speed pods." They resembled inverted canoes, and two were installed on each wing, extending beyond the trailing edge. They were supposed to smooth out the airflow and also carry extra fuel.

The first test flights showed the 990 was in trouble. The pods did increase the speed (although not nearly as much as expected), but when they were filled with fuel, the outboard engines developed a dangerous shudder at high speeds. Convair had to realign the engines, and then encountered a new headache: the realignment produced increased drag.

American accepted the twenty it had ordered, but sold five of them without ever putting them into service. Hogan wanted to cancel the whole deal, and as it was, General Dynamics paid a stiff penalty for not meeting either the specifications or the promised delivery dates. Smith was tempted to take Hogan's advice, but by then it was too late. The 1962 schedules already had been finalized to accommodate 990 service and American was dumping its pistons as fast as possible, including the sale of forty-five DC-6s to a used aircraft dealer for $30 million.

With much fanfare accompanied by crossed fingers, American inaugurated 990 service March 18, 1962, between Idlewild and O'Hare. The crossed fingers didn't work any better than the 990. The eastbound trip took one hour and forty-eight minutes and the westbound two hours and ten minutes, both identical to the 707's scheduled flying times on the same route.

The 990 had one virtue: until the 747 came along, it was the strongest jetliner in the air, structurally superior even to the 707. But battleship strength didn't compensate for its sins, and American began phasing out the 990 fleet as soon as 727 deliveries reached the point where the Convairs weren't needed. All fifteen were gone by 1969.

Yet the 990 shared one distinction with the far more successful 707: they were the first American Airlines planes to carry the new name "Astrojet," and the first since the DC-3 that weren't called Flagships and named after cities and states. This change, regretted by not a few employees, was dictated by American's new advertising agency, Doyle Dane Bernbach, regarded as the most creative on Madison Avenue. The agency had won justified acclaim for its campaign on behalf of the Volkswagen, probably the ugliest automobile ever to travel a U.S. highway. The agency turned its very unattractiveness into a sales weapon by calling the car "the Beetle" and plugging it with a series of clever, humorous ads that made owning a VW almost an anti-establishment gesture and its drivers something of a cult.

The switch from Flagship to Astrojet may have offended the sentimentalists, but it caught on with the public; Astrojet, like Beetle, achieved instant product identification. Not too long after the new name was adopted for the 707 and 990, Rosalind Russell was filming *Majority of One*. She was on a set inside a 707 mock-up; the script called for her to be afraid of flying.

The actress playing her daughter asked solicitously, "Mother, can I get you some Dramamine?"

Rosalind was supposed to answer, "Of course not. Do you think I'm an astronaut?"

But what inadvertently came out of her mouth was, "Do you think I'm an Astrojet?"

The agency followed up the Astrojet campaign with successive advertisements featuring the 707, 990, and the conversion to fanjets. American's 1961 ad budget was the largest C.R. had ever approved. But the airline got its money's worth; some of the Doyle Dane Bernbach offerings were classics.

One of the favorites was a two-picture layout, the top photo showing bumper-to-bumper auto traffic. The bottom shot depicted the identical stretch of road but with only one car, and was captioned: "If motorists were tested like our pilots, our highways would look like this."

One ad paid tribute to American's mechanics. There was a folding picture frame holding three photographs resting on a table. In the left frame was a smiling woman, in the right a little boy, and between them was a shot of a 707's nose. On the table in front of the three pictures were two mechanic's wrenches. The caption: "Give me a man who loves his work."

One of the all-time favorites was a photo of a stewardess, a Mona Lisa smile on her lips, and the caption: "Think of her as your mother."

This was institutional advertising at its best—the creation of a favorable corporate image, with no direct selling of a specific product. The agency took American's already existing standards of professionalism and conveyed them to the public via visual symbolism and with just the right touch of humor.

The dwindling propeller fleet, including the Electras, retained their Flagship designations, but it was the ad agency's feeling that "Flagship" carried too much association with older aircraft and had almost a DC-3 connotation. In fact, Doyle Dane Bernbach also recommended modernizing the corporate logo and putting the new version on all jets. The revised symbol was introduced in 1962, and it was hard to find anyone who really liked it. The rather cluttered design placed the double "A" and the eagle over the word "American" and put them inside a circle that had an elliptical appearance. The rim of the circle was red and the lettering was blue against a white background. This logo was to be used for the rest of the decade; some employees called it "the squashed egg."

At the same time, all ground vehicles were repainted a grayish-blue dubbed "Astrojet Blue," instead of the traditional International Orange. The latter color was always hard to maintain because it showed grease, dirt, and scuff marks too easily.

Some people were a little surprised that C.R. went along with all these changes. One explanation may be that his brother Bill had joined American as director of corporate design. When the ad agency was talking about a gradual visual shift to the new Astrojet "look," Bill sought the advice of Visual Marketing, Inc., a design consultant firm, which informed him American had too many variations in visual identification. It suggested a new logo and elimination of all orange markings, from the standpoint of both customer identification and maintenance economy. By 1963, the orange would come off all rudders and ailerons.

The one exception to the enforced retirement of "Flagship" was the long-standing name of the company's employee newspaper. It had been called *Flagship News* since the DC-2/DC-3 era, and Willis Player's public relations crew simply balked at changing it. The newspaper had a tradition of its own. One of its earliest editors was Frank Brunton, who later became American's p.r. representative in Washington. He and his wife Dorothy used to paste up each dummy issue of *Flagship News* on their kitchen table in Chicago before sending it to the printer.

Prior to 1960, the newspaper had been coming out every other week, and Player had vibes that in recent years it had been missing the boat as an effective internal communications tool. A consultant came up with four recommendations: publish once a week; put out a separate paper for Tulsa; publish a management newsletter; and also a separate newsletter for stewardesses. All but the last were adopted. This may have been a mistake—on any airline, flight attendants were and still are the least-informed employee group.

A Tulsa *Flagship News* was the most radical proposal, but Player felt it was essential. The base by 1960 had more than 3,000 employees, most of them strongly unionized, and Willis thought having their own newspaper would improve labor relations. There was another factor: most mechanics felt a little neglected, what with the "glamour" side of the airline—such as pilots and stewardesses—getting all the attention.

The first editor of the Tulsa edition was a short, wiry part-Indian who was in the public relations department of Oklahoma University when a friend told him American was starting a company newspaper at the Tulsa base. His name was Mack Palmer. He was called "chief" from the day he joined the airline in 1960 because of his Cherokee blood, and he was to edit the Tulsa paper for the next six years.

Mack was more than the new boy on the block, he was an outsider. At first, he was treated with suspicion by a large number of mechanics, who figured he was a management spy.

"That first week," he remembered, "I spent wandering around the base with a little notebook in my hand. Nobody knew who I was or what I was doing there, but they suspected I was someone from management checking up on them. When I came into any work area, I was the angel of death. People taking a break would suddenly start working like hell as soon as they saw me with that notebook. Until the mechanics got to know and trust me, my only achievement was contributing to productivity."

Palmer started out modestly with a mimeographed newspaper that was more of a newsletter, but later the Tulsa edition became a full-fledged publication, printed in Tulsa and inserted into the regular *Flagship News* every two weeks. Mack even gave it its own name: *Astrojet News.* The first issue carried the banner headline: FUTURE IN CAPABLE HANDS—OUR OWN. Palmer reported for work just after American had fired eight mechanics for starting a slowdown, and the Transport Workers Union was threatening a strike. It was a rude awakening for the chief; when he'd asked American's p.r. man in Tulsa, M. J. O'Brien, what he'd be writing about in the new paper, O'Brien told him, "Oh, things like the company picnic."

When Palmer started the Tulsa paper, Lucien Hunt, a former Navy captain and Annapolis graduate who had been in charge of the Navy's big Coronado maintenance base in San Diego, was vice president of maintenance. Hunt was a tall, friendly man and totally bald—the mechanics called him "Mr. Clean." Palmer went into his office to introduce himself, and blinked at the decor. Behind Hunt's desk were an American flag and the airline's own flag. "I almost stood at attention and saluted," Palmer chuckled.

But they got along fine. For all his Navy background, Hunt was surprisingly easygoing and very likable. Dissension was the last thing the company wanted at Tulsa. It had poured $20 million into the base, getting it ready to handle jets, and its importance, while less publicized, was recognized by everyone from C.R. down. Four Electras were partially modified there when the Burbank modification lines became clogged, and Tulsa also handled much of the fanjet conversions.

There was some concern among the ground crews about the jets, mostly the possibility of being sucked into an engine if they accidentally came too close. Their fears reached the status of a labor-management dispute when a company official decided that the best place to load last-minute 707 baggage was the forward cargo bin, just ahead of the number-two engine.

This would have been inconsequential except for one thing: number two was an inboard engine, and it was standard practice for the pilots to start both inboards a minute before leaving the gate. The ground crews complained to the TWU that they'd be risking their lives if they loaded baggage that close to number two.

Their protests were relayed to Jim Francis of the personnel department, who went out to Idlewild and experimented with smoke bombs, which he set off directly ahead of number two. It was like sucking on a dead cigarette: the smoke drifted upward instead of into the engine, and further tests showed that ingestion would occur only if the plane was moving.

Francis invited the union to come out and see for itself, and the delegate was Tony Rizzo, who showed up at Idlewild wearing a business suit and a felt that. Francis was worried. If the hat flew into the engine, three items would be ruined: the hat, the engine, and the new loading procedure.

Rizzo wasn't exactly the epitome of nonchalance, either, but he had guts. He came within two feet of the turning number two and bravely stood there for three or four minutes. His hat stayed on, and so did the procedure.

Jim Francis, who retired in 1982 after thirty-six years with American, was involved in another incident he could never forget. The day the Electra hit the dike at LaGuardia, the passengers were taken into a hangar where Francis and Otto Becker began handing out emergency funds for cabs, meals, and any clothing items they might have lost. Jim stopped in front of a young, attractive blonde who seemed bewildered.

"How are you doing, Miss?"

"Fine."

"Is there anything I can do to help?"

"Yeah. Where do I go for a stewardess interview?"

"Keep us the best" were C.R.'s marching orders, and his army responded.

On June 25, 1961, American's Astrojets inaugurated a new first-class service on the New York–Los Angeles flights—white linen tablecloths, new china and silver utensils, heavy glass salt and pepper shakers instead of the tiny plastic cellars, silver-finished napkin rings with engraved AA insignia, tulip-shaped champagne glasses, and a new selection of entrees from Sky Chefs kitchens. With an eye out for an historical tie-in, marketing and public relations geared the introduction to the twenty-fifth anniversary of the first DC-3 service; the contrast between 1936 and 1961 made for natural and well-played feature stories.

Curbside baggage checking by skycaps, a Walt Rauscher idea, was tried out for the first time at Los Angeles International in the spring of 1962. By midsummer it was in effect at Chicago, San Francisco, Idlewild, and Buffalo, and before the end of the year American was introducing it systemwide. Passengers loved it; curbside checking sharply reduced congestion at ticket counters. One survey showed there were 100 fewer counter contacts per day during the peak morning period. Another helpful innovation, introduced later, was the first reservations service for the deaf.

By 1962, American had become the first airline in the U.S. to install Distance Measuring Equipment (DME) on every jet in its fleet. DME may have meant nothing to passengers, but it meant a lot to a carrier. It was an extremely efficient new navigating device and an indirect contributor to safety.

More than any other predominantly passenger airline, American was still trying to make a viable enterprise out of air freight. It ordered four new 707 airfreighters, the first jets designed for all-cargo operations. When it was ready to put the first one into service, public relations decided to publicize the event by installing a regulation bowling alley in the cavernous cabin, and invited some top bowlers to stage a match between New York and Dallas.

The freighters didn't carry drop-down automatic oxygen masks so two supervisory stewardesses, Clancie Henderson and Ann Danaher, went along to man portable oxygen bottles if needed for the bowlers and a few reporters. The alley, including a regulation pin-setter, took up most of the fuselage, but a few seats had been installed.

While the match was in progress, Clancie strolled up to the cockpit in time to hear the following conversation:

Captain: "I'm a little worried about my wife. She hasn't been feeling well lately."

Flight engineer: "Sorry to hear that, Captain. Is she going through menopause?"

Captain: "Hell, she hasn't even been through Disneyland yet."

That should have given Clancie ample warning that the four-striper flying the airline was right out of the Si Bittner mold, jet age or no jet age. A few minutes later, when she was back watching the bowlers, his voice came over the p.a.

"Folks, we're expecting some turbulence. It won't last long and you can resume your game shortly. Meanwhile, I suggest you sit down and hold onto your balls."

It is possible, however, to find some technical significance in that remark—namely, the fact that at 30,000 feet he knew when to expect turbulence. By the time the jets arrived, American had established an "Upper Air Center" employing the most sophisticated weather forecasting equipment and methods available. The center's director was Peter Kraght, who in 1964 was to win ATA's Edgar Gorrell Award for his research into clear air turbulence. He had won this honor for his meteorological achievements twice before, in 1941 and 1948.

In the new environment of fuel-gorging jets, knowing at what upper atmosphere levels a flight could find the most favorable jetstream conditions might mean the difference between a profitable trip and one that lost money because of excessive fuel consumption. Weather forecasting had come a long way from the days when airmen had their own definition of a meteorologist: "He's the last pilot who flew through the weather."

But everything the airline was doing to retain its lead in everything but sheer size was minuscule compared to an event that occurred November 5, 1959.

On that date, American Airlines and IBM announced the joint development of a Semi-Automated Business Reservations Environment.

Its acronym was SABRE.

Judged by what it is today, SABRE was misnamed; the only thing "semi" in its incredible capabilities is the fact that its data and inquiries are punched in by human hands. The rest is done by 550,000 miles of data circuits linked to 65,000 terminals, including 15,000 in American's own corporate offices, reservation facilities, and ticket counters.

In its early stages of development, even mighty IBM was a mite unnerved at what American had established as its goals for a data processing system applied to airline reservations. One IBM official said it compared to the computer complexities of the DEW Line (Defense Early Warning) system then in operation.

SABRE had its genesis in the chance meeting of two men aboard an American flight several years earlier; one was C. R. Smith and the other was IBM chief Tom Watson. They didn't recognize each other, but got to talking without mentioning names.

"What line of work are you in?" C.R. asked.

"Oh, business machines, computers. How about you?"

"Airlines. This one, as a matter of fact."

"That's interesting," Watson allowed. "You must be having all sorts of problems these days. What's your biggest one?"

"Answering the goddamned telephone," C.R. replied. He went on to explain what he meant—that American was operating jets with a reservations system geared to the piston age. The airline's Reservisor system, he added, was too slow, inadequate, and outdated, but there was nothing better available then or in the immediate future.

That was all Watson needed. There were mutual introductions and the start of a long friendship between them, not to mention forthcoming years of cooperation between their respective companies.

Six years of joint research went into the project. Most of the trunk carriers had their own variations of relatively primitive electronic reservations systems. There were United's Instamatic, Eastern's Univac, and TWA's Teleflite, also used by Western—all of them roughly similar to American's Reservisor. But in each case, the fancy-sounding names couldn't disguise their weaknesses. Their display functions were limited, basically reliant on too many manual operations and lacking adequate data storage capacity.

What American sought in SABRE, and what IBM eventually provided, was a data processing system that would create a complete passenger name record in printed alphabetic and numerical characters, file those records and retrieve existing records, automatically send and receive interline space requests, automatically remind agents to advise passengers of any flight changes, make all data available on any agent's display set throughout American's system, search the files for duplicate reservations, automatically process waiting lists, supply current flight information, furnish passenger counts and manifests to every city involved, and provide meal and beverage counts for each flight.

It took Reservisor an average forty-five minutes to completely process a reservation; SABRE did it in three seconds, handling 7,500 every hour. The first city cutover was Hartford, in November 1962, and SABRE became systemwide in 1964 with a Cleveland cutover. The initial computer center, installed in 1960, was at Briarcliff Manor, New York, and was later moved to Tulsa. Even in 1962, SABRE's capabilities were awesome; it could process daily 85,000 phone calls, 30,000 requests for fare quotations, 40,000 confirmed passenger reservations, 30,000 queries to and from other airlines regarding seat space, and 20,000 ticket sales. And IBM built into the system the potential for almost unlimited growth. SABRE's capabilities today dwarf what it could do in 1962.

Just the initial research, development, and installation cost $40 million—the price of four 707s. But once again American had forced the opposition to play catch-up ball. There would be a period, as we shall see, when American allowed United not only to catch up but race ahead of SABRE temporarily —an unhappy situation that would be turned around by a man possessing C.R.'s vision and decisiveness. Until the 1970s, however, SABRE's unduplicated efficiency was a major weapon against United's size.

It was one of those numerous competitive balls C.R. kept juggling so adeptly. Another, though, was to fall and bounce the wrong way: his attempt to merge American with Eastern.

It is uncertain when the first overtures were made and by whom. The best available evidence indicates that C.R. got together with Laurance Rockefeller, the most influential director on Eastern's board, sometime in early 1961 and found him receptive. Eastern was swimming in red ink, and Rockefeller blamed Rickenbacker more than Malcolm MacIntyre, who had been president only since the fall of 1959. He honestly felt the airline couldn't survive on its own, and he was a long-time admirer of C.R. specifically and American in general.

The official announcement that a merger application had been filed with the Civil Aeronautics Board came January 23, 1962, and immediately generated the unanimous opposition of the entire industry. United's joining the solid anti-merger phalanx hurt C.R. the most. Because American hadn't fought the

Capital merger, he halfway expected Patterson to abstain from this one, although he wasn't totally surprised.

"He wasn't disillusioned," Willis Player said. "He had enough experience to expect the worst, but he was disgusted with United's position. He felt Patterson couldn't see that this merger would strengthen the industry, not weaken it."

Merger strategy was largely in the hands of George Spater, American's general counsel, and he hung his hat on the belief that under the Federal Aviation Act of 1958, regulated airlines were exempt from antitrust laws. Player, only too familiar with the Washington climate under the Kennedy administration, thought he was wrong and told him so. So did Dwight Taylor, then a vice president in American's Washington office, but C.R. trusted Spater's legal judgment. Hogan was on the fence as far as the wisdom of merger was concerned, but he disliked Spater intensely—he derisively called the balding lawyer "old skinhead"—and warned Smith, "If anyone can screw up a case, it's Spater."

MacIntyre wasn't even aware that merger talks had been going on, and when he finally was told, he predicted the CAB would never approve a marriage that wedded two of the nation's largest carriers. His lukewarm support was to prove damaging during the hearings. He was a very honest man and on the witness stand, testifying under oath, he made some admissions that depicted Eastern as a somewhat unwilling partner—only its directors really wanted the merger.

Rockefeller was optimistic, because he thought he had President Kennedy's tacit approval in his hip pocket. He did, but there was a catch: JFK told him he'd okay a merger agreement, assuming the CAB approved it, if Attorney General Bobby Kennedy's Justice Department didn't object. Justice turned out to be one of the most vociferous opponents.

The hearings, lasting through the first half of 1962, were a disaster to the two proponents. Six airlines had intervened, but Delta called most of the strategy shots. It called so many, in fact, that at times it appeared that Delta was waging a one-airline fight. At one point during the oral arguments, C. E. Woolman became worried.

"Maybe you'd better let some of the other airlines ask a few questions," he told Dick Maurer, Delta's vice president for legal and the unofficial leader of the opposition.

"We can't count on anybody asking the right questions," Maurer explained patiently.

"Just give 'em the questions," Woolman suggested.

The questions largely were aimed at destroying Eastern's contention that it couldn't possibly survive without the merger. In the belief that antitrust laws didn't apply, the case for merger was built around the same strategy employed in the United-Capital proceedings, in which both carriers argued that Capital was going to go down the tube anyway. The trouble was that neither Eastern's nor American's witnesses could prove that EAL was doomed. Both MacIntyre and even Smith wound up admitting that the "failing business" concept didn't really apply to this merger.

Delta's lawyers kept hammering away with the argument that Eastern's troubles were largely of its own making and cited such items as deliberate overscheduling, an intentional delay in ordering jets (Rickenbacker's decision), poor labor relations, and expensive efforts to improve its admittedly bad public image, the latter adding up to $57 million over a three-year period.

The backstage maneuvering could have been used in a James Bond movie. Certain Eastern employees, and perhaps a few officers as well, kept leaking confidential documents that found their way into the hands of Delta's legal staff. One of Eastern's chief claims was that it didn't even have the financial resources to spend on its showcase, the Shuttle. Delta produced a purchase order for hundreds of new Shuttle aircraft seats—an order American didn't know existed.

"We'd get such stuff mailed or delivered to us by second persons in unmarked envelopes," a Delta official said. "In the case of the Shuttle seats, it became obvious that Eastern and American weren't leveling with each other."

This was not only obvious but an indication of the merger's principal weakness: it was apparent that Eastern was the reluctant bride in this corporate marriage, its own people trying to sabotage the airline's case. One EAL employee somehow got his hands on engineering drawings showing how the carrier planned to shift its Electras over to the Shuttle and install smaller seats. He gave them to someone at National, who in turn passed them to a Delta employee so the latter wouldn't know their real source. An Eastern official was on the witness stand denying that his company was going to reconfigure the Electras when a Delta lawyer produced the name of the company that had done the drawings.

Another stolen document that wound up in Delta's clutches was an internal communication sent to EAL pilots, advising them that Eastern was going to smother the opposition with so much schedule frequency that pilot vacations would have to be postponed. It not only was evidence of Eastern's uneconomic overscheduling practices but tended to refute the claim that excessive competition on Eastern's routes was responsible for the airline's financial crisis.

C.R., sad to relate, was not an effective witness for his cause. He was at his best during one exchange with a youthful CAB attorney who asked him what kind of studies had been made before deciding on the merger course.

"We didn't have any studies," Smith growled.

"Do you mean to say that two huge airlines decided to merge and failed to prepare any studies that would justify such a merger?"

C.R. leaned back and smiled tolerantly. "Young man, if you had looked at a map of Eastern's route structure and then looked at a map of American's, you'd realize there wasn't any need for a study."

But if he could handle a wet-behind-the-ears CAB lawyer, it was a different matter with the experienced and relentless Delta staff. Maurer treated C.R. with respect, but he was tough at times. He spent a great deal of time trying to get Smith to admit that merger negotiations had been conducted secretly for much longer than American or Eastern were willing to say, and C.R.'s denials were not entirely convincing. Maurer had him on the stand for virtually an entire day, and Smith occasionally became irritated under a cross-examination that exposed too many inconsistencies. He may have turned aside the inexperienced CAB's lawyer with his rather flip dismissal of the lack of pre-merger studies, but it didn't work with Maurer, who questioned him closely on what amounted to sloppy homework.

The merger application had claimed a savings of more than $50 million in annual expenses and over $100 million in capital investment, but C.R.'s inability to substantiate such projections made it appear that they had come off the west wall. Maurer asked him about Eastern's contention that the merger would result in a $15 million saving from just the retirement of Constellations from the Shuttle, using American's and Eastern's Electras as their replacements. Smith admitted that EAL intended to retire the Connies anyway even if the merger didn't go through.

Many factors doomed the merger, not the least of which was failure to refute the chief argument against it: that it would create a giant that controlled one third of the nation's air traffic. That single point had brought Bobby Kennedy's Justice Department into adamant opposition. The word going around DOJ when merger was first proposed was, "Take a close look at it—it's a dilly." This alone made a mockery out of Spater's strategy. And Eastern's chief thrust —that it couldn't survive on its own—fell apart when MacIntyre reluctantly and rather bravely voiced the opinion that it could.

Even when the CAB examiner issued an initial decision denying the merger, C.R. still had hope. He sincerely believed in the validity of what he had testified; there was no proof that relative size, per se, could damage competitors. He had pointed out that the merged company's relationship in size to other carriers would be about the same as that of American alone in 1951. He said there was no evidence that harm resulted from American's position then —in fact, the industry as a whole was operating profitably. He argued further that United's new number-one status hadn't really hurt anyone, including American.

Smith came into Dwight Taylor's office after the hearings ended and asked how he thought the full CAB would vote.

"It hasn't a chance," Taylor said bluntly.

C.R. jammed his hat back on his balding head and stomped out. Taylor was the last man he should have asked for any sign of optimism. Months before, Taylor had spent almost an hour trying to convince him the merger was dead. He reminded C.R. that Kennedy liberals were running Washington, and to them the whole deal looked like the same kind of power deal that would have been involved if General Motors had tried to merge with Ford.

Part of C.R.'s sanguine outlook was based on his long friendship with then

Vice President Lyndon Johnson, but LBJ couldn't help one bit. American made a last-ditch attempt to win approval by offering a compromise: if the CAB granted the merger, AA and EAL would turn over fifteen cities to local service airlines and also remove route restrictions at the junction points of their systems, thus improving service to the public with more nonstop flights. It was too little and too late, and probably was like giving medicine to a dead person. It didn't do any harm but it didn't do any good, either.

Yet Spater, like C.R., thought the compromise might have succeeded if it had been submitted much sooner. "If we could have gotten started on this earlier," he was to comment, "I almost think we could have pulled it off. It proved a very basic lesson, though: it's pretty damned hard to put through a merger with an unwilling partner."

He was right in that respect, but he admitted later to Player that his reliance on antitrust exemption was the wrong strategy. "You were right," he told Willis. "I lost that merger."

CAB examiner Ralph Wiser's initial decision, released July 31, 1962, was not only negative but scathing. The CAB, with its usual procrastination, spent the next six months deliberating the case, but by early 1963, C.R. himself knew the cause was lost. The Board had yet to issue its verdict when both American and Eastern were tipped off that the vote would be unanimously against merger. Smith called in Player.

"Get out an announcement that we're pulling it," he ordered. "I've already told Eastern."

"He made the decision to kill it," Player said, "so it would not be on record as a precedent."

In that respect, it was the only strategy that worked. Faced with a no-longer-existing application, the CAB never issued a formal, final vote. And C.R., who always had a never-look-back attitude, went on to other matters.

The "other matters" included one that must have pained him. The 1962 Annual Report did not carry the name of Orval McKinley Mosier as an officer of American Airlines. His official retirement was made effective July 1 of that year.

Whether he really wanted to retire is moot, and if Smith forced the issue, it was understandable—Mosier, who had contributed so much to the airline, was no longer capable of contributing anything. Even when he was an active executive vice president and still possessing some authority, failing health had begun to undermine his effectiveness.

When Bud Wiser was put under Mosier, Wiser would find stacks of papers involving unsettled business and crucial decisions that hadn't been made. The only semblance of the old Mosier was his continued intimidation of his staff, yet to a man they retained affection for him until the day he died.

"I hated his guts at times," Marv Whitlock said, "but you couldn't help liking him. He was the greatest master of ambiguity I ever met. He developed it into an art, which was natural, because basically Red was a politician at heart. I've been at meetings with him and after they were over, his staff would hold another meeting to decide what he had said. If we couldn't agree, I'd have to go back into his office and tell him, 'We're not exactly sure what you meant or what you want us to do.' He'd sit there with a little grin and say absolutely nothing. It finally would dawn on us that he really didn't want to make a decision—he'd want you to do it your own way. I used to keep a bag packed in my office because I never knew when he'd come in and announce, 'Come on, we're going someplace.' I'd ask where and he'd say, 'I'll tell you when we get to the airport.' "

Whitlock accompanied him to Oklahoma City once and when they landed, there were more than a hundred people waiting to meet their flight. Marv looked around the cabin to see if some celebrity was aboard, and then found out it was Mosier they were greeting. It was the anniversary of the mortgage he had taken out on the City Hall years ago, and he was there for a mortgage-burning ceremony. Why he wanted Whitlock along was a mystery—probably because Mosier was a gregarious person who always wanted company.

The famous expense accounts that had gotten him into so much trouble with Hogan were no indication of dishonesty; Red simply spent money with no idea of how much he was spending and never bothered to keep any record of it. And he was an extremely generous person. His annual Christmas present to other officers and each staff member, for example, was expensive Steuben glassware, which he presented at a big party.

When Mosier joined American in Chicago, he put his Oklahoma City furniture in storage. It remained in storage for the next twenty-five years, and when he moved back to Oklahoma City after retirement, the furniture was so old and outdated that he sold it for the storage charges. The Mosiers lived in hotel apartment suites as long as they were in New York.

He was a paradox in that he could create fear among subordinates even as he inspired affection. He resembled C.R. in that respect with one important difference: Mosier would chew out people in front of others, whereas Smith did it in private. Yet he never referred to anyone as "someone who works for me"; it was always "He's one of my associates."

Mosier was in his last years at American when he contracted ulcers, so severe that he was restricted to eating nothing but baby food. For a man who loved to eat and drink in bacchanalian proportions, this was a medical edict he constantly tried to circumvent. Jerry Jacob and Bill Whitacre, then vice president of flight, used to go fishing with him in a rented boat they'd take out on Manhasset Bay. Mrs. Mosier would insist that they stay in sight of land so Red wouldn't slip off to some shore bar for a drink or illegal food.

Mosier called Jerry one day to inquire, "You goin' fishing with me and Whitacre tomorrow?"

"Sure thing, Red."

"Well, I want you to pick up a few things—pastrami, beer, pickles, and stuff like that. Put 'em in the boat before Frances drives me out there."

Jerry was only twenty-five and had just joined American, so he obeyed. When the Mosiers arrived and Red boarded the boat, he told Jerry to steer for the middle of the bay so Frances wouldn't see him consume the contraband feast. After they returned to shore, Mosier was burping, belching, and holding his sizable belly in pain.

"She knew he had beaten the system somehow," Jerry laughed, "but she couldn't figure out how, and we never told her."

Mosier died February 8, 1967, only four days before his seventieth birthday. C.R., Bill Smith and Millie Alford were the only people from American who attended his funeral. Marv Whitlock, then with United, flew to Oklahoma City for the burial services and was shocked at the slim company representation. "We were only a hundred miles from Tulsa," Whitlock recalled, "and there must have been a thousand people there who remembered Red."

Marv flew back to Chicago with C.R. and remarked about it.

"I thought it rather sad," he told Smith. "Sure, he made a lot of enemies, but he did play a big role in in American's history."

C.R. nodded and said quietly, "Yeah, it was strange, but he had a good run."

And that was Red Mosier's epitaph.

"A good run" also could apply to the man C.R. named as American's president in January 1964: George Marion Sadler.

18
The Short But Happy Reign of Marion Sadler

In moving up to board chairman and chief executive officer, C. R. Smith had named as American's new president a man who had joined the company twenty-three years earlier by answering a want ad.

It was published in the August 18, 1941, edition of the Bristol, Virginia, *Herald-Courier:*

AIRLINE POSITIONS AVAILABLE

Men and women for reservations and ticket agent work in one of the large commercial airlines. Qualifications: two years of college or equivalent, 22 to 30 years of age, married man desired. Should be willing to work in any part of the country. Write personal qualifications, business experience, salary desired. Address P.O. Box 189, Flushing, L.I., N.Y.

If anything, Marion Sadler was overqualified for the job offer he accepted, ramp agent in Dallas. He was thirty at the time he saw that want ad, just getting in under the maximum age limit, and he was not only a college graduate (Duke University) but held a master's degree in English.

Armed with an A.B. and M.A., he got a teaching position at the high school in Bristol, Tennessee, just across the state line from the Virginia town bearing the same name. He looked more like a linebacker than a teacher, a bull-necked, barrel-chested man with rugged features. It was once said that Bob Six and Marion Sadler were the only airline presidents whose profiles should have been carved into Mt. Rushmore as the fifth and sixth heads.

His vocabulary went with his physical appearance. Sadler was that rare but wonderful combination of earthy and erudite, the kind of man whose profanity could blister the paint off a wall, yet who could be smoothly articulate when the occasion demanded. He always loved good books, poetry, and classical music, and it was his writing ability that would bring him to C.R.'s attention. His hobbies included the study of Latin, Roman and Civil War history, and numismatics.

Sadler gambled on an airline career for economic reasons. He was making $72 a month teaching English at Bristol High, and the college degrees listed in his application had impressed the airline to the extent of offering him the top starting salary for agents: $90 a month. He was still working in Nashville when war broke out, and he spent the next four years as a staff sergeant in the Air Transport Command.

Actually, Sadler had no intention of returning to American after the war. As soon as he was discharged, he enrolled under the GI bill at the University of North Carolina, where he wanted a Ph.D. so he could go into college teaching. Then he happened to ask the Ph.D. who was teaching him how much he was making a year.

"Five thousand," the professor confided.

Sadler decided to rejoin American.

He was rehired at $175 a month and assigned to Oklahoma City as reservations manager. He had been there only a short time when Jack Mullins, then setting up American's new training department in New York, heard about him.

Mullins's source was Hunter Bowman (brother of actor Lee Bowman), who had worked for Jack before the war and was now with him in New York.

"I met this guy when I was in the service," he told Mullins. "Name of Marion Sadler. He was with us in Dallas and he used to be a schoolteacher. He'd be great for the training department."

Mullins called him and offered him a transfer.

"Well, Mr. Mullins," Sadler said in his slow, Tennessee drawl, "I just got to Oklahoma City and I haven't mastered this job yet. I think I should learn what I'm doing here before I take on another assignment."

Mullins was never the type to plead, but something told him to press on. "Mr. Sadler, I think this job I'm offering is more important, and it'll pay you more money."

"I appreciate the opportunity, Mr. Mullins, but I just don't think it's right for me to pull out before I've learned my work here. I thank you very much, but I'll stay in Oklahoma City."

Mullins was a little disappointed; as in most businesses, the airlines tend to frown on employees who refuse a transfer, and forget one who refuses twice. Yet there was something about Sadler that impressed him. The man had a sense of integrity, but how much integrity Mullins was to find out three months later. Establishment of the training department behind him, Mullins had gone to Dallas as regional head of reservations, and Sadler's Oklahoma City office reported to him. One Sunday morning, Sadler called him.

"Mr. Mullins, I hate to bother you on a Sunday but I feel it's terribly important and I'd like to come down to Dallas and talk to you about it."

"Tell me now."

"No, sir, I prefer not discuss it on the phone. I'd rather talk to you in person if you can spare me just thirty minutes of your time—it won't take any longer."

Sadler flew to Dallas that afternoon, and Mullins drove him to his home. It turned out that Sadler was very upset about a directive from New York to put into effect some new reservations procedures, which in his opinion were very wrong.

"I just can't ask my agents to do these things when I consider them harmful

to American," he told Mullins. "I realize that when you work for a corporation, you do what you're told. I find myself in a very awkward position, Mr.
Mullins. I can't refuse to follow orders, but I can't issue those orders to my
own staff when I know they're wrong. So I've made arrangements to go to
work for Continental."

"Continental?"

"Yes, sir. They've offered me an agent's job in Oklahoma City and I feel I
have to take it. It's a matter of principle. Those new instructions are not only
wrong, but they won't last."

Mullins could hardly believe it. Here was a guy willing to take a lesser job
with a smaller airline on a matter of principle, and as far as Jack Mullins was
concerned, here also was a guy American couldn't afford to lose. He was
thinking fast, and he remembered that Sadler was from Tennessee.

He asked, "Marion, would you be willing to go to Nashville as a sales rep
until we get this thing straightened out?"

"That would be fine," Sadler said instantly.

"Then don't do anything until I talk to Elmo Coon" (then regional director
of sales under Doc Miller).

A subsequent phone call to Coon established the fact that Elmo knew
Sadler. "He's the smartest man I ever met," he told Mullins. "Hell, yes, I'll
take him on in Nashville."

Technically, Sadler had agreed to a demotion, but sales representatives in
those days had a better shot at advancement than a reservations manager in
a minor market; their performance was more visible to superiors. Sadler proceeded to make himself known. He left Nashville to become reservations
manager in Dallas, and by 1951, he was district sales manager in Buffalo where
he scored a tour de force that justified Mullins' faith in him.

On his own initiative, he wrote a special manual for sales reps that became
a company bible—literally a small textbook of sales procedures, psychology,
and enough practical suggestions to turn the rawest rookie into a reasonable
facsimile of an expert. Up to then, the sales reps learned their trade on the job.
Sadler's manual was like sending them to college for a crash course.

He not only got a Distinguished Service Award for Merit, but in 1955 was
dispatched to New York as director of passenger sales. Two years later he was
vice president of customer service, and two years after that, vice president and
general manager.

The promotion-every-two-years schedule didn't apply this time, however.
C.R. spent the next three years carefully grooming him for the presidency,
although "grooming" also meant his performance was under a constant micro-
scope. And there was no doubt he passed inspection, as the results for 1963
showed: the best profits in three years ($17.2 million), a system load factor 5
percent higher than the industry's average, a 10.5 percent hike in sales, and
a significant reduction in costs that reflected not only the reliability of the jets
but better management.

Sadler wasn't solely responsible, of course, but that 1963 record was no accident. He was making key decisions, and making them in increasing numbers as his influence, input, and ability commanded growing respect. Furthermore, he was well liked and that included C.R.—although he did get one of Smith's famous notes after C.R. saw some correspondence signed "G. Marion Sadler."

"Either make your name G. M. Sadler or Marion Sadler," the memo ordered, "but *not* G. Marion Sadler! See Player about which is best."

The "G" was dropped forthwith and permanently; from then on it was Marion Sadler. The use of his middle name as the first led to one of those airline stories that would be labeled apocryphal if it were not absolutely true.

During the 1966 mechanics' strike that shut down five carriers and left American the only transcontinental airline, obtaining space on the nonstops was like trying to find a hotel room in a city holding twenty national conventions simultaneously. Mary Sullivan, now of the corporate communications staff but at the time a passenger service representative, witnessed one incident at JFK Airport when a man who couldn't get on a flight lay down in front of a 707 nosewheel, yelling, "This plane ain't going without me!"

Frustrated customers often resorted to name-dropping when they were told an American flight was full, and C.R.'s name was taken in vain constantly. "I'm a personal friend of C. R. Smith" was heard a hundred times a day.

(This happened frequently even without a strike crisis. Shirley McManus, skipper at the LaGuardia Admirals Club, used to marvel at the number of members who'd come in and announce importantly, "I just had lunch with C.R." She got the impression that Smith must be eating lunch thirty-five times a day.)

One weary agent got a call from a man seeking space on the late afternoon Washington–Los Angeles flight that same day. He was informed that not only was the trip full but there were thirty-seven names on the wait list. Out came the inevitable: "Look, pal, I'm a personal friend of C.R.'s."

The agent had been hearing from Smith's alleged friends all day. "I suppose you also know Marion Sadler?" he inquired sarcastically.

"Know her? Hell, I've been dating her for three months!"

Sadler was stubborn, like C.R., but somewhat more flexible. He fought Walt Rauscher's curbside baggage checking experiment, arguing that it would hurt the Sky Chefs coffee shops and restaurants.

"If people can go right from the terminal entrance to the boarding area, they'll show up later for flights and nobody'll use our coffee shops," he told Rauscher.

Walt said this wasn't true; if anything, faster check-ins would give passengers more time to patronize the coffee shops.

"You're wrong, and I'll prove it to you," Sadler insisted. "We'll go out to Idlewild and follow a few passengers after they check their bags with skycaps."

The first passengers he picked to trail were a short, stout gentleman and his companion, a tall bleached blonde. They checked several bags at curbside and walked into the terminal, Sadler following close behind to see if they'd bypass the coffee shop. A little too close, in fact. The man suddenly stopped and wheeled, glaring.

"I demand to know why you're following us," he said self-righteously. "This lady happens to be my wife!"

Sadler couldn't open his mouth. They marched off, and Marion turned to the grinning Rauscher. "Aw, the hell with it," Sadler muttered. "Let's go get a drink."

When it came to hiring, Sadler was absolutely color-blind; the intellectual in him overrode his southern background. When he was res manager in Dallas, a representative from an anti-discrimination organization came to his office and wanted to know how many blacks he had working for him.

Sadler waved vaguely in the direction of the outer offices. "Damned if I know. Just go out there and count 'em yourself."

Like C.R., he never used profanity in front of women, but he used it far more frequently than Smith, including business meetings. And uttered in his low, rather husky voice, the four-letter words gave the impression he was perpetually angry at the world. He wasn't, though; swearing to Marion Sadler came as naturally as breathing, which was somewhat startling for a schoolteacher with two degrees.

During the Electra crisis, Jim Gainer had picked up a report that Convair's chief test pilot had told his staff not to fly Electras. Gainer called Sadler, whose response almost melted the phone.

"You tell those Convair (censored) it's a goddamned lot better plane than their (censored) 990!" he roared.

The pilots loved him. He seldom got off a plane without telling the captain, "Best bleepin' flight I ever had." Bob McDaniels had him on one trip and decided to needle him a little.

"Mr. Sadler, there's a rumor going around that you use foul language. Any truth to it?"

"Not one bleeping bit!" Marion snapped.

For such a burly man, he was curiously unathletic and uninformed about sports. Fishing was his only outdoor activity, and it was the only sport he knew anything about. After he became president, he was invited to hand out trophies at the annual employees' bowling tournament in Fort Worth. He called Jack Mullins in a mild state of panic.

"Jack," he said worriedly, "I have to go to Texas for that bowling tournament. Tell me, how do you play bowl?"

It was C.R.'s policy to have American's officers fly incognito as far as passengers were concerned. Sadler was sitting next to a man occupying a window seat and after they finished eating, the passenger said, "Do you mind keeping your eye open for that stewardess? I want to get this silverware into my briefcase."

Sadler agreed, and when they deplaned, he asked the man for his business card. Back in his office, he summoned Mullins, who had become vice president of sales and services.

"Jack, I want you to send seven place settings of our first-class silverware to the name on this business card and include this letter."

The accompanying letter remarked how much Sadler had enjoyed meeting him and added:

"I was particularly pleased that you liked our silverware, but I think one place setting would be inadequate for your needs."

He never got a reply.

Marion Sadler's tenure as president came close to being the briefest in the company's history.

He collided immediately with the power base Hogan had erected, learning quickly that he wasn't the number-two man in the hierarchy but number three. A large chunk of the company was still reporting to Hogan, and that included areas in which Sadler felt the president should have more authority than any executive vice president. He accepted Hogan's tight control over finance, but refused to let him run what amounted to the rest of the airline, including management development, planning, and economic research. As Sadler saw it, he may have been number two in title but was outranked by Hogan in authority and responsibility. So he did what came naturally to Marion Sadler.

He resigned.

Sagely, he left the resignation's effective date open to C.R.'s discretion, and it took Smith two weeks to talk him into tearing it up. What transpired between the two men, neither ever disclosed, but the results were undisputed: C.R. did what he should have done in the first place and established Sadler's executive jurisdiction as number-two boss.

Characteristically, he tried hard to work with Hogan. He respected Bill, and he knew Hogan had supported his steady, unusually swift advancement. And while Hogan may well have resented Sadler's promotion over him, Marion Sadler was never really on his so-called "hit list." Outwardly, they seemed to get along, although Mel Brenner was one officer who thought Hogan did try to whittle away at Sadler's authority gradually.

"I think Marion leaned over backwards to accommodate Hogan," Brenner said, "in the course of which he gave up certain functions which I frankly argued with him he shouldn't have given up. For example, there was created under Hogan what was called a corporate planning department. Now planning is a very flexible term—it could be long range or something for next week. But the planning function became just another lever under which Hogan could get very close to current operations, and it led to some friction."

One person whose unfailing cheerfulness Sadler missed was C. W. Jacob, whose retirement was announced shortly before Marion became president. His son Jerry was appointed manager of interline sales in 1963, around the time American moved corporate headquarters from Park Avenue to 633 Third Avenue, and Jake, proud as he was, was a little uncomfortable about their working in such proximity.

His office was on the fifth floor and he told Jerry, "Don't ever come to the fifth floor. I don't ever want want to see you on that floor."

Jerry started getting his father's calls and vice versa, but one meant for Jake led to a small family argument. A Mr. Gilbert phoned Jerry and launched into a tirade about American's corporate policies. Jerry finally managed to break in and tell him he had the wrong Jacob.

"Isn't this C. W. Jacob?"

"No, this is his son."

"His son? Do you work for him?"

"No, I'm in an entirely different department."

"What do you do?"

"Interline sales."

Jerry transferred the call and five minutes later his father was on the phone.

"Goddammit, Jerry, I knew this would happen. Do you know who that was?"

"He said his name was Gilbert."

"Mr. Gilbert," Jake snarled, "is the corporate gadfly. He comes to the annual stockholders' meeting and raises hell. Now the son of a bitch thinks I'm promoting nepotism."

Jacob stayed on with American as a consultant for a few years. He never expressed any regrets to his son about leaving, but Jerry's mother thought Jake missed the airline. He had never missed a day's work in three and a half decades. He got into Wall Street as a consultant for an investment banking firm and, according to Jerry, made more money there than he ever had in his life.

His reputation on Wall Street was such that Howard Hughes, who had just bought control of Northeast, asked him to run the airline for him. Jake declined, but Hughes later asked him, "Would you be willing to sell the airline for me?"

Jacob helped put through the deal that sold Northeast to the Storer Broadcasting Co. and earned a $500,000 commission. He died of a stroke in 1974, remembered by all who knew him as a gentle and kind man whose reward at American was never monetary but the affection in which he was held.

Of all Sadler's fellow officers, he was closest to Jack Mullins, his former mentor and boss. Mullins's own career flourished under Sadler. The same reorganization that had made Sadler president already had put Mullins into the position of vice president of sales and services. The two departments previously had been combined into one with jurisdiction over all marketing activities; Mullins replaced Dick Fitzpatrick, brother of movie actress Gail Patrick, who resigned after being offered a lesser job in San Francisco.

As Sadler gained maturity and experience, C.R. seemed willing to relax the reins. There were those who noticed his spirits had been low since a tragedy that shook the whole airline—American's first fatal 707 accident, March 1, 1962. One of the passengers was an old friend, Alton Jones, who headed Cities Service.

Eight seconds after taking off from Idlewild bound for Los Angeles, Flight 1 lurched to the left, banked sharply, and continued a slow, almost graceful roll until it was on its back. Then it fell, nose down, into the shallow waters of Jamaica Bay. There were no survivors among the eight crew members and eighty-seven passengers.

The CAB investigation determined that a short circuit had occurred in the wiring of a small motor that activated the hydraulic boost system for the rudder, sending the wrong voltage through the circuits and causing an unwanted hard-over signal to the rudder that took the pilots by surprise. It was like the power steering on an automobile suddenly jamming during a sharp turn.

Examination of the rudder servo unit had disclosed evidence of pre-impact damage—scratches, punctures, and other unexplainable gouge marks on the wires. CAB technicians visited the factory where the servo units were manufactured and found several brand-new ones with identical damage. It turned out the workmen were using heavy tweezers to wrap a cord around the wiring; unless handled carefully, the tweezers could gouge the wiring.

The FAA, Boeing, and American unanimously disputed the CAB's verdict after test flights with a deliberately short-circuited rudder servo showed the hard-over force actually was moderate and could easily be overriden even if totally unexpected. On some flights, Boeing short-circuited the unit with no warning and the pilots still recovered quickly and easily.

The FAA theory was that a bolt had been installed upside down, fallen out of the hydraulic system, and rammed excess fluid into one side of the rudder controls. But American's own engineers didn't buy that explanation, either. Frank Kolk thought there had been a lateral control problem, probably stemming from failure of an aileron pushrod, a malfunction that had occurred on several other 707s but at high enough altitudes where the unexpected lurch didn't result in unrecoverable loss of control. Mack Eastburn, American's veteran director of safety, recalled:

"After Jamaica Bay, we followed every 707 accident and incident to see if any could have cast some light on our crash. I must have gone out to the junkyard where Flight 1's wreckage was and turned it over at least a dozen times looking for evidence that corresponded to something we had heard about another 707. We never did find anything, but Kolk believed to his dying day there had been aileron pushrod failure."

Marion Sadler served as president only four years, but they were four years of significant events in American's history.

In mid 1963, the company had ordered fifteen BAC-111 jetliners, a fanjet transport whose two engines were aft-mounted, with an option for another fifteen. Built by the newly formed British Aircraft Corporation, the 111 was the first of the short-range jets designed to serve the smaller airports unable to handle 707s and DC-8s.

Braniff and Mohawk had signed for the BAC-111 previously, but American's version was a later model called the 400 Astrojet, a fast, sturdy little jet about the same size as the Electra, which, along with the 240, it was supposed to replace on the short-haul routes. It never did live up to its expectations, however, and some said that only the 990 was a worse equipment decision.

Yet in 1963, the BAC-111 was the only adequate short-range jet available. The Douglas DC-9 wasn't in prototype stage yet, Boeing's 737 wasn't much more than a drawing board dream, and France's twin-engine Caravelle was considered an outdated design too small for U.S. markets. The 111's problem was not so much the aircraft itself but the woefully slow British production methods that delayed deliveries far past their scheduled dates. American didn't put its 400s into service until March 1966, almost a year behind schedule. By that time, the DC-9, a far better airplane, already was flying for Delta, and Boeing was building the 737.

Unless one stretches both imagination and truth, the BAC-111 was far down on American's list of airplane popularity. The crews referred to it as "Britain's revenge for 1776." Its high landing speed made passengers nervous, the cabin was somewhat cramped, and the galley space was almost nonexistent. The stewardesses working BAC-111 trips were invariably very junior because no one with any decent seniority would bid them. Deliveries were further delayed because American found out the plane's range was about 600 miles short of what BAC had promised, thus requiring further modifications.

But if American's first short-haul jet was a disappointment, the Boeing 727 made up for it. American was to end up operating nearly 200 of the famed "three-holer" as the pilots dubbed this first of the trimotor jets—most of them the stretched 727-200 series—and it was still serving the eagle more than two decades after its April 12, 1964, introduction on the New York–Chicago route.

It followed the Boeing 720B into service by four years. American bought twenty-five of the latter, a "hot-rod" lighter, smaller sister of the 707 with an eight-foot-shorter fuselage and the same fanjet engines. But the 720B was strictly a medium-range jet, lacking the 727's incredible versatility. The three-holer could serve virtually any airport on American's system and was a moneymaker regardless of stage length. It represented the engineering input and economic requirements of four airlines, American, TWA, United, and Eastern, all of whom had a hand in its design.

As such, it was a compromise airplane, and a rare compromise that satisfied everybody. Originally, United wanted a small four-engine jet because of its numerous Denver operations, actually a scaled-down DC-8. American and TWA preferred two engines for economy reasons. Eastern needed at least three engines because it planned to operate the plane on its overwater routes to Puerto Rico and Bermuda. And all four carriers insisted that the 727 be capable of safely serving short-runway airports like LaGuardia and Washington National.

This was a tall order for Boeing's designers. They filled it with one of the most ingenious innovations ever put on a commercial transport. They devised a unique wing flap system that, fully extended, increased the 727's wing area by 25 percent and allowed the airplane literally to float to the ground. Pratt & Whitney contributed mightily to the project with its new JT8D fanjet engine; this turned out to be one of the most reliable turbines ever designed.

And Boeing came up with a bonus design decision: the 727 would have the same fuselage width as the 707, which permitted six-abreast seating and increased the trijet's capacity from a 90-seat airplane to 120 seats. In the test flight phases, the 727 proved to be fifteen knots faster than Boeing's wind tunnels had estimated, fuel consumption 10 percent less, and payload 10 percent greater. Furthermore, the three-holer was a pilot's airplane—responsive, easy-handling, and strong. Even those who said nothing would ever equal the Electra came to rank the 727 as at least its equal.

Such a special airplane deserved a special introduction, and Willis Player's public relations team furnished one: using an old Ford trimotor to emphasize the fact that the 727 would be American's first three-engine airplane since the glory days of the Tin Goose. And the beauty of the idea was that American already had a Ford, fully restored and flyable.

Its acquisition dated back to 1962, when C.R. offered to locate an ancient trimotor, restore it to brand-new condition, and donate to the Smithsonian's planned new National Air and Space Museum. Smithsonian officials were delighted, but warned Smith that Congress hadn't appropriated any money yet for the new museum and American might be wasting a lot of time and money. There wasn't room for such an airplane in the Smithsonian's ancient Science and Engineering building.

This didn't faze C.R. one bit. He told Player there must be some way to use an old Ford for publicity purposes before the Smithsonian got its hands on it. Player got the answer from his staff: American had ordered the 727, whose introduction would be a perfect tie-in. Now the problem was locating a usable Ford.

"Find one," C.R. told vice president of purchasing Lee Glasgow, "but try to keep it quiet that American's looking for it or the price'll go through the roof."

Glasgow could have used the CIA to carry out such instructions, but he managed to conduct some undercover research into FAA's records and learned there were about a dozen reasonably intact Fords still around in the U.S. Three were being operated by Inland Airways ferrying schoolchildren and cargo between Port Clinton, Ohio, and nearby islands in Lake Erie. Two were owned by Johnson Flying Service and used under contract with the U.S. Forest Service carrying fire-fighting parachutists. A sixth, in superb condition, belonged to an Indiana barnstormer named John Louck, but he already had agreed to lease it to TWA for its own publicity stunt, re-enactment of an all-air transcontinental flight to mark the twenty-fifth anniversary of the Civil Aeronautics Act of 1938.

The search into FAA's files finally unearthed a Ford trimotor that seemed to fit American's needs. Its pedigree showed it had once been operated by American Airways as part of its Colonial Air Transport division, an appropriate ancestry. The only trouble was that said ancestry indicated the airplane's airframe had accumulated enough miles to go to the moon and back.

Its original serial number was NC-9683 and its first owner, as a brand-new bird hatched at Dearborn, Michigan, was Erle Halliburton's Southwest Air Fast Express of Tulsa. When American Airways absorbed SAFE in 1931, NC-9683 was transferred to Colonial and flew on American's East Coast routes until its retirement in 1935. A year later, American sold the plane to TACA, which flew it throughout Central America for several years.

From then on, NC-9683 was a gypsy airplane—a cargo and passenger plane in Mexico, a crop-dusting aircraft in Montana, and a freighter in Alaska. It supposedly ended its career sometime in the late fifties when it was damaged in a landing at Oaxaca, Mexico, and left abandoned.

At one time, it served as a home for a Mexican family, which occupied it for an unknown period. They installed a wood-burning stove whose chimney protruded from the top of the fuselage. When American finally acquired the plane, there was a scar where the chimney had been. And that acquisition came in a deal with the company that had located NC-9683 at the Oaxaca airfield.

The firm was Aircraft Hydro-Forming Co. of Gardena, California. It was planning to build new Fords for use in undeveloped countries, with NC-9683 as a model, but the project had run into difficulties and the company was receptive to American's offer of $30,000 as is (original cost: $55,475).

The "as is" was discouraging in itself. After evicting the Mexican tenants, Hydro-Forming had repaired the relic just enough to fly it to California and that was about all. Engines, interior, and airframe were in sad shape, and to call it flyable was stretching a point—there were several fatigue cracks in the wing spars.

Tulsa was told to prepare for the restoration job. Of the 3,000 employees at the maintenance base, only a handful had ever seen a Ford trimotor, let alone worked on one, but that didn't seem to bother anybody. Lucien Hunt told New York, "Bring it out here and hope for the best."

C.R. had promised the Smithsonian that the plane would be restored to exactly what it had been when American operated it in the 1930s. This sent researchers digging through musty files and faded photographs. Tulsa couldn't re-create an authentic cabin interior without knowing what one looked like.

It was known that NC-9683 was a 5-AT, a later model of the trimotor, and had thirteen seats, seven on the left side and six on the right, with the cabin door on the right. But Ford used varying types of seats, some with tubular frames and others wood; seat covers were wicker, cloth-covered, or leather. Then the Ford Motor Co. unearthed a thirty-year-old document establishing that the entire 5-AT series had seats with metal tubular frames upholstered in leather.

What color leather? Tulsa asked. Damned if we know, in effect was the answer.

The researchers began contacting American's old-timers for information— pilots, mechanics, stewardesses, ramp personnel. The consensus among the veterans was that the leather was green, and they also provided other facts that would add to the authenticity of the re-created cabin. The Grey Eagles, the organization of retired AA pilots, had just been formed in 1962, and these members were a good source. So was the Three Diamond Society, composed of employees with thirty years or more service, which was started the same year.

One American official had worked as a steward on Fords and he found in his attic a collection of signs that had been mounted in the cabin: washroom directions, no smoking, and the best of them all, THE CREW DOES NOT ACCEPT GRATUITIES. These were donated to the project.

An engineering test pilot flew NC-9683 from Gardena to Tulsa in two days, accompanied by the Hydro-Forming pilot who had ferried it up from Mexico. Tulsa, using volunteer mechanics who donated their time, got the plane in good enough shape to fly it to the official dedication of Washington's new Dulles Airport November 17, 1962, carrying American's old 1931 markings. Then it returned to Tulsa for the major restoration work.

Much of the structural modifications and engine replacements were accomplished before the Dulles trip. When mechanics got into the wing to replace the fatigued spars, they found the skeleton of a monkey and several issues of a Managua, Nicaragua, newspaper dated 1943. The "new" engines were rebuilt Pratt & Whitney R-985s and American was lucky to find three of them. "It was like looking for dinosaur bones in downtown Manhattan," one Tulsa veteran remembered.

But when Tulsa finished with NC-9683, it was as if American had somehow taken a time machine back to 1929 and returned with a brand-new Ford trimotor. The airline had budgeted $49,000 for the project, exclusive of what it had cost to buy the stripped airplane but including all expenses for the promotional tours that would stretch out for a year. The total expenditures were $37,000. When a few officials in New York later questioned the wisdom of spending almost $40,000 on nostalgia, Player pointed out that the whole promotional program had cost less than one full-page ad in *Life.*

The first mission of the fully restored NC-9683 was participation at the September 1963 rollout of American's first 727 at Renton, Washington. Eastern and United, ahead of American in delivery schedules, already had held their rollout ceremonies, but the visual impact of that ancient airliner standing next to the new trijet was impressive.

Prior to the rollout, NC-9683 had spent the summer touring scores of cities. Player's main goal was to emphasize the amazing advances that had been made over the past three decades, and whenever possible, the Ford was displayed alongside a jet or Electra. Courtesy flights were part of the promotion, which was officially launched May 16, 1963, when the Tin Goose was flown to Dallas for the annual convention of the Aviation/Space Writers Association. From there NC-9683 went to Memphis to take part in the dedication of a new terminal, and for the rest of the summer it flew an old-fashioned barnstorming operation, visiting cities that ranged in size from New York to Lewiston, Maine.

It was in Lewiston that an elderly lady walked up to the plane and asked Captain Ralph Long, the pilot assigned to the tour, "Is this the Northeast flight to Boston?" Long was one of the four-man traveling staff that included copilot Floyd Mace, a p.r. representative, and a just-in-case mechanic.

Smack in the middle of the tour, TWA staged its transcontinental flight and reaped enormous newspaper, magazine, and television coverage, but basically it was a one-shot effort that lasted only the three days it took its leased Ford to fly from Los Angeles to Newark. It could be said that TWA won a major battle but lost the war; over a much longer haul, American got more mileage from its trimotor than did its rival.

Thousands saw NC-9683 on the tour and hundreds flew it on the courtesy flights, marveling at the spic-and-span cabin with its surprisingly comfortable seats. (Seats on the TWA Ford were authentically wicker, and passengers had to use pillows to preserve their spines.) Various celebrities were allowed to fly it briefly; Arthur Godfrey and Joe Walker, the X-15 rocket pilot, were among them. The 1963 tour hit seventy-three cities and completed 156 courtesy flights, carrying almost a thousand guests.

The plane's major mission in 1964 was to support American's 727 introduction. After the April 12 New York–Chicago inaugural, NC-9683 flew to Newark, Baltimore, Cleveland, Oklahoma City, and other cities where 727 service was being launched. The 1964 tour totals: 117 communities in the U.S. and Canada, 430 courtesy flights, and 3,400 passengers.

Occasionally, NC-9683 was hauled out for an air show or airport dedication, but most of the time it was tucked away in the corner of a hangar at Tulsa. Its final "road" appearance was at a 1972 transportation exposition at Dulles, and American then turned the airplane over to the Smithsonian to await enshrinement at the new National Air and Space Museum, which opened July 1, 1976.

There it can be seen today, suspended from the ceiling at the Hall of Air Transportation and in the distinguished company of a Western Douglas M-2 mailplane, an Eastern DC-3, a United 247, and several other historic aircraft. NC-9683's position is too high for visitors to spot the only flaw in Tulsa's incredible restoration job: there is a patch over the hole where the chimney had pierced the top of the fuselage.

While waiting for the Smithsonian to house the Ford in the new museum, American purchased a second Tin Goose to help promote the 1964 New York World's Fair. The second trimotor was none other than N-414H, the same plane TWA had leased.

As far as is known, C.R. overruled Marion Sadler only once. This involved an incident with the Tin Goose's most frequent captain, Ralph Long.

American signed a charter contract with Senator Barry Goldwater during his 1964 Presidential campaign, and Long was assigned to the 727 the candidate used. They were taking off from Cleveland after a Goldwater speech and the tower asked Long to make a low pass over the field so people could see the new jet.

Long took the precaution of asking Goldwater for permission, but he made the mistake of not informing the reporters on the plane what he was going to do. He roared over the airport and went onto the next scheduled stop.

The next day, Sadler happened to catch a big headline in the New York *World-Telegram*, GOLDWATER PLANE NEARLY CRASHES. The story, written by a UPI reporter, was just as frightening as the headline, and Sadler, who had a hair-trigger temper, issued orders that Long be fired.

Long's case wasn't helped when the FAA denied that the Cleveland tower had requested the low pass. But Goldwater, who also saw the story, called C.R. to give him the facts.

"I've already told the FAA what really happened," the senator said. "If you take any action against Captain Long, I'll cancel the contract."

Some were surprised that Goldwater picked American for his campaign flights, considering C.R.'s long-standing friendship with Lyndon Johnson, who was running against the Arizona senator. But Barry Goldwater knew aviation, and he didn't mix aviation with politics. He considered American an industry leader and chose accordingly.

And once more, American was to demonstrate its willingness to gamble on marketing innovations. In 1966, it dusted off a Youth Fare experiment originated by Charlie Speers in 1961 and re-introduced it in a revised form as a means of filling otherwise empty seats.

The 1961 plan had offered half fares to youths between twelve and twenty-one on a space-available basis up to three hours before departure. If a seat hadn't been reserved by a full-fare passenger by then, the Youth Fare became confirmed space. Two years later, George Spater—then general counsel—happened to mention in a casual conversation with Speers that he had a son in service who usually took a bus when he was on furlough.

"He says it costs too much to fly," Spater added.

Speers was like a halfback who needs only a sliver of a hole to find daylight. From that chance remark, he conceived a special positive-space half fare for military personnel, with only two restrictions: they had to be on leave, and they had to travel in uniform. It was not only a bonanza for servicemen and -women but, like the original Youth Fare program, a lucrative revenue source at a time when load factors were down.

This also was true of the 1966 plan. The enormous influx of larger aircraft had resulted in industrywide overcapacity, and Sadler urged other airlines to adopt the same plan. Eventually, nine others did, but with considerable reluctance. The general feeling was that Youth Fares were too vulnerable to kids who would find ways to beat the system.

Originally, the plan called for a 50 percent fare reduction for passengers between twelve and twenty-two, provided that they made their reservations no earlier than three hours before a scheduled flight; U.S.–Mexico trips were excluded. But American soon changed the rules: Youth Fares were put on a standby basis only, and those holding Youth Fare tickets were boarded only after full-fare standbys were accommodated.

Sadler fought hard for the plan when it was submitted to the CAB for approval, arguing that there were ancillary benefits beyond the goal of filling empty seats. He said Youth Fares would build a nucleus of future passengers and encourage young people to travel. As for the claim that youths would try to cheat, Sadler said this "reflects too unfavorably on the integrity of the younger generation."

He was being a little overoptimistic. There were frequent instances, particularly among college students, of attempts to circumvent the rules, usually before spring breaks, Thanksgiving and Christmas holidays, and at the end of the college year. The students would make advance reservations under fictitious names, then show up at the airport knowing the confirmed space wouldn't be used. But the practice died down gradually as res agents began catching on. The most unpleasant aspect of Youth Fares was the occasional teenager demanding to be served liquor and causing a scene when he was refused. Such incidents became less frequent when captains began removing obstreperous youths at the next stop. A lesser but still vexing problem was the large number of unshaven, barefooted, guitar-carrying young hippies boarding flights and often smoking pot. American got occasional complaints about such obnoxious passengers and finally began enforcing a few minimum rules as to dress, including refusal to board anyone not wearing shoes. But offsetting these disadvantages was Youth Fares' overall success. It did fill empty seats and introduce millions of youngsters to air travel, which were its main goals. And in one sense, the Youth Fare plan symbolized what might be called the democratization of air transportation—the first solid indication that it was becoming *mass* transportation. By 1966, almost half the passengers were traveling for pleasure and/or vacation purposes. The business-to-pleasure ratio had started dropping sharply with the advent of jets.

In 1966, American and other carriers operating so-called VIP facilities were challenged by a passenger refused admittance to an Admirals Club because he wasn't a member. He filed a complaint with the CAB, charging that American had violated the Federal Aviation Act by discriminating against passengers who didn't belong to the Club.

In a preliminary ruling, CAB Bureau of Enforcement chief John Adams said all airline VIP clubs were discriminatory and violated "the public utility concept of air carriers who are required by law to serve all members of the public on equally favorable terms." It was a curious interpretation; the chief case made in 1978 for industry deregulation was the argument that airlines are not a public utility.

The airlines were shocked at Adams's decision. In 1961, the Bureau of Enforcement had asked the CAB to investigate the clubs and by a 3-2 vote, the Board decided the matter wasn't really the CAB's business. Then chairman

Alan Boyd admitted he belonged to six of them and was "damned well happy to be a member." But Boyd also had suggested it might be a good idea for the airlines to modify its membership rules, although he didn't specify how.

American responded to Adams's decision by pointing out that the Federal Aviation Act merely required that no "undue or unreasonable preference" be given to any person; there was no requirement, the airline said, that every passenger had to be treated precisely the same. Adams himself had conceded that membership involved people whose frequent patronage helped the airline, and that there was nothing unreasonable about that.

American argued that the VIP clubs were nothing more than a promotional device similar to rides on new airplanes, free calendars, and invitations to inaugural flights, none of which were offered to every passenger.

Adams suggested that the airlines either close their clubs or open them to anyone wanting membership. He seemed impressed by the protesting passenger's claim that he had been refused membership, but this wasn't true. At the time he opened this can of worms, the Admirals Club had 90,000 members and he was put on a waiting list established because the clubs were getting too crowded.

C.R. settled the issue in his own inimitable fashion. On July 18, 1967, he announced that the Admirals Club would become a dues-paying, self-supporting operation; non-paying Admirals could still be members, but they couldn't use Club facilities. It was a gutsy decision. American was deluged with protests, and more than 12,000 Admirals said they'd refuse to pay dues.

The adverse reaction began slowly; C.R. answered the first seven or eight letters of complaint, but then the floodgates opened. Smith asked Spater to take over, but he couldn't keep up with the mail, either. C.R., Sadler, and Spater had agreed that a form letter of response wouldn't suffice and that each Admiral deserved an individual answer. "Mission Correspondence" was turned over to public relations, and Dave Frailey of the p.r. staff wound up with a task that could have been included in the Seven Labors of Hercules. He wound up writing some 1,300 letters.

The Bureau of Enforcement said Smith's plan didn't go far enough, that American should open the Admirals Club to all or shut it down. But the full CAB approved C.R.'s compromise, and other carriers adopted it for their own VIP clubs. A temporary exception was United, much to C.R.'s and Sadler's consternation. It wrote members of its 100,000-Mile Club that UAL would not charge dues, but then decided to go along with everyone else when the CAB gave American's plan its blessing.

(Footnote: The man who started the whole dispute became a dues-paying Admiral.)

While jet-age passengers weren't as naive as their predecessors of earlier years, American still got its share of the wonderfully unsophisticated. Like the woman who called reservations and asked to be booked on "one of those Electrolux airplanes."

And the not so wonderful, like another woman who phoned American from

San Diego and complained that when she unpacked her bag, her clothing was wrinkled.

"I'm having everything pressed and I'm going to send you the bill," she announced.

Celebrities were always welcomed and maybe occasionally pampered too much, but so many were Personalities with certain idiosyncrasies that had to be taken into account. Even Eleanor Roosevelt, who invariably carried her own luggage, was someone to avoid on an early morning flight. If she hadn't had her first cup of coffee, she'd bite an agent's head off; once she had her morning coffee, she was charm personified.

Frank Sinatra was a well-liked passenger who usually found time to chat with employees, but he steadfastly refused to pose for pictures with them. He had a personal rule against being photographed with strangers, and American's personnel learned to respect it.

Greta Garbo was one of the more unusual passengers. She boarded an American flight traveling under the name of "Harriet Brown" and insisted that the armrest between two seats be removed. For most of the flight, she sat cross-legged, Yoga-style, in the center of the seats. When she deplaned, she backed down the ramp stairs so no photographers could snap her picture.

Oklahoma's famous football coach Bud Wilkinson took his wife to Mexico City on American, boarding in Oklahoma City with a connection in Dallas. American's Oklahoma City office sent Dallas the following teletype:

"On board Flight 459 world's greatest football coach and wife connecting to Flight 151 to Mexico City. Any assistance you give them will undoubtedly hold down the score against Texas this year."

Just before boarding 151, an American agent handed Wilkinson a copy of the Oklahoma City message and the reply from Dallas:

"Regarding Flight 459 world's greatest football coach, party of two, Darrell Royal did not arrive. Please advise."

Occasionally—but only occasionally—there was the super-honest passenger. American received a letter from a woman who confessed that years before, on a flight from Burbank to Texas, she had kept a plastic spoon as a souvenir. Enclosed in her letter was a sterling silver spoon.

One of the best stories came from Knoxville after the 727 began serving Tennessee cities. A customer walked into American's ticket office there and asked what flights were available to Nashville, which was in a different time zone. American in the early 1950s had pioneered the use of local times in timetables, whether standard or daylight; up to then, the airlines had followed the railroad and bus practice of listing all times as standard, leaving it up to the passenger to translate them into daylight when applicable.

So the Knoxville agent's answer was to suggest Flight 577. "It leaves at 5:50 P.M. and arrives in Nashville at 5:51," he informed the customer.

The man shook his head and left. He was back a half hour later, asked another agent the same question, and got the same answer.

"Can we reserve you space on 577, sir?" the agent added.

"No, but I think I'll go out to the airport and watch that son of a bitch take off."

The wonders and awesome technology of the jet age had a sobering effect on the cockpit crews. The jets were unforgiving beasts, and flight manuals became bibles of rules and procedures. The transition was easy for professionals like Tex Melden and Sam Saint, the latter a greatly respected captain whose contributions to air safety were acknowledged throughout the industry. But not even the increased disciplinary environment of a jet flight deck could quell the free souls. Such as Captain John Gatlin, who came on the p.a. one morning after a 707 takeoff and informed his passengers:

"Ladies and gentlemen, for your safety we have something new installed on this airplane: air bags." While some 100 passengers looked around the cabin for this unexpected boon to safety, Gatlin continued, "The two bags in first class are Linda and Harriet. The four bags in coach are . . ."

Gatlin was told before one flight that it was overbooked and there would be a delay until angry passengers were pacified and the confusion sorted out. Gatlin proceeded toward the field of combat, the ticket counter, with his cap pulled down over his ears, coat unbuttoned, and tie askew. In a loud voice he inquired, "Where ish thish airplane I'm supposed to fly today?"

Six passengers immediately left the counter and Gatlin said to the harried agents, "Well, that oughta take care of your oversales."

The Gatlin mystique rubbed off on one of his copilots, John "Bear" Mosley, who eventually made captain himself and established a few legends of his own. He was on a layover in Salt Lake City some years ago and bet a stewardess he could beat her at an electronics game. The stakes were unusual: Gatlin got $10 if he won, but if he lost, he would have to handle the liquor service on the return flight the next day.

He lost. The girls bought a flowery green apron for him to wear, and at the appropriate moment, he turned the 727 over to his copilot and served drinks to the startled passengers. Mosley got through first class in fine shape, but halfway down the coach aisle he had to take a breather and sat down next to a very elderly lady. A brief conservation disclosed that she had been a widow for several years.

"A widow?" Mosley said sympathetically. "Well, when we get to Chicago, maybe we could fool around a little."

A gasp came from a woman sitting across the aisle, and she glared at the Bear. "Do you always talk to your passengers like that?"

"Stay out of it, honey!" the older lady snapped. "It's been twenty years since anybody tried to pick me up."

The Will Rogers of American Airlines was Captain E. G. "Tiny" Foley, whose observations on life, the industry, Air Traffic Control, the FAA, copilots, and airplanes were so unique that one of his fellow pilots began collecting them in a notebook. Tiny's Boswell was Bill Davenport, who finally went to the expense of publishing a small booklet titled *Foleisms—The Wit and Wisdom of American Airlines Captain Tiny Foley.*

It would be tempting to reproduce the entire booklet herein, but unfortunately most of Tiny's homespun observations on life, etc., delivered in a slow-motion West Virginia drawl, were unprintable if memorable. A few less earthy samples must suffice.

A flight engineer remarked, "Isn't this a great job, Tiny?"

"Yeah. But if we could just get rid of these trips, it'd be the best job in the world."

One young flight engineer asked him for "any advice you could give me on flying the line."

"Sure," Foley agreed amiably. "Now ya gotta learn the important stuff first. And the first thing you gotta learn is how to hang your uniform coat and your topcoat on one hanger."

Tiny took a dim view of rival Braniff's gaily colored aircraft. He saw an all-green 727 and told his copilot, "It looks like a watermelon that sat in the rain too long." This was mild compared to his description of a yellow job: "A 150,000-pound canary," Foley sniffed disdainfully.

Tiny drew an officious FAA inspector for a check ride. His first question and the answer he got set the mood for the rest of the flight.

"Captain, how about explaining to me how the electrical system works on this airplane?"

"Hell, I don't know how it works," Foley confessed. "If I could build these things, I wouldn't be flying 'em."

A somewhat shaken inspector deplaned two hours later and said weakly, "Well, thanks for the ride, Captain. I must say, your kind of flying is certainly different."

"I know," Tiny acknowledged modestly. "It's kinda like horse manure in a garage: you don't hardly see anything like it no more."

He professed to have achieved much without the necessity of getting good scholastic grades. "When I used to come home from school," he declared, "my folks would celebrate if I passed the eye test." Yet under his often raunchy homilies was a man who loved flying. Toward the end of his career, he was grounded because of high blood pressure but refused to take retirement even though he was close to the age-sixty deadline. Instead, he lost sixty pounds dieting, got his pressure back to normal, and returned to the line in time to fly six more trips. Tiny Foley simply didn't want to bow out for medical reasons.

One hectic day at O'Hare, a harassed ground controller finally addressed some thirty-five impatient pilots waiting for takeoff clearance: "Okay, attention all flights! Stop where you are! I repeat, stop where you are right now. Until I say the word, nobody moves one foot!"

There was silence for a moment. Then on the tower frequency came an accusatory announcement. "Eastern moved . . . Eastern moved!"

The unidentified voice was rumored to have been that of Captain Foley, but this was never confirmed.

It is possible that Tiny's sense of humor was contagious and could afflict even the flight attendants. American had one young lady who arrived at the conclusion that pre-takeoff safety announcements were a waste of time because nobody listened to them. And she voiced this opinion to a vice president who had boarded her flight.

"And," she declared, "I'll bet you $50 I can prove it right on this trip."

He took the bet. She picked up the p.a. mike, went into her safety spiel, and ended it with this instruction:

". . . and when the oxygen mask drops from the overhead compartment, attach it to your navel and breathe normally."

The vice president looked around the cabin. Within his line of sight, not one person had looked up from his newspaper or magazine.

Tiny would have been proud of her.

American lagged behind in one aspect of marketing innovation—if in-flight movies can be put into that category.

TWA pioneered this now-accepted form of passenger entertainment in 1962 when it agreed to install in its 707s an airborne projector and screen developed by an entrepreneur named Dave Flexer. The gimmick, at first limited to first-class passengers, won instant popularity, which didn't really surprise American. Flexer had offered the system to American before he tried TWA.

Flexer owned a string of theaters in Memphis, a city where American was the dominant carrier, and he approached Jack Mullins first. His proposal was identical to the deal he was to make later with TWA: he needed seed money to finance development of the system in return for a five-year exclusivity agreement. He met with Marion Sadler and Mullins, who listened to his proposal and turned him down.

"There's no way in-flight movies would get us one additional passenger unless we could be the only ones to have movies," Mullins told Flexer, "and that five years exclusivity would last about five minutes, or just long enough for somebody to come up with a different or even better system. All it's going to do is increase our costs and get us nothing in return."

Flexer thanked them, walked across the street, and sold the idea to TWA.

"I never forgave him because what I warned would happen did," Mullins said. "Movies didn't bring the industry one more customer and increased the cost to all customers."

This was true, but what Sadler, Mullins, or anybody else couldn't deny was the public's acceptance of movies on transcontinental and transatlantic trips, where even on a jet five or six hours of flight could get boring. When TWA began showing films, American did surveys of its own passengers' attitude toward in-flight movies and discovered that to veteran customers, it made no difference. But the trouble was that other surveys showed TWA's share of the transcontinental market had increased almost from the very start of the gimmick.

One suggested counterattack was to offer good books to read on long flights, but this experiment laid an egg corresponding in size to those hatched by a brontosaurus. Sadler threw in the towel and told Mullins to find a movie system equal to or better than TWA's. Sony offered the most intriguing arrangement, small TV like sets hooked to a central projector unit and strategically located throughout the cabin so each passenger had what amounted to almost an individual screen. In its original installation, the Sonys were above the coach seats, but in first class were in the lower part of the seatback, so passengers would look down at the movie.

The Sony system had several advantages. It didn't interfere with cabin service, and passengers walking up and down the aisle didn't block anyone's view. Nor was it necessary to lower window shades on daytime flights. So it was decided to put the system on a 707 and test passenger reaction. It got raves.

"The trouble was," Mel Brenner recalled, "the passengers got on that plane not expecting anything and naturally went ape over the Sonys. So we went ahead, and the whole thing bombed. For one thing, the Sonys couldn't transmit color."

The best thing about the Sony system was the name Doyle Dane Bernbach thought up: Astrovision. The next step was to retain the name but scrap the Sonys, replacing them with a Bell and Howell color system that had fewer but wider over-the-seat screens, still visible to every two or three rows. The chief flaw was that the film was projected onto the screens by a hidden moving belt that went around the cabin; no screen showed the same picture, and the sound was synchronized for the nearest screen. For some reason, passengers would instinctively watch the action on a screen six rows ahead while they were getting sound that didn't match what they were seeing.

American eventually went to a wide-screen system, which was what Mullins wanted in the first place. But Astrovision even with its drawbacks wasn't a complete flop once color capability was provided. One survey disclosed that 14 percent of American's transcontinental passengers would wait a surprising length of time for a flight showing movies. Sadler, who hated the whole idea of movies per se, was on a Los Angeles trip with Rauscher and, when the film started, glanced around the cabin.

"Walt, look at that," he rasped. "Hardly anyone's watching the goddamned movie."

"Fourteen percent are," Rauscher reminded him.

When Astrovision was introduced in August 1964, American added a cute idea: the system was hooked to a camera mounted in the nosewheel well so passengers could watch takeoffs and landings. A stewardess once turned on the camera too soon and passengers got a great view of a mechanic giving the captain the well-known finger salute.

At one time, there was an attempt made to get antitrust exemption for an industry agreement to eliminate in-flight movies. American, TWA, and United agreed, but Continental balked—Bob Six had just installed a movie system on his planes and he refused to scrap it. The same thing happened when Mullins spearheaded a joint industry effort to stop serving free drinks to first-class passengers. As Mullins told the story:

"Free liquor involves a tremendous loss that can't be controlled because so much of it is given away. I figured if we charged for every drink, we'd have solid cost control, and I also thought it was unfair to have nondrinking first-class passengers subsidize drinks for imbibers. The fare is based on cost of service, and that includes liquor. There's no place in the world you can get free whiskey except in the first-class section of an airliner.

"So we got permission from the CAB to discuss this with other airlines— antitrust exemption, in other words. Then I approached all the major carriers and told them, 'Let's stop this foolishness and charge everyone for drinks.' They all agreed except Continental. They were competing against American, TWA, and United between Chicago and Los Angeles, and there was no way they'd go along.

"American, TWA, and United told Six to go ahead and serve free liquor, we wouldn't. But Northwest decided that if Continental was going to do it, they would, too. They didn't compete with Continental, but they couldn't stand the idea of not offering free booze between Minneapolis and Seattle. The minute Northwest bolted, so did United, they were in the Minneapolis–Seattle market, too. So the whole idea went down the drain.

"United's defection was the real blow. Bob Johnson was my counterpart there and we had worked together very closely on a free liquor ban. The CAB would have approved it because the Board considered free drinks discriminatory."

Liquor service was something of a problem during C.R.'s regime because he loved bourbon and was of the firm opinion that every flight should be well stocked with bourbon. In 1962, when Rauscher was director of sales, he began picking up reports from stewardesses that more and more passengers were requesting Bloody Marys, a reflection of vodka's growing popularity. Rauscher asked Fred Haverly, director of food service, if American couldn't start serving them.

"Impossible," Haverly ruled. "We've got nine different brands of Scotch and C.R. keeps asking for more bourbon."

A few days later, vice president of service Bill Whitney departed the premises, and Mullins summoned Rauscher.

"You know Whitney has left?"

"So I've heard."

"How would you like to be vice president of service?"

"I would."

"You've got the job. It'll be approved at the next board meeting."

Rauscher headed straight for Haverly's office, sailed past his secretary, and informed the startled director of food service, "Fred, I'm the new vice president of service. Put those goddamned Bloody Marys on the planes!"

The problem was to find a good ready-mix; stewardesses didn't have time to fool around with blending Bloody Mary ingredients. Haverly couldn't find anything suitable on the East Coast and flew to Los Angeles after hearing that Al Bone knew of a supplier.

"I never met the supplier myself," Bone said, "but I know a fellow who runs a small bar and he gets a hell of a Bloody Mary mix from a guy who makes the stuff in his garage. It's so good I've been buying bottles from the bar owner."

Bone had the bottler's address and they drove to his home. Sure enough, he had turned a three-car garage into a small plant. Before Haverly left, he had contracted to buy as much Bloody Mary mix as the man could spare. Later, a legitimate factory replaced the garage and the mix began appearing in cans under the brand name "Mr. and Mrs. T."

"American made them millionaires," Rauscher said. "After we put the mix on our planes, they couldn't keep up with the demand and had to stop selling to bars. Eventually they sold out to Del Monte."

Another beverage reform around this time involved coffee, which at first glance might seem to rank fairly well down on any airline list of things-we-should-really-worry-about. It ranks higher than one might imagine.

It used to be an industry axiom that airline coffee at its best tasted like colored hot water and at its worst like emulsified engine oil. There were two explanations: for economy reasons, the airlines often bought the cheapest blends, and even if they didn't, it was almost impossible to serve freshly brewed coffee because there was no way to brew it in the air.

Coffee-making changed little from the DC-3 right through the DC-7. The practice was to brew large batches at airports, pour it into various-sized thermos jugs, and board the jugs either at the originating station or somewhere along the route. Only occasionally would passengers get a truly fresh cup. Sometimes they were drinking coffee that had been made five hours ago, and tasted that way.

All this changed with jet-powered aircraft. For the first time, coffee could be brewed in the air, eight cups every three minutes out of three coffee makers on each 707 and DC-8 and two on American's Electras. They were no simple household percolators, either. Each unit weighed fifty-five pounds, yet had to be small enough to fit into the carefully designed, compact galleys. They also had to be capable of dispensing iced drinking water and hot water for tea as well as coffee.

That triple task required an intricate system of thermostats, heating units, a dry ice tray adjacent to the drinking water tank, plus insulation from the boiler heater, automatic valves and pumps, emergency manual valves, and timers—all in a unit two feet high and eighteen inches deep, and designed to be as trouble-free as possible.

The coffee brewing process itself was simple. The unit forced hot water, heated to just below boiling, into a cartridge containing specially ground coffee. Underline "specially"—American used separate blends to adjust for the variation of alkali in the water at cities on its system, for the only ingredient boarded was fresh water.

Price tag per unit: $1,316, which meant that American spent some $400,000 to equip its original 707 and Electra fleet with airborne coffee makers. (The coffee makers on American's later 747s and DC-10s cost more than $3,000 each, but could brew twelve cups in one minute.)

Even with the months that went into research, development, and testing, the units were not as reliable as hoped. At one point, an ATA survey showed that malfunctioning coffee makers were the leading cause of departure delays. And by the mid sixties, both Smith and Sadler became more concerned about coffee quality than reliability, which had improved. Haverly was told to do something about it.

He did. He started out by going to "school"—a workshop conducted by the Pan American Coffee Bureau, which represented growers in thirteen Latin, Central, and South American countries. It was an everything-you-always-wanted-to-know-about-coffee-but-were-afraid-to-ask course, and when he finished, he hired a consultant to prepare specifications for American's own exclusive blend.

The formula was kept as secret as the one Coca-Cola guarded for its syrup. It included three different types of coffee beans blended in about equal proportions, but Haverly never revealed which beans were used. More important were the results: the airline acquired the reputation of serving one of the best cups of coffee in the industry, if not *the* best, and the quality is still monitored carefully.

American prospered and progressed under Marion Sadler's leadership. It wasn't as dramatic and forceful as C.R.'s, nor did Smith really abdicate in terms of relinquishing total authority and influence. But he thought, and so did everyone else, he had found the man in whose hands he could place the eagle's future.

The year-by-year record of Sadler's presidency showed:

1964: A 70 percent jump in profits over 1963 to $33.4 million. Stockholders' equity increased by $23.8 million. A 2.5 percent reduction in costs. Sixteen new jets added to the fleet.

1965: $39.6 million in profits. Application to serve Hawaii and Japan filed with CAB. Twelve more jets ordered. A 9.4 percent rate of return on investment, one of the highest in the industry.

1966: A 31.5 percent increase in net earnings, to $52.1 million. A $100 million hike in revenues. Fifty-two new jets joined the fleet. American ordered ten giant Boeing 747s at a cost of $26 million each.

1967: A slightly less profitable year, but net earnings still hit $48 million.

With relentless precision, American moved closer to its goal of an all-jet fleet. This would be attained in 1969, when the last Electra was retired. The last DC-7 to operate in passenger service, *Flagship Wyoming,* was retired in 1963 and donated to the National Museum of Transport in St. Louis.

The Convair 240 bowed out June 30, 1964, with Flight 585, a puddle-jumper from Syracuse to Memphis via Rochester, Buffalo, Cleveland, Columbus, Dayton, Cincinnati, Louisville, and Nashville. Special ceremonies were held in each city, thanks to a memo Sadler had sent to Willis Player a few months before:

"By July 1, we will have retired the last of the CV-240s which served American so long and so well. Perhaps this would make a good story and, if handled properly, might get pretty wide distribution."

And with the caution so typical of Marion Sadler, the note added: "It occurred to me to say that we would no longer have any two-engine airplanes. We cannot say that, of course, because we will have the two-engine BAC-111 in the middle of 1965" (sic).

Far more than the DC-6 and DC-7, the 240's departure was an occasion for sadness. Stewardesses loved the little plane as much as pilots. Judy Judisch wrote a long poem, which *Flagship News* published (it took almost an entire page), titled "Love Dirge to a Mighty Midget." Just these two stanzas reflected the affection all flight crews bestowed on American's first postwar airplane:

> *Yes, you are still very much the pug-nosed child*
> *All baby fat and flatulence*
> *With fetal dependence on fuel's nourishing umbilical line*
> *Staunch enemy of inertia*
> *Endowed with all the exuberance of a kindergarten recess*
> *Voice as profound as the rickey-tick palaver of a*
>   *backroom piano . . .*
> *Hail to thee*
> *Empress on your sky dais*
> *Mistress of the cantilever*
> *Champion of piston's aero-decathlon*
> *Winner of the shooting match with the stars*
> *Potentate of the E.T.A. guessing game*
> *Queen of the bird's-eye view.*

No such sentiment would accompany the retirements of the 990 (1968) and BAC-111 (1972). But the DC-6's farewell December 17, 1966, an occasion on which American became the first of the Big Four domestic carriers to operate an all-turbine fleet, was marked by flying the last one over Kitty Hawk that day.

Fate dictated the inevitable; success had to be mixed with tragedy. Bill Littlewood died in 1967. Dan Beard was to follow him in 1974. Of these two giants of aviation technology, Littlewood perhaps was the better known but Beard was no less beloved. Yet few ever realized the extent of the risks he took in his never-ending quest for greater safety, or the extent of his contributions, which included the development of flashing navigation lights and reverse pitch propellers.

He took off in a DC-4 from LaGuardia on one test flight carrying the maximum gross load of 75,000 pounds. As soon as the wheels broke ground, he feathered the number-three engine and reduced power on number four, which left him with only the outboard and inboard on the left side. The odds against double engine failure on a DC-4 were extremely high, but Beard wanted to find out how the airplane would handle under such dire circumstances, so he could teach line pilots how to respond. He also once flew a DC-3 up to 29,000 feet looking for ice so he could test some experimental de-icing equipment.

Pilots worshipped this tall, distinguished-looking airman with a rare sensitivity and compassion toward others. He was nominated frequently for American's Bravery Award but never received it. The board of selection always argued that Dan was getting paid for the risks he took. It was typical of Dan Beard that he never resented not getting the honor.

"He was a real professional," Dixon Speas said. "He'd get on a problem and would stick to it until it was solved. He needed two sets of mechanics working on one of his test airplanes because he'd go through two shifts without even realizing it. And the chances he took were for one reason: he wanted every pilot to know what to expect in the most dangerous situation."

Not even the dedicated Dan Beards of aviation could plug every tiny loophole or anticipate every fatal mistake that a pilot might make. Such was the case the night of November 8, 1965, when American Airlines Flight 383 from LaGuardia to Cincinnati crashed on final approach. It was American's first fatal 727 accident, and there were only four survivors—two passengers, a deadheading American captain named Elmer Weekley, and Toni Ketchell, one of the three stewardesses.

Weekley's testimony in the subsequent hearings confirmed what investigators already had learned: Two experienced pilots—one of them a 727 check captain—had established an extremely high rate of descent into rapidly deteriorating weather conditions. The trijet hit a hillside two miles north of the assigned runway, and Weekley told the hearing the initial descent into the Cincinnati area had seemed abnormally fast.

The CAB said apparently neither pilot had monitored the altimeters during final approach which was second-guessing to the extreme. Not watching altimeters during an ILS approach was something no pilot could believe, and especially for the two men flying 383. And the CAB conceded the possibility of a contributing factor: a sensory illusion caused by the terrain.

The 727's approach to the runway involved a base leg pattern like a golf course's dogleg. After turning into the base leg, the airport was always on the left side of the airplane, and to keep the field in sight, the pilots could look only to the left as they banked.

The terrain directly to the left of 383's flight path was a river basin about 400 feet lower than the ground over which the plane was passing or the ground to the aircraft's right. Rising steeply from the river to the same level as the airport was an unlighted, wooded hillside. Only a few residences lined the riverside, providing little or no terrain definition. In the dark, under extremely poor visibility conditions, the crew easily could have mistaken the lights in the river valley as being at the same elevation as the airport. And those lights were all that could be seen from the cockpit.

Yet excessive rate of descent had been the mistake that had triggered the chain of events, and this had been a major factor in three other 727 accidents occurring around this time. There were the usual demands from headline-hunting congressmen that the 727 be grounded, but the airplane's only real sin was its own superb flying characteristics. It instilled not merely confidence but a deadly sense of overconfidence. Like any jet, it had to be flown by the book, and once pilots learned that, the 727 went on to compile an excellent safety record.

C.R. took this accident hard. The minute he was notified and told that one stewardess had survived but was badly injured, he phoned Millie Alford. He was extremely upset.

"Get the next flight to Cincinnati," he managed to tell her. "You be sure that girl gets everything she needs. Stay with her as long as you have to, and keep me informed."

Toni Ketchell would be partially crippled for the rest of her life, despite years of therapy. C.R., not satisfied with her progress in Cincinnati, had her flown to New York and put under the care of the best specialists he could find, picking up all medical bills. He issued orders that she be kept on the payroll and given a positive space pass for life.

She was one of his stewardesses, and that was all that mattered.

The most stressful time for any airline public relations man is the immediate aftermath of a fatal crash. Fortunately for Willis Player, he wasn't around to handle the Cincinnati accident.

Player had resigned late in 1964 to return to Pan Am. It was not merely the monetary offer his old airline made, but his sensing that C.R. wasn't going to stay around much longer. While he admired Sadler tremendously, he had been too close emotionally to C.R. Smith tried to talk him out of going. Player simply said:

"Look, C.R., one of these days you're going to get up and walk out of here, and you sure as hell aren't going to ask *my* permission."

His successor was an American p.r. veteran, Karl Dahlem, but he was a vice president only long enough for a friend of Lyndon Johnson to talk C.R. into hiring a so-called "big name" public relations expert. The man recommended was Holmes Brown, former vice president of public relations at the Ford Motor Co., who also had worked in Washington with the Poverty Corps. His qualifications seemed impeccable, but his knowledge of the airline industry was nil.

A short, wiry man, at American he committed every gaffe known to the airline p.r. profession. The night of the Cincinnati crash, he was on his way home when he heard a radio bulletin. Brown went back to the office and found his entire staff hard at work with the passenger list, answering press inquiries, and all the other grim tasks involved in accident coverage. Brown couldn't believe what he was seeing.

"What are all of you doing here at this hour?" he yelled. "Go on home. We've got a lot of important things to do tomorrow!"

The staff watched him leave, and then went back to work.

Brown's worst sin in the eyes of his staff was to change the name of *Flagship*

News to *Astrojet News.* He also hired a quartet of heavy hitters from various New York media, who changed the format. The paper became virtually all pictures and very little text.

One issue was a special layout in tribute to American Airlines employees who had worked so hard during the 1966 multi-airline strike. The intentions were good, but Brown was so proud of the edition that he insisted on sending the paper to every editorial writer and daily newspaper in the United States.

It took numerous days, several nights, and two weekends to compile the mailing list, along with writing nearly 2,000 covering letters. The total result was one editorial in the Dalles, Oregon, paper, which was about the farthest off-line city on the list. The other eighteen hundred papers threw it away.

That particular issue was one of the most expensive the airline ever published. The four new editors spent more than $15,000 on shots taken by professional outside photographers they had hired. For hours they waded through hundreds of prints to find the picture that would go on the front page. Finally they came across a beauty and shouted in unison, "This is it!" The one they chose was taken by an American Airlines photographer, Bob Takis.

Eventually, and perhaps inevitably, Marion Sadler and Bill Hogan had to clash.

Eastern's Shuttle had almost monopolized the New York–Boston and New York–Washington markets. C.R. wanted to get back in, and there was no argument on that score. What ignited the Sadler-Hogan confrontation was whether to start a no-reservations service like the Shuttle or invade the two markets with regular reservations and superior in-flight service on an hourly basis.

The weapon would be the new BAC-111 fleet, pitting this jet against Eastern's Electras and backup Connies. Hogan and his corporate planning group insisted that the only way to take on the Shuttle was to imitate it completely. Sadler, supported by Mel Brenner, felt American was in no position to challenge Eastern with this strategy.

"You had to have backup capability to make a Shuttle-type operation work," Brenner related. "We didn't have idle planes to use as backups and Eastern, with all those fully amortized Connies, did. The only way for us to have backups would have been to take aircraft away from valuable markets, and neither Sadler nor I thought this made any sense. The people in corporate planning just couldn't understand the importance of backup equipment; the number of planes they thought would be adequate as backups was just miserable. We'd be offering a no-reservations service and then leaving people stranded because there weren't enough planes."

The quarrel was so bitter that American came within two days of a full go-ahead for a competing Shuttle service when Sadler dug in his heels and said no. The competing service launched against Eastern February 12, 1967, was the "Jet Express," started first between New York and Boston and later extended to the New York–Washington battleground.

February 12 was a Sunday, the usual day for beginning a new schedule. In retrospect, Brenner admitted Sunday morning at 7 A.M. was a poor choice for so important an inaugural. On the previous Friday, Mel went to C.R.'s office to invite him on the inaugural flight.

"Sunday morning at seven o'clock?" Smith grunted.

"Yes, sir."

"I assume you have a lot of company non-revs to fill up the plane."

Nobody had thought of this ploy but arrangements were made quickly and the first Jet Express took off for Boston filled mostly with American employees and officials—the photographers couldn't tell them apart from paying passengers. But by the end of that first day, the BAC-111s were flying about 70 percent full, and that 70 percent load factor was maintained consistently during the Jet Express's existence, which was less than two years.

It was never a real success in that it didn't dent the Shuttle's domination of the two markets. But the Jet Express wasn't discontinued for that reason. Short-haul markets are only marginally profitable unless they're served by amortized aircraft, such as Eastern possessed; the priorities of aircraft utilization required the BAC-111 to be used elsewhere, on routes with more profit potential. In the two Shuttle markets, its speed advantage over the Electra was virtually nil.

Far more successful was Brenner's plan to extend the concept of established departure schedules—like service on the hour—to a transcontinental route for the first time. It was tried in the New York–Los Angeles market late in 1967 on an every-two-hours basis, promoted heavily, and went over. It amounted to a "Throw away your timetable—American goes to L.A. at 10, 12, 2, 4, and 6" convenience and was in effect until traffic demands didn't justify five daily flights.

But the fight over the Jet Express was Marion Sadler's last major exercise of authority.

By the summer of 1967, two events had occurred almost simultaneously. Sadler underwent major surgery for cancer of the colon, and George Spater was named vice chairman, thus establishing him and not Sadler as C.R.'s probable successor.

Those two developments raised questions that have yet to be answered definitely. Did Sadler's illness cost him what was then widely believed to be the position of heir apparent? Or would C.R. have picked Spater to succeed him even if Sadler's health had not been at issue? Some close to the situation were convinced that C.R. already had eliminated Sadler before the surgery, and there is evidence to support this. Spater was elevated to vice chairman prior to Marion's illness, and after the surgery Sadler informed C.R. he would resign.

That resignation, when it was made public, prompted speculation that it stemmed from Sadler's disappointment at not being named Smith's successor. Jack Mullins, however, didn't agree.

"Marion didn't leave American because he didn't get C.R.'s job," Mullins said. "I'm certain he was disappointed, but he was a realist. He knew the score with his cancer. He never discussed with me why he wasn't named Smith's successor, but I'm sure he knew the real reason. And fundamentally, it was because C.R. wasn't certain of Marion's health."

Actually, post-surgery prognosis was favorable, but by that time C.R.'s decision already had been made. Sadler never confided to anyone, not even Mullins, at what point C.R. was aware of the cancer diagnosis. The surgery did follow Spater's promotion, but not by much, and if C.R. knew Marion had cancer, the very knowledge could have influenced his thinking. Sadler's friends believed that Smith frankly told him after the operation that medical uncertainties had eliminated him from the line of succession, but whether there ever was such a meeting is unknown.

If there was, both men kept what had transpired between them a secret. Late in 1967, the company's officers held their annual marketing meeting and, as was the custom, it concluded with a dinner at which C.R. spoke. This time he had no speech. He simply rose and dropped a bomb.

"I want to tell you I think it's time I retired," he said calmly. "And I'm also sorry to tell you that Marion Sadler is retiring."

There was a shocked silence. Jack Mullins, who was dinner chairman, was the first to speak, and he could hardly get out the words.

"We have just learned that two of the greatest guys in this industry are leaving," he said in a choked voice. "I think they deserve an outpouring of the way we feel about them."

The room exploded with cheers and applause. And as Mel Brenner put it, "There were a hell of a lot of tears, too."

Sadler's resignation was announced officially in January 1968, although his service to American was not over. He returned in 1969 at Spater's request to serve as vice chairman, and although his health was declining, he remained in that post for four years.

He did continue as a director, however, until 1981, and his very attendance at board meetings was an act of courage. Cancer never did reoccur, but he developed serious circulatory problems, and in 1972 one leg was amputated. That was the year he moved to Tucson, Arizona, where another tragedy struck him. His wife, Joy, suffered a stroke in their swimming pool and drowned.

He was remarried, to pert Marguerite Bush, who was to be his constant companion as long as he lived.

Sadler was fitted with an artificial leg after the amputation and took the handicap in stride; he even walked a mile a day. Seldom did he discuss American with Marguerite. She would read *Flagship News* avidly, calling his attention to certain stories. Sadler would only glance at them, and once asked her, "Why do you read that stuff?"

"Because it was your airline and I'm interested in it. Didn't you ever discuss American with Joy?"

"No," Marion half-chuckled. "It was none of her business."

But he wasn't as disinterested as he pretended. One day he suddenly remarked, "You know, Marguerite, when I look back I guess the thing I was proudest of was the development of SABRE." And in his last years, he started to write a history of the airline and had a lengthy correspondence with Dave Frailey, then vice president of public relations, who sent him research material. The project, however, never got beyond a rough outline stage; he was too ill to really work on it.

In 1980, he lost the other leg, and all his natural optimism and spirit seemed to fade. He considered a second artificial leg, but decided it would be too much bother. The second operation hospitalized him for two months, and while he tried to hide his depression from his friends and his wife, she knew he was moodier than his humor and smiles would have people believe.

Sadler accepted many invitations to speak, even after the first leg was amputated, but when he lost the other leg, he declined every invitation. "If I can't stand up to make a speech," he told Marguerite, "I don't want to make it."

After the second amputation, he developed a deadly fear of fire. He was a chain smoker all his life, and he seldom wore a suit that didn't have cigarette burns. The same was true of his car seats. He smoked in bed and couldn't break the habit even with his fear of being trapped. He'd tell Marguerite, when she had to leave the house, "Be sure the doors are unlocked."

Marion would get very upset if she did not follow a prescribed schedule. When she left the house, he'd ask, "When can I expect you back?" And if she was five minutes late, she'd find him fussing and fuming. They went to Europe a few years before he died and she was an hour late getting back from a shopping trip. She got off the hotel elevator and there was Sadler, dressed and hobbling on his artificial leg, pushing the down button. He was going downstairs to ask the desk clerk to call the police.

In 1980, she threw him a surprise party on his sixty-ninth birthday at Tucson's Doubletree Inn. It wasn't much of a surprise—the minute he sensed Marguerite was planning something special, he took over the arrangements. The big surprise was supposed to be C.R.'s attendance, but this was blown when someone called Sadler a few days before the party and remarked, "By the way, I hear C. R. Smith is going to be in Tucson. Are you inviting him?"

But when Smith arrived, Marion feigned surprise, and Smith never knew he was expected all the time.

On April 15, 1981, he retired from the board, which turned right around and made him an honorary member for life. At the ceremony, Bob Crandall, American's president, drew Marguerite to one side. "I want you to make sure he comes to board meetings," he urged. "He has to be kept busy."

She tried to make him go, but he refused. He was going downhill steadily, using more and more pills to deaden constant pain. He would spend hours reading or watching television, mostly news programs or documentaries.

But he did make one final trip, to Washington in 1982 to see C.R. for one last time. Before they knocked on the apartment door, Sadler said softly, "If you don't mind, Marguerite, I'd like to see C.R. by myself. Come back in an hour."

"If you don't mind" was an expression he used all the time, even when he was issuing orders at American. It seemed to symbolize an innate decency that softened his short temper, his abrupt decisiveness that was second only to C.R.'s.

He died in September 1983, at the age of seventy-two, a blessed relief from years of pain. Fate had not been kind to George Marion Sadler. It robbed him of his health at the apogee of a brilliant career. There is no way to judge what he would have been like as C.R.'s successor, but his track record was certainly good and he would have been a popular choice.

As it was, fate was not kind to the airline he loved, either. When C.R. picked Spater instead of Sadler, he chose a good man but the wrong one for the situations that had to be faced.

19
New Look

George A. Spater looked like the kind of man Central Casting would have picked to play a benign college professor, or maybe a kid's favorite uncle.

Central Casting wouldn't have been very far off the mark, either. American's new president basically was a kind, thoughtful person with a scholarly mind far more attuned to the academic world than the daily combat of an airline.

It wasn't that he lacked airline experience—he had been associated with the industry for thirty-four years. As a young lawyer, he had filed TWA's new incorporation papers after the Air Mail Act of 1934 forced the airlines to reorganize, and he went on to serve as TWA's general counsel for many years before joining American. At TWA, he was Jack Frye's confidant and advisor in more than just legal matters. Spater, in turn, learned much from men like Frye, Ralph Damon, and Carter Burgess when they headed TWA. He was no expert in such specialized fields as marketing and operations, but his overall background was solid if not spectacularly knowledgeable.

It may well be that Spater could have made a success running almost any other carrier except American, one less volatile and aggressive, and certainly one in which he didn't have to follow such strong, charismatic leaders as C.R. and Sadler. One of Spater's earliest mistakes was trying to emulate their ability to communicate with employees at their own level without seeming patronizing or phony. The trouble was that this attribute came naturally to a C.R. or a Sadler; with Spater, essentially a gentle and decent man, communicating was painfully awkward. He really didn't understand the art, failing to grasp that attempting to be "one of the boys" wasn't necessarily effective communication.

He was too intelligent to keep trying to be something he wasn't. He was invariably polite and pleasant, but he often turned the job of communicating over to others. He once sent Walt Rauscher out to hold a series of "pep" meetings at the major stations, explaining, "Frankly, I don't do a very good job at this sort of thing." Not many airline chief executives would have admitted this failing; if there was one thing Spater did not possess, it was ego.

His rather professorial personality was not Spater's major flaw, although inability to inspire people *was* a definite weakness. That he recognized it as such was to his credit. One of the reasons he brought Sadler back as vice chairman was to utilize Marion's warmth and charisma in areas where he felt

387

he himself was lacking. Spater's major flaws were two-fold: first, he was overly impressed by men in positions of power, and second, his style of management did not work at an airline weaned, nurtured, and raised on a minimum of discussion and a maximum of fast action.

The first flaw undoubtedly stemmed from the many years he spent in Washington, when he was with TWA. Spater had learned the airline business under Jack Frye's tutelage, and no one was better at pulling political strings than Frye. His close association with Frye and the Washington scene gave Spater a somewhat lopsided perspective on the advantages and disadvantages of political ties. In effect, he saw mostly the advantages and didn't recognize the disadvantages, such as the danger of those ties turning into nooses.

His second flaw was the belief that an airline like American could be run by committee. It was no management sin for a chief executive officer to seek input and advice from subordinate officers, but Spater's trouble was that he failed to act decisively on what was discussed at staff meetings. And too often, discussion was all that went on.

Otto Becker, who became senior vice president of freight marketing during Spater's regime, used to dread executive staff sessions.

"We'd sit around a table talking about different problems and nothing would happen," Becker said. "We'd discuss one problem, then would go on to another, and sometimes I'd get so frustrated I'd ask, 'So what the hell are we going to do about it—where do we go from here?' All we'd get was a lot of talk and no decisions. Spater would tend to worry about long-range, grandiose things. He'd concentrate on one of these big projects and let everything else slide."

Most of Becker's fellow officers felt the same way, and as Spater's weaknesses became more evident they discussed among themselves the obvious question: why did C.R. choose him? Some would have preferred Jack Mullins, tough, decisive, and in many ways more like Marion Sadler than anyone else. When both C.R. and Sadler departed, Mullins had become senior vice president of marketing, which was high enough in the hierarchy to warrant consideration.

But Smith apparently never regarded Mullins as a possible succession candidate. "C.R. viewed him as a competent sales and services person," said one contemporary, "but not sufficiently skilled in the broader concepts of marketing."

In fact, Smith three years earlier had brought in Gerard W. Brooks as head of marketing over Mullins, for reasons known only to C.R. Brooks was a pleasant man, but had no airline experience, and Sadler fired him in 1965 after a one-year trial. Brooks was simply one of C.R.'s mysterious personnel appointments that turned sour.

Another thing that went sour in this chaotic period was C.R.'s relationship with Bill Hogan. They came to a parting of the ways shortly before Smith's retirement. In the summer of 1967, Hogan had gone to Korea to work out a hotel deal with the Korean government, and when he returned, he and C.R.

had a quarrel. From all evidence it was an angry one. Hogan left on vacation, and on his return was supposed to continue working for a few months until his normal retirement date in the spring of 1968. C.R. not only told him not to bother coming back, but also informed him he would not be allowed to continue serving as chairman of Flagship International, the food service and hotel subsidiary, following his retirement—something Hogan had been promised.

C.R.'s drastic action probably was influenced by the bad blood between Hogan and Spater. Smith evidently figured there wasn't room in the company for both men, and inasmuch as he had decided on Spater as his successor, Hogan had to go. It may well be that the Hogan-Spater feud was behind the quarrel C.R. had with Hogan.

Of all the officers with whom Bill Hogan had been associated in almost two decades of brilliant if at times divisive service, George Spater stood at the top of his no-respect list. Hogan used to send him memos in which he would deliberately misspell his name "Spader." There is not the slightest doubt that co-existence between these two men would have been impossible, even for the short time Hogan had to go before retirement.

In his summary of events in the 1967 Annual Report, Spater referred to Sadler's departure as "a loss" and said of C.R.:

"No words can express the debt that this company and the airline industry owe to Mr. Smith's imaginative and vigorous leadership. Whatever is best in American Airlines bears his imprint."

Hogan's departure was treated rather tersely, noting that "our chief financial officer retired at age sixty-five."

The changing of the guard had begun before Spater took over, with new names to watch and some old names no longer on the executive roster. Charlie Speers was one of the latter; he retired in 1965, having left his own indelible mark on American's history.

Gene Taylor had left to go with Allegheny, and Bud Wiser resigned in 1966 to become president of Northeast. One of Wiser's last assignments was straightening out some problems in Tulsa, a mission ordered by C.R. after the FAA fined the airline for violations of maintenance procedures, most of them minor but symptomatic of administrative laxness that cost Lucien Hunt his job.

"I don't know a damned thing about maintenance," Wiser had protested.

"I'm not sending you there to overhaul engines," Smith snapped. "You're a good executive and you know how to find out what's wrong."

Wiser cleaned up the base and turned it over to Hunt's successor, George Warde, who began his career with American as an apprentice mechanic at LaGuardia in 1940. Wiser, in turn, was succeeded as vice president of operations by Bill Seawell, another of C.R.'s recruits from the military. He was a West Point graduate who had gone into the Air Force and became commandant of the new Air Force Academy before retiring in 1963. He was a vice president at ATA when he joined American in 1965 as a vice president reporting to Wiser—an unusual tandem that found a West Pointer working for an Annapolis graduate.

Under Spater, Seawell became senior vice president of operations, but he soon left to head Rolls-Royce's North American subsidiary, and Warde replaced him.

Warde was a friendly, gregarious type and one of Spater's favorites. So was Donald Lloyd-Jones, an airline economist with Master's and Ph.D. degrees from Columbia, who joined American in 1957. He was vice president of corporate planning when Spater took over, and two years later assumed Hogan's old post as senior vice president of finance. His predecessor had been W. F. Shaffer, Jr., who hadn't lasted long under Spater's critical eye.

Spater picked his own successor as general counsel, a young lawyer named Gene Overbeck, whom he had hired for American's legal department in 1959 after hearing his name mentioned by mutual friends as an excellent attorney. The new vice president of public relations was Sylvan Barnet, Jr., formerly with *U.S. News & World Report, Fortune,* and the New York *Herald-Tribune.* Barnet had been with the Department of Commerce as director of the U.S. Travel Service and was Spater's personal choice to replace Holmes Brown.

American was a big airline, but some industry observers felt it had become top-heavy with brass. Spater's table of management organization by 1969 had four senior vice presidents, thirty staff vice presidents, and fifteen regional vice presidents. Fourteen years later, when American in most respects was even larger, a new regime had pruned the vice presidential roster to eight seniors, thirteen staff, and five regional.

In Spater's somewhat massive executive army, Warde and Lloyd-Jones stood out in terms of growing influence. Mullins ranked high for his undisputed ability, but he seemed to be regarded as an independent-minded maverick whose star was destined to fade, in direct correlation with the increasing intensity of Walt Rauscher's.

For the first three years of Spater's presidency, however, Mullins wielded plenty of clout. His marketing department embraced about half the company's nearly 30,000 employees; four vice presidents and all the regions reported to him. And into his lap fell a controversial proposal to do away with American's thirty-seven-year-old symbol:

The eagle.

It stemmed from two developments: American's commitment to a fleet of wide-body jets and the airline's being granted routes to the South Pacific, including Australia and New Zealand.

American had ordered another six 747s in addition to the original ten-aircraft order, and Spater also had signed for twenty-five McDonnell Douglas DC-10s. The huge Boeings were scheduled to go into service in 1970, and the DC-10 a year later. The 747s were aimed at the hotly competitive transcontinental market.

The South Pacific awards were a disappointment. American hadn't really sought South Pacific routes. What it wanted badly was authority to serve Japan, and the arguments it filed in the case (325 exhibits, of four volumes each) were aimed mostly at a U.S.–Tokyo route.

After almost two years of oral arguments and depositions by sixteen carriers seeking various Pacific routes, the CAB in the fall of 1968 announced a decision that left American completely out in the cold; the main beneficiaries were United, TWA, Eastern, and Western. The decision needed White House approval, and there was renewed hope at 633 Third Avenue. Lyndon Johnson, C.R.'s good friend, was still President.

Johnson proceeded to shaft Smith's old airline. He substituted Continental for Eastern in the South Pacific, and American stayed empty-handed. But as soon as LBJ left office, President Nixon first deferred all his predecessor's awards and later reached a compromise with the CAB on the South Pacific portion of the case. American was substituted for Continental at Australia and New Zealand, and also received authority to serve Fiji and American Samoa.

They were long-haul routes without much traffic potential, and as a sop the CAB granted American restricted authority to serve Hawaii with flights that could not originate from any West Coast point. At the same time, however, the CAB put five other carriers into the Hawaiian market in addition to the two already serving it, Pan Am and United. In trying to please everybody while pleasing nobody, the Board had simply glutted the market with excessive competition that was to cost some airlines millions.

The disastrous economic effects of the South Pacific awards were not immediately apparent, lost in the general euphoria over American's becoming an international carrier again for the first time since the AOA days. Overall air traffic was growing at a rate of 15 percent annually, which was the prime justification for an airplane as huge as the 747. Amid all the optimism, no one could foresee that it was going to be far too big for those South Pacific routes, and a few others besides.

Mullins wasn't the only one who thought American needed a new color scheme on its fleet. "Our old International Orange markings seemed awfully tired to many of us," he recounted. "Almost everyone wanted something that would wave the flag to go with our new routes and new planes."

He went to Doyle Dane Bernbach, which thoroughly agreed and suggested some kind of red, white, and blue striping on American's traditional silver fuselages. The agency also recommended that the airline hire a top industrial designer as a consultant.

Mullins went for the best: Henry Dreyfuss, regarded as the foremost in the world, and already well known to American. He had done the Love Field terminal in Fort Worth and the Electra's interiors; C.R. was so impressed, he had told Sadler, "I think we should hire this guy to do our airplanes, ticket offices, and everything else."

So when it came time for a drastic change in aircraft markings, Mullins turned to this unusual man. Henry Dreyfuss, who had never finished high school, started out by designing theater sets on Broadway. One never would have guessed his limited formal education; he was tall and very distinguished looking—and very expensive.

Dreyfuss was based in Pasadena, California, and flew to New York for a meeting with Mullins. Jack briefed him on what the ad agency was suggesting, Dreyfuss expressed interest, and Jack asked, "How much will you charge us for a final design?"

"I never negotiate such matters," Dreyfuss said stiffly. "My office manager does all that. Her name is Doris Marks, and you should call her. She handles all our contracts, and whatever she agrees to is fine with me."

Mullins informed Spater, who contacted Doris Marks, and a price was agreed on. Dreyfuss returned to New York a few weeks later to meet with Mullins and Spater.

"I have to tell you, Henry," Spater said, "we've agreed on a contract, but that Mrs. Marks is as tough as a boot."

Dreyfuss smiled. "She should be. She's been my wife for twenty-five years. She uses her maiden name in business."

He went to work modifying the agency's preliminary efforts and what he finally came up with was the red, white, and blue striping—a fuselage-length band below the window line—and the single word, in red letters, "American" above the windows just where the cabin section began. Dreyfuss insisted on using just "American," not "American Airlines."

"It's obvious you're an airline," he told Mullins. "The word should be removed not only from airplanes but ticket offices and hangars, too."

On the tail, Dreyfuss designed an insignia with a simple red A and blue A in large block lettering. With no trace of an eagle, however. Mullins circulated sketches of the new design and he got plenty of reaction, all bad.

It made no difference whatsoever to Henry Dreyfuss. He considered the eagle an anachronism and referred to the symbol as "the bug." He kept telling Mullins, "You have to get that damned bug off the airplane," and the agency agreed with him. Spater and others thought employee protests weren't really anything serious, but Mullins began looking for a company that had made a similarly drastic change in its corporate symbol. He found one in Mobil, which had abandoned its traditional Flying Red Horse in favor of a red, white, and blue color scheme.

Jack asked a Mobil official what employee reaction had been.

"You would have thought we just shot Christ," the official sighed.

"How long did it take you to get over the death?"

"I'm not sure we're over it yet. We're still getting protests. Believe me, it was a real traumatic experience when we got rid of that horse."

American employees had launched a "save the eagle" campaign, and Mullins felt there was no use risking a full-scale revolution. He invited Dreyfuss to dinner in the Palm Room of the Plaza and laid down the law. "Henry, we've got to keep the eagle. How do we do it?"

"Well, for one thing," Dreyfuss grumbled, "we'll make that bug as small as we can." All through cocktails and dinner, he kept doodling on a pile of cocktail napkins until he came up with a sketch showing the eagle as it now appears: a small blue bird parked between the double A, modern, streamlined, but definitely recognizable as an eagle.

When Dreyfuss decided to retire, he gave the company to his employees; there were twenty-five in Pasadena and twenty-five in the New York office. But inactivity bored him, and he decided to become a consultant with one strict rule: "I will not do any consulting on design," he told every prospective client who approached him. "I refuse to compete with my employees. I'll advise you on anything else."

He also limited his consultant work to a total of four companies for whom he had done previous work. The first three were A.T.&T., Hallmark, and the John Deere Co. The fourth would be a choice between American and Texaco.

Dreyfuss talked to Mullins about what the work would entail. They agreed he would spend one day a month sitting in on staff meetings and offering whatever comment he felt was appropriate to the subject under discussion, such as corporate plans, location of a new ticket office, fare proposals, or mailing lists for promotional material.

"It may have sounded screwy," Mullins said, "but he was a total expert in every field."

Before Jack agreed to the deal, he asked Dreyfuss what he was going to charge for his services.

"Two thousand dollars a day."

"Henry, that's an awful lot of money."

"You don't have to pay it," Dreyfuss said dryly. "I'll go to Texaco."

But when he returned to Pasadena and told his wife what American would be paying him, she was shocked. "Henry, that's disgusting. You don't need that kind of money."

"No," he agreed, "but it's two thousand more that we can give to charity."

He did verge into the area of design, albeit obliquely. American never did use Dreyfuss for uniform designs, but he was attending one staff meeting at which a new stewardess uniform proposal was being presented by a clothing manufacturer. Dreyfuss said nothing during the presentation, but when it ended, he drew Mullins to one side and pointed down at the sketches.

"This, this, and this won't work, Jack. This material won't hold up, and the girls aren't going to like that skirt."

Mullins remembered, "He was right, and he kept us from making an expensive mistake. Without him, we probably would have gone right ahead with what the designer proposed. Never did Henry Dreyfuss spend a day with us that we didn't get more than two thousand dollars' worth of advice."

The new markings were put on two 707s experimentally, to test passenger reaction, and then on eight new 727-200s that arrived from Boeing in May 1969. The rest of the fleet was repainted in Tulsa over the next two years, and all new aircraft had the new colors applied at the factory.

But the man responsible for that design died a tragic death. Doris Marks

Dreyfuss developed terminal cancer and her husband confided to Mullins, "Jack, I don't see how I can cope with her suffering."

A week later, he wrote a long letter to his children explaining that he did not want her to suffer any longer, nor could he go on without her. With his wife sitting by his side, he drove their car into their garage, closed the door, and left the engine running.

The decision to buy the DC-10 was the first major one George Spater made, and it was not easy.

The very concept of a wide-bodied jet smaller and more versatile than the 747 dated back to 1966. Its author was Frank Kolk, who at the time was vice president of development engineering—job titles kept changing more often than the men holding the posts.

The 747's enormous size, with its potential capacity of more than 400 passengers, worried a lot of airlines, including American. The only exception to this concern was Pan Am, which had been Boeing's launch customer. TWA, in fact, urged Boeing to build a smaller airplane, but the Seattle designers were committed to what Juan Trippe had specified. (It was rumored but never confirmed that the original 747 design actually *was* smaller, but was scaled up to meet Trippe's demands.)

Kolk told C.R. he thought the 747 was too big for American's route system —a prophetic judgment, as it turned out—and that it would be best used on international routes, which American didn't possess at the time. C.R. and Sadler ordered it anyway, lulled by the 707's consistently high transcontinental load factors and what then appeared to be an excellent chance of winning Tokyo. But Smith did listen to Kolk's ideas for a smaller wide-body and sent him to the West Coast with some interesting specifications.

They were handed to Lockheed, Boeing, and an ailing Douglas company that was shortly to be taken over by McDonnell Aircraft Corp. of St. Louis. Boeing, immersed with the 747 project and its 727 assembly lines running full blast, wasn't interested. Neither was Douglas; its DC-8 program hadn't recouped development costs and DC-9 deliveries were so far behind schedule that Eastern, an early DC-9 customer, had filed a damage suit.

But Lockheed, which hadn't built a commercial transport since the Electra, was. And it liked what Kolk was proposing: a twin-engine, double-aisle jetliner carrying up to 250 passengers, with a range of slightly over 2,000 miles. Kolk added a vital "must": because American's prime medium-range route was New York–Chicago, he insisted that the "Jumbo-Twin," as he called it, had to be capable of operating in and out of LaGuardia. He also wanted it powered with huge bypass engines—basically the same concept as the fanjet, but with a far greater ratio of air being used for thrust.

Kolk felt that a two-engine airplane was needed for operating economy and that only a large bypass engine could provide sufficient power for such a big airplane. Lockheed agreed, and proceeded with its design work on the basis of what Kolk had proposed. But it didn't take long for American's original Jumbo-Twin plans to fall apart.

Other airlines liked the size of the airplane but not the idea of two engines; the consensus was for three, on the grounds that two would be inadequate for an airplane so big. Kolk fought hard, but lost when it became apparent Lockheed had to go with the majority. Another complicating factor was the entrance of competition. Given new life by the merger with McDonnell, Douglas jumped into the race and pitted its DC-10 against Lockheed's L-1011. Then came the battle over the engines. Pratt & Whitney, up to its corporate ears with engine troubles on the early 747s, didn't have a suitable bypass engine quite ready to offer yet. Rolls-Royce did, likewise General Electric, and these two went to war just as hard as Lockheed and MCD.

The DC-10 and L-1011 were almost identical in their promised performance specifications. They even looked like twin airplanes, except for the location of their center engines; Lockheed's was buried in the rear fuselage, like the 727, while the DC-10's was mounted on the tailfin. This difference was to play a key role in American's selection.

On the L-1011, air to the center engine was fed through an S-shaped duct, a design that called for a shorter engine because of the space the duct took up. On the DC-10, whose center engine was above the fuselage, the air went straight into the engine intake. The bypass engine Rolls-Royce had developed for Lockheed was too short for the DC-10's center nacelle, whereas GE's longer engine was better adapted to the McDonnell Douglas entry.

The dilemma Spater faced was a preference for the DC-10 airframe and a Rolls-Royce engine that didn't really fit that airframe. Nor did Spater have any solid assurance that Rolls-Royce would modify its engine if American bought the DC-10. That one factor tipped American's choice toward MCD. The two airplanes appeared about equal in performance, price, and payload. The L-1011 was more sophisticated in some respects, particularly in its control system, but there was some prejudice against Lockheed within American because of the Electra experience and the fact that the Burbank company had never built a large commercial jetliner before. MCD had going for it the old Douglas reputation and American's long association with Douglas products.

There was general industry agreement that only one wide-body trijet would survive the competition; splitting the market between the DC-10 and the L-1011, it was felt, would be damaging to both Lockheed and MCD. When Eastern, TWA, and Delta all ordered the L-1011 with Rolls-Royce engines, everyone expected American and United to follow suit. But United wanted no part of a British power plant and announced it was buying the DC-10 with GE engines. When the unanimity-of-choice front was broken, Spater decided to go along with United.

Later, when two fatal accidents uncovered some DC-10 design deficiencies, it was only too easy to claim that American had picked the wrong airplane. Forgotten was the fact that the Rolls RB-211 engine had an astronomical rate of shutdowns when it first went into service. The problem, involving premature failures in a turbine blade component, was so vexing that the proud British company accepted help from Pratt & Whitney and GE to solve it.

The DC-10 went on to overcome its blackened reputation and now ranks high in pilot and passenger esteem. If the L-1011 is marginally superior, as some technical experts believe, the margin is so slim that Spater's decision could not be called a mistake.

Spater also took something of a bum rap in American's getting heavily involved in the hotel business, a venture that looked promising but proved disastrous. The involvement began long before he assumed command of the airline, and the idea of a hotel subsidiary was Bill Hogan's. It started on a very modest scale in 1963 when American leased a motel near the Rochester, N.Y., airport. According to Jack Mullins, some friends of Hogan's talked him into the deal. Later, American acquired a downtown hotel in Rochester, and from then on, the hotel acquisitions assumed the momentum of a snowball rolling downhill.

It must be said that Hogan had C.R.'s blessing, albeit reluctantly at first. "We'd better stay in the airline business," he warned, but two years later American was operating the Inn of the Six Flags in Arlington, Texas. Those three properties represented the extent of this diversification program until Hogan's final mission for the airline, his Korean deal in 1967.

After C.R. retired, Spater reportedly was tempted to get the airline out of the hotel business. The Korean commitments made this almost impossible, so he went in the opposite direction, increasing the involvement. By 1979, American was operating fifteen hotels and six motor inns in the U.S. and three foreign countries, a total of more than 11,000 rooms.

The biggest acquisition was the 1972 purchase of leasehold interest in several large hotels from the Loews chain, including its 1,842-room New York City showplace, the Americana. There was some opposition within the company to this deal, but Spater felt that American had to broaden its hotel base in order to compete more effectively with other chains, including the ones operated by United, Pan Am, and TWA.

Pan Am was operating a chain of successful hotels in many of the cities it served overseas. TWA did likewise when it merged with Hilton International in 1967. And United pulled off the best diversification program when it merged with the Western Hotel group (now Westin) in 1970.

Unfortunately, however, American's hotel and motel acquisitions failed to match chains like Hilton and Westin in potential, reputation, and operating efficiency. Some of them made no apparent sense. They were in cities American didn't even serve at the time, Miami being one example and Korea another.

As the man who headed the airline, Spater had to be faulted for a hotel expansion program that lacked cohesion and a sense of logical direction, and was allowed to develop with inadequately trained personnel and no articulated, common standards for all the properties. But he didn't deserve all the blame. He was under strong pressure from one director in particular, Carter Burgess, who thought the hotel venture was the smartest move American could make. And Spater did try to make it successful by hiring Bob Caverly, a respected executive in the Hilton organization, to run the hotels.

But Caverly didn't work out, and neither did Burgess, who succeeded him

—which was another mistake, because Burgess himself didn't have hotel experience. By the time Spater realized what had gone wrong, it was too late. Not even the best hotel man could salvage what was a poorly conceived project almost from the start.

What did go wrong? Jack Mullins's analysis summed up the criticism voiced by others whose views may smack of some hindsight but nevertheless are sadly accurate:

"First of all, we didn't know enough about the hotel business and we didn't hire enough talented people who did. Another mistake was not concentrating on a single type of establishment. We had very inexpensive airport inns like at Rochester and Cincinnati, and then we ended up with a monster like the Americana in New York. They were totally different and had to be operated differently.

"So we had no image as a hotel chain—we were neither fish nor fowl, with varying standards at each hotel. And that made it hard to sell to the public as an entity with a solid image of consistent quality. We needed a chain like the Westin group, where every damned one is good. Some of ours were good and others were lousy, because we never established standards applying to everybody."

Mullins thought the purchase of the Loews Americana chain was the worst boner of all. He remembered a meeting of the airline's executive council at which a final vote was taken on whether to submit the acquisition to American's board of directors. Mullins was vice chairman at the time.

The most vociferous proponent was Dick Bressler, then vice president and treasurer, who had been in on the negotiations and argued forcibly for approval. When Mullins was asked to voice his opinion, he pulled no punches.

"I just have a gut feeling we shouldn't do it," he said. "If that chain was worth a damn, Loews wouldn't be selling it—they're too smart. There has to be something wrong with this deal, and I don't think we should touch it."

He was the only senior officer who voted against it. When the acquisition was put before the board—Spater made the presentation—Mullins refused to attend. It was the first directors' meeting he had missed since being named to the board.

"I couldn't vote for it and I couldn't go against management's presentation by my boss," he explained, "so I just stayed away. It was passed unanimously, and obviously it was a mistake."

The first properties were operated by Sky Chefs, which reported to Hogan, and were called "Flagship Inns." After the Loews chain came into the airline's orbit, the hotel subsidiary became the Americana chain and was operated as a separate division. Which would have pleased Newt Wilson. He retired in 1971, but he didn't think much of the hotel venture anyway and he didn't think it belonged under Sky Chefs.

One interesting acquisition that didn't materialize was an attempt to take over the operation of the *Queen Mary,* the great British liner berthed at Long Beach and owned by the city. In 1969, coincidental with the opening of the downtown Flagship Rochester Hotel, American and the Diners Club announced that Sky Chefs would operate the ship's hotel and food services.

The Diners Club held a lease from the city for the *Queen*'s commercial development and its chairman, Alfred Bloomingdale, badly wanted American to run the operation. But Diners lost the lease in litigation, and what would have been the height of irony never took place—an airline operating one of the giant Atlantic liners that had been doomed by the jet itself.

Some officers considered the ill-fated hotel undertaking (American eventually would dump the properties) as an example of Otto Becker's criticism—that Spater tended to become totally immersed in a single major project and ignored almost everything else. Yet Gene Overbeck thought Spater's principal mistake was underinvolvement, not overinvolvement.

"If there was one criticism to be made of Spater in this regard," Overbeck said, "it was that he didn't spend *sufficient* time on the hotels. He thought Caverly could provide the necessary direction, but he was wrong."

The timing of the Loews purchase was poor. It was an expensive commitment made during an airline recession that saw American's 747s and DC-10s flying with disastrous load factors. From the historical perspective, therefore, the hotel enterprise became a black mark chalked up against Spater's administration. Whether he devoted too much time or too little time to it is a matter for debate, but there was a definite occasion during which he *did* let a single issue dominate his priorities.

For in 1968, he came up with the idea of merging American and Western Airlines—a futile dream that became almost an obsession.

Spater's first overture was made that year to Terry Drinkwater, then Western's president, in a phone call that seemed to have been initiated on impulse—at least no one at American apparently was aware he was even thinking about it.

With little preamble, he bluntly asked Drinkwater if he'd be interested. Terry just laughed and said Spater wasn't the first airline president who had approached him on the subject. Anyway, he wasn't interested. But Spater subsequently kept pursuing the matter. In March 1969, he contacted financier Kirk Kerkorian, who had just purchased a large chunk of Western stock and was moving toward control of the Los Angeles–based carrier.

Kerkorian's reaction was a rather lukewarm "maybe," and definitely no until he made a substantial profit on the stock he had just purchased. In June, Spater approached Drinkwater again, and this time Terry was more receptive. Encouraged, Spater met with Kerkorian, who mentioned an asking price for his stock that was too high. He had paid $47.25 a share and he wanted $60.

Spater went back to working on Drinkwater and proposed a straight share-for-share exchange. Terry said that as far as he was concerned, Spater had a deal. But when Drinkwater informed Kerkorian, Kirk was furious. Which didn't bother Terry one bit. He continued his contacts with Spater, behind Kerkorian's back, and on April 23, 1970, the roof blew off at Western's annual stockholders' meeting after Drinkwater had been kicked upstairs to board chairman.

The subject of merger wasn't on the agenda but it was brought up by a shareholder who asked if the rumors were true that American had proposed a merger that Kerkorian was blocking. Out of the verbal donnybrook that followed came a flat rejection of merger by Kerkorian's chief lieutenant, and Terry Drinkwater's subsequent ouster as chairman.

But Spater's dream wasn't dead yet. Between June 3 and October 30, 1970, there were ten separate contacts between American and Western officials, some of them in person, and four meetings between Kerkorian and either Spater or Donald Lloyd-Jones. On the table was another American offer: a share-for-share exchange plus an agreement that any Western stockholder could purchase American stock within a three-year period at a fixed price of $35 a share. Kerkorian accepted this, but also wanted permission for a 20 percent dividend on Western's stock before the merger was consummated. Spater said no, Kerkorian dropped his asking price to a 10 percent dividend, and Spater said he'd consider it.

By this time, Spater knew he had other suitors competing for Western's hand in marriage, the most serious being Continental. Western's own officials, if merger was inevitable, preferred Continental, and Bob Six kept raising the ante every time Spater improved his own offer.

But Six didn't have American's financial muscles. On January 30, 1971, American's directors approved a merger agreement that gave Kerkorian a pre-merger 10 percent dividend and called for exchanging 1.3 shares of American stock for every Western share. Five days later, Western's board voted for merger, much to the disappointment of virtually every WAL officer; Six said later, "I just ran out of chips."

Before the merger agreement was signed, American already had acquired Trans-Caribbean Airlines. a small carrier serving San Juan, Puerto Rico; St. Croix and St. Thomas in the Virgin Islands; Port-au-Prince, Haiti; and Aruba and Curaçao in the Netherlands Antilles, from New York, Newark, and Washington.

The TCA merger, submitted to the CAB in January 1970 and approved the following December, had been under negotiation for some time. The chief stumbling block was TCA's founder, O. Roy Chalk. Bill Hogan once called him a crook to his face, and there was ill will between Chalk and American officials even after the merger. Under the agreement, Chalk got 17.5 shares of American stock for every 100 shares of TCA. He not only netted more than $10 million from this arrangement but also received a long-term consultant's contract at $50,000 a year.

Spater had assigned Marion Sadler, then vice chairman, to head the team that worked out the merger provisions. Sadler's top aide was Gene Overbeck. The ink was hardly dry on the CAB's approval when American cancelled Chalk's personal services contract, citing "good legal reason."

The dispute involved some charges TCA claimed to have paid for television advertising. To verify them, Sadler asked Chalk to provide the operating logs for the San Juan TV station Chalk owned as a TCA subsidiary. When Chalk finally turned them over, Sadler and Overbeck noticed that they appeared to have been altered to include the disputed advertising.

Further investigation confirmed that the logs had, indeed, been altered. Sadler and Overbeck confronted Chalk with the proof, but the TCA owner argued that altered logs were not relevant to the dispute. Overbeck thought otherwise, sought outside counsel on the question, and then told Sadler that Chalk's conduct warranted termination of the consulting contract. Sadler at first demurred, but went along with the recommendation when Overbeck pointed out that "we couldn't have one code of conduct for Chalk and another for the rest of our employees."

American's board of directors subsequently terminated Chalk's contract; he sued, but at this writing, nothing further has happened in the case. The Federal Communications Commission, however, revoked the television station's license because of the altered logs.

Chalk had little reason to complain. He not only made money from the merger but was able to keep TCA operating while the merger was pending only because American advanced the airline some $5 million and guaranteed another $7 million Chalk wanted to borrow from a bank so he could meet his payroll. TCA was in bad shape. Not only was it deeply in debt, but it had defaulted on payments to its pilots' pension fund.

Chalk's airline had nine aircraft in its fleet: seven 727-100s and also a couple of DC-8s which American didn't want. But its attractive routes were to prove a bonanza. By 1975, American had grabbed 60 percent of the New York–San Juan market against Eastern and other carriers, and most of TCA's old routes have been profitable since. There were some early problems with the strongly unionized ground personnel in Puerto Rico but, Mullins remarked, "they turned out to be very loyal employees."

The American-Western merger hearings were pretty much a replay of the American-Eastern proceedings. Only some believed the deal stood even less of a chance. At least there had been some doubt whether Eastern could have survived without merger; there was none this time. In fact, by the time the CAB began considering the case, Western was doing better than American.

The opposition was formidable. Continental and United led the airline attack, supported by Western's unions, the Justice Department's antitrust division, and the CAB's Bureau of Operating Rights. Other than American and Western themselves, the only pro-merger witnesses came from the new Department of Transportation and various cities the two carriers served.

Western's pilots feared the merger more than any other employee group. American's cockpit crews had pulled out of ALPA in a bitter intramural fight in 1963, the climax of a long-festering feud between the AA members and ALPA leadership. They had formed their own union, the Allied Pilots Association (APA), and there was no way Western's airmen could win an APA-ALPA representation election—they would be outvoted three to one.

Merging of the two pilot seniority lists would have left Western's pilots holding a short stick, because of American's sheer size. When American absorbed TCA, the latter's senior captain, with a 1945 date of hire, couldn't get higher than number 400 on American's seniority list.

Spater's persistent optimism could have been called obstinate; he simply ignored all the signs of impending defeat. Opposition from the powerful Teamsters Union, representing most of Western ground employees, was crucial in that the Teamsters had supported President Nixon in the 1970 election and the White House would have either veto or approval power over the CAB's final decision.

Spater was so confident he had his officers meet with their counterparts at Western to assure mutual cooperation when the two airlines joined. Walt Rauscher, for example, was told that he should get together with Art Kelly, Western's senior vice president of marketing, because after the merger Kelly would be reporting to him. And Spater himself went out of his way to meet Western's officers whenever he was in Los Angeles. It must be said he made a good impression, although not to the extent of enlisting their wholehearted support.

He had dinner one night with Ray Silvius, WAL vice president of public relations, who happened to be married to the chief skipper of the L.A. Admirals Club. Jeanne Silvius had been telling her husband that Spater was really a nice guy who honestly thought the merger would be best for all concerned.

Even though Western was one of the smallest trunk carriers, Silvius was widely respected in the industry, and Spater dropped a hint that Ray had a bright future if the merger went through.

"Tell me," he asked, "how would you feel about moving to New York?"

"I'd rather move to Poland," Silvius said bluntly. Spater's jaw dropped, and Silvius added, "Look, I'll move any place my job takes me, but you asked me the question and those are my feelings."

The CAB examiner's initial decision, issued in the spring of 1972, disapproved the merger, but Spater's spirits never flagged. At one executive staff meeting, the unpleasant subject of possible rejection was raised and Spater said testily, "I know you guys don't think the merger's going through and that you're hearing all these rumors from Washington that it doesn't have a prayer. Well, I tell you it's going through, and you can take my word on it!"

Not everyone shared his optimism but some did, for the merger made sense. American's and Western's route systems dovetailed nicely. The unsurmountable problem was Western's recovery before the CAB got around to considering the proposed marriage. On July 28, 1972, the Board rejected the merger, and Nixon upheld the decision. Yet the 3–2 vote was closer than a lot of people expected and indicated that Spater's confidence was not that unreasonable.

Kirk Kerkorian's comment a few years later offered an interesting insight. "We felt the merger was good at the time," he said, "but we were wrong. American had many problems later that we hadn't foreseen."

Those problems, not all of which were of George Spater's own making, were enough to cost him his job.

The 747 was just one problem. It offered a chilling example of what can transpire in the four or five years that must elapse between the ordering of a new transport plane and its going into service.

American bought the biggest of all commercial airliners in 1966, a time when air traffic was booming. When it was introduced, March 1, 1970, the nation was in the midst of a recession and the airlines, so painfully sensitive to any economic downturn, were suffering from their worst overcapacity in history.

A remark C. R. Smith had made on the occasion of the 747's rollout ceremonies two years before graphically pointed up the impact of so huge and expensive a piece of equipment.

"Thirty years ago, in 1938, the market value of the airlines in the United States was on the order of $10 million," Smith said. "Today the market value of this single plane is twice that much."

Passengers loved the 747; unfortunately, there weren't enough passengers. A year after its introduction, with the 747 transcontinental flights running half full, Jerry Jacob, vice president of field marketing, got an idea.

He was in a bar one night, part of a crowd standing around a piano, and heard someone remark, "Wouldn't it be great to have a piano on an airplane?"

The next morning he called Tulsa and asked them to investigate the feasibility of putting a piano on a 747. Tulsa checked and found that Wurlitzer had a lightweight model with just the right stress. Jacob got permission to buy twenty of them at $2,000 apiece.

They were installed in the huge coach lounge American already had put into the 747 fleet, the first airline to utilize the cavernous cabin for such a purpose. It involved removing fifty seats, but load factors were depressed anyway. And the lounge turned out to be a traffic-generating gimmick that other 747 operators began imitating.

The piano bar was something extra, and its introduction, orchestrated by Jacob, was something special.

"I knew Frank Sinatra's son [Frank Sinatra, Jr.]," Jacob recounted, "and asked him if he'd be willing to give a performance on our 'Red Eye' out of Los Angeles. At the time I made the call, we had forty people booked for that flight. We made the announcement in Los Angeles at noon the day before; by the time the plane left, we had over 300 passengers on board, and there were people standing by, trying to get on.

"We spent $40,000 on those Wurlitzers, and they generated about $20 million in extra revenue during the six months we had them. We never paid any performer; they just got free transportation. Sometimes passengers themselves provided the entertainment. One trouble we didn't expect was that the lounges began attracting professional gamblers, who'd hustle passengers at the bar with blackjack games.

"There was some criticism about tearing out fifty coach seats, but before the lounges and pianos were installed, we were averaging only 120 passengers per 747 flight. We pulled them out when traffic started to upswing but they were life-savers while we had them."

The 747 and later the DC-10 were the first planes American ever bought with galleys that satisfied the stewardesses. Up to then, flight attendants had been consulted dutifully for their opinions, which were then largely ignored. Millie Alford remembered one aircraft—exactly which one escaped her memory—on which the baby-bottle coolers were installed between two ovens.

While engineers listened to stewardess recommendations, space and weight considerations took priority. On the 727, the galley proved to be too high for a 5'2" flight attendant and the shorter girls were complaining of backaches. Millie's solution was to change the height requirement for an applicant to five feet three inches. "It was cheaper to change the requirement than rebuild the galley," she explained.

With the new aircraft colors had come the first major change in stewardess uniforms: miniskirts.

They were first introduced in 1967, a radical departure from the traditional orchestrated by Walt Rauscher, who wanted something more modern and appropriate for the Astrojet motif and the forthcoming jumbos. American had always been one of the most conservative airlines when it came to stewardess uniforms. Basically, they remained unchanged from the late thirties well into the 1960s. The winter uniform was always a skirt and jacket in navy blue with a white blouse and overseas cap. Summer uniforms varied from brown to a light blue, but the only restyling every three or four years, was limited to lengthening or shortening skirts.

In 1963, American did away with the overseas cap in favor of a little pillbox hat, and also adopted a shorter, straighter jacket. There was something of a furor over giving up the overseas cap, and when miniskirts were announced, the airline braced for the worst. Rauscher's greatest fear was that C.R. would lead the protests. But Smith never objected, and with few exceptions, the girls accepted them with some excitement.

The background of the stewardess corps had been gradually changing anyway. In the forties and fifties, only a small percentage were college graduates; starting in the sixties, that percentage began to climb, until about 90 percent of the applicants now have college degrees.

Several attractive flight attendants were used to publicize the new miniskirts, but the one featured most often was Patti Poulsen, a blond beauty who was as photogenic as a sunrise over a mountain lake. She had previously won the title of the World's Most Beautiful Stewardess and played the role of a flight attendant in the 1970 smash movie hit *Airport*.

Eventually, DC-10 captains had to become reasonably photogenic themselves when American installed cockpit cameras so passengers could see takeoffs and landings on the cabin's wide screens. The camera was mounted just behind and slightly above the captain's seat, which led to some deeply resented orders from chief pilots to certain four-stripers: "Get your hair cut!"

The DC-10—it was now the "Luxury Liner" instead of Astrojet—went into service the first week in August 1971, between Chicago and Los Angeles, beating United's inaugural by twelve days. Frank Kolk's belief in the need for an airplane whose capacity fell somewhere between that of a 707 and 747 was vindicated in just this one key market where American was competing with TWA, United, and Continental. The 131-seat 707 had been too small and the huge 747 too large; the DC-10, with its initial configuration of 206 seats, was just right.

It would have had fewer seats except for a marketing decision to put the galleys in a lower-lobe belly section. Newt Wilson, who still headed Sky Chefs when Spater finalized the DC-10's cabin layout, fought long and hard against this arrangement but was overruled. The lower galleys required installation of a small elevator, which Wilson considered needlessly complicated and inefficient. He thought the way to increase seating capacity was to shrink the first-class section, rather than put the galleys out of sight.

No one heeded Wilson's advice on another matter: a food-loading vehicle for the wide-bodies. Sky Chefs already had developed a scissors-lift truck for the jets, a vehicle whose design was suggested by a company that built coal and dump trucks. The biggest Sky Chefs kitchen facilities were in Chicago, a two-story building the length of four football fields. The dishwashing equipment was on the second floor, and Wilson wanted a food vehicle that could load and unload at this level.

But Spater approved funding for development of a different loading system for the wide-bodies, again on marketing's recommendation, with Newton arguing in vain that the already existing scissor trucks were perfectly adequate. American spent a fortune on the new system, which proved so unreliable it was scrapped; the airline went back to the scissors.

Judging the Spater regime on the basis of random mistakes like the wrong food-loading trucks may seem unfair, but too many mistakes simply added up to unnecessary red ink at a time of depressed traffic, when an error in judgment couldn't be afforded. C. R. Smith, even before the jets came along, once remarked to a friend, "You know, the fun's gone out of this business. We used to make a mistake and it would cost us a couple of thousand bucks. Now we make one and it costs two million."

In 1969, the directors elevated Spater to board chairman as well as president. It could be argued that he wasn't a one-man airline—the only one pulling boners. True, but in holding those dual posts he had as much authority as C.R.; the difference was that he didn't use it to *lead*. And in this flaccid, floundering environment, at a difficult time when leadership was desperately needed, American began to sag.

In 1972, perhaps recognizing that he didn't have a firm handle on the airline's day-to-day operations, he became chairman and chief executive officer and asked the board to elect George Warde as president and chief operating officer. Warde had been named executive vice president and general manager a year earlier, at the same time Mullins joined Sadler as a co–vice chairman and Lloyd-Jones became a director.

Warde was well liked, but some officers thought Lloyd-Jones—another Bill Hogan in intelligence, but without Hogan's difficult personality—would have been a more logical choice. Mullins wasn't even in the running; his elevation to vice chairman in 1971 had been one of those boot-'em-upstairs promotions that smacked more of a demotion. Mullins resented it, too; the shift made Rauscher senior vice president of marketing, the one job at which Mullins was happiest. He left American shortly after Rauscher took over marketing, after working out a semi-retirement arrangement with Spater.

So Spater now had a new team. But it was one that would be faced with a sequence of events about to erupt in a scandal that would cost two officers their jobs and seriously hurt the airline's image.

20
Dark Days

Marion Sadler was president when it all started, early in 1966, with the hiring of a promotional expert who had been working for Pan Am.

He was Juan Homs, Jr., son of a wealthy Spanish family. Jack Mullins had gone to school with him, and when Homs expressed interest in joining American, Mullins asked Walt Rauscher to interview him.

"He came into my office," Rauscher related, "and the guy made a presentation that absolutely blew my socks off. I told Jack, 'This is a very talented man.' "

Mullins took the precaution of checking with Willis Lipscomb at Pan Am, for whom Homs had worked.

"He's no damned good," Lipscomb said. "I could tell you a few things about him."

"What kind of things?"

"Well, I don't want to get involved. Let's just say I don't think you should hire him."

In something of a quandary, Mullins and Rauscher consulted with Sadler about Lipscomb's negative report.

"I don't give a damn what Lipscomb said," Marion barked. "If Willis doesn't like him, he should tell us why. If you guys think he's good, let's hire him."

So Juan Homs became American's director of promotion. In that capacity, he was the one entrusted with implementing a new venture: the launching of an in-flight magazine late in 1966. Pan Am had started *Clipper Travel* in 1947, followed by United's *Mainliner* ten years later. American's would be the third. It began as a quarterly, the first two issues merely promotional vehicles for American. Then Homs changed the format to include a few articles of general interest, and by the time Spater became president, the magazine was being aimed at entertaining and educating passengers instead of just selling the airline.

It was called *American Way*. Homs, listed as its executive publisher, didn't actually edit the magazine. An outside vendor produced its publication under a contract Homs negotiated. The literature-loving Spater took a deep interest in *American Way* and insisted that its quality be improved, which led to the

407

vendor's hiring the magazine's first professional editor: Don Moffitt, a former *Wall Street Journal* correspondent, who took over in 1969.

There was no love lost between Spater and Homs, but their feud was confined solely to the magazine's contents. Spater used to send each issue back to Juan with corrections on language and punctuation. He wanted and didn't get more intellectual articles; Homs, somehow ignoring the fact that Spater was his boss, virtually ignored every suggestion and criticism. Yet Spater innocently trusted Homs's business judgment, as well he might. On the surface, whatever he negotiated with the magazine's vendor looked not only sound but reasonable.

This was true of other contracts Homs negotiated in directing American's promotional activities. Every project in which he was involved came in at or under budget, and he impressed everyone with his zeal for hard work. Rauscher, to whom Homs reported, said if he came in at 7 A.M., Juan's office lights would be on, and if he left at 8:30 at night, Homs would still be there.

But what no one realized was that Juan Homs was a master at squeezing kickbacks out of virtually every vendor he dealt with. In negotiating a contract, he would demand three things: absolute quality and on-time performance, an understanding that if a vendor failed to deliver as promised the contract would be canceled, and a percentage of the agreed-on amount to be paid Juan Homs. The kickback figure most frequently cited by vendors later was 5 percent.

How much Homs gained from this arrangement was never determined exactly, but American was paying the suppliers with whom Homs was involved some $2.3 million a year. Most of the kickbacks were channeled into two dummy corporations Homs established. But his whole elaborate structure of deception and greed collapsed when a vendor—reportedly one who refused to pay Homs—went straight to Spater, who ordered American's security and audit department to check out the vendor's story.

It was not only true, but the subsequent investigation uncovered another kickback involvement, though far less extensive. Melvin Fante, staff vice president for corporate design, admitted taking for his personal use supplies he had ordered ostensibly for several Admirals Clubs; chairs, lounges, and carpeting were the chief items. Fante also had received a discount on suits from Hart Schaffner & Marx, suppliers of American's stewardess uniforms. Fante wrote the airline a check for some $2,000 and resigned. Homs was fired, but made no restitution, and Spater, against the advice of several officers who preferred to let the matter drop quietly, then decided to go after him. He turned the affair over to the FBI and a U.S. Attorney. Spater would explain later that he had been impressed by a story in the *New York Times* in which that same U.S. Attorney, Whitney N. Seymour, Jr., had criticized businessmen for covering up white-collar crimes and not reporting them to authorities for prosecution.

But in turning the law loose on Juan Homs, Spater unwittingly set off a chain reaction of tragedy.

* * *

Walter V. Rauscher had come up the hard way. His father lost almost every-thing in the stock market and salvaged only enough to buy a couple of taxicabs, his sole means of making a living until he died. Walt had no college education, but he was smart and his advancement at American was steady. Shortly after the jets began operating, Rauscher spotted a curious discrepancy between confirmed bookings and actual load factors: the transcontinental flights out of Los Angeles and New York were sold out in advance, but they were departing with many empty seats.

Years before, he had noticed the same problem when he was a reservations supervisor in Rochester: the Convairs were booked full but leaving with plenty of unused space. It was the old no-show headache, again only on a large scale with the 707s, and Walt had an idea. He got American to deliberately oversell the late-afternoon flight to Los Angeles. If there was any overflow, these passengers would be put on a midnight DC-6 flight out of Idlewild, and to compensate for the inconvenience, they were treated to a fancy dinner at the airport's swank Golden Door restaurant. Even though the DC-6 took several more hours and had to stop in Chicago, American started getting letters of compliments from those who *didn't* get on the jet. With both New York and Los Angeles showing full advance 707 bookings, New York wound up carrying more passengers a month than Los Angeles.

For this, the first practice of intentional oversales to compensate for no-shows, Rauscher received the Award of Merit. Later, SABRE would accomplish this in a far more scientific manner, but in 1959 no one had thought of the idea.

Spater had informed both Rauscher and Mullins of Homs's suspected kick-backs, and they agreed a security investigation was warranted. It was at this point, shortly before Warde was made president, that Spater summoned Rauscher to a meeting in Washington at the Mayflower Hotel. Present were Spater, Warde, and Henry Golightly, a well-known management consultant.

Rauscher walked into the room and immediately noticed the absence of Jack Mullins.

"Isn't Jack going to be here?" he asked.

"No," Spater said. "And don't worry about it. Walter, you're going to be senior vice president of marketing, taking Jack's place. Warde will be president."

Rauscher was stunned. "What about Jack?"

"We haven't decided yet," Spater replied. "We'd like to do something for him."

Rauscher said, "I'd feel a lot more comfortable, Mr. Spater, if we could use him. He has a lot of talent that no one else in this room has, including myself."

"Well, I'd like to make him vice chairman," Spater said.

Rauscher left the room with his head spinning. "Here I was, a kid who had started as a res agent, and I was going to be a senior vice president of the company."

In July 1972, Spater told Warde and Rauscher, "I have information that this fellow Homs has been taking kickbacks. If he doesn't come in here and pay us back a quarter of a million dollars, I'll turn him over to the district attorney."

Confronted with this demand, Homs said, "Screw him. I'll take on Spater any day."

He was in no shape to take on Spater or anyone else. Questioned by the U.S. Attorney and a grand jury, Homs pleaded the Fifth Amendment and disappeared. Rauscher thought the *affaire Homs* was over and was sure of it when, in August, he said Warde told him Spater planned to leave the company the following February, moving Warde up to chairman and president, with Rauscher becoming executive vice president and general manager on an equal level with Donald Lloyd-Jones, who had been promoted to executive vice president a year earlier.

Then Warde added, according to Rauscher, "Within a year you'll be president."

Rauscher said Spater was present when Warde made that promise, and although Spater frankly admitted he preferred Lloyd-Jones as the next president, he also conceded that Warde felt more comfortable with Rauscher.

A few weeks later, Spater told an advisory committee meeting of top officers that he was going to ask every vice president to list any gifts they had received from Juan Homs.

"I know a number of people have gotten things from him," Spater added, "like booze and so forth. I'd like everyone here to list anything you've received worth more than a hundred dollars from *anybody*. I'm going to do the same thing myself. And I want you all to sign the form I've prepared."

At this stage of his life, Walt Rauscher had a $40,000 mortgage on his home, $6,000 in the bank, three sons in school, and his wife drove a VW. He had begun playing the stock market, needed extra funds, and had borrowed $14,000 from Juan Homs.

He listed that loan on Spater's questionnaire. He also wrote down that Homs had once made reservations for Walt and his family at a Hawaiian hotel and that when he tried to pay the bill, he was informed it already had been taken care of. Rauscher insisted on their accepting his check, but was told this was impossible because the payment already was in the computer.

The third and final item he listed was a favor Homs had done for Rauscher's wife. Her VW had been in an accident and Homs knew a Volkswagen dealer in New Jersey who loaned her a car while hers was being repaired.

Rauscher later would swear under oath that those three things constituted all Juan Homs had ever done for him. He put the list in an envelope and sent it to Donald Lloyd-Jones's office to be placed in a safe, along with the other vice presidents' questionnaires. When he returned home that same night, one of his sons told him, "Dad, George Spater called and he seemed really upset."

Rauscher, who thought there must have been a crash, phoned Spater, and his son had been right.

"Walter, a terrible thing has happened. Your paper has been turned over to the U.S. Attorney."

"My paper? Why my paper?"

"All I can tell you is one thing. Don't panic, and don't worry about your job. No matter what happens, the company will buy you a travel agency. We'll take care of you."

Rauscher exploded. "George Spater, I don't want a goddamned travel agency! I want my job! I'll be in the first thing in the morning and you'd better find out who gave my paper to the U.S. Attorney." (If Spater knew, he never told Rauscher.)

After a sleepless night, he arrived at 633 Third Avenue at 7:30 A.M. and found Spater, Warde, and director Manly Fleischmann waiting for him. It was Fleischmann who began the interrogation.

"You recognize that you had these infamous dealings with Juan Homs?"

Rauscher blew up again. "Oh, suddenly the dealings I had with Juan are infamous, but the dealings others had with him are not."

Fleischmann, one of the most respected and influential board members, said coldly, "I don't know about the others. I just know we have this paper that you signed. I think you'd better see a lawyer."

That was the start of Walter Rauscher's nightmare. Both he and Homs were indicted by a grand jury on charges of receiving illegal kickbacks as part of a conspiracy. In the indictment, the $14,000 loan was described as a kickback. Only Rauscher was tried. Homs had fled the country before the indictment was handed down.

At the trial, the judge asked Rauscher, "Did you get money from Mr. Homs?"

"Yes, I did, Your Honor."

"You say it was a loan. The prosecutor says it was a kickback."

"The prosecutor is wrong. It was not a kickback."

"Well, it's a matter of judgment, Mr. Rauscher. In these times"—he was referring to the current Watergate scandal—"we have to be certain of what we're doing. You were too close to this man. You were there, and if you borrowed money from him you received the fruits of the crime."

On advice of counsel, Rauscher pleaded guilty. His lawyer told him, "You can't afford to fight them. In this Watergate environment, they'll crucify you."

He was sentenced to thirty days but was paroled after serving fifteen days at a minimum security work farm. While the light sentence didn't erase the stigma, he was encouraged by an unexpected development—he received a letter postmarked Majorca, Spain, from Homs, whose wealthy Spanish parents lived on that island.

"I understand a lot of things are going on there," Homs wrote. "I want you to know I'm coming back to New York because I can't stand it over here. I'm going to face the music. But I'm going to have to ask you to pay me back the money you borrowed from me because if I come back I'll need it."

. Rauscher immediately wrote him that if he returned, he would arrange immediate repayment. He showed Juan's letter to his lawyer. It was too late to change the outcome of the trial, but unquestionably the letter influenced the presiding judge to recommend a presidential pardon, which Jimmy Carter issued shortly after he took office. And Juan Homs, as far as anyone knows, never did return.

It took Rauscher twelve years to pay off his legal fees. But he was far from a ruined man. Even before the pardon, the Plaza Hotel hired him for some consultant work. Then Pan Am gave him a retainer fee for advising them on computer problems, and three months later named him a vice president. ("The day I was told, I sat down and sobbed.")

He found out later that there was some opposition at the board meeting when he was nominated. One director questioned his background—"I, uh, understand he had a problem," was the way he put it.

Another director happened to be a man who had been an American Airlines official for many years. He rose and for fifteen minutes defended Rauscher as a man of ability and integrity. Walt couldn't believe it when he heard his name. It was Bill Hogan.

Walt stayed with Pan Am for five years and left to become president of the American Society of Travel Agents. Lifetime passes at Pan Am weren't awarded to officers who had served less than ten years, but the vice president of personnel told him, "You've done more for this airline in five years than some of our guys have done in twenty," and gave him the pass.

While at Pan Am, Rauscher was instrumental in arranging a deal whereby the airline was able to link its own computer system to SABRE's greater capabilities. Whatever sins he committed—and the internal investigation uncovered discrepancies in certain invoices that had no connection with Homs—have long since been forgiven and forgotten.

Gene Overbeck's summation of the whole affair is penetrating and fair:

"Spater was guilty of bad judgment. He should have fired Homs and let the matter go at that. By referring it to the U.S. Attorney's office, the episode got blown all out of proportion and brought a great deal of unfavorable publicity to the company. Employee morale was already low, and the Homs affair lowered it another notch.

"As in the case of Homs, it was poor judgment on the company's part to permit the Rauscher affair to be referred to the U.S. Attorney's office, but the board would have to be faulted here. It's probably fair to say that Walter Rauscher was not a crook at heart, but he used such poor judgment that he had no defense when he was charged as a crook."

Spater, in a sense, was as much a victim as Rauscher. The scandal broke at a time when Spater was trapped by adversities that couldn't be fought with intellectual brilliance. He had inherited a mantle of leadership that was more like a choking cloak dropped over his head. He commanded an embattled army that in military terms considered him an aloof, desk-bound general who had never heard the sound of a real war.

"I've had enough of the airline business," he had remarked to Warde and Rauscher before Juan Homs's house of cards collapsed. And under the pressures of a public scandal, added to the difficulties the airline already was having, it was no wonder Spater couldn't keep the eagle's feathers from molting, nor himself from making more mistakes.

He was erroneously, perhaps viciously, informed that Jack Mullins had been a kickback recipient. Instead of confronting Mullins directly with this unsubstantiated accusation, Spater asked Manly Fleischmann to investigate. Before the Buffalo attorney could clear Mullins, the *Wall Street Journal* published a story saying that Mullins was under suspicion for buying a car and carpeting his home with company funds. Horrified, Spater got the *Journal* to print his fervent denial that Mullins was in any way involved.

But the damage was done, not only to Mullins's reputation but to employee morale, which already had sagged with the Homs/Fante/Rauscher publicity. Denials are never read as avidly as the original charges, and the average employee was getting the impression that too many officials had been stealing everything in sight that was smaller than a 747. They had seen fellow workers furloughed, labor relations deteriorate, a succession of management mistakes, a highly touted merger go down the drain, millions spent on new planes whose outstanding feature was their consistently empty seats, and expensively promoted new international routes with no traffic potential. And they generally reacted in a way that came only too naturally: indifference, sloppy performance, and poor attitude. Management had lost their respect, and they had lost their pride.

By January 1973, service had deteriorated seriously and was further damaged by labor troubles. Hundreds of flights in late December had been canceled by a combination of weather and a pilots' slowdown over dragging contract negotiations. No airline can do anything about snowstorms, but the pilots' subtle sabotage tactics were evidence of employee cynicism that had turned into militancy.

Deliberate slowdowns lasting several weeks—some flights were delayed because of supposed dirty cockpit windshields—resulted in missed connections, mangled schedules, mislaid luggage, extra fuel costs, and angry passengers. And while it could be argued that no pilot was morally justified in hurting not only his own company with phony flight delays but passengers as well, the Allied Pilots Association was reacting to Spater's indecision and his inability to communicate.

Nick O'Connell, who led American's cockpit crews out of ALPA and into their own union, said something long after the slowdown that he couldn't say while Spater headed the company. "We never had the rapport with him that we did with his predecessors," he explained. "Pilots spend much of their lives making split-second decisions, and they don't understand an operation that has to wait for a committee to decide anything."

American's image as a professionally run carrier, literally "the business-man's airline," had been badly damaged and nearly destroyed. And the causal factors went far beyond the too-pat excuse of recession and overcapacity.

SABRE, the pride and joy of men like Sadler, had been allowed to stagnate even while United was impressing the whole industry with its new APOLLO system.

In trying to cut costs, an indiscriminate furloughing ax had cut into American's greatest strength, customer service. The majority of dismissed workers were reservations agents, baggage handlers, and airport counter personnel. Cuts also were made in another area of traditional strength, the field organization, so carefully erected and vastly admired by other airlines for its ability to operate independently and efficiently no matter how badly headquarters was floundering. Even food service was cut.

Another economy move was to slash schedules in many short-haul markets. It saved money but demolished Mel Brenner's system of backup traffic support, the interconnecting flow of short-haul traffic into the long-haul flights. And Brenner wasn't around to fight with Spater over this ill-conceived strategy; he left American in 1969 to become vice president of scheduling at TWA.

The South Pacific awards were a collective disaster. Even Secor Browne, chairman of the CAB when the final Transpacific Case decision was handed down, told Spater privately, "You're crazy to try to operate the routes. You'll never make any money, and you're going to be pouring it down a rathole. Eventually you'll have to walk away from it."

Secor Browne was one of the exceptions to the CAB's reputation for being overpopulated by members who knew almost nothing about the airline business. But Spater didn't listen to him. Although he himself had once called the Transpacific decision "nutty," he spent a small fortune trying to develop a market that wasn't there. Said one former AA official:

"George was so determined to stick his finger into the Pacific, even without Tokyo, that he wasn't emotionally able to stand back and make a coldly calculated business decision to dump the damned thing."

By the time American followed Browne's ignored advice—the South Pacific routes eventually were traded to Pan Am in exchange for some Caribbean destinations—it was far too late to recoup what had been lost.

Spater did choose a new editor to head *American Way.* Glen Walker was a former newspaperman who was then editing *Flagship News.* What may have attracted Spater to Walker was the fact that Glen was going to law school at night. He also had a reputation for honesty and directness that was to serve the magazine and the airline well. When Spater asked him to take over *American Way,* Walker suggested that it might be better to publish it "in-house" instead of relying on outside personnel. It was a pretty risky and tenuous proposal; East-West Network, the biggest publisher of in-flight magazines, had offered to produce *American Way* at no cost to the airline, whose compensation would be a percentage of the advertising revenues and a specified amount of advertising space in each issue. But Walker, while admitting the advantages to this arrangement, thought that potentially American would be better off publishing its own magazine.

"The only advantages of hiring a staff and doing the book in-house," he recalled, "were (1) we maintained control of the contents and (2) if the darn thing ever made a profit, the profit would be American's. Potential profit wasn't much of an argument, however, because it seemed then an unlikely dream. Yet I had another motive for doing the magazine in-house. I wanted to be editor, not caretaker for an outside company. Mr. Spater liked the idea of American having control, and I persuaded myself that if we failed as an in-house operation, we could always farm the book out."

Walker scrambled to organize a staff so the magazine, then carrying between eight and ten pages of advertising per issue, could be published without a break. Spater, in probably what was his happiest job in his entire American career, served as one of two editorial consultants; the other was Norman Cousins, editor of *Saturday Review.*

Walker left *American Way* in 1974 to join AA's legal staff and rose to the post of associate general counsel, where one of his duties was to advise the magazine on legal matters. But he had established the groundwork for one of the most successful airline publications in the world, and the only one published by the carrier itself.

Its growth was spectacular. *American Way* hit 100 pages in 1977 and was up to 200 pages by 1983. Its $10 million in advertising revenues in 1984 equaled American's entire 1939 passenger revenues. Its current editor and publisher, Walter Damtoft, emphasized that the magazine had never strayed from Walker's original stated objective: "To produce an outstanding magazine for passengers that promotes American by its quality rather than by puffery."

Spater's major fruit-bearing move was to hire away from a department store American's future leader. The department store background was grossly misleading; Bob Crandall had been a finance and data processing specialist at Hallmark Cards and TWA before joining Bloomingdale's as senior vice president and treasurer. Spater offered Crandall the post of senior vice president of finance in April 1973. But he was joining an airline in serious trouble.

Spater remained optimistic. In May he told the annual shareholders' meeting, "The worst is over," but he was whistling by his own graveyard. Two months later, Spater had the courage to admit voluntarily that American Airlines officials had contributed $75,000 to President Nixon's re-election campaign and that some of the money came from corporate funds in possible violation of campaign financing laws.

Spater manfully assumed full responsibility for any illegal contributions. He was the first corporate executive to come forth with such a confession, and Watergate investigators praised him for doing so. But his admission was just another punch at the airline's morale, and spelled the end of his career at American. He wasn't supposed to retire until February 1974, but he was willing, and the directors were in agreement, to leave anytime they found a new chairman.

He resigned officially September 18, 1973, and eventually went to England, where he lived the kind of academic life he really preferred. He wrote two books, the first a study of authors Leonard and Virginia Wolff, a widely praised work co-authored by Ian Parsons, and then a two-volume biography of William Cobbett, the muckracking British journalist of the eighteenth century. This, too, received excellent reviews. When he wasn't in England doing literary research, Spater lived in a small house in rural Vermont. His across-the-street neighbor was Eddie Rickenbacker's son.

Spater died June 14, 1984, in that Vermont farmhouse where he had found so much peace. He is remembered today as a gentle man who valiantly tried to do a job for which he was unqualified in temperament and style. And even before he left America, the rumors already were circulating about his successor: "Did you hear C.R.'s coming back?"

The rumors were true.

It wasn't in C.R.'s nature to stay inactive, but when he decided to retire he had no inkling he was going to become one of the people he usually referred to as "those goddamned bureaucrats in Washington."

He hadn't even had time to enjoy his supposed life of leisure. Just before he turned the airline over to George Spater, he had lunch with Jerry Jacob at the Cloud Club.

"We've got to get through early," he remarked to Jerry. "I'm going down to Washington this afternoon to see the President."

"Oh? That's a great honor."

"Honor?" Smith growled. "That goddamned Lyndon Johnson. I've known him for twenty-five years and he was born a hundred years too late. He should have been a bank robber. Johnson wants me to be Secretary of Commerce. I wouldn't get involved with a damned government job down there."

That weekend, the White House announced that C.R. had accepted Johnson's offer to join his cabinet. Monday morning, Jacob ran up to see him.

"What happened?" Jerry wanted to know.

"Well, I walked into that big office of his, with the American flag on one side of his desk and the Presidential flag on the other, and he says to me, 'Mr. Smith, your country needs you!' What the hell, Jerry, it was too goddamned hard to turn him down."

He hated every minute of the nine months and twenty days he served as a federal official. They gave him an office that Jacob said was so big "you could have played tennis in it." On his first day as Secretary of Commerce, he discovered he had been assigned four secretaries.

"What the hell am I going to do with four secretaries?" he demanded of the aide who was showing him his new quarters.

"Well, sir, one will be your personal secretary—she'll handle all your appointments. The second lady answers your phone. The third's for your correspondence, and the fourth is a backup secretary."

"Get rid of 'em," C.R. ordered.

"We can't do that, Mr. Secretary. They're civil servants."

"I don't give a damn who they are. I don't need four secretaries. Get 'em out of here."

"Impossible, sir. They'll file a grievance. They have to sit here as long as you're Secretary of Commerce. All four of them."

Gene Overbeck dropped in to say hello one day, and while he was there, Smith got a call from the White House.

"The President would like you to call him," he was informed.

"Look, sweetheart," C.R. informed *her,* "if the President wants to talk to me, he knows goddamned well where to find me."

Jim Aston visited him and commented on the size of that office. C.R. confided he had tried to get a smaller one. "Everybody told me it couldn't be done," he groused. "One guy said I'd be tampering with a national monument."

It was Aston who was largely responsible for C.R.'s return. After Johnson left office, Smith became a limited partner in the investment firm of Lazard Frères & Co. and commuted between Washington and New York. He obviously knew things were not going well at American but he refrained from any interference. To C.R., the airline was a closed chapter in his life. But Aston opened the book again.

American's directors in the summer of 1973 had instructed the board's executive committee to find Spater's successor. The committee, composed of Aston, Boston attorney Francis Hooks Burr, Charles Fisher III of the National Bank of Detroit, and Manly Fleischmann, was in something of a bind. They wanted to find the best man possible but they really didn't have sufficient time for the task. Yet they all agreed something had to be done soon; the airline was in a shambles. The board was deeply concerned over morale problems and a disastrous financial showing over the past three years. American had lost $26.4 million in 1970, made extremely small profits in the next two years, and in 1973 was running a huge deficit; the losses that year would total $48 million.

The committee met in New York one day early in September for breakfast. Those present to this day cannot recall whether it was at the Harvard Club or Lynx Club. They had met several times before to discuss possible candidates, with no success. Prospects weren't interested or were considered inadequate, and time was running out.

Aston suddenly blurted, "Maybe we should bring C.R. back."

There were immediate nods of approval, but someone wondered, "You don't think he'd come back, do you?"

"I think it's certainly worth trying," Aston said. "He can hold the airline together until we find the right man to replace him."

"Do you want to call him?" Burr asked.

"Sure I'll call him," Aston replied. Burr was staying at the club, and Aston went to his room, from where he phoned Smith at his Washington apartment.

C.R.'s first reaction: "Are you out of your goddamned mind?"

"Now, wait a minute, C.R.," Aston pleaded. "We need you. American's your baby and it's in trouble. We all want you to come back. You can pull this thing together, and we'll get busy finding you a successor."

"Let me think about it," Smith allowed. "Call me back in thirty minutes."

Aston did. C.R. said, "Okay, I'll do it for ninety days."

"That's not acceptable. I don't know if we can find anybody in ninety days."

"All right, I'll give you six months."

"That's okay for starters," Aston said. He went down to inform the others, and all four, the time of day notwithstanding, had a drink to celebrate.

Smith attached one condition to his acceptance: he refused to accept one cent of compensation. As he told Aston later, "Hell, I've already got enough money." The only thing he requested was the use of a car and a chauffeur, because he hated to drive. Jim Aston wasn't surprised when Smith specified no salary. "Very few people knew it," Aston said, "but C.R. never drew a nickel from Uncle Sam either in the Air Transport Command or when he was Secretary of Commerce."

Smith took over as if he had been away on vacation. Even the mere announcement of his return seemed to galvanize the whole airline. One typical incident: Gayle Williams heard the rumors and called Captain Ralph Long, with whom she had worked on the Ford trimotor promotion.

"What would you say if you knew C.R. was coming back?" she asked.

"It would be the greatest news anyone could give me," Long replied.

Flagship News devoted almost an entire issue to the unexpected development. If its headlines were of the size that would have been assigned to the Second Coming, it was understandable. "C.R.'s back" had the impact of a resurrection.

He wrought no overnight miracles, or any miracles, for that matter. He served only for the six months he had promised. But he accomplished what the directors wanted—the improved morale glued the airline back together and made it easier for the man who would succeed him.

He had great trust in Jerry Jacob; it was almost as though he saw in the son of C. W. Jacob the reincarnation of his old confidant. On his first day back, Smith called Jerry in, ordered, "Close the door," and said, "I want a rundown on all the new guys around here." Another man he relied on for personnel briefings was Overbeck.

He made relatively few changes during his short tenure. One casualty was John Andersen, whom Spater had brought in from Eastern to replace Rauscher as senior vice president of marketing. Andersen was experienced and capable, but making a favorable impression during the final Spater years was like trying to bail out the *Titanic* with a pail. Warde left, too; the directors never seriously considered him as a candidate for succession, although Warde felt he never had a chance to show what he could do. His major flaw was a trait he shared with Spater, according to those who worked with him: he liked to govern by committee.

Crandall, who had never met C.R. before, got a firsthand look at how the old man operated. Their first real contact involved the previously mentioned route swap with Pan Am, in which American traded its South Pacific authority for several Caribbean islands. Smith had told Crandall, "Go make a deal."

"We had done a foot-high study," Crandall recounted, "and C.R. didn't look at it for more than five minutes. He asked for the highlights, thought for a moment or so, then says, 'It looks okay to me,' picks up a phone and calls Bill Seawell" (then president of Pan Am). " 'We'll be over to your office in five minutes,' he tells Seawell. We made the swap that same day."

C.R. stayed on as chairman after his successor was named, but only for a very brief time. On his last day, Jerry Jacob happened to get into the same elevator with him. Smith was heading back to the Waldorf, where he had been staying for his six-month tour of duty.

"Well, I hope you're going to at least stay on the board," Jacob said.

"No, I'm not going to. Matter of fact, when I walk out that door today, I'm not ever coming back to this building again."

Jacob was surprised and a little shocked. "Why would you want to do that?"

"Well, if I start coming over here, and you guys ask my opinion, you have to remember I'm still thinking with a DC-6 mind and this business has changed. Yet if you don't take my advice, I'll get upset."

He looked at Jacob, a wry little smile on his lips. "You know, Jerry, an old man should know when to quit. And that's why I'm never coming back."

He never did.

21
Will the Real C. R. Smith Please Stand Up?

He had earned his exalted niche in air transportation history. Of all his pioneering peers, only United's Pat Patterson, his most respected rival and good friend, belonged on the same level as this legitimate aviation giant.

The names of other greats come to mind: Pan Am's Juan Trippe, with his accomplishments in the development of international air travel and willingness to gamble on new aircraft technology; Delta's C. E. Woolman, who turned a crop-dusting midget of a company into one of the world's best-run airlines; Continental's Bob Six, the courageous challenger of competitors who dwarfed Continental in everything but imagination and style; and Eastern's Eddie Rickenbacker, personification of the American Dream and champion of *laissez faire* in an industry whose very roots had been sown and watered by government largesse.

But they all had something in common that did not apply to either Smith or Patterson. Each won fame by what he did for his own airline; C.R. and Pat, as competitive as anyone else, were *industry*-minded, sensitive to the public's impression of overall responsibility and reputation. More than once, these two dragged the rest of the carriers along by their figurative ears, often screaming and kicking, because both recognized that some problems affected everybody. And the leadership they gave American and United simply permeated the entire spectrum of air transportation.

Smith and Patterson shared one essential quality: integrity. Yet, of the two, C.R. may well rank higher in terms of total accomplishments, if only for that gambler's instinct of his. He took chances that the cautious Patterson usually avoided. Some failed, but his batting average was awesome.

Marv Whitlock, who served under both men, compared them in these words:

"C.R. was never really close to anyone personally, but I've never known a man with more of an aura of leadership. People would follow him in whatever direction he instinctively chose. Pat was a leader, too, but he was the kind of guy who'd read a contract over four or five times and then think it over for another five days."

C.R. made a fine art out of calculated risk, and it was something that usually kept United and everyone else on the defensive. Patterson himself once said of Smith:

"I believe everything C.R. says. It's what he doesn't say that worries me."

The most accurate portrait of Cyrus Rowlett Smith has to be painted in the colors of the stories told about him. And they form the picture of a surprisingly complex man whose personality facets often were contradictory.

His shyness, for example, unusual in such a dominant person of strong convictions. Yet shyness is the one quality most frequently mentioned by those who knew him best. It may explain his reputation for brusqueness that made some think he was rude. If you asked C.R. a question, especially something personal, the chances were excellent that you'd get a one-word answer; you were lucky if he uttered three, and any wordage beyond five was considered an oration. A reporter once asked him to describe his mother.

"I liked her," C.R. replied.

Jim Bass, American's long-time chief official in Washington before retirement, visited Smith a few years ago and brought his wife along. To make conversation, she mentioned hearing that C.R. had two fine grandchildren and asked, "What do you think of them?"

"Noisy," he growled.

In truth, he always seemed a little uncomfortable around children. But in his later years, he became closer to his son Doug. The boy was big and heavy-set like his father. When he reached his teens, he worked summers for American in Dallas as an office boy and "gofer" for Tull Rea, then the local operations manager. Doug had no interest in making the airlines his career, however, and became a practicing lawyer in Annapolis, Maryland. Ironically, of all the professions he chose it was the one for which his father had the least respect. According to Malcolm MacIntyre, C.R. seldom uttered the word "lawyers" without prefacing it with "those goddamned."

He loved his brothers, but was never particularly close to them. Burck, who retired in Los Angeles, spent most of his career with the airline on the West Coast, far from corporate headquarters. Bill Smith, regarded as a very imaginative advertising man, had more frequent contact with C.R. than Burck. Bill was an amateur historian and was said to have been the family's intellectual.

In one respect, Smith's shyness was misleading. He liked being around people; he simply didn't say much and he was far more at ease sharing with others his two favorite pastimes, trout fishing and poker. At both he was expert.

Marv Whitlock, not bad with a rod and reel himself, said Smith was "the best fly man I ever saw, and strictly a freshwater trout devotee, although he did some deep-sea fishing at times."

Whitlock was with him on a fishing trip and shook his head in admiration at C.R.'s skill. "I'll bet you could hit a teacup at fifty feet, C.R.," Marv declared.

Smith grinned. "Well . . . a hat, maybe."

"C.R. is the only man I've ever known who completely separated business from personal," Whitlock observed. "He could fire you one day and call you the next to ask if you'd go fishing with him. Then he'd be amazed if you said no."

Smith used to give away expensive flyrods to his friends, a gesture not always appreciated by those grateful for the thought but who didn't even fish. It was a mystery to C.R. why everyone didn't love the sport. He asked one vice president what he was going to do when he retired.

"Damned if I know, C.R. I've got another twenty years to go and I'm not even thinking about it."

Smith snorted. "Well, you'd better start thinking. If you don't fish, there's nothing else to do."

Fishing rods weren't the only things he gave away. Some of his gifts were so valuable, the recipients were embarrassed. Jerry Jacob dropped in at his apartment a few years ago and after a pleasant chat was about to leave when Smith asked, "By the way, you still doing any hunting?"

"Not much, Mr. C.R."

"See that gun over there, in the case?"

"Yes, sir."

"Well, take it with you."

Jacob looked at the weapon, which appeared to be a pretty good shotgun. He hesitated. "I don't think I could . . ."

"Hell, Jerry, go ahead and take it. I've got more goddamned guns around here than I know what to do with."

Jacob kept the gun around his house for several months, and then on impulse took it to a gunshop. He asked the owner, "Is this a good shotgun?"

The owner examined it carefully. "I'll give you ten thousand for it."

It is impossible to put a dollar value on the oil paintings C.R. gave away through the years. He was a true connoisseur and an astute judge of a work of art's potential worth. Smith for years was very close to Father Theodore Hesburgh of Notre Dame University—they were poker-playing buddies—and gave the school a Western oil by Charles Russell. He had paid $1,000 for it sometime in the thirties and when he donated it to Notre Dame, the painting was valued at $50,000. In a letter C.R. wrote to Jim Bass in 1979, C.R. recalled making the gift and added:

"Saw Father Hesburgh some days ago and he told me he had been offered $450,000 for it plus a gift of $200,000."

A few years after he bought the Russell, he had a chance to pick up a Remington oil for $8,500 but didn't have the money. He mentioned to Bass once that the same painting is now worth more than $1 million. "Should have bought more and kept 'em," he grumbled.

Most of his seascape collection went to various Admirals Clubs; the University of Texas has a number of Western oils C.R. gave the school. American also gave Notre Dame a $250,000 professorship endowment for the school's College of Business Administration, the C.R. Smith Chair. Its first holder, Professor Lee Tavis, wanted to write a book emphasizing C.R.'s approach to management, but it would have involved lengthy taped interviews and Smith discouraged him.

C.R. never expressed much interest in being immortalized in print, and that was one of the curious contradictions in his personality. He had the large ego of a natural leader, yet essentially he was modest to the point of humbleness. Jim Bass used to invite him to the annual Wright Brothers dinner in Washington, the feature being the presentation of the Wright Brothers Trophy to some outstanding aviation figure. Except for the time C.R. received the honor himself, he refused the dinner committee's yearly invitation to sit at the head table.

When he traveled, he seldom spent company money on a fancy hotel suite, and unless he was staying more than one or two nights, he preferred a single room. Nor did he use limousines frequently; on most occasions, taxis were good enough.

He was on a 707 flight, sitting in first class, and decided to walk back to the coach section to chat with the stewardesses. He spotted a young officer he had known in ATC and insisted on moving him up to first class. The only available first-class seat was Smith's; he finished the trip in coach.

If C.R. was on a Christmas Eve flight to New York and the crew was non–New York based, he would invite the whole bunch to his apartment for dinner. And this didn't happen just on Christmas Eve—he did it on any special occasion when a crew was away from home.

Many times he flew on a space-available pass and used his positive space pass only when it was absolutely essential for him to be at a certain place by a specific time. Dixon Speas ran into him one afternoon at Washington National and was startled to see Smith waiting in a long standby line.

"What the hell are you doing here?" Speas asked.

"Flight's booked full."

"My God, you're the president of the airline," Speas reminded him.

C.R. nodded in the direction of the boarding passengers. "They're paying customers," he said softly.

Like so many of his tough-outside, soft-inside ilk, he tried to hide deeds of kindness, compassion, and generosity, and many of those he aided never knew where the help came from. He was riding in a cab with Marv Whitlock on the way to Los Angeles International and happened to mention an old-time American mechanic he was fond of.

"How is old Joe so-and-so?" he asked Whitlock.

"He's had some problems lately, C.R. His wife has been ill."

They were at the airport and Smith started to get out of the cab but paused, reached in his pocket, and from a thick wad peeled off a $100 bill.

"Whit, when you get back to Tulsa give him this—only don't let him know where it came from."

C.R. always carried large-denomination bills with him, and for only one reason: just in case the impulse struck him him to show some employee he cared. One could buy a new car with the total amount of money he slipped to stewardesses he thought had worked an exceptionally good trip. He was often seen getting off flights carrying a stewardess's suitcase, which was no surprise because the soft spot he had in his heart for the girls was melon-sized.

C.R. was on a DC-7 flight and went to the galley for a glass of water. The galley curtain was closed and Smith poked his head in, just in time to catch the two stewardesses transferring whiskey from an aircraft liquor bottle into their own flasks. They knew who he was, and turned white.

"Girls," he said sternly, "if you don't have the money to buy your own liquor, here"—and he handed them a $50 bill with one final admonition: "And if you ever need more, write me a letter, because I don't want you stealing."

He professed to be about as sentimental as a Gestapo agent, but this was pure sham. He came into an Admirals Club just before Christmas, accompanied by a large group of friends. They were having drinks when the skipper came over to tell him his flight was on time. He pulled a $100 bill out of his pocket and handed it to her.

"This is for last night," he said in a voice that could be heard throughout the club. Amid the noise of his friends laughing, he leaned toward the blushing skipper and whispered, "Merry Christmas, dear."

All women were called "dear" except for stewardesses; they were always "ladies" or "girls." He referred to any man he liked or respected as "a good man"; if he was asked about someone he didn't like, the answer would be a grunt. He never used profanity in front of women, although he had a four-letter vocabulary that could fry eggs.

He somehow found out that a stewardess named Norma Pugh always sent her salary check home and lived frugally on her expense money. She was on his flight one day and when he deplaned, he handed her one of those century notes and murmured, "Spend it on yourself."

His favorite dining spot in New York was the 21 Club and he had a lot of friends on the restaurant staff. One Christmas Smith decided to do something special for them and hit on the idea of presenting them with title to some land he owned near Phoenix. According to Joe Harty, who was in New York at the time, he gave twenty-one people 100 acres each. They were all dyed-in-the-wool New Yorkers who considered anything west of Ohio Indian Territory. The general reaction to the gift was, "What in the hell am I going to do with 100 acres of desert?"

With one exception, they sold their property as fast as they could. The exception was the maitre d', an imposing, gray-haired man who seemed to remember the name and face of every regular customer. He hung onto his parcel. Some years later, he told Harty: "C.R. made me a millionaire."

When the board held a meeting in Las Vegas one year, Smith insisted that the directors bring their spouses. Hooks Burr and his wife had just gotten to their hotel room when a bellhop knocked on the door. He was holding a bag with a hundred silver dollars.

"Is Mrs. Burr here?" he asked.

Burr nodded. The bellboy handed him the sack.

"I've been told by Mr. Smith I have to deliver it to her and not to you."
Burr found out later that each director's wife had received a similar sack.

C.R.'s generous gestures were not confined to materialistic items. When
MGM's board deposed Louis B. Mayer as studio chief, only the still-loyal
Howard Strickling of publicity was at the Los Angeles airport to see Mayer
and his wife off on their way to seclusion in Miami. But they boarded an
American plane on which they were the sole passengers—C.R. had put the
aircraft at their disposal the minute he heard Mayer had been ousted and was
leaving California. Smith, who remembered what *Three Guys Named Mike*
had done for the airline, felt it was the one last favor he could do for the
crushed, heartsick tycoon.

C.R. was not noted for a sense of humor, but it wasn't because he lacked
one. It often was sly and subtle, like the note he once sent to Larry Fritz, vice
president of operations. Fritz went into a panic anytime he had to authorize
an expenditure over a certain amount and would sit on a project for weeks,
agonizing over the decision. His procrastination reached Smith's ears and
produced one of those memos, as follows:

"I once knew a very fine poker player whose choking price was a healthy
$5,000. The game's the same—only the numbers are different."

In the DC-3 days, C.R. sent Bob Griffith to Douglas, Arizona, to shut down
American's station there because of low traffic. Griffith flew all day Saturday,
making five stops between New York and Douglas, and went to bed as soon
as he arrived. The next day he read in the local newspaper that American's
office had burned down during the night.

Griffith took the first plane back to New York and, on Monday, told Smith
what had happened.

"You sure as hell are a literal-minded bastard," Smith remarked.

The first time Mack Palmer met C.R. was the occasion of the start of jet
service out of Tulsa. It was raining hard, and when Palmer was introduced to
Smith, Mack remarked, "You know, Mr. C.R., I'm part Cherokee and we
Indians can control the weather, so don't worry about this rain—I'll take care
of it at the right moment."

The 707 was ready to depart and the rain was coming down harder. C.R.
nudged Palmer.

"Look like I'm gonna have to get me another Indian," he murmured.

Jim Aston, long-time American director and close friend, always thought
Smith's lack of loquaciousness was as much an indication of strength as
shyness. Said Aston:

"In my opinion, C.R. was the most organized person I've ever known from
the standpoint of utilization of time. At a board meeting, he was just like he
was in a one-on-one situation: a man of few words and fast action. I never had
an appointment with him when I had to wait more than ten minutes. Hell, he
had so much charisma he didn't have to say much. Everyone on the airline
loved him. He'd walk into a hangar or an airplane and it was like giving people
a shot of adrenalin. 'There's C.R.,' somebody'd say, and faces would light up."

Aston was a young Air Force officer and worked for Smith in ATC. He became probably the only associate in Smith's life who didn't call him "C.R." or "Mr. C.R."—it was usually "General."

At ATA meetings, C.R. commanded the same respect from his peers as from his subordinates at American, but he didn't always return that respect in the same proportions. He considered Rickenbacker's policies antediluvian, and he was a little contemptuous of some of Patterson's decisions at UAL, although he never bad-mouthed Pat publicly and rarely in private. He had deep reservations about dealing with Trippe, who was as indirect as Smith was direct. Trippe once called Willis Player and asked him to arrange a meeting with C.R., and Player informed his boss.

"Why the hell couldn't he ask me himself," Smith grumbled.

"To tell you the truth, C.R., I think he's a little afraid of you."

Smith laughed. "You know, Will, that may be reciprocal."

Of all C.R.'s contemporaries, only Delta's Woolman was ever known to have gotten his goat. Many years ago, Smith called him and suggested they get together and discuss a possible American-Delta merger.

"I don't know, C.R.," Woolman chuckled. "I think American's too big for us to take it over."

Smith slammed down the phone, and that was the end of the merger overture.

It cannot be said that his competitors loved him—he was too tough an opponent. But at American, he had almost a demi-god image and memories of him are spoken in terms of respect bordering on awe.

Carlene Roberts had this to say about the man who had given her a stature no woman had ever before achieved in the industry:

"He scared some people, but his very bluntness and candor let you know where he stood on any issue. He respected those who had knowledge and used it to stand up to him. I know small talk embarrassed him, yet there was an exception to this. He was at ease with employees. I remember that every morning at coffee break at La Guardia, you'd find him sitting in the middle of a group of mechanics, talking with them about their problems, business and personal. If it wasn't mechanics, it was secretaries or agents.

"He seldom thanked anyone verbally for doing a good job—it just wasn't his nature. But he'd sit at his own typewriter, in his shirtsleeves, pecking out those short notes of compliments or thanks, and these were appreciated far more than anything he could say in person."

Mel Brenner: "C.R. was an industrial statesman. The tone he set for American has lasted even to today, like a permanent imprint. He had a feeling toward the consumer and the public that characterized the entire company."

For an untalkative person, he was an excellent communicator, but usually it was via the written rather than the spoken word. He thought verbosity was one of the ailments that afflicted poor businessmen, and his standard for judging executives was usually expressed in the phrase, "He's a good businessman" or, conversely, "he's not a very good businessman." The latter meant trouble if it was applied to anyone in American's managerial ranks.

Typically, he hated long-winded speeches. He was in an audience with Art Lewis and when the speaker concluded, C.R. muttered, "He sure unloaded an empty wagon, didn't he?"

Barney Bernard, an AA mechanic from the pre–DC-3 days, used to tell a story about C.R. involving a stormy night in Newark when everything was going badly and chins were lower than the 1929 stock market. Several mechanics were discussing the possibility that there would be no more paychecks when C.R. suddenly strode across the ramp and interrupted the gloomy conversation.

"Boys, let's all have a snort," he announced, and pulled a bottle of bourbon out of his pocket, which he proceeded to share while he gave them assurances American wasn't going to go down the tube. Mack Palmer heard Barney relate that incident many times, "and every time he told it, he'd have tears in his eyes."

When Jack Mullins was in charge of Mexico operations, he wanted to build a new hangar and took the plans to New York for C.R.'s approval. Smith looked them over and asked, "How much?"

"I got the best deal I could, Mr. C.R. We could do the whole thing for $125,000."

"Did you say $125,000?"

"Yes, sir. I just can't do it any cheaper."

Smith handed back the plans. "Build ten of 'em and bring the other nine up here."

As far as can be determined, only one American Airlines employee ever called Smith anything but C.R. or Mr. C.R. and that was Captain Don Smith, who always said "Uncle C.R." D.K. was in San Francisco operations shortly after Smith had returned to American, and C.R. came in to say hello. A brand-new flight attendant was there and C.R. introduced himself: "I'm C. R. Smith."

She looked puzzled. "I know D. K. Smith, but I don't know you."

"He's my nephew," Smith solemnly informed her.

In a black period of red ink, one of the economy moves was a temporary elimination of meal service on DC-6 coach flights and selling box lunches instead. The chairman of the board of a New York bank arrived at C.R.'s office carrying one of the box lunches.

"I just wanted to show you how bad these lunches are," he said testily.

Smith looked at it. "Didn't you eat it?"

"Hell, no. I wanted you to see it."

"You should have left it on the plane," C.R. scolded. "We could have gotten two more flights out of it."

While he had an unusual command of the English language, he occasionally tripped over spelling. He once typed up a short note in which the city Cincinnati was mentioned. C.R. gave it to his secretary to mail and she noticed he had spelled it "Cincinatti."

She brought it back. "Mr. C.R., you spelled Cincinnati wrong. Want me to retype it?"

He looked at the note and handed it back. "Go ahead and send it the way I wrote it," he ordered. "From now on, that's the way we'll spell Cincinnati."

He hated paper clips and used straight pins. And his aversion to carbon copies used to drive Malcolm MacIntyre up the wall—lawyers didn't operate that way. Crucial memos involving major decisions would flow to the various departments with no record ever kept of them. MacIntyre's complaints were totally ignored, but long after he left American, he remarked, "As a lawyer I was staggered, but the more I think about it, I'm not sure but what this wasn't the best way to do it."

To C. R. Smith, American Airlines was his family and his life; except for those infrequent moments of relaxation he spent on such activities as fishing, every mental, emotional, and physical fiber in his being was devoted to the airline. Seven-day workweeks were common. He thought nothing of holding staff meetings Saturday and Sunday, and seemed oblivious to the fact that his officers had family lives and would rather be home. At one all-day Saturday session, it was almost dinner time when he announced, "Okay, let's continue this at 10 A.M. tomorrow."

Faces fell, but no one said a word until MacIntyre cleared his throat. He said gently, "C.R., some of us have families and we'd like to spend at least one day a week with them."

Smith looked surprised at this revelation. "Hell, I didn't realize tomorrow's Sunday. All right, we'll meet again Monday at 10 A.M."

The weekend meetings eventually were reduced to a tolerable level, but it still was seven days a week on the job for Smith. He often used Saturdays and Sundays to travel, invariably alone, and the Admirals Clubs were his refuge. It may well be that his passion for work was armor plate. Some of his friends believe that basically he was a lonely man and, sadly, by his own choice.

At every station he visited, he'd usually seek out the skycaps before contacting any local managers. He regarded them as the most efficient, honest pipeline to what a station was really doing, and usually they were frank without being petty or vindictive whiners. He'd say, "LeRoy, how's that boss of yours doing?" And if he got negative reports from several skycaps, he'd have a talk with the station manager.

The pilots loved to tell C. R. Smith stories. He often was Mr. Hyde to them in company-union dealings, but he was Dr. Jekyll when it came to relations with individuals, especially the older captains. He was always going up to the cockpit so he could tell them raunchy jokes.

Bob McDaniels was flying the Chicago–Acapulco inaugural some years ago and as they approached Mexico City, he banked and circled to the left so passengers could see the capital's famous volcano below. He straightened out and was just about to resume course when Jack Mullins ran up to the cockpit.

"Mac, Mr. C.R. says to go back and make a circle to the right so people on the other side of the cabin can see the volcano."

.

McDaniels didn't think it was a good idea. "Hell, Jack, we just got a bulletin ordering us to cut out these sightseeing circles—we're wasting too much fuel. You tell C.R. I wasn't supposed to do it even the first time."

Mullins looked doubtful. "You want me to tell him that?"

"Sure. It's the truth, isn't it?"

Mullins went back to report to Smith and returned a few minutes later. "Mac, I told C.R. what you said, and he told me to ask you a question."

"What's the question?"

"Do you like your job?"

Smith was not without faults. A thread of ruthlessness ran through his career, which was not surprising. It goes with the territory, a kind of psychological urge fueled by power and authority. Even paternalists like Patterson and Woolman could be ruthless at times. Yet in C.R., it was a flaw that still bothers men who were his close associates, who would have run through brick walls for him, and whose admiration and affection have never abated.

Almost all this rare criticism centers around his treatment of certain officers who were with him from American's adolescent years, in some cases even the infant years. When C.R. considered a man deadwood, he was dumped. There were exceptions like Rex Smith and Littlewood, and Red Mosier was another. But their collective problem involved health, not performance, and Mosier was a very special case—aging and ailing, he himself knew he was deadwood and C.R. kept him on out of gratitude for what he had contributed to the airline.

But there were others who had done much for American, and that didn't save them from executive extinction: outright dismissal, a requested resignation, or early retirement, the latter being in the face-saving category.

"C.R. was strange in one way," said one now-retired officer. "He couldn't bring himself to fire anybody on the vice presidential level and would almost invariably have somebody else do it. I know for a fact he told Marion Sadler to fire a guy who had been with C.R. since the Southern Air Transport days. When Marion protested, 'He doesn't work for me,' C.R. said, 'I don't care. I want *you* to fire him.' He ordered Sadler to fire another old-timer, a wonderful man, and Marion was so upset damned if he didn't send me out to do the job. It was one of those early retirement deals, but the poor guy didn't want to retire yet."

Smith once axed a veteran personnel director and Ed Hale, then American's manager in Phoenix, mentioned it to C.R. at a meeting.

"Too bad about so-and-so," Hale said casually.

"Yeah," Smith said. "The trouble was that he thought he was a personnel man and I didn't."

Hale gulped and blurted, "That makes it rough, doesn't it, C.R.?"

Except for the legendary Rex Smith, no American public relations official was closer to C.R. than Willis Player. Given that insight, his comment on Smith's reputation for ruthlessness may be the most objective:

"I guess in a sense it was true, but it wasn't that he was unwilling to let you make mistakes. He was very impatient with people who deceived him, who wouldn't correct mistakes, or who did things they knew he wouldn't like. When it came to a guy who wouldn't perform, C.R. didn't fool around like some of his peers. He didn't try to find graceful exits, either. Yet in Mosier's case, he simply removed him from stress. He kept him because he felt the company owed Mosier that much. Red had an office right next to C.R.'s and didn't do a damned thing those last few years, but we all understood that."

There were times when C.R.'s judgment of people was suspect. It ran hot and cold, from excellent to abysmal. His previously mentioned habit of stock-piling talent is a good example. He got some good men that way, but also an occasional incompetent whose recruitment could only be explained as one of C.R.'s whims or gambles. Said a former officer:

"I loved C.R., but he was the poorest judge of people I ever saw. He rarely missed on material things like planes and routes, but he couldn't judge people."

But these flaws are more blemishes than major faults, tiny imperfections in the portrait of the whole man. On the more exacting scales of history, C. R. Smith's greatness far outweighed his human frailties. His blind spots did not mean he lacked vision. Above all else, he was a visionary with an uncanny sense of what was lurking around the next corner, both good and bad.

Willis Player said:

"It's essential that to get a clear picture of C.R., you must understand his bluntness and directness. He simply got to the heart of things. He had another characteristic, one he shared with Juan Trippe—and I knew Trippe well, too. Although they were so very much unlike in many ways, they both had a tremendous power of concentration. Each was capable of shutting himself off from everything but a single problem or issue. They could disappear from you while you were sitting in the same room, locking their minds on a single subject while you waited for them to reach a conclusion they'd presumably share.

"He not only was American's leader but the industry's leader. Sure, he insisted that American be the best, but he was convinced that American couldn't be much better than the rest of the industry, not only as a matter of image but in physical and economic performance. That's why he was so active in areas that didn't directly affect his own airline.

"Remember, he consistently had American people working on industry problems. The Electra crisis was a perfect example. And Carlene Roberts used to spend as much time on industry matters as she did American's—all on C.R.'s orders. Often he'd tell me that such-and-such an airline was having problems and he'd ask me to go over and give them some help."

Player was one of several former officers who stayed in touch with C.R. long after he left center stage, flying down to Washington for an occasional lunch. Except for such contacts, C.R. became something of a recluse. He lived alone in an apartment on Connecticut Avenue in the capital. A housekeeper would come each morning to clean and fix his meals for the day. Occasionally, some old friends would drop by to take him to lunch or dinner, people like Jim Bass, Art Lewis, and Clancie Henderson (now Melton). He was his old unloquacious self, but enjoyed himself thoroughly. At one lunch, they were reminiscing and

Lewis asked him to name the most interesting period of his life. Without hesitating, C.R. replied, "The war."

C.R.'s health deteriorated after he left American for the last time. He suffered a mild stroke and walked with a laborious limp from then on. When he went out to dine with friends, he'd have to be helped into a car. His sight in one eye failed, too, but this didn't stop him from continuing to conduct his own correspondence as best he could. Granted, his typing errors became more frequent, but nobody complained—a C. R. Smith note was still something to be treasured. He wrote Player, "I'm typing lopsided now."

Phyllis Nunnery, Bob Crandall's secretary, occasionally sent him his favorite food: Texas-style chili, packed in dry ice. One of his thank-you notes contained the complaint, "a bit too slaty this time."

Mystified, she phoned him to ask what "slaty" meant.

"Salty," he growled.

C.R. celebrated his eighty-fifth birthday September 9, 1984, and his friends worried about his insistence on living alone. Several wanted him to move to the Fort Worth Club in Texas, which has residential quarters and where he would receive closer attention. The stubborn old lion balked, but early in 1985 he closed the Washington apartment and bought a small home in Annapolis close to his son Doug. At long last, the paternal gap was closed and he had a family other than American.

Please forgive this personal note. When I began research on *Eagle,* an interview with C. R. Smith seemed absolutely essential, and I wrote to him. He agreed to see me, and I heard later that prior to the scheduled interview, C.R. called Dan Henkin, vice president of public relations at the Air Transport Association.

"Someone's interviewing me for a book on American," he told Henkin. "Would it be all right if I came down to ATA's library tomorrow and looked up some stuff to refresh my memory?"

Henkin said he would not only put the whole library at his disposal but would have the ATA librarian on hand to help him in every way possible.

The next day, C.R. phoned and apologized for not being able to make it. Just before I was to leave Tucson for Washington to see C.R., he sent me the following letter, dated July 13, 1984:

Dear Bob:

It will not work. My memory is worse than I had realized. Too much time has gone by and the dates, the explanations and the names do not come readily to mind. We should have written this story some years ago.

I want to write to you early, to save you a trip to Washington. Do not come here and do not try to persuade me; it just will not work.

I have enjoyed the renewal of our acquaintance; you are a good man.

C.R.

So there was no interview. I have portrayed the C. R. Smith years through the eyes of others than himself, which is regrettable but not fatal. His refusal was one more demonstration of the man's inherent integrity, dignity, and decency. He did not want his own story told if it had to be subjected to the inaccuracies, distortions, and omissions of time's relentless passage.

Thus, we move on to the story of his two successors—one of whom brought American's slump to a screeching halt, while the other sent the eagle soaring again to the heights of industry leadership. There was a lot of Cyrus Rowlettt Smith in both men.

I have read that July 13 letter over again several times, mostly because of its last five words.

"*. . . you are a good man.*"

To an aviation historian, it's better than a Pulitzer Prize.

PART FIVE
1974–1985

22
Casey at the Bat

The search for the right man was the corporate version of a big-game hunt, and C. R. Smith was one of the hunters.

The same directors' executive committee that persuaded him to return also involved him in the choice of a successor. A head-hunting firm was hired to draw up a list of prospects along with a key stipulation: a candidate didn't necessarily have to be from the airline industry. The main requisite was top-level financial experience.

"C.R.'s return gave us time to figure out what we needed," Hooks Burr explained. "And we all came to the conclusion that American's greatest need was a financial guy. We had people who could operate the airline, but we also had to have someone who could get us through the enormous financial problems we could see ahead of us."

Throughout the fall of 1973 and into the new year, Aston, Burr, Fleischmann, and Fisher would meet every two weeks. Sometimes they would have dinner with a candidate; on other occasions they would discuss people the head-hunters had suggested or prospects within the company itself. C.R. from time to time would put forth a name; reportedly he favored Bill Seawell of Pan Am in the early stages of the search. But not until December did the committee begin to zero in on a single individual: Albert Vincent Casey, fifty-three-year-old president of the Times Mirror Company in Los Angeles.

His name was merely one on a list of some thirty prospects the head-hunters had given the four directors. Already eliminated was an interesting potential candidate one of the talent scouts had suggested: John DeLorean, who had just resigned from General Motors. C.R. told the head-hunter to forget it; "DeLorean would go nuts in a government-regulated industry," Smith said.

Al Casey certainly was not an active candidate; in fact, he was no candidate whatsoever. He had already decided to leave Times Mirror to run Conrail as a Presidential appointee subject to Senate confirmation, but without knowing it he made himself available to American when Nixon asked him to take the Conrail job without confirmation.

The Watergate tapes battle was in full swing, and the upper chamber wasn't approving any Nixon appointment. Casey, who would go from $300,000 a year to $60,000 running the government-subsidized railroad network, balked at such shaky job tenure. He was about to quit Times Mirror anyway, however,

437

and it was at this point that the American executive committee decided to approach him.

The first time the committee seriously discussed Casey, C.R. commented, "You know, the guy doesn't have any airline experience."

Burr agreed, but pointed out that he possessed a good background in transportation per se. He had been an official with Southern Pacific and Railway Express and was chief financial officer at Times Mirror before becoming first its executive vice president and then its president; finance, Burr emphasized, was Casey's strongest point.

That sold Smith, but Jim Aston was dubious. He didn't think American had a chance of landing Al Casey. In fact, when Aston initially saw Casey's name on the list, he remarked, "You've got the wrong guy," and crossed it out; he thought the head-hunter had meant John Casey, Al's older brother, who was a Braniff vice president.

"Jimmy, you're a Times Mirror director," C.R. said. "Do you know Al Casey?"

"Very well."

"What do you think of him?"

"I think he has a lot of the same charisma and ability to lead people that you do. He's an outstanding person."

"Would you call him?"

Aston, who didn't know Casey wasn't going to stay with the Los Angeles firm and was unaware of the Conrail situation, shook his head. "No, I can't. As a director of Times Mirror, I can't go around proselytizing their executives. Besides, I'd be greatly surprised if he was even interested."

Smith wouldn't let go. "Would you talk to him if he called you?"

"Sure."

In a few days, Casey did phone him. A meeting was arranged for Dallas, where Aston lived and where Casey was planning to visit his brother John. The director told him American had problems that needed a lot of hard work to solve, and that the board had confidence in his ability to pull it off.

Casey said, "Well, I'm at least interested in thinking about it."

And he was intrigued, to the extent of meeting with C.R. several times. They liked each other, but Casey kept plugging his brother John for the American job, while Smith kept insisting the directors wanted Albert Vincent. Casey finally told him he'd accept on one condition: C.R. had to quit. "I couldn't run the airline with you looking over my shoulder," he said bluntly.

This was agreeable to Smith, but not the board, which wanted him to stay on as chairman for a while. The negotiations dragged on until February 1974, when Smith established a firm resignation date as chairman. When the directors formally met to elect Casey president, C.R. accompanied him to the board room and asked him to wait outside while he talked to the directors.

"Then I'll bring you in," C.R. added, "and you can make a fiery speech about leading the company forward. You won't have much time to think about what you'll say because I'll be right back."

He didn't return for an hour and a half, apparently having had trouble convincing the directors he meant what he had promised Casey—there would be no looking over the new president's shoulder. There would be no fiery speech, nor was there a standing ovation when Casey entered the board room. "In fact," he remembered, "some guys were reading newspapers and others were just standing around talking." But Smith had a private word of advice, delivered in the form of this story:

A private walked by a general, C.R. recounted, and failed to salute. The general called him back.

"You didn't salute me, soldier. Did you know who I am?"

"No, sir."

"Well, I'm General So-and-so and I command 13,000 men and 2,000 motorized vehicles worth about $5 million."

"Well, General," the private said, "you sound like you're a very important man with a very important job, so please don't screw it up."

After telling the story, Smith smiled and said gently, "So, Al, don't screw it up."

Casey became president February 20. The directors didn't know how close they came to losing him to MGM, which just before he agreed to go with American had offered him carte blanche to run the studio. The day he walked into C.R.'s office for the first time, he found a note waiting for him:

"Dear Al: Congratulations. From time to time I'm going to send you written suggestions with respect to how you can improve the operation of the airline. The purpose of this first written suggestion is to tell you to pay no attention to all succeeding suggestions. Sincerely, C.R."

The desk itself, hastily refurbished when his return was announced, was a puzzle. On one side was the recess for Smith's typewriter, and every drawer but one on the other side was locked—Casey never could find the key. The unlocked drawer C.R. had used for a wastebasket.

A week before, C.R. had sent Casey a lengthy memo giving his appraisal of the officers with whom the new president would be working. It included this observation:

"There are dozens of vice presidents, too many, and ultimately this will need to be remedied. I can work with you on recommendations." He also suggested that Casey "recall and re-employ J. Mullins, a principal employee of American who couldn't agree with Mr. Spater."

Casey, who wanted to build his own team, didn't follow up on that advice, but he did note with interest Smith's opinion of these two key officers:

Donald Lloyd-Jones: "excellent, competent officer. No need to worry about his qualifications."

Robert Crandall: "one of the brightest young financial men I've ever met. Formerly with TWA. Entirely competent."

Casey never had much in-person contact with C.R. after he left, but they became sort of "pen pals," although Smith did most of the writing. Casey hated to write letters and seldom answered C.R.'s correspondence unless he felt they deserved a response. But he kept every note Smith sent him, usually concerning the trips he made for a while after his final retirement.

"They were classics," Casey laughed. "He'd write stuff like 'I was in a men's room in Berlin and the urinals are superior to anything I've seen.' "

Several letters commented on the service he had received flying on airlines other than American. One note, dated in October, complained that when he asked a Northwest stewardess for a magazine, she gave him an issue of *Time* dated the previous March. But the correspondence wasn't entirely in that mood. In one letter, he told Casey he had seen an excellent floor covering in the airport terminal at Frankfurt, "either a rubberoid or plastic, especially easy to walk on and much less expensive than carpet; you might like to ask PAA or TWA to get you a sample."

Through a misunderstanding stemming from a change in non-revenue travel terminology, American sent C.R. a space-available pass replacing his positive space privileges. Casey corrected that mistake in a hurry when he learned that Smith had been paying for his air transportation in order to make sure he could get on an airplane.

Only one letter contained advice, and this was written eight days after Casey took office:

> Dear Al:
>
> From the limited reports I have had, you have made an excellent start in the company.
>
> I was worried about the reaction to your limited airline experience. That has not come about with any strength. The usual reaction is that it may be time to have a businessman; losses cannot be afforded forever.
>
> One comment heard from time to time: "I hope that Mr. Casey will eliminate the internal politics of the New York office." Frankly, this has not worried me of late. There was much too much earlier, when everyone was running for office. Presumably, some of this has been carried forward in interpretation in the field.
>
> When I first came to American, a generation ago, the company was pulling itself apart with internal bickering. This was remedied in reasonable time with a policy about like this:
>
> "I do not want people in American criticizing people in American. We do have some sons of bitches around, but they are our sons of bitches. So long as they are on the payroll, we will support them.
>
> "If you want to come in and knock someone in the company, you will be welcome. I will call in the person you are knocking, while you are here, and we will get to the bottom of the complaint."
>
> I do not suggest that you need that; doubt it very much. But if there is too much bitching, it should be shut off early.
>
> Best of wishes,
> C. R. Smith

Casey didn't resent C.R.'s lone violation of his no-looking-over-your-shoulder pledge; it wasn't meant that way, and it voiced Smith's honest concern that the new boy on the block might get hurt by the intramural feuding that seems to go on in every large corporation. C.R. himself had allowed too much of that sort of thing. He took a long time to crack down on Hogan, for example, and Mosier was no exponent of peaceful interoffice relations.

Al Casey was his own man, however. C.R. may have been worried about his non-airline background, but Casey wasn't. A graduate of Harvard Business School, his notion of management wasn't anything that prestigious institution taught. After observing the way he operated at American, the school's former dean told him he had set modern business practices back a full generation.

"There are only four jobs in any company, regardless of what kind of business you're in," Casey held. "You have one guy in charge of making the product, someone in charge of selling it, the third one's a bean counter who keeps score, and then there's the boss."

And that was precisely the way he ran American, the way he turned it around, and the way he built a superb team for the future.

Casey didn't find the airline in as sorry a state as he expected. C.R. already had started the turnaround with cost-cutting moves, including the furloughing of some 1,300 employees—most of them hired in the last throes of the Spater/Warde regime—and the dumping of the South Pacific albatross. Smith had been furious when Warde gave him a 1974 budget projecting a deficit. He refused to accept it, and the '74 budget under which American was operating when Casey arrived was producing signs of recovery.

Furthermore, the airline had a healthy positive cash flow from equipment depreciation while capital spending had been light since 1972; Dr. Casey had not arrived at the bedside of a terminally ill patient. He quickly deduced that his main task was to correct past mistakes, make sure they wouldn't be repeated, and in the process convince everybody they were working on a crack ocean liner, not a Roman slave galley.

It didn't take American long to learn there was no one like Casey in the airline industry—in fact, there never had been and there may never be again. He projected enough different images to make people wonder if there were more than one Al Casey. He was a stand-up comedian who delivered one-liners with the ad-libbing aplomb of a Henny Youngman. He was the friendly Irish beat cop who knows everyone in the neighborhood, kids the mothers, teases the small fry, cheerfully bullies the merchants—and God help the thieves, pushers, and pimps who cross his path. He had C.R.'s charisma without his occasional aloofness. He shared Smith's decisiveness, but sometimes Casey's was camouflaged by his jovial, wisecracking personality. Both were patriarchs, yet in different ways. C.R.'s father image was more felt than seen, almost a state of mind rather than something visible and physically tangible. Casey was more attainable, easier to talk to; he was the bluff, hearty head of the family who handed out goodies and stern discipline in the same tone of voice. He never let anyone forget he was boss, but he also made you feel he was your friend.

In brief, Al Casey was 100-proof bourbon carried around in a bottle of after-shave lotion. He thrived on crisis, but he could laugh his way through one. He made an effort to be liked, but he never ran a popularity contest. He shook hands and slapped backs with natural ease, but he could chop off heads with the same ease. In his first four years with American, he fired twelve vice presidents.

Casey got a fast indication that his selection had bruised at least one ego. Carter Burgess informed him he was resigning from the board. Burgess, who had headed TWA, had expected the directors to make him president. Casey tried to talk him out of it—Burgess was the only outside director with airline experience—but Carter quit anyway.

Shortly after he became president, Casey received phone calls from two men in the same boat as he, non-airline types who had to overcome doubts and cynicism when they were placed in Casey's who's-this-guy-who-can't-tell-a-707-from-a-DC-8 position. One was Charlie Tillinghast, who remembered how grateful he had been when C.R. hosted a dinner for him upon his election as TWA's president. The second was Eddie Carlson of United. He had come into the airline business from the Westin hotel chain.

After Carlson identified himself, the conversation went this way:

"Al, I was new to this industry, too, and if there's anything I can do to help you understand it, I'd be happy to do it. I don't want you making the same mistakes I did when I first joined United. I'd just like to help you because I believe in our industry."

"Eddie, that's tremendous! I'd love to have lunch with you."

"You just say the word and I'll be there."

"Well, how about tomorrow?"

There was momentary dead silence before Carlson said, "That's fine," and set a time and place for the next day. Not until they met at the restaurant did Casey discover that Carlson had called from Honolulu.

Casey was elected chairman two months after becoming president, an honor which gave him some concern. American had been no exception to the common practice of splitting the jobs between two men, although C.R. at times had held both posts. Casey proceeded to knock out the wall between the president's and the chairman's adjoining offices, making them a single room.

"Since I had become chairman," he explained, "I figured everyone was wondering who'd be president, and I wanted to stop all that talk."

Like a brand-new, untried general wondering which of his officers would follow him into battle, Casey surveyed his top subordinates and arrived at the conclusion that American was well staffed except in one area: marketing. Donald Lloyd-Jones was senior vice president of operations. Finance was in Bob Crandall's hands, and Gene Overbeck was in charge of administration.

Casey's theory of good management had an inviolate rule: no boss should have more than four men reporting to him directly. He didn't have four, and for a short, time, he took over marketing himself while beginning a search for the best man available.

He interviewed a number of highly recommended airline marketing executives, but also had his senior officers talk to them. Casey would drop in during these sessions and listen to the questions and answers. One man who impressed him was Charlie Bucks of Continental, but someone else impressed him even more, and that was one of his own interviewers.

"I discovered that Bob Crandall asked the best questions in greater depth than anyone else," Casey said. "Through his instinctive sense of logic, he knew far more about marketing than the guys he was interviewing. So I called him in and suggested he take over marketing. He damned near died—he wanted the job but he never dreamed it would happen."

Crandall *had* wanted the job, and one of his prime motives was a burning desire to do something about the faltering SABRE system. Crandall had always been fascinated with data processing. His first job at TWA was putting in a computerized accounts receivable system. One of his associates and good friend was Dick Pearson, a programmer who worked with him; Pearson was to become president of TWA in 1985. He always remembered Crandall as the most persistent seeker of computer knowledge he ever met: "We'd walk down the street to lunch and all he'd do was ask me questions."

Another Crandall mentor was Otto Becker, who was sick over the way SABRE had been allowed to stagnate. He discovered the same quality in Crandall Casey had: he knew how to ask questions. SABRE was one of the first things he discussed with Becker when Crandall first joined American and Otto was giving him an informal orientation course.

"What do you know about computers?" Becker asked.

"Not as much as I'd like to," Crandall admitted, "but I do know what they should be *able* to do."

Bloomingdale's had recruited Crandall to look at their data processing, credit system, and budget control, and at TWA he had been vice president of data services. He longed to exploit SABRE's potential for marketing applications; he had spotted its sad state before joining American and had moved promptly to fix it when he arrived.

He couldn't understand why American was still using typewriter displays as part of SABRE, then discovered that the airline had about 2,000 modern cathode ray tubes (CRTs) in a basement at Tulsa. Custom-made for SABRE, they were just gathering dust until Crandall ordered them removed, refurbished, and installed.

The happiest individual at this development was Max Hopper, American's long-frustrated chief of data processing. Crandall then hired away from TWA a man with whom he had worked there, Jim O'Neill, to become vice president of data processing and communications services. Crandall, Hopper, and O'Neill formed the team that modernized SABRE and went an important step further. In 1976, American began to sell its data processing capabilities to outside clients.

This was largely a joint Hopper-Crandall idea; but the original concept was to let the nation's 15,000 travel agents (there are now some 20,000) subscribe to a joint industry data processing system, giving them fast access to any carrier's reservations information without having to use the much slower telephone.

But United, supremely confident in APOLLO's superiority, bolted from the joint effort and announced it would start selling APOLLO to travel agents. That was all Crandall needed. He had an improved SABRE all cranked up and ready to go. In May 1976, American installed its first SABRE unit in a travel agency.

Just as Marion Sadler was proudest of SABRE's initial introduction, so did Bob Crandall feel his rejuvenation of their system warranted his own pride.

"The decision to modernize SABRE and re-establish our position as a data processing leader," Crandall said, "was one of the things I'm proudest of. It has given American a very great advantage."

SABRE eventually was to serve more than 10,000 travel agents and corporate travel departments—41 percent of computerized travel agencies (United serves 39 percent). The system's center is in Tulsa, where four huge IBM 9083s handle 900 messages a second, process some 270,000 passenger reservations daily, and keep track of more than 10,000 daily fare changes. SABRE's data banks store everything from available seats to what time any flight will arrive. Passengers can ask SABRE for hotel reservations, car rentals, special meals, and seat preference. A pilot can get in two minutes a flight plan that used to require an hour for preparation. SABRE handles payrolls, credit billings, and vacation schedules. It does everything but wish employees and customers a happy birthday.

Partly, it might be said, because Bob Crandall got mad when he discovered 2,000 unused CRTs.

American ended the first year of Al Casey's "New Deal" with a $20.4 million profit, and also spent the year getting used to Al Casey.

This included his aversion to committee meetings, correspondence, memos to or from his staff (he never sent one in the 11 years he spent at American), and keeping files. He also disliked staff meetings unless there was something important to discuss. One of Casey's staff meetings was considered lengthy if it ran over thirty minutes. He preferred seeing his officers on a one-to-one basis, and his proverbial door was always open.

Casey's unconventional methods of running a multi-billion-dollar corporation were understood mostly by his patient secretary, Libby Scott. He hired her eight years before he came to the airline after telling her, "I don't care if you can't take dictation or type ninety words a minute—I'm gonna teach you how to be an *executive* secretary."

She helped him ration his time, for Casey had health problems, which no one could have guessed from his jovial demeanor. At age sixty-five, when he left American, he had suffered four heart attacks, four operations, and a stroke.

Yet if airline presidents were unionized, he could have filed weekly grievances claiming overwork. He was a human perpetual-motion machine. Until he decided to relinquish the presidency and be only the chairman, he felt he had to keep busy.

In the turnaround year of 1974, profits might have been lower if Casey hadn't taken eight of the airline's sixteen 747s out of service; two already had been sold. Conversely, it would have been higher except for a $9 million extra expense, the arbitration award American had to pay Irish International Airlines to settle a lawsuit that was one of Roy Chalk's chickens come home to roost. Chalk had defaulted on an agreement to lease the Irish carrier a couple of 747s he never acquired, and American got stuck with the check.

In 1975 there was another turnaround, in the wrong direction: a loss of more than $20 million. Shocked and more than disappointed, Casey began wondering if the twice-tried merger route wasn't the best solution after all. He began merger discussions with Bill Seawell of Pan Am, on the basis of a study done by one of Crandall's brightest subordinates, Thomas G. Plaskett, a financial whiz who had come to American from General Motors. Plaskett made the merger presentation early in 1976, but Casey decided not to proceed.

"What we found out," he explained, "was that half the benefits of the merger could be achieved without a merger, because Pan Am just wasn't doing anything. When the plan was withdrawn, Pan Am took Plaskett's study and followed our cost reduction plan. I don't blame them; I would have done the same thing."

The merger probably wouldn't have gone through anyway. Transportation Secretary William Coleman was for it, but the White House, State Department, and Justice Department were opposed.

Casey, still concerned whether American could really ever be consistently profitable, quietly began negotiations with two large insurance companies to take over the airline, Trans-American and American General. This plan came a lot closer to consummation than employees ever realized. Casey disclosed why:

"Both of them individually were in favor of it, but they were never able to sell their constituencies. I really had them convinced it would be a good deal. If you ever welded an airline and an insurance company together, you'd have a gold mine. I honestly didn't think at that point that American could stand alone as a high-cost airline which coins dough in good times but can't anticipate recessions and doesn't prune its overhead soon enough."

But when Trans-American and American General decided against acquisition, Casey told his staff:

"The hell with it. We'll do it by ourselves. We'll sell the goddamned hotels and go to work on the airline. You guys have got to learn how to run an airline. Hell, I'm not gonna learn anymore—I'll be gone in three or four more years."

He was wrong in one respect: he would stay longer than his predicted three or four years. But he was very right in all other respects, starting with the long-overdue disposition of a hotel venture that was losing $12 million a year.

When Casey arrived at American, previously committed hotel projects were already under way. Three more properties joined the Americana chain in 1974 and five more opened or were scheduled to open between 1975 and 1979, including two new hotels in Korea. Casey slammed the door on any future ventures and began disposing of the entire chain. The process was to take seven years and involve twenty-one hotel properties that were sold in eight separate deals.

The financial pendulum began to swing back in 1976. Profits that year hit $76.3 million, jumped to nearly $81 million the following year, and reached outer space in 1978 with a record $134.4 million—a figure attained despite a $101 million hike in fuel costs.

Part of the comeback in the mid seventies was another one of those innovative marketing schemes for which American was noted. This one, originating in the fertile mind of Crandall and refined by his free-swinging staff, was the famous Super Saver fares program.

In the summer of 1976, the CAB had authorized a whole new class of air charter operators who announced plans for a major invasion of the transcontinental market. They weren't airlines, but rather entrepreneurs with a foolproof way of making money: they would organize a group charter, then go to a regular carrier and buy up space at a negotiated discount, usually sizable, and resell the seats to the group at prices below regular fares but still profitable to the charter operator.

"We gotta do something about it," Crandall told his troops. "We're already selling 40 percent of our seats at regular fares, so why can't we figure out a way to sell the other 60 percent at a fare cheaper than what a charter operator can get?"

Super Saver was the answer. In simplest terms, it was a device to discount fares without diverting traffic from regular fares. This was accomplished by the industry's first real use of *restricted* discounts. Super Saver was offered to passengers who would agree to buy their tickets well in advance and stay at their destination at least fourteen days.

The industry always regarded discounted fares as self-defeating; they merely diverted full-fare passengers, who would have flown anyway, into cheaper seats. The beauty of Super Saver was that its discount was controlled. It discouraged full-fare customers by its restrictions and at the same time attracted people who normally would not have traveled.

Crandall's plan (he insisted it was "put together by a group of about twenty-five guys sitting around and hashing out ideas") introduced a whole new concept: drastically lower fares with a minimum of diversion and a maximum of new traffic generation. Super Saver fares were introduced transcontinentally in 1977 and extended to the rest of American's system the next year. It was not only a major marketing coup but the father of all the numerous discount schemes that followed. And it was so successful that charter operators filed suit against both American and the CAB, accusing the airline of unfair competition and the Board of permitting it.

The legal action got nowhere. The plaintiffs had learned, as other competitors would in the future, that Bob Crandall played hardball.

If it hadn't been for the Boeing 747, the DC-10 and L-1011 would have been considered the eighth and ninth wonders of the world—spacious, luxurious symbols of what modern air travel was all about.

But the 747 was the first-born, and every jumbo jet that followed had to suffer a little by comparison. In 1973, the Airline Passengers Association began a regular poll of its members on their favorite airlines and airplanes. The 747 finished first in every poll, while American consistently was picked as the best domestic carrier. There was a minor anomaly in this: the favorite airline was gradually getting rid of the favorite airplane.

Airlines, of course, don't measure flight equipment with the same ruler a passenger uses. American had to start phasing out its flying hotels for the same reason it began disposing of its earthbound hotels: it couldn't make any money with them. To an airline with American's route structure, the DC-10 simply was a more versatile and viable aircraft. The 747 couldn't be used on anything but high-density Caribbean routes like New York–San Juan and the transcontinental nonstop market. The DC-10 could serve those same markets, yet was equally efficient on segments like New York–Dallas, New York–Chicago, and Chicago–Los Angeles.

But on May 25, 1979, the crash of Los Angeles–bound DC-10 Flight 191, immediately after taking off from O'Hare, threatened the existence of the big trijet as a trusted transport plane. It was the Electra crisis all over again.

Before this accident, American's DC-10 fleet had flown for almost nine years with only a single serious incident, and in that, the airplane landed safely, thanks to a crew's skill and the DC-10's own flying characteristics.

The captain in this previous instance was Bryce McCormick, flying a DC-10 that on June 12, 1972, had just left Detroit when a rear cargo door, whose latches hadn't locked securely, blew off, causing an explosive decompression of the pressurized fuselage.

The blast ruptured most of the hydraulic control lines, collapsed part of the cabin floor, opening a seventeen-foot hole in the bottom of the fuselage, and left McCormick and copilot Paige Whitney flying an airplane with no rudder control, no stabilizers, extremely stiff elevators, and only his engines and ailerons giving him partial maneuverability.

They got out of this potentially catastrophic predicament for two reasons: training, and the airplane itself.

McCormick had been exposed to a simulated total hydraulic failure when he transitioned to the DC-10 at the Fort Worth flight school. He knew what to do.

"Before the Detroit incident," McCormick said, "I had learned during simulator training that you could fly a DC-10 with your hands and feet *completely off the controls,* as long as you had those three engines. I proved it to the FAA and NTSB (National Transportation Safety Board) during the investigation, when we went out to Palmdale and shot some approaches.

"I showed them how you could make an approach using just the throttles and not even touching the controls. When the copilot called out, 'Fifty feet,' I cut the center engine, added just a little power on the other two, and we greased it on that runway. It was no miracle—the simulator training had involved flying with nothing but throttles.

"The DC-10 is just a stable platform, more stable in fact than the 747. It's just the sweetest airplane that ever was."

McCormick, now retired (he and his entire crew received the Distinguished Service Award after the Detroit emergency), personified the laconic airline captain. He was based in Los Angeles in 1972, and when he returned to California, chief pilot Bob Davies asked him to write up a report on the incident.

"Well, what do you need?" McCormick asked. "You already know pretty much what happened."

"I need a full account in writing," Davis said.

McCormick composed the following account:

"We had an explosive decompression, returned to Detroit, and no further incident."

Davis rejected this as inadequate, and McCormick finally turned in a report that totaled five single-spaced pages to cover fifteen minutes of flying. Later he was being interviewed by a British author who was doing a book on the DC-10 and the writer asked him, "Did they give you your portion?"

"Did they give me what?"

"A portion. A shot of whiskey—that's what they do in England after an accident."

"No," Bryce sighed, "but I sure as hell had one later that night before I went to bed."

The crew of Flight 191 faced an entirely different and far deadlier set of circumstances. The aircraft was climbing when it lost the entire port engine and pylon, the violent separation tossing the heavy unit up and over the top of the wing and destroying part of the wing's leading edge. This impact severed the hydraulically operated leading edge slats and created an asymmetrical flap condition, like locking the wheels on one side of a car. The pilot, unaware that an entire engine structure was gone, reduced power in accordance with FAA's prescribed procedures for an entirely different kind of emergency. With the DC-10 in a sharp bank, he lost control and the aircraft stalled.

American and McDonnell Douglas had to share the official blame. The NTSB criticized MCD for an inadequate design that made the pylon structure vulnerable to cracks, and American for using a time-saving but unauthorized engine change maintenance procedure in which the entire engine and pylon were removed as one unit—pylon cracks could result from this method.

The FAA escaped official condemnation, except for some serious questions raised about its certification process, but by any objective analysis of the Flight 191 tragedy, it was far from blameless. Bill Evans, a former DC-10 captain, believed FAA's own regulations were a booby trap:

"Walt Lux [191's captain] did everything by the book, and that's what killed him. The FAA required you to come back to V_2 speed if you lost an engine right after takeoff. I don't know any pilot who didn't feel it was always to your advantage to hold whatever speed you had built up, provided you had a good rate of climb. Lux was holding at 170 knots, which was well above stall speed, but when the engine and pylon separated, he thought it was just engine failure and he dropped back to V_2 just like the book said. He didn't know the slats were gone on that side. He was too low to recover from that inadvertent bank and he stalled out. Pilots had been bitching about that procedure for years."

Even more "bitching" was voiced when then FAA administrator Langhorne Bond ordered all U.S. DC-10 operators to ground the airplane until redesigned pylon attachments were developed and the aircraft recertificated. Whether the lengthy grounding was really necessary will be a perpetual subject for debate. The airlines, including DC-10 carriers overseas, felt it was totally unjustified.

What had caused the crash was known within seventy-two hours, and most of the evidence was in before that. All that was needed to keep DC-10s flying safely was a fleetwide check of the pylons and periodic inspections until the improved attachments were available. Instead, Bond grounded the airplane in an action that demolished the schedule patterns of six U.S. carriers, including American. Quesada had refused to ground the Electra even without being sure what was wrong with it. The airlines thought Bond had shot from the hip in the case of the DC-10, and even if that wasn't true, he really fired blindly when he grounded Eastern's A-300s at the same time because he had been informed the French-designed jet also had the same General Electric engines. Bond hastily rescinded the A-300 grounding after Frank Borman blistered his ears in a phone call.

Even when the DC-10's airworthiness certificate was finally restored, public resistance to the airplane remained strong for some time. That the DC-10 was able to come back as completely as it did is a tribute to its performance after the Chicago crash.

In the courtyard rotunda of the San Diego Aerospace Museum is a simple bronze memorial plaque dedicated to the ten flight attendants who were aboard Flight 191. All were San Diego–based. It was another flight attendant, Marcia Caya, who organized the fund-raising drive.

The real father of the DC-10 concept wasn't around to witness its travails. Frank Kolk died August 3, 1976, and American lost an engineering genius in the true Bill Littlewood tradition. He may have been difficult to work with, but a gentler appraisal came from Dave Frailey of public relations, who often had to ask Kolk to translate technical terms into layman's language.

"Frank could be extremely helpful to us nontechnical people," Frailey remembered, "and also very tolerant."

                                    *   *   *

Dave Frailey became American's new vice president of public relations in 1973. Until his retirement eight years later, he had a front-row seat for some of the most momentous events in American's saga.

This was a period of the we've-got-good-news-and-bad-news variety. There was plenty of both—Al Casey could have been wearing the two masks of Greek drama. And one of his finest accomplishments was the building of a team capable of making the good happen more often than the bad.

There were many names on that team. A few stood out as individuals whose future roles would entail major input into the shaping of the airline's future. Two were originally Crandall's lieutenants, Tom Plaskett and Wesley G. Kaldahl. A third, John C. Pope, like Plaskett had come to American from General Motors.

Plaskett and Kaldahl were airline versions of switch-hitters. Plaskett was equally adept at finance and marketing. Wes Kaldahl came up through the airline ranks, starting as a res agent at Detroit with Pennsylvania Central Airlines in 1945. When PCA became Capital, he went into scheduling, and after the United-Capital merger he joined American as Mel Brenner's chief disciple. He left American in 1964 and spent the next ten years in vice presidential posts at Eastern and Pan Am, rejoining American in 1974 as vice president of marketing resources.

Pope was a finance specialist, and not even Bill Hogan compiled a better reputation in a field that requires crystal balls and the ability to assess what they reveal.

The major holdover from the Spater years was versatile Donald Lloyd-Jones. Casey thought so highly of him that he considered Jones a possible successor.

"He didn't have great charisma with employees," Casey said, "but people admired and respected him. Don had the mental capacity and training to understand anything—engineering, flight, economics. He was no great flag-waving leader, but a smart, decent guy."

Lloyd-Jones was part of the senior executive team that Casey took into the pivotal year of 1978, along with Crandall, Overbeck, Plaskett, and Becker; Plaskett was the newest member, having replaced Crandall as senior vice president of Finance. And these were the men "on duty," so to speak, when Albert Vincent Casey decided to move corporate headquarters to Texas.

It was no snap decision. He had been stewing a long time over the disadvantages of running the airline from New York. In the summer of 1978, without telling anyone, he wrote a report on the pros and cons of a move. Dallas/Fort Worth was only one possibility he mentioned; he also considered St. Louis, Chicago, and Atlanta. But Casey favored Texas by a wide margin. He had reason to believe he would get the best deal there.

He had twenty-five copies of his study prepared, but did not show them to anyone at American, not even Crandall. The twenty-five copies were handed to the directors, who were given one and a half hours in which to read and digest the contents. This was followed by a discussion and then a vote, after which Casey picked up all twenty-five copies. He burned twenty-three and took the other two home.

"I know it was brilliant because I wrote it myself," he chuckled. "No outside input, no consultants nor anybody else was involved. I didn't want to burden Crandall. I didn't want him identified with the move. If people got pissed off and nobody liked the idea, he'd be blameless because he had to support me —he had no choice. I'm a great one for sticking my own neck out and making my own deals. I don't dump off on anyone else."

Very roughly paraphrased, these were the points Casey brought up in his study:

THE PROS

1. New York was too expensive, both for the people working at 633 Third Avenue and the company, which was paying a fortune to lease the facilities and in taxes.
2. Moving to Texas would be the equivalent of an 18 to 23 percent wage increase for employees because of the lower cost of living; they'd save a bundle just by escaping New York's state and city taxes.
3. The rate of absenteeism for health reasons in the New York area was the highest of any city on American's system, a situation Casey blamed on employee use of subways and commuter trains.
4. The move to Dallas/Fort Worth would add a half hour to each workday, because Texas had a forty-hour week, which added up to a 6 percent increase in productivity. (New York had a thirty-five-hour week.)
5. The magnificent new Dallas/Fort Worth Airport, opened in 1974, was perfect for the fast-developing "hub" concept of airline scheduling.
6. A 325-acre site on wooded, stream-studded land adjacent to American's already existing training center was available on an attractive long-term leasing arrangement, and a $147 million bond issue would be floated to help finance construction of a new corporate headquarters building and other facilities.
7. Temporary facilities were available for headquarters while the new facility was being built.
8. American would save some $200 million over the forty-year leasing agreement.

THE CONS

1. The impact on employees, who would have to uproot families, change their living style, and go through the traumatic adjustment to a totally new environment.

2. The challenging logistics of a mass move, taking many officers and employees away from regular duties in the planning stages.

3. The massive expense of the exodus (not a major factor because of the estimated savings).

4. New York's expected angry public and civic reaction to the move.

Point 4 happened in spades. When Casey, on November 15, 1978, announced that American's general offices were heading south, Pandora's box was opened and out flew vituperation that shook even the usually unflappable Casey. He had expected protests and criticism, but not to the vicious extent it reached. Even *Business Week* aimed below the belt.

"Talk in the airline industry," the magazine declared, "is that Casey feels frustrated by his failure to emerge as the powerful voice in New York City affairs he planned to become and has decided to swim in a smaller pond."

Mayor Ed Koch joined the howling pack. "It's an obscenity for him [Casey] to do what he's doing," Koch told reporters. "It's like finding that someone in the CIA is working for the Russians." (That remark went over big in Texas.)

Koch was particularly incensed because at one time Casey had served on a special board whose aim was to keep businesses from moving out of the New York area, and to solve the city's financial problems. Proclaimed the mayor:

"Here he was, selected to be a member of a board to help restructure the city, and then he does this. The fact is that he should be ashamed of himself."

Al Casey was in no mood to turn the other cheek. He pointed out that moving some 1,200 headquarters personnel to Texas still left more than 8,000 American Airlines employees working and living in the New York area. He said when he informed city officials he was considering the move, they offered some concessions that in no way matched the deal American was getting from Dallas and Forth Worth.

In a backhanded sort of way, New York's semi-hysterical reaction was a compliment to American. No such fuss had been raised when Eastern shifted its corporate headquarters to Miami. Between 1970 and 1977, sixteen other major corporations moved their general offices out of New York City proper, including such big names as Texaco, Shell Oil, General Electric, Atlantic Richfield, U.S. Steel, Coca-Cola, Pepsico, Kraft, American Can, Allied Chemical, and Nabisco. They had been preceded by K-Mart, Armour, and Greyhound.

Union Carbide moved 2,000 employees from Manhattan to Connecticut almost simultaneously with American; this desertion hardly got mentioned in the New York press. An airline was a far more visible target, yet this doesn't explain why Eastern didn't suffer the intensity of the attack on American.

Petitions were circulated demanding a boycott. Boycotts were ordered or threatened by three labor unions and one large company. Warner Communications announced that its employees and officers would henceforth avoid flying American. Opportunistic TWA took full-page ads proclaiming, "TWA Loves New York."

The embattled Casey promptly announced that if the boycott threats continued, he'd move more jobs and personnel out of New York than originally planned. He was particularly angered by Warner's attack. He could understand the reaction of unions and politicians, but not that of a fellow corporation, which presumably hadn't told its employees to stop buying Nabisco crackers. Yet he couldn't resist a Casey one-liner: "I'm still going to show Warner films on our planes," he allowed.

The road to relocation was far from silky-smooth. A major problem was the housing market in Texas, affected by the rising mortgage interest rates prevalent throughout the nation. Texas had a 10 percent ceiling on mortgage interest, but this had forced lending institutions to require higher down payments. Casey knew many employees, owning homes they'd purchased when mortgage interest was lower, would balk at a relocation that might mean financial hardship.

He sent Tom Plaskett to Texas. Plaskett returned with a deal to provide up to $60 million in mortgage funds at 8.75 percent interest. Under an agreement reached with four Dallas and Fort Worth banks, American would buy certificates of deposit and the banks, in turn, would lend employees whatever home mortgages they'd need.

The actual move, which began in the summer of 1979, took about a month, with transfers staggered over that period. Gene Overbeck was in charge, aided by Merrill Lynch Relocation Management, which set up a counseling service under a $100,000 contract. Out of some 1,200 employees eligible for relocation, more than 900 accepted transfer, and even these were given one year in which to decide if they wanted to move back to New York.

For several weekends, American provided a 727 that left Dallas/Fort Worth Airport (DFW) Friday evening and carried employees to New York for cleaning up unfinished business, selling homes, and seeing families still in the area. The plane returned to DFW Sunday night.

Temporary general offices were established in Grand Prairie, Texas, in the old space research facility once operated by Vought Aerospace Corporation. It served as headquarters for three years, and on January 15, 1983—exactly five years and two months to the day relocation was announced—American Airlines moved into its functionally designed new corporate office building.

The boycotts never did materialize; there was no discernible drop in traffic out of New York, despite all the noise. In fact, a couple of prominent television and newspaper reporters who had been loudly denouncing local politicians for using the airline were spotted on American flights themselves.

In 1945, C. R. Smith had offered James Aston a job with American. Aston replied, "General, I'd be interested on one condition: that you move headquarters to Dallas. I'll be damned if I'm gonna work in New York City."

"We couldn't do it," Smith said. "New York's where the action is."

Aston instead went to work for the Republic National Bank of Dallas and eventually became its chairman. But when he came on American's board, he kept needling C.R. to move headquarters and got nowhere. After relocation was announced, C.R. phoned him.

"Jimmy, I just want to tell you this is one of the finest things that's ever happened."

"Well, General," Aston laughed, "I'm glad you finally came around. I've been working on you for twenty-five years."

The role of the Dallas/Fort Worth Airport complex in the relocation decision cannot be overstated. It might never have taken place if it were not for DFW, which gave American the ideal location for its prime hub, a 17,400-acre facility nine miles long and eight miles wide, larger than the entire island of Manhattan.

DFW, seventeen miles from Fort Worth and the same distance from Dallas, is a $700 million monument to the settlement of an ancient feud between the two cities. They had been fighting over air traffic almost since the dawn of the airline industry. They came close to a joint airport years ago when a satisfactory site was picked, but the armistice fell apart when Fort Worth's Amon Carter, Sr., discovered that the proposed terminal building would be slightly closer to Dallas.

So Fort Worth had its Amon Carter Field—later changed to the Greater Southwest International Airport—and Dallas had Love Field. The change of name didn't help Fort Worth, which saw the bulk of traffic using Love. In 1961, Fort Worth asked the CAB to force the airlines into providing more flights at its airport. It was seven years later when the CAB's molasses-caked machinery finally ground out the answer: find a site for a joint airport.

Civic leaders in both cities buried the hatchet, and DFW was the result— an airport so huge that the concrete in its runways could pave a four-lane highway more than 200 miles long. During the crisis of airline delays in 1984, DFW was one of the few airports unaffected; it can handle more traffic than any airport in the U.S. Its very size makes American's chief hub that much more efficient.

The hub concept reached full maturity as the decade of the seventies ended with the airline industry turned upside down. In 1978, Congress passed the Deregulation Act, and virtually overnight, the established carriers were playing a different ballgame under different rules: an invasion of key markets by new, low-cost airlines, an epidemic of cutthroat fare wars, and the end of the industry's regulated, protected way of life.

To meet this greatest of all challenges, threatening American's very existence, Al Casey picked a new leader. He turned the airline's destiny over to a forty-four-year-old man with the competitive spirit of a street fighter and the tireless mind of one of his beloved computers.

Robert Lloyd Crandall.

23
Shake Hands and Come Out Fighting

He became president July 16, 1980, at a time when the industry was in a shambles, hemorrhaging from every pore. It was like assuming command of the *Titanic* the day she sailed.

Deregulation was largely responsible. Casey had fought it, Crandall had fought it, and so had every airline chief in the country, except for Dick Ferris of United and Al Feldman of Frontier. The opponents conceded that the regulatory reins could be loosened to some extent, but not dropped so completely that the horse could run away.

The original intent of deregulation was to implement it in gradual stages, giving the airlines time to adjust; to open the gates to less restricted competition, but not swing them clear off their hinges as soon as they were unlocked. But it didn't happen that way, and it couldn't, not in the political climate existing in Washington during the late 1970s.

The coalition supporting deregulation was too powerful, a combination of liberal economists, consumerists, and a surprising bipartisan bloc in Congress. There were many unusual deregulation bed partners. Someone wrote Ferris, "How the hell can you support deregulation when Ralph Nader's for it?"

Deregulation's impact on American can best be measured by two figures. In 1978, before the full effects could be felt, American netted more than $134 million, and $87.4 million in 1979. The following year, when unfettered competition and ruinous fare wars flooded virtually every major market, American lost almost $76 million—and this with an executive corps regarded as one of the industry's finest.

Deregulation's timing was disastrous. It went into high gear almost simultaneously with soaring fuel prices. American was further handicapped by the composition of its fleet. The age of its aircraft in 1980 averaged almost ten years, and the 707 squadron was even older. The sixty-three fuelguzzling 707s the airline was operating that year provided 21 percent of total capacity.

By mid 1980, Casey and Crandall knew the airline was in deep trouble. It was one of the highest-cost carriers, with expensive contractual commitments to its unions, the legacy of agreements made in better years when the cost of a new labor contract usually could be offset by fare increases. And no airline had ever been able to get a union to accept a contract offering less money than it had won during the last negotiations.

As far as equipment was concerned, the only bright spot was the 1978 order for thirty Boeing 767s, a jumbo twin-jet with the promised fuel efficiency of a subcompact automobile. But deliveries were far down the path; American would have to do with what it had. Neither Crandall nor Casey—who was still chairman and chief executive officer—could see any way to compete against the invasion of low-cost carriers, nonunionized and with a pay structure that made American's look like the the national debt.

No way at all. Unless . . .

It was going to be one hell of an unless.

Crandall, like C.R., was a gambler, but a logical gambler. Al Casey always considered Crandall's logical mind his greatest strength. Crandall approached every problem from the standpoint of pure logic. If his solutions seemed daring, unconventional, dramatic, and controversial—as they usually were— it was only because everyone had missed the point. They were logical solutions, arrived at by weighing all evidence, sifting through alternatives, judging the consequences of doing something or not doing it, and then implementing swiftly and decisively with no looking back or wondering timidly if it had been the right move.

Any *Star Trek* fan could understand Bob Crandall. He became American's Mr. Spock, with logic as a religion and the self-discipline to stick with it even at the price of being considered as cold-blooded as a computer—which is what Dr. McCoy always said about the *Enterprise*'s science officer, and what a lot of people at American said about Crandall. Even before he became president, he had acquired a tough-guy image; employees referred to him as Attila the Hun and Darth Vader. Crandall himself would remark, with a touch of wryness, "My friends call me Mr. Crandall—my enemies call me Fang."

Any good executive would rather be regarded as strong than as ruthless, although the two adjectives often overlap in their practical application. Crandall was no exception, but he had the grace and maturity to accept his reputation as the dues a leader must pay. In private, he could poke fun at himself. Employees seldom saw the private side of Crandall, a warm family man with self-deprecating wit who loved to ski and resented above all the claim that officers and employees alike feared him.

When he was chief financial officer, he began an annual practice of visiting every station manager to review next year's budget, and he continued this as head of marketing. The sessions would last for hours, and Crandall scheduled them to start at ungodly times. He set one up in Tulsa for 5 A.M. and one man showed up in his pajamas.

At another meeting, the local staff kept refilling his coffee cup; the more he drank, the more they'd pour. He found out later they were trying to find out how much he could consume before heading for the men's room.

Those two incidents were significant to him. The guy who came to the meeting in his pajamas, for example. "It was a joke and everybody laughed like hell," Crandall said, "but it underscored what I think is part of this management's strength: we have a sense of humor. We work hard but we have fun.

"I don't think people are afraid of me. That's one of the crazy legends that have grown around me, the idea that I'm a terrible guy and you should be scared to death of me. The people I really work with, those who work with me every day, aren't scared of me at all. And they shouldn't be. You can't be afraid of your boss—that's absurd. You don't try to drown a boss in coffee or come to an important budget meeting in pajamas if you're really afraid of him."

Cost-cutting was his prime goal as chief financial officer and was even more imperative when he became president at a time of blood-letting losses. No cost item, however trivial, escaped his attention.

At one American station in the Caribbean, the local manager had three security guards for the company warehouse. Under Crandall's prodding, the security force was diminished to two guards and finally one. This wasn't enough, so the manager hired a part-time guard, which still didn't meet Crandall's idea of true economy measures. He suggested they get a dog for the warehouse, then proposed that the dog go on part-time duty. But if the manager figured Crandall was through economizing, he was wrong.

"I've got a great idea," Crandall told him. "Put a tape recorder in front of the dog and let him growl into it."

Someone asked Otto Becker if Crandall wrote his own speeches. "No," Becker said, "but he destroys the scripts they give him."

The relationship between Casey and Crandall was close, and it preceded the latter's presidency. For some time they had discussed ideas on lowering costs, and with 1980 shaping up as a debacle, Casey decided it was time to adopt some of the drastic measures he and Crandall hitherto had merely considered. The first surgery was performed with a meat cleaver: the entire 707 fleet, sixty-three airplanes, was put up for sale and the phasing-out process began. Within sixty days after taking office, Crandall put in motion a Profit Improvement Program—a package of cost-reduction measures, many of them moving up and accelerating plans Casey and Crandall already had agreed should be done. The 707 disposal was one; others included focusing the fleet at the DFW hub, withdrawing from a number of unprofitable routes in the northeast, and reconfiguring all aircraft to provide more seats.

The latter was absolutely essential. The escalating trend toward discounted fares had put airline space at a premium and various studies established that American used its onboard space less efficiently than most of its competitors. Moreover, fares were going down. By the early eighties, more than 70 percent of passengers were flying on some kind of discount.

It was too late to prevent 1980 from being a disaster, and the economy measures taken in the first six months of Crandall's regime were either emergency tourniquets or long-range plans that needed time to produce dividends. By year's end, American's balance sheet listed these liabilities:

- Fixed high labor costs that could be reduced only by painful furloughing, which, in turn, could affect quality of service.
- An over-age fleet with insufficient capital for modernization and expansion.
- Inflationary pressures that gouged deeply into whatever cost-control measures were taken, like trying to fill a bucket with a hole in the bottom.
- Inability to compete effectively against low-cost carriers due to any or all of the first three factors, and because any major attempt to match their fares could result in losing money even with fully loaded airplanes.

Tom Plaskett would say later that American could have gone down any of three roads, each of which would have betrayed employees and stockholders.

Highway 1: Shrink the fleet and route structure, sell as many planes as possible, reduce the payroll, and perhaps eventually peddle the whole airline.
Highway 2: Dissolve American as a corporate entity and start fresh as a new non-union, low-cost airline.
Highway 3: Seek wage and work rule concessions from employees on a do-it-or-else basis, the grim alternative being either of the first two paths.

The trouble with these solutions was that they all offended Crandall's sense of logic. With Casey's blessings and the enthusiasm of an executive team that didn't like those three highways any better than he did, Crandall went a different route. He took the airline into a jungle of virgin trails that had to be cleared with the machetes of imaginative innovations in marketing, finance, and employee cooperation.

Only four years later, American had more than $1 billion in liquid assets, a hub system second to none and expanding, new international routes, a solid diversification program, a largely modernized fleet with more new planes coming, one of the best profit records in the industry, and a revolutionary agreement with its unions that promised to make it a low-cost airline with a rainbow-hued future.

Logic had done the illogical.

Logical people are supposed to have ice water in their veins instead of blood, and all the sentimental qualities of a CIA agent.

The supposition is wrong. Logical people merely make sure that twinges of sentiment don't get in logic's way; that in itself would be illogical. Which is to emphasize that Bob Crandall should not be regarded as an unfeeling person.

After a gas explosion in Mexico City that killed almost 400 persons and injured some 2,000, American employees organized a mercy mission but needed an airplane to fly emergency supplies to the disaster scene. Crandall was informed, and didn't hesitate one second.

"Give 'em a 747 freighter," he ordered.

Liza Boyer, flight attendant supervisor in San Diego who was one of the organizers, said it was fortunate Crandall made that snap decision. "They filled that monster up so full, you couldn't squeeze in a pencil," she related. "It took us eight hours to unload it."

Crandall attended a Grey Eagles annual meeting a couple of years ago and was having a quiet drink off in a corner when an ex-pilot approached him.

"Mr. Crandall," he began, "my name's Bob McDaniels. I retired five years ago, you can't do me any good, so I don't have to kiss your butt. I just want to thank you for saving my favorite airline."

Crandall gave him a look of pure gratitude. "God, that sounds wonderful," he murmured.

He was not oblivious to how some employees and others regarded him: the quintessential tough guy, ruthless, insensitive, and uncaring. He once remarked to an interviewer, "Nobody likes to be known as the meanest man in town."

He did mellow a bit, according to some, but to change his personality just to be liked would be . . . well, illogical. For no man could have achieved what he did for American by being just a nice guy; popularity doesn't solve problems. His sometimes quick temper did get him into hot water with that well-known phone call to Braniff's Howard Putnam, but the remarks he made were on pure impulse. He simply told Putman if Braniff was in so much trouble, all it had to do was raise its fares and American would do likewise. To interpret that as suggesting a joint antitrust conspiracy, which the Justice Department incredibly did, came as a complete surprise even to Crandall's competitors. Throughout an industry that often has been knocked groggy by his aggressiveness, he is still regarded as totally ethical. Not a few of his airline peers privately questioned the ethics of the man who taped that phone call without Crandall's knowledge and turned it over to the government. At one point, the Justice Department was talking about forcing Crandall to leave American for two years as punishment. ("If that had happened," one lower management person said, "we would have loaded up the DC-10 fleet with bombs and dropped them on their goddamned building.")

But the directors supported Crandall, and the sound and the fury faded. The final settlement was a mild slap on the wrist; in effect, Crandall promised not to discuss prices with anyone.

Corporate leaders are like football quarterbacks; they often get too much credit when they win and too much blame when they lose.

Bob Crandall would have been blamed if his strategies, policies, and risks had failed. They didn't, and his name became synonymous with successful management. Someone called him the Lee Iacocca of the airline industry, a compliment that also could be turned around by calling Iacocca the Bob Crandall of the auto industry.

But Crandall himself never considered American's dramatic surge back to industry leadership a one-man achievement. In the transcribed interview with Crandall conducted during research for this history, the pronoun "we" appears ten times for every mention of "I," and this was true particularly during discussion of the brilliantly innovative programs almost automatically associated with his name: AAdvantage, Super Saver, Ultimate Super Saver, and the two-tier wage structure.

"A program has to be a joint product," Crandall said. "It starts with me, Tom Plaskett, Wes Kaldahl, John Pope, and Don Carty, and maybe a dozen other guys sitting around and talking about a problem until we get an idea that'll work. It really doesn't matter who gets the idea first, me or anyone else, it still takes collaboration to develop it into its final form."

The striking thing about Crandall's team when he settled on its composition in 1980 was its youth. Kaldahl, in his fifties, was the "grizzled veteran"; Crandall at forty-four was the next oldest, and Plaskett, Pope, and Carty (vice president and comptroller) were in their thirties. The proud Casey, who had helped form the team, said, "These sons of bitches are the best there are." (Lloyd-Jones, lone holdover from the Spater years, left in 1982 to head Air Florida.)

The first product to emerge from the Robert L. Crandall Factory of Ideas was typical of many that followed: it was so good, the rest of the industry had to imitate it. And because American thought it up first, competitors again had to play catch-up—the same thread that has run through the airline's entire history. This time it was the Frequent Fliers program, described by one industry expert as "the best single marketing innovation in the history of commercial aviation."

This, as related by Crandall, was how it came about:

"We had worked on the notion for a long time—it was one of those ideas that emerges very gradually over a period of time. We were trying to find some effective way of rewarding repetitive use of American. Essentially, how do you give somebody a discount in exchange for loyalty? We finally came up with the idea of adding up the miles a guy flies and giving him a discount proportionate to the miles he travels. Then we took it a step further. We said, why not give him the discount in the form of additional or free travel? And from this stream of ideas came the AAdvantage program [American's official name for what has become an industry generic term: Frequent Fliers].

"We did this in the summer of 1981. We had spent eighteen months working on the data processing that would have to be involved, long before I became president, because once we finally settled on the basic plan, we wanted to do all the SABRE programming before it was announced. This was to let everybody who signed up start recording mileage immediately.

"Putting the program into SABRE before it was made public was a stroke of brilliance. American was ready the minute the first press release went out. All the forms were ready, service check-in procedures were ready, and the beauty of the plan was its simplicity for the passenger. All customers had to do was provide their AAdvantage number when they made a reservation, and the trip was automatically entered into SABRE. The AAdvantage number was printed right on the boarding pass so a passenger knew his flight was being counted.

"We also had planned in advance a system by which every AAdvantage member got a monthly statement, like a bank statement, providing the total mileage accumulated to date. We really surprised the opposition. It took two years before anybody could catch up. There are fourteen versions of our plan out there today."

Crandall gave Plaskett the task of putting the plan into final form, and he did a brilliant job. AAdvantage accomplished something that had never been done before: the creation of "brand loyalty" toward an individual airline. Crandall admitted the program was expensive, because the various benefits—like free upgrading to first class and complimentary trips—amounted to a 5 or 6 percent discount. But to keep hundreds of thousands of passengers flying American (the exact number of AAdvantage members is a secret but one industry estimate is over a million) far offset the cost.

American recorded its first $4 billion revenue year in 1981 and a $47.4 million profit. But the following year was a shocker: a stunning $19.6 million loss that sent Crandall & Co. not just back to the drawing board, but to a whole new drawing board. And out of this latest crisis came a precedent-setting plan that revolutionized the industry's labor-management structure: the two-tier wage program.

The 1982 showing was not an unexpected disappointment, for all the signs of impending trouble had been plainly visible. Another national recession choked the economy, and passenger yield dropped like an elevator with severed cables. Traffic consisted largely of passengers flying on discounts, and for a high-cost airline like American, a low yield wiped out cost-saving programs.

Like AAdvantage, the two-tier idea "developed in little pieces," as Crandall put it.

"Our problem was being a high-cost airline," he continued. "So how do we go about solving it? You put the problem in front of a group of capable people and everybody starts chipping in suggestions, and gradually a consensus emerges."

For a solution with such far-reaching implications, its concept was simple: all future employees would be hired at starting salaries as much as 50 percent lower than the starting wage scales in existing union contracts. It was easy to apply this draconian measure to future non-union employees, but nearly 60 percent of American's work force was represented by labor, roughly 20,000 out of a total of 36,000. The starting wage rates actually were "market rates"—the same as or higher than those being paid by new airlines.

Crandall did not want to emulate Continental, which abrogated its labor contracts, filed for bankruptcy, and started up again as a non-union, low-cost carrier. Nor did he want to go the route Eastern and so many others had taken, asking employees to give back part of their wages until things improved. And he already had furloughed several thousand AA employees. He simply wanted to break linkage with past labor contract practices that called for high starting salaries.

Crandall placed both the problem and the proposed solution before the unions. The key group was the Transport Workers Union, representing more than 10,000 ground employees. The two next largest organizations were the Allied Pilots Association, with nearly 3,500 members, and the Association of Professional Flight Attendants, with a roster of almost 6,000. Only two other unions were involved: some 400 flight engineers belonged to the Flight Engineers International Association, and sixteen security guards were members of the International Association of Machinists.

Crandall and his staff launched a series of meetings to sell the logic of the two-tier plan to the troops. The first target was TWU, and the presentations made to this union, composed largely of maintenance employees, were the same made later to the others. In effect, this was the message Crandall delivered:

"This is a fair deal. We agree not to cut your wages and benefits. Moreover, we're going to add something to them: the best job security in the industry, we'll give up the right to furlough people. In exchange, you've got to change your work rules to give American more productivity. And you must agree to let us bring in new people at lower wages. *This is the only way for us to grow and expand and prosper.*"

The TWU approved the two-tier plan in a vote that was narrower than Crandall hoped, but it still was approval. APA was the next hurdle, and the message was similar but with an additional promise:

"We won't cut your salaries and benefits, just as we promised the TWU, but you've got to be more efficient, and that means flying more hours. In return, we promise to go out and buy more airplanes, and to fly them we'll be hiring more pilots."

APA at first balked, then began wavering, and finally went along, followed by the flight attendants. All three unions knew Crandall meant business. While the TWU was deliberating the two-tier proposal, which if turned down would have meant a strike, Crandall had a contingency plan ready to keep the airline operating. Non-union employees had been trained to take over a number of ground jobs; a chief skipper at an Admirals Club, for example, had been trained as an aircraft cleaner. And planes were positioned to ferry these emergency workers around the system to stations where they would be needed the most. Contingent contracts had been signed with fixed-based operators at every station. If the TWU had struck, every single job would have been instantly and permanently contracted out.

Crandall felt everyone, union and non-union alike but especially the former, had to realize how much deregulation had changed the industry. "We all have to accept the world as it is, not as it was," he told the pilots.

The final contractual package, including two-tier, was by no means a one-way street down which the unions had to march. Crandall instituted American's first profit-sharing as part of the deal. And he kept his promise of growth.

The 707 fleet had disappeared from American's skies. On August 31, 1981, Captain Wendy Dobbs flew the final 707 passenger trip from Newark to

O'Hare. It was Flight 194, which was supposed to be a DC-10 schedule, but the jumbo was shifted to a charter assignment so the 707's retirement could be appropriately celebrated.

The accelerated phase-out program had left the airline with only eleven surplus Boeings by mid August of '81. The Air Force had purchased twenty-five for about $61 million, including spare parts. Another eighteen went to the Boeing Military Airplane Co., which used their fanjet engines and other components to modify the Air Force's tanker aircraft.

Other 707s were sold to various cargo and charter carriers, but finding buyers was difficult. Not until July of 1984 did American dispose of its last 707. This was a cargo version flown out of Waco to the Davis-Monthan Air Force base in Tucson. By that time, the Double-A insignia on the tail was barely discernible and there was only a small strip of the red, white, and blue markings around the nose. The 707's departure wasn't really mourned, but Dave Frailey's department dug up a statistic that was a tribute in its own way: in twenty-two years, American's 707 fleet had carried 156 million passengers more than two billion miles.

New planes, not old ones, were on Bob Crandall's mind as the two-tier plan went into effect. And once again, the airline resorted to the unconventional. John Pope worked out a unique deal with McDonnell Douglas for a five-year, "bring-'em-back-if-you're-not-satisfied" lease on twenty MCD Super 80s, a stretched version of the DC-9, with fuel-efficient bypass engines and wings of a new aerodynamic design.

Pope happily described the agreement as "obnoxious." At the end of five years, if the airline had found them below expectations, they could be returned to the manufacturer with only a small penalty. It was the equivalent of a car dealer giving a customer a five-year test drive. And it kept American free of long-term obligations.

But the Super 80 proved to be so excellent an airplane that Pope leased another thirteen in an attractive deal with Bankers Trust and two Japanese leasing firms. And McDonnell Douglas was well paid for the gamble it took; American subsequently ordered 67 Super 80s, with an option for an additional 100, the largest order in American's history.

American introduced the Super 80 on its system in May 1983, less than eight months after the contract was signed for the initial twenty aircraft. Almost as large as the 727-200, it was far more sophisticated and designed for a two-man crew. It also was one of the quietest airplanes around, welcome at even the most noise-sensitive airports. Crandall envisioned it as eventually replacing the 727. But meanwhile, he had some interesting plans for what was now the dowager of the fleet—so interesting that it sent shock waves through Seattle.

He suggested that the older 727s could be modernized by restructuring the fuselage to remove the center engine, replacing the old JT8D engines with new bypass engines and giving the plane a new set of aerodynamically improved wings. This was before American acquired the Super 80.

"I don't remember exactly who first proposed it," Crandall said. "It was one of those things that suddenly turned up on the table. But I was fascinated by its potential."

Logic was at work again. The major difference between new jets like the Super 80 and the older 727 was in the wing and engine design; in effect, "If you've seen one fuselage, you've seen them all." Crandall saw a chance to modernize the three-holer by turning it into a twin-engine aircraft at a cost far less than what American would have to pay for a new plane. The price tag on a Super 80 or the Boeing 757 (a twin American once ordered but then canceled) came close to what a 747 cost originally.

Marv Whitlock was one expert who thought the idea made sense. "Basically," Whitlock commented, "the 757 is nothing but a 727 with new wings and engines, which is what Crandall was suggesting."

Nothing came of this idea. Fuel prices, which at the time of the proposal seemed heading for the moon, stabilized and never did get high enough to justify the cost of a major 727 facelift. And the cost would have been more than had been anticipated. Boeing's lowest estimate was $12 million per aircraft, and $14 million if the airline wanted a new two-man cockpit.

Abortive though it was, the 727 surgical procedure was another instance of what kept popping out of this breeding ground for originality. Some of Crandall's recommendations were industry-oriented; he may have been more like C.R. in that respect than anyone realized.

He urged the airlines to adopt a different approach to aircraft financing, suggesting that planes be standardized, with the manufacturers offering one standard for interior, engine, performance specifications, etc. He also said a financial consortium of some sort might consider pooling some maintenance and parts facilities.

One investment banker called it "a good, exciting, and big idea." United said it wasn't interested, and TWA's reaction was that it was a great concept in theory but probably unworkable. Western was one of the few enthusiastic carriers. The plan wasn't exactly new—aircraft standardization had been proposed before—but Crandall's was far more extensive.

One of American's most dramatic moves was an attack on the plethora of discounted "junk" fares, proliferating and constantly changing so fast that even SABRE found it hard to keep track. Crandall approved a plan by Plaskett and his team to put into effect a simplified three-level fare structure, the most heavily discounted level being Ultimate Super Saver. This was a new version of Super Saver, with generally similar restrictions but with discounts as high as 70 percent, and like Super Saver, it was an instant hit. Also like Super Saver, its restrictions prevented serious diversion, and its generous discount attracted people who wouldn't have flown otherwise.

Crandall expected the industry to follow suit and urged it to do so; fare simplification, he argued, was essential in the long run. But new discounted fares actually increased in numbers after American started its simplification plan.

Any tears shed over the 707's departure—and most of them came from sentimental pilots—were more than matched by the general lamentations that greeted the decision to take the 747 out of passenger service. Reducing the 747 fleet was one of Casey's first moves, with some of them being converted to freighters. Crandall speeded up their demise. He took American out of the all-cargo business by selling the 747 freighters, and traded the remaining passenger models to Pan Am in exchange for an equal number of DC-10s.

It was not one of his more popular decisions, as he acknowledged:

"Sure we got some static from passengers about substituting DC-10s for 747s, and some from employees, too. They told us it's a wonderful airplane, passengers love it, and they were right. But American couldn't make any money with it. For us, the 747 was locked into just a couple of routes. Now that's fine if you want to fly to London and you need a 747. But when you've an airline like ours, where demand patterns change and flexibility is of tremendous importance, having fifty-five DC-10s is a hell of a lot better than having thirty-five DC-10s and twenty 747s.

"The notion that people won't fly on a DC-10 is long since gone. Our DC-10 load factors exceed our system average load factors. It's a wonderful airplane, and it's the right size. It can fly nonstop to London, it can fly nonstop transcontinentally, and it can be used economically on shorter routes.

"What a lot of people didn't realize was that most of the 747s American had were leased, and the leases were about to expire. There was no way we were going to renew them. The deal with Pan Am was good for both airlines. They acquired their DC-10s as part of the merger with National and they wanted to standardize their fleet—727s for domestic and 747s international. Essentially, it was a straight trade, plane for plane."

Yet Crandall didn't do what so many other airlines felt so necessary: dump the old 727-100 models as fast as possible. It was axiomatic that no one could make money with a 727-100. Crandall didn't believe it.

"The notion that you can't make money with that airplane is absolutely crazy," he insisted. "They're terrific airplanes, and I'll tell you why. There's nobody in the world making and selling a new airplane that can be bought and operated competitively with the 727-100. People don't pay any attention to capital costs. What the 727-100 costs American is $1 million—that's what we could sell it for. So look at it as if I had just bought that airplane for $1 million. Now it costs so much to operate it, and granted it can't be flown as cheaply as a much newer aircraft like the 737-300 (Boeing's new twin-jet), but the 737 costs a lot to buy. In addition to the operating cost factor, you have to count the cost of borrowing money to pay for it. And when you look at it that way, and as long as fuel stays cheap, it's cheaper to operate the 100 series than buy a replacement. That is true until fuel goes to $1.20 a gallon. People simply don't focus on the trade-off between capital cost and operating cost."

In other words, use logic.

*   *   *

Casey retired in February 1985, with Crandall becoming chairman, chief executive officer, and president.

When Al Casey left the airline he had served so well, American was flying or about to fly from Dallas/Fort Worth to London, Frankfurt, and Paris. The eagle's wings were poised to stretch into the Carolinas with a new hub at Raleigh/Durham, and another at Nashville, thus creating two new north-south hubs. The roll call of progress seemed endless. Beefing up the Chicago hub, United's home grounds. Dallas/Fort Worth–Atlanta DC-10 service. Establishing a commuter-affiliated network called American Eagle. A $60 million commitment for a new terminal facility at DFW. The unique AAirpass program, offering future air transportation at guaranteed rates in return for a single advance payment; that gimmick brought in $10 million within months after it was introduced.

Add to the list one of Casey's major contributions. In 1982, with board approval, he created a holding company called AMR Corporation, a corporate roof over the airline and its subsidiaries. The name was derived from American's initials as listed on the New York Stock Exchange.

Another Casey contribution, of course, carried the initials R.L.C.

It is entirely possible that this chapter, written in July 1985, will be out of date six months later; things have happened that fast with Bob Crandall running the show. Yet even with the kaleidoscope of action that began swirling almost from the day he took over, with Casey's help he also created an air of stability, something of which he himself is proud.

"One of the things Al and I have done," he said, "is bring stability to the company. A lot of people on the organizational (management) chart have been here for years. Some of them either Al or I or both hired. People need to feel they have a stable group of officers who work well together, who provide some kind of cohesive direction. And then the executive group itself obviously grows more comfortable with itself."

Even the Attila the Hun image became blurred. Several employees told Crandall they were worried about his chain-smoking habit.

"Why don't you quit?" one asked. "You're doing a pretty good job and we'd hate to have you drop dead on us."

Stability, of course, is not synonymous with status quo. Reflecting his belief in SABRE's importance, Crandall elevated Robert Baker, vice president of marketing automation, to the top team as senior vice president of information systems. SABRE will earn something like $100 million in 1985 and it contributed heavily to American's record $233.9 million profit in 1984.

Two other new senior vice presidents were added to "Crandall's corps": William Shannon, who started out as a fleet service clerk and replaced Otto Becker when he retired, and Richard Lempert, general counsel since 1972. And Gene Overbeck made a relocation move of his own; he went down to Washington as senior vice president of government affairs, while Jim O'Neill took over Sky Chefs.

Some names must pass into history, but not as mere footnotes. Dave Frailey retired in 1982, and "public relations" became "corporate communications" under vice president Lowell Duncan, Jr., a soft-spoken recruit from the hectic world of television news. Al Bone died in 1970, Elmo Coon in 1977, Abe Hoyt in 1984. Abe was one of the few employees to receive the Award of Merit twice. His first was in 1945 for reorganizing military line maintenance during the war, and his second reflected his own courage. He conquered alcoholism, and established a rehabilitation program to help other employees. He was truly a beloved character and it was once said of him, "The disease of working for Abe Hoyt makes it hard to leave the job."

In men like Abe Hoyt and C. R. Smith was American's glorious past. In men like Al Casey and Bob Crandall is American's future. Willis Player, part of the past himself, once said of them:

"Under Casey and Crandall, American has retained more of its original class and style, its excellence of quality, than most of the other airlines. And going along with it, the willingness to think of new ways of doing things."

Thus, this is the end . . . of the beginning.

Epilogue

There is a time machine on the lower level of the Tulsa Airport terminal building.

This is the American Airlines museum, founded by curator and ex-AA supervisory mechanic Paul Kent when he retired in 1971. Step into a room that could fit into the first-class section of a DC-10, and you are back in time.

Back to the days of Avco and E. L. Cord . . . the air mail pilots . . . the wartime years, when so much of AA was spelled ATC.

Back to the few glory years of American Overseas and Ralph Damon. To the Condors and DC-3s and the Stinsons that flew like iron bathtubs.

It is a room with 10,000 memories brought to life by pictures, scrapbooks, and thousands of memorabilia that stir bittersweet nostalgia. Many were contributed by members of American's three major senior groups: Grey Eagles, Kiwis, and the Three-Diamond Society.

C.R.'s old desk.

A huge model of a DC-8 in TCA markings, a plane that American never flew, and a DC-10 with the old Orange lightning bolt, a color scheme it never carried.

A hand-woven rug with the AA eagle, made by a woman passenger for Captain Doc Ator.

A mannequin dressed in the flying togs of an air mail pilot, complete with helmet, goggles, and white scarf.

The food and coffee jugs off a DC-3. A lifejacket off an AOA plane.

The piano from a 747 lounge.

A collection of first-cover air mail envelopes, conservatively estimated to be worth $25,000.

A score of various stewardess uniforms.

Food trays, cups, plates, and utensils from the period when eating a meal at 10,000 feet was considered an adventure.

Transcribed interviews with old-timers for at least two AA histories that never got into print.

A photographic gallery of American's presidents.

Models of planes American flew, some of them priceless, like AOA's Stratocruiser and a DC-2.

A magnificent sculpture of the AA eagle.

As this is being written, there is talk of moving the museum to corporate headquarters someday. But it really does not matter where a museum is located. American's past is preserved in the traditions of pride and courage handed down by the men and women whose tools were pride and courage.

In 1972, American signed the famed NBC commentator Chet Huntley to be the airline's "voice" in television commercials. It became not just a job for which he was well paid, but a love affair with the airline itself.

When he was preparing a commercial, he went out and dug for ideas and facts as if he were covering a news story. He would talk to mechanics, pilots, stewardesses, agents. He made it a point to get the "feel" of the airline. He didn't have to—such commercials are written by an ad agency and usually read by a celebrity who might have a different product brand in his pocket while he extolls the virtues of the sponsor's.

Not Chet Huntley. He *believed* in what he was saying. He had become a part of American Airlines, without ever intending to. One night he was making a speech in San Diego to a system marketing meeting, an audience composed of American officials, employees, and their wives. He ended his talk with these words:

"And on those 99 percent of American Airlines flights where everything goes fine and the operation is normal, I would love to hear an American Airlines stewardess in making her final announcement, end it by saying, out of conviction, out of her heart, not reading it off a card, I would love to hear her say, *'Ladies and gentlemen, you have just flown with the best airline in the world.'* "

If It Were Not for These People . . .

My special gratitude to:

Lowell Duncan, Jr., for his support and valued advice.

Dave Frailey, for backstopping me with a knowledge of American that far exceeded my own.

Gene Overbeck, another valuable backstopper in factual verification.

Glen Walker, for helping me get it off the ground.

Mary Sullivan, my indispensable liaison.

Al Casey, Dixon Speas, Newton K. Wilson, Hamilton Hale, Bob Tuttle, Charlie Speers, John Booth, Gayle Welling, and Marguerite Sadler, not only for productive interviews but for lending or giving me voluminous material from their personal files.

Willis Player, whose interview launched the research and sent me down many fruitful paths.

Paul Kent, whose museum was a research gold mine.

Bob Crandall, for telling me right at the start, "Write the truth."

C. R. Smith, for his many letters and encouragement.

My thanks to the following for the interviews they gave me and/or aid in many forms:

Millie Alford	Glen Brink	Lee Eisel
Nick Anagnostis	Mel Brenner	Lee Elsesser
Ronnie Anagnostis	Francis Burr	Bill Evans
Kathy Andersen	Paul Clough	Ben Fidler
Elizabeth Andrew	Joe Comnillo	Chuck Foerster
Blair Ashton	Jimmy Conner	Tiny Foley
James Aston	Milt Coppage	Jim Gainer
Paul Atkins	Douglas Corrigan	Bill Gilmore
James Bass	Walter Damtoft	Warren Goodman
Al Becker	Bill Davenport	Walt Gosnell
George Becker	Marion DeSisto	Bob Gray
Otto Becker	Bill Dunn	Edythe Griffith
Charlie Billerman	Sky Dunning	Kay Hansen
Ed Boyd	Mack Eastburn	Harold Harris

Elmer Heckel
Ginny Heckel
Tex Herke
Bill Hipple
William J. Hogan
John Hotard
Robert Howlett
Mary Hughes
Jerry Jacob
Ed Jennings
Debbie Jeter
Bob Johnson
Walter Johnson
Vivian Jorgensen
Kathleen Kane
Patti Patterson
    Kennedy
Jane Kimberly
Betty Kirlin
Walt Kistler
Rita Lapka
Carlene Roberts
    Lawrence
Duke Ledbetter
Art Lewis
Patricia Long
Bob Losik
Malcolm MacIntyre
Ted Mallozzi

Richard Maurer
Chick McBath
John McCarten
Bob McDaniels
Kitty McEllin
Bryce McCormick
Nancy McGovern
Shirley McManus
Anne McMasters
Clancie Melton
Ray Metcalfe
Walt Moran
John Mosley
Jack Mullins
Goodrich Murphy
Janet Nall
Ray Newhouse
Carl Nordling
Phyllis Nunnery
Tom O'Brien
Nick O'Connell
Ginger Orlando
Mack Palmer
Richard Pearson
Art Pickell
Bill Proctor
Jon Proctor
Walt Rauscher
Tull Rea

Fay Reay
Bob "Catfish" Roberts
J. K. Ross
Sandra Roston
Ray Ryan
Barbara Schreffler
Libby Scott
Mary Selby
Leslie Shaw
Jeanne Silvius
Ray Silvius
Helen Sindermann
J. C. Sittinger
Burck Smith
Donald K. Smith
Jackie Smith
Todd Smith
Jim Stanford
Joe Stroop
Gene Taylor
Linda Timberlake
Dave Tracy
Mary Frances Vittorio
Frank Vosepka
Kurt Wallace
Dan White
Marvin Whitlock
Chuck Wilford

More than 100 individuals were interviewed during seven months of research, their recollections being recorded on some 200 hours of tape. All dialogue in this book is derived from those tapes; there are no manufactured conversations.

Inevitably, there had to be many persons associated with American's history who were not interviewed. These omissions I deeply regret, but to complete the book by its assigned deadline it was necessary to end the research and commence the actual writing. As it was, the interviewing went on a month beyond the original schedule and reduced the writing time accordingly. *Eagle* had to be finished so it could be published before Christmas 1985.

American's files in Dallas/Forth Worth and those at its Tulsa museum contained scores of transcribed interviews with various personalities from the airline's past, many of them now deceased. The identity of the interviewers was not given, but their work provided a rich lode of information for which I am beholden.

An unpublished manuscript by Stanley Washburn, Jr., *Fiorello's Futurama,* was especially helpful in relating the story of LaGuardia Airport. Another valuable source was George W. Cearley, Jr.'s fine *American Airlines—An Illustrated History,* privately published. Other prime reference sources were:

The Airline Builders, Oliver Allen, Time-Life Books, 1981.

Airlines of the United States Since 1914, R. E. G. Davies, Putnam, 1972.

Airways, Henry Ladd Smith, Alfred A. Knopf, 1944.

Avco Corporation—the First 50 Years, Avco Corp., 1979.

The First Five Million Miles, Byron Moore, Harper, 1955.

The Plane That Changed the World, Douglas Ingells, Aero, 1966.

International Airport, George Scullin, Little, Brown, 1968.

Peter Mansfield's *William Littlewood Memorial Lecture* gave exceptional insight into this exceptional man, as well as the history of the DC-3. I also found of great value Jack Alexander's "Just Call Me C.R." article in the *Saturday Evening Post* of February 1, 1941; two *Fortune* articles, "U.S. Aviation and the Air Mail," May 1934, and "Airline in the Black," Winter 1938; and Dan Beard's piece on the DC-3 in *Exxon Air World,* Vol. 30, No. 1, 1978.

Finally, a very low bow in the direction of two consummate professionals: my editor, Dick Marek, and my agent, Aaron Priest, both of whom exhibited their usual patience, tolerance, and skill throughout this journey into the past.

And to my family—wife Priscilla, daughter Jennifer, and son Jeff—my love and gratitude for putting up with those countless hours when I was neither husband nor father.

Robert J. Serling
August 1, 1985
Tucson, Arizona

Name Index